# PATTERN IN CULTURAL ANTHROPOLOGY

The doll illustrated on the
cover represents a shaman
in the Molale bands which
lived at one time in Oregon.
Their language and herit-
age vanished in recent
years.

## THE DORSEY SERIES IN ANTHROPOLOGY
## AND SOCIOLOGY

EDITOR

ROBIN M. WILLIAMS, JR.
*Cornell University*

*Melville Jacobs*, Ph.D.

Professor of Anthropology and Linguistics
University of Washington

*Pattern in*

# CULTURAL ANTHROPOLOGY

1964

THE DORSEY PRESS

HOMEWOOD, ILLINOIS

First Printing, June, 1964
Second Printing, May, 1968

Library of Congress Catalog Card No. 64-17256

PRINTED IN THE UNITED STATES OF AMERICA

# PREFACE

These chapters comprise the kind of presentation which I might offer this year in a series of introductory lectures in cultural anthropology. They presume that readers or students have already had a set of introductory lectures in social anthropology, preferably also some in physical anthropology and prehistory. Although I cherish the thought that no other anthropologist would select, omit, define, evaluate, and emphasize as I have done, I hope that I have phrased points of view which laymen, colleagues, and their students in cultural anthropology will find of interest. I have deliberately avoided designing a college textbook survey of technical papers and monographs or books. In each topic of cultural anthropology, they usually yield just a theoretical insight or two or they set forth mere fragments of a rather slowly expanding armory of methodological tools. Advanced students should track down such publications and fill in, in relation to each subdivision of cultural anthropology, the descriptive, methodological, and theoretical contributions which deserve acceptance. This book is an effort to present an orientation rather than a patchwork survey.

I wish to express gratitude to the University of Wisconsin—Milwaukee and its anthropologists for the unique and most generous opportunity given to me to spend the school year of 1961–62 as a visiting professor, to enjoy their stimulation and familylike hospitality, and to keep from rusting because of the excellent groups of students they recruited for me in several classes. This writing is one of the results of a delightful year which was far more productive than an academic sabbatical leave from my home base, the University of Washington, would have permitted. Upon return, the gracious office staff of the Department of Anthropology assisted in the preparation of manuscript.

MELVILLE JACOBS

Seattle, Washington
June 30, 1963

# TABLE OF CONTENTS

# INTRODUCTION

Before 1492 a handful of literate Europeans were electrified by books such as those by Ibn Batuta and Marco Polo, of travel to distant lands and peoples. Seaport communities of the European world occasionally enjoyed accounts of experiences of sailors and merchants who returned from Asian and African trips. But the prevailing insularity of Europeans did not suffer drastic alteration until the decades after Columbus' return to Spain from his first voyage to the west. Europeans in rapidly increasing numbers presently journeyed to the Americas and other regions of the nonwestern world. Historians have long studied and described over four centuries of post-Columbian expeditions, colonizations and their tremendous consequences to Euro-American economy and culture.

Anthropologists focus on the thousands of communities whose people could do little more than endure invasions, often bloody, of highhanded, energetic, and irresistibly armed people of lighter complexion. Descendants of survivors of European entry and colonization today total hundreds of millions. Most of them live extremely differently from the ways their ancestors dwelt during the first decades of expansion of Europe. Sociopolitical and cultural changes among such peoples have gone on to a point that over 30 new states have sent their most western oriented representatives to take seats successively in the United Nations beside delegates of older nations, some of whom include their recent overbearing masters.

What were the predecessors of these nonwestern peoples like at the time of Columbus? May anthropologists suitably term some of them primitives? Stone Age peoples? Uncivilized? Savages? Barbarians? Four centuries ago had they advanced so little, as a great many people have asserted, that it is correct to equate their intellects with the minds of children? Did they not speak crude and simple languages? Did they not believe in all sorts of gross superstitions, conduct weird ceremonies, waylay neighbors, tattoo or cicatrize their skins, and send stoical parents out into the bush to die? Were they not on just one or another early stage of evolution from which the ancestors of the bleached Europeans had long since climbed up and out? Volumes could be written on the many questions, such as these, which Euro-Americans nurtured and the scurrilous answers and vainglorious responses which they still cherish about many of the peoples outside Europe.

This one small book makes no effort to survey what the invaders and their kin who stayed at home supposed some of those darker people were like. The book discusses a few of the things, maybe important ones, that modern scientific researchers appear to have found out about the world's

1

groups of more heavily pigmented citizens before and soon after Europeans arrived with overpowering weaponry and invincible determination. A principal concern of the book is to suggest methods which ought to be employed in further conduct of those studies.

Research on nonliterate peoples constitutes a recent episode in the history of the sciences. A severely scientific rather than novelistic or unselectively descriptive approach to the subject of human beings who were overwhelmed by European expansion is even today almost a bizarre and chilling proposal. But an anthropologist's kind of approach is a full century old. Individuals who were developing it were rare, to be sure, until about the 1930's or 1940's. Before the Second World War many persons who knew there were psychologists and sociologists had never heard of anthropologists. Not many Americans have been aware that by the 1920's the United States had become the largest center for anthropological science. Here and in a few other countries a rapidly growing professional body of scientists is dedicated to toilsome analysis, without rancor or romance, of the customs, thinking, and feelings of the world's darker peoples. The commitment is to approach ever closer to complete understanding of what they were like before European penetration and what they became after Europeans established beachheads, barracks, missions, trading posts, jails, residences, and airstrips.

Glosses on the global diversity and common characteristics of culture are comically various and too numerous for citation. Other publications have assembled and even tried to make sense of them. In most instances such surveys of thoughts on the nature of culture have utility only because they reveal sentiments of those who propounded definitions of culture. Possible merit in an exegesis on culture, if one can be regarded as acceptable, is in its consequences. Can it be used descriptively, taxonomically, or to devise an edifice of scientific knowledge of sociocultural systems, or of certain facets of them? Very likely a principal utility of a definition of culture, if one can be agreed upon, is taxonomic. If culture is construed, for example, as that sector of a sociocultural system which comprises only its projective and expressive phenomena, anthropology is assisted in the conduct of operations which may build a neatly expounded system of knowledge about the sector. This book uses the term "culture" in just this manner in order to contrast one big piece out of a sociocultural system with a related piece which comprises social structural features, most of them relatively much more visible and identifiable. Expositions of cultural expressions on the one hand and webs of social relationships on the other may indicate little about the connections between social structure as cause and cultural expression as consequence. Still, the dichotomy is efficient because it limits features to be examined initially. Many anthropologists have included, under a rubric of culture or cultural anthropology, a number of topics which would have been more felicitously relegated to a category of social structure. Assuredly a dichotomy of cultural versus social is mechanical, but it may be less confusing.

The book commences with two background chapters. Most readers may bypass the first chapter because it is very likely too technical for laymen and beginning students. The second chapter deals with socioeconomic types. A novice in anthropological territories may start with it. Discussion of socioeconomic types includes material which is basic in a treatise on social organization. But the chapter offers both taxonomic decisions and a pedagogic device which allow the remainder of the book to focus upon cultural expressions, in all their variety, of nonwestern peoples who lacked writing. The socioeconomic chapter sketches, in as generalized and laconic a manner as possible, some of the ways in which nonliterate peoples produced foods and things and related to one another in their respective communities. Anthropologists might caption the material of the chapter "primitive economics and social anthropology." Today "nonwestern" and "nonliterate" are as a rule preferable to the word "primitive."

The purpose of the book is to discuss how nonliterate peoples expressed themselves, projected, felt, judged, mastered esthetic heritages, and tried to do things with excellence, including rearing children and taking care of elders. It indicates how they defended against tensions by utilizing nonmaterial kin. It points to the many kinds of things they unconsciously patterned and structured. Each chapter is a quick introduction to study of a special aspect of the cultural heritage and mentality of a few thousands of nonliterate peoples. The entire scope of the expressive forms of behavior of those groups could not be completed in hundreds of thousands of volumes. Chapters of the book amount to a starting sketch of a cluster of fields of scientific inquiry, that cluster here dubbed "cultural anthropology."

Persons who, through a variety of books, know something about cultural anthropology should be able to meet fellow members of the United Nations with a modicum of mid-twentieth century anthropological understanding of them and of their enormously different heritages. Hundreds of millions of people cry out for the compassion, respect, and acceptance for which the ethnocentric and acquisitive ancestors of living Euro-Americans had little time and temper. Practical immediate applications of cultural anthropology include assistance to Euro-Americans in making amends for centuries of brutality, arrogance, folly, and greed, and encouragement of both them and other wealthy and industrialized peoples in reorienting themselves about the worth of the multitudes whom most Victorians regarded as savages and barbarians.

Painstaking content and form analyses receive emphasis as especially important immediate means for gleaning scientific knowledge about nonliterate peoples' cultural expressions. The term "close analysis" is borrowed. Usually it is associated with an important current of recent decades in literary criticism, as represented by William Empson and many others.

Although it offers a suitable caption, its employment for several decades by literary critics has not implied their unanimity of interest in advancing toward a system of scentific theory in literature. Critics of literature who have utilized what they called "close analysis" exhibited no interest in discovery of minimal units which were appropriate because they were significant. Their arrangements of components within literatures were little or not at all structural. They simply examined written literary products with unexampled refinement and detail, sometimes also with archaic axioms about ritual to myth progressions in bygone eras and about archetypal themes borrowed from sepulchral Jungian caves. An effort to contribute to scientific theory may result in concern with details as small as those cited by literary critics, but the decisive thing about any science is that it slices, weighs, and orders items quite differently. Presumably few professionals in literature studies will object to a grateful, if not deferential, borrowing of their excellent term "close analysis."

All readers of books about the anthropological sciences should retain vivid awareness that every subdivision—social or structural, cultural, prehistory, human genetics, or anthropological linguistics—within the total field of general anthropology is a very young science. As decades unfold and increasing numbers of scientific workers make contributions to fields of global inquiry about human expressions, today's charm of immaturity or newness and the episodic excitement of breakthroughs in method and theory will transmute to satisfactions, if not awe, which arise in more secure possession of vaster compilations of descriptive materials, neater and more impressive orderings of them, and pyramidings or systematizations of sound hypotheses. Certainly cultural anthropology in the 1960's can propose little more than stumbling beginnings, false starts, and thimblefuls of tenuous hypotheses. These not especially secure rudiments are scribbled over with disorderly hypotheses, most of which will be discarded and replaced with scientific statements of superior merit and generality. Today's dime store bric-a-brac and one or two storied rickety houses will have vanished to be succeeded by beautifully furnished and towering theoretic structures which are in continuous process of renovation and addition. No reader can afford to forget that some sciences are much less developed than others in their progress toward mature systems of knowledge. It seems almost unethical to publish an introductory sketch of any behavioral science without stern admonishment that it is newly fledged.

# 1. TOWARD SUBSYSTEMS OF SCIENTIFIC THEORY
## Units, Types, Processes, and Concepts

### When Anthropology Professionalized

General anthropology treatises or college textbooks written by Americans during about 40 years have presented students with a doctrinal array of just those taxonomic, process, and other concepts which hove in sight during the first decades of the twentieth century. Some concepts, such as diffusion and culture area, were not original with anthropologists but were adapted from nineteenth century geographers and other authors for remodeling within new contexts. The seemingly novel ideological paraphernalia received only limited employment by early twentieth century anthropologists themselves. Most of their once blooming cerebral flowers show signs of having lost every vestige of former fragrance. They are ignored, if not forgotten, by many contemporary anthropologists.

Some of the early twentieth century tools for thinking about method and theory in sociocultural anthropology were patently expressions of a long period, from the 1860's on, whose orientation centered on historicism. Scientific sophistication in general anthropology about even initial procedures, such as slicing and arranging of nonwestern phenomena, was a little less than it is today.

Sound thinking in terms of the philosophy of science is neither general nor impressive in contemporary behavorial science circles. Social scientists, including the anthropologists, are members of an exceedingly malnourished, young, and inexperienced fraternity. After the long twilight, from the 1850's to the 1920's, during which many of its anthropological members were history inclined, they have surrendered in large numbers to fear-generated compulsions to engage in stiffnecked exorcisms, verbigerative prolixity, terminological gobbledygook, imitations of self-appointed and longwinded arbiters of correct method, mathematics fetishism, and interests in correlations, some of them comically petty, which are most securely attested by everything except additional field researches which they have no intention of pursuing. In sociocultural anthropology there seems to be only meager interest in speculative theory which looks promising for even tiptoed advances in hitherto superficially explored subjects.

Progress is, nevertheless, being made in anthropology since the auspicious

5

dismissal, by Professor Franz Boas[1] and many others, of nineteenth century evolutionism and its majestic global historicism. But advances in cultural anthropology are uneven or timorous. They occur in the presence of galling barriers of frequently badly trained personnel, rigidities about methodology, myopias and fundamentalism about theory, and entrapment by father figures of dwarf size. Students come to general anthropology and its cultural anthropology sector, as to each other social science, with hope that they will be presented a mature field of inquiry and that ample, if not garish, chunks of knowledge will be served on golden platters to them. The most valuable contributions which can be made to their education, apart from presentations of some postulates about the complexity and worth of nonliterate peoples and the methods of understanding them, are to show the maturity or immaturity of each facet of each social science, the necessity for recooking or further slicing the often unpalatable nutriment on the modest platters, and the preconditions for improved explorations and explosive advances.

Concepts which the earliest anthropologists possessed for identification and ordering of expressive, that is, cultural features of nonliterate societies and of their structural characteristics had become distinctive during the late 1890's. It was then that the field of general anthropology, begun only some 30 or 40 years earlier in writings by contemporaries of Darwin—Waitz, McLennan, Bachofen, Lubbock, Morgan, and Tylor are outstanding—developed its first cadres of professional field research workers, its first university curricula leading to the doctoral degree, and its first more or less professionalized university teachers of the subject. Make note of the fact that the date for multifaceted professionalization of both social and cultural anthropology was approximately 1895–1900, generations after other sciences such as astronomy, physics, and chemistry were well on their way. No distinction was made until the 1920's or later between the anthropological field's social (patterned relationships) and cultural (patterned expressive) subdivisions. Terms which stood at the start of the century for a unitary area of scientific inquiry were ethnography, ethnology, or, preferably, general anthropology.

University or professionally sanctioned departments or professors of the subject were rare before 1900, both in Europe and America, and continued to be few until the 1930's. Until the 1950's general anthropology remained an academic stepchild, a largely or wholly ignored campus epiphenomenon. In most instances its nurturing, where it gained recognition at all, took the form of one or two vagrant members of a stuffily hospitable department of sociology. This subordinate status remains in many larger colleges whose administrations do not understand the need to grant anthropological vistas to mid-twentieth century youngsters. In small colleges

---

[1] 1858–1942. He was professor at Columbia University, New York, after the late 1890's.

sociologists only too often receive the assignment to teach the subject, in almost all instances with unawareness of their incapacity to present most of its topics.

Before 1900 a layman in the United States who desired a professional statement about an anthropological question might go, to be sure, to the Bureau of American Ethnology in the Smithsonian Institution, the American Museum of Natural History in New York, the Field Museum in Chicago, the Milwaukee Public Museum, or a very few comparable non-teaching establishments. In Europe he might also appeal to a museum curator or, again, a rare individual professor in a leading university.

Before 1900 most writings on sociocultural anthropology were by a variety of persons, including ship captains, missionaries, and colonial officers, who were interested for different sorts of reasons in nonliterate peoples, not by members of a scientific association which tried to establish professional standards of training and which was dedicated to advances of knowledge in the field. Amateurism, collecting, cataloging, and historical motivations, rarely scientific inquirism as such, dominated general anthropology.

The heritage whereby any nonscientist who speaks or writes about nonliterate folk may receive a degree of naïvely confident public acceptance continues to the present day partly because commercial publishers, including some university presses, and certainly purveyors of those opiates for suburbia, the Sunday newspapers, feel no strong criticism if they print materials on nonwestern peoples by pretentious or untrained amateurs. Nonscientists' books on subjects such as nonwestern religions, folklores, and arts are as widely purchasable as they were years ago and, then as now, their principal function has been to bewilder or misinform readers. A sensible anthropologist initiates his college lecture course on general anthropology, languages of the world, arts, folklores, religions, or social structures with citations of cloth-bound and paperback books, some of them new, against which people who wish to understand the subject require resolute warnings. An area of scientific inquiry such as chemistry or physics does not need the grim and lengthy list of uncommendable publications which anthropology calls for. Its often drily written scientific presentations are almost everywhere intercepted by elegantly penned and printed trash. Paperback reprints of treatises published decades ago, some during the nineteenth century, and which were scientifically comely in the intellectual environment which had nourished them, are sold without sophisticated prefaces which phrase where they stood in the earlier history of the anthropological sciences.

What were some of the important premises held and concepts to which writers resorted from the time of the subject's beginnings in the 1850's and 1860's and up to professionalization of the field around 1900? Premises, concepts, and the like were those of Europe's own intellectual heritage and world view. But its convictions regarding non-Europeans flowed especially from rationalizations and defenses against feelings of guilt consequent upon centuries of savage manner of entry into and progressive domination of nonliterate peoples. Such peoples were of inferior races. They were brutish, primitive, uncivilized. They were savages, barbarians, dirty, like animals. They spoke primitive languages which had only simple grammars, if any, and they used only a few sounds, some of them guttural. They believed in devils and were trapped by their witch doctors. Their religions and gods were false. They had wild dances and were much too often lecherous, if not continually promiscuous. Polygamy had to be stopped. Their womenfolk were little better off than slaves. Their societies were stalled on earlier stages of evolution. They were unprogressive. It was impossible to civilize them. They lived idyllically in a state of nature and had the minds of children. Those who were food gatherers survived wretchedly and maybe even ate grubs, grasshoppers, and meat with the fur on. They had vision and hearing so remarkable that they could track like a dog and perceive things in the woods and at distances beyond the capacity of a European. Like summer session students on contemporary American university campuses, many of these shameless nonwestern subhumans sauntered forth barefoot and virtually naked.

Any reader of late nineteenth century authors, whether of novels, general anthropology, grandiose evolutionist schemes, or encyclopedic lists and comparisons of savage ways the world over, could multiply the array of horrors or beatitudes articulated by Victorian romantics and their predecessors. In an intellectual climate of such composition it seems almost miraculous that by the end of the century a few maverick thinkers felt supported by other Victorian currents of democratic, liberal, and humanitarian kinds. A German liberal such as Professor Boas could comfortably replace antiquated axioms of racist Euro-Americans' defensive world view with foundation stones of another system of much more probable as well as humanitarian formulations about nonliterate peoples.

## Boas

Future historians of general anthropology are likely to assess Boas' contribution toward undermining of nineteenth century depreciatory or idiotically romantic convictions about the worth of nonliterate peoples and their heritages as more important, scientifically, than his stimulation of students and his especially original researches in physical anthropology, linguistics, and plastic-graphic arts. The contribution can be examined in the 1911 edition of *The Mind of Primitive Man*. Decades later, Boas had not wholly divested himself of nineteenth century condescension about some nonwestern cultural expressions, although he had succeeded completely before 1911 in shedding racist conceits. What he did, however, was to make it possible for a succeeding generation of professionally trained sociocultural anthropologists to reap the harvest that he and other liberals had sown. His formulations allowed his own pupils and disciples to follow through to conclusions which the logic of his antiracist and antievolutionist presentations entailed. He regarded nonwestern music, for example, as deserving of dispassionate scientific manipulations exactly like nonwestern languages, although he had small regard for the music of some nonliterate peoples. Nevertheless his students were enabled to perceive all nonwestern cultural expressions as wholly worthy products of intelligence, creativity, and artistry. Boas, and a few of his most humane contemporaries, for the most part only pressed buttons. Their students and readers were directly released to open hitherto shut doors which had blocked understanding and appreciation of cultural output, especially so among the economically most retarded peoples. Possibly no other individual played a more decisive role than Boas in the birth of a new era of respect for all peoples' cultural potentials, complexity, and creativity, and of total rejection of premises that some peoples were genetically better than others. During the infant years of that epoch many persons were thereby freed to do new kinds of work in the set of scientific disciplines which comprise general anthropology.

It is of utmost significance that in the decades of such an offering, the late 1890's and after, groups of anthropologists who never heard Boas' compact and meaty lectures, or who either did not comprehend the consequences of his premises or rejected them, produced coteries of followers who made no important bequests to the fund of opinions and values which centered acceptance of worth in nonliterate peoples' cultural forms. Little or nothing was done to facilitate release from the strangling heritage of conceits about Europeans' sociocultural superiorities by twentieth century European protagonists of *Kulturkreis* or "culture circle" premises and method from 1900 on; by British so-called "social anthropologists" from early in the 1920's and distinguished for their antievolutionist zeal, antihistoricism, and antidiffusionist views; or by anguished resuscitators, from the 1930's on, of portions of nineteenth century social evolutionism disguised as a study of societal dynamics caused primarily by technological factors and changes. Cultural geographers, cross-culturally oriented sociologists, historians, philosophers, Marxist theoreticians, Freudians, Jungians, and a variety of other writers on cross-cultural topics likewise did relatively little in the matter. They did little or nothing to counter nineteenth century presumptions about all nonliterate peoples' simplicity or crudities. Boas' most important legacy, which was a point of view, may have come into existence and spread about anyway during the twentieth century as a result of forces and currents in the socioeconomic life of the world's peoples. It seems to be one of the subtlest, but very likely the most crucial, of ideological triggerings ever witnessed in effecting a transformation in an era's self-identity, world view, and values. In this respect the implications in Boas' classroom lectures and seminars at Columbia University, only less so in his writings, were electrifying. Most of his students sensed what his criticisms of nineteenth century stereotypes about nonliterate peoples really led to. No other social scientist or thinker of nineteenth or early twentieth century ideological rooting produced this special kind of impact upon classroom audiences. If "the idea of progress" was a fundamental ideological theme among Euro-Americans during the eighteenth and nineteenth centuries, the twentieth may be witnessing, partly because of Boas, the worldwide rooting and rapid sprouting everywhere of a theme which may be phrased something like "acceptance of the possibility of equal complexity and worth in cultural expressions of all peoples."

Especially significant today is the contrast of this nascent theme with atavistic components of Marxist thought which, in spite of much superficial defensive commentary about colonial and exploited peoples, is not really accepting of potentials or merit in their prevailingly abstract arts or other cultural expressions. Marxists have long proposed studies of such peoples more for the sake of reconstructing historical developments and of displaying operations of socioeconomic factors than for the purpose of developing systems of scientific theory about cultural products or of exhibiting worth in such creativity. Marxism, which among other things does remain a projective expression of humanitarian values of the early nineteenth century, has retained the primacy of pursuit of historical perspectives and of the consequences of technological, productive, and other material factors. Severely scientific analyses of cultural expressions among nonliterate peoples or deductions that their cultures were worthy are hardly possible for Marxists because of ritualistic intrusion of century old axioms.

Many discussants of Boas have utilized statements in his writings to show that his stress, too, was historical, and doubtless it was during earlier decades of his long career. Some of his most famous students asserted that he stood at all times for employment of the method of mapping culture traits as a principal means of offering a sound basis for short perspective historical deductions. But in 1927 Boas said to me that he then thought ultimate statements, ideological foundation stones, about the world's nonliterate peoples had to be in psychological, not historical or descriptive ethnographical, terms. He was saying, in effect, that his earlier insistence upon a diffusionist and historicist position had been only a way station to psychological formulations and that the latter were fundamental. He often spoke simplistically as everyone does in conversations. But he was clear that theory about nonliterate peoples must be many-sided. He had concluded that exorcism of psychological statements, such as characterized preachments of the English social anthropologist Radcliffe-Brown at one point in his career and which still features a number of noncultural anthropologists, is destructive to the advance of scientific knowledge. A great many feeble, if not outrageous, psychological statements are bound to accompany good ones in the course of development of cultural anthropology. Psychologizing should not be condemned but sifted judiciously to fit the most valid formulations into a many-faceted system of scientific theory.

During the first decades of the twentieth century, cultural anthropologists such as Boas in the United States and a few in England and Europe, appear to have felt that they had the conceptual implements they needed. They seem to have been little motivated to discover or devise fresh ones which would serve even better in advancing descriptive or theoretical knowledge. Concepts such as diffusion, culture area, and culture element upon which some of them then relied or, rather, which they did not use but to which they repeatedly genuflected, had been partial factors in a sensational release of a very young set of scientific disciplines from the fanciful system-building which had characterized many nineteenth century sociocultural evolutionists. The new ideological gear and some critical canons of method had also helped to expose undiscriminating ransackers, like the English classical scholar James G. Frazer (*The Golden Bough*), of comparative sociocultural items from anywhere and everywhere. After the 1890's many professional anthropologists strove to show all the features of social organization and culture that were present in a "tribe," to depict larger geographical areas and something of the multiple "tribal" heritages in them, and to cite evidences for modestly local or district spreadings of features of those heritages. Anthropologists were unaware that they were thereby surrendering a commitment which is also integral with science. It was to establish, as in any more mature scientific system, such as organic chemistry, relatively firm components of a theoretical structure, that is, a fabric of interconnected hypotheses about processes and classes of units. Anthropologists now supposed that they were making their proper and sufficient contribution by being energetically unspeculative, factual, and descriptive, and by explicitly opposing the notion that there were worldwide "laws" in the form of regularities in customs, beliefs, and institutions the world over, except for an omnipresent process of usually rather slow spread of sociocultural items. Fabrics of theory had become deservedly in disrepute in behavioral sciences, as was the so-called "comparative method" as represented by Frazer. Several late nineteenth century ventures of various kinds had been characterized by irresponsibility hidden behind grandeur of scheme and, sometimes, felicity of writing. In anthropological quarters, where innocence about the philosophy of science was rampant, and every scientific profession does contain a rank and file who artlessly parrot methodology and theory, the very terms "theory," "system," "speculation," "cultural evolution," and "comparative method" had become derogatory. Minor anthropologists of the new twentieth century vintage were not only fiercely antievolutionist and sternly prodiffusionist. They airily confused theory with methods of field interviewing, collecting, recording, and cataloging of data. Many took pride in a free-floating negativism, which they gravely called "criticalmindedness," about any premises or ideological appliances except those in the small stock of descriptive and classificatory tools which Boas had only lately offered in order to display fatal errors in late nineteenth century unilinear evolutionary schemes. Pieces in the Boasian reserve of conceptual bric-a-brac now appeared to them to supply the only solid foundations for scientific advances in anthropology. Indeed, the tiny bag of Boasian concepts did not interfere with monumental fact collecting by Boas and by his era's admirably dedicated field research workers. A salient contribution of the new concepts was that although they appear today to have been little better than mumbo jumbo neologisms in the rites of a cult, they functioned rather well, during a 40- to 50-year stretch from 1900 to the 1940's, in maintaining a nearly total eclipse of patently ridiculous evolutionist and comparativist orientations applied to societies and cultures. The neologisms, to be discussed immediately below, provided a psychological defensive system which enhanced the still few and lonely anthropologists' egos and allowed their articulators to conduct field work within a small region with magnificent energy and comprehensive theorylessness. Repugnant doctrines were held at a distance and hardly looked at with a telescope. For was not speculation as impudent or immoral as nineteenth century cultural evolutionism and the comparative method? The job was to collect and collect and collect tough hard facts about a "tribe" and list them in big batches, each batch a chapter with a familiar title like "material culture," "family," "religion," and so on.

The following paragraphs cite the principal concepts which bolstered anthropologists' defenses against speculative upsurges during an initial period of hostility to the previous century's methods, theory, and historical horizons. There was something singularly pure about Boasians' passion for irrefragable and irridescent truth by way of field fact collecting without history or theory.

## Culture Element

Units called "culture elements" were cardinal items in the new kit. The terms "elements" and "traits" appear to have been regarded as synonymous. They referred to a great many thousands of presumed units of behavior, custom, beliefs, relationships, art designs, linguistic details, and what not. They were indivisible entities usually, like little beads, although they exhibited a vast range of shapes, colors, textures, and weights. They constituted the inventory of content, the astronomical quantity of content, in a sociocultural heritage. Neither Boas nor other anthropologists vouchsafed either rough or knife sharp methods for identification of these myriad monads or for depiction of contrasts between similar ones. During unremitting field labors, Boasians happily gathered great quantities of what they perceived to be elements. Anthropologists blandly respected each other's perception or citation of a trait except in an instance where one could be shown to be more aptly regarded as a composite of smaller elements. Anthropologists did not arrange their enormously long element lists in sets or classes other than the then customary principal divisions of a "culture" such as material culture or technology, social organization, clans, religion, magic, and arts. Each such accredited, if not banal, topical division within a sociocultural group comprised, they felt, many hundreds or some thousands of their monads.

Note also that during those decades the word "culture" was all inclusive. It stood for technology, economics, social structure, and cultural or expressive sectors of a community. The definition traced back at least to Edward B. Tylor's famous introductory statement in his estimable *Primitive Culture* published in 1871. Even today many American anthropologists continue to employ "culture" in the comprehensive manner in which Tylor defined it. A culture element might be, then, a feature of social structure, an item in religion or one of the arts, or a kind of emotional response. At no time, from Boas to the most recent employment of a concept of culture traits, was there effort to classify different kinds of culture monads and to present razor sharp criteria for their identification as of one or another type. This deficiency contrasts almost shockingly with explicit phrasings by modern linguists of means for distinguishing their diverse sets of fundamental units such as phonemes, allophones, morphemes, and allomorphs.

## Culture Complex

Boasians regarded various elements as tied in with some central elements to constitute a culture complex. Illustrations which they gave included the North American Plains horse complex of traits studied by Clark Wissler, that area's Sun Dance complex charted by Leslie Spier, and East Africa's so-called "cattle complex" described by Melville J. Herskovits. Some Boasians took for granted the fact that thousands of analogous element complexes could be identified around the planet and that methodologically this ought to be done eventually. It would appear that the culture complex concept flowed partly from anxious feelings concerning the gigantic and wholly unpatterned or unarranged lists of ill-defined unitary traits. Obviously a people's way of life and beliefs could not constitute something analogous to an enormous container holding thousands of diverse beads. Some beads were strung together to constitute a culture complex. But no one suggested how many such complexes or strings of beads constituted a fraction of the container's contents, how small or large that fraction was, or what the percent might be of remaining discrete elements which were not tied with other elements into element complexes. Protagonists of trait aggregates did not offer hypotheses regarding dimensions, origins, speeds of change, or contrasts in types of culture complexes. No theoretical questions were asked or deductions about process and change facilitated by employment of a concept of culture complex. It was hardly even a rough and ready delineative tool. It was a supposed tool which really served to guard against feelings that the culture element concept was ill-defined, meaninglessly atomistic, and in fact ridiculously useless for studies of different types of processes. By the 1930's snide critics, who included some pupils of Boas, were referring to other Boasians' element lists, with their occasional clusters or complexes, as "laundry lists."

Disdain for the nineteenth century's historicist speculations about stages of social, cultural, linguistic, and esthetic evolution, and irritation over shabby genteel collecting of odds and ends by writers who had surveyed this or that "tribe," reached greatest intensity during the 1900 to 1920 period. It was then that several excellent field workers and theoreticians, including the brilliant anthropological linguist and Boas pupil Edward Sapir, wrote out at some length and with clarity a rationale for utilization of culture trait and culture complex concepts so as to permit peeks into the recent past. Short time span reconstructions of spreads of traits and complexes appeared reasonable and no other justification for mapping their distributions seemed necessary. Boas' apparent thought was that such truncated and modest historical perspectives would nevertheless help to reveal processes of change and that these would expose the superficiality of unilinear evolutionist stage sequences which had included relatively simple formulations, if any at all, about causes of change.

Functions of the mechanical notions of culture elements and complexes flowed from an essential simplicity in the new concepts. They also served, very well indeed, to expose the recklessness in pseudohistorical chimeras which had fascinated a preceding era of cultural evolutionists who had thought in grandiose time spans. Culture elements felt right, too, because they resembled somehow the then clear-cut atoms of physics and neat cells of biology. In their time, atoms and cells were magnificent conceptual advances. So too was Boasian anthropology's veiled monadism with its culture elements and complexes. During the epoch of anthropological monadism it looked as if the young science, through Boas primarily, had emerged from mists of a fantasy world of layered stages in time and forthrightly had gotten down to hardheaded scientific business. Time reconstructions now allowed legitimate vistas of only recent centuries and then merely for a few traits and complexes, some of them rather unimportant, certainly not thousands or tens of thousands of years with their breathtaking views of the most vital things in culture history. Archaeology continued to offer fragmentary insights with its pick and shovel methods and the support it received from sociocultural anthropology's understanding of food-gathering and agriculturally modest peoples.

Were not virtually all protagonists of culture elements at last digging up their neat monads with a fine question and answer technique out in anthropology's one ideal laboratory, the field situation with its very alive native informants? Neither there nor upon campus quadrangles were anthropologists pyramiding guesses and refining myths, that is, fascinating dramatic plots and pictures about evolutionary stages or anything else in top-heavy systems whose bases in secure premises had hardly been laid. Industrious field workers were talking with pride and laconicism about proper units as in more mature sciences. They were discussing "real" units, not stages of evolution which a dreamer produced out of wishful whimsies and which could not be seen, photographed, measured, or checked in a field interview with an informant. The few specialists in the philosophy of science who took note of what was going on in anthropology interpreted favorably what they saw and read. They respected the sobriety with which a small coterie of Boasian anthropologists was eschewing nineteenth century pile-ups of undocumented historical hypotheses. They nodded approvingly at an evident clearing of a forest of unsubstantiated dogmas and pseudo-historical reconstructions, and they were impressed by the healthy resort to new and simple units and to careful collecting of unitary facts at first hand, often in the very medium of a nonliterate group's language. Data gathering by ship captains, explorers, naturalists, colonial officers, and missionaries, and effusions by quixotic theoreticians on cultural evolution were being superceded. Punctilious, if not straight-laced, scientists were now sources of the most detailed and reliable knowledge of the world's nonwestern folk. Pretty dreams of historicist theory were being cleared away as so much antiscientific debris. The distinguished writer on the philosophy of science, Morris R. Cohen, revered Boas as the greatest con-tributor among the small bands of social scientists following Tylor. Im-portant contemporaries of Boas such as Durkheim, Weber, and Freud were still in the shadows and, where noticed, a little distrusted because they were not field collectors among nonwestern peoples and they wrote out fabrics of theory at goodly length, after the fashion of nineteenth century minds. For all his roots in the preceding century, Boas made no one nervous with social evolutionist or theoretical writing about long historical perspectives. He penned without embroidery and guesswork. He was like a twentieth century mathematician who offers a fine new idea in a one-page paper. Such crystalline precision and terseness were almost beautiful in an environ-ment of sociological logorrhea and following a period of flashy system building about the origins of society and culture. Boas did not erect memorial columns composed of unvalidated hypotheses about ancient civilizations and tribal peoples.

A question which is easier to answer today than in 1920 or 1930 was whether new seeds which might grow and flower in cultural anthropology were being planted in clearings burned out in its old forests by Boas. The answer is affirmative for anthropological linguistics and plastic-graphic arts, as discussed in later chapters where Boas' creative role is indicated in these special fields. In them his too-stiff or too-loose concepts of culture elements, culture complexes, and culture areas did not interfere with his formidable scientific achievements.

As mentioned in opening remarks about him, Boas was serving con-tinually as no other social scientist of the era in introducing a climate of respect for the worth and complexity of all the world's economically lowlier peoples. The dimensions of his accomplishment here may be appreciated when it is realized that Durkheim, Weber, Freud, Toynbee, and many other great names of the decades immediately after 1900 contributed virtually nothing toward acceptance of probable worth in the cultural expressions of nonwestern peoples of lowliest economy. Such a testament has become one of the axioms which guide cultural anthropology's ideology and scientific operations today. Probably it is Boas' greatest contribution.

## Culture Area

Boas and his large following operated with additional ideological equipment. From about 1914 to the 1940's American anthropologists who referred repetitively to ambiguous culture elements and complexes also spoke cheerily of large American Indian culture areas and analogous large ones of Oceania and Africa. Boas' earliest students Clark Wissler and Alfred L. Kroeber were principal purveyors of the culture area concept, Wissler in several books from 1914 on, Kroeber much later and notably in a valiant intellectual effort published in the 1940's.

From 1914 until the 1940's many American anthropologists were interested in doing something scientific, if possible, with their new culture areas. They drew wide belts rather than sharp boundary lines around seven, eight, or nine vast regions of North America and a similar number of enigmatic areas each in South America and Africa. A few professors hazarded analogous line drawing around Oceanian culture areas. Such labors were classificatory, of a kind. Anthropologists differed in the inventory of maybe one or two culture complexes and always ten or fifteen outstanding—whatever that meant—traits to which they resorted in efforts to characterize components of heritage shared by scores of intergrading sociocultural groups resident in a so-called "area." The taxonomy of areas of culture comprised selections of what American anthropologists intuited as distinctive and diagnostic traits for also intuited "most typical" groups resident more or less centrally in an area. It was appreciated, indeed axiomatic, that such diagnostic features thinned out with approach to an area's margins. Few anthropologists realized that the traits they selected were merely those which a culture-bound observer found to be conspicuous to him rather than demonstrably central in a sociocultural system.

The significant point is that protagonists of arrangements of large culture areas ignored or lacked a frame of theory which permitted a degree of objectivity in choosing and weighing distinctive or typical traits in each of their areas. From the point of view of theory about what is important in operations of a sociocultural system, an unimportant trait which caught an anthropologist's fancy might be listed by him as one of ten to twenty main characteristic features of a culture area. For example, persons who, like Wissler, cited outstanding traits of an Eskimo culture area always mentioned the Sedna "goddess" of Arctic mythologies. But students of anthropology were not told why she ranked, in cultures each of which everyone knew had thousands and thousands of traits, among the first fifteen or twenty in deservedness of citation. When Wissler and others listed diagnostic features of the Pacific Northwest Coast culture area, they always attested the vital role of potlatches, although their many functions in the region's extremely variable manifestations of economic and social life were, then as now, accorded no differential weights from district to district. In fact, anthropologists today who do not classify the world's peoples in terms of Wissler's, Kroeber's, and others' culture areas appear to have been so hypnotized by the intuitions or projections of advocates of culture area taxonomy that selections of traits of that period in anthropology usually remain uncriticized today. Who even now would deny the overweening socioeconomic and maybe also the cultural importance of potlatches on the Pacific Northwest Coast? Does anyone question that potlatching really counted among twenty most important characteristics among thousands found in the region? To be sure, the question needs asking and, then, answering.

Like culture elements and culture complexes, culture areas were so subjectively defined and of such geographically enormous dimensions that they were irrelevant for purposes of revelation of or scientific inventorying of classes of significant units, for taxonomic needs in a system of scientific knowledge, or for movement toward maturation of any portion of a structure of scientific theory. It is moot if they can help today in the small contribution which Kroeber and others were urging, during the 1940's, that they might provide: aid in determining relative ages of sociocultural features within a vast region.

The culture area concept assuredly had and will long continue to have a rough utility in assigning specimens to cases and exhibition rooms in museums and in disclosing to very young people how varied the world's nonliterate peoples were in economic and sociocultural respects. Neither of these two practical services bears implications for scientific advances or for the education of intelligences which, although young, can comprehend something of the philosophy of science. Lucubrations and exertions, such as Kroeber's belated and courageous endeavors, which are designed to squeeze pettifogging scientific dividends out of culture area classifications of the world's peoples are futile. The future of the culture area concept in scientific work is close to absolute zero.

## Culture Center and Marginal Culture

The intuitively defined micro-unit, the culture trait or element, and the several macro-units, culture complex and culture area, of the first decades of the century were augmented by a few classificatory concepts which never received frequent mention or utilization, but which served as defenses against feelings that other Boasian concepts proffered too simple a set of tools. And so anthropologists cited the culture center and marginal cultures. No one presented precise criteria by which two anthropologists might agree on "most typical" groups which were central in a culture area, or groups which partook of characteristics of adjacent areas to a point where it was almost arbitrary whether they be categorized as marginal, that is, in one or the other area or perched along a border. Obviously more of the world's peoples were marginal rather than resident at or close to culture centers.

So much for the kinds of micro- and macro-units which, in spite of strictures against their potentials to further scientific theory, constituted an advance in their era. They intercepted ethnocentric characterizations by nineteenth century evolutionist writers of sociocultural wholes as savage, barbarian, primitive, or civilized. They were a move in the direction of better scientific method.

## Sociocultural Evolution

Evolutionists had also had something to say about causes of sociocultural change. A principal dogma to which most of them adhered was that a sociocultural system at long length tended to evolve onwards, upwards, to a level or stage which was higher, whatever that approving adjective meant. And that each social or cultural sector—the family, folklore, religion, language, or art—of such a system was also inclined somehow to evolve or progress to a higher level. Boas and his group explicitly rejected such "unilinear evolutionism," as they termed it, largely because they realized that a supposed dynamic process of evolutionary change from lower to higher forms within a tribe or system was inoperative in the light of extensive borrowing of sociocultural items from contiguous peoples. Borrowing or diffusion was patent, and evolutionary change was poorly evidenced except for basic features of technology such as cutting tools. Details of unilinear evolutionist rhapsodies about stages in the "early" history of marriage, the family, religion, and so on need not interest us any more in this chapter. But passing mention is warranted of social evolution's importance, indeed dominance and radiance, in the glowing optimism and intellectual climate of the Victorian era with its new world view lit up by Darwinian rocketry. During almost two generations from the 1860's on, an enormous public of readers of nonfiction was enthralled by the brilliant vistas of early sociocultural history offered by unilinear evolutionist writers. Their portraitures suffered few blemishes from dull borrowings of culture elements and complexes. Although paperbacks on general anthropology enjoy prodigious sales today, all offer relatively colorless depictions beside the exciting fantasms of contributions to the dream world which sociocultural evolutionists were presenting as bygone reality. The several chapters to follow cite some of their special theories of stages of progress from most primitive to most advanced.

## Diffusion

During the 1890's Boas and, much later, his followers, from Clark Wissler to a considerable number of contemporary anthropologists, supplemented their new micro- and macro-units with a simplistic as well as dry formulation about a principal cause of sociocultural change. They thought it the most important, dynamic process in the history or prehistory of nonliterate peoples. It was borrowing, dissemination, diffusion of culture traits. They indicated that such spreads also featured remodeling of traits rather than unchanged borrowings. Here is a hypothesis not about units or classes of units but about process which introduces and shapes all units: there is repetitive regularity in change, it is consequent upon sociocultural diffusion, and nothing which is diffused remains wholly unaltered when borrowers accept transmission to them.

It would be wrong to depreciate the importance, for the period of about 1900 to the 1920's, of the diffusion and remodeling hypothesis. It constituted an admirable and comfortingly plausible alternative to the mystical sweetness and light of many Victorian minds with their gentle faith, recognizably a projection, in the inevitability of progress and in largely undelineated forces that were very kind to human beings because in every part of the world they made for advance from level to level, stage to stage, to ever better things and ways.

Boas had only borrowed the formulation about diffusion from various writers before him. After it had made its impact upon anthropologists, there was never a doubt that well over 95 percent of a nonliterate group's sociocultural heritage, if it could be split into minute units such as culture elements and macro-units such as culture complexes, was traceable to, although never exactly identical with, features found in each of its immediately adjacent neighbors. Therefore somebody must have borrowed from somebody. Direction of acquisition, dating of it too, remained to be ascertained. One of many troubles with this process hypothesis was that psychological or any other kinds of causes for failures of traits to diffuse— for some to diffuse slowly, for others to diffuse rapidly, for many to receive drastic reshaping after their dissemination, for many to spread together in bundles of items, and so on—were as much in the dark as ever. Obviously, citation and highlighting of a process of culture element dispersion was a valuable contribution in the 1890's and right after that because it unveiled the absurdity of some evolutionists' persuasion that most of a group's heritage had bubbled up like a geyser entirely within that group. The hypothesis also implied a need to explore the many processes of creative change that remained hidden under an exceedingly generalized concept represented by the caption of diffusion.

Although need to identify distinctive processes was quickly perceived by more perceptive diffusionists during the first decades of the century, the subject of sociocultural change among nonliterate peoples received extremely little serious examination until mid-century. After all, anthropologists were few and their main business was now field researches, data gathering, and catalog descriptivism, not theory. Some of them who were diffusionists offered lip service to correlated concepts which were, however, not really indicative of processes because they lacked exacting detail and psychological formulation. Mention was made, for example, of *independent inventions*. It was pointed out that agriculture, to cite illustrations often given, was probably invented at least twice, as were the lost wax method of casting, bronze metallurgy, hieroglyphic writing, certain astronomical predictions, the zero concept, domestications of animals, and hundreds of other culture traits and complexes. Some of these parallel inventions were so parallel that a kind of technical term, *parallels*, which revealed precisely nothing about process, punctuated anthropological writings. A similar or identical concept, with the same built-in limitation, was called *convergent development*. These were crudely descriptive not processual concepts. They pointed usefully to similar phenomena in historically unconnected districts without being able to suggest causes for the similarities. They contributed nothing to theory.

One among the few descriptive concepts which enclosed a hint about mechanisms of process and which subsumed a vast class of culture traits under it had emerged early in writings of sociocultural evolutionists like Tylor, decades before 1900. This was the concept of *survivals*, borrowed from evolutionist biology, which during the 1920's merged into cultural sociologists' concept to which they assigned the term *lag*. It is neither necessary nor fruitful to inquire why those specialists resorted to a new label, but it is advisable to warn readers that the inventiveness of behavioral scientists in coining terms during the first half of the twentieth century perhaps far exceeded all their other forms of sadomasochism and creativity. The pleasant notion of somewhat archaic items and vestigia which did not seem to wither away (like Marxists say the State will under their system) with features of society and culture to which they had once been aligned, continued to be alluded to during the era of culture elements, culture areas, and diffusion. Diffusionists respected the validity of a concept of survivals or lag when it was torn from its earlier context of evolutionary stages. A diffusionist might be heard lecturing, for example, about the harpsichord and viola da gamba as instances of miscellanea from an earlier day when they had functioned differently from their feeble modern roles in music performance. In clothing, lapel buttonholes and men's suits' sleeve buttons are seemingly nonfunctioning survivals from an epoch when they rendered quite practical services. Every sociocultural inventory, Ojibwa, Korean, or Ibo, contained such cultural lags. Diffusionists pointed out ad nauseam that sociocultural survivals were not evidences of evolutionary stages as wholes, unlike the vestigia left from earlier stages of biological evolution. Vestigia line up in extremely different classes and roles; social and biological each comprise their own classes of items. Diffusionists did not often bother to say more, or to indicate that sufficient causes responsible for an apparent lag and for psychological services still provided by a vestigial feature needed to be sought. Again, diffusionists retained a ticket for a class of phenomena, sociocultural survivals, but did not interest themselves in developing a subsystem of theory which stated multiple sociocultural processes very likely involved in the class, and their striking differences from biological processes and survivals.

Boasian diffusionism did emphasize the cumulative importance of processes that consisted centrally of spreads, with remodelings, of innumerable traits from nonliterate group to immediately adjacent group. Such diffusion was paralleled by several varieties of claimed diffusionist processes which Boas and his followers rejected as untenable. It is of great interest that at a particular moment in the intellectual development of western civilization, a set of disparate diffusionist positions appeared. Each apparently served its author or authors as means of accounting for phenomena which protagonists of sociocultural evolution had been unable to explain. Nineteenth century global historicism managed to survive in a guarded way in diffusionists' aims.

### Kulturkreislehre

One variety of diffusionism appeared in the culture circle or *Kulturkreise* coterie whose thinking had effervesced during the first decade of the century in writings by Leo Frobenius, Fritz Graebner, and other Europeans. The group's position was elaborated, systematized, and long maintained by Pater Wilhelm Schmidt of Vienna and his followers, almost all of them native speakers of German. The group seems to have disintegrated after 1945 and nobody conspicuously upholds its scheme today.

*Kulturkreis* doctrine was elaborate but, most briefly and maybe even unfairly, it amounted to a selective salvaging of nineteenth century evolutionist stage notions and their synthesis with nineteenth century diffusionist predilections. It is wholly pre-twentieth century in its presumptions. There was an extensive pyramiding of premises regarding successive amalgamations of certain kinds of sociocultural traits and their spreads over considerable portions of the world, as in great tidal waves which journey thousands of miles. Each wave or culture circle (*Kulturkreis*) tended to be overlaid by a later spreading wave so that nonwestern regions or tribes of rather advanced economy, considerable wealth, and especially complicated social structure could be analyzed into component layers. A society might resemble a six or seven layer cake. Relative datings of its clusters of culture traits were offered confidently. Peoples of lowly economy comprised fewer layers. The essentially historical and age dating directions of interest of *Kulturkreis* workers did not in the least prevent many of them from engaging in enterprises of a much more twentieth century kind than was indicated in their premises. That is, they conducted field researches among nonliterate peoples and they did not neglect the economically lowliest of all, the food-gathering regions. In fact, the field research enthusiasm of Boasian diffusionists was paralleled in the numerous field researches of devotees of Viennese layer-cake historicism.

Today an impressive percentage of the ethnographic archives about nonwestern societies and cultures comes from dedicated people whose primarily historical and diffusional orientation of *Kulturkreis* persuasion frequently did little to refine or damage their field perceptions. But the mainstreams in twentieth century behavioral sciences were little attended to by *Kulturkreis* disciples, while some of the Boasians presently directed a wary eye toward new interests of colleagues in other behavioral sciences and in the British Isles. *Kulturkreis* over the European continent remained rigidly nineteenth century in its fabric of method and historicist aims. America's Boasian diffusionists in goodly numbers shed their Boasian garb. One after another of the Boasians metamorphosed in order to appear up-to-date. The changing fashions were dictated by glamorous infiltrators from psychoanalysis, British social anthropology, and American sociology and psychology. Many or most wearers of *Kulturkreis* togas continued to accept as axiomatic the primacy of historical goals rather than scientific discovery of new kinds of units, structures, processes, and the like, in addition to techniques of validation.

*Kulturkreis* devotees did not question that there had been massive diffusions of clustered traits (culture circles or *Kulturkreise*) across oceans as well as continents. Their point of view during decades generated blood pressure and acidulous statements among both rigid Boasian diffusionists and rebels who had repudiated Boasian interests and loyalties in order to embrace new values, explore virgin areas of scientific inquiry, and acquire social status among the potentates of other behavioral sciences, including those of Britain.

### Transoceanic Diffusion

A transoceanic virus of diffusionism has been endemic in anthropological quarters since *Kulturkreis* writings and lectures vanished. Lately its effects have been duplicated, elaborated, and enabled to reach extraordinary numbers of laymen through writings by a nonprofessional, Thor Heyerdahl. Forty or more years ago a leading French anthropologist, Paul Rivet, the most important pioneer in transcultural musicological transcription, the German musicologist Erich von Hornbostel, the American anthropologist Roland Dixon, and others were spreading an ideological infection which arose in their devil-may-care deduction that a variety of culture elements, not least entire languages, had reached South America from the South Pacific. A nonanthropologist, Leo Wiener of Harvard University, was at that time claiming Ethiopian language forms in Brazilian Indian languages, doubtless after they had skipped across both North Africa and the South Atlantic. During the nineteenth century many Old World philologists had thought they could connect Old World languages, such as those of Caucasus and Basque districts, with North American Indian languages and they pointed quixotically to likely Atlantic crossings during pre-Christian eras.

This type of diffusionism seems uncommonly sick, in the sense that its zealous protagonists appear to have their eyes glued on the great briny deeps. Recent decades of anthropologists who have been inoculated with this kind of maritime ailment display tepid concern about a slow creep of great numbers of features of technology, society, and culture on land masses, and they exhibit no curiosity whatever in discovery of the multiple factors which are vital in sociocultural creativity, changes, and remodelings. Dixon was a special case, however, for his interest in such processes was strong. But it did not affect his resistance, apparently slight, to the transoceanic contagion. All writers about cultural transmission across oceans, whether amateur like Wiener and Heyerdahl or professional like Rivet and Dixon, seem to have enjoyed a fevered fixation upon supposed transmissions across oceans of a few traits—not all of which seem likely to fashion essential sociocultural changes in recipients.

We read of balsa or other rafts, Chinese junks, and heaven knows what other types of craft that transported rare souls across thousands of miles of sea, doubtless with tongues horribly parched before land was sighted, with subsequent profound impacts upon the institutions of natives who sweetly received hapless and lonely survivors into their midst. At first those unfortunates could not even converse in their rescuers' languages. Still, they presently taught the amiable recipients of culture traits entirely new ways of speech, too.

Why introductions of a few new traits should generate fundamental or episodically significant transformations is never satisfactorily explained. But we have to deduce that the heroic or unheroic relics of fabulous oceanic voyages certainly went to town after they got to the beaches. Who knows what art designs, temple plazas, potlaches, clan systems, class systems, political systems, verb conjugations, pan pipes, and inferiority complexes were installed by one or two limp gentry whose throats failed to get carved where they finally lay athirsting on the shore thousands of miles from lagoons of origin?

Sociocultural dynamisms which might be involved in changes effected by such transoceanic accidents—and who can deny the possibility despite the implausibility of many of them—are never explored with a scientist's skepticism and caution by the tiny juntas of wide-eyed sea-hopping optimists. Nor is proof or disproof of their fancies about voyages likely until far more is known of the dynamics of borrowing in different kinds of sociocultural systems. Leaders of oceanic leapfroggism, from *Kulturkreis* writers to Heyerdahl and others, have offered nothing in even feebly supported statements regarding the distinctive and many processes of creativity, borrowing, and change in the many types of sociocultural structures. They have not shown an ability to weigh the import of what they assert was shipped by ocean freight. A system of scientific theory in sociocultural matters will have to bypass claims, not about transoceanic expeditions as such, but about their impacts and significance. For a time to come, cultural anthropology, social anthropology as well, must deal primarily with phenomena which are divisible, repetitive, patterned, judiciously weighed, capable of rechecking, and based upon unimpassioned field researches. Cultural anthropology has an obligation to conduct rigorous field investigations and close analyses of collected data, although speculative fancies are sometimes invaluable. They will deal with possibilities other than those latent in expeditions by plain rafts, sails, paddles, or hurricane propulsion. The point is that laymen and younger students are vital issues for a scientific profession. They need to be advised that some unromantic adjournment of a small handful of charlatans' assertions and of perfectly serious writers' unsupported convictions about ocean-borne diffusions is the policy of wisdom. And this is not a policy that is dull or unromantic. Galvanic intellectual interests, and without question infinitely more profitable ones, may be found in researches upon and revelations of how nonwestern sociocultural systems operated and how people affiliated with them grew, acted, thought, felt, and created. Nothing is more thrilling than discovery on a theoretical level, and nothing more trivial than transoceanic cargoes which add cheap tints to some petty historical perspectives, like the trashy photographer who used to retouch family portraits.

If any one thing has characterized sea lanes diffusionists apart from their compulsion to paddle canoes or float rafts across oceans, it is their profound disinterest in people, the creativity in people, and pursuit of scientific theory about people. Migrations and waves of travel enthusiasts of the nineteenth century and lyrical salt water hoppers of recent pseudoanthropological soliloquies have always shared a kind of chill uninvolvement in their fellow human beings and a hearty predilection for great historical perspectives, agonizing journeys, and the blustery outdoors.

## Nordenskiöld

Laborious and precise mapping by Boasians of culture elements in contiguous groups was paralleled by the superlative workmanship, from about 1910 to the 1930's, of Dr. Erland Nordenskiöld, of Sweden. He conducted field investigations in Paraguay, southern Brazil, and Panama and, unlike Boasians, supplemented his spot maps of field results with painstaking library researches which added quantities of material. No diffusionist produced more fully documented statements about spreadings of traits. But Nordenskiöld supplied no increments to knowledge of the workings of sociocultural systems.

## Diffusion from Egypt

An entirely different type of diffusionism, reckless to an extreme, was advocated during the same decades by the distinguished English specialist in anatomy Grafton Eliot Smith and his ally the English geographer W. J. Perry. Unlike the unexceptionable Nordenskiöld, these historicism-oriented nonanthropologists were assuredly minor figures in the development of the anthropological sciences. But their position somehow perturbed a few contemporaries, apparently because large numbers of laymen supposed that Smith was recognized as an anthropologist by anthropologists and that he was an authority on the origins and diffusion of cultures. Smith-Perry dogmas included premises about an overweening importance of technological and sociocultural stimuli which radiated around the world from ancient Egypt; craft, paddlers, conquerors, colonizers, and the like were specifically indicated for a few districts and epochs. Protagonists of pan-Egyptian diffusion were uninterested in the thousands of peoples of lowly economy, food-gatherers, economically primitive agriculturalists, and the like, who have offered central problems in scientific work in anthropology.

Dr. Smith said heatedly in 1930 in Chicago, in reply to a barbed query by Professor Edward Sapir about Egyptian influences upon Nootkan cultures on Vancouver Island, British Columbia, "Why, I am not interested in savages!" Smith's anachronistic evaluation of higher, that is, materially wealthy, peoples such as Mayans, Aztecs, and Incas and his disdain for all other peoples appeared neatly during the exchange. Pan-Egyptian diffusionists were concerned with special inventories of features which they thought they identified in a number of so-called "high civilizations" and which they argued could have entered such groups only after a seminal Egypt had spawned and contributed the items. An issue of pan-Egyptian diffusion is long since as dead as that of Negro racial inferiority or Jewish genes.

Smith's and Perry's displacement of self-identity and arrogance from western Europe to a classical Near East group, their indifference to discovery of sociocultural processes and of psychological dynamisms in sociocultural matrices, and their clumsy historicism, too, guaranteed early discrediting. But presumptions about the civilizing role of spreads of Egyptian cultural features, some as frivolous as mummification, to distant parts of the world remain of interest because they admonish us that it is easy to slip back a mere twenty or thirty years and to think that darker and economically poorer peoples are unblessed with culture and only somewhat bleached peoples carried its flickering torch.

### Ideological Lag in Cultural Anthropology

Every scientific field exhibits successive periods each of which is marked by a special terminology and array of concepts—big ones, little ones, sharply cutting ones, duller ones. Those in vogue in sociocultural anthropology during the first half of the century require critical assessment at the same time that services they provided receive dignified acknowledgment. Present readers of an introductory work on cultural anthropology should be told about some now antiquated components of much of the paperback and other works on anthropology which they are purchasing and which were published during earlier development of the science. College textbooks have evaded important questions about the passing of five or six decades in cultural anthropology. In fact, unlike textbooks in more mature areas of scientific inquiry such as physics or chemistry, most of the modish textbooks in anthropology refer almost respectfully to rusted and rarely employed concepts and terms as if they remained rustfree and stainless tools in scientific work.

Classroom lectures of contemporary cultural anthropologists sometimes witness as extinct and useless an inventory of concepts and captions as did lectures by a multitude of older linguists, during the 1930's, when they continued to refer to harsh and guttural sounds, primitive features, and polysynthetic grammatical structures. Numerous professors of music who are assigned the course of lectures in musicology today continue to sermonize about pentatonic scales as characteristic features of nonwestern music.

Truly, much of the personnel in every scholarly and scientific field manifest ideological lags. A new textbook ought to try to help its readers prepare to be shocked as well as edified about these vestigia. An anthropologist today who would pontificate about so-called "culture elements" and "culture areas" as if the concepts were of current scientific utility would be little more helpful to his students than a professor of atomic physics who was offering in an adjacent classroom a lecture of pre-Schrödinger-Heisenberg vintage, that is, of 1926 or earlier.

It is of capital importance that people be shown the comparatively short life span of most concepts and tools which have rendered scientific services. The finest concepts eventually are superceded, even as the most beautiful Neolithic cutting tools of stone were presently replaced by sharper, if not more durable, implements produced by specialist metallurgical personnel. It is, therefore, necessary to cite ideas and tools which were employed by at least the immediately preceding generation of scientists and to indicate their survival value in a later period of advances in scientific maturity. The task is to set forth steps ahead in descriptive precision, methodology, and theory where older devices and precepts had served in their day. It is necessary to explain when, how, and why they had to be replaced by, again, only temporarily more useful means. Sooner or later all are marked for shelves of a historical museum or pages of a treatise on the history of science, instructive institutions which show progress made in various sciences. Conceptual tools and impedimenta are perishable. They are neither indestructible nor immutable like some nonwestern agricultural peoples' supernaturals.

In the early twentieth century era of rejection of hypothetical evolutionary successions of general sociocultural features, that is, of hypotheses pyramided so as to comprise historical systems little of which rested upon evidence, an understandable reaction was to surrender the search for long-range historical perspectives and to limit interest to very recent times or to a flat perspective present. It became necessary also to reduce patent complexities of sociocultural characteristics to simple, minimal, or indivisible units—the more concrete, describable, and numerous the better, perhaps. There would be no hypothetical remainder. All would be factual particulars, it would seem, rooted in the hardest soils of reality.

Boas, who had received his university training principally in the physics and mathematics of about 1880, responded almost naturally during the late 1880's and 1890's in an atomistic and hard-science manner to sweeping evolutionist summaries which lacked documentary evidence and did not account for innumerable smaller features of cultural difference. No more than two or three of the notable evolutionist writers had enjoyed his already protracted and varied field experiences, all incidentally among food-gatherers of northern North America where remarkable divergences in ideology and customs were visible from district to district. After 1900 a number of British and continental European anthropologists, many of them fairly experienced field research workers too, reacted in the same general way.

The field workers' thinking, especially Boas', was that each nonwestern society comprised an aggregate of maybe tens of thousands of indivisible culture elements or culture traits. Field work revealed them. None could be merely deduced a priori as inevitable flowerings of so-called "stages." All must be attested in field observations. Many hundreds of elements were features of technology or so-called "material culture." Hundreds constituted minimal features of family and clan customs. Hundreds more were political customs. Thousands and thousands were minimal features of folklore.

Each among even the economically simplest peoples of Tasmania and Australia had vast inventories of such culture traits. Such peoples were not nearly so simple as the colonists there thought. Each group's inventory of elements was largely duplicated in immediately adjacent groups. In other words, each community had demonstrably invented maybe less than 1, 2, or 3 percent of all its thousands or tens of thousands of culture traits.

Boas and his disciples were comparatively simplistic but not wholly atomistic in their frame of reference. They supposed that most culture elements were connected in complexes or patterns of traits, although the manner and causes of such interrelatedness would have to be discovered at later times. Nevertheless, there were a few notable pioneer studies, especially by Boas' earlier students, such as those cited previously on the Plains horse and Sun Dance distributions. These were efforts to handle with realism complexities of a world of adjacent peoples each of which obviously could not be portrayed as a special many-columned inventory of thousands of discrete culture elements. Life's complexities appeared in so-called "culture complexes," of kinds exemplified in such studies, and in extensive similarities from district to nearby districts.

As early as the 1920's the unimaginativeness and inability of listings and analyses of diffusions of composites of elements to lead to anything significant in theory about peoples was growing upon precisely the successive groups of younger anthropologists whom Boas himself had been nurturing. And so, during the 1920's, Dr. Ruth Bunzel reported on roles of innovators in pottery arts; Dr. Paul Radin wrote on philosophers and poets in non-literate societies; Dr. Margaret Mead conducted pioneer researches on childhood and adolescence in Oceanian groups; Dr. George Herzog examined structurings of features of musical expression among North American Indians; Dr. Edward Sapir lectured and wrote on the psychology of nonliterate peoples; and Dr. Ruth Benedict studied both the distributions and content of guardian spirit concepts in North America. No less a charismatic leader than Boas himself turned to an examination of processes that limited and fostered creativity and traits of style in plastic-graphic arts. The obvious features of lag in the science were beginning to be superceded by new questions and methods.

Curiously, it was during this very period of breakthroughs in the direction of wholly new problems around cultural expressions and means for solving them that Professor Kroeber engaged, as late as the 1930's and 1940's, in an undoubtedly noble twilight survey of element and area studies. In the gathering darkness of historicism and diffusionism, it was a lonely, almost nocturnal, effort to explore, as no one had done earlier, possible utilities in moribund concepts which had once seemed to support important inquiries. The result was foredoomed. The culture element granted and enjoyed no more illumination than it ever had, and the culture area clearly presented no way to specify the age of features of society and culture. Culture areas were of lessening interest because most good anthropologists had learned, unhappily, that the concept lacked a future in age dating or any other scientific applications. Indeed, a large number of very young anthropologists had already come under a spell wrought by British social anthropology's confident leader, Alfred Radcliffe-Brown. They regarded the culture area concept as possibly useful for determinations of culture element ages which only idiots, archaeologists, and benighted followers of Kroeber might want to assess. At just the time Kroeber evinced interest in shoring up the hoary culture area concept because distributions of traits in and around areas offered some fuzzy sort of age determining device, scientific personnel in the field were adopting new avocations. Indeed, Kroeber himself presently observed this trend and forsook his age-area preoccupation in order to catch up with the avant-garde battalions of his profession.

Evolutionist theory of nineteenth century sources similarly reappeared, like Kroeber's disquisitions on the age-area chimera, in a new really ghostly garb. A most articulate specter who tried to address modern minds was a man of western medicine, Robert Briffault. His fascinatingly anachronistic *The Mothers* was published during the 1920's. No scientist took a second look at the learned physician's pretentious three volumes. Like Kroeber, Briffault managed to dematerialize his ideological ectoplasm. He addressed himself to flesh and blood reality by writing novels in which he did rather well.

Much more significant among a puzzled rank and file of younger professional anthropologists has been the acerbic pamphleteering by several contemporary writers of a group located or spawned at the University of Michigan. Spokesmen for this strident clique take a position about socioeconomic causation close to that of the DeLeonites who preceded the tiny Socialist Labor Party of recent decades in the United States. The position also resembles that of the now almost defunct Technocrats who, during the 1930's, professed to have charted a plan for resolving practical difficulties in connections between modern technology, social relationships, and democratic government. The discipleship weigh favorably the technological factors in socioeconomic change, worry themselves with a compulsion to salvage selectively the best in Lewis H. Morgan and other protagonists of social evolutionist thinking, and speak of themselves proudly as neo-evolutionist. They also torture themselves and many anthropologists who respect the various contributions of Boas by lashing him as a destructive and reactionary figure, perhaps because his more naïve students could perceive little that deserved retention in nineteenth century sociocultural anthropology. One wonders why some members of this neo-evolutionist group are so superheated about a seminal worker of yesteryear who was not always well-understood by his less well-equipped admirers. The preoccupation of angry neo-evolutionists is in socioeconomic subjects which interested Boas little compared to his data gathering and creative work in methods of analysis of expressive materials in language and art.

A rather different and so-called "multilinear-evolutionist" position in writings by Professor Julian Steward of the University of Illinois principally during the 1950's is no intemperately and largely deductively offered vestigium of nineteenth century historicism. It suggests no mechanical classifications into socioeconomic and other types such as feature neo-evolutionist lectures, and it is not indifferent to cultural expressions. It seems to be an effort to depict a mesh of factors which shaped socioeconomic changes and connected with cultural manifestations. Steward's work is neither simplistic evolutionism nor abortive salvaging of something which had been long covered over. But, like other presentations of historically oriented questions, it fails to aim at methods of manipulation of expressive cultural materials and so contributes little to systems of scientific theory about them.

## British Sociocultural Anthropology

Reaction to evolutionist-, diffusionist-, Kulturkreis-, and history-oriented sociocultural anthropologists had a distinctive expressive content in England, perhaps because of special factors, whatever they were, in the backgrounds and personal histories of two men. Strategic roles in the development of modern sociocultural anthropology have unquestionably been played by Professor Bronislaw Malinowski, after his residence in the Trobriand Islands (northeast of New Guinea) during the first World War, and by Radcliffe-Brown who before that war had a relatively brief field research experience among food-gathering Andaman Islanders (in the eastern Bay of Bengal).

Malinowski was interested in sensitive depiction of everything in a sociocultural system and its people, in his case the Trobrianders. He deplored wasting time in diffusionist studies which produced doubtful, petty, and, he supposed, utterly useless items of historical depth perspective. He had no interest in social evolutionist speculations. For decades he stood for psychologically penetrating field observations. He lectured and wrote fervently about his particular brand of "functionalism," wherein he urged that the field worker report on interrelations of all components of a sociocultural system. He did not employ concepts of culture elements, complexes, or culture areas.

Radcliffe-Brown deprecated nineteenth century evolutionist historicism and the comparative method as used for purposes of historical perspectives, as well as early twentieth century diffusionist methodology. Malinowski's opinions of such policies and procedures were similar. But Radcliffe-Brown was a narrowly limited analyst of social structure who was dedicated, he said, to discovery of laws. He evidently forgot to look for them in his researches. Notwithstanding his methodological and theoretical broadsides, Malinowski was temperamentally an alert field observer and reporter of a spectrum of social, economic, cultural, and psychological phenomena. Radcliffe-Brown, who seems to have had slight aptitude for field research, nonetheless emphasized as of primary importance painstaking field work and analysis of a group's social structure. By that he meant principally its kinship, family, and lineage relationships. He preached interminably, as the great nineteenth century social evolutionist Herbert Spencer had done long before, about the need to locate "social laws." Neither sachem ever showed how one could really define or identify them. Radcliffe-Brown also had little to offer about the worth of depicting a group's cultural expressions and so he tended to leave them alone. Therefore he never emphasized the importance of efforts to deduce "laws" about cultural manifestations.

In this book on cultural expressions the principal reason for citing Radcliffe-Brown is to report that his absorption in problems of analysis and structuring of manifestations of a kinship system and his somewhat less successful ventures in transsocietal studies of government and law exerted an extraordinary impact upon a generation of younger anthropologists. He was a prime factor in shaping the thinking and field work preoccupations of many young people who were drawn from England and other parts of the British empire into sociocultural anthropology after the middle 1920's. His influence upon American anthropologists was extensive after the late 1930's. With one or two exceptions, British empire field workers who were captivated by his interests in special aspects of social structure never became much concerned, in the course of their field investigations, about cultural expressions or psychological facets of their materials. Anthropologists who identified with Radcliffe-Brown rather than with the peculiarly variegated Boas group were rarely donors of descriptive data in cultural or psychological facets of nonliterate peoples. It is as if Radcliffe-Brown's retinue drew certain blinds in the windows looking outside into the native village plaza. Apertures which might have been used to peer at religious, language, artistic, and psychological matters were fairly tightly shut for most of them, while Boas' students and followers tended to occupy themselves with just those subjects.

Not one of Radcliffe-Brown's alumnae ever published a significant paper on the language, oral literature, or music of his field informants. Boas' successors revolutionized the science of language, based on his pioneering steps in that area of inquiry. A large percentage of his liegemen published one or more ponderous collections of texts with translations or English-dictated bodies of myths and tales. Many of his partisans reported more or less fully on manifestations of native religions. A fair number published studies of plastic and graphic art. An entire field of inquiry, psychological anthropology, developed in the ranks of Boasians. The extreme confinement of interests and jewelry-like workmanship characteristic of British social anthropologists contrast painfully with the searching pseudopodia sent out by Boasians into cultural expressions. The quality of their workmanship was uneven, but they were in impressive numbers.

It can be said, maybe a bit brutally, that Radcliffe-Brown succeeded in developing sociocultural anthropologists with abilities to perceive phenomena in their social structural aspects and with other facets tabooed as improper, irrelevant, or of meager significance. Like the austere nabob himself, British field workers were essentially structure-seeking sociologists who chose to work in nonliterate societies, principally Africa. Like their teacher, they talked ceaselessly about depicting interconnections of parts of a society. They tried mightily to do just this, doubtless in proper rejection of Boasian and other contemporary shreds-and-patches delineations of nonwestern peoples. However, a principal contribution of the British may very well be in having permitted the extinction of great masses of expressive cultural phenomena about which they chose to be blind after the fashion of their sociology-oriented overlord with his Spencerian gobbledygook about laws, interactionism, and functions of the parts of a society within the whole. The substantive contribution of so perfectionist a group of analysts was in structured rather than functional or process presentations. Although they referred to themselves as "functionalists," they described the structure of a number of systems of kinship and a variety of forms of government, law, and political behavior in nonliterate groups, mainly in Africa.

It may be added that British workers often remained so long in the field, like Malinowski with his three or more years in the Trobriands, that they were able to understand and sometimes converse in the native language, even though not one of them sought modern training in anthropological linguistics. Many Boasians had such training but hardly more than two or three stayed sufficiently long in a native community to acquire the valuable tool which ability to speak in a native language would have offered. Nevertheless, linguistic research of utmost precision can be conducted by a person who cannot speak a native language with fluency. Britishers often learned to speak it, naturally with an atrocious British accent because their linguistic training was next to nil. They seem to have been paralyzed about putting their polyglot capacity to work in the close study of cultural expressions.

Radcliffe-Brown's harping upon the importance of exposing interconnectedness in the parts of a society radiated into statements, which some scientists have found ineffably corny or boring, about so-called "functional" connections between cultural expressions and everything else. Malinowski toodled the same monotonous tune. It may be thought of as the subcultural anthem of the functionalists in social anthropology.

Malinowski's more severe colleague wrote out, with Herbert Spencer over a generation earlier, what every slightly sophisticated scientist understands as an antique fallacy of analogic thinking: each sociocultural system is a special kind of organism, like an animal or plant which lives as long as its organs function interrelatedly and well. The great twentieth century functionalist's pretty borrowing of a biological analogy from the garrulous Spencer never functioned as a guide to field researches or in analyses of recorded field data. It lacked ability to produce specific questions and to facilitate analysis of special problems regarding recorded field data. It was a kind of hymn. Put differently, it was a stuffy and dramatic rationalization of much too general a kind. The biological analogy about which Radcliffe-Brown seemed to feel so strongly also had no utility as a tool because it did not point to specific means for probing and weighing, for displaying contents, forms, and operations of sociocultural subsystems within a society. Flag waving, with a band nearby playing a sacred ditty, never trained a company of soldiers in target shooting or bayonet skills. Radcliffe-Brown also exhibited an amazing, if not terrifying, survival of bad nineteenth century dialectic thinking about psychological manifestations in his contrasted opposites of community euphoria and disphoria, the latter consequent upon disfunctioning of a portion of a societal organism. No one has ever been able to follow up these extraordinary Spencerian contributions to confusion in the study of functional or psychological homeostasis in a people, at least not with observations or testing devices of kinds at present at the command of field research personnel.

Notwithstanding the Spencerian survivals in writings by Radcliffe-Brown, his analysis of Australian kinship, about 1930, was a valuable model. Indeed, it constituted a landmark in the history of sociocultural anthropology because it pinpointed minimal features in a macroclass of such features and showed their patternings in one region.

It should be understood that in the vast realms of sociocultural behavior there are at least two constellations of materials which comprise, in each instance, relatively small numbers of minimal units, simple enough to be rather easily identified, listed, arranged in sets, and accorded a patterning which corresponds somehow to their ordering in individuals' minds. These two are phonemic (minimal sound unit) structures in languages and kinship structures within larger patterns of social relationships. It is to Radcliffe-Brown's credit that he perceived, better than earlier pioneers in kinship analysis such as Lewis H. Morgan and W. H. R. Rivers, how to manipulate minimal units in a kinship system so as to elucidate that system's structure. But the student of cultural, as contrasted with social, anthropology should realize that most expressions of the human mind are far more complexly patterned than phonemes and kinship items and constitute much larger and often irregularly ordered arrangements. To put it succinctly, phonemics and kinship are among the easiest manifestations of human nature to tackle, in each instance because of their smaller numbers of units and fewer irregularities in their configurations. Numeral and color concept systems, doubtless a number of others too, are of comparable simplicity.

The history of progress in scientific work in cultural expressions cannot highlight Radcliffe-Brown, although it will cite Malinowski as an early field worker who displayed, for his time, unexampled insight in his reports of socioeconomic relationships and cultural expressions. Nevertheless, the model which Radcliffe-Brown gave for the final write-up of an analysis of a kinship system within a larger frame of societal structure offered something new and valuable. It could have been placed side by side with the model for identification and display of sets of contrastive units in languages, especially so in their sound or phonemic systems, which was being developed during the very same period. Unlike Boas, Radcliffe-Brown had no familiarity with nonwestern languages or with the science of language. Maybe he never realized that scientific linguists whom he had met in the United States were achieving precisely what he had in mind. In fact, they were doing an even better job of honing their new cutting tools and arranging the results of their slicings structurally. Although he set forth a model paper on Australian kinship, he was unable to define methods for attaining such a structural presentation, while the American linguists after Boas were rapidly turning out a goodly series of methodological statements about how to identify units and classes of units in a patterned linguistic system. They were accomplishing more than Radcliffe-Brown or Malinowski in supplying a model of method for comprehension of the several fields within cultural anthropology.

## Psychological Anthropology

Nineteenth century writers (Tylor, Wundt, et al.) had made many important statements about psychological behavior as well as about relationships, customs, beliefs, and other expressive materials among nonwestern peoples. But during the period from the 1890's to the 1920's something of an eclipse occurred in interest in transcultural psychological manifestations of human nature, with notable exceptions in Boas' writings, in the French philosopher Lucien Levy-Bruhl's guesses about prelogical mentality, mystical participations, and collective representations, and in speculations by nonanthropologists like the Viennese psychiatrist Sigmund Freud. Important factors in anthropologists' uninvolvement in psychological matters were the late nineteenth century fascination with technology, its preoccupations in discovery of evolutionary developments in sociocultural realms, its unremitting stress upon historical perspectives, and its fashioning of economic and sociological concepts. A primary commitment of anthropology's unilinear evolutionists had been in documentation of historical perspectives arranged in successive stages.

*Kulturkreis* writers until the 1950's were also primarily history directed. They too depicted details of what they supposed were stage levels. Diffusionist-oriented anthropologists in America and Scandinavia were more cautious than culture circle protagonists in deductions regarding far-flung spreadings of sociocultural features, but delineations of moderate spreads and revelations of diffusional processes were cardinal tenets of their scientific faith. Radcliffe-Brown's various influences in the 1920's and later included the molding of a clique of disciples who appear largely to have accepted his strictures against efforts to deduce the past from study of the present and who obeyed his pompous exorcisms of psychological observations and inferences at the same time that he was talking blithely about euphoria and disphoria, astounding survivals from forgotten pages of Spencer.

Although a large mesh of influences accounts for about three decades of bypassing of or triviality in transcultural pursuit of psychological questions, a very few anthropologists never surrendered appreciation of the centrality of psychological reporting and theory in general anthropology.

After all, was not anthropology interested in everything about people? Boas never lost sight of an obligation to understand the minds of people of other cultures. His teacher, Bastian, and his insightful predecessor, Tylor, had not denied that anthropology was about people in their entirety. As a result many persons refused to approve Radcliffe-Brown's declamations that the proper study of nonliterate folk was to locate sociological laws.

Boas became the first twentieth century writer to assemble in a rigorous manner probable formulations about nonwestern mentality. They appeared in his 1910–11 book *The Mind of Primitive Man*, whose very title (in an American edition published by Macmillan) attested to Boas' psychological emphasis. Still, the book contributed no new method of psychological research. Nor did Boas originate usable theoretical formulae about mental processes. Achievements in his book included a novelty in latent point of view regarding the probable complexity and maturity of the minds of nonliterate folk and manifest criticisms of other writers' statements about such minds. Boas dealt with long-standing myths such as nonwesterns' racial inferiority, child level of mental development, distinctive auditory, visual, and olfactory perceptions, and their illogical, prelogical, or other deficient ways of thinking. He threw out, as improbable, generalizations about nonwestern peoples which imputed intellectual inferiority to them. Today such a seminal work is termed a breakthrough. It was a change in total attitude rather than discovery of a method of research.

Successful descriptive pioneerings in psychological anthropology during the 1920's and later might not have been possible without Boas clearing away nineteenth century nonsense about the mentality of so-called "primitive peoples." His effort both in the book and, even more effectively, in class lectures was such as to permit his students, notably Sapir, Radin, Mead, and Benedict, and what might be termed "indirect" students (Linton, Kardiner, et al.), who presently led in psychological anthropology, to proceed upon a premise that nonliterates were psychologically as complex as persons etched in the wealthiest civilizations. During the 1920's British, French, and German writers on the mentality of nonwestern peoples were ineffective in creating interest in psychological anthropology, although Levy-Bruhl and Freud a little earlier had done much to stir reflection in the subject. It is as if their culture-bound writings goaded a later generation to do scientific work which was not burdened by extrapolations of behavioral characteristics of Europeans.

Also, during the first three decades of professional anthropology, the 1890's to the 1930's, methods and concepts appeared which later could be used in psychological anthropology. The Binet-Simon and Stanford-Binet psychological tests and other devices of the kind were being pioneered before 1920 and a few voices properly raised the question of their transcultural utility. Freud had long since offered a weighty list of psychological concepts, terms, and processes, some of which were invading everyday thinking and vocabulary. Presently, the Swiss psychiatrist Rorschach and much later Professor Henry A. Murray of Harvard contributed research tools of possible cross-cultural worth with their projective tests. Beginning in the mid 1920's, the brilliant anthropological linguist Sapir especially effectively urged development of interest in psychological anthropology. Radin, a contemporary of Sapir in Boas' classes, offered the verbatim unguided autobiography as a methodological tool, in *Crashing Thunder* (1927). A pupil of a later student generation, Margaret Mead, set another example during the late 1920's with her first intensive psychological observations of nonwestern youngsters in *Coming of Age in Samoa* (1928). She also showed that cross-cultural psychological insights pointed up the primacy of socio-cultural rather than genetic or physiological factors in the psychological behavior of youth in western civilization. Still another pupil, Ruth Benedict, stimulated anthropologists and a host of others with her concept, in *Patterns of Culture* (1934), of distinctive cultural constellations and personality determinants composed mainly of features of world view and value ideals. She showed that most members of a group internalized this kind of ideological configuration so deeply that much of their behavior and feelings could be accounted for in its terms. She spoke of such a configuration as a "culture pattern," an unhappy caption because it did not express literally what she had in mind. During the later 1930's Ralph Linton, who had been much influenced by Boas and his group, participated in fashioning a concept of modal or basic personality structure which quickly helped provide an ideological underpinning for many psychologically oriented anthropologists of the time. A psychoanalyst, Abram Kardiner, adroitly climbed on the basic personality structure bandwagon to indulge in psychoanalyzing of peoples in nonliterate societies on a basis of secondhand reports of them. The rapidly developing system of cross-cultural psychological methods and theory acquired a maladroit label, "culture and personality studies."

English and other European anthropologists in effect ignored the sprouting of concepts, research tools, and theoretical statements in the United States. Fertilization was Freudian, husbandmen were Boas' students or followers. Old World anthropologists continued tilling old ground in old ways in their complaisant heritage of surface descriptions of things, customs, beliefs, and institutions. Apart from English field workers, they were prevailingly history motivated and, indeed, seem to have remained so until the present day. Although a vital European contribution to psychological anthropology has been selected by the post-Boasians from the Freudians' pyramid of culture-bound statements about psychological processes, Boas himself was unable to accept any of it beyond the stress upon importance of early childhood learning and the regrettable need to explore sexual behavior, a most embarrassing requirement for a Victorian. Boas had the deepest distaste for psychoanalysis as a method and system of theory, for piling up of unvalidated theories, and for research on sex. He was incapable of tolerating any theoretical system building in behavioral sciences. He disdained the reckless formulations by almost all Freudians who interested themselves in analyzing, at a distance of thousands of miles, other persons' reports about nonliterate peoples. He worried about the crop of Freudianly inclined young anthropologists, mostly his own intellectual progeny, who were imprudent in their talk about psychological processes although they tended to guard their speech in his presence. He heard enough of their naughty patois to develop chronic jitters about what was going on.

Readers are referred to later sections for additional progress made in method and theory in psychological transcultural research. It is sufficient to report here that cultural anthropology received a working supply of concepts and research methods with appearance, in the 1930's, of psychological anthropology as a recognized field of specialist inquiry.

### Cross-cultural Correlations

An important method for determination of causal connections between sociocultural phenomena was pioneered during the 1880's by the justly admired British pioneer of sociocultural anthropology, Tylor, in a library-based study of correlations between certain social institutions the world over. His procedure was not pursued significantly until the 1930's when anthropologists at Yale University again tackled the problem of how to produce firm correlations and transsocietal statements of high validity. By the 1930's, mathematico-statistical procedures had become characteristic features in behavioral science researches, especially in American university departments of psychology. Devices dear to them could be adapted for special purposes in anthropology. A Yale University project called the *Human Relations Area Files*, sponsored by a sociologist turned anthropologist, George Peter Murdock, made possible such borrowing and a revamped method for use by anthropologists.

From Tylor to the 1930's, a few anthropologists slowly and painstakingly assembled in larger libraries sociocultural items from scores or hundreds of the world's groups, no two of which appeared to have had a close historical connection, and then compared and correlated them with some other possibly related items also wearisomely dredged from library materials. Cautious mathematical manipulation in this type of comparative method patently yielded highly probable statements about or pointed reliably to correlations or relationships of worldwide generality. The procedure could grant firm components for subsystems of scientific theory in both social and cultural topics. The *Files* presently reprinted data on cards which offered items on hundreds of nonwestern groups. Their beliefs, customs, and behavior were sliced, arranged, indexed, and cross-indexed in the *Files* and made available on the cards with unexampled convenience. Where earlier anthropologists might have searched along library shelves for months in order to collect scraps of descriptive data so as to solve some problem of correlation, covariation, or relationship by means of Tylor's fine comparative method, and Tylor himself must have spent a large portion of his life slowly collecting descriptive facts on pieces of paper, the printed card indexes were now available in more than twenty larger American university libraries and thereby enormously speeded up anyone's assembling of transcultural facts. A few hours sometimes yielded richer documentation than Tylor's and later comparativists' months and years of library searching. Shortly after the 1930's, a group of American anthropologists, with Dr. John Whiting and a few allies playing leading roles, began to turn out papers and monographs which contained statements about probable connections, for example, between hunting customs and shamanistic phenomena, or between childhood disciplines and adult personality characteristics, with reliabilities expressed in mathematical rather than cursive and conceivably more subjective terms. In short, American anthropology had both borrowed and transcended cruder nineteenth century procedures of transcultural comparisons with their chaotic listings. It was offering general but miscellaneous statements which eventually might be added to and then pieced together into various systems and subsystems of scientific theory.

The *Files* comprised principally older field observations obtained in periods of lesser sophistication in theory and field method, although the project drew increasingly upon recent researches. Although often rather old, facts as reported upon by field observers came from so many hundreds of nonwestern groups and were so rapidly exposed to view to a user of the *Files* that a great many strands of theory of fair or high probability became available for subsequent systematization. At the least, new field researches on a wide variety of problems could be planned in the light of mathematically propped up generalizations whose global documentation had been gleaned sometimes in a matter of days. Apart from Tylor's brand of exacting comparativism the old cross-cultural listing method of Frazer and a great many others before the 1930's had been discredited. It was evidently irresponsible and largely futile. But when correlations were made possible by the *Files* and employment of mathematical tools, Tylor's distinctive method was in effect salvaged, reconditioned, and modernized. Now it was possible to produce a chaos of theoretical statements within many, but by no means all, special fields of social and cultural anthropology. Such statements could be regarded as building blocks, not well arranged in neat piles as yet, but lying about here and there. Each offered a challenge to field research workers to get more blocks and render possible, at a future time, their proper arrangement so as to yield various edifices of theory. Such structures of course constitute major goals of scientific endeavor.

The methods devised during the century-long history of anthropology for formulation of theoretical statements include diffusionism's trait maps, *Kulturkreis'* layer cake and seven league boot spreadings, and British social anthropology's efforts to grant structural and functional depictions of single societies. These rate as almost or entirely worthless beside the refurbished and mathematically equipped modern form of the cross-cultural comparison and correlation method. The Yale group deserves praise for borrowing and then presenting such equipment to anthropology. But it is by no means fine equipment. For solutions of many cross-cultural correlation problems its source data may be superficial, fragmentary, or untrustworthy and in all instances should be rechecked and supplemented in future field researches. Hundreds of sociocultural groups still unrepresented in the *Files* ought to be added. But anthropology has at last acquired a method and an unprecedentedly convenient corpus of descriptive materials for discovery and validation of theoretical statements. The procedure also helps to minimize subjectivism of various kinds.

To summarize, anthropology witnessed three forms of the comparative method. The first, the nineteenth century listing procedure which cited indiscriminately reports of undetermined reliability about customs of one or another class the world over. This method survived anachronistically into the twentieth century in writings of Frazer and Briffault. It could not grant theoretical statements where probabilities could be assessed. The general reader might be fascinated by lists of customs and beliefs from all parts of the "primitive" world, and his reading might even draw him toward anthropology and prepare him for acceptance of the worth of heritages of formerly ill-regarded darker peoples. But public relations writing, no matter how elegant, poetical, or worldwide comparativist, has rarely if ever contributed to scientific theory.

Secondly, Tylor's special version of the comparative method, designed to determine correlations in social institutions, by contrast was quite sound. But source data which he was able to glean during the 1870's and 1880's were poor and mathematical tools available to him were only budding.

The third and contemporary form of the comparative method is one of the notable advances in twentieth century behavioral science. Still, it is very young and suffers from severe handicaps. These appear to reside not so much in the method as in the quality and number of the field reports in anthropology's archives and in the sophistication displayed at Yale or elsewhere in cutting, arranging, and indexing in the *Files*. Actually, the cutting out and captioning of *Files* items are far better for some features of social structure, notably for kinship, than they are for cultural expressions such as psychological behavior, religion, music, dance, oral literature, and others. Cross-cultural studies of humor and many other important topics are not possible with the *Files* in their present condition because those who have directed the project either ignored such cultural expressions, or they knew that field data about them were miniscule, or they did not know how to carve them into meaningful components. Expressions such as world view and ethics have been reported upon so badly for most cultures that although these topics can already be pursued in the *Files* the results might not be significant for theory. In other words, the *Files* as descriptive source materials, as the data-gathering storage warehouse or library par excellence, are not superior to the average of observations inserted in them. And, since slicings of the data are all that one finds on *Files* cards, a vital factor of possibly improper slicing must be handled at every turn. But where the items are present, their delivery to a reader is speedy as in an ultramodern large library with its elevators, tubes, and electrical equipment.

Units and sets of units which characterize a few aspects of societal organization, mostly kinship, have been relatively easy to identify. Structures which frame such units are fairly simple. But multiple variables and enormously larger numbers of units which combine as gross features of culture and psychological behavior have barely begun to be cut out or identified. Such phenomena are much more complexly patterned than kinship. The *Files* are therefore patently inept in presentations of such cultural data because materials of expressive kinds have not been cleaved into proper units either by the original field observers or by the staff which sections out the field reports into card material for indexing in the *Files*. Before much of theoretical worth can be extracted about cultural expressions from *Files* cards, advances in analyses of such expressions are required. Only later may meaningful components of expressive phenomena be cited and properly filed. Extensive returns in theory cannot be anticipated for some time in most subjects of expressive kinds, because the data have not been fed into the *Files* "library."

Assessment of the potential significance for constructing systems of sociocultural theory of various methods, developed since the 1860's, for identification of meaningful sociocultural items and perception of sets of them, and for deduction of statements about process, may take this form. The modern version of the comparative method, a cross-cultural comparison-correlation procedure, has been stimulated by the availability of the *Files* and is displayed in a few early models of workmanship by Whiting and others. It ranks as anthropology's one or two outstanding scientific tools.

Modern canons for determining units and sets or classes of units in linguistics perhaps rank as equally important methodological advances. These tools were fashioned rather deliberately during the 1930's, too, but with important precursor achievements by Boas and others. Linguistic tools for identification and arrangement of units and sets of units yielded the first models which anthropology could utilize for identification of a variety of minimal units and their arrangements in many other types of cultural expression. Today a handful of anthropologists are aware of the potential instructiveness of the linguistic tool kit and are guided in a general way by it in what they term efforts to structure other cultural manifestations.

Again, the *Files* and cross-cultural comparison-correlation method can offer only a chaos of theoretical statements, correlations, and probabilities which rest upon insecure descriptive materials and are damaged by improper slicings and index work in the *Files*. Linguists' procedures present the first carefully worked-out canons for identification, descriptively, of units and sets of units. They comprise a method which improves description and facilitates later theoretical work because it sets forth employable descriptive items. Linguistics appears to have advanced farther than other fields because its descriptive base is better segmented. It is less advanced than other fields, such as psychological anthropology, because it lacks important theoretical statements, that is, its personnel have not directed much work toward generalizations about process. They have been fascinated by descriptive perfectionism. The cross-cultural correlation method has already permitted odds and ends of deductions about process in phychological, religious, and some other cultural fields and, even better, in kinship and other aspects of social structure.

## Redfield

During the 1930's and later Robert Redfield of the University of Chicago presented anthropology with some important new perceptions. In *Tepoztlan* and later works he identified a distinctive class of peoples and thereby improved the classification of sociocultural types and made possible discovery of new kinds of processes in sociocultural life. Novel descriptive and taxonomic procedures did not accompany his offerings, nor did he operate at the almost microscopic level of minimal units and sets of units. In humanistic rather than rigorous sketchings he recognized inventories of defining gross characteristics for groups which he captioned "folk" and "peasant" societies, types which anthropologists until then had ignored in favor of food-gatherers, agriculturalists in general, and the like. Redfield listed principal economic, social, cultural, and psychological features which he supposed characterized his types. In each instance the community had been agricultural before 1492 and had been enveloped by an expanding European nation. The contribution, again, was primarily taxonomic, the items included were macroclasses of units. Redfield was also among the first, with Benedict, to emphasize need to study a people's world view, self-identity, and value ideals, cultural expressions which had been infrequently reported upon by earlier field workers. In other words, he pointed seminally to neglected systems of potential theory, although, like Benedict, he offered no methods for use in field researches and for disentangling and identifying the component strands in the expressions he correctly indicated as present in every society. Unlike Benedict, his efforts did not contribute measurably to advances in psychological anthropology. Subsequently many field workers added to descriptive knowledge of cultural heritages of the kind stressed by Redfield.

The sketch of the history of cultural anthropology has, of course, omitted a number of important developments, some of them historically rather than analytically oriented, others directed mainly to structured depictions of social relationships, still others focused upon acculturated peoples. Reason for such omission arises in their failure to add significantly to knowledge of cultural expressions in nonliterate societies as they were before Euro-American entry, or to present new methods of outstanding import in research and arrangement of data. The sketch has proceeded sufficiently to fill in a general background. Chapters to come will add those developments which need more specific citation to enhance understanding of progress that has been made in each special category of cultural expression such as language, psychological anthropology, religion, humor, art, ethics, and world view. The chapter immediately following offers a setting or background for all these inquiries in its sketch of principal types of socio-economic systems among nonliterate peoples.

## SUGGESTIONS FOR FURTHER READING

No sophisticated surveys of the history of methods or theories in social anthropology exist. Except for psychological anthropology, the history of work done in each of the cultural or expressive topics is handled, where it has been treated at all, with little more than naiveté. Segments of the chapter may be pursued, never satisfactorily, in biographies of important contributors to cultural anthropology such as Edward B. Tylor, Lewis H. Morgan, Franz Boas, Robert H. Lowie, and Ruth Benedict. Smug discipleship or hostile polemicism mars most published discussions, which are almost countless, of methods and theories. A convenient recent publication is *Resources for the Teaching of Anthropology*, Memoir 95 (American Anthropological Association, 1963). It cites some of the relevant books but unfortunately omits many others.

# 2. SOCIOECONOMIC TYPES

## Introduction

Economic determinists, especially the sects which have accorded direct homage to Karl Marx and those which have curtained such fealty, represent social structures and cultural expressions, whether Euro-American or otherwise, as more or less traceable effects of technological and economic causes. Most anthropologists take every precaution not to be simplistic, like some avowed or cloaked Marxists, but to suppose that technological and economic factors do make possible and set limits to various social relationships. In its turn, the array of basic social relationships within a society nurtures, maintains, and imposes limits upon a great many items in a wide gamut of social forms and cultural expressions.

Each specific cultural expression, and cultural manifestations are the core interest of this book, must be accounted for, of course, in a complicated web of economic, social, psychological, ideological, and other factors or variables. Each is like a thread in an ornate fabric. The many special assemblages of threads should be weighed, with understanding that an economic bundle of threads, such as production or even mere gift giving in a few of the economically simplest societies, is always both decisive and one of several skeins in a sociocultural fabric. Since cultural expressions arise in socioeconomic structures to an important extent, a survey of cultural manifestations the world over necessarily includes sections on economic and social processes—and structures too—where they can be perceived. However, treatment here of socioeconomic structures and processes of their operation is as laconic as possible. Treatises where they can be presented extensively belong to other authors, those who publish on nonwestern economics and social structures. A work on cultural anthropology, about which there is much that ought to be said, will be all the clearer and more fairly handled if it only spotlights socioeconomic structurings and processes which shape and limit cultural expressions.

For convenience cross-cultural economics may be set apart from social structure as an extremely youthful anthropological specialty which is in a culture-bound, that is, western-economics-bound, fumbling, and inchoate state. Although this is the 1960's, nonwestern economics method and theory resemble the immature condition of anthropological linguistics during the 1890's. But nonwestern economics should be regarded as a potential scientific system. Sensitive and full-length descriptions of so-called "primitive" economic establishments are rare. Sophisticated identification of minimal

43

units and sets of such units in economic behavior and relationships (production, distribution, property ownership, gift giving, markets, money, etc.) has barely commenced for nonwestern societies. Apt comments on economic processes in them are infrequent, certainly so in modern college textbooks of economics. Much too often statements on the economics of nonliterate peoples are superficial, misleading, or naïve. An analogy with writings on musicology, for example, is almost alarming: neither field has gone far toward achievement of a global perspective.

In spite of the slanted and culture-bound view which still dominates, scholarly, if not scientifically oriented, researches on the economic life of slave-based classical Mediterranean societies and on economies in feudal and Renaissance European countries have been carried on for some decades. There are also beginnings of knowledge of other wealthy nonwestern economic systems such as those of India, Japan, and China before and during modern European imperial expansion. Major knowledge of economic processes flows, of course, from studies of modern market or capitalistic and soviet systems. To the present date, construction of a transsocietal system of economic theory, one which embodies all the world's economic manifestations, has been impossible. This is because the broadest of surveys has had to rely on descriptive knowledge of a mere ten or a dozen of the world's economic systems and these include some of the wealthiest. The evidence is skewed. It contains almost nothing about the economically poorest peoples who survived into modern times.

Until recently hundreds of not so wealthy systems could have been studied and their component parts identified by anthropological field workers. These few and busy specialists did nothing of the sort because of prior commitments to and fascination with artifacts, languages, folklore, general ethnographic sketchings, partially acculturated peasant and folk societies, and other interesting and, surely in all instances, vital topics. Only a handful of nonwestern economic systems, and it is doubtless right to refer to them as systems, continue at the time of this writing, notably in New Guinean interior highland districts. Not one of them is likely to endure another decade without pervasive changes. Such nonwestern economic fabrics could be observed and analyzed in their entirety if field workers were dispatched quickly to examine them. They are a kind of last frontier for economic theoreticians who need very much to watch economic behavior which is wholly unlike kinds found in countries of most advanced technology. A balanced structure of economic theory must await inclusion of treatments of all major categories of nonwestern economic systems. Such categories include many hundreds of now hopelessly warped or shattered systems which anthropological field workers should have reported upon long ago, to the degree to which they could do this. The tragedy inherent in efforts to advance toward a mature system of transsocietal economic theory is that, to an extent perhaps greater than any other aspect of general anthropology, functioning economic networks which it should have had at hand for observations disintegrated during the first years of entry or envelopment by Euro-Americans and their superior technology. Almost all the world's nonwestern economies of so-called "primitive" types are moribund or long since vanished. And it is not possible to reconstruct parts, internal relationships, or dynamics of such systems by means of interviews with handfuls of economically inactive elderly persons who sit in western-introduced rocking chairs. Because of a lack of better information it is still necessary to piece out from these usually helpful people as many fragments of descriptive observations as one can. But a memory economy is remote from a live one. Feet must be moving, hands working, paddle blades flashing, and satisfactions recurring if descriptive and analytic efforts by anthropologists are to amount to much.

At the time of Columbus, perhaps also as late as the early nineteenth century, the variety of nonwestern economic systems was remarkable. Regard them tentatively as located along at least one intergrading continuum, from least to most productive of foods and artifacts. Then, draw lines along the continuum so as to set apart a small number of ideal economic types or models. A strategic or emphasized factor of difference in them was quantity of foods and goods produced. Procedure such as this is a standard example of orderly scientific arrangement, of the kind termed "taxonomy." It is also disconcertingly, maybe improperly, simplistic. Doubtless several other intergrading continua should be charted and subsequently connected with the first one which denotes only quantity of production. But a simple typology does serve well enough both for introductory motivations of this book and for some scientific purposes. It permits visibility and manipulation of contrasts in economic features and processes, pointed up by spotlighting a small list of oversimply stated ideal types of economic structure which are indicated by dividing lines along an oversimple continuum. In fact, traits, sets of traits, and processes in economic systems might be improperly assessed if hundreds of nonwestern fabrics were bewilderingly depicted or arranged along this kind of continuum. Indeed it would not be possible to do that because their relative strengths in productive forces can never be determined: it is too late to be giddily mathematical. The bushels of maize, potatoes, or yams once produced can no longer be counted. Still, there is no evading a necessity, certainly there is no merit in running away from the convenience, of setting up just a very few contrasted patterns of economic phenomena, a comparatively small number of ideal points or economic types along a single continuum, in order to permit sharper perceptions of contrasted behaviors and processes that once were operating. Therefore, arbitrary lines are drawn between a few wisely—one hopes—selected bunches of economic systems. A later period may bring a troubled realization that revision of such bunchings is needed. Any typology of nonwestern economic systems is dangerous because it grants oversimple impressions to most readers. In any case, a typology of things and structurings about which we know almost nothing is a precarious enterprise in a science. But it has to be attempted in order to carry on the larger undertaking which is scientific inquiry.

Readers must be warned vociferously about complexities in every pattern of economic behavior and bewildering intergradations from one to another pattern. Above all, Euro-Americans find it difficult to believe that structure and processes in a network of economic activities such as, for example, an Australian blackfellow district might have displayed during the eighteenth century, could possibly have been complicated for purposes of anthropological analysis. After all, the people there did lack houses, garments, surplus foods or goods for trading, private property in vital productive resources, markets, money, specialization of labor, or anything else which a theoretician might look for whose thinking is rooted in the endless elaborations of the world's richest economic systems.

Here, as elsewhere in anthropology, the correct decision is to extirpate the rococo concept of nonwestern primitiveness or simplicity. A cautious student of nonwestern peoples takes neither simplicity nor complexity for granted until completion of intensive researches. He does not prejudge in terms of his own socioeconomic and cultural background, or he tries not to. After all, pre-Caucasian Australian economic behavior might turn out to have been simple, however simplicity be defined at a future time when much more has been learned about what went on among nonwestern peoples. But complexity, however that be defined, is likely to turn up somewhere where Euro-Americans have least expected it, maybe somewhere in northern Australia among definitely ungarbed and noticeably disheveled women who returned home in the late afternoon, gossiping and quipping pleasantly, with a few wooden trays laden with squirming grubs for dessert to be eaten after a luscious repast of kangaroo baked in its fur.

The procedure therefore is to engage, first, in a tentative classification of a few still nearly unknown main types of nonwestern economic structures, the systems which might have been described among the world's thousands of nonliterate societies. This handful of types also serves nicely for purposes of pedagogy because they allow correlated classification of the world's nonwestern sociocultural systems, excluding the very wealthiest. In each summarization of a nonwestern socioeconomic type, its principal economic characteristics are listed first. Then some few features of that economic type's sociocultural life are added where these characteristics appear to have connected significantly with economic traits.

Related kinds of classifications, historical perspectives, too, require a passing comment. Historians, anthropologists like Alfred L. Kroeber, and others have engaged in elaborate discussions, some of them stimulated by the historian Arnold Toynbee, about changes, interconnections, and evolution (whatever that is supposed to mean) in wealthier sociocultural systems. Procedures resorted to have displayed one notable feature: they have attempted to treat sonorously, if not in the grand manner, of socioeconomic and cultural wholes, that is, entire civilizations. The different procedure of this book has two principal characteristics. One is its focus, only initially so, upon economic cores of societies for the humdrum purpose of a convenient taxonomy of the world's societies and cultures. Such artificial simplification is unsatisfactory, maybe unentertaining too. But it does lessen bewilderment and helps to avoid equally plausible interpretations when warfare, government, religion, art, and architecture are centered in the criteria for a classification. The second feature of the procedure is its emphasis upon less wealthy societies. It omits almost completely the extraordinary Europe-to-China sociocultural spreads and developments of approximately the last 5,000 years. It also stops before the great Old World river valley developments (the Nile, Tigris-Euphrates, Indus, and others) after the Neolithic agricultural advances.

Cultural anthropology has much which should occupy it. It is right that some of its representatives join hands with historians and philosophers in quests of knowledge of cultural dynamics and configurations in the richest civilizations. But in instances where cultural anthropologists have associated with scholars whose interests, like Toynbee's, were directed toward the wealthiest societies, there seems to have been some diminution in attention to processes which might be revealed quickly by close analyses of sociocultural heritages of thousands of modernly marginal and economically poorer peoples. They also came into the post-Columbian period and thereupon were caught successively in expanding whirlpools of the most advanced technologies and the wealthier peoples who had them. This book focuses upon such poorer peoples. Other cultural anthropologists doubtless will treat of the most widespread and wealthiest civilizations. There is unlimited time for efforts to reconstruct culture history after the Neolithic and its grander developments in a few areas. There is little time remaining for field study and on-the-spot analyses of the world's hundreds of food-gathering and thousands of economically simpler agricultural and pastoral groups.

To be sure, the more atomistic analyses and structurings of sociocultural features, which seem possible in researches upon technologically simpler peoples, bear exciting promise. They can supply models for analytic procedures which have been unavailable to those who have attempted to discover directly the dynamics of change and structuring in wealthier sociocultural systems after the Neolithic. Historians and anthropologists who have been favored with broad interests and unconfined intellectual curiosity may, in some instances, have been trying to arrive at important perspectives of world history before they had received basic probing tools which they needed for their reconstructions. Such tools can be fashioned even now during the course of examination of cultural phenomena displayed in Neolithic and technologically even simpler societies.

Let us proceed to a suggested typology of nonwestern socioeconomic systems excluding the very wealthiest. In the first place let us assume one over-all type, a macroclass, all collectors or food-gathering peoples. They contrast with another macroclass which comprises all other socioeconomic systems. These latter were, of course, agricultural, agricultural-pastoral, pure pastoral, agricultural-with-irrigation, agricultural-with-slave-labor-base, and so on.

Pedagogical convenience and scientific requirements may be satisfied by presentation of two principal models of food-gatherers. The understanding is that food-gatherers' systems were of a great many kinds, that they inter-graded in economic and other features, and that a revision into three or more such models may turn out to be better.

The first type is of the many food-gathering systems which were in-capable of production of economically significant exchangeable surpluses. The people did not choose to or were unable to produce more than barely kept them going each few days. "Economically simple food-gatherers" is a good caption for them.

The second type includes very few food-gatherers' systems because it is likely only a small number survived into the Christian era and fewer still into the modern period. Some of them are almost sensational in their slight but exchangeable surpluses or, better, their potentials to produce surpluses of foods which could keep the people going securely during three or more adverse months without need to walk outside the house to procure an addi-tional slice of fish or venison. A suitable caption for this type is "econom-ically advanced food-gatherers." Let us turn now to some details about these two main types of food-gatherers. And let us remark in passing that there is no good reason for rejecting alternative captions such as "hunting-fishing-gathering" and "collectors," which many anthropologists have uti-lized.

## Economically Simple Food-Gatherers

Economically simple food-gatherers include principally Tasmanians and all Australian native peoples; Toala of Celebes; Pygmies of various districts in the Philippines, Malay Peninsula, and Andaman Islands; Veddas of Cey-lon; Ainus; some eastern Siberian Arctic groups; Bushmen; American In-dians of southern Chile and Argentina and an enormous area of North America north of an uneven line drawn from the peninsula of Southern California to about Montreal. This considerable area of northwestern North America does not include, however, a long and narrow coastline of Pacific Northwest tidewater and lower river communities which comprised eco-nomically advanced food-gatherers.

Although not one economic system in all these productively most modest societies has been more than superficially sketched, some major economic traits, patterns, and processes in the type seem fairly clear. Peoples who might be placed in it were maybe universal before the Upper Paleolithic of fifteen to twenty thousand years ago, for doubtless nothing that was eco-nomically more productive had yet appeared. At that time a few strategic technological advances, especially cutting tools, and possibly food preservation and storage techniques, transformed some groups into the second type of economically advanced food-gatherers who are discussed below.

Principal economic characteristics of simple food-gatherers appear to have included the following, although it is essential to note that diversity in economic features may have been very great from district to district.

Populations were sparse except in a few naturally favored districts as in parts of California.

Bands or tiny communities which were always self-sufficient averaged less than forty and rarely exceeded eighty persons. Seasonal, temporary assemblages of a few bands were usual. Writers on Australian ethnology have referred to bands as hordes, but the merit of a special term for groups of that region is questionable.

A simple sexual division of labor supplemented some specialization among older persons, those who were even less mobile than nubile women.

Strategic production was by sexually segregated and more or less democratic work parties. Male work parties hunted or fished. Female work parties produced bulbs, seeds, fruits, honey, and smaller animals and were so assigned because of the lesser mobility, consequent upon pregnancy and nursing obligations, of females. Important, but not decisive, production was by individuals. Most bands also moved en masse from season to season, usually returning before the year was out to the location of one year earlier. Connotations of the old terms, "nomads" and "nomadism," for such seasonally mobile groups are such that it is better not to use them.

Distribution of strategic production was potentially by equal sharing. Less decisive production might not be shared as often.

Exchanges with other bands or their members were of economically insignificant gifts. No economically meaningful surplus products were made. Bands of this type lacked trade, markets, and money, although incidental exchanges occurred. Exchanges is a judicious term for the economic process. Anthropologists have spoken of silent trade in order to characterize petty exchanges in a very few regions where custom decreed that the respective band members avoid one another. The fact that some exchanges were unaccompanied by verbiage or even by the presence of participants is a matter not of economics but of stylization of anxieties about face-to-face relationships. Silent trade remains a kind of petty exchange.

Work parties visited fishing, hunting, and wild plant locales which, together with fish caught and wild animals secured, were the sole property that was economically strategic. It was utilized for production only by band members and work parties unless special agreements were undertaken or maintained with outsiders. Individuals, families, and lineages usually did not acquire special rights of use or own productive property of economically decisive kinds. Therefore people displayed no significant inequalities in wealth, or gradations in social status or class level. Although considerable differences occurred in ownership of economically nonsignificant personal effects such as gear, garments, and ornaments, decisive wealth belonged only to the band: it was in water holes, hunting and fishing resources, and wild plant sites of the area through which the band journeyed during the year.

These economic features hinged upon possession of a certain limited technology. In conjunction with many other variables, economic features shaped, maintained, or limited some important features of internal and external band relationships, government, self-identity, care and rearing of young, roles of elders, ceremonial and religion, world view, ethics, and forms of handicraftsmanship and artistic expression. It is time, then, to proceed to a second list of characteristics, those sociocultural features which were frequently, if not generally, observed concomitants of traits which have been used to denote economically simple food-gatherers.

These societies exhibited few polygamous family units. Most persons were monogamously married, although permission to be baited, burdened, or blessed by two or three wives was very likely universal. Reports of a family of three or more spouses are rare. Almost all reports of long-standing polyandrous marriages, that is, of plural husbands, are untrustworthy because of failure to eliminate an alternative possibility of fraternal wife sharing. Marriage was not often postponed long after puberty. Choice of a mate might be narrowly limited by clan, exogamic, or many other rules, or by insistent pressuring of kin. But within such restrictions partners to a marital union ultimately enjoyed independence of choice of mate and could separate at will, subject again to feelings and urgings of relatives. Females were not paid for in marriages, although gifts almost always accompanied marital arrangements and rites. In spite of quantities of assertions by field reporters to the contrary, it is apparent from their descriptions of participations and relationships that the status of the feminine sex was so high that a deduction is plausible that the sexes were, in most instances, equal in status. Indications to the contrary, such as a woman walking behind her husband or suffering indignities, are many but they appear to amount to projections or misinterpretations of that extremely subtle phenomenon, status. It is quite possible that a person whose status is high is covered with physical or emotional bruises, or crushed with shame, because of a sadistic, episodically explosive, or foolish mate.

Variability in lineage, clan (unilateral descent groups, usually exogamous), moiety (where there were two groups of clans), and other social structurings of such kinds seems to have been extraordinary, from an extreme of clanless bands in western North American districts to an opposite of elaborate lineage, section, and clan patterns in Australia.

Fighting which drew blood was usually on a small scale, either feuds between families or lineages, or squabbles limited to two bands. Men were principals in sanguine fights, unquestionably so, but one wonders if many anthropologists of yesteryear were not obtuse about reporting instances of rather bloody pugnacity of women. Socioeconomic structures of this kind may be said to have displayed warfare infrequently, if warfare be defined as large-scale slaughter engaged in by men, not women, for the sake of a community.

Government, however that be defined, was not in the hands of hereditary leaders. Its powers were granted temporarily and by majority will to one or more respected and experienced persons who thereupon took over direction of food-producing parties, religious rites, and feud oriented gentlemen. Still another problem of definition applies to law. But it can be said that every band had its hundreds of precedents about what was best in resolution of trouble situations. Adults of a band decided exactly what had to be done in terms of such precedents and their systems or sets of values.

Religious functionaries, frequently termed "shamans," were part time operators, rather than specialists, who had acquired supernatural abilities and knowledge in a variety of ways. Rites might differ for the two sexes in Australia and in some other regions, but ideology and participations in religion were essentially democratically shared.

Plastic and graphic arts tended to be less notable, elaborate, or turned out in quantities than nonmaterial art forms: dance, music, and oral literature. Nevertheless remarkable basketry, painting, and carving appeared here and there. Prepubescents received encouragement to attain mastery in all arts assigned to their sex, and creativity in each art was frequent even within a tiny band. Principal outlets for creativity appear to have been in religious ideology, music, dance, humor, badinage, and oral literature rather than in tangible forms which scholars like Spengler, Toynbee, and Kroeber tended to rely upon in their assessments of cultures and civilizations.

## Economically Advanced Food-Gatherers

Principal characteristics of peoples who may be listed under this rubric, which covers many economies and sociocultural manifestations, are illustrated by extremely varied river and tidewater hamlets from lower reaches of the Klamath River in northwestern California to southern Alaska. They are the only well-known examples of the type. It would be wrong to claim that they are quite well understood because only sample groups here and there on the long coastal strip have been subjected to rather brief periods of field research, much of it after severe acculturation and then guided by linguistic and folkloristic interests rather than by socioeconomic questions.

A possibility that somewhat analogous socioeconomic systems reached the modern period along the Amur River in eastern Siberia and among some Araucanian speaking groups in southern Chile—a district whose climate and botanical characteristics somewhat resemble portions of the Pacific Northwest Coast—deserves careful comparative study. In any case a great many economically primitive food-gatherers' socioeconomic systems and relatively few of economically advanced food-gatherer type survived into modern times. Why? Probably because the latter occupied districts which in ecological respects were more favorable for borrowing of Neolithic cultivated plants. In other words, the Upper Paleolithic very likely witnessed many fertile districts, ten, twenty, or more and exemplified in general respects by modern Pacific Northwest Coast Indian communities, which featured economically advanced food-gatherers. All such districts early became Neolithic agricultural, that is, from four or five to eight or ten thousand years ago.

Anthropology is going to be dependent wholly upon archaeological methods for revelation of even the locations of such districts, let alone for a few fragments of unsystematized information about their technologies and economics. The Pacific Northwest Coast did not become agricultural, unlike all other pre-Neolithic districts of economically advanced food-gatherers, because of an accident or pyramiding of accidents of geographical location. Middle American domesticated food plants, notably maize and beans, had failed to spread from Arizona into southern California apparently because of desert barriers beyond the Colorado River and north into Utah and Nevada, or because of the recency of arrival of Neolithic food-producing materials in the greater Southwest or because of both reasons in combination. If maize and other domesticated plants had gotten into California early in the Christian era, they surely would have advanced northward rapidly. Possibly a number of bred-up food plants, not necessarily maize or beans, would then have metamorphosed the economic life of coastal Indians northward to coastal British Columbia or beyond. In a way, sociocultural anthropology is fortunate in having had one region of economically advanced food-gatherers available for studies although few anthropological observers who had socioeconomic interests have worked in that area.

Economic characteristics of the Pacific Northwest Coast were in general terms as follows, although important local differences in economic systems along the coast seem to have been present.

Very likely no simple food-gatherers' districts had population densities as great as those found in portions of the Pacific Northwest Coast area.

Communities which averaged perhaps between thirty and fifty persons occupied a few permanent plank-, or impermanent bark- or mat-covered dwellings in all-year-round hamlets. One village or town along a valley, bay, or wider river district of twenty to eighty hamlets might contain hundreds of residents. Extremely few towns approached or exceeded a thousand persons. Some such towns, like the two beside the Columbia River near The Dalles, Oregon, functioned as slave and surplus commodity centers where especially wealthy upper-class household groups or lineages lived. It is an open question whether such towns displayed marketlike economic processes. They certainly were centers of wealth and exchanges.

Specialized older persons, slave menials, and a few household followers supplemented a sexual division of labor. A few lifetime specialist craftsmen attached to households of the wealthiest lineages. Some younger men also specialized as hunters or fishermen. A very few hamlets or villages specialized in surplus production of a single commodity, for example, pounded smoke-dried salmon or money dentalia, but it is likely that they were also self-sufficient in production of foods and goods.

Strategic economic production was by sexually segregated work parties exactly as in economically simple food-gathering bands. But in the economically advanced type, headmen or their wives recruited and dominated work parties. Upper-class household leaders also owned slave menials. There are indications, but no sufficient proof, that these leaders manipulated and profited by exchanges of surplus handicraft products of their specialist assistants. Seasonal visits to hunting, fishing, or other sites marked only some residents of hamlets and villages and the occasional work parties organized by the wealthy. All persons, slaves too if so ordered, engaged in individual or work party production which was of lesser economic significance. Distribution of strategic economic production was shared if so directed by the wealthy leaders who, normally, appropriated as much as they wanted. They then allowed the remainder to be shared within the houses of the community and responded to social pressure that it be so. Production by individuals and occasional work parties, not initiated by headmen or their wives, was usually accompanied by ostensibly token gifts of products to leaders. Apparently such donations functioned as and may be regarded as veiled tribute. It enhanced leaders' wealth and prestige.

Headmen and their retinue journeyed to other communities, especially to the few large towns, very likely to unload the factotum's surplus commodities, obtain a slave or two, explore marital possibilities, gamble, and do a variety of things. At such times trade might be effected directly through barter or with sea shell money of varying denominations. It is known that money, and the native languages apparently called it just that, was used to purchase valuable furs, slaves, and wives, in fees to shamans for curing, to persons for many different kinds of services, and as fines. Whether money also functioned in acquisition of most other things is not clear, and it probably did not.

Headmen and their wives enjoyed exclusive rights to use, or they owned, strategic productive resources. Slaves were the most valuable kind of property, and indisputably they were owned by any definition of property ownership. Other privately used or owned resources included ocean fishing areas, river fishing sites, shellfish beaches, wild plant sites, and hunting districts, all of which might be opened to co-villagers or others upon permission.

Readers should note the necessity to avoid culture-bound projection of Euro-American concepts, such as property ownership, onto another socioeconomic system. Concept and caption are to be used, of course, but with caution and thorough redefinition for each kind of economic system.

Nobility, that is, richer household leaders, received increments of wealth principally through tributelike percentages of production and taxlike percentages of fines, marriage payments, and maybe some other transactions about which little is known.

Nobility supported armed followers and conducted profitable as well as sanguinary raids upon distant hamlets, returning with slaves, shell money, and other valuables.

Kinds of investments and bankruptcies characterized leaders' dramatic give-away feasts, sometimes called potlatches, which deeply affected the statuses of households and their lineages. The importance of potlatches in operations of the region's economic systems is a moot question, one which it may be too late to answer notwithstanding the famous writings of Professor Franz Boas and his French sociologist discussant, Marcel Mauss, and statements by a later generation of field workers. But production, distribution, ownership of slaves, and valuable items which were kinds of currency were doubtless more decisive than the many give-away feasts which were only one among several devices in the status competitions of wealthier lineages. In many or most Pacific Northwest Coast districts potlatches probably were less strategic economically than many writers have supposed, although affluence and insolvency may have been consequent everywhere upon playing the game of gift giving, and it had to be played by lineage leaders.

Sociocultural features which were shared along the entire Pacific Northwest Coast are now offered in a second list. It is of importance to keep in mind that the region's heritages have long been stereotyped in one or another way so that their public "image" has had a questionable connection with reality in all its variety. Indeed, the region exhibited notable sociocultural diversity. An unfortunate, but still traditional, focus has been upon especially wealthy and by no means typical groups, the Tlingit, Haida, Tsimshian, Kwakiutl, and Nootka Indians, resident in the northerly segment of the long coastal strip. Clans, the outstandingly spectacular status investments or give-away feasts, and wood sculpturings of that district are often discussed as if representative of the entire coast north of Crescent City, California, when they actually appeared in less than half of it, that is, solely in parts of British Columbia and southern Alaska. A description of life in the pre-Civil War United States based upon industries, customs, and personalities of residents of New England would entail comparable untruth because it would not depict the whole of the North and would ignore border and southern states.

Families were monogamous except in upper-class lineages where leaders who could afford bride purchase costs and huge outlays in interlineage gift giving had as many as four or five wives. There are not even irresponsible reports of either polyandry or fraternal sexual access to wives; these piquant relationships can be presumed to have been absent. Marriages were arranged, not by sultry freedom of choice, except among the very poor and slaves. Parents and household or lineage leaders negotiated, exchanged gifts, and consummated a union with a large payment, in both sea shell money and highly valued commodities, to the bride's parents, who were always of another hamlet or town. Separations were dangerous and infrequent because of need to repay and assuage hurt feelings with money and gifts. Feminine status was a notch below men until the menopause. Women then could venture upon monetarily rewarding and ego-enhancing participations, such as shamanistic curing, usually previously difficult for them to enter. Noble, well-to-do, and poor households or lineages functioned somewhat like class strata of the world's wealthy societies but apparently much more competitively. They vied so as to rise and fall in prestige and wealth. Raid-captive or bought slaves, owned by nobles or well-to-do families, constituted a fixed lowest social class and most valuable kind of property. Slaves were few and comparatively unimportant in economic production perhaps until the early nineteenth century, at which time lineage leaders of the northernmost groups reflected their sensationally expanding economy by acquisition of a great many unfortunates. In earlier times a household or lineage headman had usually owned a few slaves, his wife one or two also, and occasionally a well-to-do gentleman or his wife owned a slave, too.

Until the present day some writers have been unable to handle Euro-American concepts with the elasticity required when extrapolating them for use upon somewhat similar nonwestern social forms and cultural features. Difficulties encountered by such writers are exhibited in almost a classic manner in their discussions of the Northwest Coast. They have gone out of their way, and perhaps they had to because of Euro-American rigidity in manipulation of conceptual equipment, in order to urge that Pacific Northwest slaves were really only symbols of status like inert badges, did not produce for their masters in any economically vital way, and were devoid of significance in accumulation of economic surpluses or in release of freemen to specialize as craftsmen. And native informants themselves nowadays stress the status-symbol function of their oldtime slaves even though they were kept busy at chores and did not escape hard labor. All modern informants must be watched closely to determine ways in which they set up defenses against criticism and fend to minimize disapproval of their native predecessors. There are signs of rationalization and whitewash in contemporary characterizations of earlier days. No evidence indicates that a majority of slaves were essentially symbols rather than perspiring, self-depreciating, and despairing captive menials or that they functioned primarily as beloved servants like favored mulattos in antebellum plantation mansions. Data on Northwest Coast slavery are so fragmentary that it precludes clarification.

A wealthy headman and his immediate family constituted a kind of nobility. Well-to-do families attached as members of a lineage to such nobles and, surprisingly to Euro-Americans, appear to have comprised the larger portion of many hamlet and village populations. Although census and statistical reports are lacking, extrapolation of likely percentages of one or another class in a European population is improper. If a European working class constituted 95 percent of its community, the Northwest Coast class of poor people less than 30 percent, and that region's slave class before 1800 less than 5 percent, we witness only the invariable lesson: concepts and terms from Euro-American society must be redefined for other social systems and used differently from ways in which they apply when referring to Euro-American relationships.

The thought that 30 to 60 percent of a European community was of nobles and well-to-do is ridiculous. Such an estimate is close to accuracy for portions of the Pacific Northwest Coast. Some families were not members of noble lineages although they were also well-to-do. Remarkable fluidity, no one today can determine how much, occurred in class status apart from the hopelessly immobilized slaves. A few anthropologists have been so pleased, alarmed, or bewildered by such vertical mobility, which did not feature European society until recently, that they have published curious statements about what they term the region's integrading statuses. Every language in the area nevertheless had forms (linguists term them morphemes), and every social system of the region had clear concepts, about the several social strata, nor is it astigmatic adherence to dogma to recognize their reality.

Ability to rise and fall in status is characteristic of stratified systems. Some have been far more inflexible than others in class demarcations. Vertical mobility of a most highly lubricated kind no more controverts a stratification which natives conceptualized and named than elevators, operating freely with ball bearings and cables, suggest an absence of superimposed floors. Since many Northwest Coast natives' self-esteem and identities were in terms of these floors, such evidence must be respected as well as the evidence of supernaturalism, potlatching, gambling, and other elevators which carried individuals up and down rather easily. It is of significance, too, that in some districts each tiny hamlet of a few households had its special status in relation to other hamlets or villages. Frequently a noble or especially well-to-do lineage resided in only one among several hamlets.

Government was undemocratic but with checks of undetermined effectiveness upon autocratic or severe decisions. The noble leader of the wealthiest household or lineage perpetuated its control of his village, maybe of several contiguous hamlets too, by handing on the succession to a son he selected. Younger men, whom he housed and aided with their marriage gifts and payments, functioned as his and his lineage's police and armed followers. He and his wife might have a few domestic slaves. He arbitrated disputes, took a cut of fines imposed, received seemingly voluntarily offered but impressive portions of everyone's production, maintained specialist craftsmen, and dispensed hospitality with unction and charity, sometimes through his gracious spouse, to the aged and needy. He enjoyed, with his wife too, exclusive use or ownership of one or several of the most productive sites or areas, and they organized village work parties which conducted major production. His status rose or ebbed with those who attached to his household, with slaves, with wealth he received from lineages voluntarily resident in his village and hamlet domain, with successes or fiascos in competitive feast giving and gambling, with fines and tribute, with ecstatic identification with beneficial supernaturals, and assuredly with other important things which operated so automatically and therefore generated so few tensions that native interpreters failed to tell anthropologists much about them. Lineages' convictions of identity and worth and their leaders' fealty to a topnotch lineage leader connected with his ability to offer armed protection and with his status as munificent purveyor of gifts, foods, and elegant, if defiantly aggressive, verbaloney upon intervillage feast occasions. Loyal leaders of well-to-do households and lineages were a check upon him and functioned as a council. One such leader might be a kind of speaker, issuing statements for him while he mumbled pompously behind his public mouthpiece. In portions of the region offenses, slights, humiliations, even the severest crimes could be resolved by fines, precedents for which determined the amount of payment sufficient to prevent bloodletting, feuding, or even grieved sentiments.

Religious ideology was prevailingly a vast aggregate of spirit-powers, the most potent of whom tended to relate to and assist wealthy persons. Individual quests secured such relationships except in the most northerly groups where supernaturals tended to affiliate, and who could blame them, with groups of wealthy lineage leaders. Poorer people and slaves related to spirit-powers also, but infrequently to outstandingly helpful ones. Even the supernaturals were reluctant to suffer social humiliation! Shamans were persons, of both sexes, who had happened to relate to supernatural kin who gave them power to cure, poison, or influence nature, always for fees. First root, fruit, salmon, marital, or other rites might not necessarily be conducted by shamans. Winter spirit-power song-dance occasions functioned to reconstitute or intensify individuals' ties with their supernaturals, to express other persons' support of another's spirit relatives, and to permit competitive displays of the potencies of their supernaturals. Spirit-powers were truly a kind of extended kin.

Each small area had distinctive basketry, music, dance, and oral literature expressions. Designs in sculpture were similar along the northerly third or half of the coastal strip. During the nineteenth century wealthy lineages of the most northerly groups had craftsmen carve commemorative house posts to heights which required placement of such columns outside; these became the so-called "totem poles" each of which, like posts inside houses, carved feast dishes, treasure boxes, and the like, depicted some of the actor-supernaturals in one of the legends which constituted something of the self-identity of the lineage of the house. Youngsters enjoyed utmost encouragement to master all art heritages assigned to their sex. Basketry, weaving, and manufacture of garments were assigned to females, carving to males.

Competition in shamanistic work, craft and esthetic creativity, gambling, and acquisition of wealth and status, and the leisure allowed everyone because of vast reserves of smoke-dried fish, venison, shellfish, and berries, resulted in societies whose inventiveness and creativity channeled principally into nonmaterial expressions, and into carving also in the most northerly groups. In a very few communities ownership of wild plant sites by women of a wealthy lineage resulted in watering, weeding, and tending of plants. Such specialist-like care and labor appear to have made possible one or several plant domestications. But a portentous advance of that nature was not achieved. The region remained food-gathering in economic type until Caucasian entry.

There can be no doubt that the late Ruth Benedict's famous characterization of the "culture pattern" as megalomaniac and paranoid was a misinterpretation of projective expressions in one Vancouver Island group's (Kwakiutl) stylized headman oratory. What some silver-tongued and affluent speakers of that group said (and had to say) doubtless expressed important tensions but by no means represented prevailing relationships, feelings, personality types among the nobility, value ideals, or world view along the entirety of the coastal strip. Dr. Benedict's Northwest Coast chapter in her distinguished book, *Patterns of Culture*, was an arresting but simplistic contribution in the 1930's. Today it requires rewriting.

## Economically Simple Agricultural Systems

This third type, if the fact of modest agricultural production alone justifies setting up another type, again comprises an abstraction of socioeconomic features. They appeared both among economically simple food-gatherers and in a great diversity of other societies probably ever since the first cereal grasses, wheat, millet, barley, and rye, were bred up 8,000 or more years ago in southwestern Asia. They or other newly domesticated plants such as manioc, potatoes, and maize in Latin America were taken over by food-gatherers of various kinds. Many hundreds of economically simple food-gathering systems must have metamorphosed into economically simple agricultural systems at one or another time during the last 8,000 or more years because of a choice to raise domesticated food plants previously possessed by and patently of benefit to neighboring communities.

A few anthropologists have asserted that so-called "mixed economies" resulted on mainlands, as well as in small island areas, directly after economically simple food-gatherers accepted agriculture. These writers have indicated that "mixed economies" sometimes long endured, that is, were of a special type characterized by equally decisive food-gathering and raising of one or several crops. Claims of this kind contain a hidden premise which assumes that an economic system, especially one on a mainland, could continue for a period of years in a juggler's balance of production from hunting or fishing and production from domesticated plants. Possibly just this sort of equilibrium of fishing and agriculture, the latter severely limited in its productivity or capacity to grant security, did feature a few Oceanian atolls and other small island areas. Indications on mainlands of a comparable parity of hunting and agriculture are not convincing because they are not supported by a single thorough economic analysis of such a half-and-half hunting-and-agriculture community. A more cautious deduction is to suppose that with adoption of agriculture by a food-gathering group —some atolls and a rare additional district or two may offer intriguing exceptions—agricultural production within a decade became decisive in economic functions, maybe in its setting new limits to social patterns, although the system long maintained hunting, fishing, or wild plant collecting in economically important ancillary roles.

A so-called "mixed" system requires especially precise definition and close depiction of how it functioned and what it did to social relationships. It is impossible to accept, for example, 80 percent of production from domesticated food plants and 20 percent production from slaughter of wild animals as a case for a "mixed" system. Unless evidence is found to the contrary, such a system was one in which agriculture was central and hunting only important. In other words, it was an agriculture-based economic system. Indeed, a great many economic systems of nonwestern peoples featured more or less vital, but not economically central, hunting or fishing production. The agricultural aspect of the system was almost always decisive because it speedily became the major factor, among several economic variables, in effecting surpluses or in pressuring and maintaining special social relationship patterns, including property ownership, specialization of labor, and elaborate gift or other exchanges. No economic system ever long endured as two systems, conjoined like Siamese twins, any more than there ever was one person who was two persons skeletally and physiologically. Anyway, instances of split personality, identical twins, and monsters are not really relevant. The problem, which is unusually difficult to handle, is to denote quantity of foods and things produced and to discover factors which shaped important social relationships and the most vital cultural expressions.

The stationary nature of tillable land and anxieties around crop production because of plant diseases, loss of fertility, rainfall, storms, and insect and rodent pests, may be numbered among factors which quickly rendered agriculture of central moment in a nonwestern socioeconomic structure which lately had accepted it. The burden of proof is upon protagonists of neatly equated hunting-agriculture or fishing-agriculture economic systems. It is up to them to show that there have been such poised dualistic structures in which social relationship and expressive concomitants of production by hunting continued to be as significant as those by agriculture.

Where a simple food-gathering system had lately adopted domesticated food plants, the new agricultural variables might not soon effect thoroughgoing changes in division of labor, ownership of economically strategic property, and other features of the economy. If the new agricultural production long continued to be severely limited by soil and climatic conditions, by an absence of irrigation techniques, or by the small tillable area available on a tiny island or coral atoll or along a narrow valley, and no important surpluses were envisaged or achieved over a period of years, the economic structure might not depart fundamentally from its traits of earlier food-gathering pattern. It maintained most of the features. As late as 1492 A.D. a few million people lived in agricultural economic systems which approximated this general kind, a total very likely surpassing that of the populations of all the food-gathering societies which had also survived into modern times.

The United States offers excellent, maybe classic, examples of economically simple agricultural systems of this type, although they also displayed strikingly diverse social systems and cultural heritages. Iroquois and Algonkin groups of northeastern North America contrasted with Hopi, Zuñi, and some other Pueblos, with Athabaskan-speaking Apache and Navajo bands, and with other southwestern peoples such as Pima-Papago, Havasupai, and neighbors of the latter. But all were agriculturalists. Every part of Oceania and many South American districts east of the Andes also offered examples of the type, although as in North America they were of a variety of kinds and many such groups were already marginal to wealthier agricultural societies. The model receives probably rare representation in Africa and was comparatively infrequent in Asia. In those two continents most peoples had long had systems whose potentials for economic surpluses were great. These wealthier systems had had fateful influences upon the socioeconomic structures of poorer ones.

During several decades the rank and file of anthropologists, from England's Marxist oriented prehistorian V. Gordon Childe to almost every contemporary anthropological author, have used the terms "food producers" and "food producing" as especially distinctive of economically simple agriculturalists who pioneered the Neolithic era. Peoples who had relinquished much of their former food-gathering, hunting, and fishing and had become agriculturalists were said to have become "food producers." Now, in recent anthropology, "food producer" is an idiom, a linguistic designation which verges on a neologism, which has been hallowed by Childe and his admirers. In spite of the circumstance that an entire scientific profession has adopted it, it is disingenuous if it is taken literally as it may well be by non-anthropologists. Agriculture was of course the most important new feature of Neolithic times. Childe's and the anthropologists' alternative term for the era, "the food producing revolution," was always inappropriate and to the merest handful of nonconforming anthropologists it has remained ludicrous. They feel that food-gatherers produced foods, too, by the sometimes less productive but not less dramatic techniques of hunting, fishing, and collecting. When you hit a sluggish porcupine on the head and take him home because his meat is tender, delicious, and nourishing, you are engaged in food producing, if you speak English. Any procurement of food, short of theft of an incidental kind, is food producing. Food-gatherers had only a different array of techniques of food production and they lacked the potential which agriculture had for production of astronomical quantities of foods. Accordingly, this book will not perpetuate Childe's economic and linguistic booboo which implies, to speakers of ordinary English, that food-gatherers did not produce foods. It will not suggest, by its terminology, that food producing commenced only in that comparatively recent epoch, the Neolithic, when a few persons began to select the seeds of better plants, poke them into holes, worry over them, fertilize, weed, and water, and presently develop specialist craftsmen, minstrels, and military leaders. In fact, if early peoples of hundreds of thousands of years ago had not been food producers in their own limited but often courageous and persistent ways, none of us would be here today.

What were principal features of economically simple agricultural systems?

Population densities may not often have been greater than in densely peopled Pacific Northwest Coast districts of economically advanced food-gatherers.

As in such Northwest Coast areas, self-sufficient all-year-round hamlets often numbered only a few score persons. However, villages or towns of from 1,000 to 2,000 persons appeared in especially favorable locations. Tillable land was adjacent or at a short distance.

Economically decisive work was by individuals or families on hamlet or village assigned plots. In some regions families received equivalently strategic productive labor in seasonal land clearing and harvesting with the aid of a party of co-residents. Economically less decisive but important production was by work parties that fished, hunted, and collected wild plants.

Foods produced by individuals on assigned plots were distributed by sharing solely when everyone was in need. Products of hamlet or village work parties outside of agricultural production were usually at once shared.

One or another among a variety of factors present the world over in systems of this category allowed some younger individuals, and older persons as in food-gathering societies, long periods of release for specialist handicraft and religious pursuits, although a simple sexual division of labor applied to most people.

Exchanges were by gifts and barter, in varying amounts depending on numbers of specialist handicraft producers and surplus products they turned out. Commerce, salable surplus commodities, and money were absent, if it be allowable to employ concepts and terms extrapolated from modern western society's market system.

Although hamlet and village councils assigned and reassigned agricultural plots to individuals, families, or lineages for long, if not indefinite periods, such decisive productive resources remained ultimately property owned by a community, precisely because it could and did reassign it. Reports on such communities have frequently insisted on private ownership in instances where words of interpreters were written down and taken literally. Although ownership has to be defined not in Euro-American terms but cross-culturally and perhaps extremely elastically, it is a difficult socioeconomic trait to establish in nonwestern societies which lacked slaves and were not wealthy. Presumably the most important property was tillable land. Communities and, only later, households or lineages owned it.

Since no one sold foods, surplus handicraft products, or land, and no individual, household, or lineage initially owned productive resources such as land or slaves, inequalities in wealth and social status connected with wealth did not soon appear. Nonsignificant inequalities featured ownership of personal effects and abilities of various kinds.

Indications of tribute, taxation, and raiding for plunder or slaves are largely absent. As among economically simple food-gatherers, people killed principally when aggrieved, angry, or humiliated, and their violence took the forms of feuds and vengeance attacks. Fighting on a larger scale did occur in defense against warlike and predatory neighbors of different socioeconomic type.

One of the most important formulations is that remarkable potentials for technological creativity which almost all food-gatherers lacked were immanent in socioeconomic systems of this type. Economically simple food-gatherers were too committed to collecting foods and maintaining gear the year round, too mobile seasonally, too attached to supernaturals who connected with their security in each food producing season and district, too needful of goodly periods for loafing, playing, and talking, and too unspecialized in skills to tinker at great length with the designs of the few artifacts which they made and which also had to be carried about. Improvements in their spears, bows, arrows, cutting tools, baskets, garb, and rituals could not change production significantly. Economically advanced food-gatherers did enjoy all-year-round abodes, especially long and secure periods of leisure because of stored surpluses of smoke-dried foods, some specialization in handicraft skills even among younger persons, and extraordinary amounts of time for ceremonial, feasting, playing, and gossiping. But their forms of specialization tended to be applied to wool-bearing dog farms, garments, basketry, religious regalia, wood, bone, and horn carving for decorative purposes, dance, music, oral literature and other interests, hardly a one of which led to an avenue of economically significant technological advance.

In agricultural systems of any kind, potentials for still more specialization of labor could develop. Rapidly fashioned pottery tended to displace slowly made basketry containers. In any case, agriculturalists of a few districts appear to have enjoyed cumulative and, over a long era, unprecedented possibilities for material inventions, artifact innovations, and sociocultural changes. Agriculture possibly did not cause directly anything outstandingly distinctive. But it seems to have been less limiting in some few places. Here and there it did offer new opportunities, more things that could be made and done. Euro-Americans might refer to this unique potential which maybe no food-gathering village with all its specialists could have had, by saying that agricultural economic systems tended to be more progressive than food-gatherers in their long range effect upon frequencies of invention of new gadgetry.

The second list of features, sociocultural traits in economically simple agricultural groups, is more difficult to assemble than for food-gatherers because of the very much greater range of social forms and cultural expressions which even these simple agricultural economies allowed.

As in economically simple food-gatherers, from which kind of economy and social structure agriculturalists had often metamorphosed not long before, marriage was ultimately by freedom of choice within customary rules of clan, lineage, and other kinds of prescriptions. Claims about plural husbands, that is, polyandry, are infrequent. As among food-gatherers, they are feebly attested because of failure to determine the duration of and sentiments in such unions. Presumably, polyandrous and polygamous households were everywhere permissible. However, households with plural wives did appear here and there. They numbered more than two wives infrequently. It is evident that large polygamous establishments developed only in wealthier societies where men purchased females, all of whom had low status. Separations appear to have been voluntary and maybe frequent in the absence of dependent youngsters.

Assertions about feminine status in economically simple agricultural groups have varied with observers' culture-shaped feelings and standards to which they resorted for such judgments. Familiar nineteenth century deductions were that Iroquois and other women enjoyed superior status, then called a matriarchate. Other writers inferred only parity with men or slightly lower status. Principal factors which long confused amateurs' and even the social anthropologists' assessment of feminine status in these societies were matrilineal reckoning of membership in lineage, clan, or other groups, matrilineal transmission of rights to horticultural plots, and matrilocal residence. Matrilineal reckoning, sometimes matrilocal residence custom too, appeared of course in some advanced food-gathering societies such as Alaska's Tlingits, where the feminine sex was of lower status at least before, if not also after, the menopause. Matrilineality in Iroquois and some Southwest Pueblo groups appears not to have connected immediately or directly with feminine status, although parity of the sexes is a plausible inference from indications which include absence of bride purchase, women's dignity, their lack of wiles or servility, and freedom to make choices such as tossing out a husband who was no longer wanted.

Class or status strata were absent in societies of this type. Everyone received a spontaneous ranking which assessed his worth as an individual, but status is something else.

Motivations for fighting were the universal ones of vengeance, poisoning, feuds, the loci of aggression which generated resolutions in individual or small-scale killings. Pacifism, with exceptions to be sure, was the theme. On the other hand, societies of this type frequently had to engage in wholesale killings because they had to defend themselves against displaced and predatory food-gatherers or wealthy agricultural or pastoral raiding peoples who lived not far away. When domesticated plants and animals appeared in a region, few peoples were so securely or marginally located that they could long continue to be pacifistic at the core and to limit their most aggressive ecstacies to small-scale feuding, kicking pebbles, and hocus pocus poisoning.

Government in economically simple agricultural groups was able to take a great many forms in spite of its prevailing democratic basis. Hereditary leaders appeared maybe only rarely in groups where a clan or similar system assigned one or several lineages to a permanent community responsibility. The common pattern was government by voluntary or democratically elected committee-like personnel, subject to quick recall when disapproved by the people. A few anthropologists have used an analogy of the early New England town hall meeting democracy, with its public elections attended by everyone and its assignments to short-term leaderships for special tasks of noteworthy value to the community.

Religion was so variable in ideology of supernaturals, ceremonials, leadership, and the like that tenable generalizations are doubtless not many or even meaningful. Supernaturals of the small-dimensioned kinds which featured food-gatherers' religious ideology may have been supplemented by ancestor spirits and comparatively minor deific beings, even by impersonal power or mana. Pantheons of titanic or supernal gods may have been largely absent. Ceremonials were perhaps more often occupied with weather and plants, with fish also where such a resource was of productive importance, than among food-gatherers. Shamans, that is, part-time manipulators of supernaturals who facilitated cures and did other unusual things for people, were usually present. But the question has often been raised about priests and priesthoods in these societies. Did more or less specialist religious leaders constitute full-time or only part-time workers? Therefore were they priests or something else? It is a matter of definition wherein the criterion must be, as elsewhere, to present anthropology with a clear-cut entity in native life and culture and, at the same time, avoid culture-bound or religion-bound extrapolations of Euro-American concepts.

As always, there is no good alternative to employment of the often frustrating resources in terms available in Euro-American dictionaries. In order to escape distortions in meanings some anthropologists have used, especially when they discussed a nonwestern religion, a great many native terms which they highlighted with italics or made to look bewitching in anguishing phonetic transcriptions which were invariably wrong, anyway, in the light of later or contemporary devices for linguistic analysis. Authors who choose deliberately to become incomprehensible and pretentious in this manner rather than commit errors of improper extrapolation are hardly aware that scientific work cannot be conducted by interested people who do not understand what is going on. It is therefore necessary to emphasize that when a publication on a nonwestern people or topic is printed in a Euro-American language, terms from that language have to be used. But they must be defined pointedly and shown to cover concepts which, in their redefined connotations, are different from those indicated in a dictionary of that language. The term priest, for example, is excellent if it is defined for special purposes of a wholly un-Euro-American kind and if, to be sure, it eventually receives a few hundred definitions which apply to the several hundred nonwestern societies in which priestlike personages were present.

Materials, expressive content, and form in arts of economically simple agricultural societies were so varied that meaningful generalizations are few. In regions where clay was available, pottery was almost certain to appear and to become the perquisite of a handful of women who were specialist potters for the community. Basketry or other materials for containers might long continue to be used although pots tended to replace other kinds of containers and to release many women for handicrafts such as weaving. Iroquois and Oceanian wood carving are now famous. All art forms appear to have been available and important to everyone. A risky impression is that few other types of society offered such favorable environments for every kind of esthetic expression, much of it attached to religion of course. Extraordinary elaborations in music, dance, and oral arts are common knowledge today among Americans who have a smattering of information about Arizona and New Mexico Indians.

No characterization of personalities of peoples of this type, or of each of the food-gathering types, is possible. Benedict's now classic stereotype, in her *Patterns of Culture*, of so-called "Apollonian" orientations and values among Pueblo Indians applied only to them and not necessarily to any other agricultural peoples. Enormous variability in psychological manifestations was almost certainly characteristic of the many member groups in each type of socioeconomic pattern.

## Economically Advanced Agricultural Systems

During recent decades anthropologists have suggested subtypes or noted points along the continuum of these numerous economic systems. Doubtless scores of millions of people, principally in Latin American countries, entered modern times as their representatives. In America pastoralism was new and limited to several Andean groups. It lagged far behind the Old

World in its few forms, in its base in slightly domesticated small camels (llama and alpaca), and in the meager socioeconomic import of such animals by contrast with Old World impacts of cattle, sheep, horse, and other animal domestications. Most Old World advanced agricultural systems were actually systems with agriculture primary and pastoralism important but secondary. Here the word "mixed" may be proper as a means of characterizing many Old World socioeconomic systems. It means that two major but new kinds of productive resource had welded somehow and that the one of usually lesser import, pastoralism, nevertheless had salient consequences upon social structure and cultural expressions. Systems in which domesticated animals were economically primary should be placed in a distinct type, as below. Pastoralism in the Old World comprised one or more of a group of domesticated creatures which includes in addition to cattle, sheep and horses, water buffalo, goats, swine, camels, donkeys, poultry, and others. In South American Andean districts, economic systems, such as the Inca polity, contained an upper class which owned the valuable herds of llamas and alpacas. No other economically significant animal domestication affected America's advanced agricultural systems. Andean highland domesticated guinea pigs and the several incipient turkey domestications, the latter found as far north as the southwestern United States, helped pleasantly in the larder in some regions but not as pervasively as potatoes. For the most part American Indians lacked economically strategic domesticated animals, unless one is prepared to macerate a conventional point of view by regarding slaves in that light. The dog was vital, to be sure, as a hunting aid to Eskimos, Kalapuyas in western Oregon, and a very few other groups, but not to economically advanced American peoples.

Some advanced agricultural societies of America may represent, as well as or better than any of the Old World, principal components of economic and social patterns which continued or developed from immediately preceeding food-gathering societies of a wealthy kind. However, few determinations may ever be possible of specific American Indian districts which had so evolved and at best the evidence would produce no more than spotty information on sociocultural processes and phenomena. Much or all of it would have to come from archaeological researches.

What are the few shared characteristics of economically advanced agricultural societies in America and in a number of Old World areas?

Populations were presently denser than in food-gathering or economically simple agricultural societies.

Villages, towns, crowded suburb-like districts, and even large urban areas appeared, a very few of the latter housing hundreds of thousands of persons.

Decisive economic production was in several types. The first type displayed servile or slave labor groups. As elsewhere, Euro-Americans' concept of a slave should not be projected mechanically into a nonwestern system. Relationships of servile workers to everyone else have to be examined in each nonwestern society and the term, "slave," redefined accordingly. Whatever they were in details of their situation, slaves were used or owned by the upper class or royal family. They were frankly private property in antebellum days in the United States. The circumstance that American Negro slaves were status symbols, offered ready at hand scapegoats, and trussed up the egos of non-slaves, is important but their role in production and domestic labor was decisive. The point is that all slaves functioned like productive property which had private owners. Secondly, there was much production by specialist craftsmen, specialist hamlets or villages, or specialist fishing, hunting, or agricultural districts. Products of specialists of all kinds might be carried to market villages for barter or sale on market days. Specialist merchants, warriors, educators, physicians, musicians, and priests often developed.

Distribution was never decisively by sharing. Wealthy owners of agricultural land and of servile workers received most. They and royalty obtained further increments of wealth from various forms of taxation and tribute exacted from those who attended or sold at the marketplace, from merchants, and others. Payments of fines constituted another source of revenue. Plunder in warfare was probably of first importance as a source of royal wealth. It was a kind of production by soldiery.

All, or almost all, these societies had neatly divisible, portable, and comparatively imperishable units, currency, as media of exchange for slaves, taxes, fines, and sometimes for the many surplus commodities produced. Sea shell money such as cowries was common. Portions of Central America apparently used chocolate beans as money, but it may be an unusual example of a currency since it was of perishable material. Groups of merchants traveled about, sometimes protected by warriors.

Upper-class men, including priests in some regions, owned wealth, that is, decisive economic resources, which included servile and captive labor in addition to tillable land.

Unequal ownership of wealth equated with class statuses which in a few regions tended to metamorphose into specialist castes.

The wealthy, including royalty and priesthoods, supported an array of specialist bureaucrats or civil servants, a judiciary, and armed followers. Warriors may be regarded both as a productive resource and as specialists in protection and defense of a regime. Conquests by soldiery gained the wealthy new productive resources in lands, captives, and slaves, in addition to valuables which at once added to wealth.

Economic systems of this kind, based as they were upon agriculture, huge servile labor forces, and men-at-arms were unquestionably more progressive, in the sense of potential to increase production further and to be rapidly changing in technology and features of societal structuring, than economic types cited above. Greater numbers of specialists, rewards and stimulation from trade, trade by specialist merchants, construction of roads by royalty, and opportunities available to specialist priesthoods, may be listed among factors which permitted, if they did not generate, ever larger numbers of material improvements and inventions. On the other hand, warfare occasionally negated material accumulation and perhaps technological advances, too, because of its massive destruction, indiscriminate slaughter, and follow-up in enslavement of the defeated.

Economic systems of wealthy peoples of the Old World are especially varied and complex, also confusing to us, because of additional problems involved in handling analyses of domesticated animals as productive resources. African, Asian, and Indonesian types of economy, with their important productive resources in domesticated animals, are many. They will not be discussed for they merge, along the continuum of types, with systems which are proper concerns of economic historians like Karl Polanyi, who has written about classical Mediterranean and other so-called "great" civilizations. However, analyses of these socioeconomic fabrics resemble depictions of the less wealthy but still advanced agricultural systems. Today, all wealthy systems of nonwestern peoples in Africa, Indonesia, and much of southern Asia may be left to anthropological field workers to study, although it would be better for economic theory if economists joined forces with anthropologists in researches on them. The day is long since over when an anthropologist could emulate a Leonardo da Vinci in his many-sided interests and competences. He needs allies in economists who are not incurably western economics-bound.

It cannot be said too often that in analyses of economic systems the greatest care must be employed to avoid naïve projection or extrapolation of western civilization's concepts and terms. Words such as slave, serf, market, money, property, rent, interest, profit, and taxes have long served in descriptions and theory of the economy peculiar to modern western society. The task is always to arrange and account for components, facets, and operations of a nonwestern system by judicious use of concepts and terms which are specifically defined for each distinctive system and which are therefore torn from connotations granted for description of operations of another society. In order to be cross-cultural it is necessary to be warily cross-terminological and cross-conceptual. The tricky, slippery foes are culture-bondedness and unconscious extrapolations. The latter enemies also have sharp horns and an uncanny capacity to keep themselves invisible. The technique for avoiding such mean adversaries is, first, to try to slice a phenomenon the way it really is and not the way in which an outsider thinks he perceives it, and again, to borrow a familiar term and concept but to redefine it for the special purpose of labeling the new segment of material.

If we now endeavor to inventory shared sociocultural characteristics of advanced agricultural systems something close to chaos may result. Some anthropologists may be right when they urge that, at present, the least distortion is effected when methodological emphasis is upon painstaking historical reconstruction of sociocultural phenomena in smaller regions, with postponement of cross-cultural generalizations until a few such intensive regional time depth studies are well under way. Archaeological techniques are sometimes helpful adjuncts to historical studies because, here and there, arid climates and great production of artifacts, garments, buildings, and religious edifices offer quantities of data.

Still, a few generalizations about sociocultural features of these wealthy groups may be safe statements and, in fact, present a pedagogically employable, although excessively simple, sketch model. It cannot serve as a guide for analysis of cultural expressions because of their variety and the multiple variables which shaped them.

Marriages tended to be arranged rather than effected by the two participants' free option, at least in upper social strata. Bride purchase and dowry sums were considerable in wealthy families. Well-to-do gentlemen were often polygamous. Polyandrous unions, possibly often of short duration, have been reported in a number of East African, Tibetan, Indian, and other districts for an uncertain, but not necessarily small, percentage of families, and in groups which also displayed polygamy. Fraternal polyandry shades almost imperceptibly into fraternal wife sharing in parts of India, with a number of factors shaping such relationships.

It is easy to oversimplify by urging that in lower-class families younger brothers resided with an older brother because the family was unable to accumulate sufficient wealth for purchase of the younger fellows' brides. It is now evident that polyandry occurs in wealthy families too and that poverty is not a decisive cause in each instance. Field researches, especially in India, have lately begun to be more sensitive than in earlier years and, although they indicate multiple factors, it is clear that one is a customary sharing by brothers of a variety of kinds of valuable property. There can be no doubt that fraternal polyandry sometimes arose in districts where such fraternal ties were close. Until recently Euro-American reporters of polyandry seem to have been in the field briefly or to have been stirred emotionally so that they were unable to perceive what was happening. They could not draw a line between permissible sexual access to a sibling's wife and the institution of polyandry. Many earlier reports of the latter may therefore have been misinterpretations. In any case, polyandrous families, usually comprising a number of brothers, seem to have been limited to a few districts.

Polyandry is a rare marital institution the world over. Even in the several Indian districts where it is well attested, it is hardly more frequently noted than polygamous households. Psychological concomitants of polyandry and sexual access, which superficially resembles polyandry, appear not to have been studied carefully anywhere. A Freudian emphasis upon incest feelings may be worth looking into, together with many other matters.

The status of females in economically advanced agricultural societies was far beneath that of males. However, opportunities for new participations for women after their menopause often were such as to bring about an older age group which enjoyed strikingly high status. A rule of thumb is that woman's status before the menopause was very low if the society had a large servile labor class. Psychological concomitants of domestic immobilization, low status, and male dominance offer a potentially extensive area of scientific inquiry which has not yet interested either psychologists or anthropologists in any numbers.

Class or caste stratification in these societies also connected with psychological phenomena of the greatest variety and interest, although rigorous researches on the latter are virtually nil. Inability to develop or later destruction of ego strength, hypocritical servility, Uncle Tom responses such as defensive identification with the master, and repressed general hostility to people but partly displaced onto out-groups may have been present in the nethermost social strata of economically advanced agriculturalists. These and other traits have been highlighted in recent studies of Negro slaves and Nazi concentration camp inmates.

Statements about lineage and clan relationships would have to be too diversified, numerous, and connected with regional or local circumstances to serve the introductory purposes of this book.

Warfare, sometimes frightfully bloody, was probably characteristic of all these societies whose well-to-do gambled with force and supernaturals to acquire additional wealth in agricultural lands, domesticated animals, servile labor, and tribute, or to effect other ends. Insecurities arising out of fears of loss of warriors and of one's own family, freedom, home, wealth, or life doubtless constituted important psychological phenomena about which almost nothing is known. The investigation of the psychology of Inca soldiers is a lost cause.

Government was, of course, sometimes by priesthoods and always by the wealthy. Except for occasional local manifestations, it was extremely undemocratic. Studies of law and government in societies of this type have, fortunately, been forthcoming, especially from Indonesian and African locales where, until recent attainment of nationhood, interests of Holland and Britain might be served by such knowledge.

Religions in these societies are, again, poorly known. Specialist priesthoods, often of considerable wealth, tended to develop and to function beside shaman-like personnel who operated in back alleys of the system. Pantheons of deities and great numbers of small-scale projective figures have generally been found. Specialists in the supernatural tended to fabricate theologies out of old myth expressive materials.

The great numbers of specialists guaranteed extensive esthetic productivity and originality. Plastic and graphic art might become more important economically and culturally than among food-gatherers or poorer agricultural groups. On the other hand, fewer individuals were able to find esthetic opportunity. Each art form tended to be limited to specialists and specialist teachers rather than available to every young person.

## Additional Socioeconomic Types

Before the expansions of wealthy agricultural and agricultural-pastoral economic systems about 6,000 or 7,000 years ago, and ever since, the major socioeconomic types sketched above, and the many subtypes within each, apply to self-sufficient systems of kinds in which an older generation of anthropologists was primarily interested. These types fit as segments along the principal continuum of economic patterns with which we started. But some other types of socioeconomic systems lie a bit off that continuum. This is partly because certain societies constituted special responses to envelopment and conquest. But only in recent decades have anthropologists broadened their interests to include study of a variety of systems generated by forces first set in motion perhaps a little over 6,000 years ago. What socioeconomic types were responses to such generative processes?

Economically advanced agriculturalists and agricultural-pastoral peoples metamorphosed into unprecedented and sometimes entirely viable socioeconomic forms, but often with shattering effects upon expressive cultural manifestations. Such results were caused by the manner of penetration and envelopment of these systems, whether in the early period of Old World alluvial valley urbanism over 6,000 years ago, during frightful slave empire expansions such as Rome's, or in the modern epoch of bewilderment, humiliation, anger and destruction consequent upon European infiltration and surrounding after 1492 A.D.

Many systems appear to have been beleaguered but not wholly crushed or disintegrated. They changed drastically into special types of marginal or not wholly self-sufficient systems. Some of them were of kinds which the late Robert Redfield denoted *peasant societies*. Each village or cluster of villages of such an engulfed group had become tied by economic, political, religious, and cultural bonds to a wealthy regime whose urban centers were nearby. Such a peasant community or cluster of communities functioned in a kind of symbiosis with a nearby city or manor where an elite, wealthy, or upper class dwelt. Characteristics shared among the subtypes of peasant community include the following.

A peasant village sold surplus products, such as foods or manufactured commodities, to cities or manors and usually received money in exchange. Villages might also send their specialist wares to markets held periodically, so that villagers bought from one another. Peasants paid tribute to city or manor or, at a later time, taxes and labor time. They borrowed money from city or manorial lord and, in consequence, paid high interest rates. They admitted merchants, storekeepers, and a few outsiders to their community. These gentry were "resident strangers" who did not relate to the peasant villagers as extended kin or clansmen. Often a representative of city power, whether born a peasant or a stranger, also resided in the community. Traveling entertainers from a city occasionally passed through and received fees from the villagers. Although most peasants remained illiterate, they respected literate specialists of the cities, priests, scribes, or other professionals, some of whom became resident strangers, too. Scribes received fees for keeping records and accounts.

The status of peasants in relation to those who had encircled them is difficult to denote. But city-bred folk, specialists, resident strangers, and priests always enjoyed higher status. Peasants' feelings about such representatives of the outside world might be mixed, as in all socioeconomic systems where lower strata bow, scrape, despise, hate, or shrewdly manipulate denizens of upper social levels. In their ethics and in order to sustain sentiments about their worth as people, peasantries have tended to place high values upon intensive industry, endurance, honesty, and many offspring.

The Old World urban revolutions often produced conquerors whose socioeconomic and cultural background closely resembled that of the peoples they dominated. Peasants were then not extremely different from their masters in religion, arts, world view, and values. Greater differences very likely featured several among the slave empire expansions such as those of classic Middle East and Mediterranean civilizations. But in Spanish Indian America and a few other regions of post-Columbian date, conquerors were utterly alien in socioeconomic and cultural heritage, especially world view, ethics, and religion. Nevertheless so-called "peasant communities" the world over seem to have displayed remarkable similarities in socioeconomic functions of villages and in ethos around family, work, and personal integrity.

An inventory of other sociocultural traits and expressive characteristics is not feasible because surrounded peoples who subsequently metamorphosed into peasantries have been of many kinds. Weldings with their conquerors have taken innumerable detailed forms. Only a handful of generalizations may be hazarded.

In marriages freedom of choice was infrequent. Arrangement or management by parents and lineage was common, with dowry and bride payments. Peasantries tended to feature male dominance and lifelong subservience of females. Despite over a century of professional historians, peasants' psychology, especially the variety of defensive resolutions, has only just begun to be depicted by the few anthropological observers who have not accepted a narrow commitment to economic and old-style sociological research designs.

Peasantries surrendered warfare, of course, while they continued to relieve aggression with much intracommunity violence.

Religion often witnessed several layers of belief and behavior, one European and really remote or superficial, the other a lag of animistic expressive figures and correlated behavior from pre-envelopment eras. Like other surrounded peoples, peasantries tended to maintain relationships to all available supernaturals, their own preconquest heritage of projections and presumably the ones which they supposed were especially effective among new kinds, such as deities and saints.

An important question regarding apparent loss, both in features of content and style, in precontact esthetic heritages is difficult to answer. Probably the trend among peasantries was to suffer severe deterioration in pre-envelopment dance, music, and oral literature, intensified in Latin America by constant discouragement by the church. Forfeiture of art forms was fundamentally a consequence of a new way of life which granted few rewards for creativity or significant self-identity.

One wonders if central cultural phenomena among peasantries have comprised permanently underdeveloped, damaged, or bewildered self-identities, attenuations in aspirations, and value systems containing contradictory ideals. An ineradicable burden of humiliation felt by almost all members of a lower social stratum is very likely vital in such phenomena.

Since defenses against peasants' characteristic sentiments may be presumed to have proliferated, it seems prudent to inquire into ways in which certain features of precontact cultural expressions became remodeled and retained and new ones created in order to serve as protective cloaks against the continued chill of peasant status in an upper-class climate. Typical and aberrant personality constellations in peasantries offer important problems of twentieth century research. In analyses of personality growth and structuring, sado-masochistic trends may deserve special attention.

The almost worldwide type of surrounded people denoted "peasant communities" may be supplemented by a number of types of socioeconomic and cultural developments which did not occur so widely. The first discussed here were mainly precontact growths. Additional types as follows were postcontact.

A few *pure pastoralists* constituted an extremely rare type. It included Hottentots in South Africa, a few reindeer peoples of eastern Siberia, and several short-lived American Indian horse pastoralist groups after Spanish advent.

Hottentot bands tended cattle and sheep and appear to have lacked economically meaningful relationships with adjacent African peoples. Eastern Siberia's reindeer-owning groups were also self-sufficient. They developed their special systems after an early Christian era domestication of that animal. Knowledge of South African Hottentot socioeconomic and cultural life is still superficial. Examination of psychological manifestations among them is virtually nil. Asia's reindeer pastoralists have been better known for half a century because several excellent anthropological observers were there, principally because the Tsarist government had exiled them to eastern Siberia as antimonarchists. The sketchings are remarkably thorough in the light of ethnographic canons at the end of the nineteenth century, although psychological treatment was superficial everywhere at that time.

Basic economic features in pure pastoral groups connected with the circumstance that they were independent of the outside world. This is unlike the much larger numbers of so-called "pastoralists" whose way of life was possible only because they had thin but nonetheless indispensable threads which tied them to an outside world of agricultural peoples. Features of pure pastoralists included small bands of a few scores or hundreds of persons, a central productive resource which was one or several kinds of domesticated animals, inequalities in individual or family ownership of them, seasonal movements of the several families of a band, extremely limited manufactures, and an absence of surplus artifacts. A sexual division of labor may have been characteristic, without much further specialization. If any societies have ever exhibited gradual intergradations in status and wealth, these may have offered apt examples. Money, markets, and trade were apparently absent and barter was limited because surplus commodities were few. Female status was only slightly inferior, if at all, a striking contrast with pastoralists who had ties with agriculturalists. Religion was animistic and much like that of simple food-gatherers. Shamans were not full-time specialists. Arts stressed were dance, music, and oral literature, not plastic and graphic, and mastery may have been open to everyone.

Several rather special modern kinds of pure pastoralists could be captioned "horse pastoralists," or perhaps "pirates on horseback." The subtype includes some little-known peoples of southern Argentina and much better known groups in the western United States. In that vast district various food-gatherers and agriculturalists took to horseback, one group after another, beginning in the late seventeenth century. Indications are that in all of them inequalities in property ownership developed rapidly and became greater when raiding and plundering became central means of increasing wealth and acquiring prestige. Among domesticated animals, the horse may be unique in its effect upon sheer speed of expansion of wealth in an economy and in rapidity of alteration of social structure. Still, the time allowed horseback Indians in the old west appears to have been too short to permit tendencies, which are easy enough to denote, to proceed far toward inequalities, predatory values, lower status of females, slavery, and other new sociocultural features. One cannot generalize on a basis of American Indian descriptive materials about the kind of system and connected cultural expressions, including personality metamorphoses, which might have resulted in response to horses as a decisive productive resource and horseback riding as a major productive technique. However, analogous Old World developments deserve re-examination by historians. Certainly Hottentots with their cattle and sheep, and the Siberian bands which had acquired reindeer, could never have displayed the spectacularly expanding economy and the cultural and psychological features which riding on horseback encouraged. Religious, ethical, artistic, and psychological developments in such a way of life must have been both rapid and profound.

The majority of the world's modern pastoral peoples warrant more consideration here than horseback pirates or pure pastoralists only because of their numbers, which were recently still in many millions, and because of their varieties of sociocultural manifestations. In spite of surface appearances to the contrary, pastoralists were not wholly self-sufficient in economy. The little they needed from nonpastoral neighbors was imperative. They required artifacts, knives perhaps, which they were unable to manufacture or raw materials, such as ferrous ore, for certain vital artifacts. Therefore they were symbiotic, however slackly, with agricultural specialists or communities sometimes many days distant. Without robbery, barter, trade, or ties of some kind to other socioeconomic systems, pastoralists could not long maintain their manner of living. Specialist tribes who were kinds of castes occupied the former Anglo-Egyptian Sudan. Here agriculturalists, fisherfolk, and the wealthiest groups which were larger than the others and owned cattle, depended upon one another in a vast areal symbiosis, a kind of caste system where the castes were geographically separated. So too, all camel pastoralists have been only specialists who depended on products of other specialist groups in or near their region. In a sense, there were no pastoral socioeconomic systems except the few so-called "pure pastoralists" such as Hottentots and reindeer-owning Siberian bands. Other pastoralists were usually a wealthier class or caste in a region whose specialist producers lived in symbiotic relationships, as all specialists do. Cattle and horse pastoralists of the Old World tended to become upper social strata, to dominate agricultural peoples in their area, and to exhibit personality characteristics which anthropologists have not begun to examine. Pastoralist women, perhaps because of a lesser mobility while pregnant and nursing, had a very low status. They could not be as responsible as men for the most important productive resource, horses, and could not participate in the profitable productive activities, such as warfare, which horses rendered possible. Women were usually purchased by a husband or his kin. Pastoralists displayed inequalities in ownership of their animals and wealthy men ran their governments. Such dignitaries usually engaged in raiding and warfare because of the considerable rewards, if successful.

Hypotheses which intimate that population pressures caused pastoralist migrations and expansions should be regarded as simplistic, careless in their disregard of multiple causes of what happened, and unenlightening as to just how the supposed pressures started and maintained such movements.

In these societies, religions and arts tended to be in the hands of specialists.

Only the so-called "pure pastoralists" seem to have been comparatively indigent and structured a little like economically simple food-gatherers. Although the other pastoralists numbered, all in all, many millions and lived sometimes far from people with whom they were tied economically, they were frequently a bit like pirates. Such gentry cannot long survive without maintenance of a system which includes both victims and pursuers. Sadists cannot be sadists without a supply of prey, and pastoralists have had to have agricultural neighbors.

Remaining socioeconomic types will be commented upon even more superficially and briefly, largely because of meager information, their small numbers, and their insignificant roles in earlier eras. They are distinctive products of the modern period of Euro-American expansion, except for some probable groups of a few thousand years ago about whom little is known. However, one must not underplay the scientific importance of analysis of any group, for populational numbers and recency of distinctive development may not correlate with value for advancement of theoretical knowledge. A language whose speakers now number a mere 5 or 50 is as rich with implications for scientific theory as a language utilized by a 100 million persons. Musical expressions of a culturally moribund Alaskan community of 30 Eskimos may be as critical for theory in a cross-cultural science of music as the music of a modern nation numbering millions and whose heritage includes a Berlioz, Delius, or Bartok.

*Enclaved groups* were those single communities or small groups of settlements which, somewhat like American Indian Pueblos of the southwestern United States during the last century, succeeded in maintaining economic isolation, self-sufficiency, and a great degree of sociocultural independence, while girdled by conquering folk or wealthy urban peoples who had penetrated the region and chose not to destroy its native enclaves. Economic changes within the newly walled-in folk might be so few as to be negligible in consequences upon much of their sociocultural system. Political change might be important but amounted largely to acceptance of one or two functionaries to communicate, work with, double cross, and damn the irresistible, although currently indifferent, power immediately outside. The group also surrendered warfare as a resolution of difficulties and acquired a comfortable unconcern about armed defense. Cultural change might be uneven. Notable alterations appear to have been in everyone's psychological security system and self-identity, and in religion and world view. Most significant features were the maintenance of self-respect, ego strength, and values. Humiliations were not consequent upon uninterrupted subjection to subordinate status. At the same time, buried anxieties about the formidable invaders probably played an important role in rechanneling and intensifying certain aspects of supernaturalism, that is, in fashioning new psychological defenses.

*Partner minorities* may offer an apt caption for those rare groups such as modern New Zealand Maoris and, it has been claimed, Chile's Araucanians which had become enveloped and their socioeconomic structures shattered by conquerors, but which remained more or less highly regarded by the victors. The defeated people had resisted so impressively, had commanded so much respect for various reasons, that the newcomers resolved feelings of guilt by frequent acceptance of the worth of individual natives and even by taking pride in some of their customs. The outcome seems to have been a minimal development of religious and psychological defensive walls, unlike the more isolated but rather anxious and subtly hostile Pueblos. Maori, Araucanian, and other cultural heritages of somewhat fortunate groups of so-called "partner minority" type received, of course, only uneven acceptance or occasional approbation. But many persons in the engulfed groups presently attained high status in the larger community and so entered it as kinds of colorful partners. Where they chose to, members of the minority managed to achieve acculturative integration, something like a number of today's Iroquois Indian men who, after almost three centuries of unhappy relationships with Euro-Americans, have discovered that they can go to the big cities to become respected and decently remunerated ironworkers in building and construction trades.

*Transplanted peoples* is a caption which applies to many kinds of modern groups. Generalizations about characteristics shared among them appear to be so few, however, that a later decision may be that it is improper to assemble them under a type appellation. However, the suggestion is that Comanches, for example, who can also be dubbed "horseback pastoralists," were self-transplanted from Wyoming to Oklahoma and Texas. Other self-transplanted groups include Gypsies who reached various European countries during the early Middle Ages after a long trek from northwestern India, Carthaginians who came from the Phoenician coast, Scythians, Hungarians, and Arizona Yaquis. Food-gatherers who have migrated en masse, like the Comanches, are rare. Large numbers of agricultural and pastoral peoples have done so.

Surinam Bush Negro people and southern United States Negro slaves had nothing to say about their transportation or transplantation. As a type, they offer examples of most divergent alterations of former world view, ethics, and cultural expressions, certainly their total personality structures too, although a very few intriguing trace components of African esthetic heritages appear to have survived. Something approaching complete change, except for language, appears to have occurred over a period of more than two or three centuries in some of the self-transplanted groups which retained socioeconomic well-being and independence. Social and cultural retentions, apparently defensive efforts to maintain at least fragments of distinctive self-identity, featured some of the involuntarily transplanted groups which became subservient or were crushed.

*Surrounded food-gatherers* have been few. Economic, sociocultural, and any other kind of reporting on a classic example, Congo Pygmies, has long been shabby and fragmentary. Psychologically sensitive observers of them have been conspicuously few. The Congo Pygmy peoples appear to have once been food-gatherers over a vast equatorial domain. Although many bands survived after Negro expansions southward into their districts, some Pygmy groups metamorphosed into specialist hunters of low status resident upon the very doorsteps of agricultural peoples. Many or most Congo Pygmies may be regarded as servants or wards of chieftains of the agricultural groups among which they dwell. Clusters of Pygmy families have often lived in environs of villages and produced elephant ivory for their taller and darker patrons. To all appearances, these Pygmies have long been deculturated and probably severely humiliated, if not prostrate, remnants of an ancient food-gathering population whose territory was overrun. On the other hand the Malay Peninsula and larger Philippine Islands had perhaps only seemingly surrounded Pygmy hunters. Some of them appear to have remained socioeconomically self-sufficient and psychologically inviolate. Therefore they exemplify economically simple food-gatherers.

The Amazon basin has revealed groups which may suitably be called *refugee food-gatherers*. These Indians were the anxious descendants of economically simple agriculturalists of a few centuries ago, before Portuguese descended upon their regions. Knowledge of the economies or anything else about these pathetic refugee societies is slight. It is possible that a proper typology of socioeconomic systems would categorize them as economically simple food-gatherers too, although it would also be necessary to account for socioeconomic and cultural survivals, if there were such, of their agricultural way of life some centuries ago. At that time they were frightened away from their home territory and gave up agriculture because it was much too unsafe to stay in one place.

The chapter may close at this point with reiterated warning about the tentativeness of the classification. It should be re-examined, revised, or rejected if too many types are omitted or errors, skewings in characterization, or compacting of complexities mar the types proffered. Undue simplification and taxonomic schema which are premature falsify reality, with penalties in incorrect perceptions and faulty contrasts, so that research problems are wrongly conceived and procedures for their resolution improperly planned. But no science can advance without some mechanical ordering of its wealth of depictive materials, even if such arrangement also effaces important complexities and irregularities.

It is time to commence the survey of the many facets of nonliterate peoples' mental, emotional, and esthetic developments.

Before linguistic science and disciplines which treat of other cultural expressions are discussed, the reader should be prepared to approach them with awareness of efforts which behavioral scientists made after the 1850's to describe and arrange their several kinds of sociocultural materials and to progress toward maturity in scientific theory. Chapter One has tried to survey the century's ventures and progress toward such ends. All these attempts must be regarded as inchoate and subject to frequent revision, of course. Nineteenth century pioneering in social sciences, linguistics hardly less so, was much affected by a compulsion to write out historical insights and to frame them in the time categories which marked the current evolutionist climate of thought. Here may be found the nub of the nineteenth century social scientist's special kind of world view and set of values, especially so after Charles Darwin's *The Origin of Species* was printed in

1859. Accordingly, developmental or historical generalizations seemed strategic in the researches of the first four to six decades of both social and cultural anthropology whose beginnings connected closely with Darwin's work. Depictive methods and canons for arrangement of data at once linked to the nineteenth century's prevailing historicism and its routine placements of everything in successive time levels, without intensive inquiry regarding causes for changes in phenomena as they passed from a lower to a later and higher level. Twentieth century social sciences became less time bound. They were increasingly analytic, structural, and disinclined to occupy themselves with evolutionist or any other sorts of time perspectives. By the 1930's the historicist interests of a long and brilliant epoch had lost out to a new analytic structuralism, especially so in the science of language. Some protagonists of the new anthropology and the new linguistics had become bitterly antihistoricist. Almost all were antievolutionist. The next chapter attempts to introduce the reader to one of these developments and to the various attempts to advance method and theory which, together, shaped contemporary anthropological linguistics. Linguistics, religions, arts, and studies of other kinds of cultural expressions may be set in larger frames of what has so far been done to build them. The effort is to locate each along the continuum of its progress toward a mature system of scientific theory within the macrosystem of sociocultural anthropology.

## SUGGESTIONS FOR FURTHER READING

Oceanian agricultural and fishing economies are depicted in various books by R. W. Firth and B. Malinowski. Leading surveys are by K. Polanyi, C. M. Arensberg, and H. W. Pearson, eds. *Trade and Market in the Early Empires* (Glencoe, Ill.: Free Press, 1957), and J. H. Steward (ed.), *Irrigation Civilizations*, Social Science Monographs, 1 (Washington, D.C.: Pan American Union, 1955). In most publications of this kind, connections between technological or economic factors and expressive aspects of a social system are drawn poorly or speculatively.

# 3. LANGUAGES OF THE WORLD

## Introduction

In order to relate to other persons, to comprehend, and to build psycho-logical defenses that worked against fears, people have had to communi-cate on a level beyond that of expression of primary emotions. The role of language in society and culture seems to have been so fundamental that it is fitting to discuss it ahead of religion and the arts. The chapter might be entitled simply "Language" or "Scientific Linguistics," "Anthropological Linguistics," or some other heading of technical connotation. "Languages of the World" sounds less severe. But treatment of the topic will try to conform with a rigorously scientific as well as cross-cultural orientation. Linguistics is moving toward its own system of scientific theory, although its progress away from narrowly historical interests and toward theoretical maturity has been much slower than most behavioral scientists who are inexpert in this subject realize. They often laud linguistics because they perceive in it much admirable, precision-tool-like workmanship which, indeed, characterizes its up-to-date descriptive labors. They are correctly impressed by its orderliness and exacting methodological requirements which are set forth in chaste statements. But advance toward theoretical sophistication in the science of language has been painfully slow. It may have to wait upon accumulation of more descriptive data from all around the planet, for indications of how language features connect with sociocul-tural and psychological phenomena, for knowledge of child learning of language in nonwestern societies, and for even finer methodological and classificatory tools than are now in linguists' hands.

Linguistics is one of the oldest behavioral sciences. Its first important modern development was in the 1790's, two or three generations before most other such sciences got under way. Additional striking advances had appeared by the 1830's. To be sure, political science and economics had begun to develop earlier. But their scrutinies then and on into the twentieth century were largely of Euro-American phenomena while linguists in-cluded in their orbit India's Sanskrit and a few other nonwestern tongues. Decades of the nineteenth century elapsed before psychology, sociology, prehistory, physical anthropology, ethnology, "primitive" plastic and graphic art, folklore or oral literature, and other fields of inquiry began to be pursued in the light of systems of theory or with methodological rigor.

Indeed, a scientifically respectable delineation of the grammatical struc-ture of Sanskrit appeared several centuries before the Christian era. In the

1790's, an English scholar's announcement that Sanskrit must be genetically related to various languages of Europe, and that each had diverged from an ancestral language, commenced a seemingly endless flow of comparative linguistic monographs and papers. During a century and a half they delved into the family of kindred forms of speech now referred to as Indo-European. Most workers who made important contributions to general linguistics before 1900 occupied themselves with descriptive, comparative, and history directed quests within the Indo-European group. Written records permitted examination of forms in many of its languages continuously for a thousand or more years back. During most of the nineteenth century, investigations of members of other language families were relatively few and tended to be restricted to groups such as Finno-Ugric, Turkic, Semitic, and Sinitic, where written records also permitted inspection of language forms of many past centuries, even millenia. Before the twentieth century, a language that was not written by its native speakers was infrequently regarded as deserving of research.

A once distinctive division of the science of language, anthropological linguistics, usually could not depend upon written records out of the past because it had available mainly the spoken languages of contemporary nonliterate peoples. It was not developed significantly until the late nineteenth century, so great was linguistic scientists' preoccupation with written languages and so complete the conviction of most of them that languages of nonliterate peoples were unworthy of study. Assuredly, they were primitive languages, whatever forms and degrees of unfitness such a characterization implied.

Nevertheless, a few excellent reports on languages of nonliterate groups, for example, a grammar of Greenlandic Eskimo, did appear during the mid-nineteenth century. The comparativist and Indo-European-oriented mainstream of linguistic science witnessed scarcely a ripple because of its protagonists' depreciatory sentiments about nonliterate peoples. During the 1880's and 1890's, decisive methodological advances, achieved by a few specialists on nonwestern languages, were again wholly ignored by pundits of Indo-European linguistics. As a result, anthropological linguistics added to its personnel extremely slowly until the 1920's. Its recruits from the 1890's to almost 1930 were principally Americans who were either trained in American Indian anthropological studies by Professor Franz Boas at Columbia University or who were influenced by him. Anthropological linguistics developed in the ranks of early twentieth century American anthropologists, not among other scientific linguistics faculties of that time.

Advances which anthropological linguists achieved in descriptive methodology and in translinguistic orientation failed to receive general recognition among the Indo-European-swaddled personnel of general linguistics until the 1920's and 1930's. A 1910 publication by the Smithsonian Institution, the *Handbook of American Indian Languages* (Vol. 1), had climaxed work on exotic languages since the 1870's. Its principal author and editor, Boas, phrased with clarity what is perceived today as revolutionary alterations in linguistics' methodology and focus. But the work did not gain immediate general recognition. Many linguists never saw or heard of it. Within another 20 years the science of language changed course and rather speedily caught up with the anthropological linguists. It became translinguistic and dropped its Indo-European and written language provincialism. Today it has explored far beyond its former mainstream. No meaningful line now separates anthropological linguistics from the rest of the science. Since the 1920's all languages, long written or never before symbolized on paper, have ranked as equally compelling objects of inquiry. There is only one science of language. Evidences from food-gatherers' forms of speech are as important for it as records of Hittite, Tocharian, Greek, and medieval French.

## Origins of Language

Anthropologists assume, although direct proof or disproof must remain forever unattainable, that prehumans over a half a million years ago who were skillful enough to manufacture chipped flints and other artifacts of stone must also have developed oral communicational media, that is, symbols and classes of verbal symbols, which were far more efficient than the meaningful devices employed by dolphins, seals, monkeys, and apes. Since there must have been rather intelligent, but in some vestigial respects apelike, populations which manufactured artifacts out of decayable materials (grasses, roots, hides, and so on) during hundreds of thousands of years before the so-called "Stone Age" or "Paleolithic," it seems likely although, again, direct evidence is unobtainable, that simpler kinds of language media were present in Pliocene times, over a million years ago. The number of such early forms of communication, whether hundreds or thousands of prelanguages, will also never be estimated even if all districts peopled by Pliocene prehumans, Australopithecenes, or others, are at length revealed.

The first weighty statement which, therefore, needs to be made, a kind of foundation stone for a system of scientific theory about language, is that initial developments of humanlike forms of languages were probably in Pliocene times, maybe over a million years back. It could be several million years ago in the middle of the Pliocene. Imagine an Australopithecus lady of Rhodesia delivering a diatribe with hefty subordinate clauses. It is possible. If linguistics could ever gather the facts it could trace all natural languages of the modern world to prehumans of such early eras, regardless of where they dwelt in Africa or elsewhere in the Old World. But all languages of our epoch are equally removed from primitive beginnings by a million or more years and doubtless by extraordinary changes in content and structurings.

All languages of our time, written or unwritten, are of equal antiquity.

There may be archaic items in any of them but there are no archaic languages. The three or more thousand mutually unintelligible natural languages which survive today, almost every one in a number of dialect variants, are of equal status in their modernity, complexities, flexibility, efficiency, and advancement beyond a primitive level, whatever that may have been like in Pliocene Australopithecus bands or later in the early Pleistocene epochs. No matter how underdeveloped the technology or economy of their speakers, natural languages or dialects of languages of the modern world appear unlikely to display primitiveness in any respects. The several Bushman or Click languages of South Africa and the many Blackfellow languages of Australia, and each of their dialects, are almost certainly as grammatical, complicated, serviceable, and elegant, although unwritten by their possessors, as the speech of literate ambassadors and representatives to the United Nations. It is, therefore, safe to state that no languages or dialects of our day, Bushman, Australian Blackfellow, New Guinean, Ibo, Yokuts, Yuchi, Algonkin, Greek, Latin, German, or Chinese offer a single clue about a feature or general characteristic of Pliocene or Pleistocene media of communication, about traits which are vestigia of days long since gone.

Some nineteenth century linguists thought that the earliest words, hundreds of thousands of years ago or earlier, were sound-imitative or emotion-generated. Include here the still familiar but, of course, absurd ding dong and bow wow theories of the origin of language. A few linguists have suggested confidently a single or monogenetic origin of all languages while ignoring the likelihood that "early man" lived in many districts of the Old World continents. Evidences for and against guesswork about remote origins are beyond reach, and all the probabilities favor multiple and geographically scattered rather than single and geographically circumscribed origins. Speculation about ancient beginnings of specific features of language also contributes nothing to a growing system of scientific theory because it explains nothing about the many facets of language (phonetics-phonemics, grammar, vocabulary, discourse units, syntax, etc.) and about processes involved in their patterning, change, and sociopsychological functioning.

It is much more important to try to find out what happened during that small and recent portion of the period of over a million or more years which is subject to examination by modern scientific procedures. It is, therefore, necessary to settle for a modicum of knowledge of language forms and processes of just the last ten to twenty thousand years and to surrender wild and futile guesses about early horizons. Still, two or three feeble statements are possible about the origins of languages. Their era can be dated as pre-Stone Age and possibly in the Pliocene epoch. They were many and diverse. Their functions, whatever such early languages were in specific or patterned respects, might have been to enhance the security and likelihood of survival of their users. That suffices for questions and an introductory handful of answers about early origins and services of languages. Little can be stated besides a vague dating, a wide territory, multiple forms, and a generalized function.

After so elusive a prologue, it is more interesting to proceed to something substantial and worthwhile for a system of scientific theory about language and its workings. First, where are the modern world's languages and principal language groups?

## Linguistic Geography

Mutually unintelligible languages with certain kinds of shared features are presumed to constitute progressively diverging forms of speech which may be traced back to a common ancestral language. A group of languages which can be so connected, and where each language is a recent or contemporary form, is termed a "family" or "stock." Today the world's 3,000 or more languages appear to align in only a few score such stocks, almost certainly less than 50. Linguistic and anthropological surveys, as well as a few atlases and encyclopedias, have presented inventories of these stocks or of stocks in special regions. Each such publication, usually with accompanying map, has been premature. Classification of languages into families or stocks is an absorbing game with rules—criteria of method—that unhappily vary from player to player unlike chess or even poker. When a player is a charismatic personality, louder applause greets his classification. Onlookers, especially anthropologists, have taken the game too seriously. Rules of method for assessment of genetic relationships of languages are much more important than tenuous maps of stocks which are offered. And exacting rules of method are not always highly regarded when results in maps are wanted more than progress toward maturity in a structure of linguistic theory.

What are the rules or criteria which, when fulfilled, justify placement of a language in a stock?

Suggested criteria are of three or more kinds. The first asks for a sufficiently large list of shared words or morphemes, that is, minimal units of distinctive meaning; second, a sufficiently large number of shared features of grammar or structure; third, a sufficiently large number of regular sound shifts, which is the most reliable criterion at hand. Some difficulties relate to a definition of "sufficiently large" and assessment of relative reliability of the three methods. A few comments on these matters are called for.

First, let us consider shared words or minimal units of distinctive meaning called "morphemes," that is, vocabulary comparison. How many shared units of this kind must there be to warrant a deduction that two languages have diverged from an ancient ancestral speech? Tentative, and not especially careful, studies suggest that any two languages which are wholly unrelated and thousands of miles apart may display 20 to 40 or more morphemes of similar sound and meaning—homonyms—and that such similarities are entirely by chance. If this kind of annoyance, consequent upon accident, turns up everywhere, and very likely it does, it forces linguistic taxonomists to resort to a criterion of required utilization of a minimal number of well over 40 morphemes or words of similar sound and meaning before they have warrant to suggest likelihood of a genetic relationship.

Since 1950, a trial balloon or specialty termed "glottochronology" (also called "lexicostatistics") has attempted to refine procedures of morpheme and word list comparisons, both to improve criteria for determining membership in a linguistic stock and to indicate approximately when languages have been diverging from one another. Protagonists of this highly touted method have accepted a dogma that speeds of morpheme or vocabulary change among food-gatherers and economically lowly agricultural folk may have been much the same as in vocabularies of agricultural Indo-Europeans during the Christian era. Glottochronology has almost foundered upon this and some other unsubstantiated dicta. Nevertheless, it has attempted to offer an improvement upon the cruder word list comparisons of nineteenth century scholars. It has contributed nothing new to method and scientific theory about matters of process and forms in language or other cultural expressions. Readers who are intrigued by glottochronologists' recent efforts to set forth refinements in word list and morpheme comparisons should pursue the subject elsewhere, with a regretful understanding that the procedure is embarrassed by undetermined merits for checking upon likely relationships and durations of apartness of related languages. At the same time it unhappily exhibits no potential for adding significant formulations to a growing system of scientific theory about language.

What about the second criterion, grammatical similarities, for ascertaining genetic relationship and stock membership? How many grammatical features or sets of features must two languages share to justify a deduction that they are kindred but perhaps long since separated members of a stock? Are some grammatical items, such as sex gender, more trustworthily diagnostic than others? In answer to these questions, linguistic science has not yet offered a firm array of canons regarding the meaning of grammatical similarities. The absence of assurance about such principles is regrettable because of indications that a very few grammatical units, also classes of units such as sex gender and noun cases, crossed stock lines within a small region in which there was much intermarriage, visiting back and forth, trade, and polyglottism. Features of grammar enjoyed borrowing so as to become part of the structure of one or more languages in another stock. However, the opinion of the late Professor Edward Sapir and others has been that the numbers of grammatical features—and sets of them—that managed to vault stock boundaries is exceedingly small. A language does seem to maintain most of its structural integrity or autonomy and to oppose ingestion of grammatical items tossed in from the outside—why, no one quite knows, although it seems possible that patterning of items which remain wholly below the threshold of perception has something to do with it. If, therefore, a theory of massive grammatical structure resistance, whatever there is in human nature and the learning process that causes it, is correct, two languages which share more than three or four diverse grammatical characteristics are likely to constitute kin within a stock. Linguistic science lacks translinguistic evidence about the willingness and capacity of speakers of one or another grammatical instrument to gulp and digest within it grammatical items supplied by other languages with which they have an acquaintanceship or even a perfect speaking command.

A third criterion, regular sound shifts, developed over a century ago by R. K. Rask and J. Grimm and everywhere referred to as "Grimm's Law," is by far the most trustworthy because it permits prediction of large numbers of words or morphemes. A list of them in one language allows prediction of a remarkably high percentage of their cognates in the related language. Consonants in one language are regularly paralleled by or correlate with certain consonants in a second and genetically connected language. For example, words or morphemes in Latin with initial *p-* (such as *pater*) are often found in German with initial *v-* (*Vater*). In such instances, it is possible to predict the sounds of words or morphemes in the second language from knowledge of words or morphemes in the first, and to set aside a small number of exceptions and to account for them in special ways. When such a high average of predictions occurs for two or more languages whose kinship, unlike the well-known genetic relationship of the Latin and Germanic languages, was not earlier shown, proof of their genetic relationship is at once provided, that is, a very high probability is indicated. Indeed, this third procedure of establishment of regular sound correspondences is so completely attested in language families the world over that it takes precedence over the first two methods of word-morpheme and grammatical comparisons, obviously too because of its ability to predict a great many specific items. The latter two methods are really only scouting devices. The method of regular sound shifts hits the bull's eye.

Most suggested stock classifications of the world's languages must be regarded as tentative and not of high probability because they have not yet been rooted in evidences obtained by the regular-sound-shift method. For the Indo-European groupings of genetically related languages, this method has been used throughout. Only a few other clusters of indubitably genetically related languages, such as Basque, are as fully authenticated. Somewhat less secure formulations apply, for example, to the Eskimo-Aleut, Algonkin, and Nadéné or Athabaskan. The latter has at least one peculiarly divergent but definitely kindred language, Tlingit. Haida is possibly genetically related to it, also. Many regular sound shifts between Tlingit and Nadéné or Athabaskan are evident. Such correspondences have not yet been extended to Haida but it has not been analyzed as well as Tlingit. Haida's grammatical similarities to Tlingit and Nadéné or Athabaskan are so extensive, however, as to indicate the advisability of closing the case by searching intensively and as soon as possible for regular sound shifts from Haida to the others. Here is an instance where the method of comparing grammatical structures is valuable and leads the scientist to resort to the one method, that of ascertainment of regular sound shifts, which will end discussion about a hypothesis of genetic relationship. Actually, the three methods can be utilized jointly or successively. Word or morpheme lists which are impressively similar constitute a stage of preliminary canvassing, grammatical similarities greatly augment the likelihood of genetic relationship, and decision is made with a display of sound shifts which allow predictions of morphemes.

During the 1930's, Professor Sapir suggested for North America and Professor Joseph Greenberg recently noted for Africa aggregates of languages or families of them upon a basis of so-called "mass comparisons" rather than by means of isolated comparison, at a snail's pace, of two disparate languages at a time. The latter procedure offers a necessary foundation for any highly probable deductions from the former procedure, which centers comparison of a mass of languages that number in the scores or hundreds. Membership in a family of languages may be indicated as rather likely when a goodly number of grammatical resemblances appear in a portion of them across a continuum. Some pairs of languages perhaps had been initially compared and also shown to be probably related. Sometimes two languages, which are so divergent that a comparison suggests little or nothing, can be shown to be probable family members that had drifted apart over a number of millenia. They are like ends of a continuum and the problem is to fill in intervening points. A convenient symbolization of the problem would be a line of overlapping circles, where the circle at the far left did not overlap with the circle at the far right. Each circle stands for a few or many languages in a division of a family. The chain of circles is a family.

Europe's major linguistic groupings, families, or stocks appear at the moment to be more firmly established than those of any other large regions. But, of course, Europe is small and for a long time linguistic science has been intensely, if not parochially, interested in Indo-European forms of speech. Scientific linguists assume that Europe contains aggregates called (1) Basque or Iberian, (2) North Caucasus, and with allowance for carelessness about geographical lines it witnesses also (3) South Caucasus unless insistence be made that on modern maps that district is a part of Asia.

Europe's two larger assemblages of related languages are (4) Indo-European and the Finno-Ugric and Turkic groups which may be subdivisions of an assortment with many members also in Siberia, called (5) Ural-Altaic. Many Indo-European, Finno-Ugric, and Turkic languages are far to the west of their bases of thousands of years ago, possibly then in southwestern or central western Asia in the instance of Indo-European. The remarkable spreads of these modernly huge mosaics are accidents of earlier location when their speakers were preagricultural food-gatherers. At that time they lived in districts benefited by early Neolithic cereal grass domestications of rye, millet, wheat, and barley and by Neolithic pastoralism with its domestications of cattle, sheep, goats, swine and, later, horses and camels. Indo-European speakers advanced westward first, then Finno-Ugric groups, lastly Turkic populations. It is possible that in later Neolithic and subsequent eras westward-moving Indo-Europeans engulfed several language aggregates which had long been native to Europe. Only Basque and Caucasus languages survived because of their chance location in peculiarly undesirable districts around which swirled Indo-European newcomers.

Movements of Indo-European speech into southern Asia paralleled its advances toward the Atlantic. Indo-European is found in Iran and in three fourths of the modern population of India. About one fourth of India's more than 400 millions utilizes (6) Dravidian and very small numbers speak (7) Burushaski and (8) Munda or Kolarian. These latter three (6, 7, 8) may be long native to India. The now dominant Indo-European group in India represents invaders who entered by northwest passes before the Christian era.

Other genetic clusters of Asia include (9) Andamanese, (10) Mon-khmer, (11) Sinitic, (12) Tai or Siamese, and (13) Tibeto-Burman. The last three (11, 12, 13) may be subdivisions of a larger assemblage. In addition, Asia numbers (14) Korean, (15) Japanese, (16) Ainu, (17) Eskimo directly opposite Alaska's Seward Peninsula, (18) Yukaghir, (19) Koryak, (20) Chukchee, (21) Kamchadal, and (22) Gilyak. A few scientific linguists believe that regular sound shifts will be discovered connecting Korean and Japanese as exceedingly divergent easterly subdivisions of (5) Ural-Altaic. There are linguists who expect that comparative studies will reveal that some or all in the set from (18) to (22) will turn out to be divisions within a Palaeasiatic aggregate.

An enormously extended group (23) called Austric, Austronesian, or Malayo-Polynesian appears to have spread from a pre-Neolithic base in or near Indonesia, perhaps on the southeastern Asia mainland. It is in four traditional modern subdivisions: Indonesian or Malay, Melanesian, Micronesian, and Polynesian. Claims of wider ties are heard. A possibility of one or more (24) as yet unrevealed groups in New Guinea, especially in the unexpectedly populous highlands, awaits reports of field studies which have barely begun. Conflicting statements which have favored (25) one or two genetic clusters in Australia and Tasmania warrant suspended judgment because the many languages of that part of the world are largely unknown.

Descriptive materials on hundreds of languages of Africa are uneven and, for the most part, oldfashioned. Classification of African languages before Indo-European entries of the past 2500 years (Greek, Latin, English, Dutch, Italian, French, Spanish) is, therefore, premature. Today it seems reasonable to some linguists to list the following: (26) Hamito-Semitic or Afro-Asiatic may have been limited to Arabia and Red Sea districts in pre-Neolithic times. Ancient Egyptian and, later, Coptic were members of a

Hamitic division. Semitic languages extended at one time from Arabia to Ethiopia and, in dialects of Arabic after 650 A.D., from Arabia and Egypt across northern Africa to the Atlantic. Berber groups, which have sometimes been tied in with ancient Egyptian under a larger heading of Hamitic, also extend across northern Africa, probably consequent upon an earlier spread westward. Cushite and Chad are divisions which were also once included under a Hamitic caption. They lie to the south and southeast. Another possible assemblage of genetically related languages, (27) Niger-Congo, is of prodigious extent, consequent upon introduction in pre-Christian eras of agricultural and pastoral techniques and, perhaps, other factors in south-of-Saharan districts. It is found now in hundreds of languages from Senegal south to Cape Colony. Professor Greenberg, who gave currency to the term Niger-Congo, a decade later has placed Niger-Congo as one gigantic division alongside a smaller division which he calls Kordofanian. He thereby supplies a new macro-stock hypothesis and offers a new label of Congo-Kordofanian. Fair-sized African groups to which linguistic taxonomists who accepted Greenberg's earlier work assigned tentative labels as families include (28) Songhai, (29) Central Sudanic, (30) Central Saharan, (31) Eastern Sudanic, and (32) the Click languages most of which have been called Khoisan or Bushman-Hottentot. Geographical pockets, each of which was formerly offered as a smaller family, number (33 to 41) Maban, Fur, Mimi, Temainian, Kordofanian, Koman, Berta, Kunama, and Nyangiya. When Professor Greenberg in 1963 presented a revision of his earlier work, he offered a hypothesis of an inclusive Nilo-Saharan family which comprises six major subdivisions: Songhai, Saharan, Maban, Fur, Chari-Nile, and Koman. His 1963 presentation of language families native to Africa is a striking simplification. It cites only four families: Congo-Kordofanian, Nilo-Saharan, Afro-Asiatic, and Khoisan (or Click). If numerals were assigned in Africa only to these four, the numbering system offered here would have to be altered and the total of families the world over much reduced.

Observe that Madagascar is Indonesian Austronesian in speech (23) because of Sumatran penetration of that great island almost 2,000 years ago.

A summary of an Old World language classification should point out that factors of chance found a small number of pre-Neolithic language groups in districts where their speakers were favored by food-producing and other changes of Neolithic and later periods. These economically (agricultural, pastoral) advantaged groups included Indo-European, Finno-Ugric, Turkic, Dravidian, Tai, Mon-khmer, Sinitic, Tibeto-Burman, Austronesian, Afro-Asiatic, and Niger-Congo or Congo-Kordofanian. Their numerical, economic, and geographical expansions doubtless resulted in envelopments and extinctions of pre-Neolithic clusters of genetically related languages and of thousands of individual pre-Neolithic languages, all of which deserved to survive as much as the forms of speech which fatefully surrounded them. Longevity of a language or linguistic stock has never been determined by its communicational efficiency, esthetic comeliness, or by anything except its location and the wealth, numbers, power, and intensity of feelings of the people who spoke it. Military, political, economic, and other factors eliminated thousands of the world's languages, never a factor of inferiority in them.

Although scientific linguistics' most intensive and up-to-date field reports are of American Indian languages, a few hundreds, especially those near or facing the Atlantic, vanished before modern descriptive and analytic methods received development. Accordingly, no classification of American Indian languages can ever be definitive because of irrevocable uncertainties regarding languages which were among the earliest to be effaced during the course of European entry. The number of mutually unintelligible languages must have been far over a thousand, with especial multiplicity along or near the Pacific shores where mountains and many short river valleys chop up terrain unlike anywhere else in the Americas. For example, California had about a hundred, Oregon about twenty-five, and Washington also about twenty-five languages, each in two or more mutually intelligible dialects.

Languages of native America constituted extremely divergent forms of a very few Asian languages of food-gatherers who penetrated easternmost Siberia and the Bering Straits coastal districts at various times between about 40,000 B.C. and perhaps 3,000 or 4,000 B.C. They presently dispatched representatives, so to speak, across the Straits into western Alaska. Their population increases and creep of frontier southward throughout the lands and islands of the western hemisphere were accompanied and followed by linguistic changes which resulted in a modern profusion of disparate forms of American Indian speech, including Eskimo-Aleut. The hemisphere's languages exhibit every major kind of grammatical structure known and thereby show that irrespective of what they were a few tens of thousands of years ago, a stretch of time of such length permitted nurturing of most of the kinds of linguistic features which Homo sapiens is capable of fashioning. In addition, it is of momentous interest that preagricultural societies were perfectly capable of fostering all those features.

Since the 1890's, studies largely on American Indians north of Mexico have produced concepts of hypothetical American stocks. Professor Sapir's thoughts on this subject shortly before 1929 were consequent upon his rough inspectional procedure of mass comparisons and observation of clusters of grammatical similarities. His views have subsequently almost hypnotized linguists who thereupon plagued themselves with taxonomic interests in a hopelessly ephemeral stock geography. Sapir pointed to (17) Eskimo-Aleut, (42) Nadéné or Athabaskan, (43) Uto-Aztekan, (44) Penutian, (45) Hokan-Siouan, and (46) Mosan-Algonkin. Old and familiar captions for possible stocks of Latin America include Carib, Arawak, Chibcha, Inca or Quechua, Aymara, and Araucanian. Nothing is more unlikely than a theory that languages of more than six or seven stocks reached Bering Straits from earlier Siberian and eastern Asiatic bases. A theory that languages of only two or three stocks arrived at the Straits looks more plausible. Claims that a language or languages of only one stock arrived there can never be proven. No careful scientific linguist is interested in the old or recent guessing game about transoceanic routes for language entry, even of one language, let alone over a thousand, into the New World. It is much more likely that a sweet potato successfully traveled so wet and salty a route than a contingent of invaders who landed along an already inhabited beach front and imposed something much more significant than sweet potatoes, namely a language, upon doubtfully accepting hosts. Only the Bering Straits avenue of original entry of a very few languages seems probable, with subsequent abundant spreads and divergings in America. The amount of time which is now allowed as likely, that is, from 10 or 15 thousand to as much as 40 thousand years, appears sufficient to account for the spectacular modern array of mutually unintelligible and structurally most divergent American Indian languages and for the stock-like groups which have only begun to be conjectured.

## Languages Vanish

The modern world's 40 to 50 so-called stocks, if there are that many, which have been granted numbers and labels above are to be regarded only as early way stations along an avenue of taxonomic progress which has been barely entered. There is no means of predicting how drastically the number of hypothetical stocks will be reduced in the course of comparative researches in coming decades. Like any taxonomy, a topic of linguistic stock determinations and geography is not itself crucial but it has minor instrumental values for progress in maturation of a general system of scientific linguistic theory. What is decisive is discovery of processes of development, maintenance, functioning, and loss in the various classes of components of language (their sounds, vocabulary, morphology, larger discourse units) and the processes of child learning of those components. Stock mappings which are as well authenticated as possible will continue to serve principally as guides for special comparative studies. They suggest to a comparativist the languages which might be most fruitful to compare. They also offer humble bits of assistance to those few anthropologists whose special interests continue to be in historical reconstruction descriptivism.

During the long Paleolithic of over half a million years, all peoples were food-gatherers, domesticated food plants were potentials of the future like space travel with hotel accommodations, and each handful of bands which shared a language numbered only some hundreds or a few thousands of people. The Old World had then spawned from 5,000 to 10,000 or more mutually unintelligible languages, each in a few or many dialects, that is, forms of speech partially intelligible to each other. The language history of the past 7,000 or 8,000 years is in one momentous respect an unrecorded story of progressive diminution in the numbers of languages. The Neolithic revolution, with its economic and populational explosions, destroyed much of the linguistic creativity of Paleolithic times because of progressive eradication of the majority of the world's languages. Thousands, perhaps a number of stocks too, and especially so in the Old World, became extinct for reasons which had nothing to do with their merits. None may have been in the least inferior to the thousands of languages which survived or the ten or eleven stock groups, such as Indo-European and Austronesian, which in recent times spread widely.

Persons with surviving nineteenth century sentiments which are expressed in slurs about nonwestern peoples sometimes look askance at scientific linguists who devote their lives to recording and study of nonwestern languages that are on the verge of extinction. For example, laymen wonder about the curious dedication of research workers who interest themselves in the many districts of North America where it is possible to find only one or two persons who recall, but no longer employ, the last remaining dialect of an American Indian language that was spoken in several dialects not long ago. The attitudes are: Why bother about something which will die out anyhow? What do you want to prove? Can the effort result in a significant contribution to knowledge? Why should taxpayers pay salaries and expenses of myopic scholars who do something which is both valueless and ridiculous? Who will ever read the eventual publications, examine the archive reports (phonemic sketches, grammars, dictionaries, texts), or make heads or tails of the tape recordings and their translations? The nonlinguist regards it reasonable that five or ten professors study Tibetan because there are a lot of Tibetans now and they are colorful and come from Communist-controlled districts. And there may be some more Tibetans for a while. But researches on Maidu, Miwok or Wiyot in northern California, Kalapuya or Rogue River Athabaskan in Oregon, Nuksak or Columbia Salish in Washington, Eyak Athabaskan in southern Alaska, and moribund bands of Bushmen in the Kalahari Desert or Australian aborigines in Queensland generate musty auras of antiquarian pedantry or of the grave. What difference will it make if multidialect languages, such as some of these, disappear without notations, even as hundreds or thousands of other languages perished in bygone Neolithic and Iron Age epochs? Of what use are records of these things? They were not ancestral to us! The psychotic survivors of nuclear holocausts will hardly be able to use card files, tapes (if not demagnetized anyway), grammars, dictionaries, or other remnants of such kinds.

This is one among several clouds under which many scientific linguists operate. Can they justify research expense vouchers and the conviction that what they are trying to do is supremely worthwhile? Realize that they are trying to do "pure" science in an age when many persons suppose that it is important for everyone to be concerned about currently popular values, world political affairs, and the coming special election which permits the voters to ventilate their hostility to anything new such as fluoridation of the city water supply.

The warranty of merit in the labors of scientific linguists who choose to be absorbed in translinguistic materials is nevertheless easily written out. It reads somewhat as follows.

In infancy and early childhood, humans learn with great speed two or three principal classes of items, apart from body coordinations. The number of items internalized in each of these classes, which include language, social relationships, and feelings around such relationships, is enormous. Processes involved in such internalization and mastery are only beginning to be examined. Arrangements and structurings of the linguistic and relationship items, as they are progressively gotten under control, are also little comprehended. But without insertion, proper arrangement, and practice in employment of various classes of units, a growing child would not be able to function in family, household, or community and an adult personality could not presently develop—one which could act as the society expected. There is no good argument against the statement that language constitutes a principal class of learned items or that another major class is behavior in customarily assigned roles or intersecting nets of roles in social relationships. Additional cultural expressions which include humor, arts, ethics, ideology, and so-called "world view" comprise later internalized classes of learned and often subtly structured materials. But language and various kinds of relationship adjustments in approved roles have to be mastered before a great many varieties of cultural or projective expressions. Only then can a child or, presently, an adult acquire classes of projective materials and eventually approach ego-satisfying acquaintanceship with them leading to potentials for play, originality, and creativity in their manipulation.

It is therefore advisable, even indispensable, to find out everything possible throughout the world about the language class of items in order to understand the many ways in which a linguistic bedrock has been laid. It is necessary to ascertain everything about adults' communication tool for effecting relationships, for continuing to learn, and for manipulating the diverse segments of an expressive heritage. Only then can that larger whole, human nature, be depicted in its total range of manifestations. Linguistics is accordingly a *sine qua non* in the modern effort to erect a science of human nature. A science of psychology without a base in a theory of linguistics is like physics without mathematics. Linguistics itself dare not ignore any of the rapidly diminishing number of languages, no matter where each one is or how few its surviving speakers. It must not lose evidence of this kind, lest a science of human behavior suffer still more from gaps such as the many that were created during and since the Neolithic when wealthier and more numerous peoples engulfed thousands of Paleolithic era languages. Every language and dialect still remembered or actively used is possibly of commanding importance for some now unanticipated element of scientific theory, whether it survives in one tiny band of dark Cape York peninsula

Australian people or in two elderly and quite toothless American Indian survivors whose ancestors employed one of the hundred native languages of California.

This is not all. The central nervous system, which includes the brain, of modern peoples possibly attained its present level or capacities 200,000 or 300,000 years ago, maybe earlier. Now, all humans lived as economically simple food-gatherers during hundreds of thousands of years. Only during the past 8,000 to 10,000 years did some of them metamorphose in economic and correlated sociocultural features into agriculturalists, that is, Neolithic peoples. Most peoples of today are descendants of little bands which transformed into economically modest agriculturalists hardly more than 4,000 or 5,000 years ago, a mere fiftieth or a hundredth of the duration of their equally intelligent Paleolithic ancestors' preagricultural way of life. Scientific linguists' researches have yielded no indications that the economic revolution from food-gathering to agriculture or to mixed agriculture-and-pastoralism effected portentous changes in the expressive content (vocabulary, grammatical classes of features) and structural characteristics (sounds or phonemics, sets of discourse features, grammar, syntax) of any languages. That is to say, basic linguistic features, in all their amplitude and variety, which selected slices of reality and thereby effected communication during hundreds of thousands of food-gathering years, continued to serve neither more nor less efficiently in the last few thousands of years of gradually and at length rapidly advancing know-how in technology and food production. The same old kinds of linguistic mechanisms, or most of them, which had worked during hundreds of thousands of Paleolithic years just kept on working and performing exactly the same kinds of services. The old kinds of languages were fine for all the new foods, military ventures, real estate, interests, purposes, feelings, worries, hatreds, supernaturals, sciences, and philosophies. Only a very few minor types of features of grammar may have vanished forever. These were some specific locational, instrumental, or other special classes of items.

But the question arises, what was happening in daily, hourly, repetitive activity and recurrent feelings during those hundreds of thousands of pre-agricultural years of brainy and imaginative humans, to shape or generate items or classes of them (sounds or phonemes, vocabulary, grammatical features) which functioned in those thousands of languages of food-gatherers? Because whatever was created linguistically by sociocultural conditions and psychological mechanisms, during hundreds of millenia of food-gatherers, provided the modern world with the kinds of languages which it now has.

It is unlikely that linguistic structures stayed autonomously so far up in the stratosphere during hundreds of thousands of years that grammatical patternings never once got a drop of nutriment from sociocultural soils beneath. Whatever several hundreds of thousands of years did cumulatively to pattern those thousands of linguistic structures, it is evident that in modern times Newton, Einstein, Charles Peirce, and Simone de Beauvoir resorted to the kind of language which food-gatherers had employed and not at all to something special in the art of communication, something created only by novel conditions of living in technologically advanced societies. Languages of the world's wealthiest peoples and most highly trained minds in mathematics, physics, genetics, or chess are languages which are neither better nor worse, esthetically more or less attractive, better or less well suited to employment in tensor calculus, merchandising, or the philosophy of the law, than languages of those who entered the modern period as food-gatherers. Charles Peirce would have done quite as well in Hupa Athabaskan, Penobscot Algonkin, Aranda, or Nyangiya as he did in English. There is not an iota of evidence that any linguistic feature of Latin, Greek, or English shaped the ways his seminal intellect worked.

Many deep changes have occurred in the grammatical structure of every language since its food-gathering users became agriculturalists, when such a technological change occurred in pre-Christian centuries. All languages have changed in salient respects during a few thousand years. The point is that the economically most advanced moderns are nevertheless really using principally the linguistic survivals, the detritus, the very patternings of communicative items, which served their food-gathering forefathers. It is as if a superlatively tooled auto of the 1960's had basic parts all of which were easily interchangeable with parts of an automobile of 1910. That is why every food-gatherer's linguistic structure, whether it reside in the head of one decrepit survivor or in 20 or 20,000 crania, is as important as English, Hittite, Greek, Korean, Sanskrit, or Scotch Gaelic for the science of language. A linguist who comments with indifference or rejection about values in the most intensive research on it is antiscientific. He is irresponsible. He is like a taxonomist in zoology who would allow whooping cranes to become extinct without even bothering to take a lazy snapshot of one of them.

## Research Method for Unwritten Languages

Although a majority of the world's several thousand unwritten languages were examined by missionaries and others who during four centuries of European expansion offered word lists and dictionary materials in phonetically inaccurate recordings, scientific linguists have transcribed only a small percentage of all these languages and then principally since 1900. Few reports as accurate as theirs about language structures preceded the twentieth century. Modern standards of analysis of nonwestern languages require intensive paper work using first-hand source materials provided orally, in each language, by a fluent native speaker who knows something of a European or other language familiar to the visiting linguist. The informant pronounces his own words and phrases in response to the linguist's queries. Research procedure is in at least these three overlapping stages. During the first days or week each translated word is noted in transcriptional symbols on a paper slip. Labor in this initial stage is scrupulously restricted to recording and translation of single words. Not until the second stage of research, that is, after four or six days, does the linguist elicit short phrases or sentences, again transcribed on slips. This stage, which yields thousands of slips, continues during many weeks, depending on the skill and experience of a researcher and the rapidity of apt responses by his informant. Six or eight weeks are a minimum for the second stage and a period twice as long may be necessary. After a number of weeks along in the stage of recording of phrases, a linguist moves carefully into a third stage wherein he encourages his informant to dictate slowly myths or other forms of connected speech. Usually he transcribes such material in lined pages of notebooks. At the end of each dictation, he reads the lines to his informant or interpreter who translates word for word and phrase for phrase. He writes the translation interlineally but continues to place additional language forms of various kinds on file slips as before. He initiates tape records of dictations of connected speech during the third stage of research. They serve as means of adding notations of special so-called "suprasegmental features" such as junctural phonemes and phrase or sentence tonal contours. At once after 1950, such tapes became a requirement of scientific method because they also allowed recheck by linguists of the future, much in the spirit of democratic publicity of reports in laboratory sciences where experiments may be repeated, at will, in scores of laboratories around the world. Since 1950, a few linguists who have been fascinated by the total fidelity of tapes have had their informants dictate connected speech directly and rapidly onto tape and have only later played it back for purposes of translation and commentary. A merit of this procedure based upon electrical gadgetry is that distortions caused by the slower dictation which was necessary before 1950 do not mar connected speech which is immediately tape recorded and only subsequently translated. However, in instances where myths, tales, and other forms of connected speech are customarily memorized verbatim, a field method of direct and rapid dictation onto tape itself slackens the speed and efficiency of translation work. In a community which has masses of verbatim memorized oral literature, direct speech onto tape need be resorted to only for a part of that literature and then mainly in order to yield a sufficient body of accurate data on junctures, melody contours, and the like. After a few months' research on a language, a competent field worker can write out a text at dictation about as rapidly and accurately as he can in his native language. As in all scientific work, a researcher is never limited to a single procedure but must apply all relevant methods as resourcefully as possible. In any case, tapes should record ultimately a great amount, if not all, the connected speech which a field worker jots on paper and the taped materials should be translated fully, sensitively, and with much commentary.

In a food-gathering or agricultural society devoid of social strata or other subgroups that are characterized by distinctive language forms, one informant-interpreter may suffice because all mentally normal adults employ the entirety of the language. In all other societies a scientific linguist accords equal acceptance of and faithfully records the speech of one or more members of each dialect subgroup. It goes without saying that full samples of each of the several dialects in a language must be secured. So-called "standard speech" in wealthy societies such as those of modern nations like England, Germany, and France constitutes only an inventory of features in an officially approved dialect. These features have been accorded homage by government, educators, or snobs during a special historical period, either because the inventory of sacrosanct items is characteristic of the dialect peculiar to an upper social stratum or because of some other circumstance. Scientific linguistics studies the vogue of such standard speech and the causes for it, also its tendencies to spread into or recede before dialects of underprivileged or rural strata in a population. But their forms of speech, whether regarded as rustic, slang, or merely incorrect, are as important for revelation of processes of origin, change, or maintenance of linguistic features as the speech which at the moment enjoys upper-class blessing or approval by haughty and anxious moguls of the country's educational apparatus. Tape recorders and scientific linguists deal with all dialects and other forms of speech in a community. Linguistic science does not kowtow before standard speech in spite of requirements by speech, drama, and other school teachers that students alter their natural dialect.

## Phonetics and Phonemics

Each language, of course each dialect of a language too, utilizes only a tiny percentage of the sounds which all humans are potentially able to articulate and which, to be sure, are futilely explored by prelanguage babies and ignored by their guardians because most of these oral forms of play do not resemble sounds in the local natural language. A virtually universal opinion that some sounds are more difficult than others is correct solely in application to older children and adults. Such unfortunate little and big people already carry burdens of deeply imbedded speech habits and of emotional blockages about sounds other than those they have often heard and experimented with. But all sounds which the oral cavity can articulate are equally easy and, in a sense, natural during early childhood, that is, before a child learns its elders' natural language. During recent centuries, hostile feelings and anxieties about foreign language learning were such that most peoples of Euro-American societies have been persuaded, from childhood, that there are really very difficult sounds in some languages. But such difficulties arise in inappropriate sentiments much more than in anything inherently difficult about production of such sounds by the oral mechanisms which effect them.

Scientific linguistics recognizes no claims regarding so-called "advanced" or "primitive" sounds. Sounds strange to Euro-Americans in New Guinean, African, or American Indian languages are sounds to which culture-bound and language-bound Euro-Americans are unaccustomed. In no instances are these sounds consequent upon racial anatomical characteristics because no linguistically significant differences in oral cavity anatomy appear among the world's races, whatever those races are. And physical anthropologists and human geneticists have by no means permanently classified mankind into so-called "races." No sounds structured into language systems are consequent upon specific features of race, climate, altitude, local bird or animal noises, splashings and bubblings and ripplings of water, or a "race's" evolutionary stage of development. Put simply, the world offers a kind of equality in language sounds in spite of people's language-bound and, therefore, parochial sentiments about inequalities and incongruities in these features. Linguistic science has barely begun to assist twentieth century citizens in emerging from humanity's perennial linguistic insularity or in its persistent provincial responses of wonderment, giggling, disapproval, snobbery, or admiration when hearing a stranger's utterances.

Even today one frequently notes that people use the word "guttural" as a means of describing an unfamiliar kind of language sound. But "guttural" correlates with hot horseradish more suitably than with a scientific linguist's identification of a special group of features in the sound system of a language. The term, with its slanderous and language-bound connotations, is one among many relics of a day when Euro-Americans had need to regard as inferior or savage certain sounds which they had difficulty in reproducing and which paralleled other characteristics of nonwestern peoples whom they had need to depreciate.

Any sounds made by a human oral cavity function with perfect efficiency as minimal units of linguistic sound, that is, as phonemes or the variant articulations of phonemes called "allophones." There are no inferiorities or superiorities in language sounds, phonemes, or allophones or in patterned sets of such units.

In languages, the average number of minimal primary units of distinctive sound, that is of segmental phonemes of two large classes or sets called "consonants" and "vowels," may lie between 20 and 40. Some languages have a little fewer than 20 such segmental phonemes. Sixty is close to the maximum found anywhere. All phonemes, of these two (consonant, vowel) and other or suprasegmental types also, become mastered in early childhood. Each segmental phoneme correctly articulated at that time may be acoustically in two or three to as many as six or seven variant manifestations which appear predictably and are called "allophones." For example, k in English key is rather different from k in kowtow. These two k sounds are allophones, variant articulations, of an English k phoneme. Native speakers of English produce them unconsciously. If a person becomes consciously sensitized to the sounds of his language, it is segmental phonemes, not their allophones, which he initially perceives and identifies. When scripts develop or are borrowed it is only certain classes of phonemes, usually the segmental ones, or those combinations of segmental phonemes called "syllables" which the native speaker chooses to transcribe. He remains hopelessly inattentive to variant articulations of each segmental phoneme, to its allophones, that is, unless they are called to his surprised attention in special instruction in the classroom of a scientific linguist or by a teacher who has learned something of modern linguistic science. On the other hand, a field research worker who is examining an exotic language early hears allophones, makes allophonic distinctions, and has the problem of tagging them as such while, at the same time, he ventures to assemble three, four, or five allophones into a single entity called a phoneme. A native speaker of the language perceives only that entity.

By the 1930's, linguistics succeeded in writing out, with a simplicity and clarity attained in no other field of cultural anthropology, those criteria which facilitated analysis and granted high probability to identification and orderly arrangement of its special kinds of minimal units. For example, two exceedingly similar sounds are really different minimal units, phonemes, like the final consonants in *sup* and *sub*, if they (1) display distinctive contrast. But if each of similar sounds in a group of sounds which constitutes a phoneme, for example the initial *b* of *bun* and the final *b* of *nub*, never occurs in the environment in which the other appears (here a matter of initial or final syllable position), then they are allophones of the phoneme; these allophones are in (2) complementary distribution. Allophones of a phoneme usually display (3) a high degree of phonetic or acoustic similarity, as in initial and final *b* in the illustration. A criterion of (4) neatness of pattern, pattern congruity, or symmetrical arrangement allows fortification of identifications of phoneme units, as in English with its set of voiced stops *b*, *d*, and *g* which is beautifully paralleled by the set of voiceless stops *p*, *t*, and *k*. The explicitness and efficiency provided by these and other methodological statements in linguistics are at present unexampled in all the many different sectors of cultural anthropology and, therefore, present a model which those areas of inquiry should try to emulate and approach.

Linguists also assert that they resort to a criterion of (5) pattern economy or rule of parsimony which states that although each fundamental unit may actualize in variable manifestations (e.g., allophones), the fewer the basic units identified the more likely that analysis gibes with reality. However, most other special segments of cultural anthropology, such as religion, law, oral literature, music, dance, ethics, and world view, probably display as large or larger numbers of fundamental units than language, although few such units have as yet been inventoried or arranged. The criterion of pattern economy must, therefore, be regarded as highly elastic and its manipulation may long be subtly affected by the subjectivism of scientific observers. Indeed, this criterion of method is not peculiar to cultural anthropology or linguistics, because a principle of economy is basic in all scientific endeavors.

Current treatises in linguistic science attempt to disclose the world's principal types of sound articulations, including both segmental and suprasegmental phonemes, in detail which need not be emulated here. It is sufficient to comment on the intriguing circumstance that every language has one or more examples of a few principal classes of phonemes such as consonants and vowels, the so-called "segmental phonemes." Each language also includes examples of several other classes of phonemes, "suprasegmental phonemes." These comprise units of stress or loudness, length or duration, pitch or tone, and juncture or pause. Each such phonemic unit also has its allophones.

Every language includes some stopped consonants, exemplified in English $t, p, d, g, k$; some continuant consonants (also termed sibilants, spirants, or fricatives), exemplified in English $v, z, s, th$; and (with possible exceptions in Caucasus districts) one or more pure vowels, exemplified in English ä (as in *sat*) and $i$ (as in *sit*). Widely, if not everywhere, found are affricative consonants, exemplified by $dz$ (English *adze*) and $ts$; and diphthongs, exemplified in $oi$ (English *oil*). Definitely not universal are many other classes of phonemes, notably the kind captioned as suprasegmental. Languages may have them in the form of stress units, that is, unitary features of greater or lesser loudness. Languages may have suprasegmental phonemes of greater or lesser length as in Italian *atta* where the $t$ articulation is maintained extra long. Some languages have suprasegmental units which are either phonemic or syllabic and which comprise features of tone or pitch level. Most of the European languages lack a class of tonal phonemes (tonemes). On the other hand, a great many of the several hundreds of languages of Africa possess phonemes of tone. Analogous tonemes appear in other continents. Many languages, if not all, have suprasegmental features which are units of greater or lesser pause or juncture.

In any one language, a linguist can account for many centuries of selection and continued presence of units of these and other classes only by resort to analyses, usually through comparisons of genetically related languages, which permit reconstruction of changes which the language underwent in recent times. Where borrowing of sounds from other languages occurred, cultural factors were, of course, responsible in conjunction with a trite factor of geographical contiguity. Most sound changes, and all patternings or orderings of phonemes and their allophones into a phonemic system or structure, are largely or wholly accounted for by noncultural processes, processes on a linguistic level which is almost ethereally aloof from the disparate processes which operate in other cultural expressions. The extraordinarily neat, almost crystalline, patternings of phonemes and allophones in all classes of phonemes seem to arise in the cumulative impact of features of human nature and in innumerable repetitions of speech units in the earliest childhood of all the members of a group. These early learnings of sounds and their patterns precede learnings of the distinctive patternings which accrue to units and classes of units in other cultural expressions such as humor, music, oral literature, plastic and graphic arts, and dance. Each of these later built-in forms of expressive behavior displays patternings of its segmentable parts too, and a generic analogy of phonemic structuring sets forth a kind of model for their analysis and pattern-like arrangements. Each of these other cultural expressions connects much more immediately and relatively more consciously with social relationships and other characteristics of a sociocultural system. Patterns of language units and classes are buried extremely deeply in the unconscious, as older Freudian writers might have asserted.

Highly skilled and modern pedagogic procedures, accompanied by sufficient practice, normal intelligence, and minimal anxiety about language learning and memorization, permit anyone to master an alien language's phonemic system and, presently, to speak it without a trace of a foreign accent except when fatigued or furious—at which point regression sets in in the very best people and their later learned patterns somehow go awry. The opera singer who performs with phonetic flawlessness at La Scala in a second language may surrender some of her superlatively well-mastered coordinations when the audience boos. If allophones, also phonemes of course, are not articulated properly, a singer or speaker exposes an alien upbringing.

Connections between a sound system (phonetics, phonemics) and a sociocultural system occur, to be sure. But no specific feature or class of features in a sociocultural system produced or maintains specific sounds, segmental or suprasegmental phonemes, allophones, or their patternings. Units which may be termed phrase-sentence melody contours, which display another phoneme-like structuring, also appear not to be the result of specific features of a sociocultural system, although connections with personality characteristics and community attitudes may be worth seeking.

On the other hand, maps of sounds or classes of sounds such as South African clicks, western North American Indian glottalized, lateral, and velar consonants, vowels too, show that they may have spread, probably over long periods of time. They certainly endured over such vast areas for protracted eras. They did so when they had found or penetrated niches in phonemic systems of contiguous languages, some of which might have been of diverse linguistic families. A familiar example is the patent borrowing in southerly African areas of click consonants which assuredly were originally only in Click or Hottentot-Bushman (Khoisan) languages. A process whereby sounds diffuse and at once metamorphose into phonemes or allophones has not been observed in the flesh, so to speak, in nonwestern regions. Something is known, however, of the process of borrowing of the originally Norman French sound in English *rouge*. Geographical contiguity presented one factor, a *sine qua non*, in such diffusion. Decisive factors in spread resided in trade, intermarriages across language and language family boundaries, in-law visits, and varying percentages of polyglot individuals. It was therefore culture, if the term is used in Tylor's broad sense so as to include social relationship features and patterns, which offered a favorable setting for diffusions of sounds. The close similarity of European

Indo-European languages' sounds to sounds in Europe's Finno-Ugric, Turkic, and Basque languages offers additional, indeed indisputable, indications that sounds spread, that they coterminously realigned in phonemic systems which they entered, and that they subsequently maintained themselves for a long time. Every continent presents the same kind of testimony in spite of obscurity in details of the process.

Phonemic structuring within each European or other language is another matter. Sociocultural causation does not seem to have operated directly in the shaping of patterns or classes of sounds.

Has there ever been a connection between culture—again use it in Tylor's all-inclusive connotation—and the number of segmental phonemes (consonants and vowels) in a language? The query needs consideration in the light of the fact that each of the world's languages contains anywhere from something less than 20 to as many as 60 such minimal units, and the percentages of vowel and consonant phonemes vary even more remarkably. Reports about languages of the Caucasus suggest few vowel and almost 60 consonant phonemes. Some northwest states American Indian languages had three pure vowel, three or four diphthongal, and over 30 consonant phonemes. Such imbalances in the direction of a high percent of consonant phonemes contrast with many languages of Oceania, Africa, and elsewhere which exhibit eight, ten or more pure vowels and perhaps no larger number of consonants. Whole areas are characterized by languages whose phonemes are largely consonants, other areas by languages with many vowels. No one has suggested good reasons for these areal manifestations although diffusional processes must have operated, no one knows when or how.

A theoretical point of interest is that an artificial language might be contrived so as to employ no more than seven or eight segmental phonemes and no allophones whatever. So small a number of phonemes would permit an adequate inventory of minimal units of distinctive meaning, that is, morphemes and words. It would number in the thousands and, therefore, could function as efficiently as any natural language. Accordingly, every one of the world's 3,000 or more surviving natural languages contains at least twice as many, in most instances far more, segmental phonemes than the minimum necessary. Linguistics has no explanation for the excess number of phonemic units with which every natural language has been burdened, if it has been a burden rather than an indication of pleasurable free play.

As far as anyone knows, conscious manipulation of phonemic units or patterns, to the point of pressuring a portion of or reshaping a language's sound structure, never transpired in prehistoric or more recent eras. Proliferation of phonemes and drifts in frequencies of their allophones occurred without awareness. Indeed, slicing a sound system into its minimal phonemic and allophonic units is an achievement of linguistic science during hardly more than the past generation. It is one of the notable successes of recent behavioral science in its immature, because theoryless, descriptive and taxonomic phases. Some writers refer to them as a "natural history" stage in the development of a science, by analogy with pre-Darwinian zoology.

Again, reasons for an invariably surplus number of segmental phonemes are not at hand. It is as if all garments required at least eight buttons but, in fact, no garments were made with less than 16 and some flaunted 50 or 60. One might hazard a supposition that when a population long possessed a kit of tools which worked satisfactorily, individuals were released to play with the tools and to devise still more of the same kind. The work shed or basement has sufficient room for both necessary and extra equipment. The human mind's so-called "unconscious" is an analogy of the surplus work space available, a vast area which people have employed for more and more excess impedimenta.

Long, long ago, when peoples already possessed or then multiplied their phoneme inventories, the units took places neatly in relation to one another, without awareness that such patterning or structuring was going on. Phonemes of similar kinds such as *b*, *d*, and *g* arranged in one group, *p*, *t*, *k* constituted another group, and so on. It is impossible to connect with culture as such these arrangements, sets, classes, patterns or structurings, call them what one pleases. But every language exhibits features of phonemic structuring, that is, a manner of operation in which members of classes of phonemes which are similar in certain respects function in almost or entirely identical ways. The fact that the human mind so patterns a great variety of items which do not rise to a level of conscious perception is a twentieth century psychological discovery of utmost import. It has also sowed seeds—few have yet grown visible sprouts or blooms of theory—throughout cultural anthropology. If those unconscious units, phonemes, which scientific slicing reveals display remarkable patterns like the crystals which physicists study, are there not many roughly analogous units and classes of units (Professor Kenneth Pike likes to refer to "emic" units, after the word phonemic) in other cultural expressions and should not cultural anthropology venture to pinpoint them, too, if and where it can? Then, will they not be found displaying their own special patterns or structural features? The answer is simple. Of course they will be found if sought in a proper manner. It is a question of devising correct methods for probing and pinpointing units and the arrangements which they have assumed.

What about the converse of the proposition that culture caused or shaped sounds and sound patterns? Did sounds, phonemes, allophones, and phonemic patterns cause, maintain, or shape anything in a sociocultural system? Did they ever determine traits in personality? Could they have influenced oral literature, dance, or music in any parts of the world?

The answer is prevailingly negative. But one can easily point to a few pleasant exceptions as in several systems of non-European music. In parts of western Africa, for example, suprasegmental phonemes of tone, tonemes, appear to have comprised factors in shaping of certain facets of scale and melody. Other suprasegmental sound features, such as juncture, duration, stress, and phrase or sentence melody contours, may have presented additional factors in a musical style. In some oral literatures, language sounds provided partial factors in special literary effects such as onomatopoeia. In a few languages, regular sound shifts, such as from *n* to *l*, functioned to express pity, diminutive, augmentative, and the like. In such instances, everyday speech might have been exactly like oral literature, so that it cannot be deduced that traits of this kind (morphophonemic) shaped only oral literature expressions.

Apart from infrequent and minor contributions, an apt summary generalization is that languages' sounds and sound patterns have molded or reinforced nothing of significance in sociocultural systems except the rare few features suggested.

## Morphemes and Vocabulary

Among its many sets of features, every language has at least a few thousand minimal units of distinctive meaning, called morphemes. They may be single phonemes or phoneme combinations, syllables, even di- and trisyllabic units. English *telegraphers* contains four morphemes, *tele*, *graph*, *-er*, and *-s*. A scientific type of dictionary, by contrast with conventional kinds, as useful as they may be, would inventory alphabetically all morphemes such as *tele*, *graph*, *-er*, and *-s* and all important morpheme combinations such as *telegraph* and *telegrapher*. It might not bother with *telegraphers*, the plural form, in order to save space and avoid frightful repetitiousness. A better English dictionary today approaches such an ideal. But in languages that have hundreds of grammatical morphemes, such as Eskimo, the problem becomes formidable, much more so than in devising a dictionary for English. In such languages, a scientific linguist's dictionary, which lists all morphemes and almost all their combinations, is necessary for purposes other than those of laymen who are native speakers and who are in a bit of a hurry and know their own language anyway.

Each of the several thousands of minimal units of distinctive meaning, the morphemes, has its special connotations. Morphemes also align in subinventories, subsystems, or classes and pattern in many ways. First, they are of two formally structural kinds, free morphemes (*one, woman, house, knife, sit*) and bound morphemes (*un-, ex- -ed, -ly*). The latter were and still are termed affixes, that is, prefixes, infixes (which are rare in languages), and suffixes.

The little that is known about the 30 or 40 jargons, such as Melanesian pidgin, Delaware jargon, Mobile jargon, and Chinook jargon which developed at various times in the period of modern European expansion, suggests that a crude means of communication, one which is unsatisfactory for expression of items in specialist occupations and technologies and which is incapable of sensitive handling of feelings, values, and ideas, requires about 500 and possibly no more than 1,000 free morphemes. It needs no bound morphemes. Therefore, as in phonemic inventories, vocabulary inventories in each of the world's 3,000 or more natural languages may include more than a minimal numerical requirement in morphemic units. A language possessed of compounding or of affixation with many bound morphemes may exhibit hundreds of thousands of morpheme combinations, that is, words. Many food-gathering peoples, Eskimos for example, have such monumental numbers of possible words. Since morpheme combinations permit vast dictionaries in languages which have lots of such coalescences, a query about numbers of words in a language is linguistically unsophisticated. From the point of view of scientific linguistics, it constitutes an improper and crass intrusion of a Euro-American value regarding sheer numbers of words. A numerical total of words in a nonwestern language tells nothing about it nor does the number reflect anything in the sociocultural system before the recent modern period.

Every language has large numbers of synonymous or nearly synonymous morphemes and words, that is, it contains excess morphemes. But there is an "if." Other things equal, the number of morphemes and words in a language may be relatively small if many of them are connotatively broad or general rather than concrete or specific in semantic coverage. For example, a language may have only one word for Euro-Americans' green and blue segments of the spectrum. European languages here use at least two words, green and blue.

A language, call it (a), reflects something in its culture when it has only one word for an abstraction whose connotations include right, proper, ethical, upperclass, and wealthy. Another language (b), such as English, reflects its very different culture by expressing in diverse words its analogous concepts with their divergent nuances. These are translated in only one word in language (a).

English refers solely to "snow" where some Eskimo groups enjoy a special efficiency in daily living in their distinctions among several kinds of snow, each with its own morpheme. But an ideal minimal or Basic Eskimo vocabulary, a kind of pidgin, doubtless could be devised. In such a Basic Eskimo, each of a small inventory of morphemes or words would range semantically over the broad territory which the natural Eskimo language had sliced into parts of more specific connotation. Every language could be pushed around in this manner, as some ambitious innovators did over 30 years ago in their Anglophilic advocacy of that artificial fabric called Basic English. It contains only some 900 words, all from English. If Basic English were to work efficiently many of the 900 must be accorded a vigorous semantic stretch, so that each receives far wider connotations than it possesses in natural English. Most of the 900 would have to do a lot of extra duty.

Just this kind of stretch, extra duty, or broad semantic coverage—it may be termed abstractness as against narrowness or concreteness of reference—characterizes a great many grammatical morphemes. Witness *de-* and *-ly* in English. In western North America the many Athabaskan or Nadéné languages, for example, display a variety of prefixed morphemes which have extremely abstract connotations, most remarkably so to a language-bound Euro-American observer.

On the other hand, many languages present bound or grammatical morphemes of almost curiously concrete, specific, or narrow connotations. For example, a few American Indian languages have a set, linguists call it a "form class," of morphemes which are body part instrumental verb affixes and which mean with the hand, with teeth, with foot, with buttocks, with head, and so on. In a proper context, one member of this special form class must be used. If it is omitted, the speaker is being ungrammatical. Nothing in the socioeconomic and cultural system of these Indians seems to have initiated or urgently pressured such grammatically required specificity in expression of body instruments. A useful statement regarding first causes of such a phenomenon is that nothing in the society and culture seems to have blocked development, whenever it happened, of a body part class of grammatical morphemes. The culture could not have deliberately seeded it but, more important, it did grant a soil favorable for its germination and growth. Most languages of food-gatherers may lack a body part form class. Among such peoples, the languages burdened with such required grammatical expression are those which responded, in this one respect, to a sociocultural setting which gently favored the evolution of the form class or its adoption by borrowing.

Grammars of a few American Indian languages contain form classes of bound grammatical morphemes which connote motion upstream, downstream, up the trail, down the trail, from beach to embankment above, from embankment above down the beach, midstream to shore, shore to midstream, into water or fire, out of water or fire, inside to outside, outside to inside, and the like. Since some of these directional morphemes patently connected with regionally somewhat distinctive kinds of daily activity, a speculative statement here might depart from the comparatively negative one submitted above regarding virtual absence of connection with society and culture. One might now assert plausibly that cultural factors did ever so slightly nudge, gently pressure, and maintain exceedingly concrete connotations of a few of the bound morphemes of at least one form class. Again, one member of this directional form class must be employed in a context where it was required. Here the culture, that is, repetitive and almost daily acts, seeded the class of morphemes in the grammar.

Every free morpheme or word stands for a thing, action, or concept which people who speak that language identify. People are unable to perceive, recognize, or translate most of their bound or grammatical morphemes, like those cited for body parts and directions. Society and culture demonstrably "caused" all free morphemes and words: for example, sputnik, telstar, Kodak, suntan, twist (in dancing). Culture possibly directly "caused," but only with most modest little pushes, a tiny percentage of the bound morphemes which is exemplified by some members of a form class of directional morphemes. Of course, very few languages exhibit such a class.

Most grammatical morphemes of English (e.g., *-ed*, *-s*) cannot be connected with English society and culture at any point in English history. Only rare items of grammar, that is, grammatical form classes and their component morphemes, can be traced to cultural seedings, launchings, or shoves and then they were usually of feeble potencies. It is as if almost all form classes of bound morphemes arose on other planets, descended to earth like humanly uncontrolled flying saucers, and ensconced themselves with utmost unreasonableness in one or another language where they had to be used in order to speak correctly before any learned academy, congressional committee, or pontificating professor could do anything about it. There they remained sometimes for millenia, required all the time and all the time logically unnecessary, functioning in order to plague or titillate scientific linguists and a few linguistically oriented psychologists, if nobody else, for additional millenia perhaps. At present those linguists and their allies in psychology have not piled up enough statements in a structure of linguistic or psycholinguistic theory to enable the intellectually curious to perceive why grammatical form classes and the lists of morpheme units in them came to be where they are.

Nevertheless, one wonders if a flickering light may be thrown on a process of crystallization of some types of form classes in a language system, if such classes are regarded not only as segments of a larger grammatical structure but as stylistic features in their own right. If it is reasonable to denote a stylistic aspect of their functioning, somewhat similar classes of stylistic features in nongrammatical cultural systems can be compared with them. Now, a later chapter on oral literature examines the expression of meaningful content and then the astonishing arrays of repetitive and other devices which comprise oral literature styles. Among the great numbers of classes of oral literature features, and they are indeed as varied and numerous as grammatical items which turn up in thousands of languages, it is possible to cite a few illustrations of stylistic traits which are startlingly like grammatical form classes. Some oral literature styles are characterized by a class of locational, a class of temporal (or aspect-like), and a class of depictive words or phrases. At a given point in plot movement, an oral literature recitalist may have to select one or a series of items from a class of locational expressions such as "they went along the trail," "they came out of the woods above the hamlet," "they looked down from above," "they went down the trail toward the hamlet," "they got to the hamlet," "they went into the first house at the edge of the hamlet," and so on. An inventory of such words, for they may be single words in certain kinds of languages, is strangely like a list of morphemes in a form class of directional affixes in each of several languages of food-gatherers. It would be possible to place the two inventories side by side and the principal difference a person unacquainted with the oral literature or the language would notice would be that the one column contained free forms and the other column bound forms. The items in the two columns, taken from a single sociocultural group, might be quite different in their content or meaning. But this is not the point. What is important is that the two columns display revealingly similar operations or functions. They include structural features which serve at different levels or in different contexts. All the same, contributions of the oral literature set of items are quite like those provided, although in a far less conscious way, by the grammatical class of items. The salient question, which assuredly cannot be answered with today's resources, is whether the oral literature form class of stylistic items was not sometimes a precursor of a grammatical form class, especially so when the literary features also marked casual conversational style.

A second class of oral literature features of style offers a similar illustration. A recitalist may have to select suitable items from a class of aspect-like (older writers used to call it "semitemporal") expressions, maybe in only one or two words each, such as "he made preparations," "it became night," "it dawned," "at high sun (midday)," "presently," "I do not know how long afterward," "toward evening," "it became dark." A recitalist may lack an item, in this class, which indicates remote time, or he may have to use one which says almost limply, "long, long ago," or "a year ago." A set of stylistic features like these in an oral literature bears a suspicious resemblance to a grammatical form class of affixes which express time or aspect. But, again, it is vital to note that the members of the two sets, literature-stylistic and grammatical tense or aspect in any one sociocultural group, may not line up in neat pairs in parallel columns. It is their similar functioning which is arresting. An anxious thought develops that the stylistic inventory of items might constitute an extremely early stage of a process of development which at long last might become a grammatical form class. Presumably, proof for such a hypothesis could be granted only in a linguistic group which comprised many languages.

A third illustration may be suggested in a class or several subclasses of depictive expressions from which an oral literature recitalist must select, in the proper context. Note, for example, "there were many people there," "there were many houses," "smoke rose from the houses," "they lived there," "every day they went away to hunt," "they were always hunting." A great many oral literatures of western North America required a recitalist to utter these nearly contentless observations as stylistic means of carrying along a plot. A speaker must use one or another of them exactly as a speaker lifted out one or another bound form of a form class to use it in order to speak grammatically. Many other oral art style classes could be cited in order to pyramid evidences that such classes functioned curiously like grammatical form classes. The same kinds of style classes also turned up in casual speech but, today, few good samples of everyday conversation are available in the languages of nonliterate peoples and so one resorts to illustrations from the many oral literature texts which linguists have obtained.

At superficial glance, words or phrases cited illustratively above may seem to imply nothing to a grammatical analyst. He may be willing to acknowledge that a nonwestern recitalist, as well as everyone in the community, had his special grammar of style, a structure of a nongrammatical kind with its own form classes of component units. But an oral literature recitalist was functioning just like a person who was speaking grammatically correctly. He was really doing the same sort of thing. He was responding psychologically to an analogously structured stretch of discourse. He must operate within a style just as a speaker must communicate both within the structure of a grammar and the structure of style of casual speech. I suggest, therefore, that oral literature style classes functioned so like the form classes of a grammar that they may offer productive analogies for processes involved in formation and maintenance of grammatical form classes. Style classes of oral literature, and all oral literatures have had their structurings and their numerous stylistic form classes, are already manageable evidences, at hand in quantity, which look strikingly like earlier stages of crystallization of grammatical form classes. Repetitive stylized utilization appears to characterize both the oral literature and the grammatical classes. It is an open chance that the one type is an early form of the other. There is no doubt regarding their similarity in unconscious functioning.

Speculations, productive analogies, and hints about processes may be of interest, but descriptive and taxonomic knowledge of languages the world over has not reached the point where it can give much support to even a few initial statements in a system of theory about processes of origin, spread, and maintenance of linguistic features. There is really a most distressing poverty in theory regarding causes and processes which may have brought about grammatical form classes. Today linguists can offer a rather nice descriptive report, too often drily laconic and rendered even more arid by terminology which almost no one comprehends, on the contents and formal relationships of classes of morphemes, in addition to proud and admiring acceptance of their presence and continuing functions in a language. In fact, one of the many great adventures of modern science has been a progressive uncovering and depiction, albeit in the most unimaginative style of presentation, of roles of grammatical form classes in hitherto unanalyzed and unwritten languages. That kind of descriptive adventure, which many exuberant people glamorize with the caption "structural linguistics" and which is curiously like structural content and style analysis of an oral literature, has a long future because there are still a few thousand little-known or wholly unanalyzed languages. There is also much that can be stated usefully, but without sophistication, regarding a system of linguistic or structural theory. But description of languages and their inner patterns without a modicum of direction from theory is a kind of fuddy-duddy natural history research. It can run into many blind alleys and sometimes important little things are not probed for. One worries if linguistics has already lost valuable time because of its fascination with exacting descriptions and the spareness of theory which is at hand for guidance. Linguistics has also needlessly alarmed some potential friends because of its formidable special terminology, much of which was never needed, and its almost unreadable phonemic and grammatical publications, which could have been rendered just a little nicer to peruse.

Recently the preoccupation with morphemes, classes of morphemes, and their arrangements has gotten a few linguists into a state of gloomy concern lest there be other important and equally meaningful units and sets of units which everyone has neglected and which have escaped the descriptive net. Segments of discourse which are longer than morphemes or words and which have their own distinctive meanings and style-like functions are being examined to see if unit values can be assigned to them. Can they be arranged in classes of units with dimensions and other characteristics different from the morphemic units heretofore recognized? The project, which in recent phases has been accorded terms such as "discourse analysis" and "transformation grammar," looks possible if not promising. It is evidently alarmingly complex or bewildering at this early stage of innocence in linguistic theory. If it turns out that it is efficient to postulate and identify such units or macro-units, they may be more slippery to manipulate than have been the neat and tiny free and bound morphemes which so far have served beautifully. Maybe linguistics will be working presently not only with phonemes and morphemes and perhaps some other micro-units, but with bulkier and less neatly arrangeable entities, of kinds which a child also perceives and internalizes. But if it appears that there is scientific profit in location, acceptance, and management of macro-units, their connections with sociocultural phenomena will also deserve close attention. First, the units have to be spotted and arranged in sets.

Grammars traditionally have described ways in which free and bound morphemes relate to one another. These not easily readable treatises exhibit extraordinary variety because grammars themselves are of the greatest variability. Chinese languages have virtually no classes of bound morphemes and are, in a sense, almost grammarless. Relationships are between free morphemes, not bound ones. The free morphemes are, to be sure, words, and ties between them are referred to as rules of syntax. Chinese, then, has syntax and plenty of structure but hardly any grammar. Since the early Middle Ages, English has drifted rapidly toward such structuring, too. It is of great interest that languages which are about as denuded of grammatical complexities as modern English (e.g., Coos and Kalapuya in western Oregon) and languages which are grammatically ornate (Athabaskan, Salish, and Chinook also in western Oregon) may appear side by side in food-gathering regions. Apparently, such contrasted structures functioned with equal adequacy for food-gatherers and any other kinds of populations. It would seem that in preagricultural eras food-gatherers explored, wholly unconsciously, a gamut from grammatical simplicity to its opposite. The important thing seems to be the suit, not the number of pounds of brocade sewed onto it. Every kind of grammatical embroidery appeared long before the portentous metamorphosis from food-gathering to Neolithic agriculture-based economies. And every such kind of grammatical embellishment survives in our time, irrespective of economy or anything else. No one has showed that revolutionary socioeconomic change had any early or later effect upon it.

A statement that languages tended to evolve from the grammatical complexity found among so-called "primitive" peoples to the grammatical simplicity of English is a survival of nineteenth century evolutionist nonsense. One reads and hears it even today. The fact, however, is that languages as grammatically dismantled as English, Chinese, and Coos have turned up in every kind of major socioeconomic level, including food-gatherers. No evolutionist trends from simple to complex or the reverse are discernible in phonetics, phonemics, morphology, discourse units, or any other structured aspects of language. Nor is anything distinctive about the languages of the wealthiest peoples apart from their innumerable specialist vocabularies and their subdialects which connect with social strata. Such peculiarities are directly products of wealth and specialization of labor rather than anything which arose in recondite linguistic processes. Languages have always changed, but directions of change in them exhibit neither regularities nor universals nor do they connect with socioeconomic levels except for specialist vocabularies and social stratum dialect features.

The remarkable advances of recent decades in methodology for identification of, display of predictable variabilities in, and orderly arrangements or placing in sets of significant contrastive units of the kinds termed phonemes and morphemes may very well connect with a circumstance of the learning process. Such minimal features in every language are perceived and internalized earlier in childhood than are other and doubtless no less important linguistic features, especially those which are bulkier and which comprise some of the sets which so-called "transformation grammar" has attempted to handle. Behavioral scientists have learned well how to treat of phonemes and morphemes, better than they have found out how to present almost all the many other types of linguistic features and certainly much more precisely and elegantly all the prodigious arrays of features in nonlinguistic expressive behavior. These latter features are the subjects which are unfortunately only too briefly surveyed in chapters to follow. Phoneme classes and morpheme sets appear to be among the easiest to perceive, list, and arrange, among the score or more principal types of expressive materials.

In linguistics itself, the topic of syntax, which attempts to examine the kinds of relationships and arrangements between linguistic free forms (such as the ties between the forms, all free ones, of the English sentence "the man bit the dog"), has remained rather puzzling to scientific linguists. Other discourse patterns, whether regarded as materials for old-style grammar, transformation grammar, or literary style study, have continued to be baffling also. Apparently, the significant contrastive features of such kinds are, in general, internalized by children after they have obtained some control and effected some structuring and efficient functioning of their phonemes and morphemes. Whatever goes in first becomes most neatly structured, regular, and removed from conscious awareness. Transformational, syntactic, discourse, and stylistic features, or some of them, and possibly no sharp lines separate such facets of a language, appear to be later acquired in childhood, less precisely defined, and less exactly duplicable, that is, they are somewhat more variable from speaker to speaker. And he is likely to have some capacity to manipulate such units, for they are closer to the surface of conscious perception than are the initially internalized units. Some aspects of a language, accordingly, are much more complex and irregular, and a speaker can be comparatively adept at play with them. He seems incapable of dislodging his phonemic and morphological structures. Therefore, no one need be surprised that linguistics has had its greatest successes, so far, in showing the way to scientific management of those simpler and more regular structures which vary hardly at all from person to person within a speech community and which no one can toss about and rearrange at will. The later in childhood the learning of patterned expressive materials, the more difficult it has been for behavioral scientists to fashion methods to recognize and set forth their meaningful units, sets of units, and arrangements of them. There need be no dismay that studies of syntactic features, for example, have languished during the period of discovery of the really simpler features. But so have studies of almost all the expressive cultural items and structurings which this volume tries to introduce. They have had to wait for the sharpening and polishing of tools for handling some of the easiest and earliest internalized expressive items.

## Language, Thought, and Culture

During the past 20 years many scientific linguists on American campuses initiated courses graced with the respectable title Language and Culture. A number of factors account for this development, among them the vogue, which has been notable among nonlinguistic academic personnel, of the so-called "Whorf hypothesis," also termed the "Sapir-Whorf hypothesis." In spite of many flushed protagonists, it constitutes a point of view which was written out in some detail by a cautious and field-experienced anthropological linguist, the late Benjamin Lee Whorf of Connecticut. It is an intriguing formulation in the arena of plausible speculations about relationships between language, perceptions, thought processes, and culture. The larger topic of language and its ties with society and culture has been discussed to some small extent. Here it is sufficient to comment on special suggestions found in Whorf's impressive papers (in *Language, Thought, and Reality*, 1956).

Relationships between linguistic units and classes of units on the one hand, and a sociocultural system on the other hand, can be discussed fully and efficiently only under several rubrics, some of which have already been employed in this chapter. They include captions such as sound systems (phonetics and phonemics), dictionary (morphemes, words and idioms), morphology and syntax, and linguistic geography.

Whorf's suggestions which, to be sure, were implicit in von Humboldt's and maybe others' thinking at least a century earlier, and which were phrased in classroom lectures by Professors Boas and Sapir or bandied about by their students shortly before Whorf wrote, included two principal and now perfectly clear statements. One related to semantics, dictionary, or vocabulary. The other applied to grammar or morphology. Each should be considered by itself and in conjunction with observations of other kinds about dictionary and grammar.

Many ardent disciples appear to have intenser convictions about high probabilities in Whorf's speculations than he professed. They are more than confident about the verity of his hypothesis that free morphemes and words, that is, the contents of an old-style kind of word dictionary, somehow limit cognitions, perceptions, or learning. They believe that words have long shaped perceptions and confined important components of the world view of a language's native speakers, those who were not bicultural and bilingual. For example, if a language has only one word for blue-green, it is implied or said that its monolingual speakers are circumscribed within a perception of just one color in that portion of the spectrum. They tend not to see blue as such or green as such, until someone, perhaps an outsider, painstakingly teaches them to draw a line between blues and greens. The claim is that a given dictionary content shapes or pressures strategic segments of a culture by defining, limiting, or confining a people's perceptions.

One question about such convictions, as in many issues which arise in the sciences, is whether the cart has not been attached in front of the horse rather than where it belongs, although a connection between cart and horse is beyond cavil.

Before showing that in Whorfians' thinking cart is improperly in front of horse, it must be pointed out that field efforts to exhibit vocabulary shapings of and long-term limits upon perceptions have so far been unconvincing. No one has been able to add to or replace a trite statement that if people are interested in or consciously aware of some segment of reality, tangible or conceptualized, such as an icicle, green color, atom, ion, or phoneme, they at once produce a morpheme or word for it. Or, let us suggest in a squeaky voice, within 24 hours.

Whenever a nineteenth century food-gathering people perceived, for the first time, a series of telegraph poles, a wire strung on them, and gadgetry which sent out and received words, they were uttering a word, maybe with two or three morphemes in it such as hair-talk or hair-listen or something of the sort, within a matter of hours. The word did for them what tele-graph did for Euro-Americans' great-greatgrandparents in the days of invention of the telegraph. It is also exactly like people who, over 150 years ago, found themselves using brand new terms or arbitrary combinations of morphemes or words such as steam-boat and rail-road, in speedy response to technological innovations which they perceived and which interested them mightily. If instead of steam-boat, a food-gathering people stumbled upon an utterance like fire-canoe, an equally efficient new word had evolved. Such evolution or inventiveness is almost instantaneous. Someone selects morphemes, others accept and repeat the suggested combination and, if no competitive caption appears, a new word rapidly receives currency. The process can be indicated tersely as culture shapes dictionary. Often, if not always, it does this with lightning speed. New perception generates new word. Challenge, response.

There is no good indication of the converse, namely that dictionary offers more than the mildest pressurings upon culture, perceptions, or world view. Therefore, the first or vocabulary half of the faith adhered to by some of Whorf's disciples may amount to no more than a wish fantasy couched in pseudoscientific phrasings.

The second part of this current cult, for which Whorf was not responsible in any reprehensible way, has offered the faith that some grammatical form classes pressure, determine, or limit perception, that is that a grammar or a portion of it is in certain respects a kind of vise which confines a culture's world view. Disciples of the cult are not necessarily pessimists or addicted to councils of despair. They may number persons who are impressed with creative individuals' autonomy, by human potential to go far in imaginative designing of a world view. Nevertheless they urge, for example, that a language which requires utilization of morphemes to express time or tense—present, past, or future—or which distinguishes with respective morphemes near-past, more distant past, and remote past time, permits its speakers the indubitable luxury, in fact in every utterance, of enjoyment of acutely clear perceptions of time. Whorf and cautious Whorfians do not go quite so far.

A language like Chinese lacks grammatical expression of tense. For all we know, a majority of the world's languages do not express it. Chinese annoyingly asserts something like wife-club-husband when we all, but not Chinese women at least, want badly to find out when she did it or when she will do it or is she doing it right now. A Chinese utterance refuses to reveal when. A speaker of Chinese is not required by his language to express time of action. Some persons who are not transfixed by Whorf's more heated if not luminous apostles may be inclined to mutter nastily that Chinese have long been culturally history- and time-depth oriented without enjoying the mechanical assistance of a set of time morphemes one of which had to be inserted into each utterance in order to speak grammatically. Would the Chinese be even more time sensitive or time bound if they had those grammatical morphemes? Would Indo-Europeans be less time sensitized if their languages were not garmented with grammatically expressed time?

Apostles of Whorf have not been heard discussing the relevent issue of cultural and psychological consequences of grammatical expression of sex gender. It features six or seven of the fifty languages of Oregon and Washington. There is not the slightest evidence that speakers of these sex-gender-ridden languages were clearer, more fortunate, or more compulsively harassed about sex than were speakers of other languages in the region. The logic of an extreme Whorfian position would require a belief that those others, poor deprived heathens, were somehow blunted in matters about which few persons wish to suffer blunting. Actually, the non-sex-gender peoples of the northwest states seem to have been about as bright eyed around sex as are speakers such as Germans, French, or Spanish for whom there is no escape from grammatical expression of it every time they open their mouths and say something more than a mere yes or no. The little sex tags which must accompany every noun in a language like French probably have no more to do with French perceptions and forms of acting out in certain respects than have buttons on French shirts, coats, or skirts.

The converse is similarly frustrating. No linguist has been able to present good evidence from the Oregon-Washington region's cultures of food-gatherers to show how a few of the languages there evolved morpheme tags, which must be employed in those languages, for masculine, feminine, and indefinite gender, at a time when five times as many other languages all around them, spoken by peoples with whom they intermarried and who enjoyed much the same sociocultural heritage, psychological make-up, values, and world view had no bound morphemes for sex tagging. Sex gender, as a required grammatical device, has pretty definitely been shown to have no effect upon culture, personality, world view, morality, or upon sex itself. Nor has any part of culture been shown to present a decisive cause of crystallization out, in a language, of a set of sex gender morphemes which function grammatically. Now this does not mean that sociocultural factors operative over long eras did not tend to bring about jelling, in certain languages, of a set of sex gender grammatical morphemes. But no one has yet revealed such factors.

Does a grammatical form class of directional morphemes such as up-stream, downstream, toward fire, away from fire, toward the outside, toward the inside, uphill, downhill, and the like, nudge or pressure or shape anyone's perceptions about directions? Does a grammatical form class of body instruments such as with hand, with teeth, with head, and with foot exert even miniscule influence upon its speakers' world view and that portion of it which is modestly perceptive of human anatomy?

These illustrations and unpleasant, possibly unfair, or philistine questions may not do the least justice to the inimitable subtleties and persuasive essences in the thinking of the more agitated disciples of Whorf. What is left for them to urge about other portions of a grammar which really do exert an effect, anyhow a measurable nudge, upon a speaker's perceptions and world view? What are those other portions? What parts of that elaborate whole, called "world view," are unquestionably pressured by parts of the grammar? Does less than one percent of the grammar effect such wee pushes? two percent? three and a half percent? No apostle, cautious or incautious, has volunteered an estimate. Still worse, no evidence from a single language has been adduced which would convince anyone that a significant segment of the perceptions or world view of the people, or some other area of their expressive heritage, has been molded or influenced by its language's grammatical features.

Let us think, again, of the many peoples the world over whose food-gathering ancestors not long ago engaged in a transformation of their socioeconomic and cultural heritage with acquisition of domesticated food plants. As already pointed out, such peoples long continued to communicate in the very language which their food-gathering predecessors had employed. Did the new agricultural way of life suffer from ideological limitations because grammatical form classes of the language really blocked them from attainment of some novel perceptions and insights? Is it possible to show that the old food-gathering epoch's language was presently a halter upon them? The answer to this question may be available for the asking in the southwestern United States where Whorf himself conducted field researches. There, many Indian peoples made the transition from food gathering to agriculture during early centuries of the Christian era. Their languages appear to be comparatively little changed in grammatical form classes from what they were before domesticated plants transformed a way of life. The languages include Tanoan, Keresan, Zuñi, Uto-Aztekan, and Athabaskan and are, therefore, sufficiently numerous and varied to grant a presentable, if not ideal, field laboratory for tests of some aspects of Whorfian ideology, if and when the same southwestern Indian peoples are thoroughly analyzed for components of their epistemology and cosmology.

Additional suggestions may be offered regarding Whorfian claims. Athabaskan languages also occurred in at least two other large districts whose sociocultural and ideological characteristics were probably about as different as imaginable from Athabaskan groups (Apache and Navajo) of the southwestern states. There was a continuous area of Athabaskan languages from central Alaska east and southeast into central Canada, and another solid area of Athabaskan languages in northwestern California and adjacent southwestern Oregon. Grammars of the languages in the three areas were hardly more divergent than the differences in various Germanic languages excluding English. Athabaskan languages were, indeed, so similar in morphological features that an apartness of little more than 2,000 years is likely. The Alaska-Canada and California-Oregon regions were populated with food-gatherers right into the nineteenth century. The southwestern states' Athabaskans were still food-gatherers, in all likelihood, at the beginning of the Christian era.

Whorf's field of special competence, the many Uto-Aztekan languages, offers another possible test laboratory whenever the ideological heritages of users of such languages have been adequately probed and intelligibly arranged in patterned presentations. And this is the key problem. Not until anthropology has hammered out a method of research upon, a schema for structured publication, and a system of scientific theory about food-gatherers' and economically lowly agriculturalists' perceptions and world views will we have much warrant to talk in any final way about pros and cons of Whorfian speculations.

But even now it is of interest to observe that Uto-Aztekan languages varied much more from one another than did Athabaskan languages. Uto-Aztekan forms of speech, which include Whorf's Hopi languages, extended in almost unbroken continuity from southern Idaho and southeastern Oregon to Costa Rica. Sociocultural systems and, it seems likely, world views of speakers of such languages varied from equalitarian hunting bands in Oregon and Nevada to Hopi mesa farmers and urban-suburban agricultural Aztecs of the valley of Mexico. It would be astonishing to find important ideological similarities among precontact peoples who exhibited these socioeconomic extremes, from poor to outstandingly wealthy, from food-gathering to economically advanced agriculturalists.

In short, although cultural anthropology is in its infancy in development of field and analytic methods for displaying a people's perceptions or world view, it is evident that Athabaskan languages of similar structurings and Uto-Aztekan languages of greater structural diversity were used by groups of extraordinary ideological dissimilarity. No one has hinted at ideological similarities in them which connect with shared linguistic features. The Whorfian cult ought to disband, temporarily anyway, in the light of such considerations. But who ever heard of a cult which sends out representatives to find evidences that would warrant it engaging in ideological bankruptcy proceedings?

This is not all. Diversities in features of socioeconomic heritage, world view, and perceptions probably occurred in many linguistic groups. Austronesian, Mon-khmer, Sinitic, Dravidian, Hamitic, Semitic, Carib, Arawak, and Algonkin were among those which patently deserve study if further research is called for in the light of Whorf's suggestions, although the extent of grammatical variability in member languages of each such group may minimize the worth of evidence adduced.

Again, the central problem is not linguistic at all. It is to secure scientifically solid materials on the perceptions and world views of these non-western peoples, a task obviously for the future and a project first to be undertaken and carried toward completion before meaningful statements about linguistic variables which affect such sectors of mentation can be ventured seriously.

All in all, the Whorf speculation about some few features of grammatical structure nudging or limiting a certain few features of perception and world view is both delightful and, to this day, unsupported by evidence which a mature science employs to document its theoretical statements. The scholar who feels strongly, that is, intuitively, that Whorf was right and must be right, has his own ethical obligations. We have no desire to rob him of his need for definitive convictions about the way in which a language structure shapes the mind of the person who thinks with the aid of the units and classes of units of that structure. But it remains clear in this early stage of development of the behavioral sciences that indications against the Whorfian cult's homilies are as weighty as the total of indications which have been cited by Whorf and others in favor of its position.

At this time, pursuit of more such tidings may be less productive of advances in linguistics' structure of scientific theory than a plan of attack upon a question which, in a way, turns the Whorf theory upside down. The question is, what were the sociocultural factors, such as repetitive journeying upstream and downstream, which as minor pressurings connected with a very few grammatical features? In any science, the wise researcher who is temporarily stymied inverts the question, maybe the research procedure too. Or he emits a long yawn and selects another topic, one which appears at the moment more likely to produce some evidence that will yield a significant addition to knowledge. Anyhow, he tries something else rather than remain exactly where he is, beating tomtoms, irritating judicious people, trying naïve shortcut research procedures, and getting nowhere. For Whorfian apostles have so far produced only continued questions and fruitless polemics, accompanied by alarming elevations in some individuals' blood pressure, without likelihood of early scientific answers. It seems prudent to place such incandescent queries, important as they are, on a fireproof shelf for a while until someone who is unusually obstinate and resourceful discovers a procedure—I suggest that it must be on the genesis, analysis, and structuring of perceptions and world view—which can throw some light on them. For most contemporary scientific linguists and cultural anthropologists, there are endless jobs to be done in other methodological and theoretical areas, apart from the theoretically sophisticated but still frank descriptivism and analysis of customs, beliefs, feelings, languages, and arts which are needed before acculturative leveling has destroyed all the world's food-gatherers and economically simple agriculturalists.

The psychology of language, for that is what Whorfian lucubrations amount to in their small way and they comprise only a minute fraction of that very large but embryonic subject, constitutes an area of potential inquiry which has extraordinary masses of factual data available for the asking in nonwestern societies. Professional psychologists and some linguists seem hypnotically drawn into the isolation chamber of the traditional psychological experimental laboratory before they dare to hazard statements about the psychology of language. Data which they ought to be obtaining include studies, which will not much longer be possible, of ways in which language content and structure are built into youngsters in nonwestern food-gathering societies. The entirety of a language is grooved deeply into a child well before four or five years of age. How it happens is little understood because most studies of the process have stressed acquisition of vocabulary items in Indo-European languages. Studies of phonemic and morphologic maturation in a child's language subsystems are just as important, and the present dearth of cross-cultural and translinguistic study of such matters is nothing short of a scandal in professional psychological circles. Cross-cultural studies of processes of language learning and use in early childhood are strategically indispensable if the psychology of language is to move far toward a mature system of theory. Imbeddings and structurings which transpire at so early an age are only first among a series of internalizations and patternings of cultural content such as humor, ethics, world view, music, oral literature, and supernaturalism. Internalization of a language makes possible incorporation of the others. Analysis of processes in the one will suggest processes of incising and patterning in the others. Study of food-gatherers will reveal how little has occurred that is really new in personality development in spite of agriculture, technology, social stratifications, acculturations, and many other drastic changes of the last few thousands of years. Only a special few problems can be resolved in the artificial and controlled conditions of an experimenter's laboratory, if the business is to advance a system of theory about what goes on in language learning. Cross-cultural and translinguistic researches can yield what is needed about phonemic and morphologic learning, and this the professional psychologists have barely begun to realize.

## Language Incongruities and Humor

Very likely all peoples play at production of incongruous connotations by substituting morphemes and words which sound familiar but have different meanings. Puns are frequent in many nonwestern groups, maybe all of them. Sound substitutions also effect incongruities and responses of amusement. Spoonerisms perhaps turn up here and there. Presumably, a universal device for laughter is to employ foreign sounds, words, grammatical, syntactic, or other features or, in a comparatively wealthy or stratified society, these features as used by a special social stratum or ill-regarded segment of the population. Onomatopoetic devices may be world-wide. Skillfully manipulated, they engender amusement both because of incongruity in a human imitation of a nonhuman and pleasure most people express in the presence of exemplary skill. In order to effect laughter, all peoples alter grammatical features, melody contours, voice placement and behavior, and phonemes of tone, stress, length, and juncture.

As with other cultural expressions, a repertoire of special units and classes of units functions as material for more or less free play. All mammals both work and play. But humans play with their very special, numerous, and structured cultural inventories of items, including units and sets of units in their language. They amuse themselves as most higher animals do, but they entertain others of their kind unlike animals who tend to be individualistic in play. Human play, and humor is one type of it, is not only inner directed. It is leveled in most of its manifestations at members of the community who are in sight or hearing. In short, sounds, morphemes or words, idioms, and virtually all phonemic, grammatical, and vocal features can be toyed with either skillfully or incongruously to produce laughter responses.

However, it would be naïve to suppose that much of the humor expressed in a nonwestern society comprised more exclusively linguistic stimuli or a lesser or larger number of them than in western civilization. Research on this subject has never been done in even one group. The chapter on humor that follows proposes a method which may disclose the cluster of component stimuli which interlace in a situation that is provocative of amusement. Purely linguistic items in such lattices are only sometimes present. Occasionally they constitute the most important strands. Field workers who have acquired a listening, if not a speaking, acquaintanceship with a nonwestern language would very likely agree that more or less conscious play with a linguistic feature is sometimes a principal determinant of a fun response. Apart from such comments, general statements about language and humor are premature. Collections of hundreds of laughter situations must first be obtained from each group studied in the field, and it appears that this may never have been done. In any case, expressive content in such situations must be cut into discrete, identifiable, and manageable items in the field, then supplemented with interrogation about people's feelings in relation to each item. Only then can there be a beginning of depictive knowledge of the kinds of language factors in nonwestern humor.

Should someone inquire about crudity, excellence, or sophistication, linguistic or otherwise, in a nonwestern group's humor, a cautious cultural anthropologist can reply only that it is necessary to agree upon a criterion and to complete painstaking research in the field. So far neither an agreement nor a study is at hand.

## Abstract versus Concrete

Decades ago, scientific linguists had showed that phonemic and morphological systems in languages of food-gathering peoples ran the same gamut of complexities and types that appeared in languages of the wealthy and literate. Linguists also showed that vocabulary size was a matter not of word count but of morphemes and their combinations; these sometimes ran into many hundreds of thousands. But nineteenth century needs to depreciate nonwestern peoples die hard. Vestigia of centuries of a heritage which comforted itself with arrogant and defensive self-flattery are many.

One depreciatory fancy after another about so-called "primitive" languages has been exposed, but individuals come right back with fresh vagaries of that kind. Persons who are themselves unable to conduct a scientific study of a nonwestern language can often be counted upon to imagine a new illusion by which to point to inferiority in a non-Indo-European language. Of late they tend to avoid Afro-Asiatic, Sinitic, Finno-Ugric, Turkic, Dravidian, Mon-khmer, and Austronesian. But it is still open season on many other groups. One trick, doubtless resorted to in all innocence, is to discuss not phonemics or morphology but solely vocabulary, and to claim that a small group of languages lacked morphemes or words to express generic concepts. The defensive mechanism produces manifestations like the following: The primitives, you see, just could not or did not bother to think like us. Their whole world centered on the concrete and specific. Only when we teach them biology, for example, in new, modern, and cozy schools or provide employment on modern technological projects can they acquire a generic term like "mammal" because previously they had words only for specific animals like dog, monkey, and horse. They didn't have a generic word for fish, an abstraction which only the superior minds of a long literate and economically advanced population would develop. No, simple primitives referred only to salmon, smelt, perch, bass, wall-eyed pike, and a hundred other concrete entities.

Is it advisable to start all over, after so many chimeras or superstitions have been unveiled, in order to exhibit principles which are relevant in such a subject? It is important to do this because of the new processions of defensive individuals who have a need to identify theirs as a superior civilization and who presently will be trotting along with fresh mythic concoctions about language superiorities and inferiorities. Maybe some readers will be helped to recognize these contemporary minds which, like dinosaurs, belong in the past, especially when offerings are set forth with pseudo-scientific twaddle.

From the southwestern states north to Alaska are about 200 languages of food-gathering peoples. Intensive and rather full grammatical investigations of early twentieth century types have been made on scores of them, although dictionary-semantic publications remain few. How many of these languages have been shown to lack morphemes or words of an abstract or generic kind? Precisely none. To be sure, one language may not have a generic word for "animal." But the same language may have a word which connotes animals *and* birds *and* fish. Is this language deficient? The illustration is crucial. If you want a word which duplicates an Indo-European's abstract or generic concept and his Indo-European word for it, you may be rebuffed. The problem is not solved by finding words which parallel Indo-European words. There must be proof that a native language did not and does not have other abstract words and cannot produce them. Such proof has never been offered. There is a towering mass of linguistic indications that it never will be.

The principle of methodology required is, in essence, one which pioneer scientific linguists adopted over 70 years ago and which also applies to all other cultural expressions: Discard Indo-Europeans' units and sets of units, painstakingly chop, slice, and classify to ascertain native ones, and find out their ties with everything else in the society and culture.

A final comment, in the form of a question: What is the degree of concreteness or abstraction in the following two verb morphemes in a Sahaptin language spoken by a food-gathering population in the state of Washington? One morpheme connotes "movement out of water or fire," the other morpheme connotes "movement into water or fire." Are these two morphemes concrete or abstract? Who possesses a calibrated instrument which would measure their specificity or abstractness of reference? Every food-gathering people's language sets forth problems of this kind. An oversimple answer is that in all instances where sedulous research has been undertaken on a language employed by such people, many morphemes have been found whose comparative abstractness of connotation is obvious to Euro-Americans. At any rate, since only a small percentage of the world's food-gathering peoples' languages have been analyzed, claims about prevailing tendencies in the food-gathering group, as a whole, are irresponsible. Some of their languages, such as Athabaskan, offer so remarkable a group of bound morphemes of extraordinary abstractness from a Euro-American's point of view that it can already be deduced, with confidence, that no significant correlation will be found between type of economy, such as food gathering, and frequency or degree of generality connoted by bound or free morphemes in languages present in that type.

Abstractions, their number in a language, and their degree of abstractness deserve study on other levels entirely, those of a people's ethics, world view, or ideology. It appears that a language system, which means five or six kinds of phonemes, a number of classes of grammatical and nongrammatical morphemes, and their relations and patternings, has its own dynamics. One-to-one connections of units and classes of units of that language system with cultural expressive content are for the most part absent except for nongrammatical morphemes. The latter include inventories of specialist words or compounds dealing with world view and ethics. Examples of specialist morphemes and compounds in English would be those which refer to organic chemistry, electronics, zoology, medicine, and the like in addition to simpler groups of morphemes which refer to everyday interests such as colors, numbers, kinship, economic activities, ceremonies, customary feelings about people, value ideals, and so on.

## Other Systems of Communication

Natural languages, that is, languages of a complexity and flexibility known to all modern peoples, served food-gathering and Neolithic peoples during the earlier hundreds of thousands of years of *Homo sapiens* populations. But trade and other developments of the last thousands of years, in those few culturally mongrelized regions where many languages were spoken, generated distinctive and unprecedented systems of oral communication, especially the simple *lingua francas* of the kind called "jargons" or "pidgins." At least 30 to 40 such jargons appeared since the beginnings of the modern expansion of Europe. Many, like the Mobile and Delaware jargons, have vanished. A few, such as Melanesian pidgin and Chinook jargon, the latter no longer a living medium of communication among younger adults, may be studied today. In each instance of a modern jargon, English or a language whose native speakers enjoyed numerical or other dominance in a region (for example, natural Chinook which provided about 90 percent of the words in Chinook jargon) was the basis for spontaneous selection of a small inventory of oft employed words, 300 or 400 to perhaps as many as 1,000, supplemented by minor lists of words from some other languages of the area. Each such jargon appears to have been almost or wholly devoid of grammatical form classes. It lacked a patterned phonemic system, too. It had no phonemes of its own. Each speaker employed only approximate renderings of sounds because when he spoke in it he used sounds of his natural language and structured them according to the pattern of his own phonemic system. A jargon's small dictionary was nonetheless flexible because each of many words in it had a strikingly wide range of connotations. Jargon words were frequently of utmost generality. For example, one word might mean feminine, woman, wife, and prostitute, depending on context. Fluency could be attained in a few weeks.

Except for Chinook jargon, structural changes in a regional jargon which survived for more than a century have not yet been reported. Alterations in it were probably in a direction of greater complexity. There might be internal movement toward crystallization of a phonemic structure, beginnings of a few grammatical form classes, semantic refinements, and multiplication of dictionary content and discourse units which were larger than words. None of these are satisfactorily disclosed except, perhaps, a few grammatical form classes in one of the several dialects or regional forms of Chinook jargon. But such developments or beginnings should be carefully sought in remaining districts where jargons have functioned.

An intriguing aspect of jargons is their impressively efficient, although inelegant, service as auxiliary media of communication in districts where natural languages continued to be used. A jargon apparently did not damage the structural integrity and richness of expression of natural languages which its speakers retained.

In a way, each jargon has been a natural testing laboratory, doubtless prematurely so in the light of the infrequent examinations which scientific linguists have made of them, for those theoreticians who, some sunny day in the future, may be asked to devise a comparably efficient auxiliary international language.

Jargons have been magnificent regional auxiliaries if one is unconcerned about their inadequacies for esthetic niceties, polemics about world view, and philosophical disquisitions in ethics. The secret of their worth resides in their short word list, semantic breadth or generality of many words, phonetic flexibility, lack of phonemic and grammatical structurings, and exclusive or nearly exclusive use of syntactic rules.

Recent centuries of European expansion also produced "creolized languages" in districts where large numbers of slaves or peons labored under colonial plantation owners. In these instances, submerged classes presently surrendered their natural languages and quickly acquired much of the basic vocabulary and phonemic structure, but less of grammatical form classes, of their masters' European speech. Each creolized language has amounted to a kind of partially borrowed or broken-down dialect of a western European language. Its processes of change and course of development subsequently resembled the vicissitudes of any modern rural dialect of a natural language.

Sign or gesture languages, so-called, as among Plains American Indians and some Australian groups, were few and never exhibited the important structural and expressive features which characterized natural, creolized, or even jargon forms. Sign languages lacked phonetic or phonemic features. They were grammarless but employed syntactic rules. Their units represented morphemes, words, and statements. Perhaps only food-gatherers, in districts where many natural languages were spoken, developed these auxiliary *lingua franca* devices of most limited expressiveness, with their small inventories of gesture units.

Theorization about employment of a gesture *lingua franca* in remote times is a product of nineteenth century evolutionist fantasying at its feeblest, since the horrendous premise is that early man lacked intelligence sufficient to produce anything more complicated in oral communication than frowns, snarls, grunts, and shrieks. Evidence for or against an inventory of items of gesture speech, and only such speech, early in human evolution is beyond reach. A burden of proof is upon anyone who would controvert a statement that oral natural languages, of wholly modern kinds and only languages of such types, enjoyed unbroken temporal continuity ever since the appearance, hundreds of thousands of years ago, of *Homo sapiens* food-gatherers in much of the Old World.

To be sure, every modern natural language has enjoyed supplementation in an inventory of expressive gesture units. As far as is known, no non-western peoples maintained poker faces, with hands in their pockets, all day long. Their gestures may connect in a very few food-gathering areas with sign language or gesture traits found there. Study of gesture units as supplements to nonwestern languages has hardly been undertaken and work upon that kind of expressive material is lean even for Euro-American groups.

One American anthropologist (Birdwhistell) appears to have offered a usable inventory of written symbols to represent gesture units employed in the English-speaking world and in European countries. Detailed and lengthy studies of these units so as to provide classes of them, if there are such, and to trace their connections with feelings and social relationships comprise the next step after bare description, transcription, and inventorying.

The past 80 or more years have witnessed over 20 scholarly fashionings, at desks, of supplementary or auxiliary so-called "international languages." The hope has been that worldwide adoption of one or another of them would promote good will, understanding, trade, and superior, if not cheerful or generous, communication among politicians, scientists, scholars, artists, and many inconspicuous citizens, not excluding less generous underground Communists. The best known auxiliaries of this concocted or scholar-produced type are Esperanto and Basic English. Protagonists of Ido, Latin without inflection, Novial, Interlingua, and other more or less buoyantly recommended auxiliaries vary in numbers and propaganda ebullience.

Deficiencies in their idealistic offerings are blatant. Most of the contrived auxiliaries display sounds, phonemic patterns, morphemes, and a few grammatical form classes selected in an aggravatingly culture-bound and language-bound way from westerly subdivisions of Indo-European. Although the proposed types of systematic gibberish might serve, if enough people agreed to adopt them, as European auxiliaries, all are cluttered with too many sounds and features of grammar. In a worldwide frame of reference they are pathetically ethnocentric devices. They have aged into anachronisms on a planet where peoples of new African and Asian nations outnumber speakers of European languages and are rapidly advancing into strategic positions in world affairs. An auxiliary international form of speech which will be acceptable perhaps should not be based upon language features which, to most persons, connote yesterday's arrogant colonial powers. The problem seems to be to devise an auxiliary whose sounds, morpheme-words, and syntax render it both acceptable in terms of bitter memories and feelings, and more efficiently constructed, with fewer sounds and no grammatical form classes, than any auxiliary so far exhibited in the international market place.

## Content and Style in Informal and Formal Discourse

Scientific linguistics today is the inheritor of several traditions of scholarly interests. The past generation witnessed absorbing methodological developments in phonetic-phonemic, morphologic, and syntactic analyses within single languages. These advances in analytic and descriptive procedure followed a century or more of comparative and historical researches largely within the Indo-European group of languages. There was also an overlapping but more recent period, since the 1880's, of increasingly exacting sketchings of grammars of nonwestern languages. A principal result of recent researches has been the establishment of methods and models for analysis of every language. Descriptions set forth various kinds of minimal units which arrange in often impressively patterned classes. These display patterned relationships or larger structurings, too. But the scientific linguists have frustrated some interested laymen by avoiding search for indications of sociocultural connections of their abstracted units, classes, and bulkier structures. In fact, many structural linguists develop a lethal blood pressure level upon the very earthy suggestion that certain classes of linguistic features ever related in a significant way to classes of sociocultural items. Today, outsiders to so abstracted and wondrously structured a linguistic analysis feel lost in the linguists' stratospherical manipulations of materials. One gets the impression of the kind of dismay, maybe a feeling of inferiority, felt by a New Critic, violinist, or dentist when he watches a mathematical physicist pouring out symbols on a blackboard. In addition, laymen tend to ask questions about facets of communication which structural linguists do not want to analyze and, actually, do not know how to segment or pattern. Laymen ask for a little light on features of living speech and hot discourse which are immediately perceptible to them, while the scientific linguist persists in operating inside a pleasantly culture-proof and very cold chamber of his own with allophones, allomorphs, and other abstracted and none-the-less magnificently predictable units which are chillingly meaningless to everybody else.

But to change metaphors, there has been a break in the dike behind which scientific linguists have been laboring with their mathematics-like arrangements of seemingly unreal entities. A few scientific linguists have lately wandered out to the break in order to look at repetitive and structured larger segments of everyday discourse. That is, they have attempted to think through some problems of methods for identification and arrangement of macrosegments as well as of microsegments of speech. Recent inquiries into such methods, called "discourse analysis" and "transformation" or "generative grammar," may be no more than trial balloons. Their merit is that they are properly scouting virtually unknown segments of communication in order to ascertain how to slice, identify, and arrange them, too. The macrosegments are partly distinguished by expressive content, partly by syntactic functions and patternings. A rough-and-ready example of a few members of a single class of such discourse macro-units might be "Ladies and gentlemen," "Gentlemen of the jury," "Friends, Romans and countrymen," "My friends," "Comrades," "Mr. President," "Mr. Chairman," and the like. Obviously, such a class of items connects with an overt feature of cultural etiquette. Study of such content-and-style discourse classes has been patently neglected, if not rejected, during late decades which witnessed the almost spectacularly jewelry-like analyses of phonemic and morphologic structural linguistics. It was possible, indeed it was most efficient for a time, to place classes revealed in such exquisitely well-sliced microanalyses apart from classes of patent sociocultural items. It was almost as if the linguistic sector of a culture had a wholly independent life and identity. However, discourse analyses and transformation grammars will inevitably produce data on content-and-style classes which will tie in with characteristics of society and culture.

## Influences of Writing on Culture

Food-gatherers lacked occasion for meticulous marking of phonemes, morphemes, words or phrases on wood, bark, or hide. Such peoples might make numerical or calendrical notations, place knots along cords, or draw in a cartoonlike style. Like gesture symbols, they outlined or made symbols for discourse units of larger sizes. But during many hundreds of thousands of years of food-gathering communities, potential forms of symbolization which are termed "writing" received no pressuring to develop. Special social relationships which facilitated the first developments in a direction toward devising a script fructified only in Neolithic and post-Neolithic agriculture-based societies. Specialization of labor, urbanization, commerce, specialist priesthoods, tax and tribute collections, and private, royal, or priestly ownership of productive wealth such as slaves, agricultural land, and domesticated animals (the latter in the Old World) first offered circumstances which favored frequent resort to cartoonlike markings or ideographic representations of things and smaller units of behavior. Many hundreds of such markings progressively became stylized and less obviously representative until a hieroglyphic script had evolved in the wealthiest districts of the Near or Middle East, entirely independently in Mayan-speaking southern Mexico and in Guatemala, maybe too in eastern China's great river valleys. Hundreds of characters in that special type of script stood for morphemes or words until, with gradual changes in the instance of Hamitic Egyptian, a few characters represented single-consonant morphemes. Phoenician peoples near Egypt borrowed over 20 such consonant characters and were thereby able to approximate consonants in their Semitic language. Further script borrowings and changes, with additions of vowel phoneme signs, resulted in the near-phonemic scripts of Greek-speaking peoples and later, the Slavic Cyrillic and Roman scripts which with a few more changes are the principal alphabet scripts of the modern world.

Observe that, as in Gregg and Pitman shorthand systems of recent times, scripts somewhat speedier than Europe's alphabet scripts contain many simple morpheme or syllable hieroglyphs. The merit of some modern shorthands is principally in their inventory of cursive hieroglyph symbols. Europe's alphabet writing, inherited by way of the Romans and, earlier, the Greeks, lacks the speed advantage which characterizes a cursive hieroglyph method or one which includes a large number of hieroglyph symbols. But an alphabet script enjoys superiority in its far smaller inventory of symbols and in approximation to a language's phonemes.

Since universal literacy and schooling, whatever that may mean, are little more than a century old in any country, writing has had slight impact upon the vocabulary content or grammar of the majority of speakers of any language and then only by slow filtration down into the general public from literate strata high in the society. Not even the few literates in any country before the nineteenth century have been affected in their sounds and phonemic structure by direct influences flowing from the script they used, if we allow for one or two rare exceptions. Among literates for a few thousand years, writing has tended to retain morphemes, words, and grammatical features which would otherwise have suffered disuse. Scientific, technological, and cultural consequences of a script have everywhere been enormous in spite of its scant effects upon spoken language. Scientific work and fashioning of systems of scientific theory would be unthinkable without a tool of writing.

## Learning a Second Language

An adult has the potential to learn a second language so well that when he uses it all traces upon it of the natural language of his childhood temporarily vanish. But infrequent adults succeed in eliminating their "foreign accent" to such a degree because they have not received guidance by a member of the still minute company of modernly trained language teachers. Among some nonwestern peoples, however, perfectionist polyglottism occurred extensively. When visits were frequent among kin of different natural languages and large numbers of intermarriages occurred, many persons spoke two or three languages without the slightest osmosis of alien flavor. Such excellence appears in Europe, too, in districts like the Rhineland, Switzerland, Hungary, and Turkey.

Wherever possible, pedagogy in a second and third language should be limited to prepubescent years, just as polyglot perfection comes to pass in learning during early childhood. At that time, acquisition of a second or third language is less likely to be accompanied by emotional resistances such as arise from many factors including concern over expenditure of valuable time, anxieties following observation of other persons' failures to learn, feelings around punishing or dull language teachers, and atrocities perpetrated in traditional kinds of introductory language textbooks. Customary assignment of second-language teaching to secondary and college years is both a pedagogical crime and an irresponsible expenditure except in the many instances where persons make late decisions to tackle other languages. The most efficient and least costly period for learning a second and third language is long before puberty. Since almost nothing of the cultural heritage of western civilization, or of any other civilization, is customarily taught in America's elementary schools and there are only lately indications that some deviants want something of cultural value taught there, it seems fair to suggest that a few elementary classroom years might be surrendered to a new crop of modernly oriented, intellectually vivacious, young, and high-salaried teachers of foreign languages and cultures. They could function at their best with prepubescent youngsters. Great numbers of children would make a competitive game of such up-to-date pedagogy by thoroughly alive preceptors who are in the fortunate position of not having to fight the impossible. Tuition would be wondrously economical. Its oral and aural procedures would supercede customary and, of course, nonsensical textbook, dictionary, and translation methods which torture the teachers and waste the time of millions of American high school and college youngsters and the money of cheerless taxpayers, even as their greatgrandparents wasted much of their years of so-called schooling in idiocies of Latin conjugations and declensions and of parsing of English sentences.

## What Languages Are Most Beautiful?

If languages are never inferior to others in efficiency of communication, potentials to express abstractions and values, or capacity to adapt to technological and social change, some may still be inferior in esthetic respects, whatever those are. What evidence is there to support statements about esthetic values in languages?

Is Italian, as voice teachers and pundits of the musical profession have often asserted, more beautiful than English? Is Haida, an Athabaskan-like language near the coast of southern Alaska, the most attractive sounding of languages? The deservedly praised Edward Sapir once wrote that it was the most beautiful language he had heard, although he never worked painstakingly to analyze it and he could not understand it. There can be no argument with a person who feels that mountains are ugly, red hair is ravishingly beautiful, and the *ch* in German *Bach* harsh. Responses such as these are frivolous ultimates on the level of taste and preference.

If one starts with an esthetic premise about language sounds, a scientific linguist need do nothing about it. From his translinguistic point of view, esthetic statements about languages may be placed in several categories such as sounds, dictionary, grammar, idioms, larger discourse segments, and features of oral style, although most esthetic options or obloquies about speech have been concerned with sounds. Careful cross-cultural research on people's responses to the acoustic effect of alien languages apparently has not been undertaken. Nor have there been exacting cross-cultural studies of vocal mannerisms, texture, tonal placement, and other important matters in generating emotions in listeners who cannot understand a word of what is being said.

It is possible to suggest, and a scientific linguist would urge, that repetitive utilization of a sound, a class of sounds, or a cluster of sounds of a certain class which is unfamiliar engenders auditors' cultural and idiosyncratic responses to the strange. If no unpleasant associations attach to an alien people, their polity, marriage habits, bathing customs, body odor, and voice placement and texture, and defensiveness in the form of rejection or disapproval of strange language sounds is not current, the response may be accepting if not ecstatic. A theoretical suggestion by a scientific linguist is, then, nihilistic: sound features of an alien language have little to do with ostensibly esthetic judgments about them. Beauty in sounds of a language is largely in the ear, that is, the sentiments or, perhaps, the starting premise of a listener, not outside in units and patterns of oral sounds to which he is attending. If he attaches positive values to classes of tonemes and melody contours, he will respond positively to tone languages. If sonant continuants such as *ž* (French *je*), *γ* (a palatal sonant continuant in Eskimo-Aleut and many languages the world over), *z, l, m*, and *n* strike responsive notes, he will be pleased again. People who find German and its *ich* and *ach* rasping may be burdened by rejecting feelings, if not stereotypy, about all Germans. If, as in the instance of the author, frequent clusters of five, six, or seven surd consonants tend to please him (for example, *łptčk*, where *ł* is a voiceless *l* with much friction and *č* is the consonant in English *chow*), he will react in a manner the opposite of that of Euro-Americans who perceive in such clusters of voiceless consonants unhappy resemblances to sandpapering or small hammers operating on tacks. Euro-Americans are the more entrenched in their feelings when they learn that this kind of clustering of consonants appears in languages of communities long suffering from ill repute because of effluvia from urine bowls and fly-blown lampreys, fish, and venison. Glottalized consonants, South African clicks, nasalized vowels, and all other classes of sounds each stir foreigners' responses which cannot be shown to connect with known principles of sound texture, pitch level, and balance in patterning, if there are such esthetic principles to which adherence is required.

Again, a major problem is to ascertain whatever is relevant in an alien auditor's background and personality because a response which he supposes is esthetic is largely or wholly something else. He misinterprets other associations. He displaces from people to sounds they utter. All this is not to say that a comparative esthetics dealing with sounds and sound systems of languages is forever beyond possibility. At present it is nonsensical because of defenses and residua of provincial feelings which skew everyone's responses of this one kind. Is it farfetched to coin a phrase which describes all of us as sound-bound, by analogy with culture-bound?

A question of beauty in a language may be shifted to its vocabulary, grammar, syntax, and various larger discourse units, but the answer is the same. Responses arise today in culture- and language-bound rootings. Scientific linguistics cannot halt pseudo-esthetic statements by laymen. As a science it has no need to. Perhaps it ought to study the subject and try to unveil the sundry psychological mechanisms, or the madnesses, which produce such assertions.

## The Future of Languages and Linguistic Science

Although all the thousands of natural languages, food-gatherers' not excepted, are equally capable of adapting to and transmitting all systems of scientific and humanistic theory which are rapidly developing during the twentieth century, pure accident, not inferior worth, dooms many languages to early extinction. One or two centuries hence, no language of a food-gathering people may survive except in tapes sealed in tins in libraries and other archives, in learned publications, and in unpublished manuscripts. Many a numerically small agricultural people of today will also replace its language with the speech of wealthier and more numerous invaders of their homeland. The sole superiorities and inferiorities in such language surrender and replacement have been and are in power, wealth, and populational numbers. Progressive contraction in number of languages has occurred since the Neolithic domesticated plant revolution of 8,000 or more years ago. Nevertheless, each of over 100 nations retains one or more distinctive languages. India and China each have many scores. Accordingly, many hundreds of natural languages will survive for centuries, supplemented perhaps by regional or international auxiliary forms of communication for use in international meetings, scientific journals, or other services. Prediction of a more distant global future as monolingual or polyglot is silly guessing.

The immediate future of scientific linguistics appears to include the following: intensified efforts to record and analyze all hitherto unstudied natural languages, jargons or pidgins, and creolized languages, not least the intergrading dialects of each, and to connect their features with sociocultural items; comparisons of natural languages in order to ascertain genetic and other relationships between them; emergence of psycholinguistics as a specialist field of inquiry, notably in infant and child language learning; development of language-and-culture as a specialist field; achievements in a variety of practical applications, especially in second language learning and pedagogy, possibly also in communications engineering and the gadgetry of mechanical translation; devising of a satisfactory international auxiliary language or of several regional auxiliaries; and construction, without an eye to applied linguistics, of a system of scientific theory which embraces all languages and the studies of language learning, a system which employs the descriptivism and analyses of today and tomorrow as source materials for documentation of its statements.

Conditioning and internalization of the broad spectrum of social relationships is almost as early in personality development as acquisition of linguistic features. A certain few almost "primitive" or basic relationships, however, are learned even before acquisition of features of language. That is, the infant early learns responses to mother or those who initially grant it food, affection, warmth, surcease from dirt and vermin, and security in various respects. Learning the larger pattern of social relationships connects with language learning.

It is now time to accord attention to all those other aspects of learning of social ties and, soon, of cultural expressions.

## SUGGESTIONS FOR FURTHER READING

Introductory reading, quite good even if occasionally uncritical, may be found in J. B. Carroll *The Study of Language* (Cambridge: Harvard University

Press, 1953), H. A. Gleason, Jr., *An Introduction to Descriptive Linguistics* (Rev. ed.; New York: Holt, Rinehart, & Winson, 1961), and in a classic of a generation ago, L. Bloomfield, *Language* (New York: Holt, 1933).

Magnificent writing and content ennoble B. Karlgren, *Sound and Symbol in Chinese* (New York: Oxford University Press, 1946), E. Sapir, *Language* (New York: Harvest Books; Harcourt, Brace, 1957); B. L. Whorf, *Language, Thought, and Reality* (Cambridge: Massachusetts Institute of Technology, 1956) and, for their period of two generations ago, the works of Otto Jespersen.

# 4. FROM BIRTH TO DEATH: PSYCHOLOGICAL ANTHROPOLOGY

## Beliefs about Babies

Euro-Americans have been fascinated by reports that some nonliterate peoples lacked knowledge of consequences of sexual intercourse. Indeed, only poorly substantiated claims have appeared about one or another people's inexpedient and therefore lamentable ignorance in that subject. No doubt there have been peoples with well-spun fabrics of theory about abodes from which babies came and with concomitant rejections of questions put to them about a simple biological significance of impregnation.

The way to look at a problem of nonwesterns' beliefs about the cause of appearance of a baby is, first, to ask how reliably a field research was conducted. Second, to understand that whatever the native articles of faith may have been about the origin of babies, import in convictions is never in their biological realism or lack of it. It is in their expressive content as a whole. It is in what they reveal about a culture's sentiments in social relationships. A society which frankly presents lies to children, such as the European myth about storks that deliver infants, expresses among other things a tenet about imbecility of the child mind and a determination to perpetuate such a state in its young people for as long a time as possible. On the other hand, a nonwestern culture's myth about a baby land where little people have their special language, live like adults, and freely make decisions about the nice humans to whom they wish to come, may thereby express respect for children, point to a value about their right to own things and to make decisions, and reveal a belief in their potential for speedy maturation. Close content analyses of such professions about babies and their provenience accordingly yield information about components of a society's world view and values. There has been little or no such research.

## Personality Development

From the 1860's on, evolutionary stage slicings in geology, biology, and sociocultural subjects offered models for later Freudian classification into stages of personality growth. Europe's intellectual mainstream from even before 1860 and on to the early 1900's was running toward stage and biological explanations. The first decades of Freudian writing, that is during the 1890's and after, offered descriptive, classificatory, and theoretical statements about growth during childhood of basic features of personality. In a simplistic manner, and pioneer theoreticians necessarily simplify, cutting of the continuum of personality growth denoted five stages to Freud and his disciples. During each of the first three stages which these inner-directed innovators posited, nuclear family parents supposedly reacted to a biological need or drive in the child, a need connected with an erogenous zone (mouth, anus, genitalia) satisfactions of which at the time dominated the youngster. The child responded to stimulation of that zone. Parents' manner of treatment of the drive, with eventual "frustration" of it, was supposed to pave the way for the next stage with its characteristic erogenous zone, especial responsiveness to its stimulation, and then a parental response. Differences in children's sociocultural surroundings received no adequate consideration in earlier Freudian studies which were inevitably culture-bound because of the intellectual climate of the era.

Freudians assumed that children's pivotal drives were innate, identical the world over, and satisfied or modified by parental responses which were everywhere of a kind. Psychodynamic mechanisms and processes of specified European types in parents occurred universally with many adequate parental responses on the one hand and botchings on the other.

To a Freudian, trouble for a child arose in parental failure to "frustrate" correctly the biological drive dominant in each level or period of personality organization. A parent should so handle a child that it presently made a healthy rechanneling or adaptation of the drive which featured the stage. For example, breast feeding and uninhibited elimination, which connected with oral needs that were natural to a youngster's first stage, could not be allowed to go on into later childhood. Highlighting of inborn urges which appeared successively from stage to stage, taxonomic cutting of the continuum of psychological growth, portrayal of results of poor responses, that is, improperly managed "frustrations" of drives by nuclear family parents, and citations of proper rechannelings of basic urges constituted, for the era, an insightful and indisputably useful outline of personality development in many urban middle-class Europeans.

Indeed, the Freudian depiction is classic in its clarity and convenience for certain purposes in psychotherapy of European people. And it soon made a profound impression. Not many Freudians quickened to a disturbing thought that their linear developmental scheme focused upon special characteristics principally in themselves and in their select group of urban European patients. Most Freudians were not prepared for a suggestion that their five-stage map was of doubtful relevance as a chart of major characteristics of personality growth in a great many Euro-Americans and in nonwestern peoples. The most learned and imaginative Freudian psychotherapists and all their retinue were unable to perceive that they were examining growth in child personality structure in a local group of Victorians and near-Victorians. There were then almost no descriptive field data or clinical psychiatric reports on peoples in other parts of the world. The specifications were culture-bound. At that time, they could not be otherwise. Psychiatrists supposed, without important dissenting opinions, that their kinds of patients were typical of humanity. A general theory about personality development was being presented for societies in which, as it turned out, important parts of the theory would have to be replaced.

To be sure, Freud was actually one of the most perceptive ethnologists of the era, although he regarded himself as a psychologist. He was studying with characteristic originality members of one class in a single "tribe" or subculture, and his psychological insight was unsurpassed. He was really observing and identifying significant social relationships in them.

Captions of the first three of the five stages in child development which he posited reflect his theory about the primary importance of body orifices as locales upon which biological urges center and around which the earliest learning occurs. The stages, which he represented as overlapping, are oral (from birth to eighteen months of age at the most), anal (from about four months to as much as four years of age), phallic (from about three years to seven), latency (from as early as five to about eleven), and genital (puberty and later).

It is unnecessary to discuss the theory of Otto Rank, one of Freud's disciples, that vicissitudes during parturition, which of course differ from culture to culture, connect as causes (the so-called "birth trauma") with characteristics of adult personality structure. Proof or disproof of such a hypothesis appears unavailable with present-day scientific methods or current ethnographic information.

## From Birth to a Year and a Half

For this period of a baby's life, Freud postulated direct cause-and-effect connections, that is, specific consequences to adult personality of regularity, manner, and duration of nursing; of time and manner of weaning; and of time and manner of toilet training, this in the few societies where it had been initiated before the second or anal stage. Freud captioned his first stage the "oral" stage. Neither he nor his immediate disciples weighed possibilities to personality of other needs, "frustrations" and handlings during this period. They did not grant comparable consideration to effects of irritations from sun, heat, or cold; disturbances of quiet and sleep; manner of cradling and of cleaning; manner and duration of daily isolation from persons; annoyances from insects, skin chafing, and sores; learning to talk—this is of decisive moment; explorations on all fours; and learning to walk and climb, followed by wider navigation and adventuring.

Since Freud's wholly urban European clientele did not suffer traumatically from insects, sores, and climate, he subsumed needs for reliability, security, and affection from older persons under a heading of the manner in which parents dealt with certain dominant drives of the stage. But a list of multiple factors and their social, affectional, and security-granting characteristics is to be emphasized. It enriches if it does not supersede a theory which accents centrality of a certain very few biologically determined needs and satisfactions around orifices.

Both in field observations and theory, an anthropologist, influenced as he may be by Freudian pioneering, which was inevitably shaped by nineteenth century biological emphases, tries to assess multiple needs, multiple responses, a fabric of causes of personality development in infancy. He does not go to the extreme of exclusion of biological factors. But he does not assert that they and the various happenings of infancy produce both specific and ineradicable consequences to adult personality. He suggests that, where present, they must also receive effective, if not continuous, reinforcement during later childhood years. At all times, he centers relationship and cultural factors. He plays down the supposition about universality of primacy of orality and its handling. He is prepared to evaluate orality as important in some societies in its role in a larger fabric of multiple factor causation of personality.

Most vital is a proposition, emphasized with fervor by later Freudians, that responses to infant needs make their impress upon a young personality largely in terms of granting of reliability, affection, and security. A robot which ministered with utmost efficiency to an infant would very likely develop a disturbed child because there would be no opportunity for the infant to learn emotional interactions which are important in personality growth. If one or more grandparents, uncles and aunts, older children, or others in a nonwestern band or village were reliable and conferred adequate affection and security, infants might have little need of biological parents. Foster parents in western civilization offer virtual proof of this suggestion. Tasks assigned to mother and father in the Euro-American nuclear family are therefore certainly sociologically demanded, although not biologically required of those two individuals. "Significant others" such as foster parents or elders may do the work if they do it affectionately and reliably. To be sure, many, if not most, nonwestern societies have displayed persons who functioned in culturally assigned roles of so salient a kind. It is impossible to understand child life and growth in many nonwestern groups without perception of roles assumed by "significant others." An anthropologist acquires, if he can, voluminous information about the behavior of such persons.

What goes on in subsequent stages of personality development?

## From One and a Half to Three or Four

Freud's second stage, which he called "anal," centered results much later in life of training in regularity and cleanliness of habits of defecation. During this period, as in others, a child appears to feel more security if learning is guided and imposition of new habits, disciplines, and horizons of tolerated behavior or, as is said, the setting of limits, is done early by reliable and kindly persons to whom society regularly grants such authority. Again as for Freud's first or oral stage, grandparents, aunts or uncles, or older children have been assigned such responsibilities in many societies, supplementing or even substituting for parents. Indeed, a question arises whether a child's socialization, especially during this Freudian second stage, is not benefited by a plurality of generous and responsible persons other than or, at least, in addition to nuclear family members. Opportunity to dilute and spread resentment which a child may feel at this time should leave him with fewer battle scars than if the entire struggle took place with only one or two "significant others." Although it might also be proposed that superior capacity to relate acceptingly to many persons is built into a child who is reared in such a larger social setting, proof may be difficult to assemble.

Freud's followers also spoke of one-to-one connections during this second stage between toilet training and the continued development of ego and unfolding of superego. "Ego" is a Freudian term for capacities for manipulation of and relationship to things and people, that is, efforts to maneuver in and successes in mastery of the external environment and especially the social relationships in it. "Superego," which Freudians asserted differentiated out of the ego, may be translated as internalized value ideals or conscience. Obviously, an extraordinary quantity and rapidity of learning occurs. Children now learn language. In the very process of furrowing its thousands of expressive items, its sounds, its form classes of grammatical morphemes, and its various structural traits into themselves, they presently build capacity to perceive and incorporate other patterned sectors of their people's heritage. Now they refine coordinations in running, climbing, walking, and in manipulations of gadgetry. They recognize, chart, and then dextrously manage most social relationships. They experience, to a finale of effective internalization, much of their culture's inventories of incongruities (humor), values, and features of world view.

Simplistic thinking by earlier Freudians tied all these complex learnings to toilet training as prime starting cause. Mid-twentieth century science prefers to arrange its charting of such elaborate behavioral manifestations in terms of multiple stimuli and reinforcings, multiple adaptations, here as in other age levels, without commitment to an unproven premise about transcendence of one above all other factors. Primacy of multifaceted patterning, as against toilet training, formerly received little attention. Freudians' toilet training dogma of a half century ago, which unquestionably accounted for many things in some Victorians, has been generally shelved in up-to-date circles among behavioral scientists in favor mainly of a willingness, and this is good, to weigh causal factors after something of the variability among many peoples and cultures has been surveyed.

Observe, too, that bowel movement or constipation anxiety has long been a notable characteristic of Euro-Americans. It is a rather quaint expressive phenomenon of their culture. Was Freud's centering of toilet matters in his second stage of personality structuring really a shrewd perception of something vital and was it, of course, a complex of cultural and biological components? A decisive factor in personality designing among Euro-Americans traces back to what the culture has done to their youngsters, not how all youngsters naturally and globally feel about defecation. The question is how children respond to parental sentiments and cultural do's and don'ts around sphincter disciplines. Children's later responses are thereby conditioned. Other and later instituted types of discipline accordingly produce similar results. The first decades of Freudians underplayed cultural factors because they knew virtually nothing about the extremely different and often far less anxiety laden sphincter disciplinings in nonwestern cultures.

Early Freudians also paid little or no attention to cross-cultural possibilities in breast feeding which, here and there, was permitted to continue longer than among Euro-Americans. Weaning occasionally transpired as late as five or more years of age in individual instances in a few food-gathering societies. In these groups, weaning frequently occurred in the second, third, or fourth years, evidently at such late times because of an insufficiency of easily masticable or digestible foods. In all cases mother's milk was early supplemented by other foods. But the psychologically significant item appears to have been a protracted availability of the breast and all that that may imply, in the first place, about security granted by mother and, in the second place, about the child's self-system. Indeed, probing psychological studies of contemporary nonwestern children who are so advantaged are conspicuously unavailable, maybe because field workers during the last three decades of researches among such peoples have occupied themselves more with kinship terminology and structuring than with the much more difficult topic of kinship sentiments. Psychiatrists and anthropologists alike have wondered, without being able to offer a satisfactorily documented answer, if capacity to be selfless and generous, as well as the security which facilitates maturation, connects with duration of breast feeding. Unfortunately only the latter may receive mathematical expression, if exacting evidence is required.

Toilet training and weaning may comprise only a small fraction of the emotional experiences and learnings during the anal stage. Feelings around personal possessions, mastery of language, eye-hand coordinations, walking, climbing, canoeing, swimming, or riding in some pastoral societies, injuries and sicknesses, and not least the internalization of values and building of kin, play, and other relationship ties may be as strategic in personality formation as the resolutions of anal and oral "frustrations." All constitute culturally designed disciplinings and learnings. If growth of personality is to be understood, many types of responses must be sharply categorized, weighed, and precisely described in broad samples of children of both sexes in single nonwestern societies.

## From Three or Four to Six or Seven

An especially striking point of view marked Freud's characterization of psychological growth during his third or phallic stage in the child. Here he struck at Victorian repressions and tabus in such a manner, indeed so successfully, that his historical contribution to the intellectual climate of later decades, to the very self-identity of many citizens of the mid-twentieth century, would be notable had he written nothing else. He startled Victorian contemporaries by claiming that, between three and seven, if not before three, every little child innately develops positive sexual feelings —underline sexual—toward its parent of opposite sex, together with jealousy and aggression, maybe to an extreme of sentiments of murder, toward its parent of same sex.

The formula in crude, one-sided, masculine-oriented form amounts to this: boy loves and wants to marry mother and is jealous of and wants to get rid of or kill his father who is the rival for mother's love. Freud used a bit carelessly an analogy with the plot of a drama by Sophocles. It offered a caption, the Oedipus complex, for a male child's sentiments. A little girl's similar love of father and hatred of the rival, mother, were later termed the Electra complex. Freud supposed that these feelings of love and hate, typical nineteenth century dialectical opposites as usual, flower in children everywhere because of their biological etiology. Such instinctive responses in children are intolerable, of course. They must soon be repressed and forgotten if a child is to mature healthily. A boy subsequently identifies with father whom he had been envying, hating, and hoping to eliminate, and he introjects admired masculine traits in that parent. He may also internalize some traits of his mother. In this manner, a boy approaches a proper and healthy masculine concept of self. A girl, similarly, after repression of comparably odious aspirations around her parents, identifies principally with mother and so achieves a healthy feminine self-image. Groundwork, that is, correct sexual identification, has been laid for admission after puberty to membership in one's sex group and for acting in terms of the proper sexual role.

As always, Freud's revelations, which are hypotheses from the point of view of science, are masterpieces of acute and original reporting. But Freud was culture-bound in his conviction that he was describing distinctive and central characteristics of a stage which develops everywhere in the specific ways he perceived in his sample of Central Europeans. He thought that biological factors, instinct, not globally encountered societal requirements, determine the phenomena which he perceived and sketched so sensitively for some Europeans.

Still, he offered a most important hypothesis about a mechanism which operates universally in child socialization: identification with trustworthy, loving, and security-granting persons who reward, punish, admonish, and establish boundaries to proper emotion, thought, and action. Today we presume that sociocultural assignments to adults have varied greatly the world over. Adults have engaged in one or another kind of role playing, depending on their social system and culture.

In the world's thousands of societies, security was conferred in diverse ways by means of definitions of boundaries and horizons. Children have internalized heterogeneous values. Some societies used fear of humiliation and shame as restraints, some used affirmations of absolute values. But the Freudian hypothesis seems to ring true in its most general respects, if one removes an improbable biological component in the premise about Oedipal responses and introduces a transsocietal perspective. A huge task for future generations of field workers is evident: to document the working of selected Freudian-based processes, such as identification and introjection in contrasted sociocultural settings, that is, to report exactly what many non-western societies have done or may still be doing to socialize and mature their youngsters.

There seems to be little if any security for children, or possibility of their emotional health and growth, without consistently maintained behavioral, ideological, and ethical boundaries. Such fencing in appears to be indispensable although its detailed features have differed extraordinarily from district to district. What is crucial is that there are firm foundations and clearly marked limits, that these are expressive cultural items, and that a society assigns persons, not necessarily a child's parents, to do the job with consistency.

Freud pointed to a threat of castration, under a heading of the so-called castration anxiety or complex, as the feared punishment for transgressing certain of a culture's don'ts. This threat and the resultant anxiety, which were real enough in many or most Victorian households, must be interpreted freely if they are to be useful in the course of building a system of cross-cultural theory. They cannot be taken literally except in thoroughly documented instances, and these have already been displayed in studies of boys in some Euro-American families. The hypothesis of a castration complex presents a useful guide to research on nuclear family relationships if rephrased so as to imply nothing more surgical than a threat of shaming or some other hurt. Whatever the potential punishment for masturbation or other misbehavior in one or another culture, it is understood by a child between the ages of three or four and seven years. He responds by internalizing the society's requirement or prohibition. It is transmitted to him by elders who are his significant people. It is necessary to repeat that significant people are often, but not everywhere, biological parents. They were almost always biological parents in the Victorian group which Freud knew so well and whose castration threat and anxiety he recognized and interpreted brilliantly.

As for masturbation, many societies are unlike Europe in their lack of concern over it. In fact, there are reports that some nonwestern peoples masturbate babies in order to soothe or quiet them. The printed verb, masturbate, is in most instances a projective expression of the European observer's alarm, disapproval, and lack of comprehension. What probably occurs is only a soothing stimulation of infants' genitals, but Europeans often have perceived it as something evil and threatening to themselves.

A child's internalization of values and need for certainties granted by significant older persons continue for almost another decade, at least they did until puberty in most nonwestern societies and on into the twenties or later among a few peoples. More of this later.

Freud's delineation of biological causation of Oedipal sentiments and their reputed blossoming spontaneously within a child turns out to be an upside-down but nonetheless magnificent picture. Where sentiments of the unpleasant kind which Freud skillfully reported for Victorian children occur, causation does not reside in a boy's chromosome- or gene-based instinct to love mother and to hate and be rivalrous toward father. Evidence for such an inherited response has never been produced. Causation is more likely to be found in a boy's parents' behavior. The child responds to his Victorian mother's seductiveness and protectiveness and to his Victorian father's authoritarianism, jealousy, and resentment of a diminutive young rival for the wife's affection. It is safe to deduce that in Victorian Europe, Oedipal behavior was and is generated by culturally shaped behaviors and feelings of parents, especially by immature ones, toward their children. It is not impelled by a youngster's innate Oedipal instinct, an explosive drive triggered and directed by a monstrous little gene or highly elaborate molecule of protein resident at a fixed point along a microscopic chromosome. Oedipal-like responses of some children in a few other societies appear to have been consequent also upon customs which produced stern male and protective, maybe unconsciously seductive, female custodians. Again, more or less anxious, limited, or just provoked adults, not instincts in children which release tumultuous responses, initiate the phenomenon. It arises in adults who are also a society's transmission lines to children.

Freud's topsy-turvy description was only too true, without its biological element, in one subculture. It resembled startlingly what was found in some other societies. In many it hardly appeared at all in forms notably like the model that Freud constructed. In all instances, causation of child behavior is to be located in adult feelings, values, behavior, and maturity, that is, in a society and culture. If a society allows relatively immature older persons, parents, grandparents, or any others to stir Oedipal responses in eight-year-olds, thirteen-year-olds, or twenty-year-olds, that pattern appears in those later years too, again not because of any continuation of an impious biological imprint in the younger person. The point is that adult behavior which institutes responses in a younger person may occur when junior is three, thirteen, or any age. Among Victorians it transpired frequently when their children were between three and seven, sometimes even before three, and it tended to recur in later years of their children's lives.

However, a discussion of resolutions of Oedipal feelings as decisive in a boy's three-to-seven period of growth is hardly of value for comprehension of the cross-cultural gamut of phenomena of socialization and personality growth at that age. It is also too simple a hypothesis to account for the whole of even a Victorian male's psychological development.

To repeat, Freud had magnificent insights but, like most pioneers, he oversimplified. Child learning, internalization of value ideals, and development of ego and of self-identity comprise many things. In all societies children in the three-to-seven stage have progressed rapidly in mastery of customarily sex-assigned skills. They could do this because the tool for communication had now been built into them. The structural and content items of the language were all there ready for instant use. Now children could learn to make things, to produce foods, and so on, but always within a network of traditional social relationships. Much of their psychological growth hinged upon what they were allowed to learn about adult social relationships. These learnings were as important as improvements in physical coordinations and in control of techniques of food production and of manufacture of artifacts. Hardly less important for maturation is what children learned, too, about their adults' panorama of the world—religion, supernaturals, geography, and the like—and about the adults' arts—music, dance, legends, and so on. Perhaps most important of all were the adults' maturity and integrity.

The learning front is broad. Every aspect of it, although its central characteristics are communicative tools (language) and relationships, enriches and consolidates personality, self-identity, and feeling of worth. Progressive maturation is as if hundreds of new pseudopodia were thrusting out, each to become a permanent feature of the organism. Let us not propose that one pseudopodium, unless it be the one that represents relationships, is enormously fatter and more vital than others, until transcultural ethnographic microscopes have been refined beyond anything we have today.

In many societies handicraft learning was patently of utmost importance in personality growth during the later phallic period, although it is generally of small moment in modern western society. Euro-American children usually do not learn techniques of major economic production. Other societies taught these techniques with signal impact upon their youngsters. Significant adults who taught them might or might not be a child's parents. Freudian emphasis upon end-of-phallic-stage resolution of Oedipal—read nuclear family relationship—feelings, with correlated building of ego and superego, must not be allowed to detract from the great significance during the same period of child life, in Euro-American and certainly in most nonwestern societies, of other learnings and vital relationships which are nonparental. Anthropology's obligation is to discover everything possible about results upon personality of all these learnings and significant people in as many nonwestern societies as can still be studied. There will be many for decades to come. Mechanisms such as identification and introjection which Freudians revealed are, at least today, of momentous value as broad hypotheses. But stress upon a nuclear family or Oedipal difficulty and its resolution, upon parent versus child feelings, and upon a castration complex, should be replaced with recognition that even among Victorians these factors were only parts of a larger network of growth vicissitudes.

Freud's achievement is not limited to discovery of the role in personality growth of a nuclear family pattern of relationships but includes his pointing to the centrality of mechanisms which connect with roles of youngsters and their elders. Causation resides in roles of significant people who relate to a child in controlling, limiting, teaching, and affectional ways. At the same time it was certainly no negligible achievement to reveal Oedipal and castration patterns when unquestionably they were characteristic of a Victorian subculture. Manifestations of similar kinds are easy to find in many societies resident upon one modest planet.

Freud also offered as a factor in a child's growth of self-awareness a sentiment which had to be repressed and the feelings around it properly resolved. This was a supposed envy of the other sex's genitalia. The notion has continued to receive much emphasis in psychoanalytic literature. But the envy, wherever found, is probably a cultural reflex. A feeling of envy felt by little girls in societies characterized by male dominance must be primarily consequent upon girls' early sensing of males' superior status and more honored roles. That is, anatomical envy is principally, although perhaps never wholly, a culturally determined envy of status and role, an envy displaced upon an overt feature which distinguishes the opposite sex. In societies such as economically primitive food-gatherers and some of the agricultural groups where the sexes were equal in status, one may expect to find envy which went in both directions. There was some male envy of female anatomical features and physiological functions, to a point possibly equaling females' envy of male genitalia. In such societies, and at a later age, a remarkable intensity of envy of women's ability to bear and nurse offspring might also develop. In some of the wealthier societies, males with strong dependency needs and marked inability to cope and compete might crave the protected, passive role assigned to females. What was operating was centrally a jealousy of respected social function, valued role, and position in relation to others. The supposed anatomical focus of interest was very likely, and only partially, a displacement from the socially generated heart of the attitude.

Early Freudian writers did not neglect still another vital "frustration" of childhood: they subsumed it under a heading of sibling rivalry. They perceived its onset as at any time when an older child became apprised of parental preoccupation with a younger sibling. Indeed, hurt because of diminished attention from elders may be felt at any stage of personality development, although it may be most painful and difficult to resolve during the first five or six years of life. An infant who is nursing at mother's breast and who, even when weaned, continues to receive a major share of parental concern often earns an older sibling's hatred. Such animosity must be buried: societies globally have supported with a variety of arrangements resolutions by suppression or repression of the older child's feelings. For example, when custom required a weaned toddler to accompany and be guarded by older children, he was at once removed from the domestic scene. Now he must work out his battle tactics at a distance from his mother and his helpless infant sibling who was still ecstatically imbibing mother's milk.

Heat which arose in rivalrous sibling feelings lessened or dissipated in a society which designed large play groups of weaned youngsters, aged on up to puberty, kin or nonkin, siblings or cousins, and where adults treated them all alike. A related phenomenon is evident in a tepidity of Oedipal feelings when parents or other elders customarily took responsibility for many children rather than only one or two. Immaturity is maintained and regression to more childish responses occurs when Oedipal and sibling intensities fail to be displaced or dissipated in one or another societally shaped way. A multiplicity of significant older persons in addition to nuclear family parents, and a goodly number of unthreatening siblings and sibling substitutes, that is, a kind of playground that is well populated with young age mates, appear to constitute excellent means by which children's needs are met and personality growth, socialization, and maturation are facilitated.

The Polynesian village, the great house of some Amazonian Indians with its hundred or more residents, the Pacific northwest states' riverine forest hamlet with its open playground area where all preadolescents spent the day hundreds of yards away from houses, the polygamous South African circle of huts, appear to have maximized opportunities for early socialization and maturation. In these societies, tart feelings received almost automatic redirection and dissolution in the very structuring of child relationships in play and learning. Correlations may be found between general type of socioeconomic system—economically primitive or advanced food-gatherers, economically primitive or advanced agriculturalists, and any other type —and manner of child maturation. But the most important influences in child development were of idiosyncratic or local kinds. Household size and playfield arrangements sometimes presented decisive factors.

Among rural Euro-Americans and in nonwestern societies, skills of value to everyone often began to be practised and mastered shortly before six or seven years of age. Nonwestern boys learned how to make toy canoes, bows and arrows, to use them, too. Girls learned to make baskets, pots, and wovenstuffs. Both sexes returned to the hut or village with small quantities of foods. Rural American youngsters participated early in farm chores. When older persons show gratitude and pride over such productive work, children early develop feelings of worth, enhanced self-identity, and responsibility.

Anthropologists have usually returned from field researches with detailed accounts of adult economic and handicraft production and have infrequently described contributions of young children because they were technologically imperfect and productively spare. Still, it is possible that fundamental factors in personality growth from three to seven years of age lie in skills still feebly learned, in petty food and artifact contributions and, above all, in feelings of older people about them. A society which disallows any child the learning of socially vital skills except taking apart a broken alarm clock, any contribution to the kitchen or storage bin except going to the store for salt or matches, any recognition of potential for economically significant production or creativity except holding father's hammer, grants the child little opportunity to develop feelings of self-identity and worth except to the extent of identifying with that segment of its parent's personality which is a socially admired role. And this is only the focus of the picayune self-system of a very small snob. A society of this kind retards a child's maturation. There have been such nonwestern societies or social strata within them. Their treatment of a child enhances the small person's considerable capability to be anxious, bewildered, and lacking in feeling of worth for, after all, diminutive size is in itself not ego-enhancing. A society does not burden a child of six or seven with more than he can handle if he is encouraged to assume small responsibilities, to venture upon practice leading toward mastery of respected skills, and if he is rewarded with praise for successes. Many nonwestern societies, possibly most of them, have done just this. The contrast in personality maturation between their children and youngsters of middle class twentieth century cities who are excluded from society's most recompensed endeavors is indisputable (reading, writing, spelling, arithmetic, and civics are hardly handsomely rewarded). Dignity, independence, and maturity in the one group contrast vividly with general immaturity in the other. Children play in all societies. But children may also work, learn, practice, and achieve when at play. Maturation is neither conclusively enhanced nor retarded by play. Children who play and who also gain access to respected and productive work suffer least retardation in maturing.

Anthropologists have frequently returned from field trips with reports of community respect accorded extremely young children's ownership of things. A modern Euro-American parent sometimes takes a toy or doll which a child regards as its own and gives it to a sibling or other child. But personal possessions, even the most unstructured chunks of wood or broken and unusable artifacts, may be vital parts of a child's self. Apparently it can be damaged by forcible or seemingly unfair removal of those parts. Nonwestern peoples, especially food-gatherers, have often revealed consummate understanding of even a toddler's, let alone an older child's, need to be a person like any adult who can have his will with possessions. It is almost as if the vote were granted two-year olds, by contrast with the world's wealthiest "tribe" which accords a comparable right of decision, possession, and privacy only to eighteen or twenty-one year olds. Episodic dislodgements of children's petty paraphernalia and transfers of their small personal effects may function as traumatic retardations.

Still another factor in child personality growth among nonwestern peoples arose in feelings about the proximity of adulthood. In western civilization, a seven-year old rightly feels a great many years removed from adult life. The vista ahead, that is, certainty of continuing to be treated as incompetent, seems almost endless. Nonwestern peoples tended to admit children to respected adult participations, including marriage, at the time of or not long after physiological changes of puberty and attainment of adult height. This point on the horizon may seem a long way off to a five-year or seven-year old, but it cannot feel nearly as far away as when entry into adult life is at sixteen, eighteen, twenty years, or later, that is, years after physical growth to adult height. In other words, awareness of nearness of acceptance as an adult augments ego strength and feeling of worth. Lack of such feeling, because of the remoteness of transition to adult life, is marked in six and seven-year olds of Euro-American civilization.

Not the least weighty factor in a child's development, at all stages from phallic on, arises in the ego strength, dignity, wholeness, and maturity of its significant elders. All the encouragement, intellectual stimulation, social participations, rewards, respect for a child's personal possessions, and love bestowed unceasingly upon a youngster only prepare him healthily for maturity. They do not confer it, like a school diploma presented at graduation. Ultimately, a child must and can internalize only what its significant elders possess. If they are poorly skilled, uncertain about some important values, overconcerned about status, and immature in a variety of ways, a youngster is going to suffer retardation in personality growth. A culture perpetuates much of its adults' immaturity from generation to generation. Only those youngsters break through the net of significant elders when new and equally significant elders appear. Here is the unique opportunity of a mature and sophisticated teacher. He has at least a chance of taking 20 or 30 partially developed little personalities and bringing them forward in spite of culturally built-in limitations in their parents and other close kin. Teachers' potentials for doing this increase greatly during children's teens because many youngsters are then sufficiently sturdy in their ego strength to transfer onto new significant elders their need for internalization of values and additional features of world view.

Again, when teachers' personalities are hardly richer or more mature than the kin, youngsters are trapped. There are now no distinctive significant elders with whom they may identify: teachers only reinforce the internalization of views and values which commenced with kin. Much of the population of western civilization is caught in such a web. But modern non-western peoples are generally in a different situation. Here teachers brought in from other lands are very different from the personalities in kin, clan, or community. Such teachers also represent the spectacular technological world beyond the horizon. Extensive personality changes in children, youth, and adults occur under such conditions, in spite of often admirably integrated and mature personalities of their early significant elders. However, these elders represent technological backwardness and social humiliation. Youngsters therefore transfer positive feelings to and incorporate thoughts and values of the wealthy, technologically sophisticated, literate, and powerful outsiders, frequently with conflicting feelings and severe guilt.

## From Six or Seven to Puberty

Like their delineations and affirmations of major factors in maturation during three earlier stages, Freudians centered biological factors once again in a fourth stage which they called "latency." They asserted that because of successful repression, healthy youngsters wholly forgot the sexual interests of the third or phallic stage. Sexuality remained latently present but would erupt anew in a later, the fifth, stage of adult genitality. Accordingly, an uneasy quiet characterized the surface innocence of the years from six or seven to puberty. As before, only a rare Freudian realized that his confreres were also describing vast numbers of sexually unsophisticated because overprotected, shielded, and more or less infantilized prepubescents of the middle class in Victorian cities, the children of one class within one sub-culture. From the vantage point of cross-cultural knowledge, which even unusual disciples of Freud lacked, it is possible to see that these prepubescents were intellectually and socially as well as sexually retarded. Extremely little of the colossal riches of Euro-American culture, except maybe music, had reached them. These were maturationally slackened children because they were permitted to partake of few of society's valued social participations and cultural treasures. Nightly they were relegated to their bedrooms hours before adults retired. The word was, "Children should be seen and not heard." Spanking, switching, food deprivations, and comments about their immaturity and incapacity were frequent and registered a consistent output of humiliations and denials of worth. Everyone thought he knew the child mind. Scholars equated it with another myth, the mind of savages of distant lands. The dogma regarding prepubescent moronity, a culture's defense, among other defenses, against insights which might have been achieved by its own young flesh and blood, shaped a century's school curricula. Today the tenet is more than a vestigial survival of Victorian belittling of prepubescents. It functions vigorously to retard the intellectual maturation and social sophistication of most children of Euro-America's schools, especially so in the United States. The doctrine has long been reinforced by rationalizations and pesudo-universals offered by the culture's professors of education and child psychology. Many of them suppose, even now, that studies within their culture furnish generalizations about psychological trends and potentials in prepubescents the world over. It is like generalizations about an orchestra based upon researches on the piccolos, limited instruments to be sure.

Assumptions which guide students of the stock markets of western civilization have about as much application to economic structures of food-gathering and nonwestern agricultural societies as do Freudian opinions on repression of sexual interests in the latency stage and western civilization's *idée fixe* about prepubescent mental limitations. These notions are expressive phenomena of a single social system. Anthropology has advanced to a point where it can no longer be expected that cross-cultural validation is ever going to be presented for western civilization's Victorian and post-Victorian mythology about the Euro-American child mind. That type of mind can, of course, be comprehended only in terms of Euro-American society and its history. Thousands of other societies had different historical vicissitudes and, therefore, produced many other kinds of prepubescents. In general, their cultural heritages contained less somber convictions about children and, what is almost alarming, they may have been closer to truth about potentials in pre-adults.

Summarily, what factors decisively shaped prepubescent personalities outside of Euro-American civilization? One, ego security and self-identity which arose in belongingness to extended families, lineages, clans, band or village groups, and the like. Two, immediate connections with supernaturals. Three, identification with experienced, if not both revered and awesome, elders, in societies whose oldest people were the main transmitters of ideological treasures and ethical canons. Four, unquestioned acceptance and internalization of elders' beliefs and standards of values. Five, imminence of entry into full adult participations, including marriage at or shortly following puberty. Six, feelings of worth consequent upon practice, acquisition of skill in, and fullness of familiarity with the society's economic, technological, social, religious, and ideological (cosmology and the like) forms. Seven, feelings of worth because of the community's intense approval of skilled young participants in art forms (music, dance, oral literature, plastic and graphic arts). Eight, reiterated commendation by elders of such skills. Nine, plaudits, too, for indications of early maturation; a lack of barriers in attaining it.

In short, a nonwestern prepubescent might have had direct contact with many parts or the entirety of the heritage. He competed creatively with age mates in mastering its subdivisions and, accordingly, enjoyed acceptance and encomia.

A contrast with the roles and status of Victorian and post-Victorian prepubescents is arresting. In many respects it is frightening. Culture, parents, adults in general, and the educational apparatus have ignored or denied children's potentials for mastery of skills, acquisition of significant forms of knowledge, acquaintanceship with world view, religion and the arts, and social sophistication. At almost every point—piano and violin virtuosity may be excepted obviously because the absence of accompanying verbalization left everyone unthreatened—learning by western civilization's prepubescents has been slowed, retarded, halted, or negated. Today elementary and secondary school teachers, who are feebly paid, respected, literate, cultured, or favored with job security outside of the cities, are rarely able to open up to their charges doors to the special repositories of the Euro-American or any other cultural heritage. It is difficult to transfer feelings of identification to such teachers because they are not often notably superior to one's kin. Because of their uncertainties, confusion, and wretched general educations, precollege teachers are incapable of phrasing or transmitting much of the ideology or value ideals of the heritage. They have had many education courses and few or no educational courses. The cultural treasure-house of western society is a complex, multifaceted, and mysterious thing. Although tiny snatches of it are sometimes exhibited in simplified, counter-feit, or disingenuous versions designed for presumably mediocre minds, its abundance and wealth lie about as concealed from youth as the gold reserve at Fort Knox is shielded from public gaze. Youngsters suffer unceasing at-tacks upon their self-esteem by reports of their insurmountable illiteracy and unglamorous IQ's. They develop subtle awarenesses that teachers as-signed to their classrooms are wanting in social, sexual, esthetic, and intellec-tual sophistication. And they are assured that little or nothing can be done to improve the quality of what they are hearing uttered in the front of the room. They are inoculated with the germs of an incurably rigid and diseased curriculum. Feelings of worth are especially fragile when children receive tagging as members of lower social strata and of disadvantaged racial, re-ligious, or national minorities. A case might be made for a theory that in Victorian and immediately post-Victorian times armies of faceless educa-tors designed an elaborate structure of destructive theory about education, watered out all of western civilization's magnificent scientific, philosophic, and esthetic heritages to tasteless opaque juices, erected prisonlike edifices and installed underpaid and ignorant sentinels in each fetid room in order to prevent the little prisoners from maturing, and so on. Whatever the in-tent, the result was and is infantilization and impoverishment of the next generation, and an almost insurmountable moat between young people and their rightful cultural patrimony. Few can envisage a successful leap across. To be sure, rare individuals are able to find libraries that happen to have some adequate books which provide fantasy personalities with whom iden-tification is possible.

In most instances, youngsters suffer both from their lower status and from the ego hurt of identification with fearful and insecure parents. The absence of other significant persons only reinforces the insecurity which can be repaired solely by parents or by sensational achievement on the athletic field. Grandparents, aunts, uncles, and cousins might display many petty kindnesses but tend to function almost as distantly and unreliably as any nonkin except the athletic coach. No groups in statuses of revered elders or respected teachers grant cultural continuities or certainties. The elderly and the assigned pedagogs alike are rejected because in this culture they are viewed as more or less ridiculous. Conflicts in values presented by multiple strata and minority subcultures generate bewilderment, rejection, and needs to defend against personal merit arising in distinctiveness. Adult-hood and marriage lie far beyond reach, certainly long after puberty. The product is a multitude of people who are lonely, insecure, bewildered, im-mature, vainly seeking relationships which cannot be granted, values which cannot be located, and ideas which cannot receive substantiation. Proliferations of religious sects function to supplement factors which render science and culture distant or unattainable, and to intensify chaos in values, although denominational congregations grant social ties, securities, and belongingness to great numbers of lonely individuals. In this one culture, many prepubescents become as predisposed to live in order to collect tangible or intangible property—money—as nonwestern people were actuated to live in order to collect or maintain tangible kin and intangible supernaturals. In Euro-American society it does not always seem likely that one can collect valuable new people and relationships.

## Puberty

Much has been made of puberty as connecting with a culturally stylized transition from childhood to postchildhood. And it surely has been exactly that in societies the world over. At the same time, generations of anthropological field workers and other observers of nonwestern peoples have very likely extrapolated western civilization's emphasis on a transition from childhood at puberty. Less accent upon puberty might have offered a more accurate reporting of nonwestern attitudes about stages of child growth. For example, few field workers have noted that at the time when children completed their permanent teeth, certainly by eight years of age, their coordinations, internalization of values, diminished requirements for adult guardianship, and ability to assume a variety of responsibilities constituted a kind of entry into near-adulthood. One wonders if some anthropologists, because of culture-bonded and unconscious extrapolating, have failed to perceive an equivalence of importance of the seven- to eight-year-old level in personality development among many nonwestern peoples with the point marked by physiological puberty in western society.

Since little is available to document the suggestion, it is appropriate to proceed with puberty itself. Freud called it a fifth stage, "genitality." The transition at the line of puberty, with its often rich expressive ceremonial which perhaps has been much more striking to outsiders than any rite around youngsters three or four years earlier, if indeed such prepuberty rites have been reported, has been included under a larger heading of *rite de passage* or "crisis rite." Over 50 years ago Arnold van Gennep introduced the concept. The terms for it headline custom-embroidered changes vital in an individual's life—birth, death, puberty, and marriage. Assuredly, these have been especially dramatic rites. That is, each society smoothed or cushioned its most important alterations in values, obligations, role, age status, and relationships. It did so by supplying outlets in time-honored ceremony, formal togetherness, art forms, and chartered utterances which functioned, among other things, to deflect from direct involvement with feelings. Freud looked upon it as a stage in which adult sexuality presently developed, if everything went real well, with fixation upon a love object of opposite sex.

In some regions neither sex was put through a puberty rite. In a few regions, only girls had the rite because of anxieties around their status and bride price or because physiological functions peculiar to their sex created deeper anxieties than did parallel functions in males. In many regions as in Australia and sub-Saharan Africa, all pubescents were objects of solemnities. Earlier generations of readers of anthropological treatises, maybe contemporary readers too, have bolstered their convictions of the over-all superiority of western civilization when they morbidly perused direful accounts of tattooing, cicatrization, circumcision, subincision, clitorectomy, installations of ear plugs and labrets, and a hundred other attacks on a person's anatomical integrity—from the culture-bound point of view of Euro-Americans. Puberty, its sexual changes rather than growth in height, is traumatic for Europeans and normal curiosity about other cultures' puberty customs is, therefore, intensified.

The usually noted descriptions of puberty ceremonials, in spite of their sometimes gory appurtenances and prevailingly artistic content in verbal, dance, and song expressions, are hardly as significant as functions, among pubescent young people, of less noticed processes of identification with elders and internalization of culture by way of supremely significant people who were mentors and custodians of heritage. *Rites de passage* expressed and revealed especially intense points of feeling along the time continuum of life. All sociocultural systems exhibited such formalities, although puberty rites were not universal. But descriptions and analyses of rites as such or attainment of adult genitality are of minor importance for a system of scientific theory about society, culture, and the processes by which youngsters have been built into adult ways. Rites were colorful, vivid externals which earlier anthropologists at once observed and photographed. Psychiatric clinicians saw the unfolding of sexual interests.

Acquisition of a sensitive record of societal, cultural, and psychological processes requires discernment which few earlier anthropologists possessed, and interrogations which few of them pursued at satisfactory length. Research also calls for judicious piecing apart of meaningful components of overt wholes of complex expressive ritual and behavior. Victorian and post-Victorian anthropology was usually able to depict them in only surface and cursive ways. Psychologically perspicacious dissection of dance and verbal expressions in puberty rites, in the many regions such as Australia and Africa where these have been found, may supply invaluable clues to the not so evident processes of maturation, status and role change, internalization of values, and the like which paralleled public ceremonials. Analysis of rituals may then constitute a means, among many, of revealing what was going on in a people and their society.

A transsocietal characteristic of a period from 10 to 14 years of age may be located in completion of fundamentals of personality structuring, character, self-identity, and the like. Of course, segments of small or larger size may be added to or subtracted from personality in later life. A question which has long confronted psychology and other behavioral sciences is its methods for delineation of a relatively completed personality structure. What does such a structure comprise? How are vital learnings of the first decade of a person's life assembled, arranged, and granted triggers so that repetitive external stimuli touch off the same kinds of responses, releases, and defenses thereafter?

Psychoanalysts and psychologists have accorded much attention to personality theory, but their discussions have always centered upon people in one society and culture, that of the West. Anthropologists took a hand in personality theory, especially during the 1930's and 1940's when Benedict wrote of so-called "culture patterns" which comprised basic features of world view, self-identity, and values. These interlocked with and governed everything else in the personality structures of all carriers of a sociocultural system. Within a few years Linton and Kardiner were presenting a cross-cultural concept of "modal" or "basic personality structure." For present purposes, distinctions made between modal and basic may be ignored. The heart of the Linton-Kardiner offering was that central features of a social system and its principal cultural expressions became imbedded in all members of a group so as to cause them to share a special and diagnostically serviceable inventory of features of relationship, world view, self-identity, and values. These were presented in more detail, in a longer set of statements, than in Benedict's culture pattern depiction. Kardiner urged that knowledge of a people's signal social institutions, manner of child upbringing, and cultural characteristics allowed deductions about central traits of personality which had been built into and were shared by all or most of the citizenry. Freudian theory about factors in personality formation in infancy and childhood were integral with the Linton-Kardiner presentations. Neither author argued about time of final formation of personality structure, whether before, during, or long after puberty, nor had Benedict earlier intimated the time when a culture pattern became set within every youngster.

During and immediately after the Second World War Benedict, an English colleague Geoffrey Gorer, Margaret Mead, and others further developed the basic personality concept. They offered methods of analysis of sociocultural materials and of interviewing people from various nations or societies with the object of displaying what came to be termed "national character." The significant thing about the Benedict-Gorer-Mead group is not an ephemeral term, "national character," but an unprecedentedly intensive resort to and development of interview and analytic methods for describing shared personality characteristics in a population. The presumption in Benedict culture pattern theory, Lindon-Kardiner basic personality structure theory, and the later national character studies was that a constellation of psychological characteristics was internalized at an early age in most or all members of a sociocultural system and that these people also exhibited wide variability of their manifestations of the constellation. Kardiner emphasized the possibility of selecting strategic social institutions, such as customs of maternal care and a society's most stressed values, such as reckless bravado, and that they could be connected, without further check-up, with resultant personality characteristics. The national character studies group was more cautious. They preferred to develop techniques for checking claims about such connections.

Kardiner's efforts to depict Marquesan (Polynesian), Comanche (Texas and Oklahoma), Tanala (Madagascar), and other societies' basic personality structures were not based upon rigorous analyses nor were they written out in an orderly way. Kardiner rested upon his Freudian convictions, dogmas perhaps, regarding invariable consequences of childhood customs to adult personality. He thereupon concocted cursive literary paragraphs which described impressionistically the psychological characteristics which he believed had to be present in a population which adhered to such customs. The Kardiner method was deduction, with a vengeance.

The contributions of all these pioneers were momentous, in spite of reservations which perfectionist behavioral scientists might have had, at the time or since, about dogmas, methods, irresponsible deductions, or lack of rigorous methods in the new cross-cultural writings. For almost the first time the mind of "primitive man" had been envisaged not in general terms as in Levy-Bruhl a generation before, as in Boas' distinguished work *The Mind of Primitive Man* of 1911, or as in Radin's impressive *Primitive Man as Philosopher* of 1927. Benedict had led the way to perceive nonwestern peoples as a great gamut of disparate societies, each of which produced a distinctive patterning of the minds of all its people. Each pattern, personality structure, or national character had arisen in its own sociocultural system and solely because of that system. Subsequently it influenced, in its turn, the system's viability, structuring, and manner of changing. Benedict and those who followed her in this group of students of group personality found no room for implications that there were primitive minds. To be sure, Boas had long before affected Benedict, Radin, Linton, Mead, and his other disciples in such a manner that it was impossible for many of them to use a term like "primitive" without queasiness. An unphrased corollary of theory in the 15 years following Benedict's *Patterns of Culture* was that each kind of personality pattern was extraordinarily complex. Each society was like a nation's currency mint which stamped out its own characteristic coinage. Kardiner was among the first to try to point to main features of the sociocultural machinery which produced the human coins and he also attempted, in a sketchily diagnostic rather than closely documented way, to describe something of the coins. Each of his depictive efforts was an oversimplification where it was not an irritating distortion of reality. But a pioneer theoretician tends inevitably to bypass most of the details and evidences which later workers collect and manipulate. Kardiner centered general statements. Later stages of work and theory always witness more exacting searching and slicing which, to be sure, might never transpire until pioneers framed some crucial inquiries and formulations.

During the 1940's many questions remained unanswered although the national character studies pioneers began to tackle some of them. There was, for example, the problem of diverse roles and status of the sexes and the utility of working with a hypothesis of two or more important culture patterns or modal personality types in every society. There was especial likelihood of multiple modal personalities in caste-stratified societies, as in extreme instances such as Sudanese agricultural-pastoral-fishing-ironworker castes and the many castes of India. Other kinds of social stratification, such as occur with ill-regarded racial, religious, or national minorities, and consequences to personality of membership in an inferior or superior subgroup, had received slight notice in the first decade of cross-cultural theorization about personality structures.

Difficulties were evident in acceptance of a premise that everyone in a society shared essential features of personality, even when qualifications were added to the dogma. For example, differences in personalities of siblings and special characteristics of emotionally disturbed persons had to be accounted for with additional theory. Nothing in the earlier culture pattern formulation of Benedict or in writings about basic personality took care of these questions. Differences in adaptability to later years of life were also not shown. Diversity within a group in capacity to relate to supernaturals or to be creative in cultural expressions remained untouched. Personality theory ought to help account for a variety of phenomena and not least the inordinate range in individuals' behavior within a tight small society. Despite the breakthrough granted by Benedict and her successors, it was apparent that comprehension of many kinds of personality manifestations had to await improvements in method, theory, and field research itself. There had been a beginning of depiction of types but almost everything remained to be done to display variability and its causes within each type.

Meantime, psychiatry was rich with theory which deserved checking in researches among nonwestern populations. For example, psychiatrists were familiar with the occasional individual in western society who when under stress displayed episodic or intermittent rather than chronic or progressive schizophrenic behavior. In such a person it is as if something encapsulated a walled-in subsystem of feeling and ideas, had cracked so as to permit acting out which normally never happened in that individual. Or, to change the analogy, it is as if strands of a sturdy net had gotten badly torn. Subsequently, the net seemed to repair itself. The formerly walled-in subsystem of feelings and notions somehow resealed. The individual returned to adequate functioning within his society's daily expected pattern of roles and relationships. If people who are emotionally sick exhibit indications of encapsulated subsystems of distinctive responses, are so-called normal persons possessed of such structural characteristics, too? Do they have lots of systems and subsystems which work smoothly, one with the other and all together, so that no one such structure ever breaks destructively apart from the others?

A question may arise as to whether a personality at puberty can be symbolized as a total system of interlocked organs, capsules, cells, or subsystems, guided and controlled by a central exchange. Radcliffe-Brown had lately thought of a society as a kind of organism, and Herbert Spencer long before had certainly been thinking in such terms. What about a personality structure? Could the analogy of an organism or elaborate structure serve here, also? Benedict's culture pattern of some central features of world view and ethical principles was her way of limning a pilot house of the personality. The Linton-Kardiner concept of basic personality structure was much the same idea, in rather different terms and with more detail.

But a distinctive method of analysis had become necessary because it was clear that there is far more to take into account than a headquarters or control center. Envisagement is of a personality built up so that, roughly at puberty, it has become a competent organism with interlocked organs, cells, subsystems, all pretty tightly glued together and responding to orders —Freud would have called these the directives of ego and superego. The result of such a cartoonlike picture of operations of personality is that component subsystems within the larger and ordinarily well-guided whole also require accounting. Identification and analysis of a headquarters from whence issue orders are insufficient. A certain type of mind and temperament enjoys tackling the nature of a whole, a configuration. Another kind of person likes probing, searching for smaller parts, cutting and slicing, and arranging small pieces. Benedict, Linton, and Kardiner presented an important configuration concept and pointed, like Freud, to a kind of control center in an elaborate machinery. They had tried to describe essentials in a whole, a constellation, with emphasis upon its pilot center. Later, Benedict herself, Mead, and others began to probe other parts or subsystems within the organism. What kind of strategy, in the sense of emphasis either upon the captain of the personality ship or upon the various kinds of machinery which he manipulates, is likely to lead to more knowledge?

A nonwestern child learned to play a number of roles which varied considerably. He learned his proper relationships toward parents, kin, in-laws, future cowives, fellow hunters, fellow fishermen, siblings, religious leaders, strangers, supernaturals, and so on. Perhaps each such relationship role was a kind of encapsulated entity, a subsystem of features of self-identity, values, and distinctive feelings. A child also learned various kinds of eye-hand coordinations as in bow and arrow, pottery, or basketry manufacture. Each constituted another learned subsystem, a kind of small organ within the larger organism. Cross-culturally, knowledge of the many different subsystems is so fragmentary that the manner in which they developed in a nonwestern childhood, ways in which they functioned for the whole organism, and manner of their interlocking and receipt of directions from the organ's headquarters are matters for future exploration, hardly subjects to present at this time as firmly founded knowledge. It appears that acceptance of an almost but not quite atomistic methodology, a probing and slicing approach, one which by contrast emphasizes all the machinery, all its subsystems, and not primarily the captain on the bridge, is proper strategy for cross-cultural researches in the next years. It will continue to be productive to regard personality as an organized and often not so neatly controlled mass of semiautonomous subsystems. But the tactics which will grant maximal returns in knowledge will be in proceeding initially to close analyses of the formation, composition, and functions of each subsystem, always with functioning of the total organism in sight. For example, research should ask when and how was the subsystem called language, and all its classes of items, internalized in a given society? When and how were all the classes of items in the subsystem of musical expressions learned and internalized in that society? When and how was its basketry manufacture and designs learned? Ambitious efforts to make significant statements about central features of the typical personality structures found in societies may, therefore, be premature when the scores of describable subsystems in personalities within these societies remain less than slightly known.

The chapters of this book, accordingly, constitute a succession of discussions of cultural systems or subsystems, for it is these which somehow interlock within individuals and comprise vital sectors of their personalities. Chapters of a book on social structures the world over should provide discussions of the various systems which deal with customary relationships and roles within societies. To be sure, internalization of such social ties and behaviors and the expressive manifestations and values around them are no less crucial for comprehension of personality structure.

In most nonliterate groups, the whole interlocking business of social and cultural systems was working in adult-like manner when an individual had reached the transition of puberty. What happened during the next stage of an individual's personal history?

## After Puberty—Adolescence

Freudians' caption for this period and its initial transition phase is the "genital stage." They observed, in Europe of course, that latent urges which were long repressed before puberty now explode. Presently, European youngsters select "object choices," sometimes initially a pal of the same sex but without essentially homosexual concomitants. Then they attach in no long time, if not immediately, to an individual of opposite sex, as indicated above.

Even among Victorians, postpuberty learning and personality growth are not well explained by a theory which stresses eruption of sexual drive, that is, one among many patterned components or systems within a personality. In many nonwestern societies, adult genitality which Freudians supposed accompanied and followed puberty was long anticipated by culturally permissible sexual behavior, experimentation if you will, but nonetheless identifiable. It happened in the years before puberty.

Permissible sexual behavior commenced in true middle-class Victorians a number of years after puberty, so that it could be said that latency continued in such luckless but well-dressed people for long periods, in many individuals throughout their life: they never attained adult genitality. Few societies around the world have exhibited such studied avoidance of sex, repression of it, a policy of resorting to it at a later time solely for the purpose of procreation, or displayed the remarkable psychological concomitants of intense emotional conflicts over such procrastination, frustration, and humiliation.

More significant characteristics, cross-culturally, of the period immediately following puberty appear to be these. In most cultures outside of the Euro-American orbit and in lowly strata of western society, the waiting period preceding full adult participations had ended. Everyone functioned economically, socially, religiously, and artistically as an adult, maybe less competent or experienced, but still an adult. Indeed, few nonwestern languages can translate Indo-European languages' words for adolescent and adolescence. Most nonwestern societies featured a transition from child directly to teenager adult.

The concept of adolescence is itself a single culture's expression arising in its idiosyncratic customs around personality development. In Euro-American civilization, especially in its middle strata, adolescence is the period when a potential adult is retarded in a variety of ways. An adolescent is a person who has the potential to be an adult but is not allowed to become one. Few other societies kept doors to adult status and roles shut so long. Emotional and psychosomatic disturbances which frequently parallel Euro-Americans' adolescent years are doubtless expressions, forms of acting out, which arise in a long continuation, a seemingly endless vista, of exclusion from society's respected participations. Administration, disciplines, values, teaching staff, and curricula of the American high school system have long symbolized to perfection American society's determination that few or no so-called students who are caught in the system be permitted even a peek at adult interests or relationships. The function of the system is cloaked. It is really a baby sitter, police, or custodial system, one which is dubbed education only because of the culture's democratic aspiration to confer a most elementary education upon all.

Consequences of Euro-American customs of postponing adulthood after puberty are almost appalling to contemplate. A thousand and one devices segregate, humiliate, and confuse the age grade which is called adolescents or, more recently, teenagers. Elaborate patterns of ideology, disciplines, and institutions maintain an almost universal postpubescent level of infantilization, fragmentary self-identity, convictions of lack of worth and defenses, as in sports and clubs, which allow special channels for expression and achievement. For decades, college and university teachers who have perhaps naïvely accepted the medieval notion of a free community of scholars have counted hordes, numbering millions, of dear little children called college Freshmen who can barely read, write, speak articulately, or think but whose physical stature is exceeded only in certain milk-and-millet nurtured tribes of the Sudan where mature males average around six feet in height.

Nonwestern peoples, especially the food-gathering and economically simple agricultural societies, usually exposed their prepubescents to much or the entirety of the heritage. Since it lacked the specialties, complexities, and voluminous content of Euro-American sciences and arts, youngsters succeeded in internalizing it. Another way of saying this is to assert that such youth, we would say children, were enabled to become cultured persons. If being cultured is rendered as successful internalization of a large amount or the totality of a heritage, no Euro-American can possibly be a cultured person. The culture includes too much. Nevertheless, most youths of the western world could sample intensively and widely if permitted. But the society interdicts broad stocktaking of its legacy. This is part of what is meant by retardation of potential adults.

The police or custodial function which characterized most late nineteenth and early twentieth century secondary schools has tended to give way to an institutionalized period of teenager play. Securities, felt by youngsters, which used to eventuate from strong discipline and authority exercised by school officials, have generally ebbed. At the same time, ideological infantilization and concealment of the culture's expressive assets have been maintained. Little can be done because the society determinedly refuses to pay secondary school salaries which would encourage ethically, intellectually, and socially mature people to enter high-school teaching. No other tribe the world over has been reported as feeling threatened by its youths' early attainment of social sophistication, intellectual adulthood, and contact with the best of the societal resources. The converse is general: nonwestern peoples have not been able to afford a perpetuation of ignorance and immaturity long after puberty. Often they pressured their prepubescents to become mature as soon as possible. They had to have a fairly full complement of skilled and cultured adults in order to survive, in order to tolerate and handle the tragic vicissitudes of life. Mass teenage ignorance, moronity, social ineptitude, and pugnacious hostility to intelligence and elders might have precipitated destruction.

## Marriage Rite and Beyond

Just as nonwestern societies' puberty rites pointed to and expressed tension-causing changes in youngsters and their roles, stylized procedures, which varied from simple to ornamental, formalized marriage and also marked role changes, status too. Not least, new ties between families and lineages received expression and sanction. It is, therefore, handy to subsume marriage formalities with puberty rituals under the rubric of *rites de passage*. Although marriages in a few groups were almost devoid of ceremony, a majority of peoples celebrated the occasion because it dealt therapeutically with an especially shattering tension. Marriage was usually a point along and not at the end of the continuum of personality growth.

The topic of marriage ceremonial may suffer oversimplification if offered primarily in terms of its function in relating two larger groups of in-laws, or of its service as one of several transition or crisis rites which functioned in processes of maturation, personality growth, and socialization. It was not simply a defense against anxious feelings of those whose roles and status were changing. Surely it was and remains many things.

Since a great number of peoples the world over paired off their youngsters at or shortly after puberty, one of the vital functions of marriage was patently to speed up maturation and other desired attributes which were wanted in adults. Western civilization has leaned toward a concept of marriage day as an end point of childhood, a beginning of adult living. Since nonwestern societies may be regarded as having tended, rather, to discountenance termini and to effect continuities in personality change throughout a lifetime, the day of marriage did not mark a kind of graduation in personality growth. Indeed, observe that in many nonwestern societies the climacteric and corresponding age in men presented less an end point than a period during which persons turned to new and often more valued social functioning, specialization, and cultural creativity. Their again altered roles and relationships assuredly nourished further personality growth.

Accordingly, the marriage rite should be located in a transsocietal presentation as only one among major way stations along the track of life. It was maybe rarely a consummation of personality development. It was generally regarded, however, as the finale of child living.

Stylized deportment of all wedding participants, and words which accompanied music or were uttered by assigned functionaries, expressed feelings about connections which were formally wrought between in-law lineages. However, little close analysis of such expressive material appears in the archives of cultural anthropology. Anthropologists have tended to examine premarital procedures, negotiations, gifts, and monetary transactions which were, to be sure, of capital significance in marital arrangements. Field observers have reported about other overt operations. These often well-delineated customs usually constituted important and necessary components of marriage formalities. But a cultural anthropologist cannot skirt psychological sets toward people. Such attitudes and responses were long since established. They continued through the marital rite and appeared again in the relationship fabric around a large number of in-laws. The research scientist may not ignore the verbal and esthetic output of the rite. It functioned, as much as bride purchase payments and groom and bridal garb, to discharge tensions and to facilitate assumption of new interpersonal roles and further adult responsibilities.

Sketching of new marital and in-law relationships and relationship changes and their social functions comes next in time. Such external description provides some basic information. But a halt after such depiction, and many recent writers in social anthropology have so limited themselves, is like production of a silent movie film of ferrous automata whom magnets are reshuffling and depositing in new positions. People have by no means been silent things which were drawn by powerful forces into new patterns. People gestured, sung, danced, talked, wept, and quipped. They created esthetically as they went. They handled in custom-granted ways their feelings about new marital and in-law relationships. A cultural anthropologist observes arm in arm with the descriptive reporter of social structures and social functions. But, in a study of a marriage rite and the months and years that follow, his preoccupation ought to be to ascertain causes, forms, content, and services of expressive behavior of the people. Such behavior included their changing feelings about themselves and their consanguinal and conjugal kin. Few cultural anthropologists have conducted such study in detail adequate for content analysis.

Since married couples frequently were of different band or village origins, marital ties resulted in periodic visits to in-law communities. Feelings about such fraternization, whether it was amorphous or highly embroidered with oratory and formality, were almost always a complex of responses. One might enjoy the days or weeks in an initially alien community at the same time that there was uneasiness about local in-laws' and others' judgments regarding one's worth. Frequently there was simple fear about local practitioners of arts of the supernatural—about bad magic, as earlier writers might have said. Since nonwestern peoples usually visited accompanied by their children, additional solicitude surrounded feelings which a host group might have toward these youngsters. Their safety might be in question if tots did not yet possess supernatural aid which could protect little people in a strange place.

Things visitors and hosts said to each other, stylized ways in which they related, and special humor, games, dances, or entertainment to which they resorted offer storehouses of expressive materials which might be analyzed for purposes of documenting features of self-identity, marital and in-law relationships, world view, and ethics. Few anthropologists have collected detailed depictive reports and virtually no one has pieced through expressive materials of such kinds. Such research is required in order to understand important segments of married and family life, if for no other reason because nonwestern people seem to have married an in-law group by the very act of acquisition of a mate. Relationship with the one was integral with tie to the other. Both kinds of relationship, with the feelings of affection, security, pride, and uneasiness which accrued, and the enriching of self-identities as experiences mounted and were repeated in later visits, require conjoined social and psychological analyses. Ignorance of psychological developments which were precipitated by marriages in different kinds of societies marks one of the many blank areas in cross-cultural knowledge today. In western civilization we know how marriage coupled with departure from parents often tends to mature long infantilized mates. We know a little about adjustment difficulties when mates come from diverse social, cultural, or religious backgrounds. What were consequences of non-western marriages to the personalities of mates? How did they handle feelings and how did their personalities adjust when backgrounds were different, as they too often were? How did they work out feelings when they were of different age levels, maybe a generation or more apart? What were the new kin relationships and sentiments which featured their lives? It would be pleasant to be able to discuss these matters. Little more can be offered than to indicate, limply, that societies and cultures have been extraordinarily different and they moulded even the married adults in many different ways.

When a young woman, in one or another part of modern India, becomes a chattel of her new husband and his brothers, as in fraternal polyandry, what happens to her and to them? Anthropology lacks usable psychological materials, which can be employed for scientific purposes, about such instances of polyandry although polyandrous relationships in a few parts of India and in rare regions elsewhere seem to be fairly well-established descriptive facts. We suppose that children in such households usually relate to a fictitious rather than a biologically certain father, without diminution or confusion in feelings of identity. But what happens to a child's self-identity because of other relationships in such a setting? How do male and female children become prepared for their own polyandrous relationships later? No one has gone far to determine how brothers in a fraternal polyandrous household relate to one another or what the effects of polyandrous relationships may be upon their self-identities and values. Nor is there good material on the ways in which pseudo and biological fathers relate to their sons and daughters. It seems impossible at present to determine what children do to the feelings of worth of the mother and the so-called fathers. Obviously a lot of research has to be done in India and elsewhere about these and other questions which arise from relationships in polyandry, whether fraternal or nonfraternal, although the latter may have been rare in any part of the world.

Similar problems arise, more important ones to be sure, because of polygamous unions which have been permissible in almost all social systems. Anthropology should long since have outgrown its nineteenth century descriptivism and its mechanical so-called "functionalism" of the first half of the twentieth century which reported, with heartrending immaturity for a scientific discipline, in almost simpleminded externality about the presence of polygamous households and their connections with features of kinship terminology and social structure. Polygamy's consequences to personalities of participants and their progeny have long called for perceptive exploration following necessary beginnings in descriptive work on kinship, clan, and the like. But little research on sentiments and personalities has been forthcoming. In societies in which polygamous unions granted prestige, and such assessment has been well-nigh universal until Euro-

Americans came in with long faces and only heaven knows how much repressed envy, what happened to less well-regarded couples who were so poor or otherwise traduced by fate that a husband could not presently acquire a second wife? The tender subject of love which cowives have had for one another—Euro-American observers have been often blandly vouch-safed such assurance—needs to be balanced with all the expressive indications, whether ventilated in eye gouging, hair pulling or not so subtle humorous asides, which might be noted about tensions between cowives.

Little is known about a tendency, if there has been one, for a polygamous husband to display high blood pressure, duodenal ulcers, migraines, allergies, or other vexatious somatization, or a process which effected in him a posture of mature and maybe worried arbitrament. Nothing is known about personality processes distinctive in half brothers and half sisters in large polygamous households. Generalizations about these and a great many other questions are hardly supported by satisfactory cross-cultural materials. It seems wise to allow the questions, for they are important if we are to acquire much understanding of some hundreds of millions of our contemporaries. It is even wiser to disallow pat answers until scientific work has started on expressive materials in words, gestures, and actions which are waiting to be collected and closely analyzed.

## The Middle Years

Western civilization's partitionings of the life span differ from those segmented by other cultures. A preceding section commented that non-western peoples frequently regarded childhood as a stage which ended abruptly at puberty. Few societies carried childhood to a point some years after puberty. Elasticity of cultural decisions about stretches along the lifetime continuum, illustrated by rarity of a segment along it called "adolescence," is shown again by various lengths of the next segment. "Young-married" in the United States means a period from late teens on to maybe early thirties. Few cultures have conceived of an analogous age grade. Euro-Americans think of the late thirties as the beginning of the middle years. This marks the end of the young-married age grade; the period of middle years ends somewhere in the fifties or, recently, the sixties. They accompany specific roles and community participations for those who are in middle age with symbolic expressions in humor, demeanor, and garb, at present much like those who are young-married. The contemporary Euro-American concept of middle age, like that of young-married, probably rarely if ever had a counterpart in other cultures. Nevertheless, in the sense of assignment of a special inventory of roles, relationships, participations, and obligations, all societies had a period which may be captioned suitably not "middle age" but "middle years." Except for a few groups that set apart an adolescent status, the period of middle years began where childhood ended. It commenced at or shortly after puberty and continued until the

climacteric in women and an analogous period in men. In other words, a
30 to 35 year span commenced at 11 or 12 to 14 or 15 years of age. An
"old man" or "old woman" began to be so during the forties, not the sixties
as in contemporary Euro-American society.

What is known cross-culturally about personality change during the
long stretch of married or middle years? Was there change which can be
thought of as growth and development, especially in its first years which
correspond to western society's stage of adolescence? Had maturation
progressed so far during the teens or twenties that further maturation did
not occur? Did self-system, ego strength, and the like improve? Did alterations take place in character and conscience?

Let us reserve for a special section cross-cultural indications, which are
still few and hardly rigorously acquired, regarding depression, regression,
personality alteration of an intolerable kind, indeed the whole gamut of
neurosis-like and psychosis-like syndromes identified in western civilization.

Societies which were comparatively wealthy and displayed much specialization of labor might exhibit less of personality change in persons'
middle years. In societies of least productive economy, where there was
little more than a sexual division of labor and principally unspecialized
individuals, personality changes during the middle years were likelier. In a
sense, the only specialized people were middle aged to older. Field observers have often been awed by the blooming of dignity, wisdom, and enriched sense of humor which seem to have appeared sometimes rapidly during middle and later years. Well-to-do food-gatherers along the northerly
half of the Pacific northwest coast (from Nootkas north through Kwaki-
utls, Tsimshians, Haidas, and Tlingits) allowed almost all middle-aged and
older citizens, but not slaves and poor people, opportunity to practice at
arts, handicrafts, and productive work customarily assigned to their sex.
Few 20-year-olds were as skilled as they were to become in their forties
and after. The suggestion, then, is that in these and doubtless other, societies
many individuals improved remarkably in competence, with resultant increments of self-esteem and dignity and with continued maturation. Other
individuals might change for the worse, of course, because of diminishing
self-regard in competitive struggle for approval. Artistry, which is still
extraordinarily valued in most nonwestern societies, often developed after
the middle years, especially so in oratory, banter and humor, oral literature
raconteur roles, and singing. Is it possible to suppose that there was such
growth and increased social worth on the one hand, or crushing recur-
rences of community disapproval on the other, without concomitants in
personality structure?

Until today, little is known about plateaus or ups and downs in personality in western or nonwestern people during their middle years. Philistine
notions of plateau-like stability in features of personality, excepting pathological eruptions, arose in a Euro-American setting which disallowed
notable personality improvement during the middle years, which needed

to veil innumerable instances of lessening capacity and worth, and which guaranteed for many persons personality deterioration during their later decades. Psychologists' culture-strapped theory of a personality and intelligence plateau expressed, accurately enough, what the psychologists' society needed to think it did to people. The theory never was relevant to other societies, if it was applicable to the society which had conceived it.

All so-called "intelligence tests" have always lacked cross-cultural validity, to put it academically. They have not been designed to tell anything about people of nonliterate societies. On the other hand, Rorschach ink blot tests do appear to be usable in nonwestern populations as in the western world. They point to a few important things about personality, but these tests have not often been taken back to the same middle-aged persons every three or five years, a requirement for objective study. Not long ago Margaret Mead revisited a Melanesian community, Manus, after a generation of absence and reported remarkable alterations in self-identity, aspirations, and value ideals. Her allegation deserves supplement and corroboration because it may be of first-rate significance in general theories of processes of sociocultural and personality change.

Nevertheless, anthropology does not yet possess enough documentation from a broad sampling of societies about changes which occurred in personalities of people during their adult and middle years. Regression and deterioration which are frequent in the middle-aged of western civilization might be exceptional the world over. Until pertinent evidence from many sociocultural systems has been assembled, no assertion is tenable that rigidity or stability in personality is a prevailing characteristic of the middle years.

On the other hand, it is more than likely that many nonwestern societies offered a way of life which encouraged crescendo in ego strength during the middle decades of a long lifetime, although many individuals in such groups stood still or regressed when ill regarded. Conceivably, an absence of extreme specialization of labor might constitute one part of a social setting that facilitated the growth which doubtless featured many individuals. Another factor which may have changed and enriched personality during the middle years was parenthood itself. Where a child's own parents were assigned most of the responsibility around him, developments in their ego strength, self-identity, and character should be sought. Where, as in some nonwestern societies, obligations in rearing offspring were spread around rather than placed exclusively upon biological parents, a principal consequence of parenthood might be minimization of status anxiety: you must have children in order to receive acceptance as worthy.

In Euro-American populations, a vital factor of a pathological kind in the plateau level of personality and intelligence of middle and later years has been assuredly a central syndrome of Euro-American personality itself. I suggest calling it a "blockage" syndrome. In this one sociocultural system people have been so anxious about their insecurity, aloneness, and self-significance; they have been so unsure of the worth of roles they played in society and in others' regard; they have been so choked by fear about their economic and status security, that they have blocked continually at new stimuli, ideas, and experiences. The open-mindedness and breadth of curiosity which anthropologists believe they have found in some economically lowly nonwestern populations were conducive to the very features of growth in personality which appear to have been impeded in many Euro-Americans. Euro-Americans who are authoritarian personalities of a variety of kinds, from Know-nothing party members and endorsers of the 1850's to haters and others in our midst today, exemplify a blockage syndrome.

Earlier, envy of opposite sex received a comment. During middle years, envy of status and roles of the other sex may be a defense against humiliations arising in vicissitudes of living. A man who fails in his sex's undertakings to amass wealth and to raise his status—a feature of societies in a number of regions—may come to envy the security of those whose role is one of dependency upon a male. Such identification with women may generate consequences such as internalization of a special supernatural or assumption of transvestite characteristics. Women may be so burdened with controls by males and dreary feminine chores that they, too, identify with opposite sex and presently act out in masculine ways. Role envy is sometimes decisive in these partial or complete switches of sexual identification. It is not primarily anatomical envy. The latter, which occurs, may contain a factor of displacement from covetousness of the other sex's role. Personality recastings of these kinds are possible during adult years. Many societies accepted such changes as inevitable consequences of special supernatural relationships, an explanation which provided an efficient defense by way of rationalization.

It is striking how little is known about any societies concerning cultural connections with the psychology of normally functioning people in their middle years. Psychologists and others have lavished attention, as they should, upon growth and learning during childhood in western civilization. Reports from nonwestern peoples about these matters have also interested such scientists although they did little of the field collecting themselves. Pathology in Euro-Americans' middle years, notably neurosis, psychosis, and alcoholism, has also been much discussed but analogous behavior is not adequately studied in nonwestern locales. Claimed connections between esthetic creativity and emotional aberrancy may apply largely to instances within western civilization.

Most people the world over settled down, a little uninterestingly to Euro-Americans perhaps, in unexciting households, reared unintriguing offspring, enjoyed themselves episodically, grieved and worried in a great many customary ways, busied themselves with traditional socioeconomic, cultural, and religious exercises and, at length, entered a new status of older persons. Alterations in their personalities during the middle years are lamentably unknown. Thirty or more years elapsed, but it has been the quick and spectacular first decade of life before the middle years which has occupied most students. Is their failure to direct a spotlight of intellectual curiosity onto the middle years an expressive cultural item which reveals smouldering concerns as well as the hypnotic influence of Freudian and other writings upon scientific observers themselves?

What were principal anxieties of the middle years among nonwestern peoples? How did people's personalities adapt to parity or inequality in sex status? In each culture region, what kinds of personality alteration and growth transpired and why? Did role change occur with concomitant modification in self-identity? Were there changes in values and world view? What functions were performed by fixity of role and status and of belongingness to lineage, clan, or community, as contrasted with western persons' much more transmutable roles and statuses and their brittle ties to specialized profession, lineage, clubs, and community?

Anthropologists have not yet interested themselves in comparative study of personalities of women either in societies where the sexes enjoyed parity or where sex statuses were unequal. Methodology for study of females within a single group can only be imagined since it is not possible to evaluate explicit procedures. It seems that no one has yet devised standard methods in such research. Satisfactory method may include lengthy labors such as autobiographical records, and painstaking collections and content analyses of projective expressions like games, casual conversations, dreams, and humor.

In societies where women were not purchased and they sensed that their roles in and worth to the community were no less important than men's, they responded to relationships with a sturdy affirmativeness, articulateness, and lack of guile or defensiveness. Their poise and dignity contrasted almost spectacularly with the self-protective giggling and other maneuvers, sensitivity to slights, passivity, servility, seeming modesty, mincing steps, and the like which characterized women in societies which maintained lowly status for them. But how are such phenomena depicted with rigor, much less presented in mathematical terms?

Women's lowly position in the middle years may have effected less pervasively self-shielding responses if, as in some societies such as the Pacific northwest states' economically advanced food-gatherers, status rose sharply to parity after the menopause or attainment of grandparenthood. Intriguing problems of depiction of personality structures of women in such societies may never be resolved because of the sociocultural disintegration that has taken place.

Does love for mate augment or diminish during middle years? The question encloses a premise about love. Is there a transculturally definable response of that kind? Love in western civilization has had a special and, it need hardly be urged, galvanic history. General anthropology has long kept a discreet silence about it as if the science favored or deferred to exegeses which clerics, poets, philosophers, novelists, and psychoanalysts have divulged. Obviously, anthropologists' initial obligations were less consequential researches on nonwestern pottery, kinship, rites, linguistics, folk-lore, and acculturational phenomena. Most anthropologists tended very well to such assigned knitting of dull introductory kinds. But maybe the time has come for cross-culturally slanted disquisitions on a most desirable, if also occasionally painful, Euro-American emotion and its analogues among nonliterate folk.

An anthropologist might elect to indicate, disarmingly, that he will at once disqualify himself as an authority on social functions of positive affec-tional responses, a dry topic in any event. But he is likely to want to suggest that love and the related concept of romantic love constitute projections or expressions whose sources, survival, and intensification in Euro-American civilization may be sought in its history. And that he would next like to adduce evidences collected by perceptive scientific linguists. Their transla-tions of nonwestern myths and other dictated texts have given rise to an alarming question about love in nonwestern societies. In many, perhaps most, instances where a stalwart corpus of texts has received close transla-tion a concept of love and terms for it have been absent. Nonwestern lan-guages always appear to have morphemes which are suitably translated as want, desire, or like. Linguists easily elicit such semantic items. Missionary linguists offer important evidence, too. When they are trying to translate the Bible into a nonwestern language, they find that a morpheme which they suspect signifies "love" is likely to be the very morpheme obtained earlier for desire, want, or lust. Frustrating though it may be, and as ener-vating as it has been to Bible translators in nonwestern societies, the deduc-tion is that cross-cultural indications of a projective expression which closely resembles western civilization's concept of love have not yet been elicited in most regions. A likelihood of finding that concept frequently is already slight.

Absence or infrequent occurrence of the concept and term is one thing. The feeling and behavior are something else. Were they missing or rare, too?

Sentiments of unmarried youngsters toward one another in nonwestern societies have probably ranged from Romeo-and-Juliet temperatures and qualities of wanting to merely proper role-playing and status aspirations acted upon with calculation. The point is that, in each nonwestern culture, variability in feeling and passions has not been segmented, with one large or small but more or less valued segment denoted as love. A variety of feel-ings, some of them blazing, characterized youngsters in these societies. But their cultures did not regularly phrase premarital groanings and yearn-ings, ideal marital consummation, and the steady affection of mates as manifestations of love. The remarkable "love" poetry of some Oceanian groups—it might furrow the brow of a James Joyce or Henry Miller— very likely centered passionate desire, ecstatic pleasure in anatomical ideals which were realized in one's object choice, and much which superficially does resemble Euro-American love. But there were vital features in it which were distinctive and there were Euro-American qualities of response which were absent. Transcultural use of a Euro-American concept and word generally means extrapolation and imposition of something onto another projective expression which has not been coterminous.

The dismal conclusion is that love and romance have been concepts peculiar to one or only a small number of cultural heritages. Partial analogues of the western concepts have been found, of course. Although the concepts were not always there in other cultures, behavioral manifestations of them sometimes were. Most of the perceptive and long experienced anthropological field workers can at once recall couples who, to all appearances, were much in love with each other by any Euro-American definition of love. And they were in love without a Euro-American concept or word for their sentiments and behavior. They might be young, middle-aged, or elderly. However, anthropologists probably would also report an especially large number of couples in their forties or older who were cemented by bonds of undemonstrative acceptance, affection, and camaraderie. If such reporting were verified somehow, it would warrant speculation that affectional ties in nonwestern societies tended to intensify in the course of living through experiences together and through prolonged sharing of sentiments of acceptance by the respective kinship and natal groups. Something like a Euro-American ideal of romantic love grew out of a long and progressively welded relationship. It grew with those who matured and learned together and who played their respective social roles correctly through the years. It did not so often precede the vicissitudes of living as married couples in nonwestern societies which stressed belongingness to extended families, lineages, and communities of origin.

An aspect of self-identity of prime importance in middle years developed from daily proper playing of assigned roles in one's community and in its network of kin obligations. Here is a principal answer to a question about crystallization of a nonwestern person's self-image. Steady daily acting out of customary task assignments and hewing to correct manner of relating to other persons, especially the extended kin, in the course of playing such roles appear to have offered building blocks in construction of a self-identity. People are what they do. What they do and their perceptions of others' evaluation of it, especially the responses of kin and in-laws, gives them their awareness of what they are. A society always grants assessments of the worth of their behavior and of the things they make. But western civilization usually offers conflicting evaluations so that an individual selects ones he wants. The judgments uttered by kin are comparatively uninfluential. Nonwestern peoples were not often able to have as much lonely freedom to select values, nor were they bewildered about alternative possibilities, about a choice of one among many ideal identities. Nevertheless, they frequently discussed values publicly and thereby secured some freedom to choose among a small variety of possible judgments of worth, probably without painful puzzlement until advent of Caucasians.

Nonwestern people had deep relationship roots in kin and in-laws of goodly numbers, constancy in role, certainties about values, and a small array of ideal identities from which to select. Modern people of western civilization have had much shallower relationship roots, lesser durability of role, and much bewilderment about values. Fixity or tight cementing of social relationships may connect with absence of anxiety about one's self-identity. Many people of the modern west can never be sure who they are, because there is always a potential threat that they will be torn from the surface roots which nourish them in their shifting soil. Among nonliterate peoples, belongingness in and riveting of relationships, definitiveness of role, and lack of confusion about values before the modern epoch of accultura-tion were crucial factors in persons' self-identity during all their years, not only middle years. Threats to such stability characterize middle years of many people in western societies and in all peoples who have been sucked into maelstroms of aliens, geographical mobility, and technological mod-ernization. Permanence, extended kinship ties, and certainties about values were undermined centuries ago in many Euro-American areas.

Another crucial factor in nonwestern peoples during their middle years was the busyness of their days, that is, if their social system remained unscathed by an approach and entry of Euro-Americans. In a functioning nonliterate society, there was always something which was traditionally performed such as economic production and distribution, visiting, loafing, entertainment, ceremonial, perhaps, too, the care of children. Food-gatherers or economically lowlier agriculturalists suffered no periodic un-employment. In periods when economic production suspended, everyone who belonged to a status or community engaged in visiting, rites, entertain-ment, or leisure together. No temporal pauses which were wholly empty occurred except where a culture conferred hours of openmouthed vacuity with utmost approval. Men's sweathouses or clubhouses in food-gathering western North American Indian settlements functioned in culturally styl-ized dawdling and chitchat. Few men assumed special self-identities as con-sequence of apartness, exclusion, nonbelonging, or rejection of others' value judgments. Chores, duties, holidays, togetherness, and gossip filled the middle years.

What about creativity during 30 or more middle years? The answer is that among nonwestern peoples transcendant creativity might be hoped for, looked forward to, as a terminus which loomed ever nearer as the middle years drew to a close. A person practiced at or improved proficiency in a craft or art form through the middle years until, presently, he attained mastery. Command of knowledge, of legal decisions, and the like also in-creased. Superior performance, wise reflection, and assurance in value judgments occasionally became habitual but were more likely to mark older years.

Each person enjoyed progressive consolidation of self-identity founded upon awareness of increasing worth, higher status with aging, and intensifying respect overtly expressed by others. Since elders were not usually regarded, as in contemporary western countries, with hypocritical defenses against feelings of horror around them, by frank and unhibited distaste, or by rejection of their old style ways and values, middle years might witness no diminution in self-respect, no damage to and scarring of self-identity. Anxiety about approach to later years might be absent except for a worldwide reluctance and fear of being cut down by an incurable ailment, accident, or intransigeant enemy. Need to appear and act twentiesh without let-up has never been reported from a nonwestern group.

Augmenting distinctiveness, merits and, of course, demerits in each person of middle years ticketed and deeply imprinted the image which everyone had of him and the reflection of that image within himself and stirred defenses, frequently by way of manipulation of supernaturals. Each person became ever more sharply engraved in the minds and feelings of extended kin and community. Presumably discussion of his activities, virtues, and faults were interminable throughout the district. Small groups gossip inexhaustibly about their members and neighbors. Appreciation of a person's growth and cumulative evidences of it over the years functioned to enhance everyone's security because of the extent of identification with him. It was as if everyone in a small face-to-face society blended into everyone else. Persons both blurred and enriched their self-identity by internalizing others' qualities and, by extension, the ancestors' too. Citizens of western civilization now tend to reject everyone, especially ancestors and the aged, and pay a dire price in aloneness and lack of feeling of distinctive worth.

Tenuousness of self-identity in moderns of western countries often is defended against by acting out in aggressive, sadistic, incongruous, or childish behavior. It may appear to warrant a stamp of distinctiveness, as when a middle-aged driver of a car shows everyone what a great fellow he is and hostilely terrorizes them by deftly skidding on an icy or snowy road, or when a middle-aged and hopelessly unemployable lady garbs or otherwise demeans herself ridiculously. Such acting out is not just Euro-American misbehavior. It occurs wherever a recently functioning social system has been shattered, people are bewildered as to who they are and what they can or should do, and are incapable of resolving repeated humiliations visited upon them by Euro-Americans who have entered the land.

Happy anticipation of community rewards, granted during later years, for productivity and growth during middle years, is slight in the western world because of its crushing rejection of aged persons.

A principal characteristic of western society's personalities during their middle years is their awareness and fear of intensifying aloneness. Another central characteristic is the repetitive evidences they observe of their insignificance and lack of worth. Neurotic latching on to others, especially onto one's own children, is an especially well-known defense against mounting anxieties around loneliness, nonsignificance, and aging. Another especially familiar defense is in accumulation of things as if they were admirable extensions of self. Still another defense, widely present, is controlling of others. It is available to great numbers of persons in a wealthy society which can produce, distribute, educate, and govern only in elaborate enterprises with hierarchical levels for the arrays of employers, foremen, supervisors, bureaucrats, and administrators. In western society, neurotic defenses of a great many kinds appear, not least those which involve ego props by way of private or group pipe lines to a deity or social reform cult. Many writers have discussed these and other means of defending against sentiments of aloneness and worthlessness. Such defenses operate inefficiently against anxieties of the special kinds generated in middle years of citizenry of modern western civilization. Middle years among nonliterate peoples usually excited wholly different anxieties, less often or even rarely those arising in sentiments of aloneness, worthlessness, and rejection, that is, not until shattering acculturative changes transpired.

A few anthropologists have observed that their native informants appeared to have both detailed insights in and much capacity to accept, as the natural order of things, distinctive or quite aberrant traits in other persons. The amount of ratiocination which even now goes on in a nonwestern lineage and community about each of its lifelong members doubtless accounts for much psychological sophistication, except where culturally stylized avoidances operate so as to taboo conversation, if not thinking, about certain classes of persons such as in-laws. Many anthropologists have sensed but almost none have publicly reported nonliterate individuals' insights into motives and defenses. On the other hand, a principal factor in the seeming psychological acuity of some nonliterate peoples is only a contrast with the innumerable extremely infantilized products of western society. Still, it would be interesting to learn how many widely respected anthropologists have had their noses put out of joint by psychologically adroit and probing natives who especially enjoyed analyzing the highly scrubbed and sometimes hirsute visiting deviants. And every anthropologist has been at least a deviant, often a little pathetic and not very competent either, in the eyes of his informants and interpreters.

Unluckily, psychological concepts and phrasings informants employed have rarely been written out for later publication. One wonders if some anthropologists were equipped with less psychological insight than that had by natives they were professing to study, or that psychological concepts which were workaday tools to natives were so alien, like a native color term which embraced the whole green-and-blue segment of the spectrum, that the anthropologists failed to perceive anything worth noting. Nevertheless, it should not be deduced from these comments that all or even many nonwestern peoples necessarily exhibited a great degree of psychological sensitization, a proliferation of psychological concepts and terms in a kind of theoretical system, and an ability greater than ours to accept difference and to live with it without hostile acting out. But it is inconceivable that such characteristics were absent from a number of small closed societies where everyone lived with utmost intimacy with everyone else for a lifetime. On the other hand, lest a reader deduce that millions of insightful food-gathering Sandor Ferenczis, agricultural Sigmund Freuds, and agricultural-pastoral Harry Stack Sullivans were waiting to be studied by psychologically obtuse Euro-Americans, it should be stressed that a majority of nonwestern peoples very likely explained behavior not in a theoretical frame of psychological concepts but almost entirely in terms of displacements. For example, a person did what he did because he had to, he could not help it, that was how he was because of one or several supernaturals, or because of his ancestors, or because all his people were like that. It is such thinking which connects with an often almost total absence of psychological concepts and vocabulary terms among nonwesterns and, no doubt, many or most food-gathering and other economically lowly peoples reasoned in such a manner.

An interesting topic which anthropologists have bypassed with a cliché or two treats of feelings nonwestern people had toward other persons' children, values set by a culture in shaping such sentiments, and effects of such feelings upon the middle-aged themselves. Many writers have correctly noted multiparental settings in nonwestern groups. They were writing from the point of view of an effort to discover how children developed and matured. But there is a reverse side to this old Oedipal coin. It involves a need to examine how middle-aged persons and elders felt because they shared responsibilities and concerns for many children who were not their own. Little trustworthy reporting is likely to be found today in a search for answers to this question.

## Old Age

There is no need to discuss external aspects of the very terminus of old age, dismal topics which generations of anthropological writers centered: voluntary exposure and death of the aged among a few of the world's most economically handicapped peoples; handling of corpses; funeral rites and processions; stylized caterwauling by widows and other mourners; mortuary customs—cremation, canoe and tree "burial," shallow graves, grave markers, and so on. Such cheerless subjects are legion and, to be sure, reveal important attitudes and institutions. But it is more meaningful to inquire how nonwestern peoples lived, felt, and made autonomous decisions in their later years before bells tolled, mourners forgathered, and maggots began their awful work.

Date of inception of old age, roles, status of elderly folk, and their self-identity in nonwestern societies have almost everywhere differed greatly from modern Euro-American designing of that somber period. In western society today, it is almost unvaryingly a lamentable and vexatious age. It is a period when one is hopelessly hemmed in. Until the 1920's much of the knowledge of nonwestern peoples had been gained from older natives by field workers whose background rendered them confused, to put it mildly, about the worth of elderly persons. The harvest of information accumulated little about services, relationships, roles, status, stature, and tenor of sentiments of oldsters however such persons be defined. Pioneer field investigators found much of what they were looking for. It was what they called "ethnography," a thing of unconnected strands, shreds, and patches of surface phenomena. Elderly people could remember far back in time, could they not, but what else would most Euro-American observers think of these ancients? In a setting of drastic acculturation, nonwestern elders often appeared as inactive and useless as inmates in a dilapidated nineteenth century county poorhouse. How was it possible to reconstruct precontact times when elders had indeed played outstanding roles among their people?

The technique of autobiography introduced in ethnography during the 1920's by Dr. Paul Radin required so many weeks of dictation from each elder that in a single society a proper sampling of their age group demanded long years of recordings. Anthropologists do not appear to have been interested in devising other means, if there are any, of securing comprehensive information on old age. They did not try to work up an inventory of significant queries to be directed to elders which would display essentials of their status, social functions, feelings, and opportunities to do significant things. Anthropologists did not interrogate with sufficient sensitivity to reveal causes of these phenomena.

Nevertheless, probable portions of a beginning of a system of cross-cultural theory about old age can be suggested. First, when does it start? At 45, 60, or 70 years of age? Few 60 year olds in the United States today accept, as did their great-grandparents, relegation to a nineteenth century category of elderly. If medicine presently conquers various heart and blood pressure ailments, arteriosclerosis, periodontal difficulties, and beaten up spinal discs so that many people remain dapper, ebullient, vigorous, pink cheeked and toothy, in their nineties and later, the Euro-American concept of old age, the roles played by centenarians, and their images of themselves will again enjoy revolutionary change. The status will no longer apply to 60 or 70 year olds. Middle age may accordingly extend into the eighties and later. In other words, elderly has to be defined for each culture and in western lands it has already been redefined several times during less than a century.

A second question is that of perception of decrepitude. When do people respond restively or sadly to skins that are no longer taut and unlined, bags under eyes, missing teeth, bent backs, and other more harrowing indications of aging? One society's reaction of distaste may be paralleled by another's responses of respect and romantic affection. A bad odor to some may be an autumn evening perfume to others. Stigmata, even mutilations, are relative to each observer who perceives what his culture has taught him to denote. He suffers at what he has learned to suffer. The answer to the question is that culture provides most of the important perceptions which signify aging.

Perhaps only a few languages and their cultures have a term and concept for middle age. Probably every language has terms for children at various growth levels. It always has a term for old person. The problem is to ascertain exactly what each term connoted in its cultural context, and why it did so. Often "elder" implied any age following the menopause. Or it was the age when a person might have his first grandchild. In some regions people in their later thirties were already categorized as old persons. Who was elderly was determined not by wrinkles and warts but by a culture's segmentation of the life span and by a special complex of roles, status, relationships, and attitudes. A complex of one or another inventory of items of content was universal and each heritage's language had one or more morphemes for it.

Some Buddhists and a very few others may be excepted from a statement that all peoples appear to have suffered from cheerless sentiments about their certain death. Since older people were closer to it, a nearly universal disconsolateness among them about its proximity cannot be doubted. But in most, if not all, nonwestern societies elders, whoever they were, were granted exceedingly sturdy defenses against this feeling because they were allowed most respected statuses, valued roles, and opportunities for continued or enhanced self-regard. These commitments on the part of society functioned for elders in various ways and, not least, as shieldings against a heaviness of heart which modern western civilization reinforces and does almost nothing to lighten.

Earlier writers accentuated the bolstering granted by assurance of a pleasant afterlife in those infrequent instances where nonwestern people projected an attractive afterlife. Maybe our pioneer writers were overimpressed because of their sentiments about an unlikelihood of an agreeable nonmaterial future, a Heaven, for themselves. Some few cultures tranquilized citizens in their terror of corpses and of personal extinction by means of purple fantasies and diaphanous tableaux of a life beyond. The question is, how effective were such fantasy screens? Probably slightly so. A seeming equanimity which some extremely aged or dying people exhibited may have been consequent upon a combination of other factors: long familiarity with sickness and corpses; belongingness which related to the many kin who were present and the many survivors who would mourn sincerely; a life lived with relatively few thwarted expectations; sheer wisdom and courage so that the inevitable was met with both distaste and forbearance. If there was an imperturbable countenance, it was probably a cultural stylization which functioned to cloak feelings and so to lessen tensions.

Intriguing theoretical questions arise. What were the status, roles, and opportunities to be autonomous accorded to nonwestern elders? What were the psychological consequences?

Western civilization's progressively lessening regard for and rejection of significant community and family participations by elders have become almost complete. The very concept of retirement is modern Euro-American although its veiled sadism is being uncovered by the still small groups of pioneers in geriatrics researches. Few, if any, sociocultural systems outside of the West had a fixed retirement age. Some, however, had functionally similar phenomena, like the older Comanche men who were no longer sufficiently athletic for piracy on horseback and who accordingly sat around griping, citing past exploits, and envying and disliking younger men.

In the sense of changes of status, role, and self-identity in a direction of greater dignity, food-gatherers probably did most among nonwestern peoples to "retire" their elders. They might not accompany daily food-producing parties as regularly as before. But elders' fresh contacts with supernaturals, whatever the psychological factors might be, increased utilization as specialists in manufacture and repair of artifacts, heavier responsibility in child tending, education, and ceremonialism, and opportunity for leadership because of greater experience and wisdom effected a wholly unwestern concept of retirement. The word, therefore, has to be construed so as to apply to nonwestern social systems. Retirement among them was usually only a change to valued new participations from formerly pressing economic obligations and, for women, pregnancies and nursing. Such retirement was a release to be creative in new ways. Psychologically and in roles granted, it was entirely different from the shelving of people and the guilt responses characteristic of western civilization. Nonwestern retirement tended to effect an opposite of ego deterioration and diminished self-regard. Nobody felt guilty about the fate of nonwestern elders. Even those elders who were passive and inactive tended to shine in the light which came through open doors of opportunity to choose to be active, productive, and revered. It was helpful for ego strength to belong to the subgroup regarded as unique and most valued, even with awareness that other individuals in that age grade were worthier.

Among nonliterate peoples, specialist skills and channels leading to creativity in later years depended, probably to a great degree, on conditioning, building of confidence, and fashioning of ego integrity during middle years. That is, almost all persons other than slaves and slave-like strata reached elder status with a sufficiency of personality assets. These were such that favorable environment and newly opened opportunities granted to elders offered stimuli to creativity or at least allowed maintenance of ego strength. Nonliterate people prepared for later growth in personality stature during their middle years by means of continued internalization of items of world view and value ideals. They experienced intensification and reinforcement of self-confidence because of successful productive work, fulfillment of parental, lineage, and community obligations, and occasional contacts with supernaturalism. Upon entry into oldster roles they, therefore, had good foundations of, let us call them again, personality assets.

It is necessary not to glamorize nonliterate peoples as generally possessed of such perquisites and opportunities in old age. Among economically advanced food-gatherers—the Pacific Northwest Coast—disadvantaged social strata and slaves must have neared old age with severely damaged self-identities. Such people had few potentials for an old age characterized by ego strength and autonomous creativity. Most peoples of Middle America and the Old World were stratified so that lowlier social levels must have been pathetically unequipped, psychologically, for continuations of rejection of worth and exclusion from creativity which had plagued them all their earlier years. Today cultural anthropology sadly lacks materials depictive of the later decades of personalities of such people of socially devalued identity. Only beginnings of knowledge of the catastrophic personality readjustments following enslavement have been gleaned recently in the course of reassessments of historiographical attempts to depict the vicissitudes of Africans brought to the coast and transported under appalling conditions to the Americas. A very few survivors of Nazi concentration camps have written about themselves and their fellow unfortunates. Earlier it seemed plausible to state, maybe a little oversimply, that captives who were destined for a slavery from which escape was unlikely were afflicted with a kind of paralysis of initiative.

But a person does not remain impotent and rudderless psychologically and continue at hard labor over a stretch of decades. Slaves and other captives fortified themselves, almost in order to stand up, with defensive readjustments. They retained these into old age. At present it seems more efficient to subsume the many special responses under general headings of drastic change in self-identity, regression to childish responses, defensive identification with sadistic guards, masters, owners, and so on, and some other altered personality traits. The old age of slaves is really unknown to social psychology. One wonders how well novelists have granted a kind of cross section of such people. One wonders if old age in slaves often featured intensified regressions or an opposite of changes toward dignity, maturity, and wisdom. The slavery once integral with social systems along the entire Pacific Northwest Coast of advanced food-gatherers is almost a blank in respect to its pitiable victims' psychological and personality manifestations. But it seems a fair speculation that harrowing severance from kin, lineage, and community and the indescribably humiliating coup de grace of slave status produced personality alterations as extreme as those which social scientists lately delineated for America's African slaves and the tormented prey of Nazis. Captives of Incas, Aztecs, Greeks, Romans, Egyptians, Mesopotamians, and other wealthy agricultural groups doubtless changed in personality structure profoundly but it is possible only to extrapolate and, therefore, fantasy what such woebegone folk were like in their middle and later years. Little survived in writings about feelings of these wretched people because in all parts of the world their masters had to defend against caring. Realistic perceptions of what happened psychologically to captives would have brought about identification with them. Pain and guilt would have been unbearable. Defensive and incessant rationalizations that slaves were inferior, like animals, or benighted in some other respects have been reported almost everywhere. Data from most districts of Pacific Northwest Coast food-gatherers are extremely spare but it is evident that slaves were rated as dogs, at least in some places, and dogs were the filthiest animals. The mechanism of rationalization is beautifully clear.

In western civilization, many persons manage to reach the portal of old age with extremely sturdy personality props. A majority, however, enter old age after decades of meagerly rewarded repetitions of limited skills, with conflicting values, bewilderment in perceptions of the world, and chronic anxieties about security and worth. Often their roles as parents have been only partially ego enhancing. They have not had opportunities to develop sentiments of worth in either lineage or community because of society's attenuation or elimination of meaningful belongingness beyond the nuclear family. They have had few valued community participations. Infrequent individuals had enjoyed membership in a choral society or rewarding participation in a church or charitable organization. Only rare individuals arrive at old age with personality equipment so strong and a self-identity so flawless that they can continue to feel worthy or creative. In western civilization, destructiveness of old age is so extreme, like the shattering consequent upon enslavement, that even those few who come into their later years with powerful psychological assets tend to undergo extensive change in personality. Many of the others retrogress long before severe organic deterioration sets in. An analogy with slaves is haunting.

Changes produced in elders by western civilization's customs around the age grade exhibit a confusing variety of manifestations. Maybe classification is possible into a list of newly wrought personality types found in old age. Or it may be more efficient to inventory only tendencies such as bare maintenance of self-identity, deterioration in value ideals, cracking of ego integration, and retrogression toward childish adjustments, even toward infantile dependency and vegetating.

At any age level, drastic alteration in status, role, and opportunities for respected participations produces new constellations of personality characteristics. These configurations connect, doubtless, with patterns of personality assets that have been brought to the point when the social and role modifications occur. The impact of such changes can be devastating. It can be remarkably stimulating and for the better. In a few nonwestern societies, elders might be accorded new opportunities which resulted in further maturation, in supplementations of ego strength. If the outcome of new relationships and other social alterations was sufficiently shattering and undermining, no earlier personality configuration or underpinning could long hold up. Many persons defended against what had happened to them by taking a dive toward childish or infantile behavior. Drastic acculturation, warfare, massacre, community decimation because of epidemic disease, and envelopment by callous, although not necessarily murderous, invaders have triggered metamorphosis in personality structures, even as in the instance of enslavement.

The kind of pattern of living granted persons who must wander about in the dark alleys of old age in western civilization is somewhat analogous to the societal settings which are caused by frightful circumstances of the kinds just listed. Resolution by exit to childish patterns is only one way out. In extreme instances, as in slavery and Nazi concentration or extermination camps, avenues out may be consistently self-destructive or suicidal.

In western civilization, most older old people function as useless creatures who literally wait for death because they continue to serve themselves and society only in a bleakly anonymous exercise of voting on an infrequent election day. Writers of western civilization not long ago set forth myths about early man, even modern primitive peoples, who put out their old people, venerated ones at that, to die! Here and there, principally in a seasonally mobile group of food-gatherers, a feeble or badly crippled elder was an impossible burden to the others. But Euro-American society may be the sole system which in effect has conducted a special form of mass genocide for its status of elders. It may be the only society which has institutionalized humiliating rejection of the worth of an elder's self-identity. It may be the outstanding example of a society which offers no new or alternatively respected ego-enhancing activities which an elder may pursue. In addition, it has made principally token efforts to permit elders to live at the level of physical comfort and security which they enjoyed in their middle years. The retirement pattern is a fully revealing feature of the society. It is one of several materializations of a hushed decision to shovel all elders into refuse heaps where manner and speed of decay are matters of overt indifference to their younger successors. A related expressive phenomenon appears only in western society because only there do younger persons long sustain a conviction of indestructibility. They are the only people in the world who approach complete incapacity to identify with and accord unselfish generosity to the aged. Their feeling of indestructibility consists of a number of defenses, one of which appears to be founded upon a cultural horror reaction toward elders. Nonwestern peoples usually lacked a presumption of personal indestructibility, both because they saw corpses much too often and they needed no protection against even the slightest identification with aged people.

Western culture's manifest insensibility to the feelings of elders is really a disdain for the wretches. It is only slightly veiled. Everyone reacts with something approaching horror at their physical characteristics. Tens of millions of elders function as valueless vestigia who sense the discomposure caused by the circumstance that they are still alive, visible, disagreeable looking, and burdensome. They sit decomposing and unwanted in rocking chairs. They do nothing of value for the community because there is nothing they are permitted to do. Or, they perform unskilled and unrespected household chores like baby sitting, knitting, and dishwashing. Productive work, creative activity, and fun are for younger people, who seek no competition or companionship with them. Increasingly, kin expel and lodge them in cheerless cubicles and wards in so-called "nursing homes" where presently they die in an environment of urine, lysol, carrots, rutabagas, and guilt rather than in one of dignity and love. Fame may indeed accrue to an exceptional elder, to a Grandma Moses who is permitted both to remain in the home and to execute creative work, and to a Chancellor Adenauer who functions in a manner which the culture expects of politicians years younger. Grandma Moses' role in the culture was so unorthodox as to generate mass stupefaction followed by recoveries in almost ritualized two-column obituaries and editorial page gushings. The culture decrees, unavailingly in a solitary instance in upstate New York, that elderly ladies are at best sharp-tongued has-beens. A crowd always gathers and cackles when convention is flaunted as spectacularly as in this instance. The exception throws a vivid light on customary roles and status of the aged in western civilization. Their assigned role is to rot and then die, preferably out of the house.

On the other hand, every anthropological field worker has long known that in nonwestern societies persons of grandparent level—reference is not to old old but to younger old—generally enjoyed releases from economic or other directly productive participations which had drained most of their energy since their wedding week. A caption for this section, then, might fittingly be something like "Cultural creativity begins at 40." A frequent expectation was that 40 year olds specialize in new skills or practice with additional intensity in familiar ones so as to attain technical mastery and achieve in original ways. Artists and creative intelligences emerged in pottery, basketmaking, sculpture, weaving, metallurgy, music, dance, oral literature, supernaturalism, religious rite and theory, wit and humor, worldly wisdom, and values. These were the people who might be assigned roles of preceptors of the young and custodians of the heritage.

No wonder that the most creditable citizens, in their forties and fifties and as vigorous as ever, although no longer as agile as youths, felt that they were attractive and often appeared prepossessing to younger persons. Nor is it remarkable that in a few societies regard of younger people and acceptance in roles and relationships were such, and affectional needs of elders were such too, that a special kind of romantic dallying was culturally permissible. Probably the younger old rather than older old applied themselves to such gamesmanship. Abundantly ego-enhancing liaisons might develop between persons 20 to 40 or more years apart, without abatement in mutual or community respect. Euro-American value judgments must not be imposed upon disparate chronological ages or age levels of two persons who expressed, either in a marital tie or an illicit or allowable union, positive feelings toward each other.

It is important to emphasize favorable characteristics of the status of older or elderly persons in most exotic societies. It is indispensable to display opportunities accorded them and rewards they received for creativity and participations of significance to their community. It is necessary to find out about personality changes which accrued to them as they grew in stature. It is equally important to balance the depiction in such a manner as to exhibit equivocal feelings toward many elders because of roles which

sociocultural systems assigned to them in child training, property ownership, and religious and political leadership. Masters, authorities, and disciplinarians, no matter how dignified and admirable, are never loved and
loved alone. At deep psychological levels they are both identified with and
hated. In a great many societies, elders, not parents, were principal transmitters of skills, knowledge, and values. Whoever praises and withholds
commendation, reveals horizons and imposes boundaries, and pontificates
about moral rectitude may become at once deity and ogre.

A sociocultural system which richly utilized grandparents served them
better than one which dismantled and dismissed them. Although anthropology lacks data to prove the statement, it seems safe to assert that fundamental change in role, rise in status, and newly inaugurated opportunity for
admired creativity caused nondeteriorative change in personality structure.
One cannot assess its extent. Western civilization's and earlier Freudians'
supposition that personality structure is completed in childhood, or before
20 or 25, is evidently a sticky rationalization in pseudopsychological garb
by a society which limits its middle-aged people and impoverishes its grandparent group so that only fortunate older individuals long stave off personality decay or regression. Where Euro-American younger oldsters are
at best on a plateau and older elders are on a downgrade in self-esteem,
competency, and feelings of belongingness, old age groups in nonliterate
societies were often on an upgrade in productivity, self-regard, and awareness of positive feelings toward them. The crescendo might continue until
physical handicap or organic senility caused a halt. At such a time an elder
might be hurt, too, by dislike, indifference, or rejection comparable to
sentiments which Euro-Americans lavish indiscriminately upon older people. Euro-Americans' senility almost always arises where organic factors
are absent, in putrescence in self-esteem, that is, a special kind of decom-
position produced wholly by the culture.

Victorian diminution of sexual expression in middle and older years appears to be not biologically but culturally determined by crumbling self-
regard of individuals and sometimes their lessening appreciation of one
another. In exotic cultures, sexual activity might well have continued or increased during later decades because of intensified acceptance of and mounting affection for persons who were advancing in status and worth.

What could have caused a culture to produce social enzymes which
guarantee rotting, especially in the light of ripenings which other cultures
effected?

Many factors make for emotional, intellectual, and social infantilization
of teenagers in Euro-American civilization. Also, there are many causes for
its complex of rejecting sentiments around elders. One wonders if there
is not a simple positive correlation in Euro-American culture, a causal nexus,
between its monstrous infantilization or retardation of the young and its
relentless repudiation of worth of the elderly.

Were there societies each of which displayed the two phenomena?

Actually, little is known about instances in nonliterate societies of infantilization, retardation, or prolonged exclusion of youngsters from adult participations. Even less has been reported transsocietally about disfavoring of grandparent level or older people. But it is as if Euro-American society expressed itself by putting into the minds and mouths of its people statements such as the following: (Elders speak:) "Let those cheeky youngsters take a long, long time before they are allowed to behave in an adult manner, so that we can delay our horrible fate of being rejected, discarded, and destroyed by them." And the reverse of the coin: (Youngsters speak:) "I will get even with you at the time when you become weak. I will throw you out of everything that was once meaningful for you, for you long held up my progress toward adult strength, power, and creativity." There is no gainsaying the mutual distrust, resentment, or animosity between the two contrasted age grades of western civilization, even though few members dare to phrase their feelings. Sentiments engendered in the one age grade appear to be a reciprocal of sentiments arising in the other.

Comanches, lately resident in Oklahoma and Texas, again provide a suggestive example. There seems to have been some connection among them between retardation of maturation and shelving of elders, between rejecting feelings toward older men and hostile feelings of older men toward younger persons. A peril in correlations and polarities as simple as these is that they seem so apparent as to discourage study of the totality of sociocultural and psychological processes in a community. Many of the correlation studies popular today among behavioral scientists are inherently dangerous because, while appearing to offer admirable short cuts to possibly important formulations, they are silent about further intensive researches of novel kinds which are needed, too. These alone may permit weighing all the variables in complex sociocultural phenomena.

Although a substantial number of cross-cultural instances that might render probable the nexus are still lacking, an anthropologist can be certain that almost all food-gathering societies, very likely most economically simple agricultural and pastoral societies too, which encouraged a crescendo of creativity in elders and which valued the productive work of all adults, accorded younger people opportunity for early maturation. They also respected idiosyncratic traits and wants of children much more than does western civilization. It appears that people who are not hemmed in have little need to strike out at others or to tighten nooses around them. Envy then receives neither impetus nor sustenance.

## Dead People

Every nonwestern culture has resembled the Euro-American world by having some kind of picture of what happened after breathing ceased or the heart stopped beating. A myth recital might set forth such a representation. Whoever depicted it, it offered a projective expression of culturally important needs, defenses, and relationships.

Some nonliterate groups supposed that the nonmaterial replica of the body, that is, a vital something which has been loosely translated as "soul" or "soul-ghost," departed from the body weeks or months before discontinuance of breathing and had long since gone where such incorporeal things go. What may have been the function of such a portrayal of death? It may be that a culture which projected each person's self-identity into a hardly tangible ghost or soul which left the body long before the heart stopped, provided a defense against the horror and shock of abeyance of life. If one were really dead weeks or months before, that is, at the time when the soul quit the body and refused to come back into it, feelings of identification with the deceased were ameliorated. After all, he had not been alive for some time. He had already gone. His self was somewhere else. The body had merely kept breathing and going about, by blind habit, for a time longer because there was still breath in it. It was not really a person any more. It did not die, for it was long since dead.

It should be understood that concepts which Euro-Americans employ for behavior which is termed "unconsciousness," or even merely for sleep, may be regarded as an area or class of behavior which in other cultures equated with death although only temporary death. Doubtless in most nonwestern languages, an utterance which an Indo-European language translates "death" or "he died" has to be qualified in some manner in order to reveal whether the connotation is of drunken stupor, unconsciousness from some other cause, sleep, temporary soul loss, or permanent soul loss and irrevocable death. A nonwestern equation of sleep and death is familiar to many anthropologists. Here is a class of behavior which displays and includes several special forms in sleep, stupor, unconsciousness, and death. Observe, therefore, a repeated premise of cultural anthropology: every concept which reflects something in Euro-American society and culture must be handled gingerly if it is to serve in representing something which seems to be but actually is not analogous in a nonwestern cultural system. Concepts and terms like "unconscious," "sleep" and "death" do not serve without painstaking redefinition when a Euro-American leaves the familiar realm or class of bunched-together items assembled by his own heritage. In order to communicate with and understand a carrier of another heritage, his classes of items must be located. It is often difficult to do this without persevering interrogations in addition to close analyses of different kinds of expressive materials.

As is well known, a great many cultures portrayed the deceased's nonmaterial replica as loitering about the household, community, or nearby grave. A single projection of this kind may have arisen in or enjoyed maintenance in many psychologically different responses to death. One was the wish that the loved departed remain. Another was fear of the dead arising out of various anxieties about death and the unknown. Hostility to a person who was gone but lately had power or higher status was another. Still another was the desire to believe that there was a something which remained of oneself and so, of course, displacement onto a person already departed.

Whatever these and many other processes may have been in causing and sustaining a projection of a soul or ghost who was close by, anthropological researches may not often be able to assess which factors or how many of them operated. The important formulation is that ghost-souls have been projective figures universally. Things these spooks did and said reveal wishes, anxieties, anger, and the like which people entertained toward kin, themselves, and the great unknown. That is to say, ghosts serve anthropologists efficiently like dreams, myths, and value ideals because it is possible to use them, always in conjunction with deductions independently arrived at in close analyses of other kinds of projective expressions, to point to probably important feelings and tensions generated in a social system.

In a great many heritages ghost-souls took off on one or more journeys and wound up, for a shorter or longer period, in a community or region above or below the earth's surface or beyond the horizon. These souls reached what anthropologists and others have often referred to as a "land of the dead." Why were these myth-like adventure plots embroidered so as to constitute a special kind of journey? Why these myth-like descriptions of a special abode or land where ghosts resided? What determined the kinds of things ghosts did in that land? What details of that dismal or resplendent country were projected and what did each such detail signify? Clearly, a tremendous amount of projective material of these kinds is available the world over for analysis which, to be sure, can yield invaluable information about relationships, tensions, and feelings of the living. Whatever people have supposed about their dead both veiled and exposed how they felt about themselves. An attentively diagnostic look through the web of that veil offers fascinating insights about a sociocultural system and the kinds of people who lived in it.

A journey to a land of the dead, whatever its special depictive details constituted in each culture, appears in general to have functioned as a means of explaining why the ghost was no longer close by. So, it went somewhere else. It was comforting to know where it went and what it did on the way. It was even more consoling to know that it was irretrievably gone. Stay-at-homes always wanted to hear about the travels of both their dear ones and their enemies. Identification occurred with them both, guilt around hostile sentiments toward them, too. Terrible experiences which a traveling ghost underwent en route to limbo doubtless connected with many concerns including anxieties about one's own demise and guilt feelings of various sorts. A soul's eventual arrival in a land of the dead again offered reassurance, perhaps also sadistic satisfaction in many instances. Many hours of question and answer field procedure are required in each culture to elicit evidences which may assist in supporting or erasing hypotheses of such kinds. Often little can be deduced without such interrogation.

Depictions of a region where the departed still lived are of most diverse kinds. Hostility toward kin and dead alike might be indicated by shocking, topsy-turvy, or incongruous behavior in that land. Its residents might be putrid mutilated corpses or bleached skeletons in the daytime, bored dancers all night long, loving but unoccupied couples, or what not. They might eat only maggots, which people abhorred; they might receive sustenance by passing a feather under the nostrils; they might never eat, which was tragic to be sure; or they partook of magnificent fare, which even a furious anti-Freudian may be willing to identify tritely as an old style wish fulfillment. Ghosts might engage in normal economic and craft tasks or they might sit or lie about with nothing to do. It was horrible when there wasn't much to talk about. Ghosts might survive endlessly or vanish after a short term of years. Even a concept of immortality must be translated with care when attention is directed to nonwestern convictions about duration of souls. Euro-American belief about enduring immortality may not often be duplicated. It must be replaced for many nonwestern heritages by concepts of short term soul survivals in other and bleak vales. Each small component of a representation, each feeling had by the dead, each utterance, occupation, relationship, or value they expressed, connected as the projection it was with something important in the society, usually with a relationship or activity which created emotional turbulence or friction. Close analysis of successive items in a journey to the dead people's haven and of items of behavior and worth in that fantasied realm is as revelatory of important emotional tugging in a society as is close analysis of expressive content in recital myths, supernaturalism, or humor situations. Research on the one need be pretty much a duplication of manner of research called for in the other, except for an especial need for caution, tact, and generous acceptance in eliciting answers on subjects as fraught with anxiety as mutilation, sickness, maggots, death, souls, and ghosts.


## SUGGESTIONS FOR FURTHER READING

Topics of this chapter are covered in an enormous range of books and articles. M. Mead's volumes, some in paperback, are original and invaluable. A few other excellent readings include C. DuBois, *The People of Alor* (paperback; New York: Harper, 1961); E. H. Erikson, *Childhood and Society* (New York: Norton, 1950); A. I. Hallowell, *Culture and Experience* (Philadelphia: University of Pennsylvania Press, 1955); V. Barnouw, Culture and Personality (Homewood, Ill.: Dorsey, 1963); F. L. K. Hsu (ed.), *Psychological Anthropology* (Homewood, Ill.: Dorsey, 1961); B. Kaplan (ed.), *Studying Personality Cross-Culturally* (Evanston, Ill.: Row, Peterson, 1961); J. W. M. Whiting and I. L. Child, *Child Training and Personality Development* (New Haven: Yale University Press, 1953). J. J. Honigmann, *Culture and Personality* (New York: Harper, 1954) served for some years as sound textbook coverage, as did C. Kluckhohn, H. A. Murray, and D. M. Schneider (eds.), *Personality in Nature, Society and Culture* (New York: Knopf, 1953) but they needed a dynamic classroom lecturer to brighten them.

# 5. PRODIGIES, GENIUSES, MEDIOCRITIES, AND MORONS

## Who Is Potentially Creative?

If linguists were to ask interpreters in several thousand language groups to supply translations of Indo-European words for "prodigy" or "genius," answers would probably not be forthcoming. Concepts of this kind may have developed in a few wealthy societies outside of Euro-American civilization. Its traditional convictions about prodigies and geniuses are such that the culture's professional or academic psychologists have turned handsprings, more recently. They have purchased computers in order to supply both explanations and measurements of the phenomenon. In the twentieth century it was easy enough for psychologists to borrow genetics' concept of mutations and mathematics' tools such as the bell-shaped normal curve of distribution. Supposedly exceptional inborn talent could be expressed as a segment far to the right on that curve. To be sure, there is no warrant for skepticism about a distribution of innate capacity in a variable human population. But it is the old Euro-American form and functions of the belief in genetic superiority, not evidences in favor, which require consideration.

What is a prodigy or genius? Is it, in every instance identified as such in Euro-American society, a person whose genetic constitution contains the salient cause of his uniqueness? Is it the rare Euro-American youngster who just happened not to suffer retardation or intellectual suffocation after the manner of all his age mates? Or is it both?

For the moment, consider acceptance of an initial premise that most geniuses are the least retarded or blocked individuals of western civilization and that their innate equipment is no more than normal or slightly superior. Follow-up of such an uncanonical premise is heartening because a number of disparate facts have been allowed to fall into line and receive the same plausible accounting. One fact is the comparatively small number of Euro-American female geniuses, or persons customarily called such, since Classical times. A second fact which is abundantly clear is that in the wealthiest of societies more doors of opportunity for creativity outside the household have been closed to females than to males—one refers to the lower status of the feminine sex. Another fact, possibly the weightiest of those which are pertinent, is the percent, which astounds Euro-Americans, of persons, women especially, who have been found doing creative work in the arts in some of the food-gathering societies. Still another fact is the conviction, among many anthropological field workers of Euro-American origin, that a remarkably large number of persons in the smallest and economically simplest nonwestern societies display impressive intellectual stature. Women of such a kind may be as frequent as men.

The rarity of markedly original Euro-American minds, men or women, may therefore be no consequence of extra special genes, gene mutations, and the like. It may be the manner of operation of one sociocultural system which appears to have granted opportunities for creativeness to very few males and almost no females. Frequency of geniuses may therefore be culturally determined. So too the content and style of what they achieve. Their behavior, ways in which society develops them and then relates to them, and consequences of their seminality are in each instance cultural products. Knowledge of these matters is meager for nonwestern peoples beyond indications that some of them have produced many fertile minds.

Psychologists, intelligence testers, psychoanalysts, psychiatrists, professional educators, and others have expressed, in their special ways, another conviction about inborn general intelligence. This belief is also a significant component of Euro-American civilization. They have supposed that their tenet, a kind of very short myth, is bolstered by historical and other sufficient evidences. The myth is that it is natural for intelligence and personality to display an upgrade in childhood and all through so-called "adolescence," that there are biologically modulated plateaus in intelligence, levels of varying length, during the middle years, and that a downgrade occurs inevitably during later decades of a lifetime.

Myths of highly generalized representation may be regarded as dogmas and this one is peculiarly Euro-American. Similar tracings of supposed ups, levels, and downs in personality or intelligence may have been explicit in a few nonwestern cultures. The important thing is to identify the Euro-American dogma and, then, try to explain why it appeared and how it has functioned. It is necessary also to examine sociocultural systems whose beliefs about intelligence, if they expressed any, were different and whose institutions produced other manifestations of growth, plateau, and senescence. Cross-cultural indications are that childhood upgrade in intelligence has almost always been speedier than modern western civilization has perceived as likely in its own so-called "normal" children. In other societies, adolescence as a period of deliberately manipulated retardation in personality growth has almost always been absent. Middle years in nonwestern societies often have begun in the late teens and offered opportunities for important changes and improvements in personality. Old people were usually counted among those who were fortiesh and so on. Frequently their sociocultural system then granted them new or enhanced opportunities for personality development. Euro-American civilization's views about potentials in children, adolescents, persons of middle years, and elders are, in each instance, punishing or destructive. In addition to its calumnious dogma about extreme rarity of geniuses and great leaders because of biological circumscription, a notion embroidered with pseudoscientific silk threads by Francis Galton in Victorian times and by hosts of others since then, western civilization succeeds in limiting people's potentials for rapid maturation, steady growth, dignity, and creativity. Few food-gathering and agricultural societies of primitive economy have been able to afford the questionable luxury of so much undermining or sacrifice of human potential or of cultural expressions that denoted and reinforced devastating hostility to persons within one's own group.

Geniuses and prodigies themselves therefore constitute a distinctive expressive phenomenon of western civilization: they are those rare individuals who were permitted to be creative and, by one or another accident of their childhood, escaped the retardation which the society has long seen as inevitable in and required of most of its younger people. The rarity of genius is one of the most vicious dogmas of the West.

## The Average Person

The mathematical concept of average is, of course, one of western society's exemplary ideological products which was fashioned in the course of nineteenth century mathematical and scientific work. People of that civilization presently adapted it crudely to represent all sorts of undistinguished persons who might be amusing but who never made anyone anxious by being unusually bright, stupid, distinguished, obnoxious, or filthy.

Perhaps no anthropologist has returned from a field research with evidence that he found a similar concept among his informants, no matter how sophisticated or imaginative they were about details and patternings in their social system. It is foolish to underestimate the dexterities and insights informants might exhibit in such sociological delineations of themselves. In modern western civilization, with its deep currents toward democratization and urban inconspicuousness, many people are satisfied about being nonvisible, that is, average, using that term in the popular sense which embraces a large majority of the citizenry. People of the West appear to want to be unharrassed or unrevealed as having any outstanding distinctiveness. Most of them project their fate of inconsequentiality into others. Therefore like Sinclair Lewis' Mr. Babbitt they find aberrancy or nonconformity irritating, even unbearable. They do not want to be subjected to the glare of publicity or the sadism they want very much to be accorded to others who are mavericks. A layman's concept of average, therefore, functions nicely to protect those who are fearful lest they be thought of as not especially competent, disagreeably different, or an object of interest to an unkindly and large public whom they do not know. To such persons average comprises a crowd in which to hide and remain unfrightened. Among nonwestern people comparable concerns might not have developed and so the source or support did not arise for a concept of average citizens. Among people of the West it functions defensively.

A factor among many which operated in some regions of stratified societies to block development of a concept of many persons who were average may be found in the larger numbers in such societies who were members of upper and lower social strata. In the United States of the twentieth century the extremely wealthy are few. The poor and pathetic are still in tens of millions but display decreasing numbers in relation to the whole population. A concept of average people, therefore, functions as an expression of feelings of a majority who occupy neither upper nor lower rungs of the status ladder. Since such numerical relationships of social strata were never closely paralleled in stratified nonwestern societies, a concept of average persons could have received less or no nourishment among them. It is indeed difficult for citizens of western countries to realize, for example, that well-to-do lineages in some, if not most, of the thousand or more Pacific Northwest Coast food-gathering hamlets and villages numbered a majority of the populace. A wealthy citizen might have constituted an average person, if western civilization's concept of average had also germinated in Northwest coastal populations. It did not, to be sure. Each stratified system has had its special arrangement of statuses. Those which characterized modern western society, notably that of the United States, supported the bromide of an average citizen perhaps much more so than in other parts of the world.

## Morons and Worse

Doubtless every group identified, at least in some indirect way, a few individuals as not so bright. But the many nonwestern languages which lacked morphemes for brilliant, bright, stupid, or idiot and which, therefore, appear to have lacked the very concepts might have had morphemes for clever, resourceful, or tricky, and dull, clumsy, or gauche—the latter almost but not quite signifying "stupid."

It is not yet possible to determine which societies perceived or conceived of intelligence, stupidity, moronity, and the like. One wonders if perceptions of such kinds tended to accompany defensive hauteur and disparagement of the lowly in wealthier agricultural and pastoral systems which had extensive social stratification. There is meager, if any, evidence of concepts like high intelligence, an opposite of it, stupidity, or moronity among advanced food-gatherers of the socially stratified Pacific Northwest Coast. But they did perceive a batch of able and clever persons who were like that because of their good supernaturals. They also knew an assortment of character disorders, clownlike personalities, clumsy codgers, supernatural-less unfortunates, and other ignominious or preposterous persons. That is, community nuisances or troublemakers also received characterization. People had to accept their presence and to help them from time to time. Moronity appears to have constituted behavior which, without sharper identification, was included in behaviors of some members of that larger group of persons who were bothersome because they were poor and did inept or absurd things, usually because they lacked good supernatural allies or had uniquely bad ones. It never occurred to anyone to comment on an abstracted element called "intelligence" or the lack of it. But everyone identified trickiness and cleverness and regretted its absence.

Recognition of superior and inferior intelligence may, then, have connected with and been included, wholly implicitly, in relationships to good and bad supernaturals in economically lowlier and, in some instances, unstratified societies. Concepts of intelligence and the converse, stupidity, appear to have connected with long or extremely stratified societies and to have functioned as defenses, on the one hand as a means of characterizing and justifying upper social strata, on the other hand as characterization of social inferiors. Beliefs about superior and inferior brains appear, then, to have been abstractions and projections which, if one were able to pursue evidences into Greco-Roman centuries or earlier, trace to needs to justify relationships and protect self-regard. The circumstance that modern science offers, doubtless with fine objectivity and evidence, a normal curve of distribution of intelligence in a population is not relevant to operation of mechanisms which generated or sustained any analogous concept in nonwestern societies.

In economically lowly societies, morons often survived because their lineages accepted their incapacity and tried to live with it. These unfortunates were likely to be accounted for on a variety of bases such as lack of supernaturals, poisoning or bewitching, and relationship to bad supernaturals. A concept of lack of intelligence might not often be present. Nonwestern peoples could hardly connect head or brains with a concept which they did not even possess. But capacities and wishes might be tied in with heart, stomach, eyes, or other organs which were the very ones likely to suffer penetration by supernaturals or things sent by supernaturals. A person thought, of course. But he thought with his heart, for example. He certainly did not think with a sticky spongy mass which, obtained from crania of person-like four-legged creatures who had eyes and heads too, was excellent in some regions in the preparation of tanned hides.

No satisfactory cross-cultural data are at hand regarding the point along a continuum of intelligence where morons blend into idiots and imbeciles and what nonwestern peoples did and felt regarding them. If such pathetic individuals survived they were probably explained as having been affected adversely by some supernatural, not as having been brought into the world with a handicap of low intelligence.

# 6. FEMALE AND MALE

## Introduction

Progress in sociocultural, currently captioned "behavioral," sciences, has been characterized not only by more and more descriptive reporting and by orderly arrangements of extremely few portions of it. There has been increasing employment of methodological shortcuts, such as questionnaire, sampling, and correlation techniques, and of theorization about processes in sociocultural life. Need to arrange fresh data neatly and augmenting sensitization about many things that go on in societies have generated taxonomic tools, concepts, in goodly numbers, often with accompanying puzzlement of both laymen and some anthropologists. For example, the taxonomic concepts or macroconcepts of status and role, ever more frequently employed since Professor Ralph Linton popularized them for anthropologists in his *The Study of Man* during the later 1930's, continue to serve as headings for facets of phenomena which connect with intimacy. The two concepts may or may not be efficient classificatory tools both because they overlap and each covers a multiplicity of behaviors, feelings, values, and other matters. On the face of it, it would seem that each concept ought to be cut into classes of units which could be handled with superior precision. It is proper to comment briefly on status and role, whatever their likelihood of survival in a sociocultural and psychological anthropology which advances knowledge of nonwestern peoples only when its cutting tools are sharper than rubber and its slices are not too bulky for handling. Role may be translated as the bundle of things a sector of the people is assigned to do. Status is a community's ranking of the group which does those things.

A simple or primary sexual division of labor among economically indigent food-gatherers brought about their adult males' and females' roles. Each such package of roles continued with important changes into older males' and females' roles. A food-gatherers' society's own assessment of the relative standing and worth of each such four groups denoted the group's status. And what a person customarily did in his roles, and what everyone thought accordingly about his social ranking and position in relation to all other persons, contributed to determination of his self-identity. That is another classificatory concept, obviously much too comprehensive also because it likewise covers a complicated array of items, some of them psychological.

Frightfully ethnocentric, naïve, and patently projective thinking, in a variety of forms, has long characterized modern writers' depictions of adult and older women's bundles of tasks, participations, or roles in nonwestern sociocultural systems. Still worse, females' status, the regard a culture had of their position vis á vis men, has been portrayed and assessed for the most part with scandalous irresponsibility. Painstaking field investigations designed to elicit people's own statements about females' status are still almost nonexistent.

## Evolutionist Theory

Nineteenth century theorization about virile, if not volatile, cave men and passive or inert cave women was mythic or projective thinking, too. It was obviously enjoyable because it was wishful thinking. It offered satisfying if not titillating daydreams to some repressed Victorian folk. Evidences of prolonged residence inside caves by early peoples have never been forthcoming although a myth of cave residence, and of women's lower status in and out of caves, appears in writings by uncritical anthropologists to this day. It is unlikely that populations of remote eras could have lived efficiently if they resided inside caves during even a part of the year, in districts blessed with an abundance of caves. Interiors of caves have always been visited periodically, although not used as permanent or seasonal residences by food-gatherers except for a handful of hard-pressed Bering Straits Siberian Eskimos. Only visits can be deduced from art and artifacts found within any kinds of caverns in other preagricultural locales. Rock shelter residences doubtless go back, here and there, to a great antiquity. Even a few modern food-gatherers such as the Veddas of Ceylon used them. It is curious that few suggestions have been offered about the aggressiveness of men and passivity of women whose families lived beneath rock shelters. There seems to be something far more fetching about those dark cave interiors for so much printer's ink, if not emotion, to have been expended upon women's status inside and beside them. Let psychoanalysts speculate about this question, if they so wish, and explain why many Euro-Americans supposed that ancient women had so uncomfortably low a status when their families dwelled inside caves, another status when the little bands loitered under rock shelters, and maybe still another status when everyone snored outside in grass huts and other manufactured habitations. The only interest in such suppositions is in their possible use as expressive material whose analysis may reveal psychological and sociocultural characteristics of Victorian Euro-Americans and their still somewhat fettered descendants in our midst.

## Status of the Feminine Sex

Nineteenth century protagonists of the matriarchate, a few early twentieth century ones too, sketched and forthwith slobbered over a fantasy of a remote era when females assigned vital tasks and roles to themselves and thereby enjoyed something more than parity of status and bloated self-identities. Such writers varied in their specifications of wondrous advantages once accruing to the curvaceous but not necessarily gentler sex which presently lost ground to males and, accordingly, surrendered a firm but gracious and cultured dominance. Anthropologists today find no evidence in their field researches of a society which displayed feminine economic, political, religious, or status superiority. Women have enjoyed, so it seems, status parity in a number of sociocultural systems, but no more than that. There is, therefore, reason to extrapolate into a remote past, of course without direct evidence to support statements, and to suggest that in the light of everything learned about food-gatherers, a herculean burden of proof is upon an advocate of an ancient era of feminine superior status, the matriarchate. Anthropologists prefer to leave the question with a formulation that women enjoyed equality in many groups visited or studied in modern times. It may have been *The Mothers'* lot during hundreds of thousands of years, right up until the last ten or twenty thousand.

Few phenomena in sociocultural anthropology are less clearly defined than sex status. Few topics display less consensus about the nature of the behavior under scrutiny. Excellent anthropologists have often remarked, usually in the course of comments about something else, about a lower status of the feminine sex among Australians and Eskimos, for example. Actually there is no definitive determination of feminine status in these two food-gathering populations. An assertion that women's status among them was low is more doubtful than some anthropologists suppose. Correct method requires, first, tactfully procured collections of native judgments, noted verbatim, about women's social position in relation to men; second, exacting comparison of specifically relevant components of the sexes' behavior.

Anthropologists of Euro-American origin face a problem of examining their projections of ideas and feelings about women's status into another sociocultural system. To put it baldly, judgments by anthropologists about the status of the feminine sex, when the provenience of such scientists is in western civilization whose women occupied a low status throughout the Christian era, are at once suspect if they have not obtained word for word native comments and then closely analyzed both them and overt behavior. And this is not a kind of research which can be completed in a day or two. It is of interest that only a few North American Indians who constitute a minute percent of the members of a worldwide anthropological profession grew up in a heritage, such as that of southwestern states, which is unquestionably characterized by equality of status.

There is only a possibility of a lower status of females in societies which lacked social stratifications and status differences of kinds other than age grades. No stratifications or status differences appeared in the male half of the adult membership of Eskimo or Australian groups but, again, a host of writers have asserted that women's status among them was not on a level with men. If it was lower, what marked it as such? Men's humor? But humor has not received close analysis in these groups. Religious ideology? The little known about it reveals nothing relevant. Wife lending? A custom of that kind, shocking to Euro-Americans except in decadent corners of their civilization, has been claimed *ad nauseam* for Eskimos, but no one seems to have bothered to study carefully, by obtaining a large number of cases each of which is depicted in convincing detail, whether a woman herself broached it or gave smiling or sour permission when someone else such as her sadistic husband or a shaman urged it. Did an especially effulgent aura around hunting and fishing debase women and lower their status? No anthropologist has offered such a criterion of status. Documentation to support an allegation about such glamor would be unconvincing until it were also shown that nothing a woman did was ever as lustrous. Did freedom from pregnancy and nursing elevate or depress the status of males? This question can be skipped because no one has claimed that such incapacity automatically generated higher status. Freedom from menstruation? Curiously, just this has been asserted as a decisive cause of superior standing of males. Anxieties around so-called magical contamination with menstrual fluid have been widely reported. But the contamination theory begs the question of why the status of females was extraordinarily inferior, by almost any definition of status, from India to the Atlantic during at least 2500 years, while women in many nonwestern heritages were obviously enjoying much more of acceptance and participations in the very societies, as in western North America, where menstruation was enveloped with impressive taboos. Additional factors in status would have to be noted in order to make sense of a contamination theory.

What about property ownership rules? If this criterion be allowed, Eskimo and Australian women could not be regarded as of lower status because differences in significant, because productive, forms of property were absent in their homelands. What about exclusion from important ceremonials? Early indications from male missionaries and male anthropological observers that Australian women had to absent themselves from vital rites were balanced later by strong suggestions that those reporters had not been allowed to observe comparably momentous rites from which men were excluded. It begins to look like six of one and a half dozen of the other. Among Eskimos the criterion cannot be used to exhibit a lower status of women because there were no such banishments.

Status of the feminine sex in a native community might be efficiently assessed by noting, in four parallel columns, its judgments of values of participations into which its women entered and those from which females were excluded and its judgments of values of participations into which its men entered and from which they were excluded. But very likely there is no such careful analysis of Eskimos, Australians, or other groups where women's status was high if not on a par with men. The uncomfortable conclusion is that many scientists have been playing leapfrog with method and evidence. They have been jumping ahead of their data. They have been too ethnocentric to do more than offer slapdash judgments which are projections of something within themselves about the worth of womankind.

Short of a rigorous analysis in any part of the world, it appears that the status of women has been extremely high or on a parity with men among economically simple food-gatherers, even those whose wives stayed at home and chewed winter boots to make them soft, or whose wives trudged along the trail behind the men, or whose wives received more frequent beatings than the stylized clobberings to which they subjected erring and irritating husbands.

Among economically advanced food-gatherers of the Pacific Northwest Coast, the status of premenopausal women was demonstrably, by any criterion, on a rung inferior to but not a big step beneath males. In several districts along the coast, such females were convertible into currency at the time of and for years after their marriage. Their participations outside the household were long severely restricted. But once they passed the climacteric their status rose to something that now looks like parity. A deftly probing survey of this facet of the region is needed, together with indications of differences from district to district.

Among economically simple agriculturalists such as Iroquois, Navajo, Apache, and Pueblo peoples, to name a few regarding which the field data are extensive, the status of women appears to have been on a parity with men.

Among all other socioeconomic types women's status has been variably low, extraordinarily so in societies where large numbers of peon- or slave-like persons were found and where well-to-do men possessed more than two or three wives. The contrasted power of a few sub-Saharan older women, as of some European queens and noblewomen, does not controvert the fact of lowly station of females in such societies. Indeed, a rather efficient rule of thumb may be that feminine status has connected with severity of the peon or slave system, the numbers of such unfortunates, degradation of the lowest castes or classes, and size of polygamous households. The more crushing the slave system, the more cruel the exclusion, poverty, and hopelessness of the lowest social strata, and perhaps the larger the polygamous households, the lower the standing of women. If this imprecise formulation is correct, a nexus is likely between feminine status, the kind of social stratification, and the extent of polygamy. It seems that depreciation of the worth of any large segment of a society encouraged its men to undervalue and belittle their wives similarly, although in far more veiled ways. Certainly wherever a woman was equated with currency and valued property, her status fell short of parity.

The question of status merges into that of work assignments, social participations, or the conglomerate of behaviors which Linton and others have subsumed under a heading of "role." The following section accordingly discusses adult male and female roles.

## Sex Assigned Role

Work tasks, participations, or roles assigned to the two sexes among all modern peoples sometimes varied signally from society to adjacent society. A familiar example is in Arizona where Hopi Pueblo men weave and, nearby, Navajo women weave. Although these peoples have lived virtually side by side and had agriculture and similar arrays of features of sociocultural heritage for many centuries, the arbitrariness of their divergent handicraft assignments in weaving is instructive.

A few writers have supposed that vital customs of modern food-gatherers resembled, in general respects, strategic customs of peoples of remote eras, the very mores regarding whose ancient operation no one is ever going to learn much. One surmise is that modern food-gathering folk offer clues to causes of the ancient sexual division of labor, if not to sex assigned roles of other kinds in those bygone eras. Nineteenth century evolutionist conjectures already cited may be characterized as the voice of the Victorian unconscious. It projected an ancient matriarchal epoch when gentle females, mothers to be sure and ample ones unquestionably, dominated family, household, and community while males snarled, fought, and were disagreeable at a distance in the bush and did not have roles in work or social assignments during most of their unpleasant lives. The matriarchate was a wish fulfillment for downtrodden and petticoated Victorian ladies who did not know enough about scientific method to counter a projected image with trustworthy evidence. A delightful aspect of the fantasy of a matriarchate is the fact that during the middle of the century reputable and surely most masculine gentlemen such as Bachofen, McLennan, Morgan, and others more or less independently depicted it on their reverie screens. One wonders how much guilt these Victorian intellectuals had around their sheltered and controlled middle class women and how it was assuaged by so lovely a flight of profeminine fancy.

Not a few writers of recent decades nodded favorably in the direction of another and gruffly masculine projection onto the fantasy screen, a muscle theory of history, evidences for or against which are unobtainable. The unconscious of its protagonists, if enough were known about them, might make spicy reading. Their thesis states that possession by males, on the average, of somewhat superior brawn and speed was anciently the cause of their customary assignment to hunting, fishing, and any other physically demanding labor and, of course, higher status and dominance. In reality, skill has often been as important a factor as athleticism in hunting and fishing, if not in local government. It can be acquired, after sufficient practise, by women as well as by men for all purposes of food production.

There was comment above on writers who offered a magical danger theory, a rather insidious projection of Victorian anxieties about and perhaps even hostility to women. Such authors urged, in effect, that in many nonwestern societies activities of central moment to family and community were not to be endangered by magical contamination and that, therefore, early peoples were especially fearful of females' special physiological functions, menstruation and parturition. Maybe breast feeding figured in the mélange of such Victorian feelings, too. The result, so reads the doctrine, was that females tended to suffer exclusion from hunting, fishing, and other vital work and sociocultural participations, not least those which had to do with supernaturals and leadership.

A few decades back, academic voices from gruff basso to high tenor and castrato were audible on the subject of the implications of modern history, to wit, its paucity of great women especially in the fine arts and humanities. The sybilline testimony of art history was supported by mathematical and, therefore, irresistible indications from intelligence tests which, naturally because that was their caption, were supposed to test and score intelligence. Questions included in such so-called tests were so manipulated, assuredly wholly unconsciously, as to show a superior average intelligence of males and their greater numbers of geniuses. The superior male brains theory must be summarily dismissed as fraudulent analysis of history. It was also allowed to rest upon misinterpreted evidence because it used incompetent tests. It was culture-bound. It seems to have been an expression arising in or maintained by masculine anxiety about remaining in a dominant status in a rapidly changing society.

Obviously evidences of remote origins of productive and other assignments, as of sex status and roles, are forever lost. Theorization about such matters is both futile and ridiculous. In addition, magical danger, muscle, and feminine mental inferiority theories of remote origins of the sexual division of labor and of exclusion of females from certain facets of social life look suspiciously like variably knit fabrics of rationalizations, defenses, and projections which can be accounted for in the inner life of alarmed males who were carriers of nineteenth century feelings about women's proper place.

Although remote origins of rejections of women or men from certain activities cannot be observed, customs of many nonwestern peoples can still be examined for factors which continued to support such exclusions. A plausible theory about women's roles and status in food-gathering societies is that females' natural responsibilities in pregnancy and nursing long upheld customs of exclusion of men from tasks which did not connect efficiently with productive contributions which only females could render. In addition, according to the most trustworthy reports, men have never succeeded in becoming pregnant and their nursing activities even now are to a degree limited to handling of sterilized products sold in supermarkets.

Nubile females among food-gatherers were long necessarily somewhat less mobile than males, if the community was to survive. Therefore the tendency among food-gatherers may everywhere have been to preserve within the more mobile sex assignments of especially important economic kinds which required some journeying and athleticism. The men's responsibilities were those which, during a woman's nubile years, did not gibe with maximal safety for infants when she was pregnant and nursing her young. Factors other than difference in mobility account for most remaining assignments such as cooking, sewing, weaving, scolding, and art criticism.

The greater freedom of movement of males, not male musculature, skeletal frame, freedom from magical contamination, or intelligence is as plausible an explanation as any for men's acquisition and exclusive ownership of economically vital productive resources such as slaves and the most important domesticated animals. It accounts, too, for their domination of trade, acquisition of wealth in premodern societies, and maintenance of roles in government, military, and police. It explains their higher status in all wealthy societies. On the other hand, advanced technology achieved in western civilization in the twentieth century has eliminated the factor of lesser mobility of females as one which should longer impede their entry into all roles hitherto dominated by males. As for modern men, two important roles alone cannot be sought by them, those of giving birth and nursing infants at the breast.

Whatever theorization may suggest about historical or other factors which maintained a society's special labor and role assignments to one or the other sex, it is of much greater importance to understand how such assignments operate in the lives of all peoples today. It is parents who directly determine their children's learning of sex linked roles, except in the many societies where other persons are identified with or accept responsibility for such teaching. Parents or others admonish, approve, and grant rewards to a child during his learning of etiquette proper to his or her sex. A child similarly learns right posture, toys, dolls, games, relationships to children of opposite sex, and the like. Where a youngster's principal identification is at two or three years of age with the parent of the same sex, the child at once adopts adult-like posture and ways of relating to people, of kinds which he has observed in and been maybe only subtly rewarded for by that parent. Where persons other than parents relate closely to, manage, and approve youngsters, identification may be principally with such individuals.

It is of first importance to understand that biological or foster parents are not omnipresent as a child's significant elders. Anthropologists have often reported on special ties with aunts and uncles and have unnecessarily captioned such institutionalized relationships the "amitate" and "avunculate." The neologistic inventions of amitate and avunculate have contributed nothing to knowledge. Such relationships, minus peculiar terms, are also documented for grandparents and a variety of household and small community elders. It is evident that the world over there are many distinctive relationships with kin and others beyond the primary family.

Although identification with some significant person or persons of the same sex has been universally encouraged in the child and the way it has been done deserves cross-cultural study, an important problem remains. It is to account for each sociocultural system's ideal posture, ideal voice mannerisms, ideal behavior, and roles of that sex. The model girl or boy, the standard adult female or male, the correct voice placement, posture, and pattern of expected relationships were in all instances expressive products of a sociocultural system. What maintained these images, these constellations of desired behavior and values, these role expectations? It was a person or persons with whom a youngster identified and who, at the same time, exercised some authority over him. Uncle, aunt, and grandparent often played such a role.

## Male and Female Ideal Types

Euro-Americans are no different from carriers of any distinctive sociocultural heritage of the past or recent times in having their own special tensions. And so Euro-Americans tend to peer into another society's children for particulars such as the pregenital seductiveness, wiles, gait, and posture of its little girls, and the cocky directness, assertiveness, and dominance of its little boys. In western civilization, a cluster of traits which spell seductiveness is often remarkably built into girls and reinforced a thousand times by one or both of their parents. Boys, on the other hand, are supposed to be boys. That is, our kind of boys, thoroughly masculine but in a preadult way.

Girls who lack a Euro-American kind of feminine complex of acquired characteristics are sometimes later handicapped in acquiring a mate in a society which requires parental noninterference and supposedly romantic but anxiety laden freedom of choice. Euro-American boys who lack another complex of acquired traits built into them and constituting an expressive cultural feature that unfailingly spells masculinity may find themselves unable to obtain the siren type and are forced to settle for ability, bones, or blubber.

Nothing is more agreed upon among anthropologists than the flat and trite generalization that western societies' trait clusters which mean attractive female and attractive male are not at all biologically pressured, at least not largely so. There is too much of learned items in them. These two clusters of expressive features function as a Euro-American mother's extension of herself, and a father's extension of himself. They serve, too, as kinds of art products, things of beauty in themselves, although they are images of desirable female and masculine male. In western society, parents of youngsters, with other elders in supportive roles, try to shape the little products according to such cultural images and values. They take pride in what they suppose are results of their household handiwork. It is like nonwestern parents who, in some few cultures, "molded" their babies' limbs with nightly massage in order to shape them so that they would grow into approximations of the culture's images of what adults should look like.

In Euro-American society much of what is poured into a child, in its learnings about sexual identification and expected sex role behavior, is a kind of dress rehearsal of a person's later physical appearance, posture, gait, gestures, etiquette, and culturally assigned maneuverings in premarital and courtship years. It is not wholly, at any rate not since frontier days, in preparation for a later role as a married person. On the other hand, non-western elders were more likely to emphasize how one should behave as a married person than as a seeker after a mate. Elders often planned mating, anyhow, so that a principal anxiety was around mates' behavior after the wedding when elders were no longer able to do much of the managing.

Some nonwestern peoples, maybe those who were rather sure about their own sexuality and marriageability, waited until daughters or granddaughters were on the verge of the menarche before venturing to fashion girls' demeanor. Very soon after, in pubescence, these maidens played the expected female role well enough in the presence of potential mates. If a society was wealthy and stratified, its feminine sex had lower status, and a girl was manipulated in marital negotiations as if she were a purchasable commodity—in a sense, she was—she might be taught model deportment and ideals which required inarticulateness, passivity, modesty, and ways in which she could veil her cunning.

Among most food-gatherers, where sex statuses were equal or virtually so, expectations seem to have included primarily themes and realization of ideals which accented occupational competency. In such instances, anatomical sexual attractiveness was minor, productive and relationship roles were decisive. The ideal was to develop skill in one's own sex's food production and other work assignments, especially manufactures such as basketry, weaving, and preparation of hides and garments. Industry, modesty, and dignified passivity were stressed, as were principles of how to get along acceptingly with husband and in-laws. In such societies similar ideals which stressed competence in hunting, fighting, manufacture of gear, reliability, resourcefulness, courage, and intelligence were, when actualized, traits that rendered youths sexually attractive. It appears that in some of these societies only extremes of mutilation, or anatomical aberrancy such as loss of an eye or albinism, nullified an otherwise alluring person who almost measured up to the female or male ideal images which centered abilities and tact in relationships.

Winsomeness to opposite sex, the community, and a mate's kin, the latter of capital importance in many nonwestern societies, was phrased in terms of values which were a culture's expressions around sex status, role, and identification. The roots of such values and images, if it were possible to probe historical and social factors which developed and maintained them, connected with the following among perhaps many more in an elaborate web of causation. One basic factor, of course, was the relative statuses of the sexes. Another comprised rules about freedom of choice in courtship or parental or lineage arrangements in marriages. Another included standards regarding occupations and community roles expected of newlyweds. Still another arose in rules for proper manner of relating to new in-laws.

Since such characteristics of social systems were extraordinarily variable, patterns of items which constituted amenity as male or female were extremely variable, too. Each sex's self-identity and, more specifically, its tonsure and cosmetic efforts, posture, and etiquette in social relationships were shaped by a sociocultural net of factors. In birds causes of secondary sexual characteristics such as plumage lie immediately in biology, in genes. But in human beings each sex's proper personality, behavior, and plumage have been culturally manipulated. The products, the desirable young man and woman, may be regarded as expressive features, structures, or patterns if you please, most elaborate ones, which have segments and arrangements like designs painted on pottery vessels. One might efficiently digress in order to employ this analogy of graphic art. The first step in a method of delineation of everything that had gone on in such art work would be to analyze out the component features of expressive content. For self-identity these could include, perhaps, awareness of competences and relationships, and inner convictions of self and worth. The second step would disentangle features of style. These are, again to offer only a few suggestions, forms of speech, dress, cosmetic materials and procedure, and etiquette rules. The beginnings of cementing of such a complex of ideals and learnings, all of them expressive features, into the child ought to be revealed painstakingly in each culture. They present one of the most important and interesting opportunities of new kinds in transcultural studies. The incessant maintenance and reinforcement of these ideals and conditionings, so that youngsters continue to behave in line with them and at length perceive themselves as examples to the last felicitous details, are only a follow-up of research on childhood initiation of such items and, to be sure, are of equivalent importance. Few anthropologists have been able to achieve success with field reporting on these successive sectors of the learning process and on their long range impact on people after they have internalized the values. In a nonwestern community many children and older persons would have to be observed, photographed, and interrogated. Observations and replies would then be subjected to close analysis. Field research procedure of this kind probably has never been employed in its every aspect, although Margaret Mead and maybe a few others who were psychologically oriented have indicated the way in their expeditions and write ups.

In spite of indications that most of the content and style in those cultural constellations which are male and female are elaborate expressive items that are inked indelibly into a child's personality structure, psychoanalytic theoreticians and others have tended to suppose that masculinity and femi-

ninity arise in biology. Some writers who have asserted acceptance of cultural factors in sex identification have insisted that there is a biological
remainder, an ultimate given by genes in female personality and behavior,
a biological remainder of another kind in male personality and behavior.
They might urge that these remainders are immutable and arise in genes
which some day can be revealed by biology. Haven't you seen a two-year
old boy walk like a little bantam? They allege that this is biology. Perhaps
it is at that early age. But the point is that a scientific field should not spend
valuable time trying to settle a question that cannot be answered in the
near future, especially when there is not much time left to probe sociocultural factors which are the only ones responsible for expressive manifestations that differ from region to region. If biological factors still lurk
significantly in style if not ideological content of adult sex role, measuring
equipment available today cannot be placed alongside them nor probes
touch them. But it is still possible to obtain mountains of cross-cultural information about culturally caused and implanted displays of sex role and
identity. Here is where work is needed at present. Meanwhile, sociologists
and social psychologists may continue to observe the tens of millions who
strive to internalize an image of the desirable female represented at the moment by a Brigitte Bardot or the most fetching male represented by a
Marlon Brando.

If a combined observation and question-and-answer procedure is indicated for the field research worker, how will he itemize and order his data?
In general respects the method may be like that of manipulation of other
structured expressive materials. Under a heading of "Content in Feminine
Image and Behavior," itemize value ideals in relationships: modesty, obedience, subservience, and the like, to each set of persons who are siblings of
opposite sex, parents, in-laws, upperclass persons, potential mates, and so
on. Under a heading of "Style in Feminine Living," itemize posture, facial
expression, direct or turned aside gaze, sectors of anatomy exposed and covered by garments, ornaments, cosmetics, and so on. Then, connect each such
item or unit with everything else to which it related in the social system
and ethics, again by means of fresh observations and interrogations. These
are only hints about a method of research which might be tried out and
developed in a few among hundreds of still partially viable nonwestern
social systems. Field workers will in no long time agree about most productive field methods and means of analyzing data, especially the very
words of the natives. The need is to obtain some of the data at the same
time that increasing sophistication develops about method.

Value judgments about nonwestern peoples' varying images of desirable
male and female or about their roles are like a Euro-American musicologist's
assessment of the esthetic worth of Choctaw, Menomini, and Makah music
before he has analyzed his tape recordings to determine contrastive features
of both content and style. Judgments of esthetic worth before close analyses
are necessarily culture-bound. They are skewed because a cultural outsider

initially perceives only small parts of a phenomenon and he responds to them with items taken from his alien pattern of content and style. So, too, judgments about male and female identifications and ideals in nonwestern societies are inappropriate. Their values to which Euro-Americans react approvingly reveal the little that was initially perceived and values which long before were etched upon the outsiders' minds. The anthropological preference is to study, observe, find out, analyze as closely as possible, and attempt to understand. Is this posture satisfactory only for a scientist and unseemly for civilized and compassionate citizens?

If an anthropologist reports rapturously about the attractiveness of the native girls we can deduce, helplessly, that he is assessing their charms only in terms of his culture's and his own values. For purposes of advancing scientific knowledge, his contribution in this one respect is about himself rather than about the exotic objects of his optical gymnastics.

## Sex Differences in Self-identity

Role connects with self-identity. Each person's awareness, judgments, and feelings about himself comprise his self-identity. Comparisons of self with the culture's ideal of a feminine female, or with its stereotype of a masculine male, are factors which determine both the identity and its attached self-regard. What, then, is the feminine core of a female's self-identity and her regard for her worth, and what is the masculine core of a male's self-identity and self-regard? Answers are available for only a handful of the world's wealthiest societies.

In spite of masses of ethnographic reports about peoples of food-gathering economy, what it feels like to be feminine or masculine in such societies is a matter of guesswork by outsiders rather than of quotable statements gleaned painstakingly from sample individuals within. In parts of food-gathering western North America an individual Indian's feelings about her femininity appear to have been less centered on factors of anatomy and garb than on awareness of her voice, demeanor, modesty, manner of relating to men, competence in sex-assigned skills, responsibility, and loyalty to kin and husband. A man's feelings about his masculinity seem to have been centered in his appraisement of his own competence and reliability in sex-assigned roles, perhaps also in the kinds of animistic beings to whom he had made relationship.

Stress on femininity and masculinity appears to have lessened for many nonwestern persons during their middle years. After the climacteric and in so-called old age, some people seem to have exhibited only tepid awarenesses of sexual concomitants which had been important in their self-identity during their younger and earlier middle years. But in the very same groups there were often a number of widowed older women who might maneuver into tingling romances with young blades who found them exciting. Some older widowers might engineer marriages with young girls.

Great variability in self-identities probably marked many societies by contrast with the wealthiest regions, certainly western civilization, which appear to have preferred a narrower stereotypy of middle-aged and older female and male identities. Cross-cultural research is very much needed on this subject, which is peculiarly intriguing to Euro-Americans because of their malaise about their own self-identities. Field methodology employed by aliens should include acquisition of autobiographical data and techniques of interrogation, these in native groups where rapport with outsiders is good and where the ethnography is comparatively full and sensitive. In such groups it might also be possible to employ short cut devices dear to the many thousands of experts in the behavioral sciences who are in a frightful hurry, like to work with questionnaires and mathematical gadgetry, and whose professional self-identity is allowed to remain unpunctured because of a kind of passivity and gracious cooperation of those who answer their laconic, often ill-phrased, and almost always culture-bound inquiries.

## Courtship and Freedom of Choice of Mate

Little is known about premarital etiquette in economically lowly food-gathering societies. Although exogamic or other rules often severely limited the numbers of possible mates, youngsters enjoyed a fundamental freedom of choice in a remaining list of persons among whom they could procure a consort. Very little has been reported about their responses to advice and pressurings by older persons. Such guidance may have been less irritating to them than it has been to most young people in modern western civilization. One wonders if family, community, and childhood had not internalized capacities to respond positively to people, even those who pompously tendered counsel, while in western civilization a mate selected democratically and without pressurings by others has sometimes constituted one of the few persons toward whom one retained positive sentiments or whose advice received kindly attention. In any case romantic love or freedom of choice intertwined with attitudes of kin, lineage, and community. One might almost say that courtship was a composite of etiquette maneuvers and responses by both future mates and everyone else, although ultimate decision might reside democratically in the pair to be betrothed. In societies of this kind, weldings with gifts accompanied but did not govern bonds which were being forged during the premarital period. Unstratified agricultural societies of simpler economy probably operated in the same general manner.

World distributions of physical manifestations of premarital feelings have always been of concern to Euro-Americans who have wanted anthropologists and, lacking such authorities, pornographers to provide details about fondling, hand holding, necking, kissing, eyebrow chewing, tongue explorations, toe tickling, and the like. Foreplay has doubtless been universal. It has ranged from etiquette which seems affectionally or sexually arid to Euro-Americans to items which provoke feverish responses in most of them. It is sufficient to note a world variety of exploratory and affectional play, its essentially etiquette character and complexity which require, of course, content and style analysis, and its relationship to respect which persons had for one another and for their kin. It might be private or in view of other group members. Community values, feelings, and anxieties about relationships with potential in-laws doubtless connected with each inventory of permissible amatory devices. Few if any serious studies of such techniques of courtship have appeared. Publications of erotica are as worthless as they are numberless. Their distortions, sensationalism, and avoidance of plausible scientific theorization serve principally the vast numbers of emotionally sick, repressed, and lonely persons in western society.

Among the Pacific Northwest coast's economically advanced food-gatherers, pubescent youngsters theoretically accepted parents' and lineage's decision about the marital future. It need not be a cynic who might suggest that courtship etiquette was socioculturally displaced from youngsters to their elders. Those worthies enjoyed manipulation of premarital protocol once denied them years earlier because they were then too young. They had a fine time regally discussing assignments to and reports from marital crossers, agents, or emissaries who shuttled back and forth between the potential in-law groups. The now controlling parents and elders enjoyed the gamble and tension of successive payments, agreements, status advances and retreats. They were more involved than the young couple in the dickering and approach to the grand finale. Then, rather like some other societies, the girl's people brought the passive child with downcast eyes and garb covered with money beads to her future husband's hamlet and household for the wedding feast, oratory, and games. One might say that in such a society courtship etiquette was determined by courting of status. It was reserved for families, households, elders, and entire hamlets. Precious little except a case of jitters, maybe some furtive and embarrassed meetings too, was left for the young pawns in the competitive gamble between their lineages and villages. The couple's role was to accept. They must react with impassivity, as few whispered queries as possible, and no audibly salty observations. Everyone knew or supposed that the youngsters were tense, frightened, or embarrassed, also proud in instances of highborn lineages. Summarily, the game was a status game and the pawns were marriageable property owned by older persons of extended kin groups.

Bride and groom in such societies might initiate their roles as active married folk only when the drama, that is, the period of four or five days of feasting, dancing, games, and visiting, was over and in-laws and guests had departed to resume the status game at some later time and perhaps in other ways.

Where patrilocal residence was customary, a bride began to participate in chores in the household of her parents-in-law, her husband to participate as a married man with other married men of his own community. Premarital etiquette, which might include speechlessness and immobilization of the feminine betrothed, had concluded. Sexual courtship might begin only slowly, maybe fearsomely, because the stakes and dangers of lineage humiliations continued. Huge payments which had linked—not with chains of gold but with valuable possessions or strings of money beads—two status-proud and hypersensitive lineages must never be returned, if avoidable. In other words, sexual roles in early months and years of marriage connected in every act, nod, smile, gesture, and tone of voice with portentous financial and relationship commitments and with in-law tensions and potentials for sensing intolerable humiliations. When newlywed roles and behavior were etiquette expressions of lineage status, finances, and anxieties, marriage and sex were not quite like two birds upon a branch or two squirrels in a field.

Culture has everywhere overlaid plain universals in human nature to a point where it seems that some very special equipment is needed to find out what of such universals may have been there at all. No one, questionnaire and mathematical statistics specialists in psychology least of all, seems to have had a good idea about how to devise such equipment. Therefore, it is better for the present to find out what various cultures projected and required than to speculate about biological underpinnings or common human items which cannot be probed or trapped with mathematical bait. A scientist's immediate obligation here is to account for items, fabrics, and district-to-district differences in cultural manifestations. Once a system of theory is available concerning them, it may be opportune to look for biologically shaped universals in sentiments and behavior.

In a society of economically simple food-gatherers or agriculturalists, a young couple who had paid court to each other actively with finger tips, teeth, and eyes, maybe with poetry too as in Polynesia although within limits set by the culture, continued to relate to one another after their wedding in their culture's terms of nonmonetary and nonstatus values. Such young people usually retained a degree of freedom of choice to separate if they ran into stormy waters, especially so before their first baby was born. But even they, too, connected with their respective natal households, families, lineages, and communities in ways which have all but vanished in western civilization. Since their relationship was also fraught with obligations and tensions around kin, values, and etiquette, their self-identities as married and nubile female and married and virile male tied in with many other persons' feelings.

The comparative extreme of isolation, independence, privacy, and shutting out of extended kin, parents too, by married couples of mid-twentieth century urban western civilization is novel. It contrasts with an indefinite continuation of tight nuclear and extended kinship belongingness to many other persons in nonwestern societies. In terms of society's requirements, each Euro-American partner is relatively free to select from a bewildering miscellany of values, images, and stylizations of behavior in order to maintain relationship with the new mate. Actually, Euro-American mates tend to act in accordance with values and etiquette style which they long since incorporated from parents, fiction, and screen. If their parents were always overtly tender they may relate in a tender manner. If parents squabbled and made up they may do the same. If mother was fat, waddled, and was devoid of manifest interest in sex, daughter may presently repeat some of mother's history. In western civilization permissible etiquettes in married years are often confusingly varied, much more so than in premarital courtship. The latter has more standardized etiquettes of petting, necking, midnight door-step kisses, worried and furtive experiments in reproduction, and other requirements of what is necessary in behavior in order to be an attractive girl and a youth who can enjoy his peers' as well as a girl's approval.

## The Middle Years

Many ethnographic reports have implied or frankly asserted that among nonwestern peoples a strategic component of self-identity in a woman's middle years were the extensions of herself and of her lineage in the children she had borne and reared. Her principal role was to contribute them. The emphasis upon lineage is vital for comprehension of the proper identity and role of many nonwestern women during this period. To be sure, each such woman supplied very much for her husband's self-identity, too. She and their babies had enabled him to function as a married man should. At the same time, she had served her own kin, especially so if her offspring were reckoned matrilineally as members of her clan, by increasing and perpetuating her extended kinship group. This was one of the decisive sectors of her total role during her middle years. Her attractiveness hinged on successes in that wifely and maternal role which redounded to the prestige of her kindred, as well as on efficiency in chores, intelligence, management of her husband, graciousness when his relatives turned up, or whatever other values the culture had established. The west's recent intensification of concern about retaining physically youthful appearance during middle years has witnessed few if any parallels among nonwestern peoples. Their narcissistic supplies and attractiveness resided in ways they played their sex-assigned roles of wholly different kinds. A value which supported continuation of premarital youthful appearance and garb after marriage may have developed first among females in recent western civilization. A similar value has been accepted by men even more recently.

Values around extramarital courtship play and liaisons during middle years have varied the world over. Even in western civilization, a modicum of acceptance of such dalliance has been easier to find among some Latin Americans than among most other Euro-Americans.

## Personality Differences

Margaret Mead's researches in several Oceanian agricultural societies have provided some of the important documentation now available on global variability in masculine and feminine types of personality structures and in manifestations of male and female roles.

As far as one can ascertain with current limitations of descriptive knowledge gleaned in field researches, male and female personalities appear to have displayed greater variety in agriculture-based societies or other comparatively sedentary communities than in food-gathering groups which moved about from season to season. Food-gatherers, most of whom required such mobility, sometimes a good deal of athleticism or endurance, have not been reported to have displayed in their men an average personality structure which was passive, tender, and, from the point of view of Euro-Americans, feminine-like. Nor have reports of women in food-gathering societies indicated a very strongly masculine-like average personality—masculine only through the eyes of western civilization—although individual women among them, especially the older women, sometimes did exhibit such a character. The most sedentary food-gatherers, those along the Pacific Northwest Coast who occupied year-round hamlets, possibly exhibited no more tenderness and passivity than food-gatherers who were far more mobile.

Maybe it would be feasible to try out a number of intersecting continua such as the following, for one kind of crude and maybe ingenuous ordering of data about value ideals and group personality norms in relationship to sex: activity versus passivity; crudity in relationships versus sensitivity; courage versus timidity; arrogance versus modesty; callowness and narcissism versus tenderness and compassion.

It might still be possible to observe numbers of personalities that would offer documentation about proper sex role in societies in a later state of acculturative change than the agricultural groups which Mead visited in Oceanian regions. Probably the natives in communities which Euro-Americans enveloped and progressively crushed during a century or two have internalized to such a degree Euro-American male and female personality ideals and have so accepted western values that precontact ideals, values, and personality characteristics are difficult to reconstruct. A chance of such depictive restoration arises in improvements in close and independent analyses of projective materials such as legends, historical narratives, humor, and casual conversation. In long enveloped and severely acculturated agricultural groups, which Robert Redfield captioned "folk" and "peasant" societies, an obvious problem is to determine factors in and degrees of incorporation of Spanish or other colonial masters' images of male and female, in retention from precontact days of the original culture's images, and in processes which shaped current roles of males and females. In Latin American countries lower status of the feminine sex in wealthier precontact groups, apart from some rather different societies of lowland districts, may have coincided remarkably with Spanish values.

## Old Age

Problems in cross-cultural understanding of the total self-identity and range of roles of an older person have been discussed. Here it is sufficient to indicate that in nonwestern societies male and female identifications in older people were often weakened and in other instances fully retained. In many instances they were intensified. Since an older person might be tagged as such in the forties because of grandparent status and new roles, it was of course easier to continue to be attractive sexually as an "older person," so-called, than in modern western society in which the middle years continue to 60 or more.

Anthropologists have encountered a number of societies, viable or lately moribund, in which postmenopausal women, sometimes only those who were widows, actively sought sexual liaisons. Earlier in their careers such women had done nothing of the sort. Because of intelligence, artistry, long success as respected married persons, and other approved attributes, they were sexually attractive to men, not least to youths, until their seventies or later. A proper role of an older woman might be, then, to enjoy a freedom of choice in affectional relationships which was limited or denied her when she was marriageable or the valuable property of her kin and her husband's kin. Her pursuit of sex and love might not be, as in western society, a last hour effort to recapture or improve upon her youth. It might be many other things such as an expression of desire to be of continued worth and importance to people. After all, young men might want her very much, by contrast with young men who would not desire her in western civilization. Doubtless, there were societies where the word which a Euro-American would translate "grandmother" carried an important additional connotation of romance. Many Juliets have been much more than 14 years of age. Shakespeare's denotation of the youthfulness of his drama's Romeo and Juliet is a delightful projective expression of values in European society of his era. The sexual attractiveness of able and intelligent, albeit somewhat wrinkled older men and women in nonwestern societies might be such, precisely because of their endowments, that younger people enjoyed positive affectional responses toward them, of a kind that has hardly occurred anywhere in western civilization in recent centuries. The sexual repugnance felt by most modern western youngsters toward elders is supported by the culture's total rejection of the aged. A displacement mechanism, from disrespect to sexual unattractiveness, seems evident.

Characteristics of personalities of nonwestern elders may be pointed up by a few comments on what has happened to older persons in western society. During the Victorian period, middle class elders tended to be regarded as long since finished with sex, if they had ever participated in it for purposes other than solemnly planned procreation. The sly thought that a "middle-aged lady," let alone an older woman, a grandmother, might still be sexually active would have outraged if not threatened most middle-class Victorians. Feelings of dirtiness and distaste around any interest she might continue to have in sex survive widely today. Victorians expressed visibly their sexual and other forms of repudiation of attractiveness or other merits in middle-aged and older women by requiring special garbs for them. Old ladies wore black half-hats, gloves, shoes, and clothes, and carried only black umbrellas. Since black was also the color worn by those who attended funerals and by close kin who survived long after burials, older women who had to wear black, or felt they had to, were expressing or validating society's wish that they be completely dead, not merely partially dead, unwanted, useless, and sexless. Obviously a person, of either sex, whom it was correct Victorian etiquette to assist upstairs or downstairs or across a thoroughfare merely because he or she looked eightiesh, or was made to look it by special garb and other accoutrements, was really being projected onto the very threshold of death. Such a person could not conceivably be any longer significantly male or female except in a nostalgic memory of what had happened long, long before. When older persons such as a widow and widower married in Victorian times, no middle class person supposed that their motive was other than to minimize loneliness in a sexually sterile companionship. Few nonwestern peoples regarded liaisons or late marriages of older persons as so aridly contrived or maintained.

Personality consequences of such feelings and frank expressions of rejection are familiar to western readers of these lines. Since comparably complete repudiation has been found nowhere among nonwestern peoples, a cultural anthropologist engaged in field work is alert to discover complex manifestations of sex as well as of craftsmanship, leadership, and other qualities in the personalities of older persons.

## SUGGESTIONS FOR FURTHER READING

M. Mead's *Male and Female* (New York: Morrow, 1949) is perhaps the most notable among the many books which parallel portions of this chapter. Some of Mead's other books also contain important materials or repeat portions of her *Male and Female*. It is curious that our heritage of sex-assigned roles and status in western civilization effected an inversion of the proper alphabetical order of the words in the title of her book.

# 7. SLEEP, DREAM, AND FANTASY

## Sleep

Manner and duration of sleep among nonwestern peoples are topics regarding which the data are scattered and virtually devoid of meaning for a transcultural system of theoretical statements. Not long ago, for example, Professor Cora DuBois commented on the all-night noisiness of an Alorese village on Timor. People might wake up and talk at any time of the night without concern for a presumed need of children to remain undisturbed. But neither Alorese nor any other nonwestern communities have been described in terms of the average and variability in duration of a night's sleep, and the sociocultural meaning of such behavior. Euro-Americans' anxieties of at least a century about getting regular sleep, at least among persons who are older than the middle twenties, probably contrast with a general absence of compulsive concern among nonwestern folk about sleep regularity. Alarm about loss of a full night's repose may be peculiarly Euro-American and may tie in with something important in the civilization. Anyhow, no one has reported meaningfully, except for comments about dreams and supernaturals, on what nonwestern people do or feel when they wake up in the middle of the night and cannot get back to slumber. Valuable expressive materials, including data about spirits, may be present in their explanations of their wakefulness.

The recent history of psychiatry and psychology accounts for Euro-American intensification of interest in and, perhaps, greater knowledge of dreams. Let us turn to glance cross-culturally at these expressive manifestations.

## Dreams as Personal and Cultural Expressions

Freudian theoreticians and psychotherapists have long stressed the mechanisms and defensive functions of dreams and have availed themselves of the considerable utility of dreams as indicators of processes operative in their clients. An assumption was that images and causes for their appearance in Euro-Americans' dreams were examples of what occurred universally: everywhere dream images of bowls, dug-out canoes, hills, and mountains were symbols or disguised representations of female anatomical parts; pencils, telegraph poles, and things of such shape represented the male organ; a terrifying pursuer was a hated parent. Psychotherapists tended to accept a standard and fairly long inventory of such universal symbols and interpretations and applied them almost mechanically in analyses of dreams, auditory and visual hallucinations of psychotics, and folktales irrespective of cultural provenience. A Filipino, Pueblo, or Zulu who reported a dream plot which included an image of a pole was at once presumed to have a special emotional involvement in a phallus, his own, his father's or someone's.

Evidence which might permit estimations of probabilities about the world-wide occurrence of such dream symbols, images which appear in psychotics' hallucinations, and folktales too, are few and scattered. Reports which comprise unannotated dictations of folktales are in profusion, but published materials on dreams and psychotics' fantasies are lacking for large areas of the nonwestern world. Until a sampling of nonwestern dreams is obtained with correct controls, from many more districts than have been studied so far, claims about a universality of dream symbols and mechanisms are premature if not improper. On the other hand, a few skeptical or cautious anthropologists have already been almost shocked out of their wits by their informants' dreams and dream interpretations which suggested the accuracy of some Freudian statements, especially those dealing with so-called universal dream symbols of the kinds cited.

Although individuals within a community differ in the frequency, complexity, and vividness of their dreams, it is safe to state that a projective screen of shared dream images, feelings, and plots characterizes the members of each community the world over.

Among nonliterate peoples the common although not necessarily universal tie-in of dreams with supernatural beings introduces special field method and interpretative problems. These have to do with the often considerable cultural role of dreams and with ideology, values, and tensions which shaped dream content, if not form. In many parts of the world, dreams functioned as much more important cultural expressions than they do today among any Euro-Americans outside of Los Angeles where doubtfully qualified practitioners of psychotherapy abound or used to. Dreams were so vital in a number of nonliterate societies that omission of discussion of the dream from a cultural anthropology survey is perhaps as incongruous as deletion of plastic and graphic arts, language, humor, or oral literature.

How are dreams studied in a nonwestern setting? What are some cultural barriers to research on them? What did dreams express? What repetitiveness and stylizations of form occurred in them?

## Method in Field Research on Dreams

Contrasted extremes of near absence and fullness of involvement of supernaturals offer decisive factors in research method on dreams. In some societies, projections of supernaturals entered infrequently into dream content. Euro-American culture offers illustrations, especially among its numerous citizens who are irreligious and calm about such aberrancy. In society where everyone had culturally stylized dreams which also contained projections of supernaturals, and where people maintained secrecy about their dreams, field workers may be unable to conduct research which elicits earlier or contemporary dream experiences. They may be able to record only dreams which were culturally standard and where people were not loathe to expose them to fellow members of the community or an outsider. That is, some parts of the world may remain nearly blank in a final compilation of descriptive materials. In other regions the harvest may be poorly balanced, with vital dreams unrevealed or distorted because of natives' qualms.

Because of the peculiarly personal quality of dream reports, rapidity of defensive forgetting, frequent privacy of religious experiences, and cultural pressure to garble or stylize each dream no matter what it actually was, excellent rapport with informants may be of utmost importance. Cross-cultural research on dreams is peculiarly dependent upon ability to minimize skewing and secure full materials. A requirement of proper sampling means that many dreams are needed from each of a sufficient number of persons of both sexes, all age grades, all social strata, and the occupational specialties. These persons should be revisited at later times so that social, personality, or other changes may be connected with changes in dream content. A great many hundreds, if not a few thousand, dreams should be noted for each society studied. So severe an order also implies a remarkable degree of rapport and completeness of knowledge of the sociocultural heritage. Today the numbers of such adequate collections of dreams are doubtless few.

As in researches on other expressive materials, mere verbatim recording and collection are insufficient. That method is about as dessicated in conception and conduct as the collecting of a century's folklorists who never tried to find out all sorts of things about tales they were recording at dictation. Like oral literature, ethnomusicological, and linguistic researches, investigations of nonwestern dreams must be conducted with a question and answer procedure. There must be daily slicing and identification, where possible, of all likely segments of each dream in the field situation in a matter of hours after dictation. Then a quick return, preferably within a day, both to the dreamer and others who can be approached about such matters, with questions about their feelings concerning and interpretations of components of each dream. The indispensable procedure of interrogation about dream content may be risky to manage because whenever an anthropologist intimates or suggests, during his querying, some underlying dynamic which he appears to be persuaded is present, he may unwittingly stir up discomfort and resistance to volunteering of dreams and of associations around them. He may thereby damage a research irretrievably. There is a chance that pioneering investigations on dreams and myths several decades ago by a distinguished psychoanalyst, Geza Roheim, in Australian and Melanesian groups were injured by the manner in which field interrogation proceeded. No anthropologist watched Dr. Roheim's technique in a field situation and so a cloud of uncertainty hangs over interpretations which he elicited from informants.

A scientific approach to dream analysis very likely requires listings of each of the following kinds of materials: (1) persons, personality stereotypes, and fantasy beings on a dream screen, (2) social relationships between those dream figures, (3) their acting out of feelings, and (4) items of patent unrealism and incongruity. Plot themes and several other kinds of features, depending on a culture, have to be noted, too. Frequencies of items in each of the inventories of kinds of dream content connect meaningfully both with stresses in a social system and a dreamer's personal history. Each dreamer should also be depicted for as much of his biography as is obtainable.

A few dreams from a culture, especially the first ones volunteered, may offer as skewed a reporting as the first few myths recorded in an oral literature research. Almost all published data on nonwestern dreaming are of this skimpy and therefore unreliable kind. They contribute no more to a scientific system of cross-cultural theory about dreaming than the first two or three large so-called origin myths which were volunteered display much about content, style, and functioning in a large corpus of myths and tales.

Requirements of thorough sampling and sensitive question and answer follow-up are a large order. But advances in basic theory in "hard" sciences depended on monumental quantities of laboratory research by a multitude of people during many decades, apart from all the cerebration of a theoretical kind. Comparable headway in systematic theoretical knowledge of cultural expressions cannot be expected to require less devotion, reflection, judgment, time, descriptive details, and research personnel. Hurry will get cultural anthropology nowhere if it lacks excellent cross-cultural materials. Sophisticated but voluminous data gathering is indispensable.

## Dream Content and Style

Projections onto dream screens display some distinctive differences from those which appear on oral literature screens. Even in nonwestern societies in which adults' dreams tended to approximate stereotyped content and forms shared throughout a community, individuals' idiosyncratic stresses and needs very likely effected additions or substitutions of projected beings and relationships. Conscious control might not be as strong as in art forms such as myths and tales. These arts were often of materials which received word-for-word memorization. They tended to constitute community property. They were invested with authority. They were statements by revered ancestors, maybe. Changes in art forms made by individuals were often items which, to be sure, gibed with community needs but also arose in borrowings from neighboring peoples. There were changes in frequency of selections in an array of permissibly employable alternate items of content or style. But dream content was usually more variable and idiosyncratic than myth or tale content.

Stylistic frames of dreams, rather than their expressive content, are so little studied, even suspected, in Euro-Americans that it seems at first thought almost discreet to bypass them as a topic. They are nearly unknown as yet among nonwestern peoples, but no anthropologist doubts that in some peoples, such as Mohaves, such structures were important.

Anthropology's contributions to a system of cross-cultural theory about dreams may now take several directions, all of which concern projective content.

One direction points to cultures which granted dreamers ready-made or official dream content, as it were. In such instances, analysis of content, not of its social and psychological functioning, is really a duplication of oral literature content analysis. In each ready-made dream, freedom to select from a class of items of expressive content was perhaps no greater than that of a raconteur's. Principal differences in his selection of what to project resided in immediately preceding stimuli, presence or absence of an audience, option to be entertaining, motivation to offer a performance of admirable craftsmanship, and the like. Even so, in a few cultures a dreamer might repeat his dream to an audience within a few hours, if not almost at once. Probably he did this in a style of presentation which is analogous to the structure of an oral literature genre.

In some cultures only wanted types of dreams were attended to. Generic characteristics of these desired or official dreams were cited by elders so that a younger person created, or at least selected from a list of possible items, a goodly portion of the content, but not the frame, of each dream which he could recall. For example, many western North American Indian cultures transmitted to the younger generation, through elders, an outline of information that in a dream, a dream which was culturally meaningful and wanted, one "encountered" (1) an animal, fish, bird, insect or plant "person" or maybe some mythic ogre who forthwith (2) metamorphosed, appeared in the very garb and anatomical characters of a human being, (3) sang and danced one or more song-dances which were his very own, (4) offered money, help, or specific skills, (5) presently sermonized about the dreamer's desirable future behavior and (6) vanished. Here is a series of content centered steps or scenes, of which I have suggested six for one small region, in a kind of one-act play. The repetitive sequence was a matter of oral dramatic recital style. The encounter as such, the actor who was met, his appearance and personality, the song-dance or several song-dances which he performed, and his little lecture to the dreamer were projected items of content. The dream, therefore, had both content and form. The over-all types of possible content and the form were fairly rigid internalizations from cultural authority. Selection of specific items of content in any one dream was idiosyncratic. Its principal causes were a dreamer's anxieties and defenses against anxiety. Experiences of a previous hour or day might trigger these. What the dreamer projected into each little scene in his one-act play, if it was in only one act, was a matter of more or less unconscious selection out of an enormous range of possible content. His personal history accounts for what he selected and projected onto the screen of his dream play. This type of dream content and structure was found in a society whose theory and practice of supernaturalism offered experiences with supernaturals which were identical with dreams. Dreams and contacts with supernaturals were one and the same, in content and style. If, in this culture, the same dreamer experienced any other types of dream content, framed in other ways or devoid of frame, information about them is absent and maybe beyond acquisition. Chances are that a dream—call it a free dream—which did not have a certain kind of intensely wanted content and a form of the type noted was not even recalled upon waking. A dreamer was either indifferent to it or rendered mildly anxious. It was ignored or dismissed as inconsequential because there was no reinforcement or intensification from the hard core of cultural anxiety over supernaturals and from the authority wielded by a society which was explicit only about its official dreams. Preceding experiences of an extremely traumatic kind such as fishermen, hunters, or travelers underwent, and which set off dreams, were likely to effect dreams whose content and form were those of a traditional supernatural kind with their neat stylization.

Cross-cultural theory about dreaming, then, must accept the fact that in many, if not most, nonwestern cultures a dreamer projected his own selected smaller details of dream actors, relationships, and situations within culturally granted inventories of them (classes of content) and in a culturally granted sequence of them (style). This is another way of saying that in nonwestern peoples dreaming was to some extent culturally shaped. It might be so fully shaped and consciously internalized that it verged on a kind of art form. In western civilization, who but a television script writer, contributor to the New Yorker, opera librettist, or political theoretician is likely to have a dream which, when he later writes it out, smacks of a work of art?

Even in western civilization, instances may be found of highly structured dreams consequent upon internalization of beautifully structured materials. For example, physicists and mathematicians have reported that they solved scientific problems during sleep. The mechanism appears to amount to internalization and later projection of both content and frame of materials which have been sanctioned by scientific authority. In response to emotional triggering, wanted materials receive projection in a dream, fit into needed relationships and lo! a scientific problem is solved.

People who have studied dreams of Euro-Americans have observed that a sequence of images in a dream plot is often beyond restoration by a dreamer when he wakes up. He remembers only people, relationships, feelings, funny or alarming incongruities, and values in a formless whole. He is not clear about time order in the scenes of his little play of fantasy images. This is patently because most Euro-Americans have not internalized even one type pattern with a customary sequence of scenes. On the other hand, it is likely that many nonwestern peoples internalized one or more such patterns. Their dreams had stylization, form. Upon waking they might be unable, at least reluctant, to repeat a dream without according it such a form, although images which they experienced might not have been so arranged. They were vague about, dismissed, or quickly forgot whatever could not be perceived as a part of a stylized whole.

Tactics of field method and of analysis of dreams have been suggested. But strategy in cultural anthropology at this time would suggest that variables in dream projections and mechanisms are so many and data elicited from informants are sometimes so spotty or elusive that other types of research on projective expressions, from which anthropology may learn much with relative ease, ought to be pursued first. When it has laid foundation stones in these much more accessible fields of inquiry, it may be better equipped to tackle the dreamer's evanescent creations, internalized in precise ways and stylized as they still are in many or most cultures outside the western world. Strategic considerations, therefore, suggest that cultural anthropology despatch its earlier scouting parties in the direction of researches on some of the arts and on humor and religion. In these territories, barriers to clear-cut and accurate reporting, and to proper segmentation of recorded materials, appear to be fewer.

## Functions of Dreams

The familiar theory that a great many dreams occur near waking time and function to preserve sleep a little longer, that is, by permitting tensions to have projective outlets on an image screen, is both good theory and culture-bound. Let us not concern ourselves with the question whether it is accurate for most Euro-Americans, apart from their occasional nightmares which, of course, do not preserve anything but only intensify the jitters. Indications are that dreams in some other cultures did not often if ever operate protectively for sleep. They might function in several other ways. They might awaken the dreamer in order that he, in turn, awaken everyone around him so as to be able to relate to them at once his shut-eye experience. Dreams might function as wanted safaris into a land where supernaturals dozed and where they were awakened and presently acquired as kinlike helpers. Each region's dream life had its special functions, one or several, to be ascertained by careful research without looking back over the shoulder at causes for and functions of dreams in western civilization. As in linguistics, one must not project mechanically into another culture's manifestations.

To be sure, nighttime consequences of especially upsetting stimuli such as a sour stomach, mad dog, or threatened enemy raid may also be what we

call a dream. There have been billions of dreams, and they have functioned
in numerous ways. Mechanisms which connect with their content, forms,
and services are fully known only when their cultural frame is comprehended, that is, when anthropology has ascertained what people feared,
wanted, and internalized from their culture.

In a number of cultures, a native theory of somewhat psychological
turn developed about the function and meaning, that is, the interpretation,
of dreams. It was an explanatory code, maybe with precautionary or therapeutic uses. No one such psychology-like system of theory and practice
has been subjected to close analysis, if it has ever been disclosed in all details
to an outsider. Little can, therefore, be said about such indigenous theorization, reasons for, and manner in which a native dream analyst or therapist
acquired his knowledge, procedure he employed when accounting for
someone's dream content, and steps thereupon taken for the sake of client
and society. The intriguing revelation is that Euro-American psychologists
and psychiatrists have been merely recent pioneers in dream analysis or
"depth psychology"! Independent, conceivably a handful of rather insightful, ventures into this psychological specialty dot the world map. Such
nonwestern explorations possibly examined only sectors of the total phenomenon. Study of dream theorization and determination of its tension
relieving or other functions, in instances where we can find such lucubrations and secure satisfactorily extensive information about them, may be as
rewarding as study of any other cultural expression. Everything known
about nonwestern peoples warrants expectation that sophisticated insights,
partial as well as ranging ones, will be found beside premises concerning
animistic beings. It would be naïvely simple, and not especially useful, to
suggest that anxiety about supernaturals who appeared in dreams generated
psychological interest and a compounding of theoretical assertions. Origins
of a native theory of dream analysis cannot be observed. After all, most
societies lacked specialists in dream analysis although shamans were often
functionally close to such professionalism. In most societies many members
of a community, including shamans, developed some skill in interpreting
details of dreams in terms of supernaturals but without deductions or insights about mechanisms and universal symbols such as mark modern psychiatric theory.

## Fantasy

The line between a dream and a fantasy may not be the same in different
cultures. In any case, most cultural anthropologists have been far too busy
obtaining field materials on traditionally sought sociocultural materials to
permit themselves the luxury of investigations of the fantasy life of their
informants and interpreters. But the more one examines cross-culturally
the riches of content expressed in a variety of projective materials such as
oral literature, humor, and dreams and the diverse and complicated designs

around each of them, the more the appetite is whetted to canvass non-western fantasy expressions and to tie them in with larger bodies of socio-cultural materials. Do fears about strangers, in-laws, or supernaturals more often determine the content of fantasying than aspirations and wishes, as so often in western society? Does free floating fantasy ever occur or is fantasy almost always shaped, maybe only a little, by dream genres and supernaturalism?

Obviously the descriptive materials, supplemented by probing commentary, secured in field situations will disclose anthropology's most successful and sensitive field research people, the ones who have effected extremely accepting relationships.

## SUGGESTIONS FOR FURTHER READING

Although book-length cross-cultural discussions of the subjects of this chapter are either not at hand or suffer from certain limitations, Freud's system of theory offers decisive beginnings, for all its restriction to clinical data obtained only in western civilization. D. Eggan has written excellent short papers, but her close analysis of Hopi dreams is not yet in print.

# 8. SICKNESS

## Curable and Lethal Ailments

The most important concepts regarding sickness and therapy comprise projective expressions which connect with world view, ethics, and other macroclasses of cultural features. All feelings and ideas about health require close analysis in much the manner to which cultural anthropologists should resort in explorations of any classes of expressive materials.

In the first place, injuries and minor ailments whose causes were visible and obvious and whose consequences were not likely to be lethal comprised a category of difficulties which people often resolved with material means and in ways comparable to therapeutic procedures resorted to in western medical science. For example, splints set broken bones. Poultices, salves, and wrappings assisted healing of wounds, skin infections, boils, and other surface exigencies. Plants whose leaves, bark, or roots had medicinal properties were used realistically. The telling point about ailments handled in this manner is not that people maintained a store of prescientific information for their treatment, but that people were not fearful lest they be fatal because of their connections with the soul or supernaturals. Appropriate remedies, therefore, involved little or no resort to nonmaterial helpers.

Every nonwestern culture drew a line somewhere along a continuum of ailments. Up to that line an indisposition was unthreatening and a material cause was known or suspected. Healing proceeded without recourse to projections endowed with humanlike qualities and powers. Beyond the line an indisposition was scary, deadly if untreated, and maybe lethal anyway, very likely because one or another especially unfortunate supernatural or the soul itself was involved. Here was where people summoned projective beings and part-time or full-time specialists who had excellent pipelines to those beings. These specialists were shamans, of one or more kinds depending on the culture. Shamans were expert in making contact with projective figures of notable power. Feelings of aggression were projected into other persons, nonmaterial individuals, who supposedly poisoned, shot deadly worms or bits of sharp volcanic stone, splinters, thorns, or other objects, sent their own or other supernaturals to remove internal organs or one's soul, and so on. The dimensions of a nonwestern culture's system of theory about potentially or always mortal illnesses, many or most of them caused by soul loss or malevolent others, could be monumental. A heavy volume might be printed for each of many food-gathering groups about its projective expressions which were compounded or embroidered into

pantheons of beings and theories of diagnosis, prophylaxis, and thera-
peutics. The volume assuredly would be just as large for each of hundreds
of agricultural peoples. No anthropologist has come within reach of exhausting such stores of theory and practice in a nonwestern community.
It would seem that apart from ordinary interpersonal tensions the more
severe the pique between lineages, in-laws, bands, villages, or social strata,
the greater  the proliferation of theory and therapeutic practice around
supernaturally effected ailments of most serious kinds.

The trouble with such cultural data is that they often lurked in the
shadows and darkness of shamans' private worlds. The ideas and mechanisms, sometimes the sentiments felt, were only partially public. Extraordinary amounts of bloodchilling gossip, polemics, and theorization might
swirl around in the citizenry before a shaman who had been summoned
arrived at the patient's side, announced his diagnosis, and proceeded with
therapy. A Euro-American anthropologist who can penetrate all the arcana
of shamanistic theory, medical practice, and terrors in a nonwestern community may never be born. Field research appears to be limited to mini-
mizing distrust of an observer, who is usually a Euro-American, piecing together sample disclosures from various informants, trying to obtain everything one can from shamans, and securing case history after case history.
In time, galling frustration in field work is recompensed by a yield of enormous amounts of case and other information. Like any types of expressive
materials, data on deadlier sicknesses and therapy comprise quarries rich
in psychological ore for anthropologists to mine. With their diggings and
a skillful breakdown of the raw descriptive stuff, they may build an important system of theoretical knowledge. At the same time they can turn up
quantities of additional items or byproducts for systems of theory on world
view, ethics, and other topics.

## Magic

Readers may note that magic—witchcraft goes under this rubric—has
not yet received discussion. Surely a lot of nonwestern sickness was ascribed
to and cured by magic. All sorts of respected writers have said so. It is
necessary to indicate, and to state again in a following section on supernaturalism, that the copious writings on magic, Sir James G. Frazer's and
others, have largely failed to pinpoint what magic is and how it arises and
works. Frazer and other early writers discussed an inventory of supposed
actions by supposed nonmaterial beings, or actions which somehow followed one another and were, therefore, plausibly presumed to be connected.

But it may be that knowledge of such beings and actions is not in the
least advanced by employment of a traditional covering concept of magic
as described by Frazer and others. Nineteenth century and later writers
projected Europeans' special heritage of so-called magical beliefs and de-

vices, and a European concept and name for that heritage, into other cultural systems, much like grammarians projected a Latin declension or an Indo-European form class of tense into a grammar of a non-Indo-European language.

Like any science the fewer, simpler, and more precisely defined the rubrics, concepts, and hypotheses, the better. That is why anthropology may not need resort to a concept of magic in analyses of cultural expressions among nonliterate peoples. It has a simpler and more precisely defined concept. In cross-cultural studies of sickness or religion, it is usually sufficient to identify special classes of projections, whether supernatural entities or beliefs about cause-effect connections, and to account for their origins, forms, and factors of maintenance and effects upon people.

Like earlier writers on magic, Frazer took for granted that it constituted a large and scientifically manageable class of phenomena. He suggested that it was a kind of early science or prescience because, like science, it rested upon a fabric of interrelated statements about cause and effect relationships. Unlike science, such statements were not publicly available for repeated checks. There is nothing profoundly objectionable in this simplistic statement. But it is faulty because of its failure to arise in close analyses of a probable macroclass of phenomena. Therefore, it was impossible for Frazer to assist in building a system of knowledge about the phenomena which his statements about magic only ventured to pinpoint. Written works on magic could not go on, in Frazer's or most others' treatises, to account for distinctive kinds or classes of so-called magical concepts, kinds of magical processes, why they were believed in, their origins, roles of supernatural beings and substances, and so on. The grammar which Frazer and others supposed they had contributed to understanding of the structure and functions of magic was a superimposition from a sector of the ideology of western civilization, not the consequence of analyses of differing items and structures and their detailed workings.

Today it is possible to see that the term "magic" is, in general, not needed transculturally although western civilization crystallized various of its own beliefs and practices into such a concept. When nonwestern phenomena are under scrutiny, magic can almost always be replaced by a simpler and more sharply descriptive concept and term such as "spirit-power" and by operating with well-documented psychological processes such as projection and displacement. Frazer's oft-quoted distinctions of "contagious," "sympathetic" and other types of magical procedures offered only a gross and mechanical classification, not a report of significant types of phenomena and processes of magic-like kinds found in thousands of cultural systems. He did not point to or classify projective figures such as spirit-powers, the ways they made people sicken or die, or reasons why people believed in and utilized them. Briefly, Frazer offered a few crude labels, old style notions about psychological causes and dynamic processes, and no useful suggestions about differences from culture to culture. He defined nothing which could be utilized and he then classified into worldwide types such as "sympathetic" and "contagious" magic, which were also unusable. Early linguists had done much the same with categorizations into "polysynthetic," "inflective," "agglutinative," and "isolating" language structures.

Sickness, world view, humor, dance, ethics, ceremonial, and religion offer fairly sharply characterized areas of cross-cultural inquiry regarding which systems or subsystems of scientific theory will be built, although they will also interlock. "Magic" may not find a niche anywhere in a total architecture of theory except in those special regions or societies which somehow set magic apart with its own distinctive items of content and their patterning.

Anthropology's rapidly growing public need not weep over devaluation or loss of a hallowed nineteenth century cross-cultural concept like "magic." The scientific rule of parsimony should console grieving folk. The history of every science which had advanced farther along the road toward maturity than sociocultural anthropology could be cited for evidences of concepts, terms for them, or entire systems of inquiry which served valiantly during a few generations of research and then had to be discarded or suffered inclusion in a broader fabric of scientific knowledge. Concepts are dropped, with sincere thanks for services formerly rendered, because they fail any longer to assemble usefully both old and new kinds of data. The concept or topic of "magic" may have outlived its cross-cultural usefulness, if it ever had one. Today it seems reasonable in many regional cultures to allow "magic" to bow out, or to discharge it, in favor of more comprehensive, apt, and simple concepts such as spirit-powers and projections.

Magic which has been connected not with sickness but with religion can be treated with superior clarity under rubrics which also point to spiritual entities and projections. A variety of psychological processes functioned in supernaturals, incantations, rites, sacred formulae, and the like, and the obligation is to ferret out such processes.

Magic which was once connected with love and love potions may be subsumed simply under shamans, projections of supernaturals, and several psychological mechanisms. Magic which was read into fertility rites, garden magic, and the like is again suitably subsumed under various headings including projections of supernaturals.

To return to the topic of sickness, a suggested generalization is that among nonwestern peoples the more threatening sicknesses connected with a variety of special projections which were supernaturals. Persons who effected relationships with supernaturals, or groups of people who worked together to manipulate their supernaturals, could counter such sicknesses. No concept of magic need be intruded in analysis of such beliefs and behaviors.

Methodological and classificatory problems are always vital in scientific work. At this time they are decisive for advances in cross-cultural knowledge of sickness. They include questions such as how best to obtain information about each culture's medical system. Then, what were the main classes of items in each such system? And how did they operate and serve the people?

Procurement of information about a culture's medical system requires cases of sickness numbering into the hundreds or, preferably, thousands. The good research worker will itemize and arrange the case data in distinctive classes such as ideological materials, practitioners, and therapeutic procedures.

## Cross-cultural Psychopathology

Few behavioral sciences possess an elaborate system of theory which has held up in its entirety for more than a generation or two and continued to guide research. Economics long had such a structure of hypotheses. Psychiatry has enjoyed one since the 1890's, principally in writings of Freud, his disciples, and revisionist successors. In each instance, the system of theory has been culture limited because of applicability to and evidences secured in only one sociocultural group, that of western civilization. However, early Freudians did not question a global validity of their structure of hypotheses. Indeed, important components of it may presently receive support in evidences from nonwestern peoples.

Even before the recent rooting of edited versions of Freudian theory among most psychiatric therapists, psychiatry had taken an initial step ahead before 1900, with Dr. Kraepelin, from descriptivism of the mentally ill to orderly arrangement or classification into a few principal types of mental ailments (such as dementia praecox, manic-depressive, neurasthenia, psychasthenia) found among Euro-Americans. Kraepelin taxonomy has had many alterations. Today no one supposes that psychiatry, any more than any other science, is close to a classification which will endure even in the sociocultural system which gave birth to it. Nor is any current arrangement into types of mental ailments accepted in all details and in all quarters. But for purposes of brief introductory phrasing of cross-cultural psychopathology, some statements are needed about such generally accepted types.

First, injuries, tumors, and drugs often cause severe mental aberrations, briefly or for long periods. Some drugs, alcohol, peyote, and several others, generate responses which vary from culture to culture and from individual to individual, depending on socioculturally and idiosyncratically induced needs, aspirations, feelings of hostility, and the like. Alcoholism in one society evidently displays an average, variability, and types that are manifested differently in other societies. Some alcoholized sailors see snakes where equally besotted American Indians perceived supernaturals and were delighted about it. But for our purposes, we can bypass discussion of the many kinds of mental disturbance which are largely or wholly caused by evident physical factors. Sociocultural factors skew manifestations here

and there, as in peyote and liquor, but in this large and varied class of abnormal mental behaviors a decisiveness of organic causation is without
question.

A prodigious variety of Euro-American mental illnesses, which can be
segmented unsatisfactorily into six or seven principal types, has not been
shown conclusively to connect with organic or physiological causal factors.
As far as known, there may be contributory, reinforcing, or other minor
components of a physiological or organic kind that are likely to become
perceptible, especially in manic-depressives, years after onset of the disease. But major variables appear to be located in relationships, situations,
emotional conflicts, and the like, in nonorganic factors, not in chemical,
anatomical, or physiological factors or in anesthetized or severed nerves.

How are these principal nonorganic ailments characterized?

There is, first, a group of nondeteriorative paranoias, in which a Euro-
American patient represses an enormous amount of hostility until, some
day, it erupts against a scapegoat whom the patient supposes is persecut-
ing him.

Secondly, there is a group of so-called "character" or "personality disorders," in which a Euro-American patient displays disturbed relationships and acts out his maladjustment in codgerish or eccentric ways, sometimes with episodic compulsions, obsessive ideation, or paranoid streakings,
but always without progressive deterioration.

A vast third and most varied array of Euro-American ailments has long
been subsumed under one class heading which of late years is schizophrenia. Patients have a long individual history of difficulties in relationships,
apartness or isolation from people, delusions and hallucinations, severe
disturbance in self-identity, and regression to responses of dependent, childish, or infantile kinds. Some patients are paranoid, too. A common denomi-
nator is withdrawal from reality.

Four, a group of Euro-American ailments comprises severe depressions,
psychotic types of depressions, where there is also some break away from
reality.

Five, another group, manic-depressive manifestations in the classical
typology of Dr. Kraepelin, is characterized by a period of uncontrollable
excitement and spectacular hyperactivity. Sometimes it is followed by a
period—days, weeks, or months—of extreme depression and slowing of
responses, then of manic behavior again, and so on until remission to seemingly normal personality. Repetitions of the cycle of manic and then depressive behavior, with remission to normal living, may produce over the
years an individual who is more schizophrenic than manic-depressive.

One more catchall category, to be contrasted with the personality alterations of the first five types, is subsumed under a heading of neuroses or
psychoneuroses. Their types and subtypes are legion. But all display an
awareness of and contact with reality, that is, an ego which does not de-
teriorate. The difficulty is that ego and self lack adequate defenses against

anxieties or stresses which have arisen in interpersonal relationships. By contrast with the five psychotic types, neuroses exhibit no fundamental ego damage or changes in perceptions of self and others. The external world and relationships in it are understood fairly objectively, if not reacted to with fine realism. The ego or self is suffering but it is not on the rocks. A Euro-American neurotic is, then, more or less upset, maybe constantly upset. He feels terrible. He experiences disabling, even unbearable conflicts of feeling. But he knows what is going on around him even if he cannot handle the sentiments and anguish within himself.

Victims of one or the other of the main classes of psychotic maladjustments are less burdened by conflicting feelings and more by some basic damage to self-identity. They, too, lack good defenses against interpersonally generated stresses and anxieties but maneuver by way of withdrawal, escape, denial. They retreat from social relationships. In severe psychoses there is virtual paralysis of ability to handle the real world, that is, relationships with people. Psychotics resolve difficulties with reality by breaking away from it. They set up substitute fantasy worlds in which wishes and fears are realized. Self-identity changes and identities of other persons are altered. In some instances, psychotics regress in behavior to child or infantile level.

Now, do these many kinds or macroclasses of nonorganic sicknesses appear in the nonwestern world? Some few years ago a number of psychiatrists went so far as to assert that certain nonwestern populations are not subject to neuroses. In each instance of such a report the psychiatrist had relied upon secondhand field indications because he could not speak or understand the native language!

Today cross-cultural observers are satisfied that neurosis-like manifestations are likely to turn up in any population. The problem is to report with exactitude on such behavior, but this has rarely been done among nonliterate peoples. A further problem is to locate socially induced stresses which precipitated neurosis-like responses. This, too, requires researches of kinds which have not yet been conducted in nonliterate groups.

It is important to set apart a most variable class of neuroses that are socially caused and produce chronic consequences, from a great class of phenomena that are behaviorally somewhat similar but not chronic. They are more or less abnormal behavior which was decisively tipped off by external situations of a traumatic kind. Reflection about the yearly round of activities and an inevitability of stressful situations among food-gatherers, for example, results in conviction that tumultuous emotional responses of a nonchronic kind were present, even frequent, among such peoples. Field evidences in proof have only begun to be assembled. Acute reactions which have been observed must be differentiated from repetitive neurotic manifestations which were responses to familial and interpersonal stresses, in western civilization usually of childhood. Anxieties in the presence of real dangers or community disasters are, in a sense, normal. In these respects, technologically primitive agriculturalists and pastoralists were not much more secure and serene than food-gatherers. How could it be otherwise? All of these peoples were hard put, at least occasionally or seasonally, to survive with their meager technology, weaponry, and supernatural resources.

Consider the devastating attacks of cougars and grizzly bears upon trail-goers in parts of the food-gathering Pacific Northwest. Terrors which were realistic, indeed as inevitable as death and taxes, have been reported among Eskimo hunters who must go out in fragile kayaks in turbulent waters. An Eskimo hunter who, after he returned, developed a hysterical paralysis was possibly that individual who was burdened with a chronically neurotic kind of response to life; of course most hunters returned with no such paralysis. The completely neurotic Eskimo would be that individual who could potentially suffer from a hysterical paralysis without triggering in an actual situation such as a dangerous solo trip in his kayak. What is especially needed is study of those Eskimos whose responses were apparently caused not by a crisis situation but arose in their personal history of disturbed relationships. Indeed, both types of disturbed behavior require documentation with a great many clinically responsible case histories and presumably this has not yet been forthcoming from an Eskimo district.

Periodic famines, surely wholly real, plagued almost all food-gatherers and economically lowly agriculturalists. Again, case histories in large numbers are needed to indicate which kinds of emotional disturbance witnessed during famines were essentially psychotic episodes or, secondly, neurosis-like reactions consequent upon an appalling situation and, thirdly, which disturbances were reactions of chronically neurotic individuals whose sickness was exacerbated by an external circumstance such as the likelihood of starvation and cannibalism. There are no sharp lines along the continua of emotional disturbances but types must be set up in order to reveal contrasts in features.

Pastoralists sensibly anticipated possibilities of animal epidemics and total loss of herds. Everywhere there was fearful mortality in childbirth, both of mothers and babies. Skin afflictions and internal ailments were utterly beyond control all over the world. Psychosomatic, hysterical, and other defensive maneuverings against external horrors of such kinds are feebly reported and then only from a few nonwestern groups. In all instances, it is indispensable to distinguish defensive behavior in response to crisis situations from those chronic neuroses which arose in disturbances in interpersonal relationships and which were not initially set off by external events.

On the next level, then, contrast a tremendous range of classes of more centrally neurotic manifestations where anxiety was not rationalized by justifiable anticipation of disaster in the external world. Observe the universal intimidation caused by supernaturals and by a variety of mechanisms which older writers subsumed under the merely descriptive heading of magic. Here we have interpersonal difficulties not grizzlies, kayaks and gigantic waves and breakers, famines, locust destruction, headhunting, slave raiding, and other relatively external terrors of real life.

No sociocultural system ever produced and institutionalized designs for gentle living which guaranteed every person absolute security, indestructibility, and certainties about never being faced with situational frights. But individuals who reacted in most upset ways such as hysterical paralyses or psychosomatic symptoms such as allergic or nauseous responses were the ones who were burdened with built-in neurotic responses which traced back to familial or interpersonal stresses of special kinds. Each nonwestern social system had a goodly machinery of kinfolk, supernaturals, rites, customs, and authority which functioned to handle Oedipal difficulties, sibling positions and rivalries, confusions over authority and affectional figures, and a hundred other sorts of tensions. But it is plausible to deduce that there was always a large residuum of familial, kin, and community relationships which were accompanied by creakings and that unlucky individuals got hurt along the way. They included the society's sufferers from neuroses.

Today the world's most secure adolescents who live in America's sanitary and perfectly manicured slums, that is, suburbia, are remarkably well shielded or anesthetized against external frights and traumas, even against threats of intercontinental ballistic nuclear missiles. Unlike nonwestern youngsters, most of them never anticipated famine or saw a severe mutilation or a corpse. Nevertheless, they are often deeply uneasy. Many of them exhibit neurotic symptoms because of uncertainties about limits, bewilderment about self-identity, inability to surmount immaturity, convictions of incompetence, and what they suppose are rejecting feelings of relatives and others toward them. Many of these infantilized, diffident, scrubbed, and vitamin-balanced illiterates act out feelings about interpersonal difficulties and about themselves in neurotic ways and, of course, such ways are legion. Nuclear weapon anxiety, low grade in school, loss of a parent or even a football game can perhaps be immediate triggers for overt neurotic responses in them but are never the entire or even the principal causation.

No matter what the sociocultural setting, true neuroses are caused by bundles of precedent interpersonal stresses. These arise in a society and its culture although fuses responsible for especially explosive neurotic expressions may be found in external events. Causation is multiple although the central factors in a neurotic manifestation are social, relational, and their effects are cumulative and chronic, even if long latent.

In a nonwestern society where almost everyone normally saw and heard supernaturals, an individual who was never able to do that was certainly not normal. He was a true neurotic. His feelings were cumulative and his ailment was chronic. The form it took was also culturally shaped and constituted a selection of one or two among many possible reactions.

A basic problem, then, is to find out what kinds of behavior are neurotic from the point of view of the sociocultural system. Likelihood that there was or is a neurosis-free population is minute because no social system can protect all its young from all possible kinds of interpersonal hurts. What is needed is a special theory about kinds and etiologies of neurotic manifestations in each sociocultural group, a solid sampling of clinically respectable depictions of each type of neurotic behavior found in that group, and studies of ways in which each community produced and later handled the sufferers. It is necessary that externally impelled neurotic manifestations, like kayak anxiety or behavior in famines, not be centered, although it is important to have scientific data on such episodically neurotic behavior, too.

In Euro-American society, an individual who eats and eats and eats and becomes a three hundred pounder who is unable to reduce his weight is a comparatively simon-pure neurotic. No external situation was decisive in producing and maintaining such behavior. Royal Polynesians ate and ate too, but it was fashion and status not neurotic conflict. The problem is to find analogous neurotic individuals in nonwestern societies, and in such societies neurotic disturbances were likely to take wholly different forms such as inability to commune with supernaturals. Special training, including thorough knowledge of a sociocultural system and its cultural heritage, is needed for any meaningful research.

Psychiatrists have asked about psychotic as well as neurotic syndromes that are found in nonwestern groups. Surely, they have said, schizophrenia occurred the world over in as many forms, if not exactly the same in kind, as in western civilization. Anthropologists have responded helpfully by burrowing into their published archives. They have come out in dusty despair with extremely few even probable instances of schizophrenic-like cases. Their reports of paranoid or depressive syndromes are scarce, too. They fail to depict character disorders in even those instances where the society itself recognized them. But in all cases behaviors which these syndromes manifested were shaped by culture, at least in some external respects if not in basic dynamisms, and these latter tended to be badly veiled or ignored in the publications. However, anthropologists' professional literature does list, for example, "arctic hysteria" among some Siberian pastoralists of Tsarist times; windigo psychosis around the northern shores of the North American Great Lakes among Algonkin food-gatherers; Japan's much discussed and maybe not so well understood stylization, hara-kiri, of a suicidal depression which contains, to be sure, central themes of extreme upperclass gentility and ethics and of violent aggression turned in against the self; and Malaya's running amok, an apparently similar set of dynamisms but with far less gentility and with aggression acted out in a publicly frightfully gory onslaught against others first and then against the self.

In recent years, ethnographers were able to note additional but still badly reported upon "ethnic psychoses," so-called. Each seems to have been a culturally stylized form of acting out against self, others, or both. A sufferer's capacity to continue to relate to people was so damaged or weakened that he must retreat, or the society did what made him retreat from the reality of customary social relationships. Perhaps he withdrew in a stylized finale of suicide, or in semi-finales of exile or hermit-like isolation. He might resort to transvestitism, where he assumed garb and roles of the opposite sex so that he did not have to tackle difficulties, for him, of relating to people in ways customarily assigned to his sex. He might adopt a shamanistic role or other socially permitted devices.

It is likely that exotic social systems long provided precise roles into which most persons with trends toward psychotic withdrawal and regression could retire. Western civilization has done so, too, for many persons. But it long offered most of its psychotically, that is, most intolerably disturbed people a straightjacket in an asylum or, recently, hospitalization, hydrotherapy, insulin or electrotherapy, and psychiatric treatment. Apart from western civilization, an outstanding recourse for individuals who were breaking with reality was to offer them a sanctioned but divergent role in social life. In it their hostility, paranoia, hallucinations, need to change self-identity, and the like were permissible. They could receive acceptance in that new role at the same time that their urge toward aggression, for example, was maintained. But it was held by a kind of cultural leash. This way out for a schizophrenic, paranoid, or personality disorder-like set was to assume one or another kind of shamanlike role.

If this theory is right, the leash and the role outlet were both worldwide and an admirable way to beat a retreat. It was extraordinarily efficient since most or all societies provided it without friction or doubts. Neither straightjackets nor hospitals, not even tranquilizers, were needed. Only a special profession and role were called for and, above all, acceptance by a great many or, more often, by everybody. A potential patient merely altered his self-identity and reinterpreted his relationships to everyone else. Everyone thought this was according to Hoyle. Nothing was more therapeutic to a sufferer than unanimous acceptance of his new role, even if his community granted it with misgivings and tension. A new shaman was usually cause for rejoicing in all quarters except the medical profession itself. Already established medical gentry, that is, shamans, might become alarmed at fresh competition. Some interesting pulling, tugging, and hauling might ensue among jealous medicos, especially the entrenched older ones, with the community standing by with mouths agape and, in most instances, delighted at a shamanistic contest about to develop. Who wouldn't enjoy watching two of the less comely psychoanalysts, one old and the other somewhat younger, in a public wrestling match?

Shamans have certainly not all been psychotic in one or another way, any more than all surgeons, chiropodists, and psychoanalysts are upset individuals. But no one can doubt the availability, in thousands of societies, of a shamanistic or medical role for a person with psychotic trends. Nor can there be doubt that some shamans who were extremely aberrant in personality found a haven in the role. They could live out their lives in it with episodic sadistic and masochistic satisfactions and with security arising in community fear and acceptance of them. If a trend to withdrawal from reality were deep in a shaman's personality, he could dwell somewhat apart and keep defensively occupied under his eyebrows with his fantasies. But freedom to remain withdrawn without hurtful criticism or resentment, and the ultimate circumstance of acceptance of him in his professional role, account for his stabilization in a new network of social functions and a new fabric of self-identity. This was how an occasional shaman maintained receipt of satisfactions where these were too stressful to obtain before his assumption of shaman role. From the point of view of his society, he was not becoming sicker and sicker and, in fact, he was not sick at all, although much the same bundle of mechanisms in him produced a recognized class of syndromes in modern western civilization. In other words, many psychotic-like individuals resided in nonwestern societies before the advent of Europeans. But often such persons were not tagged as sick. In a number of regions, shamans were not sick by any overt clinical criteria such as change of self-identity, regression, and withdrawal from social relationships. It is almost astonishing to realize that most of the world's societies were able to put some of their most cantankerous or hostile people, mentally extremely ill only from the standpoint of a Euro-American who perceives the mechanisms of defense operating within them, into roles which society welcomed as acceptable, productive, or creative.

This is not to say that in nonwestern societies no people were identified as mentally ill. There are reports of psychotic-like individuals who, for reasons about which data are insufficient, failed to receive a union card of enrollment in the shaman's profession, or who were already too removed from reality to negotiate a culturally prescribed initiation into shamanism. These were very likely frightfully sick people and recognized as such in their society. Recently, the few anthropologists who have found such individuals said that they might be isolated, for example, in huts apart from a community or otherwise tolerated, fed, and watched at a distance, but hardly lived with.

A principal difficulty in fashioning a system of cross-cultural theory about mental pathology is not only that reports of syndromes are poor and few. Indeed, syndrome reports alone are insufficient for devising a structure of theory. An undetermined percentage of syndromes and cases which, in constituent mechanisms and patternings, paralleled syndromes and cases clinically known in Euro-American psychiatry, were handled quietly and efficiently in other cultures by channeling sufferers into stylized and acceptable, even wanted, roles. Euro-American society, of course, does precisely the same thing. It does not identify, much less hospitalize, all those who by modern psychiatric criteria have a full-blown psychotic syndrome. Euro-American society also permits great numbers of persons to resolve tensions or to stalk away from reality, even regress, in special roles which are widely tolerated or approved. In fact, everyone really appreciates the circumstance that psychotic trends are evident in a few individuals in many respected professions, indeed in just the professions where the nature of the work offers channels for sadistic manipulation of other people, for ventilation of aggression, or for withdrawal into cubby holes. This is not to say, for example, that all men who apply for jobs as electrocutioners, cyanide manipulators, or hangmen in state prisons have potentials to be psychotics or are psychotics. Or that forest lookouts, lighthouse tenders, and night watchmen generally display such characteristics. The point is that the society does allot professions and roles which are especially suited for such individuals should they apply. When they take on the roles, they can enjoy a long equilibrium, raise a family, and manage a checking account at the bank. The role and community acceptance tend to protect them against further deterioration. They stabilize or get better.

Psychiatry, then, is really hopeless if it aspires to a cross-cultural theory based upon reports of neurotic and psychotic syndromes as such. This is because many syndromes get lost, in a manner of speaking, in accepted roles and ways of living. The matrix of the society hides the syndromes.

On the other hand, a cross-cultural theory based upon close study of neurotic and psychotic single mechanisms, not syndrome types which are visible and publicly labeled, is both needed and possible. Careful studies of all kinds of people in a nonwestern society, not merely the few who have been set aside as sick, will reveal much about withdrawal, regression, displacement, projection, and so on. What has to be done is to explore and report upon these and other mechanisms operative in various societies, no matter how culturally accepted the individuals who are studied. Then psychological anthropology will find out where stresses existed in social systems, how people responded, what were the causes of and ways of pulling away from reality, in what circumstances the mechanisms operated, and, later, how they wove together into patterns something like one or the other of the familiar Euro-American syndromes. There is no easy shortcut, by way of listing syndromes like arctic hysteria, running amok, or windigo, to a cross-cultural structure of theory about psychopathology. The road is a long one and requires field investigations of mechanisms in many persons who have been functioning in intolerable and accepted ways in their societies.

## SUGGESTIONS FOR FURTHER READING

M. K. Opler has edited a relevant volume, *Culture and Mental Health* (New York: Macmillan, 1959). See also his *Culture, Psychiatry, and Human Values* (Springfield, Ill.: C. C. Thomas, 1956). Pornographers and their publishers have long tortured or titillated sectors of the reading public with culture-bound nonsense dispensed in profitable volumes. It purports to deal with sexual aberrancies but is only a mass of projections generated in guilty minds. The cross-cultural pornography literature reveals much about sickness in its authors' society and little about any other society.

# 9. SOCIAL BEHAVIOR AND APPEARANCE

## Etiquette

Proper manners comprise important expressive materials to which few ethnographers have paid attention and upon which almost none have reported in detail. A method is necessary for analysis of a culture's heritage of stylizations of expected public and private social demeanor, of etiquette rules toward supernaturals, too. The problem is to identify their meaningful units or segments and connect them with a culture's positive, anxious, or defensive sentiments about social relationships. There may also be ties with its values in esthetic excellence and creativity. Maybe it is trite to observe that every nonliterate society had a repertoire, a big one, of etiquette rules, if they can be called rules. Most likely, few were translated out of actions into so many words except when aliens exhibited different etiquette.

Etiquette always embodies several kinds or classes of behavior. Each should be examined separately so that meaningful units of a class are exposed with clarity and their expressive functions displayed.

One kind is postural. It includes closeness to or distance from another person; standing in one or another posture, sitting, squatting, or snuggling; facial posture—averting gaze or looking at the other's middle or feet, or his face, mouth, or eyes; handling of lips, nose, arms and hands, and the like. Age grade, sex, status, and kind of group assembled are factors connecting with each unit of postural expression.

Another category of etiquette covers speech. Conversational rules among nonliterate folk varied with proper talk to mate, children, parents, elders, headmen, in-laws, non-kin or visitors, supernaturals, and the dead. One must not omit a connection of each speech rule with sex of speaker and of person addressed.

Some distinctive units of postural and speech etiquette have been especially easy for outsiders to observe early in their field work. For example, a visitor might enter a house and be properly received only by seated residents of the house (postural rule) who said precisely nothing (speech rule) until some time after the visitor had also sat and arranged himself comfortably (postural rule). After what seems to a Euro-American like a remarkably long, if not exhausting, silence (speech rule), a house elder might say some completely stylized nothing such as "So you have come." Again, by requirement of a speech rule, the visitor might be able to respond only

232

with another stylization which was virtually of zero expressive content such as, "Yes." In conversation with close kin, speech etiquette might allow interruptions before completion of an utterance; with elders, visitors, or non-kin, a person must be allowed to finish what he was saying without interruption. Whereupon an auditor sensed the etiquette rule which permitted him to pontificate in his turn, without the slightest likelihood of verbal interposition or distraction short of an earthquake. Or, etiquette might require that an auditor repeat verbatim every phrase, maybe in a stylized monotone. Or, each utterance must be responded to with some stylized vocable, something like "Aha."

If a host spilled food or drink over a visitor, the host's kin might be required to utter delicate laughs, or turn their heads, or dash about seeking materials with which to clean up the mess, or speak apologetically. It depended on the etiquette rule, and there was always one available in the storehouse of prescribed, indicated, and proper actions.

Manners might require complete avoidance of certain persons by means of physical distance; avoiding of disrobing or eating in the other's presence; partial avoidance by not looking, responding, or conversing except through a third person; and exceedingly mild avoidance by lowering the voice, substituting monotone for tonal rise and fall, or using pseudo-elegant or somewhat hypocritical speech style with distinctive phrase melody contours. Possibilities seem numberless. So, too, were prescribed joking, teasing, buffoonery, and badinage requirements, all of them etiquette centered, and both nonwestern and western peoples possessed them. It appears that etiquettes which required an opposite of drollery, that is, out-and-out avoidance down to prescribed embarrassment about exposure of portions of one's anatomy, and resort to mild-mannered speech, applied especially often to in-law relationships where sexual tensions and anxieties about acceptance and resolution of humiliation were potentially great. Etiquette, then, offered classes of stylized means of defending against possibly troublesome situations. Each means may be regarded as a minimal unit for purposes of scientific analyses.

Rules of manners, of course, receive categorization which cuts across the postural and speech categories of etiquette units, in terms of age grade, sex, kinship, and other relationship, friendship, and visitor boundaries. Additional behavioral stylizations featured ceremonial occasions, council meetings, and raconteur sessions. Siblings frequently adhered to rules of manners which determined just how they played, dressed, and bathed together, or looked at or spoke to each other at various ages. Prepubescents from nine or ten years of age and on might have to behave in special ways in the presence of the opposite sex of the same age grade. Here a defensive maneuver which a culture stylized rather obviously resolved intensification of sexual relationships which might become difficult.

All etiquette rules were stylizations. Therefore, they were already prepared, one might say precooked items, each with accompanying dressings and condiments. They functioned in many ways but, as already indicated, notably as defenses in relationships which effected tensions. They also functioned to release people from the effort of thinking afresh through each moment's relationships and tribulations. If one had to cerebrate every minute about what to say or when not to say it, what to feel or not to feel, how to grimace or when to look sad or stony faced, when and how long and how firmly to hold another's hand, arm, neck, or what not, the day would be about as fatiguing as it is to the American school teacher in a fourth grade class of infantilized and hyperactive ten-year olds or the ultra-conscientious psychoanalyst who is on the alert lest he mishandle a single petty detail of relationship with his patient. People have to be guarded in a thousand ways about other people, especially their closest kin and mate's kin. Such care might be all the more necessary in societies of lowly economic level. Relationships are easier and tepid, even possibly in smaller numbers of minimal units, in cities where few persons know each other or are related as kin, in-laws, or close neighbors.

Etiquette items, then, are those culturally readymade rules and niceties, perhaps thousands, which regulate posture, voice, utterance, feeling, serving of foods and drink, giving of gifts, exchanging of commodities, and the like, which minimize gaucheries or downright dangerous errors in relationships, and which maximize each person's comfort, privacy, and feelings of being respected and accepted. All the items, the whole elaborate language or grammar of them, connect with tensions, immediate or potential, created by a social system and in a broad sense function to ameliorate or ward off those tensions. They are applications of anesthetic, topically administered and inexpensive. Where a social system is highly stratified, additional categories of manners put each social level in its place, enhance the security and ego-identity of those who are at higher levels, and express with veiled sadism the often irrevocable subservience of those who occupy lowly stations.

If these discussions were addressed to thoroughgoing rather than only partial Victorians, it would be necessary to add that there is no known connection between petticoats, G-strings, and other items of dress or undress, that is, customary nakedness or its opposite, and elaborateness of a culture's catalogue of manners. Modesty is culturally labeled. It exhibits no universals. Food-gathering peoples of tropical locales might exhibit as complex a structure of etiquette as do any other peoples, although bowing and kowtowing stylizations constituted units in classes of etiquette forms which appear to have been especially magnified in the most stratified societies.

Just about nothing is known, at least from direct field reports from non-western peoples, regarding causes and functions of changes in manners. In western culture such modifications have evidently been rapid since the Industrial Revolution, the burgeonings of cities, generations of democratic frontier relationships, rapid rise in the status of women, and other social factors of new kinds. A person need not be eightiesh to report upon many metamorphoses in manners. For example, the 1910 and earlier rule of rising for an adult female in a crowded public conveyance all but disappeared within a generation. Now elderly women often hang grimly and with much self-pity onto posts and straps while young men comfortably seated read sports, the funnies, *Playboy*, or the *Manchester Guardian*. A Victorian requirement that a male doff his hat to a passing female adolescent or adult survives for older adult females but exhibits severe weakening even toward them. No American any longer lifts his hat to a teenager. Who has heard of a modern Sir Walter Raleigh who hurled his fine topcoat into a slushy street for the sake of a lady's threatened opera pumps? The etiquette of sexual segregation in privately endowed schools and colleges appears to be in its final decades; it disappeared in publicly supported educational institutions in recent years. Lavatories for Ladies and Gentlemen are obsolescent; the verbal rule now requires only Women and Men. A volume could be written on the innumerable units of behavior and speech in the winged changes of etiquette of premarital courtship and sex, their historical causes, functional connections with a rising status of females, and expressive significance.

Studies of alterations in manners among acculturating food-gatherers and economically primitive agriculturalists are absent in the archives of anthropology, although other kinds of acculturational research in such societies have been numerous.

Deserving but still ignored topics treating of cultural expressions are embarrassingly many. One wonders why so many research workers are fascinated, rightly too, by analysis, for example, of phoneme and morpheme patterns in linguistics and kinship structures in social organization, but block at analysis of manners and many other types of expressive units and their patternings. Maybe because it is easy to show overt designs of linguistic and kinship units at a time when almost no one exhibits a need to probe deeply in order to connect them with psychological processes for the sake of exploring covert matters. But it would be manifestly ridiculous to work at a structural-functional-expressive analysis of etiquette without manipulation of psychological variables. At this point in the mid-twentieth century, it still looks forbiddingly difficult and so almost no one has tried intensive study of it in a nonliterate society.

## Wearing Apparel and Body Decoration

There is a nice continuum in problems of analysis and theory from etiquette through wearing apparel and body ornament onto plastic and graphic art. Changes in all of them, that is, fashions in garments, ornaments, and designs require study, too.

During and since the nineteenth century, museum collectors played a noble role in efforts to collect apparel from every part of the nonwestern world. They also obtained dolls, which usually represented adult dress and ornaments. But a system of scientific knowledge is only spurred and facilitated, not effected, by dedicated gathering, delivery, cataloging, and exhibiting of things. Every collected item calls for a question and answer technique in the field before packaging for delivery to a museum, a requirement which professional museum personnel have fulfilled only spottily. That is, museum acquisitions of apparel are tangible enough and that is good. But they are too often unknown in their functioning and expressive features. A system of theory about wearing apparel still awaits proper field interviewing in a good sample of the world's societies. It is, indeed, late to start working toward such theory because acculturation has almost everywhere weakened craftsmanship and altered functions, sentiments, and standards. Museum holdings and a kind of myopic analysis of materials, craftsmanship, and designs can provide little of the pyramiding of statements to comprise a structure of scientific theory about apparel as a cultural expression.

Methodology in the devising of systematic theory about any cultural expression calls initially for prudent, not blindly atomistic, segmentation into its principal kinds of content, then determination of relationships of each kind to everything else in the heritage, and finally study of formal or stylistic matters. For apparel, kinds of content in wearing apparel may be suggested as follows. First, materials employed (fiber, fur, hides, shells, quills, feathers, etc.). Second, implements used (clam shell and stone knives, ferrous cutting tools in Africa, awls, needles, scrapers, looms). Third, eye-hand coordinations and rhythmic or other manipulations. Fourth, types of apparel—headgear, headbands and belts, footwear, larger garments, and so on.

The concept of apparel should serve in its broadest sense. It should, therefore, include hair tonsure or styling; ear, nose, and lip ornaments; rings, anklets, bracelets, and necklaces; tattooing and scarification; face and body colorings, and doubtless other classes of things. Materials, technique of manufacture, and expressive design units or motifs of each type of body ornamentation should be ascertained exactly as for caps, belts, headbands, footgear, and garments.

Each unitary item of material, artifact, and manipulation must be connected with a society's technology, economy, sexual and other division of labor, and with relevant features of social organization and religion. Each must be linked, too, with the handling of childhood learning about manufacture and design of apparel.

There is need to study the way in which a culture encouraged approach to mastery of manufacturing technique, and to release from technical difficulties with materials, techniques, and management of expressive content so that a producer was especially stimulated to change and invent.

There is need to collect field data on a culture's value ideals about apparel, and on its own artists' and craftsmen's judgments of quality, excellence, or artistry, in partially or wholly finished items.

Study is wanted of factors making for imperceptible change and conscious or creative change in materials, implements used, manipulations, development of craftsmen, and values in products. That is, there is need for analyses of changes in fashions in apparel together with special studies of borrowers and creative innovators.

Comparatively speedy changes in apparel—so-called changes in fashion —probably featured well-to-do and urban classes of the past four or five centuries of western civilization and recent centuries of acculturation in nonwestern societies. Causes for such rapid fluctuations in fashion resided in a complex of factors which include successive technological innovations, European expansion over the planet, extraordinary increments of wealth in Euro-American society's upper classes, and decline of guilds with development of burgher entrepreneur, wage-labor, seamstress-dressmaker, and hired-designer apparel production for a market. Continued, although ever veiled, sexual-commodity and subservient status of women, and maintenance of tensions around her social participations and permissible behavior in courtship, have resulted in or reinforced emphasis upon competitive creativity in her apparel. Progressive approach toward equality in status of the sexes, lessening female subservience and passivity, and women's increased capacity to be rejecting of beaux may comprise factors, apart from devices of manufacturers themselves, in a developing variety and speed of change in men's garb. Pre-Renaissance societies and nonwestern cultures, in general, were comparatively slow to change both sexes' apparel, at least over time stretches such as a number of decades.

Feelings of embarrassment attach only to lack of items or designs that cover or decorate parts of anatomy which, at the moment, carry a tension load. When custom and fashion have long exposed breasts, navels, or buttocks, shielding them may be incongruous, embarrassing, or humiliating because such hiding has become socially disapproved or unfashionable. The converse operates, too. Exposure of a portion of anatomy when it has long been unseen because of internalization of elders' values at once generates tension; it is embarrassing or humiliating.

Anatomy as a field of scientific investigation defines primary and secondary sexual characteristics. A nonwestern culture's definitions were not necessarily identical with those of western science. Western civilization's ethics around sex defines what is permissible, impermissible, or sinful in exposure of parts of the body such as nipples, nose, mouth, navel, or toes. Nonwestern cultures may define them as sexually charged features. Western civilization lately allowed public display of earlier concealed anatomical areas. Earlier nonvisible portions of anatomy are seen in urban and stylized situations provided by lavatories, locker rooms, pools, burlesque houses, red-light districts, special kinds of parties, college summer sessions, and at beaches and dances. Here a culture's former values which contained non-scientific definitions of sexual features have become limited or shelved.

Esthetic responses to nonwestern peoples' garb, hair styling, ornaments, cicatrization, or tattooing have been familiar phenomena in western civilization. An anthropologist's assessment of such Euro-American reactions is that they contribute nothing meaningful regarding esthetic values in nonwestern apparel. They reveal only current attitudes in western culture. For example, sculptured head hair in a Melanesian group may be reacted to by analogy with contemporary Euro-American canons of utilization of masses and surfaces in wood and stone sculpture. On the other hand, a body of reliable theory regarding esthetic values in nonwestern apparel and appearance will be possible only after intensive analysis of both such nonwestern expressions and the elicitation of much critical commentary by natives themselves.

## Cleanliness

One of the most dangerous things in contemporary western society is to be in a small plane which has nonwestern travelers whose body odor may cause the pilot to faint. Not long ago, Euro-Americans produced similar reactions in those parts of the world where custom decreed frequent bathing and where the food intake was distinctive. Recent ancestors of Euro-Americans lacked the indoor plumbing which rapidly, during the last century and a half, made it easy for those people to become addicts of soap and water. Of course, body odor is partly a consequence of diet and diet is often a more decisive factor in body odor than washing. Various foods such as milk, butter, and cheese are responsible for exudation of butyric, valeric, and other volatile acids which present appalling odors. A population whose members share these or other atrocious effluvia becomes unaware of them so that only outsiders who carry a different array of odors respond unhappily.

This is not the place to discuss psychoanalytic or other hypotheses regarding compulsive or other feelings around aliens' body odor or reactions to cleanliness as such. It is sufficient to suggest that customs of daily immersion were unlikely in desert, subdesert, or arctic areas, and that until lately the world's most frequently wetted bodies were not Euro-Americans'. Many Amazonian, Caribbean, and Oceanian peoples endured olfactory tortures, apart from other pains they suffered, when the infrequently washed and hideous smelling Europeans first arrived in their midst. Even today Americans, who are extraordinarily more pressured to bathe than were their great-grandparents, build defenses against feelings of unworthiness by means of utilization of dry cleaning establishments and, therefore, often find highly cultivated Europeans' clothing unpleasantly odoriferous. An anthropologist of middle-class origin by no means enjoys a completely delightful field research, contrary to surmises of laymen about him. Research in an environment of uncustomary and redolent vapors may produce estimable advances in a science but at some cost to the research worker's appetite and waistline. A reader who doubts this and assumes that field research is wholly romantic is urged to climb or stagger uphill or just trot along after a file of contemporary natives whom this author feels should remain anonymous. The point would have applied also to Euro-Americans' pungent ancestors of not many generations ago. Internalization of values about halitosis, hair pomades, body odors, armpit shaving, washing, and cleanliness occurs early in a person's life and such values root deeply. Anthropologists need to find out how and why they develop and how they function in the nonwestern world.

# 10. HUMOR AND TRAGEDY

## Introduction to Humor

It is trite to say that all peoples enjoyed the luxury of verbal sallies that were funny. It is not yet a commonplace to observe that many nonwestern peoples appear to have chuckled more often, in reaction both to pleasantries and situations, than masses of Euro-Americans. Language and cultural barriers in addition to grumpiness, sullenness, incapacity to relate acceptingly to other persons, and an obstinate brand of culture bondedness hinder Euro-American awareness of other peoples' outlets in humor. Even Americans are relatively so fearful and serious that it seems as if they have perpetuated an almost classic projection in their grim-faced great-grandparents' stereotype of an invariably dour Plains Indian. Ethnographers have learned, the time consuming way, that Plains and almost all other American Indians were as prone as any peoples to quip and giggle except in the presence of those whom they distrusted and disliked.

Smiles and laughter are customary responses to an enormous range of situations. They appear after milder accidents and hardships, mistakes, clumsiness, and petty failures, silly pretense, pomposity, and a thousand other incongruous kinds of behavior. They are stirred by snores, sneezes, and innumerable types of posturings and situations in addition to their generation by means of wit. But it is evident that all peoples smile after observations and in circumstances where others do not. Humor responses that patently serve needs in one society often fail to receive employment for those needs in another.

A handful of modern writers, notably Henri Bergson, Sigmund Freud, and Max Eastman, whose outlook and cultural heritage were wholly Euro-American have attempted to locate factors which everywhere generate a fun response. Like many other initiators of systems of social and psychological theory, especially during the nineteenth century, pioneer thinkers on humor at once grappled with the subject as a totality before evidences had reached their desks regarding worldwide manifestations of the phenomenon. Statements appeared that rested on no more evidence than what went on in the neighborhood, that is, in western civilization. Still, they had merit as starting hypotheses because they pointed to some of the psychological mechanisms and to incongruity as a noteworthy feature of humor. Whatever a cross-cultural comparison, which is not yet possible, may reveal, devising of a system of scientific theory about humor, its causes, forms, sociopsychological services, and changes among the world's peoples has hardly commenced. One wonders if almost all among some tens of thousands of behavioral scientists since the mid-nineteenth century found the subject too difficult to handle even for humor of western civilization. Or, a comparative long-facedness of Euro-Americans and their anxiety about lusty forms of laughter blocked development of interest in significant exploration of the topic. Possibly it is the mathematical compulsion of positivist cohorts in academic psychology and sociology which stands in the way of their engaging in a frontal transcultural attack upon a kind of behavior which, on the face of it, does not look like promising material for such as they. In humor what, indeed, can be counted reliably apart from frequencies of audible laughs?

As in many instances of omissions in their field work, even the most sensitive and accepting among the cultural anthropologists, persons who might have been expected to have written some notes about this subject, almost always returned with nothing about it. But their oral testimony that informants and interpreters were often full of fun has been unanimous. Since the 1890's, when subjects such as native technology, social structure, cults, languages, and acculturative processes constituted important topics to pursue on field expeditions, humor remained unimportant and ignored. There is something almost alarming about such refusal to examine a kind of behavior which is as evident as kinship, cult, or phonemic patterning.

Although ancestors of modern peoples were sufficiently brainy to devise artifacts of stone over a half million years ago, knowledge of psychological characteristics which had developed in those early eras is so infinitesimal that speculation about the earliest time and manner of employment of humor is unbecoming. We can be sure only about the validity of a generalized kind of statement that laughter has resolved feelings for many tens, if not hundreds, of thousands of years. There is no likelihood that advances such as those from food-gathering to agricultural ways of life, or basic changes in family and community forms, introduced significantly new classes of traits that stirred up fun.

As in most considerations about features and processes in cultural expressions, advances in their scientific knowledge hinge upon partitioning them into distinctive chunks and contrasting slices which most fruitfully reveal how they operate and structure. For humor, that also means field researches in the many nonwestern cultures which survived into the twentieth century.

## Research Method

Therefore, since such research has not yet been undertaken, what is left to say at the present time? What can a pioneer scientific observer of the phenomenon do? As everywhere in scientific procedure, apt selection of and accurate depiction of probably pertinent descriptive material comes first. Literary materials which contain humorous items from the past are unemployable because audience and reader responses were not also written out. Grins, smiles, and guffaws were not cited. Therefore, only twentieth century peoples deserve initial study. A perhaps too simple suggestion is that it is necessary during many days of field research to make note of relevant features of the setting preceding each occasion of laughter, to characterize participants, to record exact words they employed, and to relate their varying responses. Every day scores of such fun situations may be delineated. Where sound on film can be used a report may be repeated and analysis corroborated or corrected more easily. Children's humor should be recorded, also humor generated by and responded to by adult males, adult females, older men and older women, by members of different occupational and class groups, too. Different ages, sexes, and social strata may laugh at different times. Any anthropological field research of some weeks or months, even without sound on film, could yield detailed notes on hundreds if not a few thousands of fun situations for pioneer scientific purposes, although recorded in longhand.

Dissection out and arrangement of component contrastive features of such materials should proceed at once in the field, with further interrogation of informants about their feelings and responses. Subsequently, mathematical manipulations of components of each fun situation would corroborate, perhaps also sharpen up, deductions about causation, humor content, and its social functioning. This is a counsel of what might be done. But it has never been done. No anthropologist appears to have gleaned field notes of such a kind, of such needed quantity and variety, much less with the always requisite follow-up questions. Cross-cultural differences in humor responses and services cannot be seen and a system of scientific theory of humor advanced very far until field reports and analyses of such a kind have been made on several peoples of distinctive sociocultural heritages.

## Patterns and Components of Humor

Still, the humor of western civilization is sufficiently well known, and a bare beginning of examination of nonwestern humor has been ventured, to warrant tentative deductions and starting formulations.

In every fun situation causes of laughter are multiple. No laughter response arises in a single cause or combination of only two or three. A cluster of sufficient stimuli precedes each laugh and it appears to number six, seven, or many more parts. In every instance, they comprise a fabric of extremely rapidly woven items: these are kinds of minimal units most of which are presented or manipulated without conscious awareness, that is, without ability to pinpoint and denote them in words. In addition, and doubtless in most fun situations, lack of fit, irrelevance, or incongruity of such a pattern, or of parts of it, in relation to reality or to the customary provides a special and over-all laughter-causing factor. In a way, it embraces the several units in the pattern. The causal factors, units, and over-all incongruity function as a total stimulus, an unanalyzed perception, which briefly relieves a spot of tension in human life in general or in a local social setting. Some factors, especially the element of incongruity, in a fabric of humor appear to be universal. Other factors are not universal but arise in anxiety-producing features which are peculiar to a culture or region.

One example of a laughter-provoking fabric from western civilization may help to clarify these observations. Ivan asks Dmitri what he will do when nuclear bombs fall. Dmitri says, "I'll put on a shroud and stroll slowly toward the nearest graveyard." Ivan asks, "Why go slowly?" Dmitri says, "I don't want to cause a panic." This fun situation (or did you fail to grin?) contains at least the following minimal units: (1) a defensive response of laughter lessens the unimaginable *horror* of a nuclear explosion and carnage; (2) defensive laughter occurs again but at the hardly bearable prospect of *personal annihilation*; (3) laughter develops as a release with realization that one has improperly identified self with a *corpse* in a shroud; (4) laughter occurs at *ghosts* which terrorize only backward people; (5) laughter is generated by *ineptitude*: observe the deliberate and *incongruous* reference to a slow pace when speed is needed and, indeed, inevitable; (6) *incongruity* appears again in the notion that the victim is responsible for panic when the bomb itself would create panic; (7) *lack of fit or appropriateness* arises in the question "Why go slowly?" when a more likely question anyone might ask would be, for example, "Why go toward a cemetery?"

Global laughter-generating units enclosed in this pattern may be 1, 2, 5, 6, and 7 above. All peoples the world over may respond similarly to these five stimuli. On the other hand units 3 and 4 are culturally created. They could appear in societies which believe in ghosts of the special kinds projected by people of western civilization. Of course, a shroud is a cultural artifact which may not be found among many peoples.

Again, every fun situation reveals universal and culturally idiosyncratic components. This is why many of the things, people, customs, or situations which one sociocultural group laughs at may be only slightly or not at all funny in another. Therefore, humor can be translated only if it is sliced into units and the culturally induced, hence locally distinctive, ones are carefully annotated in order to render them intelligible to bearers of another heritage.

Numberless specifically cultural items in nonwestern societies weave in with universal ones to produce laughter. There are peoples who tend to laugh, forthwith, at mere mention of certain animals and insects, females, elderly persons, feebler deities or supernaturals, blindness, amputations and other disfigurement, drowning, and imminence of murder. Examples from western civilization of laughter units that are cultural rather than universal include stuttering, hunchbacks, belching, senatorial bombast, and a vast array of personality types, each of which requires further analysis, such as Mr. Micawber, Mr. Magoo, and Stepinfetchit. Incidentally, the last-named individual of movie fame stirs less amusement in audiences than he did 20 years ago: values and tensions modify rapidly in swiftly changing cultural heritages. Sometimes a laughter-breeding factor of a generation before seems only tragic and provocative of guilt feelings a generation later. After the nineteenth century, disfigurements and hunchbacks also rapidly lessened as laughter formative items.

Like a scientific linguist's lengthy lists of possible consonant and vowel sounds, some few of which function as phonemes in the phonemic structure of a single language, the following lists suggest possible laughter-creating stimuli. The first table cites likely worldwide stimuli, each of which may also be colored by local cultural factors. The second table suggests stimuli, a great many of which occur in western civilization, that set off laughter in one or more culture regions and are probably not universal. They are patently more concretely defined than items inventoried in the first table.

Phonemic systems range from something less than 20 to as many as 60 segmental consonant and vowel phonemes and possibly average, for the world's 3,000 or more languages, somewhere in the upper twenties to lower thirties. So, too, discrete units which weave into the distinctive fabric which comprises each humor situation probably range from 6 or 7 to as many as 13 to 15. The world average of components within each laugh moment may be somewhere in between.

To be sure, statements about such matters are premature, if not naïve, in the light of absence of efficient segmentation of a satisfactorily large and properly annotated sample of humor situations found in a nonwestern sociocultural system. There is a question whether units listed in the tables are truly minimal. Doubtless many comprise combinations of items. Indeed, it remains to be seen if the kind of analysis sketched, and kinds of units suggested, can serve to advance knowledge. Perhaps it is efficient to treat of classes of units as in grammatical sets or form classes. For example, slapstick may be a good caption for one set, language error for another, anality for still another, and so on.

## Jokes and Other Stylizations

Jokes are no more universal than cartoon drawings of kinds found in the *New Yorker*. Jokes constitute a special social procedure, an oral form of variable structurings. This form functions in and is indigenous to western civilization. Something like a few of its variant genres may be found in nonwestern cultures, possibly infrequently. Components of jokes are not distinctive, only the social occasions for them, the manner of their presentation such as at parties, when friends chat and pass the time, in speeches, and their employment in one or another stylized manner in such social situations.

## Table 1: WORLDWIDE FACTORS

a. incongruity, lack of fit
b. slapstick
regressive behavior
unusual physical prowess
cleverness
foolishness

faulty perception
forbidden behavior
evil-doer comes to grief
falsehood
hypocrisy
irony, sarcasm

understatement
exaggeration
language error
language misunderstanding
pun
vocal mannerism

musical error
dance error
repetition
progression
saturation
mimicry
onomatopeia

## Table 2: CULTURALLY CONDITIONED FACTORS

special animal or special insect: donkey, mule, camel, monkey, flea, etc.
anal reference
bad odor
body odor
feces
diarrhea
halitosis
flatulence
odor of urine
belching
drooling
sneezing
nasal mucus
hiccups
burning
choking, loss of breath
drowning
darkness
death
fright
fear of height
horror reaction
escape from danger
fainting, unconsciousness
resourcefulness, skill
sleight-of-hand, Houdini-like trick
female

older woman
older man
vanity, narcissism
clown
naïveté, gullibility
ignorance
stupidity, incompetence
immaturity, childishness
timidity, cowardice
lower class, lower caste
slave, servant
scapegoat; racial, national or cultural minority; Negro, Irish, Mormon, Catholic, Protestant, Jew, Swede, Greek, Italian, Mexican, Chinaman, professor, boy scout, music teacher, Salvation Army, missionary, revivalist preacher, beggar, male beautician, social worker,

politician
tenor, coloratura, soprano, basso profundo
beatnik, "Bohemian"
unfamiliar musical instrument
eccentricity
sexual reference
eunuch
large genitals
pendulous breasts
"perversion"
rape
Don Juanism
virginity in adult
disguise in dress
unconventional dress: pigtail, zoot-suit, long fingernails
unconventional item of diet
supernatural or miraculous transformation
pigmy stature
diminutive size
giantism
mutilation
disfigurement
physical pathology
unusual posture, gait
unusual gesture

physical unattractiveness of specific kind
shivering
hysterical behavior
finding valuable object
greed
loss of personal possession
futile search
penuriousness
compulsive orderliness or cleanliness
disorder, disarray, sloppiness
personality or character disorder
hermit, rustic
be lost
drunkenness
overeating, excessive orality
humiliation
victory
thieving, dishonesty
stammering
foreign language
special linguistic form, e.g., diminutive, augmentative

Western civilization's joke form functions, too, in competitions between friends who vie in recital of the largest number and most comical of fun situations, many or most of which are contrived rather than real. Emphases in joke inventories and recitals appear to change about as rapidly as fashions in dress. The so-called "sick" components (mutilations, tragic ends) of jokes of a few years ago are less frequent today. Joke recitals and competitions have rarely or never been reported upon outside of western civilization. The stylized over-all form itself is certainly a distinctive projective expression found in one society which employs the form, with its variant and ever changing genres, as a means of ventilating a variety of feelings. It also effects certain special relationships between members of a group who tell and listen to jokes.

Western civilization is so markedly distinctive in its technology, wealth, subcultures, and specialization in production and distribution that it is subject to efflorescences of forms of many expressive kinds. No wonder, then, that in western civilization joke genres are supplemented by many other genres of humor, especially those dependent upon writing and printing. Newspaper and magazine cartoon artists are specialists in a form of humorous expression which is already over a century old. Comic strips of newspapers are not quite so venerable but also precede the twentieth century. The humorist writer-commentator of nineteenth century and later books and newspapers is a familiar phenomenon of western culture, from long before Mr. Dooley to those who have followed James Thurber. Specialists in this form or macrogenre have provided a heterogeneous inventory of humor styles or genres.

Farces and comedies have featured the European theater during a period of over 400 years. Predecessors of these intergrading macrogenres trace back to pre-Christian eras. The American minstrel show of two or more generations ago was a farce genre which exhibited novel features of content and stylization in the black-face comedian, incongruously made up and played only by a Caucasian. The American burlesque theater genre contained its special stereotypes of funny personalities, especially the comedian who referred to homosexual interests in himself and whose several appearances on the stage provided a none-too-subtle, incongruous, and, therefore, humorous contrast to feminine choral nudity and solo strippers who generated only heterosexual responses in the predominantly male audience.

Circus clowns offer an ancient genre. Its antiquity is suggested by the great range of cartoonlike personality stereotypes represented, a variety that could have developed only over a long period and in a venerable heritage of specialists. It is of remarkable interest that female circus clowns are unknown in recent generations. In the few other settings in which clowns of feminine gender arose, they lacked the notable stylizations which characterized male clowns. A rapidly rising status of females during the past century appears to have been paralleled by an increase in numbers of mildly clownlike comediennes, especially in variety, vaudeville, and light opera genres of the period. Tension around feminine rise in status may be a principal factor in comedienne humor. Clownlike actors were frequent in nonwestern rituals, dramas, and other forms of art.

A recent humor genre, with accompanying idiosyncratic personality stereotypy established by each of its few specialists, is that of the monologue entertainer, from Will Rogers over a generation ago to Mort Sahl and many minor practitioners of the 1960's. Some of these humorists and would-be humorists express themselves in gentle social criticism, as Rogers did. Others resort to much saltier commentary on the political scene as Sahl has done. During the last generation, night clubs succeeded the Broadway theater as the principal setting in which this genre functions.

Humorous Euro-American music, or spots of humor in such music, offers a variety of expressive forms. It is sufficient to cite a few compositions by Haydn and Mozart almost two centuries ago, and to observe that composers up to the present have engaged in moments of musical incongruity, that is, of humor in musical symbols. "Popular" music and performers have also resorted to incongruous, because harmlessly unconventional, features of musical content and style.

Humor in Euro-American dance forms is old, too. In recent decades one might cite Angna Enters and many others who have resorted to a genre of humorous expression with symbols fashioned by gesture, posture, and garb.

## Humor Forms as Plays

Western civilization's professional humorists who write and its clowns, comedians, comediennes, monologue performers, and other specialists who act in public before large audiences may offer stylizations which are, in each instance, a kind of theatrical play within a genre. Each specialist, whether the late Fred Allen of Allen's Alley or Jack Benny with the stylization characteristic of him and his troupe, creates or adheres to a special design. Each such design frames distinctive themes, personality stereotypes, or other components of content. It would be of interest to analyze formal beginnings, endings, rhythm and pace of speech, posturings, vocal mannerisms (for example, those of Fred Allen and Rochester), repetition-saturation devices (which are distinctive in Jack Benny), incongruous halts (again, Jack Benny and Mort Sahl are contemporary examples), and other stylistic features of performances of these specialists in humor, apart from content analysis of their verbal expressions and projected personalities. Each actor evidently offers a skit or play whose content and style are partly his own because they are congruent with the special personality structure which he has projected into his play role. The uniqueness of each public performer's play personality and of some features of the content and framing of his play is an indication of the newness of the audience humorist styles of our time. They have been replacing clown genre stylizations of earlier days, although older stylizations have tended to reappear in numbers of clown specialists.

## Functions of Humor

The world's many kinds of humor, and crystallizations in innumerable distinctive genres or styles, appear to serve principally as means of ventilating anxious and guilty feelings by way of placing together things which do not really fit. Some means of ventilation are mere punctuations of discourse. Except in literature forms, contrived jokes, and in a variety of actors like clowns and monologue performers, they are spontaneous. It is possible that in societies of least economic productivity and specialization these breaks in discourse are principal outlets of a humorous kind. In societies of great wealth and specialization, there is spontaneous humor too. But there are also a great many more or less prefashioned designs, genres, which frame humorous content. Some of them almost amount to one-scene skits or one-act or even longer plays.

Other designs, found in oral literatures of the economically lowliest peoples and in a variety of contexts in wealthier societies, are personality stereotypes which comprise incongruous juxtapositions of just a few selected traits, with one or more of which identification is possible. The class of art forms here offers various kinds of oral cartooning.

Apparently nothing in a sociocultural heritage provides so much of immediately available bits of emotional release as does humor. This in spite of kin and comrade ties and all the many kinds of projective expressions in supernaturals, world view, ethical inventories, oral literature forms, dance, and music.

It should be understood that in nonwestern societies religion and the arts functioned importantly, much more so than in Euro-American countries, to effect distractions from and release from anxieties. Nevertheless, humor was the one outlet which was available to nonwestern peoples at all times and with almost lightning speed, often in the thick of religious and esthetic situations which in western civilization would be accompanied by high seriousness and long faces. That wealthiest of societies does not always seem to serve its people as well in a quick availability of relieving banter, impromptu joshing, and impulsive commentary on people and situations. One almost wonders if the manner of living had by food-gatherers and the poorer agriculturalists was not more conducive to conversational expertese than in any wealthier and more stratified societies. Only a nice sampling of tape recordings, skillfully translated, annotated, and secured in the very next few years may ever provide a trustworthy answer about such a moot point. One formulation may be set forth: food-gatherers perhaps everywhere had a most active sense of humor.

## Excellence in Humor

Euro-Americans who are addicted to boring their acquaintances are frequently heard uttering pontifical statements such as that punning is a low form of humor. The same self-constituted authorities on what is slovenly in humor rarely clarify what they believe to be elegant or refined in that art form. A pun is that fraction of a humor situation where a lack of fit applies to employment of a homonym or a morpheme which is nearly homonymous. The linguistic incongruity is never alone. It is enclosed in a cluster of laugh-provoking factors. The reason for repetitive deprecation of punning components in humor must be sought in Euro-American sociocultural history, because a scientific posture about humor allows only disentanglement of strands in humor fabrics and determination of all their connotations and connections. At the risk of seeming to take a nihilistic or barrenly relativistic position, it may be urged that no cross-cultural measuring devices are available for assessment of worth or excellence in classes of humor units or in humor genres or styles. Each culture's estimate of excellence in its own kinds of humor offers expressive characteristics of that culture and, to be sure, they deserve study too. Apparently, each culture has fashions in the kinds of humor fabrics to which it responds with especial approval. It would seem that such fads are principal factors in the well-known incapacity of Americans, for example, to contribute a smirk, much less a smile, to many of the stimuli and styles of fun to which Burmese, Germans, Sioux Indians, or Zulus respond with howls of laughter. And, of course, Europeans and nonwestern peoples find much of the humor enjoyed by Americans to be similarly flat if not obnoxious.

A criterion of value about which everyone may be able to agree is in the sheer numbers or especially complex pyramiding of incongruities and other factors in a laugh situation. On the other hand, it seems judicious to urge that verdicts of the worth of fun situations, whether puns, simple or ornate fabrics, slapstick centered or any other kinds, have no important place in a scientific approach to humor. Since evaluations are culture-bound and relate to a culture's current tensions, ethical ideals, and fashions in humor, they also reveal only things that need study. In short, a scientific approach disallows evaluations of humor although it examines them. Scientific responsibility is primarily to discover laugh-provoking units, classes of units, styles in fabrics of them, and their connections in a sociocultural system. And when it is said, for example, that a pun caused laughter or that an amusing observation was sick humor, the denotation of the kind of humor is an emphasis or selection, coupled with a veiled evaluation, of a part pieced out of a whole. The emphasis or kind of recognition—of a pun or of sick humor—is itself an expressive phenomenon which requires explication.

## Tragedy

At the opposite end of the continuum of feelings is a response of extreme sadness. People weep wherever their culture lacks a stylized behavior to replace tears and where the culture does not have values which interdict their display. Tears of another kind are, in a sense, stylized. A culture almost automatically requires them, produces them, in a set of situations. Readers of anthropological treatises have been familiar, for example, with weeping which in some societies marks a widow's duty to mourn audibly and at appointed times of the day her recently deceased husband or child. Where peoples differ in their tears when relatives or friends depart, cultural factors may be more decisive than psychological or personality variables.

The behavior is primarily a cultural requirement and it may vary from frozen countenances to faces wet from crying. At both extremes and at points between, the proper way to act is a matter of etiquette.

Social scientists were reading 50 or more years ago that anxieties about important transitions in an individual's life are publicly ameliorated by means of *rites de passage* or crisis rites in which formalized togetherness, supernaturals, and artistic behavior combined in patterned ways to tide participants through emotionally especially difficult times. Few peoples have lacked some sort of rite to carry them through or to lighten the tragedies, indeed the horrors, of epidemics, tidal waves, forest fires, famines, fighting, and deaths. Whatever the many causes of feelings of a tragic kind, it can be said that, unlike laughter responses which are much the same in their visibility the world over, responses of a sad kind are often difficult to perceive. Sadness is easier to veil than a smile or guffaw. Required etiquette may decree keeping a stiff upper lip. It may even dictate smiles.

Overt expressions of sadness, such as the formal daily wailing cited for widows, may not always or even often represent feelings. Public simulation of tragic sentiment may be mere etiquette, custom which sometimes functions, perhaps, as a defense against anger which would arise if a mourner's emotions were made obvious.

There seems to be no reason to doubt that moods of tragedy have ensued everywhere upon injury, serious illness, or death of a person with whom one has identified or who constitutes a valued possession or extension of oneself. So positive a relationship may be with covillager, headman, master, child, mate, sibling, or respected in-law. In addition, deprivations of innumerable kinds have produced dolorous responses—loss of status, self-identity, valued possessions, home, supernatural relatives, or skills. Nothing except slavery was more tragic along the Northwest Coast than a social humiliation or loss of a spirit relative. Humor is often a response to that which is threatening and at once perceived to be only slightly or not at all injurious. Stylized laughter which equated with but constituted a publicly expressed protection against display of tragic feelings or of feelings about other tensions occurred in a very few societies. It was not fun laughter but, rather, an assumed overt fun response and it functioned in a stylized way to hide or assuage grief or to cover embarrassment or tensions of other kinds. Possibly the very incongruity in the stylized smiles or pretended hilarity arose in the veiling of the sorrow or rending ambivalence which was present beneath.

Sadness itself follows irremediable hurt, loss of something important, or continuing concern lest that which happened to another may happen to oneself. Incongruity which envelopes a fun situation is absent from a tragic situation which is unrelievedly real and insoluble. There is nothing more real, threatening, terrifying, and inescapable than the feelings consequent upon our uncontrollable process of identification of self with a person who has just endured a mutilation or agonizing pain, or with a corpse of a person who is kin or some sort of surrogate kin. A sociocultural system offers no complete defense against agonized identification with others in their misfortunes, only formalized behaviors which do a little cushioning of feelings and repressions which mask the fact of identification. Patterned customs hide and help to defend against a total awareness and shattering profundity of tragic sentiments, especially those that surround war, severe sickness, loss of dearest possessions, and threat of one's own death. An anthropological observer can only rarely ascertain and make note at once of what is really going on behind an overlay of customary defensive devices—imperturbability, cool deportment, rituals, mourning sessions, shamanistic performances, requirements of haircutting, wailing, mourning garb, and the like.

It is worth belaboring the point that during 70 or more years of field researches, anthropologists have much more often written down in a rather external way what they saw people doing than they have ransacked, tactfully to be sure, people's verbalizations of feelings about what was transpiring. Furthermore, occasions for amusement and laughter are frequent. Incongruities rear their silly heads every day where tragedies develop at far longer intervals. Still, it seems methodologically right to suggest that just as fun situations are, in essence, lightning quick structurings which contain universal stimuli on the one hand and culturally idiosyncratic factors on the other, so too the factors that effect great sadness are both universal and culturally special. Cultural items include, of course, things such as loss of community regard, status, wealth, car, distant cousins, supernaturals, or some other highly valued extension of or prop to one's self-identity. The scientific task is to locate, for each culture and as accurately as possible, universal and culturally particular causes of tragic feelings and to represent the ways in which customarily available protective devices ameliorated such emotions.

Unlike laughter, which may function to ward off certain sentiments, a visible or audible response of sadness hardly protects a person who grieves although it may serve as ventilation and purge of guilt feelings. A system of theory about tragedy the world over may have to wait some time for descriptive gleanings, preferably in natives' own words, their analysis, and cross-cultural comparisons of sets of items pieced out. But tragedy has been frequent enough, both under aboriginal and acculturational conditions, especially so under the latter, to warrant a thought that rapid progress is possible in understanding sadness in its worldwide manifestations and in the many classes of devices such as etiquette, rites, and myth recitals which have functioned to project, displace, cushion, and alleviate.

## Stylizations of Tragedy

The ancient Greek theater produced a stylized form or genre of tragic drama which doubtless had precursor forms in the Near East. The tragic drama of modern western civilization's theater is a lineal descendant. Other wealthy civilizations, such as modern China and Japan, have also developed dramatic forms which express feelings of tragedy. Poetry, novels, short stories, court reports, journalism, even oratory, possibly some commencement addresses too, and certainly articles in social work journals and liberal weeklies of political commentary offer additional stylizations for expression of sentiments of a tragic kind. All such forms may be punctuated by spots of fun to ameliorate a preponderance of gloom. Nonwestern peoples' oral literatures often included myths and tales which functioned for recitalist, audience, and year-around discussants almost exactly like the tragic drama of western civilization's theater. The oral literature chapter discusses such nonwestern stylizations.

The processions and public funerals of most nonliterate societies constituted dramatic stylizations of still other kinds. Needless to say, cultural anthropology has so far gleaned little but external descriptive items regarding them and, perhaps, a few statements about their social functions. Close analyses with sensitive psychological inquiries and responses are almost entirely lacking, of course. It is very late and cultural anthropology still has many important things which its protagonists have hardly thought of studying!

## SUGGESTIONS FOR FURTHER READING

These culture-bound pioneers in the study of humor deserve reading: S. Freud, of course, in his brilliant essay *Wit and Its Relation to the Unconscious*, which has received various printings; the French philosopher H. Bergson, *Laughter* (London: Macmillan, 1911); M. Eastman, *Enjoyment of Laughter* (paperback; New York: Simon and Shuster, no date given but a reprinting of a work of the 1920's). A stimulating work of more recent years is M. Wolfenstein, *Children's Humor* (Glencoe, Ill.: Free Press, 1954). Anthropologists have granted no close analyses of humor or tragedy in peoples they have studied.

# 11. RELIGION

## Introduction

Anxieties of Euro-Americans around religious beliefs, practices, and denominations have long been so extreme that no observer of a nonwestern people has failed to interest himself, to a degree, in their religion although he might unconcernedly and entirely ignore their humor, oral literature, or aberrant individuals. Certainly no anthropologically trained observer ever returned to western civilization with a claim that religion was absent in the nonwestern sociocultural group in which he had been resident.

But definitions of religion, religious person, and the religious experience are as many as patent medicines. Writers on cross-cultural manifestations of religion have emphasized belief in a deity, multiple deities, nondeific supernaturals under a caption of animism, a nonindividualized nonmaterial substance called "mana" which also operated in material ways, ethical tenets, mythology and theology, magic, group rites, specially flavored emotional reactions of the greatest intensity, and even more. Some writers have selected just two or three of the foregoing as constituting a *sine qua non* in religions, even though only a handful of faiths were sketched more than superficially in the century during which cultural anthropology developed. The descriptive sample of religions remains tiny in a world of thousands of them. It seems easy to define what is universal when printed data comprise less than a tenth or twentieth, maybe a hundredth or thousandth, of what ought to have been written down. Nevertheless, few authors have been willing to forego the quest of certainty regarding pivotal characteristics of religions. A search for a tight cross-cultural definition of religion has seemed right in view of the different and much more advanced stages of development in "hard" and biological sciences. Most collectors of the unripe fruits of cross-cultural inquiry in religion have equipped themselves prematurely with cursive presentations under a series of arbitrary subheadings such as monotheism, animism, shamans, magic, rites, and so on. The topic has not often been treated in a rigorously scientific manner, except in incidental items. Any effort to structure it in classes of units which function almost interchangeably, and whose causes and behavior can then be shown to be similar, is inevitably crude. However, suggestions about operational merits of such a taxonomic approach are already timely.

Awareness of the juvenile stage which the twentieth century is in in progress toward systematic theory about the planet's several thousand religions justifies a supposition that contemporary effort to achieve a rigorous delimitation or commitment to statements about religions' most basic characteristics may be deceptive. It may mislead later researchers. A definition now would amount to arbitrary selection or stress of some and omission of or obliquity of judgment about other often vital characteristics. We do know enough to state, for example, that in languages there is always a macroclass of consonants and almost always if not absolutely always a class of vowels. Such formulations receive strong support in a few hundred sound systems which have been rather carefully examined. Too much is still missing in the annals of reporting of nonwestern religions to permit similar setting forth of universal classes of minimal features. About all that is necessary, anyway, to get scientific labors under way is to agree regretfully and goodhumoredly to go along for just a little while with the many observers who, in their culture-bound or religion-bound ways, have pointed to what they sensed was a sector of all nonwestern heritages and which they accordingly called religion. Euro-Americans have always referred as religion to that sector which contains a nonwestern people's beliefs about powerful beings or substances which most persons of western civilization seem unable to see or hear without benefit of a few tumblers of brandy. The sector has also witnessed formulae, rites, and a variety of individual and group observances. It has numbered individuals, called shamans or priests, who stepped forth and temporarily, occasionally permanently, took over certain duties. It has been paralleled by a bewildering array of emotional responses. It has exhibited esthetic behavior, always in poetry, music, dance, and often in plastic and graphic representations. It has emphasized behavior which earlier writers captioned as "magic" and which effected deeply wanted ends such as recovery of lost souls, cure of the mortally ill, bringing about or stopping rain, poisoning enemies, and doing a thousand other things which prosaic technological devices did not quite manage to execute. All these and maybe more, too, have been regarded as located in a portion of life which Euro-Americans have labeled as religious. Their extrapolation from western religions, which determined what they perceived as religion in a nonwestern group, is satisfactory enough for a preliminary or rough and ready captioning, definition, and choice of where to look in a nonwestern sociocultural system. A principal hazard is in reliance upon a too simple definition such as the familiar assurance that religion equates with belief in God. A nonwestern religion is always much too elaborate in its multiple classes of items to bear out such easy generalization.

Much more efficient than a starting definition is some discussion of method of data gathering which can be applied to this crudely defined area of cross-cultural inquiry. How is it going to be possible to progress toward a mature system of scientific theory about a fuzzily delimited sphere of life when it is also necessary to commence with shocked or puzzled observers' depictions, when these may not be many or descriptively trustworthy, and when even the best of them do not display a wanted completeness? For there is little published in transcultural study of nonwestern religions which proffers knowledge or advances beyond a fragmentary descriptivism. Classification, a later stage in a science and one which presents an apt and orderly arrangement of descriptive data into at least their major classes of units, has hardly been developed for religions of the world. And well-founded statements to comprise parts of a scientifically mature cross-cultural system of theory about them are indeed spare.

How does a cultural anthropologist conduct field research on a religion of nonliterate folk? He never has the slightest difficulty in identifying some major parts, such as shamans and rites, in such a religion, although he may long be imperceptive about certain aspects which, at length, turn out to be important components. In any case, an exotic religion, or segments of it, is always evident even to the ill-equipped because culture-bound and poorly trained Euro-American observer. Then, how study, describe in minute detail, and account for the multifaceted content and forms of a religion? Is it correct method to seek out, forthwith, the community's religious leaders and to interrogate them? What about interrogation of a sample of citizens who are religiously inactive, indifferent, or comparatively passive observers of religious activities in their community? How tactful, and how damaging to scientific work, is it to importune people for information about personal and maybe private or secret supernaturals? especially so where people have suffered bitter hurt because of disdain, criticism, and rejection by invaders who grandiloquently referred to them as heathens and their deepest certainties as superstitions? Is it correct method to identify with people to the extreme of seeming to accept their beliefs? of participation, although without inner conviction, in their rites?

No simple answers can be given to such questions. Perhaps the most reasonable general statement is that the closer a written report is to verbatim recording of everything an interviewer asked and everything a people, religious leaders and others, said in explication, the more trustworthy the research. If a religion comprised, among other things, hundreds of supernaturals, statements about each should be recorded from a number of informants. Cosmology which connected with supernaturals should also be recorded verbatim from several informants, preferably in native text, close translation, and appended commentary elicited by imaginative interrogation. Public rites should be recorded, when permitted by a people, on sound film and, if possible, written up in notebooks at the same time. Biographies and autobiographies should be gotten, too. Myths, music, dance forms, initiations, games, curing, and anything else that connected with religion should also be recorded with equipment offered by modern technology and with rich annotative commentary obtained in tactful interrogations. Question and answer commentary is sometimes the most decisive descriptive material because it may permit deeper probing of feelings, by way of finely cutting content analysis, than even a faithful sound-on-film record yields.

Now, all this provides only raw descriptive stuff, but it is so well secured and reliable that later generations of scientists can accord the materials confidence. They can re-examine everything.

The next step is orderly arrangement, taxonomy, or classification of items obtained in the field. But arrangement is neither possible nor meaningful until tentative theoretical leaps have led to decisions as to where and how to slice the descriptive data into contrastive units and meaningful rather than picayune or irresponsibly arranged classes of such elements. Here is the rub, indeed. Cultural anthropology's progress in study of nonwestern religions does not seem to have advanced taxonomically as far as has linguistics. It has not moved along to the point of knowing how best to cut up relevant beliefs and behavior efficiently into usable minimal units. More important, it does not really know how to locate such units serviceably in sets. Until there are right decisions about such groupings of items and they are charted in their connections with each other, few tenable deductions can be ventured about processes of origin, maintenance, functioning, and change.

Assessment of methods of cross-cultural research requires examination of a doctrine, to which few anthropologists have accorded assent, that trained field observers who have had soul-stirring experiences of a religious kind in their own culture are best fitted to perceive what transpired in a nonwestern religion. The trust is that their capacity to accept supernaturalism and to identify with deeply religious persons opens portals of insight. Are these barred against a cultural anthropologist who has never been moved poignantly in the presence of a supernatural or in the course of a rite? Are such emotional experiences prerequisites for scientific research on nonwestern religions? Are religions everywhere so similar in emotional content that the love, wonder, awe, or anguish felt by a believer in one are almost transferable to another? In order to perceive, arrange, and generalize about a nonwestern religion, is it necessary to feel about religions as believers do?

Answers to these questions, which are important in consideration of the manysidedness of problems of reliable scientific method, may be clearer after a pause for comments upon one or two relevant analogies. Is a psychotherapist who suffered from neurotic symptoms at an earlier time thereby better fitted to identify with a neurotic patient and to accept the genuineness of that patient's difficulties? Some psychotherapists have pulled out of a schizophrenic quagmire in their personal history. Are such therapists better able to understand and treat schizophrenic patients? Resolution of these queries perhaps resides in the following considerations. A psychotherapist who has experienced mordant feelings in the course of enduring and resolving his own emotional perplexities is doubtless advantaged in his capacity to comprehend the overwhelming involvement of a patient in his system of defenses. Such a psychotherapist may have unique ability to perceive a patient's entrapment, his incapacity to break through and advance to more mature structuring of his relationships with people. In other words, this psychotherapist may apprehend, by identification and *in a general way*, a patient's fullness of emotion, depth of suffering, and difficulties in redirecting himself. On the other hand, such a therapist does not necessarily have information, which is superior to any other therapist's potential to acquire it, regarding specific components of ideological and feeling content of his patient. To be sure, he may be more accepting, more sympathetic, more inclined to be resolute and pertinacious, no matter how long a time it takes for the patient to surrender a cluster of immature defenses. But he may not be better apprised about causes for the defenses, symptoms, and regression to a less mature level of responses.

The analogy with a scientific investigator of a nonwestern religion is suggestive. Intensity of emotion around supernaturals, ceremonials, shamans, healing, and the like may be sensed in a general way by a research worker who has experienced comparable magnitude of feeling in his own culture. But supernaturals and ceremonials, certainly the religious functionaries among nonwestern peoples, are of most diverse kinds. So, too, are social and psychological functions of religions and the very kinds and amplitudes of emotions which are stirred in them. Capacity to feel with utmost intensity in the presence of a nonvisible being or substance, to relate completely to a supernatural, to accept ministrations of a religious leader, offers no toeholds of comprehension of an array of distinctive items of ideological, emotional, or other content in a religion which is wholly outside a Euro-American anthropologist's Judeo-Christian heritage. A Pentacostalite's glowing sentiments about his God may not parallel sentiments of a Yakima who is dreaming about his rattlesnake spirit-power. The contents and forms, certainly the psychological features, of the two sets of phenomena are much too unique, too idiosyncratic. It is possible that sentiments around a mathematical experience of a hard-bitten professor in his campus office are about as similar to those of a Yakima in the throes of identification with his rattlesnake brother as are the feelings of a devout Christian. Feelings in the two religious systems, Judeo-Christian and nonwestern, are distinctive and one begs an important question in a claim that such emotions are similar. Intensity, repletion, unconditional surrender there may often be, in both. But very little has been pinpointed in a nonwestern religion if that is all that a formerly or presently profoundly religious research worker really shares, antecedently, with subjects of his field study.

Another analogy may be found in the potential of a Euro-American cultural anthropologist who has approached mastery of one or more music, dance, or plastic-graphic heritages of his culture. Is such an anthropologist uniquely equipped to study a nonwestern art because he knows much more than the rest of us temperate and clumsy folk about ways an artist feels? The answer is much the same. Other artists may not have specific sentiments that parallel those of Euro-American artists who are in a celestial or Left Bank agony of esthetic creativity. An anthropologist-artist may be able to identify peculiarly well with some nonwestern artists in a few most general respects such as pride in craftsmanship and virtuosity, thrill in creative play with components of an art heritage, and pleasure in audience applause. But probably he is not the least superior to another anthropologist who has done no more than incorporate values of respect and acceptance, capacity to perceive maturity, and the like. Such internalization is a requirement of anthropological field work method. The scientifically necessary procedure of cutting and slicing an art into its unitary features and its component classes of units is equally severe for esthetically untrained and trained cultural anthropologists.

The advantage enjoyed by a scientific observer who has had a religious experience in his own culture is not at all in his enhanced capacity for recognition of the many different units and classes of units which comprised a nonwestern religion. It is only in his potential to grant acceptance of worth to that other religion and to identify with its most perfervid surviving communicants, perhaps especially so in those very many nonwestern religions where Dionysian-like violence of feeling was and still is allowed overt expression.

Another question arises. Is a cultural anthropologist whose religious background has been tepid or superficial, or a psychiatrist who has never had a severe emotional disturbance, or a field worker who never danced the two-step, sang beautifully, played the violin with distinction, or carved a block of wood so as to please a Cubist really less able to grant a nonwestern person acceptance of possible merit? Are these researchers handicapped to such a degree that they might be advised by vocational counselors to try to enter another profession, such as experimental psychology, accounting, or electrical engineering, which appears to have no need for personnel with capacity either to identify with or accept the worth of people?

Quite likely, the answer is that competent field workers in cultural anthropology must have embraced certain values. These include the deepest convictions about potentials for complexity, psychological maturity, and functional, if not other, merits of beliefs and institutions in nonwestern peoples, including all food-gatherers. Each field worker must have built into himself a capacity to accept sociocultural and psychological differences and an aspiration to add to scientific knowledge about them. He must be sensitized to detraction or repudiation of nonwestern worth such as arises, without awareness, in extrapolation of one's own culture's values onto an alien culture. An anthropologist whom a nonwestern group learns to regard as a person who does not spurn their heritage, and who is obviously capable of accepting their equal merit as persons, may suffer from few handicaps in research on their religion. Sincerity, integrity, genuine curiosity, linguistic aptitude, and psychological insights only supplement capacity to recognize others and their heritage as complex, worthy, sensitive, and adult.

A modern cultural anthropologist's further involvement in mastery of correct method is to know a lot about scientific method in general. For nonwestern religions must be approached primarily by scientific workers if all parts, fabrics, and functionings of those faiths are to be revealed and made to contribute to a growing system of scientific knowledge. A torrid, pulsating, intuitive onslaught on data can offer little more in construction of a theoretical edifice for the world's thousands of religions than it may facilitate those who seek to move progressively toward maturation of systems of knowledge of nonwestern music and nonwestern political structures. There is no alternative to accurate depiction of everything and to judicious slicing, orderly arrangement, and properly documented deductions about process. Personnel who do this require special training and values, not ecstatic experiences, memories of them, and capacity to swoon at the right time.

## Believer and Disbeliever

If Euro-American culture were not so riven in sects and in functionally related but more or less unorganized groups such as nonbelievers and aggressive atheists, an interest in contrasting religious with irreligious persons might never have arisen. Occasionally, Euro-Americans who have concerned themselves with cultures of nonwestern peoples have projected outward their discomfort, maybe loneliness, actually their very selves because of their a-religious aberrancy. Accordingly, they have inquired, with hope and sympathy, about those other nonbelievers or heretical dissentients among nonwestern peoples. The question is of slight importance for a cross-cultural theory about religions. But it seems pressing to persons whose ties to one or more of the surviving Western religious denominations are more angrily rejecting than loyal or respectful and who thereby suffer from disapproval by a majority of the populace. A person who has had a vexatious struggle to tear loose from a denomination and who is still tingling with guilt about it seems to want to know if there are others with thorny problems such as he may suppose he created for himself. He might feel just a shade less uncomfortable if he could receive assurance that large numbers of Zuñis or Zulus had been heretics, too. A few kindred cranks among them would help a little.

Now, disbelief, truculent heresy, or mere questioning by nonwesterns of tenets of their people's world view are familiar to anthropological field workers. But reports of such heterodoxy issue largely from nonwestern groups which have long since suffered uncompromising envelopment by western civilization. Skeptics and apostates appear almost automatically and usually rapidly among younger natives upon penetration of their society by the impressively wealthy invaders. Missionaries' converts require inclusion in such a category of apostates. However, the unorthodox backsliders, even converts to Christian denominations, are usually only partially so. Segments of their old orthodox ideology had become undermined at different times. The question is not about these iconoclasts of the modern period. Everyone knows that when native seceders are supplemented by many Christian converts or Communists the religion which an anthropologist wants to study sooner or later goes out.

The question here is about precontact sociocultural systems. It deals with a functioning sociocultural heritage and whether or not it contained a built-in permissiveness to reject some or all supernaturals and other classes of features in the religion. It deals with the possibility of variant beliefs regarding the reality of supernaturals, efficacy of ceremonials, prayers, and offerings, and merits of religious leaders. Unfortunately, few anthropologists penetrated a nonwestern system well before other outsiders had entered. Questions about a dead weight of orthodoxy, about permissibility to be a skeptic or sheer ideological opportunity to become one, would be puzzling if the sole means for replying were founded on direct reports of disbelieving and disbelievers. There are probably no such reports from cultures not yet balefully contacted by Caucasians.

However, take into consideration the fact that almost all, if not the entirety, of nonwestern peoples have had religions whose content included, among many other things, an enormous class of small scale supernaturals, that is, animism, rather than a small assemblage of hulking deific beings, that is, polytheism. A pure monotheism may not have developed anywhere except in small leadership groups in the wealthiest societies, as in the pre-Christian Near East. In precontact nonliterate groups, the congregation or district population of miniature supernaturals usually numbered in the hundreds, assuredly so in most food-gathering cultures. Nonconformism and striking out against kin and established ways, therefore, were likely to take the form of rejection of only a few supernaturals. A large remainder survived unquestioned and undisturbed in their customary haunts. They felt no hot blasts of rejection from a human heretic in a band or village some miles away. Apostates' anger was satisfied by displacement onto a few puny nonmaterial beings who could also do exceedingly material things. All other supernaturals could remain uncriticized, unscathed, and as potent as ever. Very likely, then, relentless and complete repudiation of an entire class of diminutive supernaturals occurred rarely, if at all, in precontact eras, if these general theoretical considerations are plausible because of consistency with everything else that is known about precontact peoples.

On the other hand, since few, if any, such folk believed in only a few deific beings, a small and really stingy class with an inventory of, say, three or six or seven burly gods, a question about ideological nonconformism in such probably nonexistent kinds of heritages seems academic, to put it mildly. A religious ideology which comprised a small class of titanic gods, without supplementation by numerically much larger classes of small-scale supernaturals, has never been reported. If there had been such an ideology, there might very well have been impious freethinkers in the population. The fewer and larger the gods, the easier to consign them to exile and limbo. A pure monotheism, belief in only one god, may be easiest of all to undermine because its one supernatural is unspecific and remote. Evidences of work done and help given by it appear far-fetched in comparison to the concreteness of contributions of plural small supernaturals each of whom has a specialist talent. No nonwestern peoples of lowly economy ever simplified their ideology of supernaturals to such an extreme as that of pure monotheism. Such people needed numbers of animistic relatives and could spare only a few of them.

Disbelief in the efficacy of ceremonials, prayers, or offerings and doubtings of the talents of religious leaders are other matters entirely. Such sectors of religion tie in more directly with flesh and blood people than with populations of nonmaterial people who are especially potent kinds of supportive and fearsome kin. It seems probable, then, that hostile feelings could be directed at once, without ideological complexities and puzzlement, against real people and what they really did. Heresy, therefore, may often have taken the form of sneering at a few leaders and their public performances and at maladroit contributions of leaders and others in prayer, offering, or curing.

Another factor of possible import in a question about frequency of ideological nonconformism is the circumstance that nonwestern people witnessed, discussed, and, to a degree, accepted some of the sociocultural differences which characterized peoples resident in the environs. However, a class of rationalizations usually took care of, accounted for, and reinforced confidence in the reality of one's own group's supernaturals and rites in spite of many different convictions and customs a few miles away. Intellectual comparisons of supernaturals and customs with slightly foreign beliefs and rites of adjacent groups may have constituted no important factor in production of heretics.

## Animism

The term "animism" covers the one class of projection figures which appears to have occurred universally in nonliterate peoples' ideology of nonmaterial beings. Animistic beings were usually humanlike. A question remains whether such beings were absent from any nonwestern people who were both literate and economically most advanced. Probably all such societies exhibited animistic beliefs.

Edward B. Tylor was among the first to identify "animism" as a class of ideas. He treated the topic with exemplary efficiency for the 1860's in his famous and widely read two-volume work *Primitive Culture*, printed in 1871. The term "animism" and the concept for this type of nonmaterial beings has survived in the technical writing of behavioral scientists. But Tylor's presentation, both descriptive and causal, has decreased in utility for scientific purposes with growth of knowledge of the range of animistic conceptions, of multiple factors which must have brought about beliefs of this type and, especially, with increasing sensitization to the variety of psychological and social functions they served. Note that Tylor's achievement was both in identification of a class of beliefs in comparatively modest-sized supernaturals and, on a more mature scientific level, in indication of causes in dreams, hallucinatory episodes, echoes, and reflections in water. In other words, he was one of the earliest behavioral science writers to go beyond mere fact gathering, classification of facts, and suggestions about their temporal succession in evolutionary stages. He was enough of a scientist to offer highly plausible statements of a theoretical kind about causes for a class of items. Until the 1890's, few generalizations by a nineteenth century social scientist may have been more useful in providing momentum for advance toward maturity in a field of inquiry. They constitute a noteworthy historical landmark. But knowledge of nonwestern religions has long since progressed beyond Tylor's work which was, to be sure, an expression of the best in nineteenth century perceptions of certain external facets of behavior, here the class of animistic beliefs found nearly everywhere.

Several decades ago anthropologists were wont to assert that Tylor's and his contemporaries' treatment of nonwestern cultural items was intellectualistic, that is, he and other workers of his era were unable to probe below surface levels of behavioral phenomena and tended to present highly rational choices and decisions as characteristic of people. The criticism was true, but it helped little because of the scanty additional insight exhibited by the then equally intellectualistic critics. It would have been more useful to show just how much farther Tylor had gone in the direction of fashioning a system of theory about religion. It would have been valuable to show how far his professedly, but not so successfully, psychology-oriented critics and others of their era had cut with still extremely blunt scalpels.

Animism means beliefs in many small nonmaterial beings, spirits as everyone says, which are too diminutive and too lacking in powers to be members of a class of comparatively grandiose and usually remoter projective figures called gods. But no sharp line separates animistic spirits from polytheistic deities. The two concepts cover only ends of a continuum of supernaturals. Two important things feature all of them. First, they constitute portions of an all-inclusive class of supernaturals. Secondly, all display humanlike psychological characteristics and are patently projections, as if on a movie screen, of human beings. Supernaturals feel, think, and act, some or all of the time, like people and, with exceptions, they have eyes, heads, bodies, limbs, and, not least, sex. They also appear part or all of the time as ghosts or souls, fauna, flora, or nightmare figures. Some of them change appearance or behavior upon occasion. For example, a spruce which speaks in a certain situation may not take on all lineaments of a human. Still, its function, its speaking to a human and power it can grant, places it in a class of supernaturals.

Actually, an accident of the history of classical Mediterranean ideology of the supernatural resulted, in that cultural heritage, in distinctions between a class composed of one god only, a pantheon or class of gods, and a class of spirits. Writers on ideology of the supernatural have until now sought to make similar class distinctions in descriptive data about supernaturals projected by nonwestern peoples. The line, drawn by Tylor and many others, between two classes of animistic and deistic or polytheistic beliefs should be recognized for what it is: projections imposed by culture-bound European writers. The continuum of beliefs in the supernatural should now be segmented according to what field workers have found in nonwestern cultural heritages, not what Euro-Americans have superimposed upon field reports.

A comparatively decisive line segments that continuum, a line not perceived until a number of field workers' accounts of beliefs were assembled between about 1900 and 1915 and were then shown to contain new kinds of concepts about the supernatural. The line separates a large class of concepts of animistic beings, ancestor spirits, and deities from a strikingly different and also large class of concepts of impersonal, wholly unfaunalike and unfloralike nonmaterial power. Projections of the former, in familiar guises of people, animals, plants, and ogres, can be accounted for with relative ease. It is extremely difficult to account theoretically for causation, maintenance, or functions of a category of beliefs in unindividualized fluidlike or electricitylike power. That kind of projection, that kind of supernatural power, has been termed "mana" because Bishop Codrington used his transcription of a Melanesian word for it in his classic description of a belief which he had encountered before the 1890's in the South Pacific.

Evidently, the individualized projections, animistic or deitylike, that is, small or large, have connected in origin and reinforcing pressures with persons. Fundamentally, all such supernaturals have been projections of humans. When, as in the hypothetical instance of a spruce spirit, indeed in any instances of animal, bird, insect, and ogre-fantasy beings, these supernaturals have seemed to differ from humans, ego-protecting distortional mechanisms such as displacement can be invoked as the most plausible hypothesis. If a belief in a mana kind of nonindividualized power enjoyed similar origin and continued reinforcement, evidence for such development and maintenance may not be easy to find. That is, mana does not appear to have connected so directly with individual humans, the one projected into or a displacement of the other. One wonders if, as a projection of a special kind, mana related to felt community forces rather than to individual personalities such as parents, lineage members, or community leaders. More of such speculation about mana elsewhere, where Emile Durkheim's contribution is also cited.

The effort here is to hazard a segment of theory whose premise is that all members of the class of individualized supernaturals, irrespective of sizes, shapes, or potencies, have tied in with individual humans. Now, which humans? parents? siblings? shamans? kin? chiefs? aliens? The most plausible hypothesis may include the methodological requirement that each nonwestern religion's ideology of animistic or deific supernaturals be accorded its own analysis in terms of special operations of the sociocultural system and everything else in the heritage. In one region, stresses and relationships of various kinds were such that supernaturals, however they originated, appear to have enjoyed continual reinforcement from sentiments arising around parents. In another region, relationships to and feelings around extended kin, in-laws, and lineage or community leaders may have provided ignition and more strategic support for projections which continued to be fueled by societal stresses. The theoretical formulation is that a complex of needs and relationships determined the support for, if not origin of, the projections. To be sure, pursuits of beginnings or origins, a kind of interest which preoccupied nineteenth century theoreticians, including Tylor, is truly futile because pertinent evidences in favor of or in disproof of hypotheses about such processes are almost always beyond reach. For the same purpose of exploration of origins, some recent writers have resorted to mathematically sophisticated dressing up of the nineteenth century grab-bag comparative method, with its extreme of methodological awfulness in writing by Sir James G. Frazer. Instead of citing, as Frazer was wont to do, superficially similar instances of some phenomenon from peoples of all kinds the world over, a typology of societies from economically simple to complex is ventured, then a few presumed sample societies are taken as examples of each type and the author concludes with correlations which display frequency of something or other within each type. The demonstration terrorizes into belief persons who are unaware of the scantiness or spotty unreliability of descriptive data, especially on religion, from nonwestern peoples. It also impresses persons who cannot perceive the faulty premises which vitiate most classifications into socioeconomic and sociocultural types. Anyhow, an unassailable system of theory which can be fashioned will largely ignore first beginnings. It will offer statements about a class of units. It will point to them in terms of specific needs and relationships, pinpointed and linked within each sociocultural system or small region, and supported by sensitive descriptive documentation and close analyses of verbatim recorded expressive materials. The theory will center maintenance and functions, including psychological processes, not origins in remote times of classes of religious features.

Although a central task is to reveal stresses and needs within each region, to connect them with the manifold content and forms of the region's supernaturalism, and to show how it worked for its devotees, a broader approach serves as an introductory guide. Cultural anthropology already appears able to show that all peoples, not merely the food-gatherers and economically modest agriculturalists, have supplemented parents, kin, and other "significant people" with pseudo-parents and pseudo-kin in order to feel more secure, comforted, or reassured in threatening situations or sheer crises which, of course, occurred universally. These included mortal sickness and death, epidemics, natural disasters, weather, and enemies. But there is no immediate scientific utility in such observations. They delimit only an area of life and point to general causes and responses. Processes which have to be formulated carefully in building a system of theory about supernaturalism may be deduced only with intensive "tribal" and areal analyses and their subsequent comparison. One eventually gets back to a controlled procedure of comparisons, indeed, but a solidly rooted method based upon reliable expositions of what is compared.

Social structures of economically primitive food-gatherers certainly tended to connect with elaborate animistic ideologies. Cultural projections generated and maintained in such societies were often wholly lacking in large-sized supernaturals. For all their variety, food-gathering communities exhibited meager or no interest in either deific or mana concepts. They were so intensely involved in small-dimensioned supernaturals that, it appears, few, if any, skeptics who doubted the existence of a population of such beings could have come forth. The larger and more remote a supernatural, the easier it was to become anxious about whether he was there at all. If six persons in a community of 49 saw a nonmaterial dog near the huts, it was difficult to counter their perceptions. Disbelievers about the entirety of an ideology of simon-pure animism were probably infrequent. Cynicism and hostile responses about single items in the ideology were rampant and did not in the least weaken the ideological structure. The class of projective items was virtually impregnable as a class.

Just what was it in societies of lowliest economy that so securely sustained an ideology of hundreds of small supernaturals and failed to produce, bolster, or center, if it had them, a class of concepts of gods or a class of ideas of mana? Tylor's suggestions about causation of animism may be useful here but, perhaps, in a manner different from the way he intended. When he singled out dreams, hallucinations, echos, reflections in water, and other experiences as first causes for animistic beliefs, the stress was on ultimate origins, as in most evolutionist-oriented and intellectualistically slanted writing of later decades of the nineteenth century and in some of the correlation-compulsive efforts of contemporary sociology-oriented workers. But it is a minor because invariably futile task of a system of sociocultural theory to account for ultimate causes or first origins. Much more must be described, arranged, and explained. Principal tasks are to account for persistence, patternings, and services, that is, for continuations of ideological content, their shapings, functioning in relation to everything else, and changes, that is reshapings, growth, proliferations, or diminutions. No one can expect to offer evidences for or against any theoretical statement about initiation of a segment of ideology which developed tens or hundreds of thousands of years ago, especially so at a time when cortical structures may have been somewhat different from those of all modern human beings. However, it has been possible to observe ways of life which reinforced and changed animistic beliefs among modern peoples of primitive technology. It will also be possible to add quantities of field observations for a short time to come in a few remaining food-gathering and economically lowly agricultural communities. No more exciting field research awaits an anthropologist or his sociologist allies during the next decade or two than study of connections and services of animistic supernaturals in relation to all the rest of the heritage of a nonliterate community of simple productive capacity.

Tylor's intellectualistic suggestion about origins of animistic beliefs in dreams and the like directed attention only to possible and plausible early causes, among others which have remained unknown. Tylor and most of his contemporaries were unable to appraise circumstances that made people who lived in an unproductive economy need to continue to believe in and relate to a population of humanlike supernaturals. No matter how a belief in a spruce, rattlesnake, dog, or ogress supernatural originated, it is clear that it helped or threatened in much the manner in which some fellow human being helped or threatened.

During the 1920's, when Dr. Ruth Benedict commenced her career with a bookish diffusionist survey of so-called "guardian spirit" beliefs among North American Indians, she correctly emphasized services of spirit-powers as helpers. The very title of her work employed the term "guardian spirit." But she did not highlight important maleficent functions of the continent's spirit-powers, that is, its animistic beings. North of Mexico, they functioned demonstrably as parents, extended kin, siblings, elders, in-laws, and aliens. At any psychological level below the visible surface such supernaturals were people, camouflaged people of a special kind because they were often intangible and only a few persons saw and heard each individual spirit. They were people who both supplemented flesh-and-blood people and who often could do things, good and bad, which real people could not do. They were, then, supplementary kin, supplementary headmen, supplementary aliens, supplementary enemies. Only some few of them were guardians in a literal sense. A North American Indian who saw and heard a grizzly supernatural really perceived, not necessarily in a visual perception, another kind of person, kin, elder, alien, or whatever it really was to him, one whose capacities and motivations were grizzlylike and horrible, to be sure. The grizzly accoutrements of this supernatural were not a disguise. They were only an alternative garb. It was consequent upon a displacement from horrible person to terrifying animal. The displacement functioned, among other things, to protect the recipient of a relationship with a grizzly supernatural from shocked recognition of its latent identity with a living or recently deceased person. Since grizzlies were kinds of people who were fierce and feared anyhow, because they ran fast, growled, clawed, and killed, the spirit vision and connection displayed fit. They offered a wholly appropriate displacement. Once a person made relationship to what he supposed was an individual grizzly supernatural, that is, to a special kind of person, he was released to incorporate every bit of frightfulness which culture tradition applied to any and all murderous spirit-persons of that kind. It helps only us to term them grizzly supernaturals. An Indian was released to identify with the cultural stereotype of a person who was integral with a grizzly being. Every awful and destructive thing which such an individual perpetrated was explained by his helplessness, because he was now partly or wholly a grizzly kind of person himself. One behaved as one was. Mechanisms witnessable in such a religious phenomenon included anxiety, aggression, displacement, internalization or introjection, identification, and rationalization. Obviously, such a composite of psychological mechanisms, projected image or belief, and behavior was no simple matter of acquisition of a guardian spirit, underlining guardian. It was not acquisition, either. The total phenomenon requires carving into all its significant psychological processes, ideological segments, and their connections with needs and social relationships.

If an Indian supposed that some other aggressive and sadistic person had a grizzly kin, that is, had related to and then incorporated characteristics of a grizzly being, an explanation or rationalization had been made. It was entirely plausible. In the absence of a more likely accounting for the disliked person, its reasonableness functioned as reinforcement of the general ideology of relationship to and introjection of supplementary nonmaterial people.

Vital questions arise in a conviction held by most students of religion that animistic beings were everywhere regarded as immortal: they did not get sick, senile, or die. Actually, evidence is not everywhere clear about the indestructibility of supernaturals, least of all these relatively modest ones who were the stuff of animism. Why should they have been indestructible when people were not? Would wishful thinking everywhere have conferred an infinity of years and perfect health upon all spirit-powers, all deities too, even the malevolent ones? It looks as if once again a lot of persons have been projecting Mediterranean and western civilization's thoughts out into nonwestern ideologies when the perpetual durability of nonwestern supernaturals is regarded as axiomatic. The point is that painstaking field interrogations about matters such as this are almost impossible to find. Indeed, it seems likely that in many districts spirit-powers appeared, got hurt, suffered, fought, changed abodes, and vanished rather like people. The fact is, they *were* people. It is projection of Euro-American notions to regard them as immortal, except when natives insist upon that.

In certain types of society, persons could account for their own needs and for others' personalities only by employment of premises of animism. It was either the sole psychological theory, or an important one among several, which worked for peoples of lowly economy, albeit it constituted their religious ideology, too. Very likely it had served them for tens of thousands of years in both respects, in a unity which only from a Euro-American point of view contained discrete psychological and religious portions.

Once a person acquired nonmaterial relationships, he had more kin than if he was confined to the daily familiarities of tangible people. Life became at once more private and less lonely. It was certainly more secure. An animistic ideology provided intellectual plausibilities and thereby granted at-homeness and security. It operated safely in the total absence of alternatively plausible thoughts. And it was extraordinarily bolstered by its supplementary people because their capacities ranged beyond those of immediately visible and audible family, community, neighbors, or enemies.

## Beyond Animism

This caption serves to avoid artificialities and errors which arise when religious beliefs about ancestor spirits and deities are brusquely segregated from spirit-power concepts as if distinctively different in kind. Deities must not be discussed as if they lacked vital similarities to animistic beliefs. Deities differed from spirits principally in dimensions, geographical or space remoteness, and theological embroiderings which special religious functionaries in wealthier nonwestern societies sewed on them. Where distinctive classes of beliefs in supernaturals appeared, it was because cultures which featured them treated them as discrete. An anthropologist discovers the class which is in the data. He does not impose it on the data.

Tylor's evolutionist orientation, a nineteenth century historicist's compulsion to assess cultural phenomena as simple or complex and, therefore, remotely or recently evolved, resulted in a statement that a generalized animism was the first stage of development in religious ideology and that it was succeeded by later stages. The second, higher, more complex stage was graced by a profusion of ancestor spirits beside surviving spirits of the first stage. Tylor offered a later, still higher, polytheistic stage in which some of the ancestor spirits had taken on attributes of deities. Unlike other writers of evolutionist persuasion, he was sufficiently cautious to avoid specification of kinds of socioeconomic structures which tended to connect with his successive stages of religious ideology.

A good case can be made for a position that simon-pure animism, animism plus ancestor spirits, and these plus a handful of deities, so-called polytheism or a kind of mixed polytheism, were really only different kinds or classes of content which are most suitably subsumed under a single macroclass heading. "Multiple supernaturals" or simply "animism" and "beyond animism" might be appropriate rubrics.

It is moot if the three types of ideological emphasis or three classes of units are well described as classes. It is also uncertain that, if really types, they connected with distinctive socioeconomic levels. Currently published data on religious ideologies of nonwestern peoples, such as the oft referred to Australians, are far less reliable than many writers on the subject have suspected. It is not always certain if supernaturals which have been reported upon as deities were anything more than animistic beings. Exceedingly careful, perceptive, and repetitious field research, in which there is the finest kind of rapport with a variety of native informants, is sometimes necessary before a report upon religious ideology can be read with confidence. Native informants will employ captions, which they have learned from culture-bound missionaries and other Euro-Americans, in such inappropriate ways that the meanings of their concepts fail to get across to those who interview them. The danger of twisting native beliefs is less when an interviewer employs morphemes and words of a native language. Even then a period of missionary and acculturative influences can produce disastrous distortions in statements by non-European language speaking informants.

If a writer refers solely to a macroclass of supernaturals and avoids distinctions between supposedly different sets of nonmaterial beings, less maceration of the phenomena may appear in the write-up. After all, each kind of supernatural, small, large, below, high above, ancestor, monster, generous, or murderous, was both a projection and a displacement of important people or of sentiments about such people. It arose in feelings about relationships and it functioned to effect wanted relationships. No system of theory about a district's religious ideology can get off the ground without acceptance of such premises. Most of the remainder of such a system deals with depiction, arrangement, and explanation of particulars and classes of them.

Ancestor spirits were significant people, projections of feelings about those people, or displacements onto them, exactly like animistic grizzly, antelope, or spruce spirits and without faunal or floral disguises and distortions. Deities were also significant people, but projected onto a much larger screen and, usually, a more distant one. The fact that deities dwelt at a distance in space rather than in time was, nevertheless, not a significantly distinctive trait in them. What were significant were the psychological mechanisms, feelings, relationships, and identification. These operated in much the same manner for all kinds of supernaturals.

Only in the phenomenon of mana do we encounter perhaps somewhat distinctive projections, displacements, feelings, and other responses. That is why a special discussion of mana is required, while the seemingly kaleidoscopic variety of other concepts of the nonmaterial world can be lumped and disposed of in one big class.

## Mana

This concept of impersonal, nonindividualized, fluidlike supernatural power, sometimes referred to as "animatism," which pervaded and was the essence of all substances, including living beings, has sometimes been difficult to elicit from informants in nonwestern groups. The concept has, nevertheless, been supposed to have been present in every continent. One wonders how careful some of the field researches and reports about it have been. The suggestion has been made that mana was an old as well as widespread concept. But its appearance among modern surviving food-gatherers is poorly attested. The universality and great antiquity, if not primacy, which protagonists claimed for it not long after the turn of the century therefore seems to have been almost a wish fulfillment. At that time, theorization that it constituted the earliest stage in evolution of religious ideology was a consequence of uncritical and simplistic retention of nineteenth century unilinear evolutionist orientations and of the enthusiasm which greeted reports of its discovery, between about 1890 and 1920, in widely separated agricultural districts. These included West Africa, Melanesia (by Bishop Codrington), and Iroquois and Algonkin Indians of North America. Additional field reports on mana concepts thereupon poured in, although earlier writings, for example on Polynesian royalty and the nonmaterial power which they could grant their people, would have revealed the concept. Anthropologists were sometimes a bit slow about perceiving things which were in nineteenth century travel and other writings.

After people became fascinated by its seeming ubiquity, theoretical import, and resemblances to physicists' concepts of electricity and magnetism, mana was quickly connected with so-called magical processes—more about them follows—because of a logical plausibility in the tie. But there was little, if any, follow-up in probing field interrogations which might have supported assertions about a mana-and-magic relationship. A further similarity of mana to cosmological concepts developed by professional philosophers and protagonists of some new religions only intensified an impression that the mana concept was of capital importance in the world view and religious ideology of nonliterate peoples. In fact, they were not as benighted as evolutionist writers had supposed. They had achieved something which great philosophers as well as modern physics and Mary Baker Eddy had later worked out. A case might be made that the furor around the discovery of mana connected with a changing climate of opinion about the mentality of even the poorest among nonwestern peoples. Such a change was rather obvious at the very time (1910) when Boas had written his *Mind of Primitive Man* and the French philosopher Lucien Levy-Bruhl was trying, in a series of books, to find specific respects in which so-called primitive thinking differed from his own or what he supposed was characteristic ratiocination in western civilization. Before the 1920's, so little was known about the mentality of nonwestern peoples of lowly economy that receipt of scraps of information and misinterpretations, too, about mana almost electrified scholars and theologians. With accumulating and ever more sophisticated cognitions about nonliterate folk, a discovery like mana will recede into a more suitable niche as just one among vast numbers of concepts and awarenesses once present in the nonwestern world. And there can be no question that it is necessary to cleave the over-all mana concept, with which some contemporary writers still naïvely deal, into specific expressions and shapes which appeared here and there.

Whatever the frequencies and absences of mana projections among food-gatherers, and doubtless such notions will never be found among some of them; whatever the occurrence of mana beliefs among economically more advanced folk; and in spite of a likelihood that such fantasies are more varied than any writers on mana have suspected, the discovery of the concept among nonwestern groups was of more than passing interest. Without it one might have deduced that all manifestations of the nonmaterial or supernatural were members of a macroclass whose central characteristic was wishful and fearsome projection of human beings into the environments of earth, water, and sky. The reputed diffuseness and impersonality of the electricitylike power which Codrington and others after him reported seem to warrant locating it in a second macroclass of religious beliefs. It was a major discovery, no doubt.

Bad guesses about origins datable long, long ago are easy. It is always impossible to support such conjectures with on-the-spot evidence. A venture at depiction of manner of origin of some feature of culture is usually simplistic thinking anyway. A mana concept might be surmised as having evolved in projections of breath, a pulsating heart, blood, saliva, perspiration, or what not. It might have connected somewhere with storm, wind, and water. It might constitute philosophical reworking of animistic, ancestor ghost, or other concepts. It might have connected with society, social forces, or the network of perceived limits instituted by the society. Theorems of such kinds can never be bolstered with evidences because they stress first beginnings in bygone eras which left no writings. Invariably such long shots lead nowhere, as a century of sociocultural evolutionist theoreticians and their failures, superficiality, and culture-bound guessing sadly reveal.

Animistic beings and deities were so like humans in overt appearance, psychological traits, and social functions as to warrant assertion that they connected both in origin and maintenance with projections of people. On the other hand, mana does not seem to have connected so closely with the shapes or capacities of people. One wonders, again, about the possible tie of mana with a class of substances such as breath, perspiration, or winds or with that awesome power structure, society. Polynesian royalty, for example, exuded mana and extended it out for their subjects' use. Who can say if the projection was of them, of their social class, their ability to impose their will by use of force, or their social structure as a whole?

A much more aggravating difficulty is consequent upon unimaginative eliciting of information about mana in groups where it appears to have been present. Field research on the content, form, and functions of canoes has been far easier than research on the content of mana ideas and their links with many other features of a heritage. Few ethnographers, indeed, have been able to work directly through a native language for purposes of clarification of fine points of epistemology and cosmology. Interpreters who were alert about subtleties in their elders' ideology of the supernatural have often been unobtainable, to the misery of bewildered anthropologists who would like to have things explained when no one can be found who can furnish just the right answers. Again, no one may doubt that mana-like principles have been frequent and of the greatest variety, globally. But anthropologists have not begun to locate either the distinctive features of different mana propositions or their innumerable ideological threads extended through religion, social life, and world view.

At the moment, a vital problem is to ascertain where and how mana notions operated among food-gatherers because, other things equal, the amounts of musing, deliberation, and tossing about of ideas which must have characterized daily life in such groups appear to have constituted gigantic reservoirs of opportunity for ideological creativity. It is not at all paradoxical to indicate that nonwestern peoples of lowly technology appear to have had much time and motivation for philosophical mentation. It is foolish to underestimate the lucidity of their largely ephemeral, because unrecorded, intellectual exercises, whatever they were. At the same time, elaboration of classes of animistic beings in such groups, and services psychologically rendered by these often recalcitrant kinfolk of the dream, jungle, waters, and hills, may have been such as to allow supernaturals of animistic classes to account for everything that transpired and to serve for every needed speculative purpose. The result may have been that a mana theory had little chance to obtain currency among food-gatherers, with its sufficiently potent but unspecific features of content, with the impossibility of seeing or hearing it, and with heaven knows what other handicaps implicit in its daily utilization. The immediacy of large populations of animistic projection figures of greatest variety may have blocked comprehension, acceptance, or spread of mana perceptions. They were not needed. There were no functions for them.

When societies supplemented animistic beings so as to develop relationships to less immediate projection figures such as deceased kin, ancestor spirits, or a small class of deities, a mana concept perhaps had a little chance to be born, survive, and toddle around. There were fewer on-the-spot helpers to intercept it if animistic spirits had diminished in numbers and services. It is possible, then, that the more remote or the smaller the numbers of humanlike supernaturals, the greater a likelihood of development or acceptance of a mana projection and consequent elaboration of theory and practice regarding it.

The question whether mana was a more sophisticated concept than projections of animism and polytheism, and the search for causes of its startling similarity to notions such as life force, élan vital, electricity, nirvana, all-matter-is-spirit, and pantheism, remain intriguing problems. Speculation about these matters should profit from intensive researches among remaining food-gathering peoples. If mana is not well attested among them, it may be deduced that it connects in origin, and surely in functions, with something special in the way of life and ideologies of peoples who had left food-gathering behind and had taken over agricultural food producing techniques.

Research on mana is of capital importance now because of near extinction of every food-gathering sociocultural system. Field evidence about mana beliefs is usually crude and bewildering in its lack of specificity and because of the psychological, philosophical, and cultural unsophistication which features most writers, and this includes the anthropologists, who encountered it in field situations or thought they did. Sometimes they did not understand what was being asserted to them. They did not know what more to elicit.

Two primary categories of beliefs about supernatural beings and forces have now received comment. Each may be regarded as a larger structural set of features in cultures, like classes of nouns and verbs in languages. The macroclass of animistic and deific beings has been universal, although some cultures projected only a class of animistic beings. Wherever there was a class of deific projections, the animistic class continued to be present. Universality of the mana class is improbable. Current indications are that elaborations of mana ideas occurred more often in agricultural societies when status strata, royalty, priesthoods, and maybe eggheadlike specialists had developed.

Additional distinctive sets of ideological units, large and extremely important classes, must now be accorded discussion because they have been often or universally integral with religious structures. The first class, doubtless global, may be captioned myths or theology. A second class, apparently found tied in with supernaturals in wealthier nonwestern societies and dubiously so among food-gatherers, is ethics. Discussions of a third class, magical ideas, involves, first, consideration of the very tenability of a concept of magical processes and, secondly, the operational propriety of setting up a class of unitary premises about such processes—all this in spite of massive writings by Frazer and others on a fearfully muddied topic. Lastly, a supposedly worldwide class of concepts denoted the "sacred." It requires treatment and, note immediately, elimination because it is a naïve extrapolation from western culture's own ideology. Even Durkheim, who enjoyed repute because of his persuasive contrast of sacred and profane (in *The Elementary Forms of the Religious Life, 1902*), perpetrated many a culture-bound error, here one which damaged anthropology severely for decades. Dialectical opposites, such as sacred-profane, at termini of a lengthy continuum of highly variable behavior sometimes are of little value in advancing knowledge. Durkheim would have been more useful had he proffered analytic delineation of examples, from sample societies of different kinds, of the kinds of beliefs and behavior which he had in mind when he referred to sacred and profane.

## Mythology and Theology

Dramatic formal recitals in season and casual commentary during conversations and work sessions all the rest of the year featured the life of myths among most nonwestern peoples. Usually myths presented events and vicissitudes of people, ogres, or supernaturals who lived long ago. Among peoples who lacked much specialization in occupations and roles, repertoires of myths were handed on from generation to generation with comparatively small changes applied here and there to actor-personality

delineations, expressions of humorous incongruities, feelings in social relationships, items of cosmology, and so on. In such societies, a larger integration of content and a more uniform stylistic design were not placed over a
large segment or all of the myth repertoire. Internal contradictions were
often numerous. Different styles or genres of myth drama might coexist.
Principal characteristics of a mythology among food-gatherers and other
socially unstratified societies might have been its episodic light touches or
humor, its frequent inner inconsistencies in certain facets of content, its
variety of play or dramatic frames, and the fact that change in it flowed
from its manner of handling by many adults and elders.

In wealthier socioeconomic systems which had developed secret societies, specialists, or priesthoods, such groups were entrusted with or controlled portions or all of the myths. The result appears to have been a tendency to check, criticize, rationalize, reformulate, and impose more stylistic
and play uniformity of design upon myths. A related result may have been
a larger fabric of connected myths which contained fewer contradictions
or inconsistencies. Genres might receive unification. The cosmology episodically or incidentally expressed in a mythology was reformulated and
centered. A product of remodeling of such content and style by a specialist
priesthood may be termed a theology, to borrow a term for special purposes
of cross-cultural researches.

Myths obviously comprised distinctive classes of beliefs, expressed in
both dramatic and, it must be emphasized, sometimes hilariously entertaining episodes in formal recital sessions, and bandied about in incessant citations and conversational amusement. Mythic beliefs depicted, as on a movie
screen, personalities and occurrences of a past era. These were, as urged
in the oral literature chapter, projections and extrapolations of items in life
around which there were special tensions. Dramatic delineations functioned
to sanction or ventilate selected and especially anxiety-ridden components
of a people's supernaturalism, customs, social relationships, economic activities, environment of neighboring peoples, value ideals, and thinking about
the universe. In some regions, myth actors equated with supernaturals and,
in a way, gave additional references to and support of such vital classes of
religious items. A theology was perhaps no more impressive than a mythology, maybe less so because of its transmission by supernaturally potent
specialists who lived somewhat apart and thought differently from ordinary
folk. But a theology served much like a mythology in its rich supply of
associations, references, and explanations of earlier people and contemporary supernaturals. Priestly custodians of such valuable materials ministered
to the people, too, in various ways at the same time that they lived off them.

Cross-cultural knowledge of theological systems in societies of wealthier
economy is slight. It is much too late to salvage any but the tiniest chips of
the Aztec, Maya, Inca, Chibcha, or most other American Indian ideological
edifices of this kind. It seems futile to try to analyze the scraps, ideological
superimpositions, and misunderstandings which colonial era Spanish writers

displayed. However, much could still be done in a hundred Old World districts, from Africa to Oceania, although no striking signs of interest in field research projects on theological systems are evident in anthropological circles of the present moment. Field work would have to be characterized, of course, by philosophically sophisticated and peculiarly flexible interrogations, through indigenous languages, of native religious thinkers at the same time that phrasings secured from them were subjected to close content analysis. Requirements for conduct of field researches of such a kind cannot be met by many people who are receiving training today in sociocultural anthropology because most professors are tending to emphasize inquiry into social and political systems and exacting techniques for ascertaining correlations. Almost none of the current crop of younger anthropologists know how to proceed with an analytic investigation that is conducted in a nonwestern tongue. The anthropological linguists of today are motivated completely toward minute refinements for purposes of general linguistics. They are almost valueless in training cultural anthropologists for efficient field research which is little concerned about allophonic and morphological neatness because it centers sensitivity in translations of materials which are psychological or deal with world view and ethics.

## Supernaturalism and Ethics

Food-gatherers and economically lowly agriculturalists usually failed to connect principles about good and bad conduct with their many small-scale supernaturals. Beings of this kind were unlikely to judge and evaluate, although they dispensed security and abilities, sometimes almost for the asking. They were not especially parentlike or elderlike people. They had capacities but, perhaps, not extraordinary ones. Another and mechanical way of saying this is to state that classes of ethical statements usually remained unconnected, at least in any fundamental or intimate way, with the class of animistic supernaturals.

On the other hand, wealthier and stratified societies tended to project parents, elders, or leaders into supernaturals who were perhaps aptly referred to as ancestor spirits, deities, or both. A parent or other significant adult, maybe any adult, is almost gigantic to a little child. Deities, if not deceased ancestors, have been large, rather difficult to convince, extremely controlling, withholding, judgmental, and castigatory upon occasion. They might partake of characteristics of those who fed, nourished, imposed limits upon, and punished youngsters. Prestigeful elders of a community functioned like western civilization's parents and as sources, therefore, of ancestor spirit and deific projections. No wonder, then, that in wealthier nonliterate societies, ancestor spirits and, maybe more often, deities were sometimes the impressive projective figures who also purveyed ethical principles, exercised authority, and used force. They too were disciplinarians, judges of right and wrong, and punitive. Nevertheless, nonwestern populations, usually those which were fundamentally animistic and even some of those which had projected deities into a select district in their cosmos, tended to keep ethics apart from supernaturals. Ethics was, therefore, not necessarily or often an integral part of nonwestern religions. Again, a more technical way of stating this is that classes of ethical principles only sometimes connected with classes of ancestral spooks and deific figures and had thereby entered the larger structure of religion.

Although the macroclass of animistic supernaturals in food-gathering groups may have been little or not at all conjoined with ethics, supernaturals who were also myth actors did express values. In other words, ethics connected with mythology and accordingly with religion, but only indirectly. Ethics did not tie undeviatingly with current supernaturals in such societies because those beings did not sanction or require standards for the populace.

## Magic

Preceding pages have commented on the question whether cultural anthropology needed to set up a macroclass of items of belief and behavior called magic. Every anthropological writer and treatise has implied such a requirement. If magic constituted what many people have said of it, it should receive mention in several places, that is, in each of several subsystems of theory in a survey of cultural anthropology. It would suffuse discussions of supernaturalism, sickness, law, rites, ceremonials, and maybe other topics. Actually, much confusion and contradictory statements galore appear in the literature on magic. Earlier writers said it had nothing to do with religion or that it had everything to do with it. They cited magic in discussions of crimes by so-called magical shootings and poisonings. They defined it, however, in various ways. They connected it with impersonal supernatural power, mana, and implied, if they did not frankly assert, a lack of tie with any kind of humanlike supernatural. On the other hand, modern field researches show that magiclike behavior was effected in some societies by means of the cooperation of animistic beings who had great abilities, this in cultures which knew nothing of a mana concept. Anyhow, older authors wrote about magic endlessly. It is perhaps impossible to find a responsible scientist or scholar who has dared to question its universality, however it be defined. It would appear that it embodies a subsystem or macroclass of features.

Whatever its definition may be, where does magic fit in an over-all structure of cross-cultural theory? What are its origins, causes of maintenance, functions, and anything else that is meaningful about it in each cultural subsystem? Is magic always or only sometimes an area which may be manipulated, for scientific purposes, as a structured system of classes and items? And is that macroclass one of the several arrays of features which comprise a religion?

A first duty of an anthropological theoretician is to take a critical look at each concept he has inherited or which he employs. He should check on whether or not he is improperly extrapolating or projecting onto non-western peoples something, or some set of items, which is real enough in Euro-American ideology or relationships. The circumstance that Indo-European languages have sex gender and verb conjugations does not warrant chapters on sex gender and verb conjugations in every survey of languages of the world. Extrapolation, without extensive qualifications, into one cultural system of a characteristic feature, class of features, or system peculiar to another sociocultural heritage is both natural and improper. Accordingly, magic may turn out to constitute something rather more distinctive of the Euro-American heritage and less distinctive, in the sense of comprising an analogous system of units, in nonwestern heritages than most anthropologists have supposed. Western civilization is peculiar because most of its magical beliefs do not rest upon animistic premises. In nonliterate groups, some magical ideas and devices may connect with a belief in an impersonal kind of supernatural power like mana. Others, like means of making the rain come, may tie in with a deity or animistic being. The vital point is that in many, if not most, nonwestern societies magiclike beliefs and procedures which an anthropologist has found, for example rain making, so-called garden magic, and bewitching, may be subsumed with greater simplicity and aptness under headings such as animism, mana, polytheism, shamans, priesthoods, or rites. The question is whether there is justification for a separate rubric to take care of a special system of magic beliefs, behaviors, and social functions. The very same query applies to so-called witchcraft. The problem is to ascertain just how a sociocultural system operated and what were the many subsystems within it. It is already clear that in some food-gathering societies an anthropologist's identification of magic, also witchcraft, in them may amount to an inept reading in of a Euro-American concept, that is, extrapolation of a class and arbitrary depiction of it where it was nonexistent as a class of structured items. A test of operational efficiency of the concept of each form class is crucial.

Only close analysis of examples of each main type of sociocultural system will suggest a possible universality of a decidedly distinctive class of units called magic. It is sufficient to have questioned its universality and to have repeated the methodological requirement of caution in extrapolation of sets of items familiar as sets to Euro-Americans. Such questioning and caution are necessary no matter how numerous or revered the protagonists of magic's universality. But they are correct if they imply only that magiclike phenomena have been everywhere.

If, to use some food-gatherers of western North America again for an example, every rite around fish was directed to fish supernaturals, every rite for berries was addressed to berry supernaturals, each method or trick of a curing shaman was effected by one or another of his personal supernaturals, any effort to control weather was by means of special personal supernaturals who could do that, it begins to appear that people in that vast region did things only in two ways. One was materialistic or realistic, the other animistic. In other words, magiclike behavior in this type of sociocultural system appears to have constituted only a facet of animistic supernaturalism. The outsider perceives or reads in such a facet, the native perceived only supernaturals. The question in such an instance is, then, when is an outsider's perception of magic as a patterned phenomenon a consequence of improper extrapolation?

The psychology of magic is little explored among nonwestern peoples, possibly because there was less of magic and more of animistic and deistic projections among them than almost everyone has supposed. Nevertheless, magiclike convictions about the efficacy of bone pointing to kill enemies miles away, of throwing salmon bones in streams in order to ensure salmon runs, of doing thousands of things in order to effect all sorts of ends, appear to have adhered to a mechanism of wishful thinking which was stirred by stressful features of daily or seasonal living. When a magiclike procedure was followed by a failure, rationalization bolstered security by accounting, with some verbiage, for supposed causes of the failure. The magical process itself was left unrefuted. It remained a resource and prop to everyone's security system. Rationalizations protected the integrity of each of the units in the class of wishful beliefs. Rationalizations guarded the entirety of the class of cause-effect statements. They protected members of that class against cold blasts of cumulative evidence. They kept it hidden from public examination. For the class of magiclike processes was always maintained, like animism, in a kind of walled-in world, one in which public examination and check-up could not often enter.

Now, such statements and psychologizing about magiclike items may or may not be nice. They certainly are much too generalized. They invoke only a very few and oversimple statements like walled-in systems of ideas about causes, irrelevance of evidence, taboo of rechecking, wish fulfillment, defense against insecurity by means of unexaminable dogmas, and automatic rationalizations to account for failures. Methodologically required analysis involves exploration of each nonwestern group's magic system, if it really had one, by the kind of painstaking observations, decisions about minimal units, and interrogation for which the term "content analysis" seems apt.

## Sacred and Profane

Until lately, transcultural study of thousands of nonwestern religions had arrived at about the same degree of development which the science of languages had reached in the 1890's. It then lacked sharply dissected materials from each of a sampling of nonwestern forms of speech. It was then acceptable to characterize nonwestern language structures, about which almost nothing was known, with extrapolated concepts, such as inflection, which seemed to apply to large classes of grammatical forms in familiar

European languages. The history of linguistic science is instructive as a guide to those who would refine methods and advance knowledge in other sociocultural subjects. Thinking today about thousands of nonwestern religions or other expressive systems must, therefore, rest upon a premise which emphasizes utmost caution in gross characterization of such systems or of big segments within them. Analytic knowledge is less than meager except for a very few of them. In spite of the great name of Durkheim, one accordingly questions if his and others' venerable dichotomy of sacred or holy and profane, secular, or unholy is any more operational, that is, employable in scientific work, than pre-modern linguistics' once generally extrapolated concepts of inflection, polysynthesis, and agglutination. Long ago it turned out that no classes of linguistic units were usefully identified, arranged, or predicted by these hoary if not hallowed constructs. They had to be shelved although they had served over a period of decades with gross descriptive utility for students who lacked close analyses and good structurings of materials in nonwestern languages. Does this example offer an efficacious analogy for the antique concepts of sacred and profane which doubtless classify religious phenomena of certain kinds in the Judeo-Christian heritage?

Are sacred and profane too broad or unwieldy in their coverage of and contrasting of classes of data from nonwestern religions? Does a concept of the sacred cover so vast a macroclass of beliefs, ceremonies, and functionaries that it is not especially useful for understanding of specific operations within any one nonwestern religion? Is it any more employable for operations shared in a group of such religions? Is the supposed quality which some writers have dubbed "the sacred" capable of manipulation in the manner of other organizing concepts? Is it a concept which encloses a single class or several classes of particular items? Is it necessary or useful in any way in fashioning a structure of scientific theory about differences as well as similarities among nonwestern religions?

All the same, is there not an over-all quality or characteristic, the sacred or holy, which accrues equally to each of the many classes of beliefs, rites, and personnel in every western and nonwestern religion? And what does sacred really mean? Is it, possibly, only an alternative term for a variety of supernaturals, a wide range of feelings about them, or for persons and activities which connect with them? Indeed, is it a veiled synonym used in a prepsychological era for a nonspecific anxiety and multiplicity of tensions?

It seems, for example, that like earlier linguists' agglutination concept which disintegrated with disuse and additions to knowledge, the more questions asked around the meaning and the more relevant facts gleaned around possible cross-cultural utilization of a concept of sacred, the more it melts into other concepts such as anxiety, supernaturals, or religion itself. These and other constructs appear to provide all that is presently needed to forward a system of scientific theory. Extrapolation of the Judeo-

Christian concept of sacred into nonwestern phenomena, as in Durkheim's library-based research on Australian religions, evidently bears a troublesome resemblance to the long discredited procedure of projection of features of Indo-European language structures into languages which do not exhibit such structures. In addition, the extrapolation at once reveals myopia, inevitable in Durkheim's time and for a while after, concerning a variety of psychological operations around supernaturals: today it is possible to perceive workings of general anxiety and of defenses by means of displacement, identification, and projection. These psychological concepts may be on the verge of becoming dated, too, because they themselves cover too many classes of religious features and responses. But, for the moment, they have the virtue of escaping condemnation on the score of constituting blatant extrapolations from one ideological heritage to all others. The sacred appears to blanket a generalized anxiety and kinds of religions which have been defined principally for a few wealthy societies and sociocultural heritages. Its employment for other heritages and their religious phenomena seems to contribute confusion, duplication of terms, an emphasis which results in ignoring of psychological processes, and zero dividends in pointing to features of religious difference and in arrangement of contrasted classes of significant items. It is likely, then, that Durkheim, one of the most seminal thinkers at the turn of the century, improperly projected concepts of sacred and profane into his reading of surface descriptions of Australian religions. He overestimated the completeness of those delineations. Many other and more recent writers on religions have unwittingly subscribed to the same fallacious method. They have also respected source materials which were superficial and burdened with culture-bound extrapolations. They projected a sacred-profane contrast where probing researches which might uncover it are lacking. Comprehension of the phenomena remains unaffected by pious citation of a dialectical sacred-profane antithesis. Further scientific research may not everywhere or often receive assistance with it. The binary opposition approach should be reserved for use in linguistics and in those cultures and cultural expressions which unquestionably codify items of ideology and contrasts in feelings in that manner. In many spheres of expressive materials sets of units do arrange as binary opposites. But it is necessary to find out where such opposites appear before they are unhappily regarded as present.

### Shamans and Priests

There has been sufficient citation of and comment upon principal classes of beliefs or ideological units which integrated with a nonwestern religious system. What about functionaries and behaviors which meshed with it?

A familiar formulation is that along the continuum of persons who had special contact with supernaturals and distinctive capacities in employing them, shamans were only part-time workers. They were primarily laymen who most of the time were indistinguishable from the rest of the people. Shamans characterized food-gathering and economically poorer agricultural societies. They participated in economic and other social relationships like everyone else. Female shamans were rarely as numerous as male practitioners. On the other hand, the term priests, a label borrowed from Judeo-Christian sociocultural systems, has served anthropologists as a convenient caption for those full-time specialists, usually well-to-do gentry of male sex, who in nonwestern societies dealt with supernaturals and who functioned differently in economic activities and social relationships from the remainder of a population. Terms like witch doctor, soothsayer, seer or seeress, and sorcerer have been used to cover special sets of persons in wealthier nonwestern societies who operated at social levels lower than affluent priests. An evolution-oriented writer might suggest that legatees of the black arts in such societies were survivals of an earlier period when their predecessors had been wholly respectable shamans who had functioned as the only persons who made important contacts with supernaturals. Origins of specialists of such kinds are obscure if written records are absent. Evolutionist guesswork is as futile as elsewhere.

It has generally been supposed that priests, in the technical sense of the term as employed by some anthropologists, tended to crystallize out of a community in wealthier nonwestern societies which also had, of course, specialization in occupations, superior status of males, and surpluses portions of which were allocated to support of priesthoods. These functionaries were likely to take part or all of a mythology out of the hands of laymen and refashion its content and its style genres so that it could suitably, although a bit loosely, be captioned a theology, another rubric borrowed from western civilization. Often a priesthood became the topnotch group of pedagogs. It might acquire productive property, even slaves, secure tribute, specialize in cosmological, astronomical, and calendrical inquiries, become an arm of government, and carry on artistic work.

A system of psychological statements about shamans and nonwestern religious functionaries is embryonic. The psychology of priesthoods in nonliterate groups is all but unknown. Indeed, the phenomena are of bewildering variety and complexity. Psychological and psychiatric theory may be inadequate to cope with them today, with an apparent result in field observations which have received little usable direction from theory. There are no case studies of a satisfactory sample of shamans or priests within a nonliterate community. Claims have been made that shamans comprised some of a society's persons with schizophrenic trends and that the status, responsibilities, and contributions in health and religion of such individuals so contained their pathology that it remained more latent than manifest in them. Regression and deterioration into an intolerable emotional state did not often develop in these people. Evidences for or against such judgments need to be gleaned in each district the world over. It seems judicious to withhold opinions until new and better field evidences, principally in case study form, are collected. An assertion that a high percent of part time or full time specialists in the supernatural displayed potentials for schizophrenic break with reality may constitute an expression of hostility toward religious functionaries by dereligionized social scientists of our era. It certainly ignores the absence of satisfactory cross-cultural psychological data gained in field researches. It flies in the face of a likelihood that abler and more realistic persons, rather than individuals who were prone to sever connection with reality because their minds tended to be off-beat, may have been the very ones who inclined to enter and succeed in prestigeful pursuits such as those offered by supernaturalism. In some food-gathering societies where shamans surpassed all other persons in station, emotionally disturbed persons, particularly those who were prone to regression and unrealistic adjustments, may have been little likely to become successful shamans. The ablest people are invariably capable of doing what is necessary and possible, even when it requires hallucinatory raptures.

It appears that in advanced agricultural societies, priesthoods, which again very likely contained some of the most competent, mature, and imaginative citizens, tended to unify ideological content, integrate mythology into theology, subject rites to ever more elaborations, and engage in educational efforts for children of the wealthy. It seems that in such wealthy societies, religions which competed with each other, attempted to engulf other faiths, or strove to maintain themselves in a rejecting environment tended to structure their ideology of the supernatural, their world view, and maybe the ethics of the people in ways not found among food-gatherers and economically simple agricultural groups.

In the latter types of society, some regions or communities appear to have known consciously only their own beliefs and customs and these functioned integrally with all other segments of the sociocultural heritage. What Euro-Americans identify as the entirety of a nonwestern religion perhaps exhibited little encapsulation. It is possible, indeed necessary in accordance with scientific method, to dissect out of all nonwestern religions components of rather well structured systems such as the annual round of ceremonials, the status, roles, and functions of shamans, and the mythological core of the oral literature. Somewhat patterned clumps of primarily religious, because supernaturally connected, materials were always present. They were only slightly amorphous subsystems, each with its special classes of units, and they adhered so as to comprise a macroclass which is properly captioned religion. In less wealthy societies that macroclass had not been remodeled, parts excised, rationalizations added, or the subsystems pieced together in a vast integration. Priests or other specialist thinkers were not there to do it. They functioned as such integrators, creative thinkers too, in wealthier and stratified societies. Means to which they resorted and webs and novel insights which they wove require special study in each region.

## Ritual and Art

Even in modern western civilization only a few so-called "progressive" schools conduct rituals such as assemblies or commencement day solemnities without a split second intrusion of citation of a supernatural. University masters and doctoral examinations, in addition to state examinations of certified public accountants and intelligence testing by psychologists, offer examples of rites which also usually lack such reference. Nevertheless, these formalities arise in features of the sociocultural system which produce much anxiety. One wonders why the supernatural is not then invoked. In spite of rapid increase in numbers of nonbelievers in western civilization, most of its ceremonials include survivals from an era when nonbelievers were almost unheard of. These vestigia resemble the retention of final accusative suffix -*m* in *whom* in English sanctioned by high school teachers. Rituals need to be regarded for purposes of content and style analysis as having their elaborate grammar, too, with form classes, syntactic and discourse patterns, and the like or, rather, analogues of such sets of items. These are woven into structures, call them rituals, whose parts require connection with other structural and stressful characteristics of the sociocultural system. Some few parts are leftovers of former classes of items and are retained because they also function to grant little crumbs of security, assuage guilt, and stir other mildly pleasant feelings.

All nonwestern societies presented rituals of various kinds at intervals through the year. Among food-gatherers, almost everyone participated or attended when customarily assigned elders or special groups of persons took over. Sexual segmentation into subclasses of rituals, men's and women's, appeared in a few regions, notably Australia.

It would be fatuous to underestimate potentials for elaboration of features of expressive content and style in song, dance, and verbal forms in such preagricultural societies. Sound-on-film records and satisfactorily full commentary about them have so far been rare in any part of the world.

Many of the rituals of nonwestern agricultural societies functioned in relation to crops and weather. Groups to which fishing was economically strategic invariably expressed themselves in ceremonial around such production. Specialists, clans, priesthoods or other sectors of the population might carry out assignments to conduct rituals. No one can doubt a nexus between communities' seasonal insecurities or periodic dangers and resort to invocations of supernatural kin who granted favors as consequence of esthetically modeled rites. Feelings of security and belongingness intensified during such ceremonials. Esthetic responses reinforced these sentiments.

The richer and more stratified a socioeconomic system, the greater the passive audience role of most persons. Sometimes, too, the greater the numbers of rituals.

Speculations and assertions during recent decades about rituals as sources of mythology have been regarded almost as scholarly gospel among groups of professors of literature, few of whom have disregarded Frazer, Jane Harrison, Lord Raglan, Joseph Campbell, and Stanley E. Hyman as responsible pundits in these historical questions. But anthropologists and scientific workers occupied in cross-cultural research on oral literatures are in virtual agreement that, in spite of the stature of its protagonists, a ritual-to-myth dogma is inapplicable to food-gatherers or the economically simpler agricultural, pastoral, and fishing societies which have long been a special province of field workers in cultural anthropology. Rituals in such groups and concomitant dances and music have no more cloud-seeded their torrents of myths than they did anything else. In most, if not all, societies rituals have been esthetic and psychologically satisfying results, not historically precedent causes of classes of items.

Rituals constituted macroclasses of expressive phenomena whose dynamics and functions cannot be depicted in a simplistic statement. Each macroclass such as myth, cosmology, dance, poetry, music, or supernaturals, portions of which were woven into a ritual, had its idiosyncratic correlates in a society. Each such class must be further pieced into unitary components which have to be exhibited, with full commentary, in all their connections. There is, therefore, no more warrant for a few terse statements about origins, principal characteristics, and functions of complex cultural manifestations such as rituals or myth repertoires than there is excuse for simplistic statements about origin, characteristics, and functions of a nonwestern dance repertoire. Ritual, mythology, and dance are each a macroclass which contains distinctive classes and smaller sets of features. The latter should be identified in all their multitudes, arranged with other members of their class, and manipulated with a precision which a scientific linguist employs in identification, ordering, and depiction of functions of each unitary member of a set of instrumental, tense, or gender affixes.

As art forms, rituals, like Europe's opera, have usually been most complex aggregates of their component sets of esthetic items such as music, dance, poetry, and plastic-graphic expressions. Poetical declamation and myth recital, each present in some rituals, had their special esthetic merits. Dance and music in ritual offered other esthetic attributes. There might be plastic-graphic and body ornament sets of items too. Impact of an entire ritual might not amount to more than a mathematical total of its class segments and the units in them, if mechanical counting has relevance in treatment of this kind of artistic expression. For the present, scientific research may have sufficient to do, initially anyhow, in separate analyses of features of expressive content and style within each such esthetic segment. But rigorous content and style analysis, that is, structural method is not yet standard procedure in such research.

Outsiders' esthetic responses to ceremonies of nonwestern peoples are as fatally culture-bound as are the ecstatic reactions of European musicians to Navajo songs or New York sculptors to Pacific Northwest Coast carved houseposts. That is to say, perceptions of features of content and style in a nonwestern ritual are hardly more than those which a western observer has already learned in his own sociocultural system. He inevitably fails to perceive most items in each array of expressive or style features which is included in dance, song, or other facet of a ritual. In a way, a nonwestern ceremonial is a kind of supermacro-art because it contains several macro-classes of arts. It is ridiculous to expect a western observer to respond with discretion or taste to so elaborate a tapestry before he has studied it at great length.

Presumably it is exceedingly accepting, respectful, and sincere to attend faithfully to successive details of a Hopi Pueblo or Watusi dance ritual. Thousands of gracious or merely curio-minded Euro-Americans do so each year. But there is no escaping the fact that they cannot comprehend most of what is going on. Their reaction to the elaborate proceedings is expressive of a rapidly widening and deepening mainstream in western civilization of acceptance of worth of nonwestern peoples and concern to divest itself of yesteryear's racism and cultural arrogance. But it is not a sensitive or informed esthetic response. It cannot be. Obviously, an esthetic evaluation of a nonwestern ritual or of its components, such as music and dance, is naïve before publication of rigorous analysis and commentary made with rich knowledge of the sociocultural heritage.

## Stability and Innovations

Supposition that the considerable realm occupied in a nonwestern society by religion comprised one of its most conservative areas is of course an extrapolation from one sociocultural system's experiences. It is not a generalization which has flowed irresistibly from a reservoir of cross-cultural studies. Sampling within each of the world's socioeconomic types is required to substantiate a belief that religions were prevailingly slower to change than other facets of culture. An a priori case might be offered to support a probability for the opposite of the belief, at least in some types of societies. It might be urged that since supernaturals were resorted to in order to alleviate tensions and to tide people and communities through crises, alarming new situations might rapidly engender resort to both traditional and novel supernaturals who thereupon served in wanted ways. If supernaturals were responsive in such a manner, that is, if mechanisms of projection, especially of new supernaturals, operated so quickly it might follow that nothing in a sociocultural system changed more rapidly than religion. However, only the recent profusion of descriptive materials on post-Columbian nativistic or revivalist developments, commented upon in the next section, is available for such theorization. The statement exacted here is that change in nonwestern religions might be fast. A dogma about religious conservatism is unsupported by cross-cultural evidence.

Nor is the question of stability resolved by treatment solely of the totality of religion. A faith within an economically simple society may have been amorphous to an extreme of its classes or parts merging indistinctly with almost everything else. In wealthier societies, it may have been somewhat encapsulated and managed by specialist functionaries. But each religion was unquestionably a most complex hodgepodge or structure of classes of units. A decisive issue is the determination of factors, also well-measured speeds, of change in one or several such classes while other classes remained unaffected for a time. Questions such as the following must be asked. What occurred with causation and rate of change in religious dancing? music? memorized incantations during rites? myths? ethical statements, if there were any that tied in with supernaturalism? Not least, with numbers and kinds of supernaturals? Actually, change in religion does seem to have operated unevenly, certainly so during an initial and sometimes long period while the whole complex of classes, that is, the structure as an entirety, presently displayed readjustment, too.

In some parts of food-gathering western North America, the earliest changes after Euro-American entry affected customary hideouts or locales of spirit-powers and tended to emphasize relationships with very much weaker ones, that is, with almost humiliating ones, and this in a region where social hurts were almost worse than massacres. People were no longer "finding" and relating to strong and wealth-giving spirit-powers. People were obviously expressing in this projective manner their lessened self-confidence and feeling of worth. Native theory was that their potent, but not wholly human, kin had fled the districts into which invaders were pouring. Presently, more and more natives were encountering a few remaining spirit-power kin close by rather than at a distance and the populations of spirits available were no longer numerous or endowed with great abilities as of yore.

Naturally, there was no stability in the religion of a surrounded, crushed, or disgraced people. Every class of items in their earlier religion changed more or less speedily, defensively of course, under such acculturative conditions. Often it was fear and misery rather than wholesome aspirations which determined what people "saw" and wanted. They could hope for little more than a violent elimination of the Euro-American cause of their misfortunes.

Since projections of and relationships to supernaturals, especially in animistic cultures, may have been among the most sensitively responsive classes of items when socioeconomic changes or crises occurred, an interesting theoretical possibility follows. It is that in food-gathering societies portions of religion which centered about classes of kinlike beings, who were extremely close by and in virtually daily relationships with all the people, were among the most rapidly alterable segments of a sociocultural system. They were so because of a mechanism of projection which was basic to generation and unconscious designing of supernaturals. It is, therefore, conceivable that vital parts of religion were most unstable among food-gatherers. Projections of supernaturals were progressively more solidified as societies became wealthier, stratified, and with religion entrusted to a property owning and politically controlling priesthood. Such societies stressed less easily cajoled and remoter deities and allowed priests a major share in their manipulation. It is as if people in time displaced from flexible and kinlike supernaturals to a small array of distant surrogates for those supernaturals. Deities, like priests, were also more slowly affected by needs and feelings in the rank and file of the populace. Therefore, if these speculations are tenable, the wealthier a society the more stable or rigid the religious structure and most of its classes of features, especially its bigger supernaturals who now had institutionalized protectors. In such societies a variety of responses to socioeconomic changes might have been more rapid than changes in the religion.

## Revivalist and Nativistic Cults

Anthropology and history will never be able to reveal fully the extent and profundity of nonliterate peoples' religion-centered responses to socioeconomic changes and European entries since 1492. In large districts of the Americas, even minute parts of religious heritages of entire populations of culturally distinctive peoples vanished after completion of processes of their acculturation. Many of these groups had witnessed adaptive cults that functioned temporarily to take care of feelings engendered by disastrous alteration in their life. Short-lived religious developments of such kinds were only larger community responses which paralleled endless individual religious reactions that, very likely, displayed similar psychological behavior and services. But anthropology has records principally of cults not of adaptive individual experiences. Comprehension of the psychology of new cults which were responses to Euro-American expansion and penetration might have been furthered by information on individual innovators who led and participated in a cult. In the world's economically backward districts, new cults appeared almost every year for centuries, although a mere handful became even superficially documented for the behavioral sciences. Anthropology has taken note of a few examples of processes of great diversity. There are published items on western North American Ghost Dance cults of the 1870's which spread northward from California into Pacific Northwest states, a so-called Ghost Dance Religion which became visible from Nevada to the Mississippi in the early 1890's, a curiously named Shaker Indian religion which appeared in Washington State in the late 1880's and which had spread into northern California and British Columbia by the 1940's, recent Cargo cults of New Guinea, and a meager catalog of others. Only a small percentage of the cults which flowered during the past 470 years are known by a name because most of them were too small in scale, too rejected by the few Euro-Americans nearby, and too transitory to be written up.

Characteristics of revivalist and nativistic cults may be accorded crude summarization in the following major steps. They offer an initial classification of the many things that occurred in each cult. First, there was drastic change in ways of living. Euro-Americans or others introduced technologic and other innovations. There might be slave raids, hangings and shootings, massacres, venereal diseases, tuberculosis, epidemics, or forced removals to strange locales. There were always augmented mortality, tragedy of new kinds, despair, hopelessness, conflict in lineages and families between elders and youngsters, and other wretched circumstances. The crisis was socioeconomic, cultural, health, and psychological, all in one. Second, people strove to meet their crisis as realistically as they knew how and they always employed their traditional religious devices. But whatever they did was to no avail. Recourse to guerilla warfare, migration, appeals for help from invaders or supernaturals did little or nothing. The Euro-Americans were invincible, brutal, arrogant, and callous. Third, a few people presently turned to familiar supernaturals for aid of new kinds in resolution of individual, lineage, or community frustration. In some regions such recourse to supernaturals was effected, as in precontact eras, by fasting, trance states, or native drugs. Spirit allies vouchsafed results if certain requirements of new kinds were fulfilled, usually by means of rituals of modified content and styling. Fourth, one or more persons reported distinctive supernatural experiences and played prophet or seer roles from the invaders' point of view. Other persons accepted organizer-emissary roles, still others public relations or missionary roles. Fifth, "seers" so-called, organizers, and missionarylike natives cooperated so that their cult spread in the district. Converts or joiners found many specific things to do in building the cult and, for a while, were in remission from earlier depression and despair. It was a kind of group psychotherapy. Sixth, wishful ideological products of the cult included items such as miraculous elimination of invaders, acquisition of their skills and material possessions, return to life of murdered or other prematurely deceased natives, and return of decimated food resources (game, fish, food plants). Often syntheses of precontact and Christian ideology and ceremonial appeared. Principal functions of such cults included mass remission, usually only temporary, from depression consequent upon realistically insurmountable tragedy, and ego therapy, also often only ephemeral, which facilitated participations and acceptance in a changed and Euro-American pervaded environment.

Research method in reporting and analysis of such cults has been largely old style journalese descriptivism. Scientific sophistication displayed in field researches has amounted principally to concern about fullness and accuracy. As in study of any sociocultural expression, a cult phenomenon should be dissected into its probably distinctive classes of items such as dances, music, supernaturals, rituals, organizers, and leaders. Each member item of such a class should be accorded precise description, electrical transcription too, if possible, and granted commentary following sensitive interrogation of informants. No thorough structural and functional analysis can be managed after return from a field situation because it has to be done, at once, with a variety of informants at hand. Only then can ties between classes of items be perceived, components of the fabric assessed, and the totality of the phenomenon portrayed.

## Perspectives

Although art critics have insisted upon their moral right and professional capacity to judge merits in nonwestern esthetic products such as wood sculpture, pottery, dance, or music, cultural anthropologists today encounter few comparable claimants, except missionaries, to roles as umpires of nonwestern religions. And a growing, but still extremely small, number of missionaries have been moving in a direction of emphasis upon respectful comprehension rather than evaluation based upon conviction about their own superior faith.

A current obligation of cultural anthropology is to employ every device of scientific method which will facilitate advance in knowledge of specific religions and district types of them. The goal is the building of a system of scientific theory about all religions of people of simpler technology. Since such theoretical knowledge is in its infancy, employment of it now for purposes of estimation of the worth of nonwestern religions is irresponsible. Eulogy and dispraise appear to arise in compulsions felt by culture-bound or religion-bound persons.

The future of religions of peoples of lowly economy is as opaque as anything in cultural expressions. No one can doubt that whole classes of features, individual items too, in some few of the thousands of such religions will long survive sociocultural changes consequent upon acceptance of twentieth century or later technology. Holdings of classes of features such as music, dance, and mythology may be especially frequent. A romantic or esthetic reader may wish for or approve these or other retentions. But he is going to suffer disappointment about survival of unchanged religions as entireties among any peoples of simple economy.

### SUGGESTIONS FOR FURTHER READING

Outstandingly deserving treatments of the religions of peoples of lowly technology are few. The following include some of the more important writings. B. Malinowski, *Magic, Science, and Religion* (paperback; Garden City, N.Y.: Doubleday, 1954); E. B. Tylor, *Primitive Culture* (2-vol. paperback; New York: Harper, 1958); E. Durkheim, *The Elementary Forms of the Religious Life* (Glencoe, Ill: Free Press, 1954); R. H. Lowie, *Primitive Religion* (New York: Boni & Liveright, 1924); S. F. Nadel, *Nupe Religion* (Glencoe, Ill.: Free Press,

1954); E. E. Evans-Pritchard, *Nuer Religion* (Oxford: Clarendon, 1956) and *Witchcraft, Oracles and Magic Among the Azande* (Oxford: Clarendon, 1937). A fascinating old classic is J. Mooney, *The Ghost Dance Religion* (14th Annual Report of the Bureau of American Ethnology, 1896). There are many others.

College textbooks and related kinds of writing are largely unsatisfactory for cross-cultural insights and the internalization of criticalmindedness about the world's religions. Recent textbooks that are often assigned to college classes include E. Norbeck, *Religion in Primitive Society* (New York: Harper, 1961); W. W. Howells, *The Heathens* (Garden City, N.Y.: Doubleday, 1948); W. A. Lessa and E. Z. Vogt (eds.), *Reader in Comparative Religion* (Evanston, Ill.: Row, Peterson, 1958). I think that if I were to give an entire course on the world's religions I would prefer to assign the Lessa and Vogt *Reader* and then resort to a variety of other readings and to classroom lectures in order to fashion a frame of theory to hold everything together. The layman needs a stern warning that J. G. Frazer's much touted writings were uncritical and are long since out of date.

# 12. THE CULTURED PERSON, THE ARTIST, AND CREATIVITY

## Who Is a Cultured Person?

One among numerous reasons why people in western civilization ask this question arises in a somewhat apprehensive effort to contrast the few who are learned, skilled, and display breadth in their interests and the many whose abilities and interests are extremely limited. A definition of culture skulks behind and is a response to the question.

Concern over persons who are cultured and those who are not is quite another matter and requires fresh premises and additional definition. Many, although not necessarily all, nineteenth century evolutionists would have reflected the self-identity of people of their own society and culture in a conviction that they and the humanistically educated (Greek, Latin, European history, European philosophy, Indo-European languages) classes of Euro-American civilization were cultured persons compared to populations stalled on lower stages of sociocultural evolution. "Savages," that is, the very intelligent people we now call food-gatherers, and the peoples of agricultural and pastoral systems who once were termed "barbarians," the latter on higher rungs of the economic evolutionary ladder, were, of course, not then regarded as cultured individuals. How could they be compared favorably with Europe's mathematicians, astronomers, operagoers, and art gallery addicts? Centers which were full of evidently cultured people were Vienna, Budapest, Florence, or Paris. Only an uncultured near-barbarian from Brisbane, Toronto, Sauk Center, or St. Louis might doubt it.

Anthropologists no longer think of themselves or their kind of western civilization in these adulatory if not eulogistic terms. Cool winds have blown in, perhaps even from the primeval woods, coral islets, and lagoons which Jean Jacques Rousseau and Gauguin exalted. Sentiments loudly uttered about one's superior civilization, heritage, and cultivation have come to be regarded as suspiciously racist, chauvinistic, nationalistic, or ethnocentric ranting. Culpability, perhaps outrage, has been building over the destruction and atrocities committed in homelands of darker peoples who lacked numbers, firearms, and social organizations adequate to put a stop to what was happening to them. Field workers are often awed in the presence of the humanity, dignity, adaptability, wisdom, and creativity of some native informants. More than one anthropologist has departed from a session of field research and from new native friends with notebooks in briefcase, file box under arm, and tears in his eyes. Upon return home, an anthropologist might be overheard purging himself in grave avowals that "the most cultured person I have ever known" was this or that native informant, and "the worst savages I have ever known" were Caucasian intruders in the district. Beatitudes of such kinds are sufficiently frequent to indicate change in the intellectual climate of the West. An expressive feature, among a vast number, which denotes such alteration in attitudes is to be found in the content of twentieth century discussions about the cultured person, the person who is truly rather than fragmentarily cultured.

Anthropologists have long perceived that before the middle years, often in the teens, food-gatherers and many of the economically simpler agricultural peoples incorporated their elders' world view, mythology, religion, ethics, and skills assigned their sex. Only sex differences in assignments and specialization after the middle years constituted some division in labor and interests. It was possible to internalize almost all of a cultural heritage and to participate to the full in every cranny of the society. Few or no participations, social or cultural, were exclusive.

If fullness of participation is a criterion for a person who is cultured, a deduction is that in western civilization individuals can proceed only a short way toward being cultured because of social strata and multiple specialist participations which they lack opportunity to enter and because, too, of the vastness of the heritage itself. Completely cultured, that is, fully participant people could, therefore, be found only in the economically simplest and least stratified societies. Australian Blackfellows, Bushmen, Andamanese, Veddas, Eskimos, and an array of American Indians and Palaeasiatics were among the small numbers of modern human beings who permitted all their citizenry to be rounded, completely participant, learned in all that could be learned and, accordingly, truly cultured. There is no hidden joker in such a statement, given a premise about fullness of participations and possibility of internalization of all of a cultural heritage.

Late nineteenth and early twentieth century European thinking about cultured or civilized persons offered a special pattern of values which comprised competence in one or several of the then more respected art forms; wide reading in poetry, literature, history, or philosophy; adherence to middle or upper class etiquette, garb, and residence; addictions to "great" music, opera, and art galleries; and travel to other cities. Urban residence was required, too, short of a mansion or cluster of summer cottages for intelligentsia in the countryside or at Carmel. It was then possible to have a self-identity which contained maximal self-esteem about one's degree of personal cultivation. At the same time, a "cultured" individual could be as ignorant as an Orkney Island fisherman about the "hard" and biological sciences and about how anybody lived or thought outside of Euro-American civilization.

The late twentieth century is witnessing drastic change in that civilization's concept of a cultured person. The trend seems to be this. A person who is culture-bound or persuaded that his own culture is superior may presently not be thought of as cultured in spite of his range of participations. Although a few decades ago a learned humanistic scholar was unquestionably a person of culture, his ignorance today of every scientific field stirs incertitude about his being a cultured person. Tomorrow a lack of knowledge of every behavioral science may impel similar perplexity, if not severe rejection. A value ideal is in process of alteration. Definitions of a cultured person may soon change almost as rapidly as fashions in cravats and home architecture.

Perhaps it is most efficient and meaningful to think about the cultured individual in terms of portals and possibilities rather than realizations of them. A suggested value ideal points to open doors of opportunity to participate in any sectors of the sociocultural heritage, with understanding that in technologically advanced societies of our era no individual can live long enough to enter many such doors. Freedom to select which to penetrate may, however, be regarded as crucial. It may shortly be urged that a society which fastens padlocks on many gates of opportunity produces few or no persons who are cultured.

When a nonwestern sociocultural system has suffered surrounding by irresistible numbers of persons of western civilization, the criterion for a cultured person in the enveloped society must be revised. Is a person who is now a cultured individual merely one who has acquired a fine western education? Is it an individual who has sturdily resisted western civilization in order to remain fully conversant with his prewestern heritage? Is it an individual who has internalized both the old native and the new western heritages and has done so with humor, courage, and creativity? At this time, efforts to answer such questions about values may be more impulsive than useful. An anthropologist who studies processes of change in personalities in an acculturating group avoids value judgments about their successes and failures in identifying with people of their own or another heritage.

## Who Is an Artist?

No matter how art be defined, everyone has long agreed that ethnographic and other museums contain estimable plastic and graphic art from nonliterate peoples besides quantities of examples of their handicrafts. Magnificent specimens—that is an alien's reaction to them—come from food-gathering groups whose members were denominated "savages" by evolutionist writers generations ago. By the 1930's, Euro-American painters were in ecstasies about South African Bushman drawings and paintings on rock surfaces. Choral approval of European Paleolithic food-gatherers' cave engravings and paintings preceded the twentieth century. The same theme has been long maintained without dissonant notes and with occasional intensifications when new discoveries, such as those at Lascaux in southern

France, occurred in more recent years. Euro-American laudation of non-western dancing as unimpeachable art, especially in agricultural Oceania and agricultural-pastoral East Africa, is now decades old. By the 1960's, Watusi dancers had become appreciated so widely that their name was enshrined in the annals of rock 'n roll and the twist. Acclamation of non-western music and oral literature has been comparatively less frequent. But the direction of the mainstream of Euro-American sentiment about all the kinds of nonwestern art is evident.

"Primitives," so-called, are rising in the esteem which palefaces have for them, so much so that rapidly mounting numbers, especially State Department and United Nations personnel, are worried about the propriety of referrings to "primitives" when any darker peoples are meant. Terms like "savages," "barbarians," and "primitive peoples," long employed for special technical purposes by kindly anthropologists, are at best uncomfortable, if not glaringly parochial, utterances today. Apart from college and high school classrooms, they often have to be suppressed, most certainly so when highly literate, articulate, and acute persons who know their Shakespeare and T. S. Eliot arrive to represent new states at the United Nations and in national capitals, or to register as students on Euro-American campuses. The rapid decline in even unintentionally defamatory references to nonliterate peoples deserves study as an important expressive feature of the mid-twentieth century. It connects with enhanced respect for so-called "primitive art."

Assertions that Greek and Renaissance esthetic achievements were the world's greatest increasingly sound like repetitious mutterings of culture shackled silver-haired professors of history who never heard of Benin bronzes and who need no longer be taken seriously except when they grade examination papers. Admiration for classical Greece and the Renaissance is not diminishing, but it is accompanied by augmenting appreciation of darker peoples and their creative expressions.

Since it is no longer necessary to work hard to persuade people that in nonwestern societies artistic creativity has been abundant and of several kinds, problems arise to find out about native authors of such products and to probe sociocultural backgrounds which fructified them.

But first, it is necessary to suggest how anthropologists think cross-culturally about art if their art friends do not mind being told, by indirection, that writers on art have not yet agreed very well upon concepts which can be borrowed as a matter of convenience by anthropologists. Anthropologists feel pressure to have some presentable thoughts about the subject, so as to get to work in a definable area of problems of scientific cast. Most Euro-American philosophers of art, writers of art criticism, and discussants of "primitive art" seem preoccupied with plastic and graphic expressions. These may comprise only a small percentage of a total output of esthetic creativity in nonwestern cultures. Special problems unquestionably arise in oral arts, dance, and music. Anthropologists are obligated to include such matters in an integrated view of a people's esthetic life.

Every food-gathering and economically lowly agricultural or pastoral group transmitted a number of heritages which a Euro-American will accept as arts without preliminary bother about a careful definition of art. Almost all peoples have done something with plastic and graphic forms of expression. Apparently all peoples have danced and expressed themselves in musical symbols. There is every indication that all peoples have had one or several oral forms of expression which approached excellence, especially so in those economically impoverished societies which most of our Caucasian great-grandparents regarded as only a stage above animal existence. In each of at least four categories of artistic expression (plastic-graphic, music, dance, oral) we descry (1) materials or instruments which were employed, (2) a heritage of ways of handling or manipulating those instruments, (3) a heritage of patterns, designs, or classes of units from which selections were made and to which meanings—often religious and legendary —might apply, (4) months or years of practice with (1), (2) and (3) until (5) mistakes made, in the light of requirements accepted by most of the citizenry, were so few that, it can be said, a point of mastery of materials, techniques, and knowledge of the art had been attained. Such mastery or virtuosity in performance was mere technical perfection. Artistry, however, means (6) capacity to go beyond mechanical perfection. In addition, it means ability to play with some or all the materials of an art heritage, to manipulate and produce creatively, originally, and upon a basis of technical virtuosity which itself releases a performer to be original. The perfectly produced pot or basket, the errorless myth recital, song, or dance is not necessarily a work of art or performance of artistic merit. It becomes that if it is both technically fine and something more, that is, it is distinctive or original in some respect. At the least, these comprise a Euro-American anthropologist's criteria for assessment of artistic achievement. This formulation appears here because it seems convenient or efficient to adhere, as a starting axiom, to something definitive which is also in agreement with Euro-American thinking about technical mastery or excellence and release for originality in craftsmanship or performance. An anthropologist must start somewhere. He cannot afford to become so global and nonwestern in orientation that he has not a single question to be answered at the beginning of his transcultural journey. Actually, words such as art, artistic, or great art may not be translatable into most nonwestern languages. Nonliterate peoples knew what they greatly admired and they were almost always able to pinpoint technical or other features in a performance which they regarded with approval. But they might not be able to subsume that which they greatly esteemed under a category of art. That class of behaviors and products in the West is patently a derivative of European and Near Eastern historical developments and of unique kinds of speculations by philosophers in classical Mediterranean cities and continuously thereafter until art critics of today.

But art criticism has been universal. All nonwestern people judged and paid a kind of homage, maybe rather calmly, to what they thought was admirable work or performance. They knew that Smith was their finest dancer and Jones their best oral literature recitalist, without getting super-heated about their recognition. They knew who made magnificent pots, baskets, woven belts, and head bands. They selected, without blood pressure, what they most admired. They had morphemes or words for good and bad, sometimes too for beautiful and ugly. But one may travel far in the nonliterate world with its thousands of languages to find a morpheme or word that signified art, artistic, or artistry. There was not the Euro-American compulsion to single out and heap ecstatic praise upon the exceptional or finest, to set it apart in a special class. It was perceived but not with the distinctive raptures and paroxysms which have become familiar, if not required, in Euro-American culture.

Although the point of view about art which is offered here is essentially Euro-American and is denoted almost dogmatically, a merit in such decisiveness is that it works nicely to get cross-cultural study under way. It allows a modicum of initial agreement among field workers about important sectors of their research designs. It tells them what to study. For example, it stresses a need to examine in nonwestern societies the period of study and practice leading toward technical mastery in an art. It emphasizes a field worker's obligation to ascertain from natives themselves the point at which they supposed that such mastery was reached. It insists, whether or not older Euro-American art critics want or like it, upon the indispensability of a field worker's painstaking, accepting, and resourceful interrogations of natives regarding originality which they perceived or presumed was achieved. It emphasizes the necessity of finding surviving natives who are indicated as admired or reliable assessors of their own art, and the importance of preserving and analyzing just what they said about performances or art products by their people. It directs attention to a striking ideological theme and value ideal in Euro-American civilization: its compulsion to select and respond with a required intensity of appreciation to a small percent of expressive products as "works of art."

No one ever demonstrated that nonliterate groups lacked large numbers of articulate, finely perceptive, well-informed, and respected critics, that is, esteemed discussants, even arbiters, of their own arts. It is just as important to learn about people of this type as about witch doctors and polygamous wives, although anthropologists have so far sought out principally the latter, maybe because of the West's greater preoccupations with death and sex than with creativity. Nobody has yet displayed evidence that would indicate that native critics are as useless for comprehension of art as the current drama reviewer employed by the Podunk, Iowa, Daily News. It is probably a distrust of the objectivity of Euro-American art critics which has been projected into the nonwestern world and has brought about a view, supported by antique prejudices of course, that native art discussants were and are absent, negligible, insensitive, or irrelevant for assessment of the higher things in life and, consequently, ought to be ignored. They were primitives anyway, never fully conscious of what they were doing, and how could they have been verbally facile like the West's art critics and art philosophers? Surely the great writers on art from Aristotle through Tolstoi and on to Berenson are not to be subjected to invidious comparisons with vulgar, illiterate, and unverbose savages. But a Euro-American who dismisses nonwestern discussants and philosophers of art throws away potentially significant scientific materials, expressive source data too. He imperils advances in knowledge. Today, no one can claim that natives' tasteful responses and critical judgments are useless for a scientist's perceptions about what transpired in the life of a nonliterate people.

For over half a century, Euro-American art critics, notably those who specialize in painting and sculpture, have been identifying African sculptures as great art, almost always without consulting an African who had approached or achieved mastery of his heritage in sculpture. What was the non-African arbiter of taste and values really doing? He was imposing his own or his culture's criteria of technique, form, and excellence upon nonwestern specimens. Frequently, he was discovering that they fulfilled and even surpassed requirements which he accepted. He never inquired if pieces of sculpture failed to meet or also succeeded in meeting requirements defined by the people from which they came. In brief, a piece was glamorized as a work of art in terms solely of an outsider's perceptions and canons. A western reader had no means of knowing what it was by its own people's feelings and esthetic values. A delightful and even deeply moving performance to an outsider might be old hat, conventional, or not especially excellent to a native audience.

At this juncture, an anthropologist may elect to stand aside or retreat from further disputations about worth or greatness in art products. Some so-called "cultural relativists" in the ranks of anthropology appear to have inclined toward such escape from esthetic responsibility. Actually, they do not want to decline responsibility. They want only to avoid superimposition of canons from an alien art heritage and to judge merit by native canons which assessed expressive content, creativity, and originality. Evidences about such standards are not available to an outsider unless he has studied intensively within a nonwestern culture and has painstakingly interviewed individuals among its craft and art personnel.

In the light of Euro-American art values, that is, those of contemporary professional critics who are uninformed about the arts of nonliterate societies, exemplary products turn up with astonishing frequency in collections from nonwestern folk.

No anthropologist lacks admiration for nonwestern art work, no matter how ridiculously relativistic his dogma (a dogma can be relativistic) or how reluctant he may be to play the deity and make pontifical esthetic judgments like his western art critic friends. An anthropologist is distinctive only in wanting to dredge up every bit of evidence within a nonwestern social system and ideological heritage about what goes on in its art work. An anthropologist also feels that the question whether a nonwestern art product is great art, by its own culture's standards, is silly until anthropological knowledge has been granted by field workers about esthetic canons within that culture. It would be shocking, would it not, if yesterday's so-called "uncivilized" peoples or "savages" and today's poised ambassadors, emissaries, and visiting foreign students of dark complexions turned out to have esthetic standards more demanding than those of the former master race?

Anyhow, a cross-cultural anthropologist's commitment is not to function as an art critic or arbiter. It is not his task to tell people what is beautiful or what they ought to like. People should be free to like what they want to like. An anthropologist's work is not in the State Department, Peace Corps, social uplift, or art criticism unless he elects to leave scientific work and enter into contractual obligations to help out in workaday and art gallery problems of our time. A scientist who acts in his role as anthropologist is a pure scientist and only that. When he enters service or applied work, even art criticism, he is a former anthropologist or an anthropologist on leave of absence from scientific labors. His obligation in a role of pure anthropologist is solely to conduct comprehensive or specialized descriptive studies, to apply orderly arrangements to very full data, and to move ahead cautiously but imaginatively in the direction of building systems and subsystems of theoretical knowledge. Whether he study nonwestern art, kinship terminology, polyandrous marriages, or beliefs about sneezing and deities, he is a scientist. He must find out what has been going on in nonwestern societies and cultural expressions. He has more than enough to do without wasting time and energy in quarrels with western-culture enraveled critics over their pet prejudices and anxieties. Their compulsion to assess has to be met for what it is. Let them worry and froth about whether wood carvings from New Guinea are as great as the handiwork of Phidias of ancient Athens or Michelangelo of Renaissance Italy. An anthropologist as anthropologist needs to do unprecedentedly intensive field research on how natives learn one or the other of their arts, on what happens at a point of attainment of mastery, on how a community rallies around, encourages, and recognizes originality, on the status, role, and self-identity of creative artists, on their feuds, competitiveness, and esthetic values. If anthropologists and their confreres do not attend to these and related scientific interests, a cross-cultural system of knowledge of art is beyond attainment. Critics in museums or on staffs of metropolitan newspapers who vouchsafe judgments about excellence in Melanesian woodwork or Peruvian textiles contribute nothing to a system of theoretical knowledge, although they may be the nicest people. They are only expressing something which is pressingly important in western culture. Incidentally, they are admirably widening the circle of those who have some little understanding of cultural anthropology and of those who will grant a new kind of respect to nonwestern peoples. An anthropologist who works in art topics is concerned that, at present, little more than descriptive odds and ends and largely meaningless treasures in museums are available about the arts of nonliterate peoples. The long, long interrogations of native learners, virtuosos, creative artists, critics, and audiences have hardly begun.

Many recent Euro-American critics of painting, sculpture, music, and literature have been exceedingly gracious, for which they deserve thanks, in their acceptance of nonwestern arts as worthy cultural expressions. It is also painful to reflect that these occasionally garrulous, if not polemical, gentry have so far done nothing to erect a structure of knowledge which is other than culture tied. Has a single critic who has discoursed learnedly about merits and beauty in sub-Saharan African sculpture published a page, let alone a score or more of pages, which report his interrogations of native sculptors or critics? Of course, many field workers have been active interrogators. But the essential point is that natives' replies to them have not been broken up into classes of projective, psychological, and formal items so that advances in knowledge could be made. Interrogation has been without guidance from proper theory. Merely asking this, that, and the other question is not scientific work, although bits out of a mass of responses may be salvaged for purposes of building a system of theory. People should be interrogated in terms of problems which arise in the course of efforts to obtain evidence to support inadequately documented statements in a theoretical system. What is really being said here is that study of art cross-culturally is as much a task for scientific workers as anything else they do. Art critics also can do such work. But their writing is valueless in the advance of knowledge if their research is not conducted exactly as a scientist operates.

Many Euro-American critics care little about anyone's arbitraments or even descriptive statements but their own. Why, then, does anybody bother to pay attention to such opinionated narcissists? They chatter about what they like and dislike, and they have a free citizen's right to such vocalizations although these are not contributions to knowledge. It is right to accord freedom of expression to generous or truculent gentry whose business is pontifical art criticism. But it is also sagacious to remain unserious about their deductions about expressive content and form in arts of nonliterate societies. Some anthropologists, maybe the ones with more rugged sense of humor or greater sweetness of disposition, will continue to enjoy Euro-American critics' culture-bound groanings, heavings, ecstasies, adjectives, crotchetiness, and frequent unreasonableness. After all, some of them have become anthropologists' most supportive and often stimulating friends. But an anthropologist better make haste, wave an affectionate greeting in the direction of less dogmatic art critics, and get some long sessions of field research done. Few Euro-American critics appear to want to do that sort of thing. Almost none were trained to do it. Their dedication is most certainly not to advance knowledge.

It sounds puerile to ask if a run-of-the-mill anthropologist is ipso facto a reliable judge of some nonwestern art. Is an art oriented fieldworker presently more capable of sound esthetic judgments about Nigerian sculpture or dancing than his critic friends in London or Chicago? A field worker may find out many important things about which other persons may only speculate. His extra sensitization to expression of content and to features of style may render him a better judge than stay-at-homes, but only if he has worked at analyzing out such content and style items.

The question of who can and should make esthetic judgments ought to be allowed to gather dust on the shelf. The question has been asked before responsible answers are available. Today's job is to learn, as never before and, indeed, in some haste, everything possible about each nonwestern art and the craftsmen and artists who expressed themselves in it. Anthropologists may acquire a bundle of good answers rather soon, if they begin to watch the fortunately large numbers of remaining nonwestern craftsmen and artists and, somehow, work to construct a system of knowledge in an orderly and rigorous manner. Such a system will be based upon field research findings and analyses of what natives believe and do, and, above all, what they say about what they believe and have been doing.

## Who Is an Inventor or Creative?

Few writers have treated the topic of invention in terms of frequencies of invention and novel cultural expressions in different types of social system, or in terms of creativity outside of technological innovation. Cross-cultural theorization about innovation must first classify sociocultural systems into principal types, then ascertain special factors which have generated innovations in each such type. And innovations must not be confined to gadgetry. Innovations in music, dance, humor, poetry, cosmology, perceptions and, indeed, every other aspect of social organization and projective or cultural expressions require integration into a system of theory about invention.

The very first statement or cornerstone of such a theory, in its present immature form, is that field descriptive data relevant for theory are absent from reports on most nonwestern sociocultural edifices. A second statement is that a system of theory which can now be fashioned is culture confined because it applies, unfortunately, largely to the wealthiest of sociocultural heritages, that of western civilization. The theory cannot reliably indicate either dynamics or frequencies of creation of novel items in nonliterate groups.

In spite of a lack of hypotheses or designs for field research on inventiveness among food-gatherers, a few special statements about them are both plausible and necessary. Since everything they made or thought about tended to receive incessant community discussion, novelty in their heritage might flow less from lonely or prima donna innovators than from conversational buffetings. It is shallow dogma to claim that food-gatherers' sociocultural heritages were necessarily more stable in all respects than those of wealthier societies. On the other hand, absence of significant specialization, a technology based upon cutting tools of stone, and requirements of seasonal mobility imposed insurmountable limits. Food-gathering societies were stable in their inability to transcend food-gathering procedures of production and to accumulate large surpluses for leisure months. Interconnected areas of interest which were fortunately not so confined in such sociocultural systems were in some arts, humor, supernaturalism, sickness, and poisonings. Here the inventiveness of food-gatherers might run riot.

For all its severe limits imposed by technology, food collecting habits, and values, the way of life permitted much originality in basketry, for example. To be sure, the varieties of basketry techniques and art styles among western North America's food-gatherers have long been noted. Sample specimens are in many museums. Furthermore, perhaps every district in the western states and Canada which had a distinctive basketry style exhibited mastery of technique and creative esthetic play among many of the middle-aged and older women. In fact, the frequency of innovators in this single form of expression, from which men were customarily excluded, may be unparalleled in any specialized craft or intellectual specialty in western civilization. It is as if 10 to 50 or more percent of the women, for example, in northern California's Pomo Indian groups were geniuses, if the term which Euro-Americans like to employ for their outstanding father figures and corporeal pseudosupernaturals may be permitted to equate with valued innovators. No concentration of so-called geniuses, comparable to that found among Pomo basketmakers, seems to have been reported from another sociocultural system, not even from the free citizens of Periclean Athens. An irresponsible theoretician might deduce from Pomo evidence that women more often than men have potential to be geniuses and that Pomo bands constituted a unique gene pool which turned out the highest percentage of geniuses in any "race" the world over. That is, Pomo women were biologically far superior to Pomo men. And if one forgets about those men and the fact that they comprised half the Pomo population, the Pomos were racially superior to any other population anywhere! The point, of course, is that special sociocultural processes, not gene pools, must be invoked. Such processes, which require discovery in an economically lowly food-gathering society such as Pomo, produced a notable return in perfection and novelty in one handicraft. The Pomo evidence is irrelevant to either the race or the woman question, but it does suggest the following problem.

If creative artists and innovators constituted a majority of older persons in a food-gathering group, why the comparative infrequency of innovators in wealthy civilizations? Why does a Maxwell, Mendel, Rutherford, or Picasso turn up so rarely? There is no reason to suppose that the wealthiest populations are biologically inferior to economically lowly food-gatherers. The place to ferret out answers is in sociocultural dynamics. It does appear likely, in fact Pomo evidence is overwhelming, that under optimal conditions, whatever they are, a great many people could be innovators. Such conditions have been absent in western society for 2,000 or more years. Pomo women seem to have enjoyed such advantages, at least in sculpture and design based upon root strands and grasses. There is another important aspect of the Pomo case. It suggests that people direct their potential to innovate only into channels or in media offered by their sociocultural system. To be sure, this statement is trite, if not deadly. Nevertheless, observe that among food-gatherers, outlets for creativity were different from those available to a few persons in a very wealthy sociocultural system. One very nice outlet for talent among Pomo women was basketry. Among most nonliterate peoples, a vital channel for innovators was the dance. Another, supernaturalism. Another, deft conversation. No matter how meager its economic productivity, every sociocultural system has offered a goodly number of opportunities for creativity: supernaturalism, humor, singing, dance, basketry perhaps, and doubtless many others. Who knows how innovative many, if not all, food-gathering peoples may have been during a few hundred thousand years? The unhappy aspect of it all is that such inventiveness could not be cumulative and survive into modern times until the crucial invention of writing which was, to be sure, a product only of stratified advanced-agricultural systems. Forms of creativity available to food-gatherers were in speculations regarding supernaturals, in music and dance, in crafts which employed perishable materials such as grasses, woods, or hides, or in oral literature, poetry, humor, and rituals. But anthropology cannot expect to find traces of inventiveness in such expressions among thousands of peoples who lived during hundreds of thousands of years. Their achievements shortly spluttered and went out like American children's sparklers on a Fourth of July evening.

Since few food-gatherers remain unscathed by western envelopment, dynamics of invention among them may never be fully revealed. Nevertheless, it is impossible to build a case for paucity of creativity among them, especially in nonmaterial outlets, that is, in cultural expressions which have not survived into later eras for evidences to be gleaned. Again, only important technology and notably valuable methods of food production were ever cumulative because people did not often renounce achievements which increased material comfort and security. Usually these were jettisoned when still better devices were hit upon.

A number of economically simple agricultural peoples, notably in highland New Guinea, survived into later decades of the twentieth century and, for an extremely brief period, remain available for research without the destructive blurrings consequent upon surrounding by an expanding and penetrating western civilization. Thoughts hazarded about inventions among food-gatherers may apply to these agricultural peoples and some pastoralists. Impressive diversities are apparent in cultural materials within comparatively small districts such as the Arizona-New Mexico Southwest and sectors of New Guinea and thereby suggest a great amount of inventiveness, how recent is anyone's guess.

Innovations in western civilization may arise in specialization, and in sociocultural and personality factors which are different from those of many nonwestern societies. Competitiveness, monetary reward, status aspirations, and like motivations can produce novel results in one sociocultural system. In another, community discussions or play with techniques that everyone is encouraged to master generate novelties. An important premise of a theory of innovation would, therefore, be that a variety of social, cultural, and personality factors stir creativity. Each sociocultural area requires its own subsystem of theory to account for distinctiveness in it. The rarity of inventors and creative people in western civilization is, of course, a consequence not of inherited intelligence quotient limitations but of a complex of special social factors in that heritage. A dogma about rarity of geniuses is not well supported even if one seeks indications of innovation principally in science and technology. Actually, innovation should be sought in every cranny of a sociocultural system: frequency of innovation may be considerable in its nonmaterial sectors.

Probably very few innovations appeared only once. Similar sociocultural factors usually operated upon a number of individuals who, thereupon, utilized similar gadgetry or ideas to produce novel results that were alike. For example, it is probable that procedures or techniques which effected plant and animal domestications were achieved at least twice. The same deduction holds for bronze metallurgy—the latter in Peru and the Middle East. And the same for the Old and New World methods of lost wax castings. It is much more difficult to compare similar features of content and form in nonmaterial expressions. But anthropologists have often cited examples of parallel developments, such as sex gender form classes, in some few Old and New World languages, and Old and New World yodeling as a style of utilization of the voice in music. It is pointless to offer long inventories of virtually identical achievements in technology, social forms, and projective expressions where historical connections can be ruled out as improbable. It would be simple to cite columns of parallels of ideological kinds, such as orthodox Freudian interpretation of dream symbols, and the elderly and quite nonliterate Tillamook Indian woman on the Oregon coast who indicated that in a myth which she had dictated a little bent-over man in a canoe of course symbolized clitoris and vagina.

Simplistic, if not stupid, theories such as the popular phrasing that necessity is the mother of invention, the one that invention can be ascribed to aberrrant or neurotic personality structures, and the one which asserts that frustration engenders inventive efforts to lessen tension, are in each instance a nineteenth century hangover of a stuffy attempt to account for phenomena which have not been properly probed so as to reveal their many facets. Again, each type of society and each region must be analyzed afresh in order to work out a subsystem of theory which contains statements of those several variables peculiar to it which, combined with other variables, created novelty.

# 13. ETHNOMUSICOLOGY

## Introduction

It is commonplace today to observe that every one of the world's thousands of language groups expresses itself in musical forms. Each group possesses a repertoire of many hundreds, if not some thousands, of musical compositions, vocal, instrumental, or both. People of a food-gathering or economically simple agricultural community perhaps categorized their repertoire into types such as work songs of several kinds, war songs, ritual music of a number of kinds, songs connected with individual supernaturals, lullabies, canoe travel songs, welcome, greeting and farewell songs, fun songs, game songs, and so on. Nothing prevented the technologically simplest of hunting peoples from recognizing and captioning 20 or more such noninstrument types, probably on a basis of their differing expressive content and social functions, although stylistic traits might be similar in all.

Probably millions of nonwestern religious melodies, lullabies, compositions used in rituals, and the like are potentially available for study. But almost all remain unknown to science. Ethnomusicology has long been confined to a minute handful of research workers whose storage shelves of field recordings total only some tens of thousands of musical items and these from very few groups. While intensive studies of nonwestern sociocultural heritages and of languages have mounted into the hundreds since the 1880's, there are not many comparably revealing musical researches. Almost elementary descriptive, analytic, and question-and-answer field procedures must be developed before much of a system of cross-cultural musical theory can be initiated. In spite of its obvious importance for understanding the activities, esthetic creativity, and emotional releases of every people, ethnomusicology has suffered from astonishing neglect, although cross-cultural areas of inquiry which are similarly or even more completely evaded are still many. They include, surprisingly too, dance, emotional aberrancies, plastic-graphic arts, humor, child development, and old age.

Laymen have exhibited wonderment or annoyance about the absorption of a few scientific linguists in salvaging records of nearly extinct food-gatherers' languages which, to all appearances, no one can either use or comprehend. Of course, exotic languages do not offer a universal language. No one can or need understand them for utilitarian purposes in the contemporary western world.

People's feelings about music are evidently less surprised or fearful. Thousands of writers and teachers have parroted the comforting statement, which arises in nineteenth century and earlier beliefs that hark back to classical antiquity, that music is a universal language. Is not the symbolism of music universal? If its symbolism and everything else about it are really universal, and almost everybody agrees to such globoloney at the drop of a hat, then all people can listen to any and all music and appreciate it. Unfortunates who nurture reservations about the intelligibility, to them, of the Bartok violin concerto, still feel that music is a global medium of expression and that, somehow, they are not quite adequate in their response to so modern a concerto and so peculiarly intellectual a composer. They console themselves in the thought that each of us suffers from limitations. When a matter is of no great importance, it feels especially good to adopt a posture of humility and respect.

Such a stance by no means always extends to auditions of nonwestern music. Musicians of Euro-American training listen raptly, and with much understanding, many of them suppose, to disk or tape records of Nigerian orchestras, Balinese gong ensembles, Navajo or Siouan singers, and Moorish recitals. Nor does anyone offer a querulous observation about the worthwhileness of expenditures incurred in ethnomusicological field researches, dubbings onto copies, and technical analyses of rhythm, scale, and melody. No one seems to be as unmanned by exotic music as by exotic linguistics, nor is this a matter of the absence of four-letter words in the one and their undisputed presence, in translation, in the other. For music, not phonemics or linguistic morphology, equates among Euro-Americans, especially central Europeans, with respect for culture. They know they must respect culture, especially cultural performance. And so the social psychologist finds aggregations of the culture hungry listening intently to performances or playbacks of nonwestern music. They may be indifferent to or question values in other exotic cultural forms, excepting sculpture. Performance of exotic music is, of course, a Euro-American ritual. It verges on religious ceremonial. It begets in the generous minds of auditors and participants a response of belongingness to the faithful band of those who keep burning the small flickering fire of culture. Ritual of this kind frequently concludes with some member of the group volunteering a climactic blessing, which contains the knowledgeable asseveration that the recording just completed exhibited a pentatonic scale. No evangelical religious group of modern western civilization ever conducted a service without some uneasy awareness of disbelievers along the avenues, but the devout who pay homage to disks and tapes upon which are imprinted the supposedly universal language of music have no reservations regarding their vespers.

But one must not depreciate ethnomusicology, least of all the musical performances which its protagonists record in the field and replay at home to sincere and deferential supporters. Such community respect and approbation are useful in spite of ceremonialism, parrotry, pretense, and incongruity which often accompany them. Ethnomusicologists are luckier than scientific workers who conduct researches on dying languages and oral literatures of the world's nonliterate peoples. Public sanction always facilitates support for the devoted, altruistic, and lonely who would advance theoretical knowledge which laymen often think they understand.

Of course, ethnomusicology is much more than field expeditions which bring home lovely musical recordings. Although it is only slightly beyond its starting line, it may soon be on the way to becoming a special scientific inquiry which moves in the direction of construction of a system of theory. And that is its principal justification, for it is good to advance a frontier of rigorously acquired knowledge. The respect which the esthetic multitude now have for nonwestern music is a happy accident of Euro-American history. An astonishing paucity of scientifically sophisticated research upon such music is another matter.

## Origins of Music

Just as languages constitute equally evolved end points or, rather, patterned termini following continuous changes during a million or more years, so each of thousands of musical repertoires is to be regarded as an enormously structured array of items which could be traced back, if ethnomusicology contained sufficient information, through a comparably long period. Every modern food-gathering people's language has been patently most elaborate. Seriously offered statements about their music's extreme simplicity are puzzling in instances of some small collections of songs. Reports have asserted, for example, that such compositions exhibited only two-tone scales. To be sure, these look crude or simple by comparison with scales in music of wealthier peoples. But are any or all other facets, that is, patterned sets of items, of a musical repertoire equally simple in a group which is said to have had only a two-tone scale? Inquiry remains open until completion of full analysis of the various classes of expressive and formal items enclosed in a musical genre and the repertoire which always comprises a number of genres. In no instance has such range of analysis appeared in print.

It would be curious if, after changes of a million years, Australian Blackfellow music, which some observers have said contained ultrasimple scale patterns, retained an unusual number of simple Pliocene or earlier Pleistocene features and patterns of expression while Blackfellow speech did nothing of the sort. Therefore, it seems safer to assert, much as for analogous features of language, that musical origins may be Pliocene and that the earliest features of scale patterns or tonal intervals, melody line, rhythm, vocal behavior, and the like are unknowable. However, it is reasonable to assume that in Pliocene and early Pleistocene eras rhythm was supplemented by percussion, the human voice was the one richly expressive instrument, and dance accompanied singing and percussion. Note that nothing specific is stated about early musical units and patterns.

Some writers, especially Karl Bücher in *Arbeit u. Rhythmus* (1902), have suggested musical origins in rhythmic work, that is, the earliest music developed in work singing, canoe paddling, trail walking, and the like. Evidences for or against such nineteenth century twaddle about forever invisible origins are, again, unobtainable. The statements evoke nothing meaningful about the always diverse sets of items in musical content and form. Like conjectures about remote era origins of concepts of the supernatural or of linguistic features, surmises about origins of expressive classes of elements in other complex cultural systems such as music, dance, or humor contribute nothing to the structures of scientific knowledge which need to be developed regarding those systems. Origin hunts in instances of cultural systems, and specifically in music, are so much nineteenth century waste motion, although they might have been fun in their time, like the pleasant memory of an Easter egg hunt in the old family home. The sooner a twentieth century science faces the fact of inutility in much of the charming prehistory guesswork of earlier authors, the sooner scientific work can be gotten under way.

It is, therefore, correct to proceed directly to examination of materials, methods, analyses, and classifications which bear promise of yielding significant classes of expressive and formal units that can constitute cornerstones of a transcultural structure of scientific theory about music.

## Method

From the 1890's to the end of the 1920's, some thousands of small Edison, Columbia, and other wax cylinders were brought back with fresh field recordings cut on them from nonliterate groups. Scientific descriptive study was hardly possible before Edison's invention of the wax cylinder phonograph because each musical composition must be performed many times in order that its significant features be identified and transcribed. A composition must also be available for others to play and replay so that they may examine, check, and make improvements upon the transcription: this is a minimal requirement of scientific procedure. Although the 30-year haul of small cylinder recordings of nonwestern music was infinitesimal and many large regions remained unrepresented by a single song or other composition, several central European scholars were sufficiently stimulated to start ethnomusicology on its way, principally by means of their recommendations (Carl Stumpf, Erich von Hornbostel, et al.) of transcriptional symbols which stood for musical features that were both significant and unrepresented by symbols such as were used to write musical expressions of western civilization. These pioneers offered a few score more symbols than the small kit of them then at hand. In addition, tiny groups of field collectors appeared, men like Bartok and Kodaly of Hungary, and collectors of North American Indian music like Alice Fletcher and the indefatigable Frances Densmore.

Between about 1925 and 1950, a few thousand more compositions of nonliterate peoples were recorded on sturdy Dictaphone or Ediphone wax cylinders and presently electrically on discs, the latter at awesome financial outlays when done for musicologists by commercial recording companies. Further important advances were not made in the armory of transcriptional symbols for nonwestern musical features, although such new symbols were much needed. A small number of wire recordings were contributed between 1945 and 1950. Since then, ethnomusicology acquired probably thousands of tape recordings which, happily, are inexpensive, easily copied, and exhibit a high degree of acoustic fidelity. At the same time, possibly important advances have been made in fresh identifications of musical features and in approach to recognition of fundamental musical units.

Methodological and correlated theoretical problems arise only superficially in recording equipment and materials, important as they are. Fragile small wax cylinders of the 1890's to the 1920's remain usable in spite of their rude noises arising in surface scratch, tinny nasal quality, pitting by moths, and only two-minute duration of singing, where moths have not wholly destroyed them. Such cylinders are good for purposes of scientific analysis providing they were recorded with a concern for various other matters of method, but this was rarely the case.

What, then, are methodological considerations which attach to all ethnomusicological collecting, archiving, study, and development of theory?

First, let us learn what we can from pertinent analogies. Little systematic knowledge, that is, a structure of supportable theory about plastic and graphic art, is possible upon a basis even of millions of sculpturings, pots, baskets, and other collected items stored in museums, as pleasant as it may be to look at all these specimens of handicraftsmanship and esthetic creativity. Far more is needed, not least, a body of hypotheses about basic sets of features in each type of plastic or graphic art. Linguistics would hardly be able to progress toward a mature theoretical system were it to acquire untold thousands of magnificent tapes of many hundreds of spoken languages, if the tapes were unaccompanied by fine transcriptions, a variety of annotations, precise translations, and, above all, a body of hypotheses about the basic units and classes of language units (phonemes, morphemes, etc.). If anthropology had superb sound and color films of scores of thousands of the nonwestern world's dances they would avail little, too, if the dances were not painstakingly transcribed and annotated. Anthropology still could not advance knowledge of the dance if it lacked, as it does, a set of starting hypotheses about fundamental segments, component units, and classes of units in dance expressions. A collection in beautiful phonemic transcription and sensitive translation of 100,000 laughter generating situations in hundreds of nonliterate peoples would reveal little, indeed, about those peoples' dynamic processes in humor. Anthropology must start with a bundle of hypotheses about significant classes of items which may be represented in a fun situation. In any case, a great many of the 100,000 examples might not even be funny to a Euro-American.

The point is that when examples, prodigious quantities of examples, of cultural expressions are collected, brought back from nonliterate societies, accurately presented in electrical recording or other perfect sample specimens, and placed in fine archives, scientific knowledge is never meaningfully advanced *ipso facto*. So, too, superb fidelity in tape recording and purely musical analyses of great numbers of excellent field-obtained compositions contribute only partially to a system of cross-cultural musicological theory. They serve as documentation, as source materials which can be rechecked by scientists. In a sense, they are crucial experiments, parts of which can be repeated over and over. They comprise collecting and archiving, but these alone are of small value.

In field researches on nonwestern music, it is necessary to secure alternate versions of each song, in Africa or Southern Asia of each instrumental performance too, from the same performer and from others, in order to display esthetically permissible variability and limits. There must be pertinent information about these informants, their social relationships, and their own commentary about what they are expressing and how well they have done it. There must be a good sample of compositions of each type or genre recognized by the people: lullabies, work, play, fighting, gambling, and other songs. Nonmeaningful or nonsense syllables (like *tra la la*) and words which attach to music must be transcribed and the latter translated: to do so, a field ethnomusicologist must also have had linguistic training. He observes and, with an imaginative question and answer procedure, elicits from performers and community the widest possible range of commentary and criticism about each performance. That is, every musical piece must be exhibited in its permissible variability, its relation to others of its type, and its sociocultural connections to religion, world view, the ethical system, and the total esthetic world of a people, especially including their canons of esthetic criticism. A quickie version of a song can be put on tape in just a few minutes. Its variants take longer. Other songs of the type, and variants of each such song, lengthen the task greatly. The many kinds of required annotations take a still longer time but comprise indispensable data. To secure them, the experience, skill, and scientific sophistication of an ethnomusicologist are decisive.

The history of ethnomusicological field collections and their archiving is, therefore, tragic. Requisite variants are few. Each type of composition is often poorly sampled. Linguistic notations are almost always frightful. Sociocultural annotations are usually superficial, naïve, or skewed. Most often, some or all of the needed information is absent. Above all, lack of clarification or agreement in ethnomusicology about minimal musical units and principal classes of units means that a proper question and answer procedure was neither devised nor pursued in the field.

In addition, purely musical transcription and analysis have usually been attempted only upon return from a field trip, just as linguists long tended to leave completion of structural analyses to later months and years after return to their homes. But postponement of analysis means that insights and tentative hypotheses cannot be supported, eliminated, or revised with the aid of native informants. The lesson is, therefore, to proceed as far as possible toward completion of analysis of musical, linguistic, or other cultural expressions while still in residence in the field. Modern cultural anthropology patently has much to learn about method of conduct of its specialist field researches. During 70 or more years, field investigators invariably returned to home base proudly and prematurely with stacks of inadequately analyzed and rechecked field notes. They rarely went again into the same field situation. They thought that they must carry out obligations to collect facts elsewhere, too. The rare ethnomusicologists were no more guilty of a kind of innocence in this facet of field method than were any other of the few specialists in researches upon cultural expressions.

Another requirement of method in ethnomusicology is that each recording be dubbed speedily onto a number of tape copies which can be made available for recheck by other specialists. This requirement also applies to field notebook annotations. Each article and book which delineates some scientific research must be granted public access the world over. Researches in ethnomusicology, specifically, must enjoy a comparable public pickling and distribution in at least several strategically located repositories so that anyone may reexamine all earlier work accomplished. A research which remains long buried in files, cartons, or a steel safe in a professor's office is research which for purposes of advance in knowledge was not even carried on. Free, democratic, and unrestricted availability is a central characteristic of all sciences. When efforts to recheck depictive or theoretical materials are made difficult, or the data lie in "classified" niches, an outrage has been committed against science. Only dire need for national security may diminish such mischief.

## Content and Style

Minimally distinctive features which constitute the building blocks of a musical literature's structure need to be identified one by one, arrayed in classes, then placed along a continuum from almost wholly expressive features of content at one terminus to features of content which at the other end effect structure and stylistic embroidery. Mandates of rigorous analytic method are fundamentally the same in dance and oral literature: sensitive, even though subjective, selection and identification of principal and minor minimal units; establishment of sets or form classes of such units; and depiction of their functions, whether largely expressive at one end of a continuum or, at the other end, more or less lacking in expressive content and serving purposes of ornament or formal style. A sharp line never separates all features of content from features of formal style because many of the former, or sets of them, serve functions of a stylistic kind.

In ethnomusicology, a customary approach is to segregate larger divisions or macroclasses of items. Each macroclass receives a rubric such as scale, rhythm, melody, manner of singing or vocal technique, musical forms, and harmony and polyphony.

Since mechanical instruments shape and limit meaningful content that can be expressed and, to a degree, determine features of style, initial discussion of such music producing devices is needed.

### Instruments

In North and South America, few, if any, instruments were capable of complex melodic expression. Vocal music, therefore, dominated. Stringed instruments were virtually or entirely absent. A great range of percussion devices can be described, from handclapping, thigh slapping, and use of sticks on planks to a large array of drums and rattles.

Old World technology and, in pre-Christian eras, the devising of a simple stringed instrument—a taut string over a resonator or sounding board—opened up possibilities of instrument inventions which were never available to peoples of the western hemisphere. The result was that increasingly elaborate melodic expressions which were produced anciently with multi-stringed instruments in many Old World districts importantly supplemented, where they did not replace, vocal expression. In some districts the very melodies, scales, features of style, and acoustical qualities of instruments reacted upon and shaped features of the style of sung music. Various books list the reed, wind, and other kinds of instruments which were invented. Instrument ensembles, actually kinds of orchestras, are notable in parts of Africa.

### Scale

Customary patterns of tones in a kind of horizontal line, that is, in succession, constitute features of melody. Vertical arrangements and relationships of tones in a composition or group of compositions constitute a scale. Almost nothing has been reported reliably regarding native singers' and discussants' capacity for abstraction of scale patterns and so, at the present, ethnomusicology relies upon its own personnel for knowledge of tone systems of this kind. An ethnomusicologist notes numbers of tones in a scale, intervals between them, and tonic or base tone—that is, the tone of greatest frequency and length or the one in terminal positions. A few musical styles, in each instance from peoples whose music remains insufficiently sampled, are reported to have employed extremely simple scales. A great many peoples had some songs, or one or more types of song, which were sung on a single tone. Two- and three-tone scales appeared in many regions. More elaborate scale patterns were widely present. An important descriptive problem is the determination of the number of different scales in each group's musical system, and the kinds of compositions, lullabies, ritual songs, or the like which were expressed with one or the other scale.

Lack of grammatical form classes does not make Chinese a primitive language and so it is necessary to be chary of animadversions regarding musical systems whose scales were seemingly simple. Linguistic complexities in Chinese are many, but not in grammatical features. A nonliterate group's musical repertoire usually displayed extraordinary elaborations in sets of features which had nothing to do with a scale class.

The problem of rigidity of interval relationships in musical scales reminds one of the long since discredited notion that in languages of so-called "primitive peoples" consonants and vowels are not sharply articulated and arranged in classes as in a pattern. Nineteenth century writers used to imply that such language sounds were muddied, mixed, or inconsistently variable. But researches have long since shown how pointedly, accurately, and predictably each speaker utters one or another allophone of a phoneme. The question regarding seeming permissiveness in flexibility of scale intervals may presently be solved in favor of an analogue of linguistics' premises about phonemes and allophones. That is, nonwestern singers probably sang in terms of a series of tones, a frame of tonal intervals, a scale, which in a rough way is structurally analogous to phoneme and allophone units of a language system. Apparent flexibility of a nonwestern scale system may have been essentially no more than the reaction of the outsider who had not yet perceived actual tonal units and relationships. It took a long time, many decades and researches, before linguistic science refined its concepts of phonemic and allophonic regularities to the point which they are at now. Obviously, analyses of nonwestern musical styles have been too superficial or rare and specialists themselves too few for ethnomusicology to assemble evidences that might establish a comparable theory about tonal interval regularities.

## Melody

Horizontal series and patternings of tones offer an infinity of units and frames for melodic expression. Ethnomusicologists depict different types of melodic movement and contour in a musical system, whether level, ascending, descending, arc-shaped, undulating, cascading, and, of course, more complexly patterned. Melodic movement was naturally almost level when a scale was only two-toned. Some regions, notably American Indian districts in parts of the United States, displayed downward patterns of melodic movement. Connections between each kind of melodic movement and psychological or other sociocultural factors are matters for study at a future time.

## Rhythm

Music among nonliterate peoples ranged from an extreme lack of regularity of beats, stresses, or rhythmical patterns, that is, arrangements in bars and measures were relatively free, to another extreme of repeated and uniform beat patterns. In addition, a frequent feature was a pattern of variable rhythms within a composition—one rhythm for some measures, another for the next measures, and so on. Lengths of measures might change during a composition or remain uniform throughout it. Altered lengths obviously effected contrasts in expression and stylistic variety—they were common in musical styles the world over. Classical written European musical compositions before the twentieth century utilized simple rhythms and very few of them such as four-fourths, three-fourths, six-eighths, and so on. Folk music in modern southeastern Europe exhibited a much greater range of possible rhythms, to as complex as seventeen-sixteenths and twenty-one six-teenths. Such intricate rhythms and changes of measures, so as to effect extremely complex rhythmic structures, appear to have been common among nonwestern peoples, too. In some regions, rhythmic patterns effected by a percussion instrument did not parallel or, seemingly, even relate to the different rhythms of measures of the melody which was sung. The voice, which was the principal musical instrument of nonwestern peoples, patently offered no barriers to rhythmic complexities in either sung melody or percussion accompaniment. The greatest variety of rhythmic patternings may be found in the world's nonwestern musical systems. Rhythms located in written European music comprise an extremely limited array of possibilities. Classical European music itself displayed little variety in rhythms compared to unwritten European folk music and to African and other nonwestern musical systems. In other words, possibilities in structurings in rhythms and measures are many. Euro-American written music was long almost primitive or backward in this one class of features by contrast with complexities which arose in rhythms in many other musical systems.

## Manner of Singing and Vocal Technique

The voice was manipulated very differently from region to region. Vocal chord tension and strong pulsations were widespread in the Americas, although lack of tension and relaxed vocal chords, at the other extreme, offered a stylistic characteristic of music in a number of American Indian districts such as a part of Arizona, northwestern Washington, and southern Alaska. While possibilities in vocal techniques are many, similar or parallel developments may turn up in several regions over the world. For example, use of falsetto in yodeling was not restricted to a handful of Swiss. It appeared among some south-of-Sahara Africans, Navajos, and perhaps a number of other groups.

## Harmony and Polyphony

Nonwestern music was sung principally in a single melodic line even when a choral group followed a soloist. If harmony or part singing, which is a melodic line supplemented by subordinate voices, appeared anywhere in preconquest America, it was restricted to extremely few and only wealthy groups. Harmony developed especially elaborately, of course, in Old World areas which had devised or acquired a variety of musical instruments. Technological advances in instruments patently tended to encourage proliferation of features of style in harmony. On the other hand, part singing was notable south of the Sahara in districts where musical instruments offered few, if any, factors in supporting its development. Polyphony, wherein more or less independent melodic lines weave together, is related to harmony. Possibly it was absent in the Americas.

## Instrumental Music

Music produced by one or more instruments other than the voice was rare among nonwestern peoples except in comparatively wealthy societies such as those in Indonesia and districts south of the Sahara. In American Indian areas, simple flutelike instruments served for romantic expressions, if not in other styles, but sung music generally characterized the western hemisphere. In the Old World, performers of instrumental compositions sometimes were specialists, even full-time specialists in wealthier societies. And it is possible that such specialists enjoyed opportunities to develop more analytic sophistication about components of content and style than singers acquired.

Instruments which had fixed tonal intervals such as flutes, drums, and other percussion devices sometimes tended to limit and stabilize vocal music's scale patterns. Vocal style, in a sense, followed the leadership of the other instrument when it was a fairly expressive one. Instruments also stimulated vocal developments in harmony and polyphony.

Again, stringed instruments were not a native American Indian development and a possible exception or two only points up the distinctiveness of the Americas: they did not have the many stringed instruments which developed in the Old World even before the Christian era.

## Musical Form

A musicologist can analyze gross structure in compositions much as an analyst of style in a verbal art may make note of lengths, repetitions, and relationships, that is, structuring of successive lines or verses in oral poetry (if there is such) or successive "scenes" in a myth. Musical compositions have a roughly analogous kind of architecture or gross structure. Lengths and repetitive features of musical lines or melodic phrases offer regular patternings, too. Indeed, repetition of short musical lines is a principal feature of musical architecture. Over a wide area of western North America, for example, a spirit-power song might display five, ten, or more repeats of the initial melodic contour or line, with minute distinctive embroiderings of, or variations within, each successive line to break monotony, provide emphasis and climax, and so on.

African musical compositions south of the Sahara are now well known for their gross architecture of a pattern of solo melodic lines often of great variability, in successive repeats, followed by a pattern of choral lines which might repeat the solo lines but with little or no embroidery. The solo refrain and choral response architectural form appeared in other parts of the world also. A simpler solo response pattern appeared in North American spirit-power singing where choral response was sometimes identical with a soloist's series of lines.

In each region, then, a musicologist arranges compositions according to patterns of smaller and gross forms. Numbers and variety of such architectural patterns the world over were legion, something like the great numbers of oral literature genres and subgenres.

Just as analysis of style in oral literature may treat of acts, scenes, and other gross structural traits, smaller structural features in oral literature require identification. Introductory and closing words or phrases, and prologues and epilogues in myths or tales, may be somewhat paralleled in musical genres by classes of initial phrases and phrase-finals from which a composer selected. As in sculpture, every performer made choices of single items in a class of design units. He took the unit he wanted, at the moment, from a class of permissibly employable units.

A concept which in its broad functioning has excellent analogues in dance choreography, oral literature, and other expressive arts is denoted in music as the group or class of main types of melodic contours. That is, each one of the special styles or categories of musical expression within a group might be characterized by a small number of basic melodic contours. Each such stable melodic configuration or pattern had a shape which a composer retained as a frame for his next new composition. His creativity was a kind of expressive embroidery upon it. It limited him at the same time that it offered a form. He created within its confines. Hundreds of songs, an entire music genre, might be modeled and filled out with no more than special little details around a single fundamental melodic contour or frame. For example, the melodic structure or contour, with its successive phrases of equal length, which characterized "Home, Sweet Home" and "Way Down Upon the Sewanee River," served a great many composers. Over a century ago it provided America's Stephen Foster with a stable core or frame of melodic design for his compositions. The frame can be witnessed in hundreds, if not thousands, of melodies in Europe for centuries before. Comparably stable and basic melodic contours doubtless constituted a worldwide structural feature in musical styles and systems.

A similar stable design or frame functioned in the short story form as developed also over a century ago by Edgar Allan Poe. In nonwestern oral literatures, comparable basic structurings were, to use a western North American Indian example again, the subgenre of four or five successive acts or scenes in which siblings proceeded to their destruction and only the last sibling managed to survive. Such a phenomenon in oral literature may be referred to as a play structure. Scores or hundreds of myth or tale recitals in a small region and a variety of contiguous cultures might contain such a basic frame. Musical genres or subgenres each of which was characterized by a distinctive structuring of this generic kind must have numbered in the thousands the world over. Minor changes of content and style were, in effect, the principal creative embellishments around such stable structural frames which, in most instances, endured for centuries or longer.

## Functions of Music

Cultural anthropology and its handful of specialists in ethnomusicology have not begun to develop a system of theory which includes a set of statements about ways in which musical expressions served nonliterate peoples. It is commonplace that music functioned in secular and religious situations, in work, play, nursery, war, curing, and funerals. An intriguing thing about music is that it was as universal a form of expression as humor and language itself, and that it resembled them in its elaborateness of structuring and variety of ideas and feelings which were symbolized in the special kinds of units used. Emotional services provided by expressive utilization of musical units offer an unexplored area of inquiry. Music soothed, pleased, stimulated, excited, irritated, or released, all depending on an external situation or context and music's own expressive and formal features. It produced responses because of its auditory impact—how can one speak more tritely?—but just as much so because of its many patternings, that is, its intersecting classes of expressive and formal units. An ethnomusicologist can pursue the topic of functions of music among nonwestern peoples only by resourceful interrogations during and after musical performances. This type of research has been barely initiated. Collectors have wanted to collect music more often than they have exhibited intellectual curiosity about its manner of operation among a people. Almost no collectors were dedicated primarily to the building of a broad, multifaceted system of scientific knowledge.

## Evaluation of Nonwestern Music

Commercial disk pressings of nonwestern music which, during the 1920's, were coming in in the hundreds, especially compositions performed by West African singers, found a market largely in their native areas. Such disks augmented into the thousands during the 1960's and represented many regions. Although sales of recordings of African, Indonesian, and other nonwestern music have been principally in their countries of origin, Euro-American musicians and others often purchase them and in few instances refrain from ejaculations of esthetic appreciation. Patriots and the culture-bound in general are not often heard objecting to passionate internationalism applied to art forms, providing that such exuberant affection for dark aliens does not spread into benevolence about their sociopolitical and religious heritages or into accepting and democratic social relationships.

Canons for assessment of nonwestern music are subject to exactly the strictures which apply to evaluations by Euro-Americans of nonwestern oral literatures and plastic and graphic arts. The totality of content, style, and achievement in performance in an art is only fragmentarily perceived by a nonnative and, usually, parts recognized are very small. Approval and disapproval of art products increase in validity with analytic knowledge of them. A Euro-American professional critic of music has little that is meaningful to offer in evaluation of Navajo, Tlingit, Ifugao, or Togo music except his own culture-bound, shall one say art-bound or music-bound, reactions. He descries a few features which resemble components of his own culture's arts. He misses almost all the other features. In music, he is unable to assess a composer's effort or performer's success in manipulation of instrument, voice, structurings in rhythm, melody, or smaller and larger architectural designs. Nor is he able to discern expressive content which connects with competitive games, supernaturalism, warfare, or intercommunity relationships. Truly, there are no trustworthy western critics of the music of nonliterate groups. There are western pretenders or self-appointed arbiters who have little or nothing to contribute to advance in a cross-cultural science.

## SUGGESTIONS FOR FURTHER READING

The one attempt by an American author to provide an introductory survey is B. Nettl, *Music in Primitive Culture* (Cambridge: Harvard, 1956) but it was much too hastily written and its utility for pedagogy or orientation about method and theory in the topic of ethnomusicology is slight. Another reference survey which also offers little is J. Kunst, *Ethnomusicology* (The Hague: Nijhoff, 1959). Many volumes of studies of North American Indian peoples' music by Frances Densmore, which appeared as bulletins of the Bureau of American Ethnology, display remarkable pioneering. Their cursive sociocultural commentary marks them as the work of a descriptivist who wisely perceived much more than sets of purely musical features. The musical transcriptions of Helen H. Roberts, who worked with wax cylinders of Coronation Gulf Eskimo, Hawaiian, and other music, may be technically somewhat better than Densmore but are probably not as detailed as transcriptions by various disciples of von Hornbostel. The best ethnomusicologists, a small group which includes workers like von Hornbostel, Kolinski, Herzog, and McAllester, wrote no important books.

# 14. ORAL LITERATURE

## Introduction

Fragments of plot and motif content in myth and tale recitals, penned by scribes and authors and doubtless, in many respects, different from oral versions offered to live audiences, are available from a few wealthy civilizations such as China, India, Mesopotamia, Egypt, Greece, and Rome, in some instances for as much as two millenia before the Christian era. But not one oral literature, whether from ancient cultures or modern food-gatherers and other nonliterate peoples, is represented in a large and reliable sample of its content until about the 1880's. If little content expressed in perhaps thousands of orally transmitted literatures survives, just about nothing remains of their features of style before the 1880's because missionaries, travelers, and other scribes embellished and censored without concern for content and canons imbedded in spoken originals. Until later decades of the nineteenth century, literate people of western civilization regarded dramatic recitals, orations, rituals, or prayers by unlettered elders of less wealthy and, therefore, less glamorous civilizations as worthy of recording only if fitted out in the style of written Euro-American literature of the time.

Today, faithful written and tape records of stylized verbal expressions, together with a fairly wide range of recorded recitals in each culture, offer insufficient source materials for development of a structure of oral literature theory, although they permit its initiation. Such a structure will exhibit features both of content and style, fabrics which they display, probable causes of their origin and maintenance, and ways in which they operated in the lives of their recitalists, audiences, and society.

Professional folklorists, so-called, of the past 80 or more years interested themselves in setting up new standards of accuracy in recording and sampling. They stressed analysis into plots and macrosegments termed "motifs." They also dedicated themselves to archiving and cross-indexing such materials. And they studied, with devotion worthy of a more revealing pursuit, regional and world distribution of their plots and motifs, the latter largely in order to attempt deductions about centers of origin and routes of dissemination. They were completely accepting of the merit of such historical reconstructionist ventures and never questioned the meagerness of contribution which historicism of that kind could make to a system of theory about oral literatures. But they were not really interested in a scientific theory about any one or all of the verbal arts. They were interested in history or, rather, historical perspectives in folklore, and in problems such as discovery of paths and times of diffusion of tales and components of tales from the Middle East or India. This is, in unfair brevity, the historico-geographical "school" of folklore. Its scholarship has already provided perhaps millions of field notebook pages of accurately recorded tale texts, mostly from modern European raconteurs but also from some nonwestern peoples. Hundreds of monographs and maybe thousands of papers, in a variety of folklore and other scholarly journals, set forth historico-geographical studies that have been made.

In spite of such monumental and, in many respects, admirable production, a structure of scientific theory about content, forms, and processes in the world's oral dramatic literatures and other oral arts has progressed little farther than it had developed in the 1880's. So little theoretical advance is curious in the light of universal fascination in myths and folktales and in the numbers of cautious scholars who have been collecting and examining them. Surely, 80 years and thousands of devoted field workers and students might have produced something more than literal reports, plot, tale type, and motif catalogs, stacks of maps, and guesses about routes of plot and motif borrowing. Unlike the miniscule amounts of effort applied to study of ethnomusicology, nonwestern dance, and humor, numbers of admirably painstaking scholars did work in folklore. They labored in an era of great progress in so-called "hard" and "behavioral" sciences. But it appears that since most of them were trained in history, languages, and literature, they rarely became acquainted with developments of method and theory in more advanced fields of scientific inquiry. They were essentially perspiring collectors, drudging archivists, and aspiring historians, not scientists in pursuit of adequately validated statements designed to fit into a theoretical system. The devastating thought is that the motifs, plots, and tale types which interested them had extremely little to do with a developing scientific theory about dramatic oral literature. Meaningless macrosegments of content were the be-all and end-all of almost one century's specialists in folkloristic researches. Oral literature is, then, backward as a science, although it possesses extraordinary amounts of descriptive, catalog, and comparative items. Their utility for construction and validation of a system of theory about oral literature is no longer a moot question. There is no doubt that they are largely waste effort. Not much is known about nonwestern oratory, rituals, and other oral art forms. A majority of historico-geographical folklorists had little interest in them.

To be sure, a number of theories, spun during the past hundred years, have purported to account for ultimate origins of oral literature plots, themes, motifs, tale types, and actors. Historico-geographical folklorists maintained a nodding acquaintanceship with these theories, occasionally cited and criticized them graciously, but in effect ignored them. Let us comment about them briefly after a glance at anthropological folklorists who valiantly supplemented, in researches among nonliterate peoples, the European folklorists' accumulations, catalogs, and maps.

## Anthropological Folklore

After the 1860's and until about 1940, numbers of anthropologists and linguists, principally Americans, who were conducting field studies among nonwestern peoples recorded folktales. They perceived that texts recorded in a precise transcription of sounds of a nonwestern language were not only required in scientific linguistics but produced superior results, in most instances, for purposes of folkloristic studies. There are over 100 published volumes of such texts and many more are still unpublished notebooks. Well over half of them are from a small percentage of the groups of American Indians north of Mexico, a circumstance which arises from leadership given in such researches after the 1890's by Columbia University's Professor Boas. Most nonwestern language groups, thousands to be sure, in Asia, Oceania, Africa, and Latin America are wretchedly, or not at all, represented in this form. Recordings made directly from interpreters who were able to use English, Spanish, or other European languages are many for Indian groups north of the Rio Grande and spare for most other parts of the world.

Little of all such data gathering, in nonwestern language text-with-translation or in a European language through interpreters, offers the richness in alternate versions which characterizes notebooks and publications of historico-geographical workers in their field collections among European storytellers. Alternate versions are potentially important but enervatingly time consuming for field workers. And such versions have slight use in a vacuum of theory regarding processes of origin, maintenance, remodeling, and the designing of projective expressions which relieve tensions and conflicting sentiments.

Oral literature collections by anthropologists and linguists usually offer admirably recorded single versions of only an extremely small percentage of a repertoire of myths and tales. In most instances, the fate of work done by such field workers is that it yielded far too small a sampling for purposes of advancing oral literature theory.

Almost all collectors ceased their field effort after recording and translating dictated words. They did not know what else they ought to do. After all, they faithfully recorded a recital itself and they supposed that their work as collectors was then done. During a century, no field collector appears to have operated with a kit of tentative hypotheses which required elaborate question and answer follow-up to elicit correlated matters in a society and culture. Questions later put to interpreters were usually linguistic and sometimes, more recently, on Freudian matters, but did not go far toward supplying answers which helped in the progress of oral literature knowledge.

The most dedicated and precise field collecting is accompanied by an aura of ineffectuality when it is not guided by questions answers to which may shed light on sociocultural and psychological correlates of recitals.

Hundreds of linguists, anthropologists, and Europe-oriented folklorists recorded tale dictations with an exactitude and integrity which, if oral literature had possessed a system of theory, might have granted spectacular scientific returns. As it is, most collections are small, lack variants and, above all, are devoid of relevant commentary elicited in question and answer follow-up. The key to scientific progress is in use of judgment, as well as resources of theory, during interrogation of informants and interpreters.

Assessment of what has been achieved, therefore, amounts principally to the following. Anthropological folklore discovered—a most important finding—that oral literatures, whether collected among economically backward food-gatherers or in any other kinds of societies, possessed features of content and form which warrant acceptance of merit and suggest intensive studies of new kinds. Complexities which require unraveling probably exceed those which scientific linguists have been exposing in the world's nonwestern language structures. Features of content and form were often manipulated with excellence, projected with subtlety and imagination, and responded to with critical and mature understanding. Accumulation of indications of such kinds may have provided one of the notable achievements of the past century's work in behavioral sciences. It serves no purpose to assert, nor is it longer plausible, that there was something distinctively primitive, in the sense of simple or inferior, about any or all oral literatures. Affirmations of such a kind are patently defensive mechanisms which operate to bolster the often diminishing self-regard of protagonists of so-called "higher civilizations."

## Folklore's Theory Fringe

Few active field collectors have offered hypotheses regarding origins of oral literature content. Contributors of such theories were principally students who examined Classical Mediterranean and European mythologies and reports published by modern field workers. Historical and literary scholars, that is to say, amateurish observers whose perceptions were unaffected by field research experiences, originated most of the speculations regarding ultimate beginnings of oral literature expressive content. From the point of view of scientific method, results of their efforts have been as petty as the writings of most persons who brashly characterized themselves as chemists and had never passed over the threshold of a chemistry laboratory. It is difficult to find an area of scientific inquiry in which publishing houses have printed so much presumptuous guesswork couched in elegant and lyrical measures or so many postulates that have been unusable for purposes of advancing knowledge. Science fiction authors have very likely offered more constructive stimulation to scientists than have all the psychoanalytic and literary bibliophiles who have presumed to tell a large reading public about the nature of mythology and folklore. In addition, a culture-hungry public which would enjoy some enlightenment about folklores the world over finds little in even the best university and large city bookstores which serves a function other than to mislead them.

A few nineteenth century scholars proposed that folklore plots and motifs originated in one or another impressively luxurious center such as the Near East or India. They indicated that the rest of humanity, less favored by wealth, slavery, military power, and temple plazas with great stone structures gradually accepted, by a process of borrowing, plots, motifs, and tale types supposedly spawned in environments of enchanting urban living, dancing girls, priestly processions, mysterious rituals, earth goddesses, and commerce. One might almost come to the conclusion that plots, motifs, and tale types traveled arm in arm with merchants transporting herbs, cosmetic ointments, spices, and dyes, and were greeted with gusto by heathen bards in many Old World regions.

Satisfactory reasons for the literary seminality of a certain few homelands were never forthcoming. Indeed, publications of oral literatures from other regions, especially from North American Indian districts, presently showed that every country was arrestingly creative in oral literature content, style too, although Pan-East Indian diffusionists appear not to have concerned themselves with what, to them, were very likely only lowlier kinds of creatures, savages, and barbarians. Nor were they often interested in items of folklore content which were found in the Americas but not in the Old World. Spreadings of features of content from the wealthiest Old World centers and from economically least impressive districts, that is, from areas of food-gatherers, remain to be assessed, a task not yet possible because field reports are too uneven.

Some decades ago, a phalanx of writers argued that "primitive peoples," a term which everyone then employed without a quiver of misgiving, projected human and zoomorphic figures into phenomena of nature such as sun, moon, stars, meteors, eclipses, storms, tides, floods, and forest conflagrations, and presently wove plots about these figures and occasions. Such a naturistic theory of origin of content assumed folklorists' ability to speculate plausibly about first causes of components of content which thousands of persons had subsequently transmitted and remodeled during long periods. But neither proof nor disproof of naturistic origin was ever possible for a single actor personality, social relationship, or other expressive feature. Probably, the widespread stylistic trait in oral literatures which is an explanatory accounting for heavenly bodies persuaded protagonists of the theory that they were on the right track. A naturistic theory of origins soon lost support because it patently violated principles of scientific evidence and it seemed improbable to most scholars whatever their canons of thinking. Few active field workers were able to regard it seriously at any time. Today, it is also evident that plot, tale type, and motif origins are only the smallest part of the business of a scientific theoretical structure for oral literatures.

Members of the early twentieth century group of Freudian sectarians, perhaps only one of whom, Dr. Geza Roheim, entered upon nonwestern researches which provided oral literature from field sources, also engaged in scholarly disquisitions upon ultimate beginnings of folklore content. Many of these psychoanalytic writers had had humanistic kinds of education in European gymnasia and universities and, therefore, were familiar with Greco-Roman mythology and religion. These theoreticians proposed that expressive items originated—once again the nineteenth century compulsion to fixate upon beginnings—in much the manner in which dreams bubble through from unconscious wellsprings into conscious awareness. Latent drives and conflicts, with an especial frequency of feelings around Oedipal situations, were disguised by a variety of distortional mechanisms such as rationalization and displacement. Nevertheless, manifest dream and myth content may be analyzed to reveal mechanisms and originating drives. Content in both dreams and myths comprised manifest expressions of latent feelings and conflicts. Again, proof or disproof of merits of such generic theorization about origins, as well as evidences for processes of maintenance and remodeling of content down through the ages, cannot be obtained for items which are more than a generation old. Most oral literature material is, of course, of indeterminable antiquity. A system of theory regarding which relevant observations and evidences cannot be provided is of small value unless its plausibility is superior to any other theoretical system. Obviously, validation or disproof of statements of the theory may be expected for mechanisms of dream work. But oral literature displays distinctive content, far more numerous or elaborate stylizations, a wider range of religious and other social functions, maybe some special mechanisms, and doubtless a great deal more than dream portrayals, for all its surface similarity to them —which Freudian writers rightly perceived. Many myths of nonwestern peoples do exhibit arrestingly dreamlike characteristics.

A group of literary, historical, and psychoanalytic scholars, with virtually no allies who conducted folkloristic field researches, have made a remarkable impact not upon workers of scientific bent but upon mid-twentieth century literary critics, principally in that spirited sect of facile arbiters known as the New Critics. Their deities or father figures include the Zurich psychoanalyst C. G. Jung, the famous and prolific protagonist of the long discredited nineteenth century form of the comparative method applied to religion, magic, and folklore, Sir James G. Frazer, and some recent essayists and writers in literature itself. The group have urged that myth plots, and some of them have thought principally about Greco-Roman mythology, might be traced, if data were available, to rites practised by earlier peoples. This ritual-to-myth evolution-oriented theory, of course, explains nothing about origins of rites, reasons for processes in embroidery and remodeling of plots around them, or causes for their retention. Most myths and tales recorded in text and translation from nonwestern peoples exhibit no signs if superficially read, and no indications if deftly probed, of ritual origins. The theory patently tells little or nothing about origins and subsequent fashionings of actor depictions, social relationships, humor, features of world view, ethical items, or other components of oral literature collections. The theory asserts nothing about the many features of style in each such collection, a curious omission in a portfolio of postulates which comprise the faith of the New Critics whose alleged interest in close analysis of style in verbal arts of western civilization is almost their most distinctive attribute. The theory offers no statements about functioning of an oral literature in a people's daily conversations or in their formal myth recitals. One gets an uneasy impression that protagonists of ritual-to-myth theory are little interested in any myths except creation and other highly esoteric or dreamlike materials. But when an anthropological folklorist ill-advisedly permits himself to be drawn into a discussion of their theory with them, they seem impelled to be severely consistent with the theology of their cult, to bow reverently in the direction of Frazer (who stimulates few genuflections among scientists), and to insist that all folkloristic data must be assumed to constitute a kind of detritus laid down long ago by rituals of ancestral people. Nineteenth century kinds of unverbalized premises and habits of mind are obvious in the cult: evolutionary stages for which evidences are unobtainable, survivals which cannot be demonstrated, disinterest in minutiae of behavior, fixation upon creation myths, and failure to attend to patternings and stylizations. In spite of wholly anachronistic premises of the theory, thousands of literature professors who are unacquainted with methodological or other advances in the behavioral sciences since the Spanish-American or Boer Wars are lecturing today in favorable terms about an unproven, unprovable, and wholly improbable doctrine. It itself appears to offer a solitary available example of a ritual-to-myth process.

The same literary rank and file have managed to intertwine a pseudo-psychological premise with their ritual origin surmise. The splinter sect of Freudians created by C. G. Jung a half century ago later identified a limited number of themes or plots, so-called "archetypes," which supposedly received development at the hands of folklore recitalists everywhere. The postulate is that native raconteurs just could not resist formulating out of dark racial-feeling fabrics. They got started by some kind of biological jet propulsion and one after another archetypal plot poured out of them. These archetypal plots or themes have fastened, like a series of polyps on vocal cords, upon the heartsprings of great numbers of contemporary specialists in literature criticism. Some of the cultist professors are confident, although they are acquainted principally with Old World myths, that the properly centered interest of folkloristic theory, whether it apply to Eskimos, Fuegians, Ilocanos, Zuñis, or Zulus, is the discovery of such archetypal elements, even as the probing revelation of them is the virtuous professional obligation of a critic who subjects novels or poetry to close content analysis. The critic then examines how an author, or a raconteur in the instance of an oral art, has manipulated his archetypal themes. Close analysis is, of course, admirable, if that which is analyzed out is not principally, inevitably, and invariably one of Dr. Jung's archetypal social relationship conflicts with its early hypothetical ritual expression in some pre-Greco-Roman or other vanished tribal groups, preferably indeed groups which basked in the silvery light of Bachofen's matriarchate. Scientific workers in anthropology long ago relegated that state of feminine dominance to the scrap heap of bad guesses, but not so the New Critics. In spite of the awesome irresponsibility and absurdity of the New Critics' theology and their pathetic loyalties to Bachofen, Frazer, Jung, and a cluster of living idols, their support of close analysis stands as a valuable contribution. Ritual-myth and archetypal premises, Jung, and other deities of the New Critics receive no acceptance in scientific quarters.

When Boas, that most assiduous collector of precisely recorded anthropological folklore, suggested somewhat weakly about 45 years ago that a folklore collection mirrored the life of a people who had expressed it, he meant only that ethnographic items of technology, economy, social organization, and religion sometimes received verbalization in myth and tale recitals. He never sought an answer to an important question why some groups projected a great amount of their sociocultural life into myth recitals and other groups projected exceedingly little of it. He observed that there were such differences in amounts of what was mirrored, but he was unable to explain why the differences occurred. Today, a social scientist might state simply that the contrasts appear to be effects of multiple causes. In certain instances, it is a matter of different literary styles rather than something on a level of varying kinds and quantities of content expressed, although items of content functioned as stylistic features. More of this later.

Apart from a rigorous professional field worker such as Boas, dabblers in theorems about origin of content presented statements to which cross-cultural evidence could not be applied in validation or criticism. Unfortunately, Boas resembled others in leaving most features of content, style, and connected sociocultural phenomena untouched by theory. A grievous consequence for oral literature in the 1960's is its spare system of scientific hypotheses, one which is almost embryonic by contrast with growth achieved in other specialist fields in the behavioral sciences. Oral literature theory now contains principally evidences about the fact of dissemination of content, and it had mountains of evidences of that kind 50 or more years ago, provided both by careful European workers on folklores of Old World peoples and by Boas and his followers in their work on nonwestern oral arts. There are few correlated evidences or even thinly supported statements about processes of any kind in oral literature creativity, maintenance, and functioning. In other words, 150 years after pioneering by the Grimm brothers in recording European fairy tales, a theory of oral literature content and style has barely begun to be fashioned.

However, a group of mechanisms limned by Freudians and called by now familiar terms such as "projection" and "displacement" can be salvaged from the grandiose structure of psychoanalytic theory to become central components of a special theory for oral literatures. These mechanisms can be set beside the process of dissemination. In fact, diffusion requires a vast amount of reexamination in order to determine what different kinds of processes are lumped clumsily, in fact concealed, under the gross heading.

## Content Analysis

Within the past century chemistry, zoology, linguistics and other fields of inquiry were released to forge ahead, in some respects with sensational rapidity, toward systems of mature scientific theory after judicious appraisals and selections of their most likely minimal units and classes of units had been made. Elements and, later, the isotopes of elements in chemistry; chromosomes and, then, genes in zoology; phonemes, allophones, and morphemes in linguistics have so far served reliably and radiantly as hypothetical conceptual units which, in the current state of knowledge of each such field, permit devising many statements regarding structuring, process, and change.

Composites such as tale types, plots, and motifs which professional historico-geographical folklorists long cited, cataloged, and reified, paralleled if they did not effect a garroting of interest in process other than who borrowed what and when. The end product has been a kind of immature historicism, not a structure of theory about content and style, certainly not a step toward a mature system of theory about oral literature. Sound historians venture to locate major and minor factors, psychological and otherwise, which account for events they record. Legitimate scientific curiosity about causes, development, and maintenance of oral literature content was left to simplifications and guesswork by dithyrambic origin hunters who lacked awareness of scientific method and whose conceptual units of tale types and motifs were much too bulky. Before 1930, perhaps only one folklorist, Vladimir Propp, had stipulated that motifs, plots, and tale types were not the segments of folklore recitals with which to conduct scholarly researches. He failed to offer sets of superior units for content analysis, although, in a remarkable study of the structure of Russian fairy tales, he anticipated a modern kind of analysis of one aspect of oral literature style. He was able to do this because of his discovery of one class of smaller content units which had stylistic functions. His units were successive scenes in a fairy "play" and he called the scenes, curiously, "functions." Alan Dundes calls them "motifemes."

The avenue leading to selection of proper segments or units of content is indicated only upon discovery of what was expressed in an oral literature. For example, it is surprising that historico-geographical scholars perhaps never disclosed the many indications that oral literatures phrased and copied from neighboring literatures items that concerned social relationships, behaviors, and feelings which the borrowing sociocultural system failed to handle comfortably. Where there are written literatures, authors evidently select for writing out and printing discussions of relationships, personality types, values, and other interests concerning which they and their society are bothered: these are matters which are not otherwise customarily disposed of, adjusted, or tidied up with an extreme of efficiency in sociocultural life. In Western culture, script writers and directors place on the movie screen relationships, personalities, and values about war, love, and loneliness which represent infelicitous areas of contemporary life. That which receives projection onto the screen, for purposes of ventilation and emotional release, is often deeply disturbing. In every modern industrial nation, many different things are so projected onto printed pages in novels, short stories, or poetry, into newspaper cartoons, joke forms and other kinds of humor, song lyrics, and phrases of rites and rituals. Myth and tale screens of nonliterate peoples functioned in analogous ways. The basic processes, which appear in emotional needs and conflicts and their resolution by way of projection, displacement, identification, and ventilation, are universal.

The variety of materials which have been placed in many guises on oral literature screens, that is, which were expressed in oral literature recitals, require segmentation and classification. Plot, tale type, and motif concepts of folklore scholars have long impeded such classification because each encloses voluminous content of expressive significance. "Motifemes" are also overloaded with content. Such content must be further sliced into clear-cut small units and groupings of units that are meaningful because they point to processes that explicate oral literature behavior. Each such unit, and each such set of units, can then be shown in its connections with stresses and discomforts in the social system. A scientific attack upon processes which determined structurings, complexities, and vagaries in millions of myths and tales the world over must commence with the most promising expressive units and classes of units, those which can be tied in not with the entirety of a society and culture as in the Boasian mirror reflection theory but with sectors of sociocultural life which operated unsatisfactorily for a people who recited, discussed, changed, and listened.

Main classes of items of content included a great range of social relationships, usually hundreds of actor personalities, humor, cosmology and world view, religion, value ideals, and almost always some interspersed songs. Each of these classes, and others too, has to be arranged in subclasses. Literary readers are herewith asked to note that archetypal themes do not comprise an employable class or subclass of content items, if for no other reason than that each such Jungian agglomerate is ridiculously massive. It is much too complex for possible scientific handling.

Each principal class of expressive content receives brief comment in paragraphs which follow.

Almost all myths or tales, other oral arts too, cited one or several types of *social relationship*, each of which may receive further subdivision in terms of behaviors and feelings expressed in the relationship. A tentative list of relationships includes these: premarital maneuvers; marital (monogamous, polygamous, polyandrous; deserted mate; tricked mate); incestuous; parent-child; siblings; leader-people; uncle or aunt-child; kidnapper-child; religious functionary-people; ogre or ogress-people; upper class-lower class; freeman-slave; in-laws-people; comrades; community-community; elder-people. Eliciting of full ethnographic background is a requirement for comprehension of these relationships and reasons for their placement on an oral literature screen.

Unlike other oral arts, a corpus of myths and tales contained a small group of principal male, another small group of principal female *actor personalities*. Their labels and lineaments as animal, bird, flower, fish, ogre, or other kinds of creatures served in various ways which included expression of animistic supernaturals, totemic animal ancestors, and so on. Basically all of them were human or humanlike. Human thinking, feeling, and relationships were projected into each of them. Each of these principal actors might appear in two or three to a dozen or dozens of myths. Community perception of the personality of each such actor constituted a composite of that actor's behaviors in all myths or other recital forms in which he appeared. Artistry in recital arose in selection and manipulation of facets of that perception. And a recitalist himself ultimately responded to year-round discussions within his community about such matters.

The small groups of leading actors were supplemented by many times as many minor actors, a few of whom sometimes constituted effective cartoonlike caricatures. Most of the minor actors were mere stage props. An oral literature field worker must elicit as extensive as possible commentary on every actor, leading or minor, in order to fill in otherwise unphrased perceptions of them had by a community. For it was just such unverbalized perceptions, the many things which a recitalist did not articulate but which his community understood very well, which contained fundamental features of an oral literature and which permit unraveling of its processes of expression of content. Verbal presentation by a recitalist offered only a stylized selection of actor personality traits. In analyses of expressive content, elicitation of commentary after a recital is methodologically almost more vital than the record of words of the recital itself, although the latter is indispensable, of course, especially so for style analysis.

Actor personalities did not necessarily, or perhaps even often, mirror personality structures in a society. Oral literature actors tended to be composites, stereotypes, incongruous eccentrics, caricatures or projections, anthropomorphizations indeed, of value ideals. It is, therefore, impossible to deduce average and variability in a society's personalities from its oral literature's actor personalities. Only intensive ethnographic research permits assessment of similarities in oral literature actors and real people. Behavior and feelings in relationships exhibited by actors also were no mirror reflection of daily life. They appear to have comprised a selection of facets of life which stirred emotional turbulences. The realistic novel of modern western civilization is only to a degree realistically accurate in its depictions of how people live, feel, and relate to one another. But it is far closer to the reality of its society than any body of oral literature from nonliterate peoples. A decisive characteristic of content analysis is, then, determination of what was selected for placement on an oral literature screen, why it was chosen, and why everything else was passed over. Actually, much was.

The next principal feature of oral literature expressive content is *humor*. It was manifested in funny songs, comical vocal mannerisms, humorous features of physique and personality ascribed to actors, clownlike and other actors who were ipso facto amusing, laughable archaic verbal expressions and expletives, and funny situations. These and other types of humorous expressions punctuated myths and tales, although not all of them. In some regions, myths were much more laughter generating than tales. The opposite may have characterized other regions. Humor attached to expressive content which was itself incongruous and it functioned stylistically to lighten tragedy or ease long-continued tension. It, therefore, served for purposes of both content and style. The chapter on humor offers an introductory discussion of that many faceted topic which, until the present day, has been accorded slight attention by behavioral scientists and almost none by anthropologists. Roles played by humor in other verbal arts remain almost unknown.

*Values*, another long-neglected area of inquiry except among religionists and philosophers, received oral literature expression in many ways. However, in some cultures very few myths or tales constituted centrally materials which were referred to or recited in order to offer sanction of an ethical principle. Myths might be wholly devoid of moralistic motivation. Or, ethical content in them might be no more than latent. Tales might constitute frank lessons in ethical precepts. An idealized actor personality might function as an example of an ethically most attractive person whose worth was highlighted by his tragic destiny—a kind of existentialist manipulation of plot.

The method of eliciting value ideals which received covert or manifest articulation is primarily by interrogation after a field recording. But significance of those values was in their relationship to a larger body of ethical statements and it can be gleaned only in ethnographic research. A principal task is to determine causes for expression of some values and omission of others from an oral literature. A starting hypothesis is that ideals which received inclusion, in one or another manner, in myths and tales dealt with those especially tense spots in maturation, relationships, and behavior which a sociocultural system failed to handle smoothly or to internalize fully in people. Expression of values in other oral arts very likely arose in the same way.

The next main kind of expressive content treats of portions of *world view*, that is cosmology, attitudes toward alien peoples and their sociocultural systems, and history and prehistory—pseudohistory from the point of view of scientific historiography. Items of such kinds usually received expression incidentally in things actors said and did. After a dictation and its translation, a field worker ought to direct questions which draw out native commentary so as to fill in depictions of perceptions of the universe or multiverse, of space and time, propinquity and worth of alien peoples, supernaturals, deities, districts from which humans and other creatures came and to which they departed upon death, and so on. Partial expressions of world view which were latent or explicit in oral literature recitals require comparison with full perceptions yielded in ethnographic and other expressive analyses. Only then may it appear why certain components of world view were present in oral literatures and other items were left out.

At this point, a reader, a traditional folkloristic collector too, may be inclined to protest that oral literature research as conceived here is not primarily tale or other oral art collecting at all. It seems to be regarded as a special kind of ethnographic research. Orientation is in a direction of scientific theory rather than the folklorists' traditional data-gathering and historico-geographical perspectives. A reply to such a complaint is affirmative, except that in oral literature field research which is conducted as it ought to be a great amount of sheer recording of myths, tales, and other oral art forms does go on. Folklorists and ethnographers have done little of the many sided kind of collecting which is demanded, doubtless because they lacked time for it. And naturally ethnographers had self-assigned problems for which they had to harvest masses of evidence, without exhausting themselves in oral literature interests.

Let us continue with remaining kinds of content which received expression in oral literatures.

*Religious content* need not be discussed for those sociocultural systems where the topic can be subsumed under world view. On the other hand, it is prudent to suggest that items of religious ideology and behavior which were projected onto myth and tale screens constituted, in all likelihood, unconscious selections of precisely those portions of religion which stirred deepest concerns. Where rites do not appear to have tied in with a people's greatest anxieties, a myth and tale screen was almost a blank in its depiction or even citation of rites. A notable example of this phenomenon is in Boas' collections of myth texts from northerly Pacific Northwest Coast peoples. It is not possible to reconstruct ceremonies of those societies from their myths. On the other hand, animistic supernaturals constituted most provoking problems and such beings were cited endlessly.

In most myth and tale literatures, *musical compositions*, usually solo songs of actors, interrupted narration. Close analyses of words, vocal mannerisms, and purely musical features of songs may reveal significant things. In any case, each song must be accorded commentary in subsequent interrogations, and a folklorist does not have to be a practiced ethnomusicologist to ask most of the relevant questions. Incidental employment of myth or tale songs in everyday life has been common the world over. Their functions in such roles may be of interest, too. In instances where a field worker lacks a tape recorder and is doing research in the manner of most anthropological folklorists before 1950, that is, a phonetic-phonemic transcription in long-hand, it is still indispensable that each song be recorded mechanically. If a tape recorder is unavailable, it is necessary to use some other mechanical device, maybe even old-fashioned equipment such as a wax cylinder Dicta-phone. Songs can be dubbed onto tape for musicological analysis at a later time.

## Style Analysis

No hard and fast line separates content and style because most classes of features of oral literature style constituted repetitive or other manipulations of items of expressive content.

Scientific linguists who have lately professed interest in literary style seem to be outraged at a suggestion that linguistic factors in oral literature styles were sometimes petty or negligible by contrast with nonlinguistic expressive devices. However, since not one linguist has offered a full-length stylistic analysis of a nonwestern oral literature, a preference by linguists for kinds of factors which they descry and highlight is intelligible, if not praiseworthy. Actually, large numbers of kinds of phonetic, morphological, and semantic items have functioned for stylistic purposes in nonwestern oral arts, a great many more of such linguistic items in some literatures than in others. An important theoretical point is that there were oral literature styles that were marked by few linguistic features which effected distinc-tive stylistic results.

Familiar linguistic devices included sound changes to express pity, di-minutive size (e.g., *an eeedle bit* for *a little bit*), large size, and duration; duplication and reduplication to express them too (e.g., *big big* for *very big*). Classes of melodic contours or intonational patterns, also special vocal mannerisms and timbres, might be limited to myth or other stylized utter-ances.

Morphological devices which served stylistically were of the greatest variety, although only a tiny number may have received selection, so to speak, in any one oral art form. Obviously those which were selected and distinctive for literature style were classes of items whose members ap-peared in a literature in a frequency different from their frequency in every-day speech (e.g., *thee, thou, ye,* archaic pronominal vestigia in English). Moribund or archaic grammatical form classes or individual forms may have offered fairly frequent features of style. A grammatical feature which now may be familiar to many scientific linguists was a special tense for remote eras or the age of myths. Classes of special honorific or personifier mor-phemes might attach only to humanlike beings who were myth actors.

Unlike some oratory, myths might feature especially abbreviated discourse units, without subordinate phrases, such as successions of short staccato-like subject-predicate-object sentences. Syntactic features might display frequencies in oral literature performances different from their frequencies in informal discourse.

Classes of vocabulary and semantic features which were reserved for oral literature references and recitals were legion. There might be special names for myth actors, archaic morphemes for things and actions peculiar to myths, and almost always inventories of idiomatic phrase or sentence expressions (e.g., *once upon a time*) which belonged properly to myth recitals although referred to, in addition, in casual speech.

In brief, each oral art co-opted and assigned, in customary locations in individual myths or types of myths or in other oral arts, a limited array, sometimes an extremely small one, of purely linguistic traits from the great numbers of structural features and semantic units at hand in a language. Texts and translations of both recitals and conversations permit identification of linguistic traits which served in formal recital style.

Years hence, it may be possible to generalize warrantably that distinctive linguistic features of food-gatherers' recital styles (myths, tales, oratory, ceremonials) were much fewer than in some wealthier societies which included literature, governmental, juridical, and priestly specialists. Too little text-and-translation resource materials from wealthier and socially stratified societies are available to warrant that deduction today. In any case, its service would not be so much a statement integral in a system of theory as a reminder to ascertain contrasted processes in oral expressions in the two very differently structured classes of sociocultural systems. The statement, which is of a kind dear to the heart of sociocultural neo-evolutionists, is too broad in its coverage to point to important dynamics within those sociocultural systems. Scientific theory deals with such dynamics, preferably in a temporal or historical frame if that frame is meaningfully specific.

All remaining characteristics of oral literature style involved selections, placements or orderings, and repetitions of items and classes of content, or other features. Most of them were vividly expressive, possibly surprisingly so. Brief comments follow on each of a limited selection of them, although the types presented constitute a list which could be multiplied. Recitalist-audience behavior; beginnings, pauses, continuations, and endings; pattern numbers such as three, four, or seven; a class of items that expressed location; a class that expressed time; explanatory devices; plot devices; structuring of act, scene, or episode sequences ("motifemes" are included here); headings, titles, or manner of ready reference; depictive inclusions and omissions; selected items of psychological commentary; speed of action, vocal technique and mannerisms, repetition, rhythm, and intensity. Again, many other kinds of mechanisms which employed expressive content served stylistically.

It is important to understand that all accurately and sensitively recorded oral arts, not least those in technologically simple societies, have displayed a great many classes of stylistic features and each such class might include a huge array of unitary items. The task is to identify every one of the classes and its component units and to attempt to determine their origin— usually a futile pursuit although the effort is worthy—and their functions— a difficult business sometimes. But they can and must be pinpointed by means of close content and style analyses, especially those conducted in a field situation because necessary interrogations are possible only there.

Paragraphs which follow take up those stylistic classes which are comparatively most expressive, and with only brief comments because the subject is sufficiently big to justify a treatise. However, there is one class of stylistic material which is distinctive in its breadth of content coverage. This class treats of the several genres found in each oral literature. A genre is, to be sure, an over-all structural or architectural type which has characteristic classes of content and classes of stylistic features. Genres will be spoken of after comments on other classes of features of style.

A formal recital of a myth or tale in a nonwestern society usually differed from protean everyday references to myths and tales in requirements regarding physical and vocal behavior of recitalist and audience. Children, adults, or both in an audience might be required to sit or recline in prescribed fashion. Audience members, maybe only the children, might have to intone each phrase after a recitalist, or utter an affirmative or other syllable after each phrase or larger segment of discourse. Some styles of oratory and ceremonial had similar canons.

Almost all myth performances had stylized beginnings and endings which functioned like English's "Ladies and gentlemen" and "Once upon a time," and "Thank you for your kind attention" and "Then they lived happily ever after." Many, maybe most, such formulae were in familiar morphemes or words but were not otherwise functionally meaningful. Some were as meaningless as abracadabra. Myths that were so long that they must be halted and resumed the following night might be accorded stylized junctural phrasings at the close of the first evening and the beginning of the next session. Dramatic literatures might have stylized prologues in addition to formal initial phrases, and stylized epilogues with a stylized closing phrase.

Pattern number appears to have constituted a stylistic feature or class of features in most oral arts the world over, although districts here and there omitted it. Where it occurred, a myth or tale actor had, for example, three wives, shot three arrows, took three steps, crossed three streams, or was one of a set of three siblings. Persons and actions had to be cited in threes or, in other literatures, pairs, fours, fives, or sevens. A literature might have two, three, or more pattern numbers, that is, a class of them, each member of the class tied to something distinctive. For example, in one small coastal Oregon district, recitalists in Tillamook Salish hamlets had to enumerate four items if female actors or actions by females, five if male actors or actions by males.

The next few classes of items from which a recitalist must select were locational, temporal, and depictive. In the chapter on language, comments were offered regarding a similarity in function between these oral literature classes of stylistic features and some of the grammatical form classes from which individual morphemes were comparatively unconsciously and with lightning rapidity selected in casual speech. Languages which displayed a locational or directional (upriver, downriver, inside, outside, etc.) form class were rare.

In an oral literature, references to locations might comprise a class from which just one or two items could be or, rather, must be selected. For example, a recitalist of a tale might have to say "he left the village," or "he paddled into the stream." He might have to follow with "he went along the trail" or "he went upriver" or "he went downriver." If travel was on land, the next required phrase might be "he came out of the woods and into a clearing." Classes of such locational words or phrases were as watered out in expressive content as "and then" in English. But its stereotyped members or units, and one or another of a class of them often had to be used, functioned to move action along from place to place.

A class of features which expressed time was common, possibly even universal, in oral literatures. "Pretty soon," "after a long while," "the next morning," "presently," and a great number of others may be cited. Some oral literatures might have lacked a specific item such as "long, long ago," others required it. Some lacked "a long, long time afterward" but might require the recitalist to say only "presently," no matter what the context. The point is that a literature style usually offered a recitalist a readymade kit of time expressions and depending on context he used, indeed he must use, one or the other item in that set.

One might go as far as Whorfians to deduce that a recitalist was so hemmed in by special temporal or other required classes of items available that his own and his audience's perceptions of dramatic action were somehow shaped by this one segment of the style. Did oral literature style ever really shape perceptions, just as grammatical form classes have been claimed to have been determinants of perceptions? On the other hand, it is possible that fullness of knowledge of a way of life, heritage, and oral art itself must have been such, in both recitalist and audience, that restriction to stylized temporal items probably functioned only as a convenience for purposes of steady utterance. Although a speaker or recitalist cerebrated intensively, his readymade devices permitted him to move along frictionlessly. Anyhow, no Whorfian seems to have come forth with a claim that thinking was molded by oral literature style classes, which were remarkably like grammatical form classes in their structuring and functions. Maybe it is injudicious to suggest another neighborhood for exploration and lucubrations by such philosophical souls.

A linguist might elect to speak of classes of "zero" items, that is, potentially depictive allusions which a recitalist never mentioned. For example, if context pressured a recitalist to say something about a myth actor's good looks, he was able to select only one or two items from a small inventory of anatomical features, the only ones which were ever explicitly commented upon in that culture and its oral arts. Features of anatomy which remained unexpressed, unselected, possibly not even thought of, were always legion in every culture. Most peoples the world over ignored long eyelashes, although Europeans have long been rather sensitized to them and have had them mentally at hand for citation. The inventory of anatomically depictive items which could be referred to differed remarkably from culture district to district and, of course, from oral literature area to area. In one area, a recitalist might be able to mention light complexion and one or two or three other body characteristics like high forehead, buttocks, ankles, or feet. In another area he alluded to height. In another, to long straight hair; in another, wavy hair. In another area, to thickness of lips. In another, to long eyelashes, of course. A culture's selection of anatomical items which were tension generating, highly regarded, or to be verbalized in a given context connected with the class of beauty items which were available for mention by myth recitalists.

Allusions to weather and landscape were also rigidly set. Most things that might be said about them were not said at all. It has to be ascertained if people perceived them without a cultural outsider's prodding. Many oral literatures lacked a style class of items which referred to "nature." And so their recitalists never mentioned foliage, flowers, brooks, or waving grass. Oceanian districts displayed styles which did pressure recitalists to cite particulars of "nature." Most western North American Indian recitalists never alluded to a single such feature. In each region, oral literature style analysis must not merely structure, that is, enumerate and arrange items in this facet of style. It must venture to account for their presence and maintenance, a task likely to be foredoomed to failure although, at least, it must be tackled.

Explanatory items have a long history in folkloristic writings. The familiar European "and that's why" there is a rock, waterfall, or mountain, and the widespread accounting for sun, moon, constellations, and stars by metamorphosis of tale actors into such celestial figures, have resulted in assertions that myths developed to account for features of nature. But secondary or tagged on functions of most explanatory items are now well-established. A recitalist's statements about the origin of this or that were primarily stylistic. They interrupted a plot so as to break suspense. Or they served to underpin components of world view or, on a smaller scale, supply some sort of security-granting account of items of local botany, geology, zoology, or geography. Explanatory elements were often of utmost unimportance for world view or security. But they served, primarily so, as stylistic punctuation. They functioned, too, as a special kind of plot device, of which more, presently. They broke continuity as digressions which distracted within plots. Or, when appended at the close of plots, they offered releases of another sort by weakening identification with people who had been plot actors and by lessening empathy for such actors' feelings in intense social relationships. Summary formulation about so-called "explanatory myths" themselves and about all explanatory pauses, asides, or closings is that their principal role was stylistic, their secondary role explanatory.

Plot devices in myths and tales suffered the sad fate of being construed by generations of folklore epigoni as central kinds of content for purposes of their scholarship. Innumerable monographs have assembled examples of one or more plot devices, which folklorists have called "motifs" and which number many hundreds around the globe. As noted above, the dedicated savants of traditional folklore scholarship exhibited interminably the geographical distributions of motifs, principally from the Atlantic Ocean to India and beyond, in a vain conviction that they were adding something of worth to knowledge. What are these motifs, which are far removed from the expressive core of oral literature although they constitute fundamental classes of stylistic machinery? An example or two will suffice. In several regions a myth actor ascended to the sky on a ladder made of arrows which connected. This motif has been primarily a plot device, one might almost suggest a short cut, although a spectacular one, which allowed a hunter or archer to get from below to above. Expressive content hinged actually upon his unexampled skill in archery or his supernatural ally or capacity.

A second example of a motif which is better treated as a plot device, and which, incidentally, has turned up in every continent, has been the so-called "magic" or "obstacle flight." A principal actor, with whom audience might identify, fled a hateful or terrifying creature but must quickly devise obstacles, tremendous ones, to slow up the evil one's pursuit. A thimbleful of water thrown back over the shoulder became a lake or sea. A rock or some dirt cast back became a mountain or range of mountains. A stick became an almost impenetrable forest. The plot device functioned to slow pursuit of an Oedipal or other feared being, to build and relieve tension around him.

Plot devices of many kinds might be collected under a generic heading of "magical" or "miraculous resuscitation." For example, corpses returned to life by merely stepping over them or uttering a stylized formula. The function of the device was evidently to get the deceased back to the living, quickly and excitingly so for the sake of the plot.

Folklorists who have been preoccupied with these and a hundred other plot devices and their geographical distributions have not perceived more essential content which was expressed in social relationships, actor personalities, and features of humor, world view, and ethics. Materials with which they should have been dealing largely evaded their scrutiny. A great many overt stylistic items such as motifs, which in each instance included expressive content too, became their main business. Almost a century's professional folklorists never comprehended that they were writing about components of style rather than about what they supposed was the most vital content which was expressed in oral literatures.

Additional characteristics of style are of importance, too. Many, if not most, oral literatures contained myths and tales which displayed comprehensive structurings—in his study of Russian fairy tales, cited above, Vladimir Propp called the components in one type of structuring "functions." However, gross or architectural structural matters can be managed nicely by borrowing captions such as skits, acts, scenes, entr'actes, prologues, and epilogues from Euro-American theater. Propp was really citing a single type of play, a genre, which always had seven scenes, each a selection from a set of possible items. Structuring in terms of acts and scenes may be inappropriate for some myth and tale repertoires and, naturally, it is unlikely to fit nonwestern oratory, incantations, prayers, and other types of oral arts. But it does constitute demonstrable stylistic segments, expressive content segments of course, in many or most dramatic myth or tale recitals. A recitalist might not be able to point, in so many words, to act 1, scene 4, or act 7, scene 2. Nonetheless, he had to frame his presentation in successive segments or macrosegments which were much like acts and scenes of Euro-American theater.

Distinctive genres in the corpus of oral literature of a nonliterate people present as troublesome a question as other contrastive features of style because folklorists, anthropological and others, have almost entirely ignored genres. But nonwestern peoples were always sharply aware of their genres and maybe always had names for them. Natives usually could indicate some of the main structural characteristics of each genre, kinds of content which tended to be included in it, and its special social, educational, or religious functions. Manifestations of genre are, in fact, easier for an outsider to identify than many other facets of style because traits which marked a genre comprise, even to him, visible and gross rather than hidden and small features.

Recitals might include a genre of myths about remote eras and another genre of myths dated as less remote. Ascription of lesser antiquity might be the solitary distinctive feature which marked this second genre. In all other stylistic respects, it might be identical with the first. Another genre might include formally recited tales distinguished by absences of a group of stylized devices which had to be employed in myth recitals. A global count of genres which could be characterized would doubtless add up to a huge total. A single society might possess as few as two oral literature genres, myths contrasted with tales, but genres of other oral art forms, as in rites, always appeared, too.

Just as nativistic cults effervesced in hundreds of nonwestern locales after the threatening advent and entries of Euro-Americans and the compulsive certainties which sometimes rendered missionaries attractive to people who had become unsure of themselves, so, too, new genres quickly boiled and bubbled through myth, tale, ritual, and other oral art forms inherited from the precontact era. Euro-Americans and missionaries were precipitating factors in the puzzlement which accompanied undermining of world view, values, relationships, and humor. Accordingly the Bible itself, or rather the perceptions and misunderstandings of Christian religious ideology and practice, provided features of new oral literature content. These introduced ideas stirred imaginations with resultant rationalizations and defenses in frequently impressively skillful efforts to reconcile native with Euro-American orientations. Such defensive maneuvers effected new projections on oral literature screens. And so an old myth genre might be supplemented by a kind of genetically related genre whose structure was much the same, but whose expressive content included novel features, especially some altered actor personalities and behavior and features of world view, ethics, and humor. For example, actors who were startlingly like older myth dramatis personae might be captioned Jesus and the Devil and only in some respects resembled Christians' delineations. New items of world view might depict a heaven and a hell, although the sketchings might by no means be similar to Dante's. New humor might include a lack of fit in citation of a supernatural who paused for his five o'clock tea.

Other postcontact genres might contain borrowed West African, French, or Spanish tales, depending on the provenience of new arrivals and how they presently related to original inhabitants of a district. Expressive content borrowed from tales told by such newcomers might become quickly remodeled and offered in the stylistic garb of a precontact genre. For example, early nineteenth century French Canadians told tales of French origin to western Oregon Indians. The tales were rapidly and completely remodeled in style so as to be presented in the tale genre of the Indians. Expressive content was extremely mangled and the medieval French stresses and depictions largely lost.

Literary critics rightly seek stylistic devices of a great many kinds. They also look for what they call "texture." They enumerate and account for effective utilization of metaphors, similes, and symbols. Analysts of nonwestern oral arts have much to learn from pundits whose literary world is one in which solitary authors express themselves in writing and whose creative efforts do not tie in as directly with community discussions as do recitalists who record for anthropologists. The dynamics of creativity in content and style differed considerably in the diverse social settings which produced expressive forms. But classes of features which appear in a literate society's written arts should be sought in oral arts also. It is correct to presume that most such classes will turn up, at least in a few districts.

## Prose versus Poetry

One wonders about propriety in setting up a topic of prose and poetry because the two concepts are patently drawn from Euro-Americans' quota of generic literary categories. Would an anthropological folklorist prefer to place proselike and poetrylike styles of expression, where such contrasted forms appeared, simply under headings of one or another nonwestern oral literature genre? A few generations ago a characterization of poetry, and its then definitive contrast with prose, might have been acceptable. A dichotomy of prose and poetry did not then have potential relevance to nonwestern myths and tales because no one supposed that a folklore from a nonliterate people exhibited literary excellence. Nonwestern folklore was as right for children as Grimm's fairy tales, if in translation and suitably censored. Meantime, kinds of expression and forms utilized for Euro-American literary prose and poetry altered so remarkably, like changes in Euro-American plastic and graphic arts and music, that a continuum from prose to poetry is no longer neatly divisible in the minds of literary critics although, no doubt, it once was precisely definable in that community of self-appointed judges. Oral arts of nonliterate peoples unquestionably contained diverse genres which were relatively proselike or poetic, that is, compared with nineteenth century Euro-American genres. Actually, danger of extrapolation of old Euro-American concepts into nonwestern literary phenomena is such that discussion about differences between prose and poetry is valueless cross-culturally. Correct procedure is to analyze out kinds of expressive content and features of style in each nonwestern genre, to show its grosser structurings too, and to avoid, as much as possible, superimposition of culture-tied concepts of over-all kinds such as prose and poetry. However, markedly poetical features, features similar in general respects to those in Euro-American poetry, do appear in nonwestern oral art genres, perhaps especially so in rituals and song verses. In some instances, it is important to put a spotlight upon them for the sake of enlightenment of an opinionated Euro-American who remains confident that no savage could express himself as beautifully as Heine, T. S. Eliot, or Katherine Anne Porter. But the demonstration is for practical and pedagogical purposes. It should not be accompanied by a statement, for example, that such a nonwestern food-gathering or economically ultrasimple agricultural group had a genre of ritual poetry. An apt way to make the point about poetrylike features is to indicate, with scientificlike specificity if not acidity, that a genre which characterized certain rituals was poetical in some features of expressive content and maybe in some features of style, but only so when compared with similar features in so-called poetry of Euro-American provenience. Here an adjective, poetical, and a noun, features, in a phrase "poetical features," are more appropriate than a lone noun, poetry. But it is sadly evident that the adjective, poetical, refers to nothing with exactitude. There is no escaping the necessity of slicing a total expressive phenomenon and indicating, in a dull enumeration, component features of expressive content and style that are poetical, that is, that have characteristics which Euro-Americans have long looked upon with favor and in special ways. Short of such careful slicing and inventorying, nothing is really well said. It is certainly not said in a manner so as to permit its employment in an orderly array of scientific statements.

If poetical features are definable, poetical traits of expression and style have been universal, as far as one can perceive at present. Food-gatherers appear to have had as much motivation and capacity to resort to them as anyone else. Poetical items have turned up in nonwestern oratory, songs, rituals, myths, and tales of all kinds, and always in casual conversation. The latter, in fact, appears to have been intriguingly well phrased in nonliterate societies, if current indications from field research experiences are trustworthy. Still, a statement that poetical features of expression are worldwide functions to warn an inexperienced oral literature analyst that he must not forget to look for such expressive and stylistic traits in each oral literature, at the same time that he pinpoints everything else in it. He needs to be especially on his guard for the poetic only because Euro-Americans have long been supercilious about the superior worth of their oral art heritages and ought to be taken down a notch or two, every so often, for their own good. A statement about universality of poetical expression does not tell an oral literature analyst how to slice instances of it out of a nonwestern literary product. Nor does it reveal how such parts of the fabric wove in with all the remainder. It does not tell him how to look for origins or factors of maintenance and change in its poetical or other strands.

Analysis and criticism of nonwestern oral literature forms have much to do. Disquisitions on poetry and prose facets of expression help in such work only in muzzling culture-bound delegates from western civilization who otherwise waste everyone's time with their compulsive raising of special issues that have developed in studies of a few written literatures. Much of cultural anthropology has been written to provide gracious replies to queries, anxieties, and snobbery of the culture-bound. In the future, efforts should center upon fashioning systems of theoretical knowledge about all the world's peoples. The culture-bound may then have become as undesirable as vocal segregationists in Honolulu, and in no long time such well-intentioned creatures may be safely ignored.

Finally, every oral literature had a kind of grammar, a special sort of grammar of two contrasted facets, content and style, which connected on a continuum of features. Emphasis should be upon such facets, not prose versus poetical. It turns out, surprisingly, that a grammar of oral literature content, that is, the patterns of form classes of relationships, major and minor actors, and features of supernaturalism, world view, ethics, and humor, is always prodigiously complex. Possibly even more unexpected to the culture-bound is the discovery that a grammar of oral literature classes of stylistic features is always complex, too. Scientific linguists' grammars will enjoy no monopoly in descriptive structural presentations over the decades. To be sure, theirs have been pioneer efforts, somewhat naïve, of course, because linguists largely supposed that they could and should make their descriptive and taxonomic statements without tying them into sociocultural or psychological phenomena. Whatever their worth, linguistic grammars have been of one general type. They have yielded extremely rough reading at best. But they have rather marvelously showed the way in which expressive phenomena must be sliced and arranged before anything else of noteworthy scientific significance can be done with them.

Now it is evident that all arts have grammars, that is, structures or fabrics of content and style classes. These are of almost wholly different kinds from the classes of items which make up linguistic structures. What most scientific linguists today do not appear to realize, and few sociocultural anthropologists suspect, is that structural elaborations in a nonwestern oral art may exceed those found in linguists' most involved grammars. Indeed, a suspicion develops that each of the distinctive kinds of expressive manifestation of a sociocultural system—religion, music, and humor are reasonable examples—displays structurings which are at once more complex and ornate than those laid down in very early childhood in speech forms as such. And just as each language cannot be examined in a scientific spirit without a basis in a close depictive analysis of its structural characteristics, so too nothing else which people express, esthetically or prosaically, can be fully understood except in the way in which a scientist comprehends reality, that is, with a comparably close structural analysis.

## Esthetic Evaluation of Oral Literature

A foregoing section commented about questions proffered by the culture-bound, and there seems no way at this point in the twentieth century to duck them. Anthropologists usually live rather intimately with Euro-Americans who insist on rating oral arts. Anthropologists have to adhere to a principled policy which is to smile acceptingly, or as acceptingly as they can, in all cultural directions. Laymen keep hammering away at esthetic evaluations of Benin bronzes, Kwakiutl wood sculptures, Peruvian effigy jars, and what not. Do anthropologists join in such games?

Now, Euro-American principles of assessment have long been the same for each kind of art, Euro-American or nonwestern. But there is a special history to Euro-American thinking or feeling about worth in nonwestern myths, tales, or other oral arts. Historico-geographical, evolutionist, naturistic, ritual-to-myth, and archetype obsessed folklorists made no claims that achievements of Pindar, Lucretius, Dante, and Shelley were comparable to those of nonwestern oral literature recitalists. But a maverick dispositioned pupil of Boas, Dr. Paul Radin, began writing in such a vein during the 1920's. His contribution, in *Primitive Man as Philosopher* (1927), was epochmaking because he directed fire at literary people most of whom, until that time, indeed until the present day, were unwilling to concede that voluminous outpourings of outstanding excellence in oral arts were possible without pen and paper equipment. Radin's evidences for his position were unannotated and elegant translations of Eskimo, American Indian, African, and Oceanian text recordings, that is, as geographically wide a sampling as he could obtain. He set forth no close analyses. He was certainly no structuralist in method, although he had a strong interest in grammatical analysis, did considerable field work on grammars, and published a grammar or two of American Indian groups. For oral literature, he merely republished translations apart from Winnebago and other texts. Indeed, translations he made available were of notable merit. Few questioned their accuracy or suspected undue polishing. Doubtless he deserves credit for breaking the dikes or trying to. Because Radin argued effectively, a small group of people in philosophy and literature now believe that many so-called primitive peoples reacted with great insight, compassion, wisdom, maturity, and poetic phrasings to life experiences. Radin's approach to the problem of assessment of a nonwestern oral literature was that of a romantic humanist, an excellent plan for purposes of persuasion of nonscientists, a valuable practical procedure, too, at a time when most nonwestern peoples are entering upon active participations in world affairs. A drily structural design, with items of content and style arranged almost mechanically, might have been less persuasive during Radin's decades. It might not be especially convincing to a great many humanist scholars today. Who ever heard of a grammar or structural analysis generating a rebel yell?

But presentations of worth in exotic oral arts are likely to slip into polemical and sophistical dithyrambics. Orderly and terse itemization of merits is not frequent in journals which print literary criticisms.

Nevertheless, it is timely and sufficient to report on the descriptive data already available in oral literatures, on possible methods of research and structured analyses of their content and style, and on the current state of theory about them.

In summary, each body of trustworthily recorded and translated nonwestern texts and the few close analyses of such resources display extraordinarily large numbers of expressive depictions of social relationships, a few score personality actor depictions supplemented by hundreds of stage prop actors, great numbers of humor situations, large inventories of value ideals, features of world view and religion, and other kinds of expressive content. In other words, a vast amount of expressive content is present. It is classifiable in a large number of categories or classes of items. Again, stylistic features of several categories and many classes are even more unexpectedly elaborate. They include recitalists' and audience behavior, dramatic play structures, and scores or hundreds of motifs which serve as devices to symbolize time, location, and explain nature. There is a wide range of additional formal features, including linguistic ones.

A possible deduction from such expressive and structural evidences is that every nonwestern oral literature which has been properly collected constituted a complex fabric with a great many intricate subordinate fabrics and contained often insightful expressive content. It was both complex and, at present, remains so poorly related by its recorder to the sociocultural setting within which it appeared that assessment of it as an esthetic achievement is premature or irresponsible. But it displayed a variety of merits, if Euro-American art values alone are brought to bear upon a problem of assessment of worth. Evidence, therefore, supports a contention that it may well constitute an admirable esthetic achievement, one even comparable to that of outstanding creative figures in the history of written literatures. Radin may have been right. But it is not necessary to leapfrog with him ahead of evidence from sensitive and close structural analyses which are connected with sociocultural materials. There is doubtful merit in ecstatic commentary about an African poem which intuitively equates with Pindar's noblest lines, until a great deal more has been displayed about that African art product and the achievement of its creators. At present, a scientific worker's obligation is to withhold evaluations, add to knowledge, present finely cut analyses, tie in all items and classes of items with everything else in a sociocultural system, and request trained estheticians to withhold for a little while longer their value judgments in cross-cultural comparisons.

This is not all. A burden of proof that nonliterate people created great literatures comparable to those produced by literate peoples is unfairly placed upon anthropological folklorists. Their immediate task is certainly not to offer esthetic reactions. It is solely to prepare superior translations, close analyses, and unprecedentedly full commentary, all obtained in kinds of field research which are much more protracted and exacting than those earlier undertaken by anthropologists or linguists.

A literature professor who cannot believe that nonliterate people ever had an esthetically outstanding oral art is in exactly the intellectual position of an 1870 physicist who claimed that human beings would never fly heavier-than-air vehicles. There was some rationale for such a position, just as, today, published oral literatures so lack translational qualities, analyses, and commentary which might offer satisfactory evidence of their esthetic values, that a cranky disbeliever that such worth will ever be revealed might present a feeble case to support his doubt. The question may be closed with the observation that no long-experienced and linguistically oriented field worker in oral literatures among nonwestern folk would cast his ballot with the anointed who have voted heartily, before the evidence is in, against esthetic excellence in nonwestern oral arts.

## SUGGESTIONS FOR FURTHER READING

Works on mythology or folklore by G. L. Gomme, J. G. Frazer, C. G. Jung and C. Kerenyi, L. Spence, A. Watts, J. Campbell, A. H. Krappe, Raglan, and a great many others are out of date, pretentious, culture-bound, or rooted in untenable premises. The market is inundated with books of such kinds, to such a degree that few persons who are interested in the topic even stumble into reading which can provide them with a scientifically respectable or cross-culturally proper orientation.

S. Thompson, *The Folktale* (New York: Dryden, 1946) has much too long been the standard American college textbook for an introductory course. It speaks solely for disciples of the Finnish diffusionist method and it centers their largely useless assemblages of features of content such as tale type and motif. It is valueless for oral style. Sadly, no better textbook survey is available. Partial criticisms of various speculations about origins of oral literature content appear both in Thompson and in M. J. and F. S. Herskovits, *Dahomean Narrative* (Evanston, Ill.: Northwestern University, 1958).

Respectable modern studies, some of them shaped—or warped—by what ought to be a defunct diffusionism, include writings by K. Luomala in *Voices on the Wind* (Honolulu: Bishop Museum, 1955) and W. A. Lessa in *Tales from Ulithi Atoll* (Berkeley: University of California, 1961). Especially well-regarded writings on North American Indian oral literatures include F. Boas, *Tsimshian Mythology* (31st Annual Report of the Bureau of American Ethnology, 1916), R. Benedict, *Zuñi Mythology*, Columbia University Contributions to Anthropology, 21 (New York: Columbia University, 1935), and several too long unappreciated monographs by R. Bunzel, also on Zuñi.

Note V. Propp's structural analysis of one aspect of style in Russian fairy tales in his *Morphology of the Folktale* (American Folk Lore Society, 1958) which some younger folklorists have touted out of all sensible bounds. Nevertheless, every student should read it because it is superb for its period of the middle 1920's. A pioneer and much too purely linguistically oriented analyst of style is T. Sebeok, who writes excellently on Cheremiss folklore. A structural-functional analysis of a Chinook oral literature, with especially detailed examination of style, is in M. Jacobs, *The Content and Style of an Oral Literature* (Chicago: University of Chicago Press, 1959). His *The People Are Coming Soon* (paperback; Seattle: University of Washington, 1960) treats of the same Chinook group but is pleasanter reading.

# 15. DANCE

## Introduction. Method

Ethnomusicology remains largely an aspiration to become a field of rigorous descriptive inquiry and firmly founded theory. Comparative studies are premature without such a base. The closely related field of inquiry, the dance, is in even worse plight. One may seek to no avail to find trained or experienced research personnel who are engaged in analysis of significant smaller segments and sets of them in nonwestern dance repertoires. A transcriptional notation which represents a successful effort to supply economical means of rendering units and classes of units in various styles of body expression, so that analyses of them can be undertaken, may be more of a wish than a reality. It is not clear that the recently offered Laban transcription can serve.

Only about 35 years have passed since rigorous analytic work in this field of investigation became even possible. Sound on film, perfected by late 1926, had to be made available because dance almost always connects with musical expression. An analyst must be able to repeat a native performance over and over, both dance and musical portions, to permit identification of meaningful segments of compositions. But there are difficulties. Sound films are not usually processed in areas where anthropological informants are in goodly numbers. Films must be sent to and processed in the biggest cities. A field worker must receive his developed films quickly, replay them, analyze them into their meaningful contrastive units, and then interrogate native performers. Field requirements are therefore like those which weigh heavily upon scientific linguists, ethnomusicologists, and analysts of humor and oral literature. A consequence of improper limitation of analysis to groping and frustrating homework on sound films after return from the field is that uncovering of many significant components cannot then be achieved. A field worker must analyze compositions quickly and return, preferably tomorrow, with innumerable new queries to performers and other informed persons in the community. Speedy processing of lengthy sound films appears to be necessary for such research. A type of study which cannot do this, in fact which can hardly afford the field expenditures, is not going to progress very far toward a system of theory. That is, it will not soon offer much of a stark descriptive kind upon which interrogation, structuring, and deductions can be based. In addition, a specialist in nonwestern dance research must be able to identify and handle at once, in a field situation, linguistic, musical, and ethnographic correlates of performance data. Few areas of scientific inquiry institute so many mandates in preparatory training of their personnel. Anthropologists have rarely mastered more than one or two of these prerequisites, with the result that a most important area of cross-cultural inquiry has languished.

Still worse, the very sound films that might have been collected incidentally in the course of anthropological field investigations which had another orientation or direction of problem have not been brought home. Unannotated films would have been better than nothing at all. They would have helped to chart problems. The sad report is that most anthropological field investigators have returned with nothing about dances except their dates and comments on their social and religious functions. Actually, extremely few such workers after the 1920's felt able to concern themselves with either music or dance recordings because of self-imposed pressure to secure facts solely on one sociocultural problem for which they had acquired research funds. In the absence of music or dance specialists who were also in the field, they were the very workers who should have obtained music and dance materials as a scientific sideline because they were in a perfect position to formulate pointed questions and to provide explanatory annotations to accompany tapes and sound films. Problem-oriented research has been a mixed blessing when by problem many anthropologists have read "a single problem and no other scientific curiosity or contribution allowed."

A woeful consequence is that in recent decades as in earlier times large districts of the nonwestern world became extinct for purposes of knowledge of their dances. Natives rapidly became too acculturated to display deceased elders' dances. Here and there, deaths of three or four performers meant a blank in knowledge which never again could be filled in.

As in other types of art among food-gatherers, dances were learned and participated in by everyone except for certain lineage or upperclass groups on the northerly Northwest Coast. Specialist dancers received emphasis in wealthier and more stratified social systems.

## Content and Style Analysis

Ideas, acts, relationships, personalities, incongruities, and feelings projected into and represented by body postures and movements comprised units taken from sets of units. Doubtless that which was so represented was analogous to the several items selected by a sculptor, the two or three or eleven which together customarily stood for a myth personality or symbolized an action. Like a graphic design, plastic representation, or citation of characteristics of a myth actor, a dance performer in every successive movement selected from classes of units. Such choice and consequent compacted utilization of items is often called symbolism, for in no art expression was reality merely duplicated with detailed narrative realism. Every dance composition or performance must, then, receive that chopping up into its temporally successive sculpturings, the component units of each of which an informed native perceived, identified, and discussed upon interrogation. Dance films unaccompanied by such notations provided by the best informed natives and native dancers are, therefore, of exceedingly limited worth for scientific purposes. At a later time, component segments of a dance and the purport of each segment cannot be guessed. Legends, rituals, supernaturalism, or other connotations which attached to each dance must be obtained, preferably in text and translation. Musicological analysis of associated music has to be completed, too.

A dance genre might contain, in a sense, a goodly number of form classes of items in addition to designs which comprised successive segments like scenes and acts of dramas. It is evident that content analysis may yield extraordinarily complex expressive materials. In architectural characteristics dance compositions doubtless resembled music and oral literature forms. Each genre received its special frame and embellishment with, for example, prologue and epilogue stylizations, successive acts and scenes, rhythms and pattern numbers, crescendo and diminuendo, and great numbers of other formal items. A line between classes of content and classes of style items is as arbitrary as in any other art, although it is efficient to denote contrasted segments of a continuum from content to style.

Some time ago, Curt Sachs in *World History of the Dance* (1937) ventured to introduce a bundle of concepts and terms which would serve in stylistic characterizations of dances of peoples of differing socioeconomic and Kulturkreis stage levels. He intimated that Lower Paleolithic dancers performed individualistically within an unstructured circle or group of dancers; he offered statements about stylistic features of Mousterian and Upper Paleolithic dances. Obviously, neither proof nor disproof can accompany assertions about dance forms prevailing among thousands of long since vanished societies. Sachs went so far as to connect features of the dance with round and square or rectangular house construction. Although a few terms such as close and open, introvert and extrovert, which Sachs employed for binary opposites in stylistic traits of dances may find utility, his historicist and dialectical offerings must yield to thorough analyses of dances which can be observed and in which modern field workers may locate significant features of both expressive content and form. Certainly no full length structural analysis of a nonwestern dance repertoire of a people of lowly economy has appeared, nor have Sachs' and others' terminological contributions been shown to have far reaching utility for such analysis.

## Functions of the Dance

In recent decades, movies and, lately, television have offered tantalizing snatches of dances especially from Oceanian and East African regions. The meaning and function of each dance have remained unexplained so that little more than body behavior could be perceived, like a small excerpt from a tenor solo without intelligible words, without piano or orchestra accompaniment, and certainly without informative program notes.

Since every known nonwestern people danced, and religious and other functions of their dances were to all appearances important to them, little need be said again apart from a few repetitious statements about minimal requirements of method for study of content, design, and functions of the phenomenon. Careful interrogations of performers, choreographers, teachers, and well-informed members of a native audience are clearly indicated needs. The task is to obtain commentary about each segment within a dance as well as explication of the meaning and service of the dance as a whole. Such commentary should include psychological processes which were integral with every dance.

Oral literature analysis offers a relevant analogue. Audience members identified successively with myth or tale actors or reacted to them with compassion, hostility, or humor. Very likely, similar identifications and other responses occurred in quick succession in members of a dance audience and among performers. If at all feasible, the sound on film record of each dance should be played back, segment by segment, for native comments and for interrogation to elicit as much as possible of the psychological insights needed.

Performers' gratification in technical mastery of a dance composition, and their zest in creative play with its segments of content and style, provided them with esthetic satisfactions which were supplemented by flattery of audience applause and pride granted by community and visitors.

Many writers have supposed that all dances among nonliterate peoples tied in with expressive representations of supernaturals or with other aspects of religion. This was not so. Many, if not all, cultures had at least one or two genres of dances of primarily fun-performance content. Children's play dances might be of this kind. Adults often had kinds of skits or plays which expressed people, relationships, and incongruities, which lampooned, expressed tragedy, or offered imaginative representations of fauna. Fun or dramatic performances of such kinds were not merely secular. They might function as entertainment when one band visited a nearby band or as virtuoso showmanship in intra- or extra-group competitions, like youngsters playing compositions one after another in a student music recital. Feud or war dances always contained supernatural content, but sometimes a principal function was to heighten or drain off feelings rather than to utilize supportive or protective supernaturals.

A contrast between the feeble religious and social roles of dances in western society and their importance and elaboration among nonwestern peoples continues to offer one of the especially striking discoveries of cross-cultural observation. Untrained observers noted it centuries ago, but it remains for anthropologically sophisticated personnel to present orderly statements about it at some future time.

## Esthetic Evaluation of the Dance

Points made regarding esthetic assessment of plastic-graphic, musical, or oral arts apply to Euro-American responses to dances among nonliterate peoples. But there is a difference. Nothing is more reasonable, even today and in all our ignorance of nonwestern dancing, than an inference that many nonwestern peoples had as large or larger a repertoire of meaningful units of body behavior and of ornate structurings of them than do any Euro-Americans. Even the rather elaborate European ballet genre already appears to be simpler or more meagerly equipped with classes of meaningful and stylistic body movements than some genres from Southern Asia, East Africa, and Indonesia. But there is no reason why non-Europeans should not have had extensive repertoires each in a number of genres. Euro-Americans possess bodies which are neither better nor worse than the bodies of any other populations for purposes of the dance.

Every gesture and movement had a content or style function. It had meaning, or it served as embellishment or as a device to connect successive dance phrases. Again, expressive content and sets of items which functioned as style cannot be plucked off a film by an anthropological observer or by a Euro-American specialist in the dance, any more than a first-rate critic of Greek drama can analyze a Cherokee myth from Georgia or an Ibo tale from Nigeria. Therefore, outsiders' esthetic responses can be only culture-bound or dance-bound reactions, and then to a solitary facet of a dance art, its body behavior. Such responses contain no perceptions of all the other culturally packed classes of expressive items which were also integral with body movements in each dance. Until all these classes have been identified and connected with one another, no evaluation of a nonwestern dance is other than gawking at little understood masks or other accoutrements, unintelligible acrobatics, meaningless pantomimes, or most un-Victorian body movements. The impossibility of a just critical assessment does not preclude enjoying what one can. Let there be no doubt that many nonwestern dance styles have been profoundly moving to western observers.

On the other hand, nonwestern dances can be studied and, presently, appreciated in all their components of content and style. Presented on sound films with written commentary, that is, kinds of voluminous program notes, they may become fairly intelligible art treasures for everyone to enjoy in exactly the manner in which it may be possible, years hence, for a cultivated Navajo family to understand and enjoy a fine reading of Greek poems, an album of LP recordings of Tamil music, or a performance of a play by Shakespeare. But without full ethnographic and esthetic commentary, there is only pretense or amusement which is so special and truncated that it seems essentially shameful to a cultural anthropologist.

## SUGGESTIONS FOR FURTHER READING

The prevailingly dismal writing on the dance from a cross-cultural point of view is topped by C. Sachs, *World History of the Dance* (New York: Norton, 1937). Since there appears to be nothing else in English in book form, people who want to know about this most regrettably undeveloped area of inquiry require admonition that Sachs was an uncritical disciple of Kulturkreis method and his book has had slight value except as a historical curiosity. Sachs apparently was unaware of the possibilities in close analyses of features of expressive content and form. Bits of sound writing in journal or other short statements have been contributed by G. Kurath, Franziska Boas (a daughter of Franz Boas), and a few others.

# 16. PLASTIC AND GRAPHIC ARTS

## Approach and Early Method

Interest in nonwestern handicrafts and plastic and graphic arts was inevitable in the wake of burgeoning nineteenth century nations and empires, widening appreciation of collections of art work from the classical city states and empires, and the impact of social evolutionism after Darwin's breakthrough of 1859. People who treasured pottery vases and sculptures from so-called "great civilizations" of the Mediterranean, Middle East, southern Asia, China, and Japan were likely to develop interest in specimens from other wealthy civilizations such as Inca, Maya, Aztec, and Benin, and not long after that, from more remotely prehistoric societies. To be sure, the latter might be referred to as "Stone Age," in the characteristic terms of early twentieth century muddlement and stereotypy about premetallurgical peoples. Reference to a Stone Age people never told anything of value, but seems to have satisfied a need for historical pigeonholing. Presently, that is, during later decades of the nineteenth century, national and municipal museums acquired curators and world-traveling enthusiasts who vied in acquisition of hauls of plastic-graphic specimens from every region and supposed evolutionary stage. Nevertheless, these institutions and personnel maintained intense interest as before in the rich city states of antiquity, in temples, stone plazas, and ancient ruins, in Egypt, Mesopotamia, and Rome. But food-gatherers, benighted though they might be and patently wearing a Stone Age label, did produce artifacts of apparent excellence like Pomo and many other groups of basketmakers manufactured along the west coast of North America. Such peoples began to be accorded massive representation on storage shelves in museum basements, if not in sample specimens in exhibition halls upstairs.

Many museum collectors fancied themselves not as salvagers of lost or dying arts but as scientists. Was it not the essence of a science to collect all the facts and to preserve and arrange them so as to illustrate every stage of sociocultural evolution? It was necessary, too, to photograph and measure pieces obtained and to find out about tools and materials used in their manufacture, the hand manipulations and techniques, possibly even the personal names of natives who had created fine artifacts. By 1900, food-gatherers' baskets and the most modest agriculturalists' pottery were being treated almost with the respect granted a painting by a Jackson Pollock today. Soon, wood sculpturings by Melanesians, Africans, Iroquois, and Pacific Northwest Coast groups were also exciting Euro-Americans.

Later decades of the nineteenth century and the first decades of the

352

twentieth which saw a new dedication, resolve, and orientation in its humble curators of ethnographic arcana might be characterized as a natural history stage in cultural anthropology. It bore marked resemblance to bird walks and butterfly collecting. The theory implicitly adhered to or fairly explicitly worded by such collectors, guardians, and admirers of plastic-graphic arts was an almost comically unimaginative adaptation of evolutionary stage classificatory procedure. It was not really theory. It was descriptivism, collecting, and arrangement. But respect for specimens, techniques of manufacture, and esthetic successes connected importantly with a new kind of acceptance of merit in nonliterate people who had done such work.

## Evolution in Art versus Close Analysis

It was obvious enough to late nineteenth century evolutionists that decayable materials and artistic products of labors with them could not be secured from early peoples. Therefore, stages of evolution in technical processes could be denoted only for imperishable substances, stone and pottery, of course. But at the same time several writers had suggested, and they were granted serious attention in the first decade of the twentieth century, that the earliest stage in evolution of a plastic-graphic art witnessed efforts at more or less realistic, true-to-life representations. In a later stage, such realism changed to abstract, geometric, conventionalized, or symbolic figures. Seeming support for an hypothesis about such repetitive regularity in successive kinds of esthetic embellishment was found in recent discoveries of Upper Paleolithic (from 10,000 to 20,000 or more years ago) ceiling and wall drawings or paintings in French and Spanish caves. Stylistic characteristics of such Upper Old Stone Age materials were not closely analyzed. They were summarily misinterpreted as early graphic art, unquestionably indicative of a very early, maybe the earliest, evolutionary stage in esthetic expression. They represented characteristics of such a stage in every other part of the world. This was the way food-gathering peoples everywhere had expressed themselves in graphic media. This was how they had decorated objects they made. A maddening thought apparently occurred to few enthusiasts about Old Stone Age art that there were hundreds of groups of food-gatherers still strolling about, very much in the flesh, and that hardly a one of them expressed themselves like the cave artists of western Europe had done during visits to those dark and silent caverns 10,000 or more years before. An evolutionist orientation was so simple, pretty, and satisfying that a great range of variability in plastic-graphic expressions among living food-gatherers was not properly noticed. Anyhow, there was much less romance about unwashed modern hunting peoples than about gentlemen, whoever they were, and their appellation was "Cro-Magnon," who did obviously magnificent art work inside western European caves long, long ago when humanity was young. Not least, the extraordinarily symbolic rock wall drawings of nineteenth century South African Bushmen had not yet been made available in copies. The already well-known symbolic or cartoonlike carvings and incisings on ivory of Eskimos were almost ignored. It seemed impossible for most nineteenth century minds to face already available evidences of a great variety of expressions in a single type of humanity, hunting-fishing-gathering savages. Stereotypy, simplistic thinking, and nineteenth century sociocultural evolutionism seem to have been bosom companions. The prevailing intellectual climate produced quite a lot of difficult people. They had their pet stages one after another in this or that, and when they were willing to perceive new data it was principally materials that fitted as documentation of their already cherished stages. It was like true believers in matriarchy.

By 1910 Boas, who was very much a product of the most positivist, antitheoretical, and anti-social-evolution currents in the late nineteenth century intellectual climate, had already displayed interest in scotching a few of the most outrageous claims which flowed from convictions about innate inequalities and nineteenth century evolutionism in questions of primitive mentality, race differences, folklorist stages, and linguistic forms. At a relatively advanced age, he turned his attention to the mainstream of evolutionist statements about plastic-graphic art history. Among others at the close of the nineteenth century, the British ethnographer, A. C. Haddon, had written an evolutionary stage fantasy about design and embellishment into his *Evolution in Art* (1895). Boas perceived at once that the sequence of stages claimed by Haddon must be turned upside down for plastic-graphic art on the northerly Pacific Northwest Coast strip where he was continuing to occupy himself with field investigations.

Boas stated succinctly that realistic representations, which evolutionists had indicated as an initial stage in plastic-graphic art work, could hardly be achieved in basketry or other woven items in their earliest stage of technological development because of coarseness of fibers and crudity of surface texture. Not until extremely fine strands could be made and woven, especially so in basketry, was there a minute possibility of recognizable realism in design representations. Therefore, if there were any gross trend of an evolutionary kind in decorative work in handicrafts, the delimitable stages would be the reverse, certainly so for wovenstuffs. That is, abstract, symbolic, or geometric representations would be first and realistic ones later as consequence of technical improvements and finer eye-hand coordinations. An evolutionary stage depiction must accordingly be inverted for wovenstuffs. Boas stressed the elementary point that theoreticians who proposed regular processes which led early peoples from one to another stage in style of embellishment in plastic-graphic arts had not taken into account decisive factors in manufacture in those arts: kinds of materials, mastery of control of them, techniques of manufacture and embellishment, eye-hand coordinations, and simple borrowing from neighbor groups.

Boas did not effectively make the point that the general approach of evolutionists to plastic-graphic arts rested upon a dogma which was veiled from their own eyes. They were actually thinking in terms of an assumption about the inferiority of the mind of the Old Stone Age savage and his gradual progress up through a succession of stages toward the respectable mentality, that is, the ability to carry on abstract thinking, of modern urban humans. Sheer realism in designs was supposed to be primitive because it had appeared in those eerie western European Upper Paleolithic caves, therefore abstract or symbolic representation, its opposite, was not primitive. Boas paid no attention to Paleolithic cave data for purposes of his criticism. But he knew that possibly hundreds of thousands of years had preceded the Upper Paleolithic, and that western Europe comprised only one or two so-called culture areas in an Old World that must have had dozens of Upper Paleolithic culture areas. Therefore, he emphasized limitations of form, design, and embellishment which arose in areal heritages of materials and tools which were used and in eye-hand coordinations which were achieved and then passed on from teachers to learners. People did what they could within confines of what they had and learned, and what they learned was no more than a heritage present in a single district. People did not learn the heritage of a culture stage. Accordingly, Boas eliminated an unnecessary hypothesis of primitiveness, dropped another unnecessary one about automatic passing through a stage of development, offered a common sense one about limitations in materials and known manipulations of them, introduced no new psychological or sociocultural processes into the system of theory about processes in esthetic embellishment and, then, without theoretical sophistication about what he was really doing to advance knowledge, proceeded to analyze closely several different kinds of plastic-graphic arts in northwestern North America. He tackled Alaskan needle cases, northerly Northwest Coast sculpturing, and northwest states and adjacent types of basketry. During the 1920's the net result was something which he never really perceived as an achievement. It is of interest that his pioneering in physical anthropology from the 1890's on was never recognized adequately until 1960. His methodological refinements in linguistics during the 1890's took 20 to 30 or more years to be appreciated and then placed in the mainstream of linguistic science, largely by Edward Sapir and Leonard Bloomfield. The advance during the 1920's in plastic-graphic art analysis is still hardly recognized after 35 years and a paperback printing of his *Primitive Art*.

But cultural anthropology has long numbered extremely few analytic-minded specialists in studies of nonwestern plastic-graphic arts. Reasons for their rarity connect with the large numbers of disciples whom a few leading writers and teachers of social structure recruited during and since the early 1920's and with a general unconcern or anxiety among anthropologists, ever since, about applying scientific methods to analyses of expressive materials other than those in languages. Perhaps there was a feeling that research in them implied esthetic dilettantism on the one hand or a necessity, on the other, to master mathematico-statistical tools. Indeed, a creeping paralysis from sources in the touted validation, mathematical, and correlation procedures of contemporary psychology and sociology also must be perceived, together with some social anthropologists' antiscientific exorcising of researches which were focused upon expressive cultural topics. Anthropologists who are concerned over a barrenness of thinking about method and theory in many unexplored areas of cultural anthropology need to find out why the neglect or aridity has been of such long standing. There are indeed sufficient reasons why these areas are left almost untouched by contemporary field workers. In addition to social anthropologists' distrust of cultural subjects, there was intellectual infection and concomitant anxiety consequent upon overweening respect for highly technical methods. Upon reflection, these bear little immediate promise. There was also a familiar kind of provincial American awe in the presence of British intellectual royalty which was unrestrained in its snobbism and hoodooing, in instances of men like Radcliffe-Brown and a small percent of his disciples.

Boas' interests in plastic-graphic art studies long preceded animadversions by the Radcliffe-Brown cultists against research in cultural anthropological topics. Everything that is known about Boas would suggest that the British oracle's pronouncements about the merits of research in a few facets of social structure would not have frightened him out of intellectual growth or a pursuit of his curiosity in the arts. Boas' plastic-graphic studies certainly amounted to no dilettantism. Interestingly, they made no use of his mathematical talent. They offered an original contribution to scientific method simply in the degree of painstaking analysis of significant components of a projective expression which enjoyed content, form, and frame and which was distinctive in its involvement in habitual eye-hand coordinations learned in childhood and the production of substances, such as clays, grasses, and bark, which were employed in the artifacts devised.

In a sense, Boas previsioned similar methodologies in close analysis of data in both linguistics and plastic-graphic arts. Linguists today rather naïvely refer to their method as that of "structural linguistics," as if structuring the units that were dissected from a mass of extraordinarily variable materials was something special to linguistics. Structuring is, of course, indispensable method in any science as it pulls away from an early crudely descriptive, natural history, or surface fact-grubbing stage. If knowledge is to be advanced, materials about which a web of hypothetical statements is sought have to be rightly chopped, sliced, packaged, and most neatly arranged. Then it becomes possible to exhibit contrasted stuffs, types, and processes. Boas was the American who laid the necessary foundation for structural linguistics, that is, for scientific advances of unprecedented and unanticipated kinds in the science of language. He did essentially the same thing for plastic-graphic arts: he prepared the ground for scientific inquiry in them. A few people saw what he did in linguistics. Again, almost nobody, not even some of his reverent disciples, perceived what he had done for plastic-graphic arts. From the late 1920's until rather recently, the panjandrums of social anthropology and hundreds of correlation-awed and otherwise hypnotized souls in the ranks of American anthropology found nothing that was worth following up in Boas' seemingly atomistically analytic procedures or in areas of inquiry, other than linguistics, that had interested him. And only a handful of linguists appreciated his originality in their specialty. The bellwethers of social structure researches easily led the nonlinguistic and unesthetic sheep, few of whom dared to nibble at a native language or plastic art in districts in which they were attempting to do field research.

Apparently the reason for Boas' successes in advancing methodology was that he was a dry and mathematically skilled scientist whose training and compulsions led him to cut up, count, and arrange things, especially the very cultural expressions which the self-anointed priests of social structure later regarded as undeserving of scientific work, if their output and disciples rather than their verbiage be considered. Boas' slicings of features of materials, finger and hand coordinations, and design elements were offered in an orderly manner, perhaps as a defense against elephantine system building and bizarre pyramidings of unsupported statements about art evolution which were customary in his earlier period and which he had found distasteful. Many other careful laboratory workers of his time felt the same way about pyramided hypotheses. And so they worked painstakingly in chemistry and biology laboratories in order to present small but valid formulations. Boas merely worked with other data. His scientific laboratory was on the Pacific Northwest Coast among Indian informants. He had sliced up languages there. Now he began to make note of hand manipulations and to examine fibers and count strands and shell beads; he studied possibilities in working with the Northwest's soft woods and sharp stone adzes; he slit every Northwest design into its probably meaningful parts, interrogated Indians about them, and tried to relate each design unit to legends, supernaturalism, and anything else it represented or symbolized. He liked to talk about esthetic worth, but he hardly dared to write a publicly visible line of such assessment. The scientist kept his esthetic preferences for laconic conversational comments. He identified Northwest design units with natives' help and he depicted various ways in which such units were employed on surfaces. This was elementary but still quite new method. It was not new theory. For Boas was a man who developed methods and only criticized others' theories. His work cleared out a jungle of false theories, revealed some design variables and units in native arts, and opened the door to possibilities of accounting for the units. He, therefore, prepared a field of inquiry for later venturings toward a system of theory. His bent against massive theoretical systems which were omnipresent during his first decades of professional work was such that he built defenses around himself. A principal defense constituted what he felt was a firm foundation of carefully depicted elements, properly arranged, geographically located solely in the Northwest or some other district. In his time, such an approach to behavioral science data constituted a methodological choice of a rare, if not original, kind. He disdained irresponsible, premature, and global generalizations about stage sequences and about world distributions of gross aspects of culture such as appeared in Spencer, Frazer, and other protagonists of the so-called "comparative method." He countered with his own atomistic but ordered analyses of stuffs, hand movements, design elements, and their unstable meanings in one region. This is what he did for designs and embellishings in plastic-graphic arts. The need in behavioral sciences of the period after 1900 was exactly for this kind of readjustment in method and humility of approach. Theory had to wait until some of the classes of items about which theory could be ventured had been pinpointed and their changes and recombinations noted within small districts. No important advances in any sectors of cultural anthropology have been possible, or are likely today, without adherence to a Boaslike severity and closeness of analysis of small sets of data within a modest region. Boas exemplified such method for all behavioral sciences of expressive kinds in his pioneering in linguistic work outside of the Indo-European group and in studies of plastic-graphic arts of a few food-gathering peoples. During the 1920's and later, Radcliffe-Brown, Malinowski, and other leaders of British social anthropology effectively decried some of the weakest sectors of the Boasian heritage, its atomistic, diffusionist, and historical reconstructionist interests to which Boas had resorted in order to display deficiencies in evolutionary stage systems. The criticisms made of Boas, which degenerated into incomprehension and irresponsible slander in some instances, were most effectively displaced onto his diffusionist and anti-evolutionist interests. The result was that in American anthropological circles only linguists, led by Sapir and Bloomfield during the 1930's, and a few of Boas' most loyal disciples paid further attention to what Boas had done for research method in cultural anthropology. But they could not see that it applied to anything except languages. The percent of American anthropologists who were interested in nonwestern plastic and graphic arts dwindled while growing numbers of research workers, in the 1940's and later, proceeded into studies of social structure, peasant communities, acculturation, and other matters that carried little or no taint from a Boasian heritage, although Boas had attempted early in his career, not especially successfully, to depict Kwakiutl social organization.

It was one of the first pupils of Boas, Alfred L. Kroeber, who never surrendered an interest in the tangible crafts and arts. Kroeber had gone from literature to anthropology during his student days. He turned up during the 1930's with a borrowed neo-evolutionist point of view, stimulated apparently by historical cycle generalizers, Spengler and Toynbee. He resurrected their approach in altered garb by way of global impressionistic assessment about changes and levels of worth in plastic-graphic arts. Boas' emphasis upon limitations in materials and learned manipulations and his atomistic methodology which offered solid ground upon which theory could be erected seemed to some persons an undiscerning, lackluster, positivist, and sterile deterrent to insights and theory. Kroeber, always a man of literature who also had intellectual curiosity about the sciences, did not consistently perceive how sedate identifications and solemn dispositions of meaningful units and classes of units of manufacture and heritage of design in each art might foster the very theoretical knowledge which he tried to provide in gilded insights and culture-bound evaluations of excellence. He offered sweeping depictive strokes about trends toward crescendo, climax, and decrescendo in a cluster of arts in a high civilization although the dynamics of such cyclical phenomena, if concepts of historical cycles were ever valid, could be disclosed only after methodical piecing apart of significant component elements in each art and display of their connections with sociocultural phenomena. Kroeber tried to describe historical cycles in art, but he charted no method by which another scientist could independently arrive at them. The approach was that of a humanist and historian, not a scientist.

Instead of formulations in impressionistic, evaluative, and other general terms about clusters of arts in wealthy societies, knowledge of a theoretical kind may be forwarded solely upon a basis of patient, atomistic, close analysis of each art, its classes of materials, techniques in production, expressive and design elements, and their multiple bonds with everything else. A base of orderly descriptive knowledge has to precede theorization about processes of maintenance, change, and patterning.

For example, think of an aggregate of food-gathering bands that produced ladles of bone or horn, ten or more distinctive kinds of tight and openwork basketry, soft bags, woven belts and head bands, a score or more types of garments, carved canoe prows and sterns, and incised wooden food dishes. An inescapable scientific requirement, although many persons would regard it as dull, plodding, and intellectually unrewarding labor, is to subject each of those many arts and crafts and all their sociocultural tie-ins to careful depictive analysis and only later to summary statements about the entirety of a community's artistic life. Short cuts to understanding are largely valueless outside of mathematics and some of the "hard" sciences. Linguistics and oral literature obviously can enjoy no theoretical fostering without pedestrian but clarifying preliminaries which display many of or all the materials, forms, and variables in them. Every other expressive category in a cultural heritage must also be faced in so prosaic a spirit. Slow disentangling and patient identification of whatever is present in an enormously complex phenomenon do not spell stupidity or lack of vision. They alone nurture advances in knowledge in conjunction with hypotheses and insights which guide the work.

## Esthetic Assessment of a Plastic or Graphic Art

It is unnecessary to repeat principles stated in chapters on music, dance, and oral arts about canons of worth. Nor is it worthwhile to poke fun at pseudolearned critics of wovenstuffs, pottery, Congo house painting, and Papago basketry. It is correct only to grant people a right to enjoy anything to which they respond positively in a plastic-graphic heritage of a nonliterate people. Efforts by cultural outsiders to judge African wood and bronze sculptures, Peruvian pottery, Navajo and Australian sand paintings, and South African Bushman rock wall paintings produce no ideological contributions until they are rooted in full ethnographic knowledge and replies of native craftsmen, if any survive, to dextrous interrogations. Otherwise, assessments point principally to an outsider's esthetic canons and thereby reveal something about him. In instances where twentieth century Euro-American artists received stimulation in their perceptions by examination of Bushman paintings or West African sculptures there has been no meaningful evaluation except in terms of a Euro-American's receipt and incorporation of something which he had not earlier seen. Values in a native art are neither revealed nor affected by its impact upon Euro-American artists.

It is presently not at all important to try to evaluate a nonwestern art. But today a capital consideration is to inculcate respect for nonliterate peoples' plastic and graphic arts. Such a response may shortly displace onto the people themselves and the rest of their cultural heritage. Inevitably, they learn about outsiders' feelings and sense them as acceptance of integrity and worth, an experience very different from Euro-Americans' earlier responses and nonliterate peoples' awarenesses. Consequences in native emotional health can be easily underestimated.

### SUGGESTIONS FOR FURTHER READING

A sensitive lecturer will very likely warn his students against reading the L. Adam paperback *Primitive Art* (Penguin, 1949) although its pictures of plastic art are good. But hundreds of books have magnificent reproductions of nonwestern plastic and graphic arts, with an accompaniment of commentary that, more often than not, is bloodcurdling in its compulsive evolutionism or historicism and in its culture-bound assessments. Works which can be recommended with gratitude are extremely few. They include, for example, several books or monographs by L. M. O'Neale and P. S. Wingert, or writings in which they collaborated with other authors. Towering above acres of published nonsense is the old 1927 classic of F. Boas. It would be curious if anyone were to use another textbook than his *Primitive Art* which, happily, has been available in paperback by Dover since 1955. Every generation in a science somehow forgets or ignores a few classics of an earlier day: no college library should lack R. L. Bunzel, *The Pueblo Potter* (New York: Columbia University Press, 1929) which, in my judgment, was a more important advance for the 1920's than was Propp's fine monograph in the related art field of folklore.

# 17. GAMES AND PLAY

## Adult Play

Play and amusement are certainly universal. Games are only stylized forms which belong under a broad heading of "amusement." World ethnographic literature on these facets of expressive behavior is superficial and fragmentary like most transcultural treatments of expressive manifestations. Recent examination of data on amusement the world over reveals uneven and usually slight interest by ethnographers in securing even partial reporting, in spite of salient roles which play and games often had in the lives of people. Published materials deal principally with externals such as paraphernalia and rules, not often social and emotional components of the phenomenon.

A continuum requires segmentation in each society or region from its comparatively unstylized play to games which, in a few nonliterate cultures, might have been as complexly structured as chess or bridge. Then each form of play or game needs to be further sliced into meaningful component parts. Each connected with socially pressured needs or tensions, feelings in social relationships, ideology around supernaturals, or other means of succeeding or winning, childhood disciplines, values, personality characteristics, linguistic forms, and the like. Complete sound-on-film records to supplement scattered observations and interrogations are rare or nonexistent. In spite of such handicaps, it has seemed possible to initiate a global survey of the spotty data in order to offer a few tentative statements which may have some utility for later field observers. However, an immediate need is less to provide such a survey than to obtain full materials within sample communities, exactly as such data are required for other expressive forms like languages, religions, oral literatures, and music. A world survey of nonwestern music is already possible but would yield only a petty handful of starting hypotheses. An intensive study of a single musical literature which survived in only 20 or 60 compositions when perhaps thousands were once present would, nevertheless, allow statements about problems in scale units, rhythmic patterns, melodic forms, and voice behavior although it would reveal little about the totality of that literature. Rules in a very few games, like the widespread hand game among hundreds of food-gathering peoples in western North America, have received fairly complete listing in three or four groups, but such inventorying of rules is only a beginning in scientific work on games because of its patent externality. Other games in the same cultures remain almost unknown. A gamut from all kinds of play to all the

games is nowhere thoroughly reported or analyzed. Nor is the kind of seg-
menting of such data offered, that is, main classes of sliced-out items of behavior and ideology. Classification of all data around a single game has
never been suggested.

Although anthropologists agree that amusements are universals, there is
a question whether a few peoples have even a single structured or stylized
form called a "game." Obviously, reports about nonwestern peoples have
been such that no certainty is granted about total absence of games in rare
groups.

Speculation about remote origins of play—a typical compulsion of nineteenth century minds—has been both frequent and, very likely, profitless
for a system of theory. Everyone's familiarity with solo and group play in
mammals helps to document a starting statement that play constitutes a
kind of expressive behavior which doubtless antedated language and humanlike technology. The problem of time of origin is of slight significance
compared with the importance of piecing out needs, cooperative, narcissistic or sadistic actions, and kinds of resolutions of feelings in modern
primates or other nonhumans. Classes of components of play among humans are surely far more numerous than among even the surviving apes.
None of these creatures possess stylized play forms or games, unlike the
structured or designed play, humor, and many other kinds of expressions
whose complexity characterizes only humans. The question of what is play
brings up some fundamental considerations about the very nature of human beings in societies and cultures. Anthropologists who have stressed
language, technology, culture, symboling, or something else as the most
distinctive characteristic of humans have usually failed to direct attention
to humans' varied slicings and patternings, including the resort to binary
or contrasted opposites, in what they express. No one cluster of traits such
as symboling should be pointed to as the most decisive feature of human
behavior, unless symboling be defined in a special way. If the definition of
symboling implies that a principal mark of humans is their capacity to cut,
select from a set of cuts, and arrange such sets in patterned relationships,
for purposes of both efficient communication and pleasure or play, then
something rather basic has been offered. The utility of the ability to slice,
arrange, and structure experience and thoughts or projections may early
have had survival value. But that which is structured is still played with,
and the play of humans is unique in the many ways in which it is structured.

Very likely, field methods which can be used to find out about play and
games in a nonwestern society permit, if they do not require, fullness of
participatory observation which is hardly possible in study of other types
of expressive behavior such as music, religion, and oral literature. Anthropologists can often play with youngsters and can receive willing instruction in games, even those in which supernaturals supplemented moves that
were made. But lengthy observations, participation, and sound on film are
never sufficient. When materials have been cut into hypothetical units

which are forthwith ordered into sets, interrogation of native informants must follow. It alone can expose a range of relationships, values, and supernaturals which connected with game or play moves and which can be had if asked for dextrously.

## Major Types of Games

Different principal classes, macroclasses, of games have been categorized tentatively although their shared features are many. There were vast numbers of games of physical skill like relay races, staying under water without rising for air, hockey, shinny, running, and wrestling which need categorization into sets of components. Strategy and chance factors might also be present in such contests. A second macroclass, games primarily of strategy, varied from a type which, as in poker, contained a component of chance to games like chess which were relatively purely rational. A third macroclass, games of almost pure chance, an example of which is roulette, may be segmented into sets of units, too. Depictions of attributes in the macroclasses are, however, of less significance for a system of theory than a requirement to exhibit each game in its many classes of expressive components. Games of physical skill had relatively few, perhaps.

Preliminary cross-cultural surveying, with use solely of published data on extremely few groups over the world, has lately suggested an intriguing formulation that games which were centrally characterized by strategy rather than chance or physical ability appear to have received especial development or elaboration in sociocultural systems which were comparatively rigorous about obedience training in children. Similar superficial surveying suggests another entertaining thought that games of chance and physical skill connected with socioculturally shaped feelings around responsibility and achievement. Such initial correlations are typical of the tantalizing, chaotic, and unstructured bits of probable formulations which are spawned by contemporary social scientists who prefer to work initially with world surveys and a dubious typology rather than with close analyses of single heritages. Even if validated in later decades after superior field reports are in, correlations of these kinds gained now may serve principally to point to needs for new research that will expose causal factors and dynamic processes in games. Correlations of so tentative a kind, and which present only a spare generalization or two, do not exhibit the configuration of variables and the net of processes in a complex social phenomenon. Close analyses of the many sets of ideology, relationship, and behavior items in all the types of play or games in a few intensively studied social systems offer more solid foundations for a system of theory.

Indeed, current efforts of anthropologists to conduct cross-cultural surveys of two or three possibilities of relationships in phenomena, when closely cut data within the total phenomena are miserably few, are bound to yield disappointing results about materials concerning which they seek generalizations. Correlation studies today are usually simplistic, overgeneralized, and inutile in a system of theory. There are no reliable short cuts to knowledge of expressive behavior. A most disturbing trend in American anthropology is its unimaginative imitation of American psychologists in use of mathematical manipulations without careful investigation of the expressive significance of items that are entered in the research design. Before correlations and validations with mathematical tools are ventured, and it is of crucial importance that such tools be employed at appropriate times for support of theory, it is first necessary to hazard hunches about significant classes of items.

## Participation

Of course there were children's, adolescents', women's, men's, oldsters', and lower- and upper-class forms of play and types of games. The wealthier a society, the greater the likelihood that it contained specialized personnel who made up game teams and who were watched and applauded, as in professional baseball and football, by audiences whose members participated by identification with the players. A portion of such a process of identification connected with pleasure in mastery of technique used in the game. Pleasures in participation itself and in identification with participants arose in several classes of factors. These classes included expressions of values internalized in childhood (for example, obedience, self-reliance, strength, intelligence, trickiness), ventilations of tensions (Oedipal, sibling, marital, leaders) integral with intragroup relationships, acting out in displaced forms of anxieties integral with interband, intervillage, or inter-in-law relationships, and security and capacity granted during the game by means of resort to or identification with nonmaterial allies, supernaturals. The latter is often a decisive sector of the amusement pattern of a nonwestern people.

## Dolls, Toys, and Pets

There is no trustworthy report of a culture in which children lacked dolls, toys, or pets. Animals and birds served almost universally as childrens' pets and older persons often presented them to children. Such gifts constituted, at the least, indications that a giver wanted a child to have whatever other children also possessed. When a child played with a doll or a stick it made relationship on a fantasy level. When a child had a pet it effected a more satisfying relationship because the pet was responsive. It made relationship, also.

Ways in which nonwestern youngsters played with their toys and dolls offer rich materials for cross-cultural study of personality development in childhood. Clinical psychologists and psychotherapists have long utilized observations of western society's children playing with toys, dolls, or in games, but comparable observations by anthropologists in nonwestern groups have been few since Jules and Zunia Henry's classic study of a Brazilian group a generation ago.

Ways in which both children and adults related to bird and animal pets are also potentially replete with information about relationships, personalities, and spots of tension in nonwestern groups. Each culture had its techniques and values around each type of pet. One society's torturing of its pet dogs, for example, may contrast with another society's pampering and reiterated demonstrations of love for dogs. Although thoroughly stylized, such customary behavior can be shown to connect importantly with vital features of ethics, personality, and maybe supernaturalism. But until recently, most anthropologists have preferred to take field notes of pottery, kinship, and revivalist cults rather than to make painstaking observations of the daily life of a dog and the ways in which the people related to it and felt about it. Domesticated work and food animals have more often been discussed.

## SUGGESTIONS FOR FURTHER READING

An important contribution is in J. and Z. Henry, *Doll Play of Pilagá Indian Children* (New York: American Orthopsychiatric Association, 1944).

# 18. WORLD VIEW

## Introduction

A familiar German word for this multifaceted sector of a cultural heritage is Weltanschauung. What does it mean in its many components? How do they operate in people's lives? Philosophers' definitions and discussions need not detain an anthropologist, although it is of much interest that peoples of lowly economy sometimes reflected about matters which specialists in philosophy have discussed in writing under headings such as epistemology and cosmology. Many people have been unable to believe that non-philosophers, certainly those in nonliterate societies, could do as well in their thinking about world view, at least spottily or episodically so, as philosophers of western civilization.

All peoples possessed an inventory or structure of tenets about their world view in addition to creative thinking about it in which they sometimes engaged. The nineteenth century conviction that darker peoples had mentalities which are to be equated with the minds of unthinking pre-pubescents may presently give way to realization that the Euro-American child mind itself, from three or four years of age to puberty, is only an infantilized or retarded product of a special Euro-American kind.

All nonwestern peoples lived in a manner which allowed them to mull over and discuss, usually at much length, problems of life, death, and humans' role, if any, in the universe, and what the cosmos was like. Not all peoples spent notable amounts of time in such speculations. A world view was a bulky code few of whose axioms received explicit phrasing except in contexts such as discussions about sickness, weather, and distant communities. But one can no longer question that many peoples found time for asseverations and wrangling about problems which the West's philosophers and poets have considered. Inquiry into these questions was, of course, limited not by a childlike immaturity of ego but by a kind of coercion of references, which everyone in the community could make, to a corpus of oral tradition, most frequently its myths, and to remembered utterances of revered elders. In addition, everyone was held in line by dogmas regarding history and time, the structure of the cosmos, the nature of matter and substances, the identity of self and power, the nature of birth, death, sleep, and sickness, essential characteristics of the animal, fish, plant, and insect populations, and religion's projections of supernaturals and their habitats. Note that world view means not merely cosmology, nor does it comprise cosmology primarily. Among nonliterate peoples it consists of thoughts about the self and about projections of the self and the familiar. Much of it was projected from base lines of self-awareness and social relationships, although it comprised other things too.

It is of merit to attempt assessment of the intellectual sophistication with which nonliterate peoples discussed and cogitated over beliefs which were inextricable from their mythology and supernatural faith, in order to handle epistemological, cosmological, and psychological problems. But it is not correct to place their solutions for purposes of evaluation beside the critical questionings and repetitive examination of dogmas and systems of theory which have been possible for professional philosophers. The two types of people asked similar questions. They arrived at very different answers. Although comparably burdened by ideological heritages from which it was difficult to secure releases, philosophers of Europe during many hundreds of years enjoyed luxurious resources in libraries and had an enormous advantage in heritages of other and unique kinds, those today termed logic and scientific method. In addition, Europe's philosophers during some centuries have been able to communicate and check on errors through personal correspondence, publications, and, recently, periodic conferences. Since the Protestant Reformation they could function without the confinement of a former supernaturalism and its theological frame.

Contrasted ideological resources and other facilities must be noted for nonliterate peoples. Their philosophical materials could be worked through not with the help of deceased and living specialists at a distance, but principally within a household and small community and solely in face-to-face communication. Preservation of original intellectual achievement was rarely possible for much longer than a generation. Philosophical insights of novel kinds were intermittent. They were retained only for a time and had to be achieved independently again and again where they failed to receive memorization in myth and formula or structuring in a system of beliefs. One wonders what chance any anthropologist has to encounter significant intellectual accomplishment of recent date among nonliterates when its manifestation was perhaps only transient, when it was blocked or speedily nullified by oral literature and an inescapable supernaturalism, when feelings of guilt and disloyalty inhibited thoughts that controverted the postulates of elders, and when it left few, if any, traces except those which somehow penetrated one or another type of oral tradition. Verbatim memorization of esthetically compelling lines which preserved nonwestern myths, rituals, and poetry nevertheless allows hope that fragments of the intellectual life, at least the achievements, of a few nonwestern peoples have survived, in addition to gleanings in reports of commentary and humor from interviews with abler natives, in case citations about instances of theorization around sickness, and in discussions about unusual events.

## Method of Research

Before nonwestern philosophies and intellectual exercises receive discussion, it is proper to ask how an anthropologist obtained information about them. Who were his informants? How acceptingly and articulately did they relate to an alien questioner and observer? How well did he understand them, in the light of his partial command of their language or his exclusive utilization of unphilosophical, if not bewildered, interpreters? How did he proceed in his research? We even need to know if he was so naïve as to elicit information in imbecilic terms such as, "Please tell me about your world view." A nonanthropologist must not assume that persons who long before wrote doctoral dissertations and now enjoy Ivy League professorships were invariably adroit or resourceful in field researches. Because of different cultural and ideological backgrounds, the most experienced and nimble-minded anthropologists committed innumerable errors or faux pas in field situations. They asked informants all sorts of things which seemed stupid, maladroit, silly, or just uninformed, things about which a native child already knew. And most anthropologists had so spare a background in philosophy that they really did not know what to look for in this portion of a nonwestern heritage. Nonliterate people everywhere have been dismayed by the intellectual blind spots of their questioners from universities.

It is easy to follow in footsteps of hundreds of field workers, ever since W. H. R. Rivers wrote on kinship almost 60 years ago, to adopt their method of obtaining something of a household and community census, and to elicit kinship terms and relationships by inquiring, for example, how John Doe referred to Joe Doak and related to him. It is also a simple matter to imitate procedural steps of anthropological linguists who obtained initially only words, a few days later and for a number of weeks short sentences, and eventually dictations of connected speech. No imagination is necessary for management of field recordings of musical compositions on tapes, although discretion and skill are called for when eliciting significant information about each musical performance.

But what can an investigator do about research upon only one of those many and prodigious tapestries of world view which nobody has assembled and defined in each of their important designs, themes, or classes of items? An anthropologist who in the first week uses a questionnaire is only employing a blunt tool which expresses culture bondedness, anxiety, innocence of productive field method, and awe in the current academic environment of mathematically addictive psychologists and sociologists. A questionnaire in any early stage of research in a nonwestern group is as premature as the procedure of a linguist in the 1880's was improper because he asked questions about dative case, subjunctive mood, and other Indo-European features of grammar in a language which almost certainly had nothing of the sort.

Professor Paul Radin used to say that somehow an anthropologist soon found those few natives who were endowed with a philosophical turn of mind, if the inquirer were oriented toward such people rather than toward potters, basketmakers, merchants, and young blades. Radin once asserted, perhaps in a careless and optimistic moment, that it was no problem for him because, since he was philosophy-directed himself, philosophical intellects naturally gravitated to him. The description of his success, if true, was of slight help to students whose personality structures lacked such a magnet.

Philosophical-minded natives have been excellent for eliciting manifest materials, the phrasings which people are able to provide. But covert orientations, axioms, and main ideological themes which people have lived by have not always been easy to elicit. Even a philosopher might be so inclined to rationalize, embroider, or cover over that he was little better as an informant for some parts of the work than were more inarticulate natives who acted almost automatically in terms of premises of their world view.

If informants long failed to volunteer portions of their world view apart from what was imbedded in ritual and myth dictations, stylized pedagogical sermons, and disease theories, an anthropologist could resort satisfactorily to a roundabout approach. For example, he could examine myths in conjunction with expressive materials which ostensibly were of other kinds. In addition to myths and historical narratives, he could probe various dictated materials such as lessons to youngsters, autobiographical data, and direct statements about causation, sickness, and ideology of the supernatural. He could also sift through humor situations and responses. Close content analysis of some or all such data, not only myths and bits of explanations offered by elders, shamans, and priests, is likely to provide starting points which permit a degree of release from Euro-American orientations, such as a dichotomy of animate and inanimate and a concept of causality, which clog a field worker's mind. He can utilize what he finds in early content analyses of verbatim dictations on a small range of topics and so work up direct queries about world view. To be sure, such circuitous approaches are required methodologically in any deft field work in cultural anthropology. Frequently the problem is to recognize items of unique value when data are being phrased on a seemingly unrelated topic. An oblique approach is often more efficient than direct interrogation, certainly so in initial stages of a field research. The method by no means implies fooling secrets out of natives. But it is a means of finding out whatever was really there, especially matters which informants were unaccustomed to putting into words. Interrogation on a single topic such as shamanism, mythology, humor, sickness, or music invariably opens doors to other topics if material recorded receives close content analysis at once and an anthropologist returns, within hours, with new questions to confound his thinking informant.

In recent years, a most destructive development in anthropology issued, as noted above, from simple-minded emulation of indisputably admirable tactics in more mature sciences. Nothing is more mischievous in a very young science, in any science to be sure, than inflexible adherence to and pursuit of a single model or design for a research, where a variety of immediately alternative procedures not encompassed in the model has not been granted. Many younger anthropologists, even those who went out in the company of a specialist in a related discipline, have returned from the field with blank notebook pages and feelings of worthlessness because their instructions had been to secure kinds of information indicated in a questionnaire or much too tight model with which they began their field project. At present, no investigator should venture upon a research, even a multidiscipline project, on world view if the design for the work excludes recourse to painstaking content analysis of any types of oral expressive and dictated materials. No one can anticipate the worth of native statements which are responses to direct queries on world view. Indirect procedure must be permitted, too. Content analysis includes, of course, reading between lines and hazarding deductions about what may be latently present and is not manifestly so worded. It is impossible to overestimate the potentials for insights into native ideology which such flexible tactics in field research can yield. At the very beginning of an investigation a modicum of close content analysis maximizes release from one's own culture's orientations and offers a usable basis of items for question-and-answer procedure. Preliminary field desk scrutiny of most probing kinds, subsequent interviewing which is studded with clarification by informants of items which desk work has suggested, may turn out to be maximally efficient in researches into nonwestern ideological expressions. In other words, if a field worker cannot at once elicit an outpouring of native explanations of world view, he should elicit something else such as songs, games, myths, or instances of illness and shred that kind of material into all its parts. Pretty soon, bits of world view come forth. A start has been made. In cultural anthropology, an oblique beginning is frequently more productive in field work than a direct onslaught upon an area of inquiry.

Amplification of materials on world view may, therefore, hinge upon a kind of counterpoint of question and answer returns and content analysis of a variety of projective expressions. Deductions from one type of source material always receive supplementation and checking in independent deductions from source materials of other types, precisely because of an interconnectedness of parts within every sociocultural heritage.

Possible headings, that is, main classes of items, of world view itself are many. It may help to list a few, with understanding that overlappings may obscure them.

A difficult class for a Euro-American to comprehend comprises an inventory of items in a nonwestern group's perception of human beings and humanlike beings. The single inclusive class might be summarily characterized as people and animate and inanimate things, all of which share capacities of intent or purpose, feeling, and action. To nonwestern peoples, they had a common core which was essentially human. An anthropologist might slice this generic class of "nature is people" into component units of large numbers, a few illustrations of which follow. Each unit, and a reader may add many more, requires documentation in myths, for example, and in data gleaned in question-and-answer procedure. The class might then include units such as people, plants, insects, animals, fish, sun, moon, stars, comets, meteors, thunder, sicknesses, money beads, winds, sleep, and forest dwarfs. The point is that each was humanlike. A correlated subclass might include the semen which was the thunder person's rain. Another might be the infants who lived in another land and had not yet been born. Still another, the dead who went to live in a special land.

A second class might comprise items of belief about an impersonal cosmos. Unitary components might be a belief that the land is round and surrounded by a universe of water; the land lies on the back of a being of a certain kind—when this being moves, we have an earthquake; the sky is a land above, with special kinds of people dwelling in it; and the land of dead persons is in a certain direction.

Another class might comprise origins during remote eras, with unitary beliefs such as people originated in clay; they transformed into rocks; they also transformed into fishes, insects, and animals; they arrived from elsewhere; and a traveling hero dispensed customs, rituals, and productive tools to the newly arrived people.

A class of mythic premises might apply to major stages in world evolution, to include unitary elements such as a creation, an early myth era, the mid-portion of a myth era, a later myth era, transformation from a myth era, early modern times, and recent modern times.

A class of items of geography, directions, and space might number these and many others: dwarf people live in the north, a land of wealthier people is in the east, and there is a land to the west across a vast ocean.

A class of principles of a kind of prepsychology, with unitary statements about capacity, ability, intelligence, and wisdom, might include items such as these: abilities are consequent upon acquisition of nonmaterial kin; insanity is consequent upon acquisition of special kinds of nonmaterial kin; and people are clever or lack shrewdness.

A class of convictions about what was clean and dirty might number the following among many others: nasal mucous equates with decay and death, urine is cleansing, feces are dirty, lizards, frogs, and snakes are loathsome and inedible, and toasted larvae are good, clean food.

A class of items which phrased what people feared might contain these and hundreds more: in-laws, angry nonmaterial kin, shamans' nonmaterial kin, alien bands or villages, dead persons at dusk, nonmaterial cannibal people who dwell in the hills, humanlike water monsters, grizzly people, other persons' nonmaterial gambling kin, ogresses who live at a distance but kidnap babies, slave raiders, and sadistic and raping youths on a district tour.

Determinations of interrelationship of units within a class, decisions about their relationships with units placed under other class headings and, one hopes, a patterned arrangement of classes and their component units, comprise challenges which are almost without precedent in cultural anthropology. Like Benedict's pioneer effort in *Patterns of Culture*, writing on the world view of a nonwestern people has been impressionistic, selective of one or two central themes, discursive, and, above all, so sketchy and brief as to be deceptive or valueless for precise work. It was part and parcel of the nineteenth century humanistic heritage of cursive and superficial descriptivism in history, biography, travel, and other writings. In no instance has analysis of a nonliterate group's world view been as atomistic, judiciously selective, orderly, and replete as even the initial procedures in analyses of phonemic and grammatical patterns. During the 1930's, linguistics worked out a descriptive method which is far out in front of other aspects of cultural anthropology because it specified the necessity of stating all the contrastive items in each class of items and established criteria for determination of difference or contrasts in those items. Only such fullness of citation allows something more than pursuit of a few incidental processes in language. It is reasonable, therefore, to expect that progress in knowledge of world view may be forthcoming when each culture which is studied is subjected to an unprecedented beginning tactic of linguisticslike atomistic selection, inventorying, and structuring of items, later tied up with everything else to which they attached in a sociocultural system. So much for the most promising method of descriptive and structural research.

## Premises about People as Expressive Materials

Among many or most food-gatherers, one of the hubs of their world view already appears to have been a variety of projections of people. An interesting problem for the future is in determination of whether this personalization or anthropomorphization of much of reality applied to agricultural peoples to the same degree. Did they too have an unshakable cognitive "set" that most of nature comprised people of several kinds and of a variety of powers and capacities?

Economically simple agricultural peoples expressed so many disparate principles of world view that it is rash to generalize about them. But pantheons of especially potent supernaturals were frequently, if not always, present among agriculturalists in addition to more modest because human-sized supernaturals. Tensions around storm and rain, extremes of weather, locust or grasshopper plagues, rodents, the very earth, and not least the food-producing domesticated plants, sustained new projections of human-like, but often expanded, supernaturals who were identified with such things. In many instances such modified projection figures had to be mollified or managed, as if they were powerful kin or other people of high status or authority, with gifts, offerings, and even more severe sacrificial self-deprivation to express intensity of dependency, self-debasement, or surrender to them. These deities or subdeities would then take pity. Psychoanalysts might offer their own frame of theory with its emphases upon guilt, masochism, and the like. A psychological equation often appears to be wealthy leader or ruler equals deific figure, almost as if concern around crop and monarch had synthesized into a single deific projection who was feared but rendered tractable with presents and obsequiousness. Food-gatherers appear not to have related to deities with sycophancy, possibly because extremely authoritarian regimes, social strata, and life-and-death dependency upon crops did not characterize them. Important projection figures were, therefore, not regarded as mighty and aloof, although they might be brutal, churlish, even murderous.

Origins of religious and other beliefs of these kinds cannot be found. Speculations about such matters, common indeed in nineteenth century writings, cannot be bolstered with evidences nor can they be effectively countered. But it is possible to collect indications of the functions of beliefs for those who accepted them as valid. Some of the factors which probably sustained and reinforced such notions can be shown.

For example, a belief in a personal supernatural who conferred longer life or skills was patently supportive. It was like the comfort, warmth, or security received from a close relative who was always ready to assist. Belief in a detailed prehistory, offered with elegance by a myth recitalist in the presence of people important in one's life, granted security of another kind, an at-homeness in nature, vicinity, kindred, and band members. Beliefs about causes of illnesses allowed practical follow-up. A patient knew exactly what to do. These and other ideological items summed up to a total of unequivocal knowledge. A person did not live in a world of unknowns or little understood matters like most citizens of the most bewildering of sociocultural systems, that of western civilization today. Insecure Euro-Americans include rigorous scientists themselves, who know absolutely only that absolutely definitive statements are wish fulfillments. Scientists operate on a premise that although no kind of knowledge is more trustworthy than that which is encased in a well-knit and supportable system of scientific theory, it comprises only hypotheses of variable probability. A probabilistic world is not as warm and cozy a location for permanent residence as one which was indubitably peopled with spirit helper kin, family- or lineage-like supernaturals, and monarch-like gods who had their kin too. A world of projection figures offered more anchorages than a world of impersonal hypotheses bolstered by mathematically phrased likelihoods and undercut by skeptical reservations.

## Assessment of a People's World View

Euro-Americans have often expressed admiration for nonwestern cosmologies which display resemblances to those of the ancient Near Eastern, Mediterranean, and other so-called high civilizations. At least one food-gathering group, the Bella Coola of the economically rather advanced northern coast of British Columbia, appears to have achieved something of the sort, including Euro-American plaudits. Such approval is of the same order as value judgments of nonwestern music or ethics. Books such as the famous *Mythology of All Races* series of 13 volumes of about 50 years ago have been written on nonwestern cosmologies which impressed Euro-American minds, especially those who enjoyed the undoubted merits of a nineteenth century humanistic and classical kind of education. When such a cosmology appeared in a wealthy and stratified society which also constructed monolithic religious edifices and plazas, whether or not the stones were cut, hauled, and lifted in place by wretched slave gangs, the response has been laudatory and the phenomenon regarded as indicative of a high civilization. Nineteenth century evolutionist writers, V. Gordon Childe and Toynbee in the twentieth century, are representative of the many who have judged civilizations by gross material achievements in spite of elaborate defensive rationalizations which also cited other values such as complex cosmologies. Evaluation of esthetic or other merit in nonwestern cosmologies has little interest for an anthropologist as scientist, although he may be forgiven if he slyly includes a reference or two to such matters when he addresses the local Commercial Club on Main Street. Normally he limits himself to dispassionate analysis of items and processes in a cosmology. He postpones handclapping to an unstated time when people understand far more about sociocultural systems than they do at present.

## Nonconformism in World View

A question of religious nonconformism among nonliterate folk is perhaps quite different from a problem about degree and kind of disagreement with their customary features of world view. In spite of Durkheim's emphasis upon group participation, much of religion among peoples of simplest economy was intimate, personal, and no matter of interest in controlling others' wholly private ties with beings of power. A nonwestern community tended to accept variety in kinds of supernaturals. It was apprised of other distinctive beings among the nonmaterial retinue which succored and armed neighborhood peoples.

World view may not be regarded as just cosmology, epistemology, prepsychology, theory of disease, logic, and the principal topics that have been of interest to professional philosophers. World view in nonliterate peoples functioned as and constituted a more inclusive network of perceptions which included those cited and, in addition, very different classes of awarenesses. Supernaturals were a principal class, to be sure, and so a world view overlapped religion. World view embraced classes of beliefs regarding geography, climate, history, the zoological and plant world, the heavens, biological functions, health, mentality, and so on. In a way, it comprised knowledge, excluding technology and expressive heritages such as myth, music, and dance. It also embodied convictions about relationships between self and other selves and the very nature of individuals' identities.

Where was nonconformist opinion ever permissible or possible concerning each of the classes of ideas and perceptions which merged into a total world view?

When Euro-Americans entered districts of nonliterate folk, some sectors of native belief suffered early and occasionally nervewracking undermining, especially among younger people. The class of items termed geography was quickly shattered when distances evidently reached out across oceans and great expanses of territory. Animals and plants introduced by the invaders at once added to lore on fauna and flora. Cosmological notions had to be dropped or reconciled somehow with the outsiders'. Nonconformist thinking was at once consequent upon culture clash and presumably always has been. An invasion has impact upon the self-awarenesses of those whose homeland has been entered and whose security has been undermined.

But what could have touched off significant bits of nonconformist thinking and feeling before the advent of Euro-Americans? An obvious suggestion of a somewhat surface intellectualist kind is that persons who traveled were likely to do some critical comparing of disparate features of world view. Anthropologists have so far learned almost nothing about ideological consequences of interband and intercommunity visiting before the modern European contact period.

Summarily, it would seem likely that important over-all heresy in world view was never generated in food-gathering and economically simpler agricultural societies. Only portions or a few classes of items in world view, not the entire net of axioms, could be queried with a traveled and jaundiced eye. But in wealthier nonwestern societies tensions between social strata, in addition to competitive or power seeking specialists such as practitioners in religion, appear to have been productive of questions and novel thoughts about many specific classes of ideas. In spite of their rivalrous shamans, poorer peoples of the nonliterate world perhaps lacked social characteristics which tended to generate disagreement with most classes of items in the weighty fabric of convictions called "world view." Probably no precontact peoples could have countered the totality of their world view with an alternative whole tapestry of ideas. Only segments were vulnerable to examination and restatement. But anthropology lacks orderly studies in the field of these phenomena.

## Primitive Man as Philosopher

This is the title of Paul Radin's minor classic of 1927. In it he tried to show with recorded and well-translated oral literature materials that some nonliterate peoples exhibited a variety of poetic perceptions and philosophical insights. He did not define a professional philosopher and contrast such a specialist with authors of kinds of creative thinking which indisputably appeared in nonwestern cultures. But the appellation of philosopher ascribed by Radin to an occasional nonliterate thinker or deviant mind has been of value in the transformation of western sentiments about darker peoples. However, an error is committed if a category of philosopher of western civilization is left in an equation with creative thinkers in other societies. The two types coincide only in part. Classes of materials dealt with by professional philosophers did not often parallel thoughts by non-literate sages. Nor have philosophical systems reared in the course of the intellectual history of Greco-Roman and western civilization resembled closely a nonwestern community's world view as articulated by one or several of their interviewed pundits. The latter are unlikely to have done more than to reshape slightly classes of ideas already integral with their people's world view. And it is fundamental to note that utilization of a body of principles of logic and scientific method seems to have been possible only among philosophers of the west. In other words, the west had philosophers many of whom ranged broadly through heritages of many classes of ideological components and who applied, of course often unsuccessfully, critical methods to hypotheses and inferences. A nonliterate philosopher was a narrower gauged thinker, sometimes a maverick, who had intermittent insights, maybe remarkably original ones, in one or two special classes of materials of world view. Probably he was no system builder although a succession of individuals like him may have produced, for their culture, a kind of philosophical system.

## Chance, Fate, and Destiny

Few field workers have elicited and almost none ever recorded, at length, phrasings of nonliterate people who were interrogated about the topics of chance and fate.

Although much of what happened to food-gatherers received ultimate accounting in terms of decisions and acts by supernaturals, a residuum of human experience, such as tripping over a fallen log, might have been laid to pure accident without involvement of a human or not quite so human projective interloper. Therefore, a concept of chance could have been latent or explicit in a food-gathering group, although there is likelihood that no important event or noteworthy development in a community was ascribed to accident.

In wealthier societies which projected deities, intervention of such purposive beings in mundane affairs might have eliminated possibility of acceptance of a doctrine of pure chance, even if it were restricted to petty occurrences such as stubbing a toe. To be sure, close analysis of a community's lucubrations on questions of causation would reveal if a little bit of chance was allowed in between acts of deities. There seems reason to believe that a doctrine of accident will be elicited frequently among peoples who lacked deific projection figures and who made do with hordes of animistic gentry.

Euro-American concepts like fate and destiny may have received infrequent articulation in nonliterate societies. At the same time, a research worker may observe feelings about the plight or good fortune of an individual, family, household, or larger group. He may properly refer to such sentiments by saying that the people had awareness of fate or destiny.

Indeed, where myth dramas, as among Pacific Northwest food-gatherers, evidently contained themes which pointed up individual actors' and families' destiny, it can be assumed that common folk in that region also had some kind of sensitization to these themes and spoke, however laconically or indirectly, of such characteristics of mundane life. They might say no more than "That is the way he was," and were thereby putting an identifying finger on a theme of tragic destiny. No language in the northwest states has been reported to have a morpheme for a concept of fate, but plots in myths indicate manipulation of the theme.

## Historical Perspective

The ability of Polynesians to name lines of ancestors in unbroken chains which extended a thousand or more years contrasts with most nonliterate peoples' indifference to or ignorance of names of ancestors who lived a century or more before them. But names are almost empty labels which, in the instance of Polynesia, denoted upperclass lineages and there was supplementation by only bits of proud reference to military and other exploits. Names and a few deeds of ancestors offer tiny components of historical perspective. Nearly everything about ancestors that would be meaningful to a behavioral scientist was unimportant to nonwestern people. Notation of names of Pilgrim, Puritan, DAR, or other colonial predecessors is a most restricted kind of historical perspective which is analogous to a proud Polynesian nobleman's highly selective recitation about his forbears. Genealogy fixated Americans rarely display additional accuracy in knowledge of significant aspects of colonial society and culture.

Historical perspective depends, then, on how it is defined and how much is asked of it. One might question whether historical scholars of many decades ago possessed much breadth of perspective in the light of their compulsion to treat principally of political and military affairs of the past and their disinterest in most other aspects of a former manner of life. Granted that western civilization has long been history oriented, time perspective sensitized, a cardinal question remains regarding characteristics of that orientation and sensitization. A few generations ago, children in United States schools acquired microscopic pieces of a time perspective which excluded most of the world, including next door neighbors such as Canada and Latin America. Children received details and historical interpretations of the ancient Near East, ancient to modern western civilization, and the United States which were closer to the verities in Navajo mythology than to evidences scrupulously gleaned by professional historians. Sunday School classes added odds and ends from small portions of the ancient Near East.

A case may be made that Levy-Bruhl's characterization of some few people of the west as logical and most primitives as wholly prelogical was as accurate as a fantasy that a few school children and adult Americans acquired historical perspective and nonliterate people did not. In short, historical perspectives are of a great variety of kinds, but one worries about the veracity of details, sequences, and emphases presented even in the most sophisticated historiography. If historical or time perspective receives translation as any heightening of awareness of people, happenings, and customs before the present, then all peoples had a perspective of history or of past time. Since most citizens of western civilization and almost all their children have had their special types of perspective filled in with as many absurdities as truths, they have little justification for convictions of superiority over nonliterate folk who also believed in silly odds and ends about the past.

A principal difference between the world views of nonliterates and the west is the presence in the latter of a most admirable but generally ignored heritage of methods and values for public recheck of statements about the past. A handful of inquiring specialists accept self-imposed assignments to seek out with utmost care what happened in earlier days, and to correct errors made by preceding specialists. Nonliterate societies lacked that kind of corps of specialist historians. Without archaeological methods, library depositories of written records, and a trained research personnel, there can be only feeble or intermittent appraisal of assertions about the past. Until lately, western civilization was alone in its possession of means for determination of probabilities about portions of its background, although actually it was interested in certain special facets of that history. The remainder which dribbled out to the general population was largely an inventory of myths.

Among nonwestern peoples, myths and other orally transmitted sources of knowledge of former times served to build in some sort of remoter time perspective, one supplemented by elders' less stylized narratives of a recent period.

A methodologically correct way to pursue examination of different cultures' time perspectives is to analyze out exactly what people selected as worthy of citation regarding bygone persons and events. Then, to try to ascertain why such selections had been made and why everything else about the same period of yesteryear had been waived as undeserving of memory and mention. Western civilization's professional historians perennially singled out stylized slaughter, politics, and government, together with leaders in those noblest of endeavors. Nonwestern cultures usually set forth different classes of citations such as experiences of supernaturals, migration routes, and events crowded with the miraculous.

## The Idea of Progress

Few, if any, peoples supposed that things were always as in the modern era. The historical perspective classes of items in a cultural heritage usually depicted features of earlier eras as inferior to contemporary ways. Food-gatherers and others often presented myths of stupider or incomplete creatures who lived in an epoch of yore, generations before the great great-grandparents. Images of such a kind included, of course, projections of humans around whom there were tensions. Changes which these projective figures at length underwent in a direction of becoming things, animals, or persons functioned as a kind of theory of progress. Once they had become familiar features of the modern world, progress ceased. In other words, a characteristic orientation was rather like that of evolutionism with its successive stages. The last stage might be regarded, in order to defend against doubts, fears, and discomforts, as the stage which would endure—although in recent centuries all nonwestern peoples had to face drastic current change and the advent of western civilization which their world view had rarely anticipated. An eighteenth and nineteenth century kind of idea of progress is not closely paralleled in nonwestern ideologies. The evolutionary stage ideology of the late nineteenth century is in over-all structure comparatively closer to the thinking of many nonwestern groups who, to be sure, often portrayed earlier stages as less desirable times than the modern era. A theme of progress was thereby a facet of a vista of stages.

## SUGGESTIONS FOR FURTHER READING

At the beginning of the present century the French philosopher L. Levy-Bruhl published a number of books in the genre of the old comparative or worldwide grab bag method. He was among the first to tackle the extremely tricky topic of nonwestern peoples' world view. A method of close analysis of two or three peoples seemed less productive at that time than the tried and true procedure of assembling file slips of the observations of ship captains, army colonels, and missionaries. Sir J. G. Frazer's voluminous writings also adhere to this pathetic and deceptive genre of sloppy comparativism.

P. Radin, *Primitive Man as Philosopher* (New York: Appleton, 1927), and lately in a paperback, was a notable advance in orientation. It is certainly one of the classic writings in the early development of cultural anthropology. Radin, *The World of Primitive Man* (New York: Schuman, 1953) has had much less impact. Radin's was only a programmatic and impressionistic effort. He offered little more than general contrasts and he never came to grips with a method of close structural and functional analysis. Nor did R. Benedict in her early *Patterns of Culture* of 1934 (in paperback since 1946). It was the first effectively and widely dramatized presentation of the topic of world view. Radin's and Benedict's classics are must readings in any college courses which specialize on a cross-cultural handling of world view. Benedict did even better, in methodological respects, in her study of Japan, *The Chrysanthemum and the Sword* (Boston: Houghton Mifflin, 1946). Robert Redfield's excellent books can all be recommended enthusiastically, with the understanding that they followed the tradition of compassionate, accepting, insightful, cross-cultural but wholly pre-structural writing.

# 19. ETHICS

## Method of Research

Explicit items in moral codes or formalized cores of ethics of nonliterate peoples constitute selections of principal values and their corollaries. Implicit ethics comprised many additional items which were somehow below a threshold of attention which had resulted in pontifical formulation. But prodding and discussion might result in later verbalization of such items, too. If these comments are well taken, a lesson about methodology is clear. Research by a direct method, such as a questionnaire, on a nonwestern people's ethics may be artificially selective and limited. Proper method requires at least two procedures following acquisition of a rounded ethnographic picture.

If an anthropologist queries informants about their people's ideals and standards of ethical behavior, notations are likely to consist of a comparatively small inventory of commandments or proscriptions of kinds which pointed to principal zones of social tension. Interrogation of a direct kind is only one procedure. The anthropological record will be less full than if social behavior is observed at length. Still more productive is analysis of a variety of expressions, in myth, ritual, humor, biography, and so on, including answers given in response to questions. This is the second procedure and often it is rich in returns.

In the first procedure of direct confrontation about ethical principles, a field worker ascertains ideals or core standards about which people, or at least some of their most articulate representatives, were initially explicit. A question and answer technique follows in order to determine feelings around each expressed principle and its religious and other associations. There should be accompanying documentation as in case study of the law. Each principle ought to be supported by as many real-life cases as possible, whether merely recalled by some persons or, when feasible, observed by the anthropologist if he remains long enough in the field situation.

A question arises as to why there were selection and maintenance, by the people themselves, of principles which were easily verbalized and, it sometimes also appears, of statements which were subjected to some formalization in a kind of logical system. Solution may be found upon determination of those many especially tense spots in social life which were accorded definitive and quick handling by means of application of relevant ethical principles. This is not to say that handling was invariably successful. People murdered when they shouldn't. But because of availability of a moral code, doubts and anxieties about what was right and wrong arose less often. Explicit ethical principles served a function of stilling doubts and facilitating coercion against offenders without resort to agonized discussion about what ought to be done.

People did not bother about thinking of or phrasing values in relationships which infrequently or never generated difficulties. Items in a body of explicit ethical principles, as in the law, connected with potential, frequent, or excessively threatening trouble situations. Whatever caused infrequent, slight, or no trouble was no matter for anxiety or for formal rules to guide and expedite decisions. That is, the core or explicit moral code, which in only a few societies had something of logic and almost visible structure, did not comprise value statements that covered all minor trouble situations.

Now what was this logic or structure in instances when it has been found? It consisted of as few as four or five main premises about values in behavior, something like the few principal poles of a Plains Indian tipi. Everything else rested upon the foundation structure provided by the poles. Values consisted principally of corollaries. An ethical system might be constructed upon a much greater number of value axioms, each with corollaries.

Another structural analogy is a phonemic system, where each phoneme has its several allophones. Those who sermonized or admonished children about right and wrong singled out principal ethical abstractions. These are analogous to main tipi poles or phonemes. People did not often document with many instances or illustrative cases analogous to the lesser gadgetry in tipis or to allophones. Still, in ethical matters people were able to perceive corollaries, although a speaker of a language was unable to discern acoustic distinctiveness in his or others' allophones.

The second procedure in study of a nonwestern ethical system directs attention to its greater numbers of principles which were inexplicit usually because they related to minor spots of tension. They might connect as corollaries with major tenets of an ethical code. They might be extremely difficult to elicit apart from illustrative cases. Where did such principles lurk? How can they be pulled out of the shadows, identified, given verbal form, and documented in cases? The procedure may be painfully slow and indirect for an impatient anthropological field worker who has not been trained to accept the diamond hard facts of infinite complexity in sociocultural systems and psychological anthropology.

One means of eliciting minor principles is to approach a people's veiled projective expressions of them exactly as in close content analysis of an oral literature. To be sure, an oral literature itself contains clues to many minor as well as major principles of ethics. An anthropologist who has identified minor values follows with a question and answer checkup and further emendation from informants. Recordings of certain kinds of spontaneous conversations, if secured on tape or in careful notebook transcriptions, may be even richer with judgmental statements than an oral literature. Situations and principles applied to them can be dissected out and, as always, further discussed with informants. Recordings of native pedagogical sessions or of formal admonishings of pubescents by band or village elders are important to obtain, when possible. The purpose of such procedure is, of course, to allow close content analysis. Masses of prescriptive and proscriptive concepts can be dredged from a people's structured oral literature, elders' sermons, case law, biographical depictions, and unstructured chitchat, after which informants should be asked to try to formulate values tersely. Then they should be asked to supply additional illustrative cases and commentary.

## Rigid Sanctions versus Lip Service

Controls upon conduct exerted by explicit statements in a moral code on the one hand and by an inventory of latent values on the other hand varied from society to society. Certainly western civilization presents an intriguing instance of a code which displays neither logical consistency nor neatness of structure. It is an example of a hodgepodge of ethical statements, a potpourri perhaps consequent upon rapid sociocultural changes in recent centuries, whose function is largely not to constrain but to bolster convictions of worth of self when one mouths a portion of it. It enhances personal conceits of those who insist on others behaving according to it. All its standards are episodically negated. For example, the commandment against killing is daily flaunted by customs of resolving politico-economic disputes with mass slaughters and of responding to murder, rape, and treason with capital punishment. Opportunistic rationalizations serve as ethical justifications of such customs. The society's religious specialists who play a unique role, as sociocultural systems go, in their complementary assignment as guardians of the moral code seem to be among the foremost rationalizers about permitting exceptions to the moral rule against killing, at least during and after armed hostilities.

A problem, therefore, arises regarding the impact of an ethics, whether or not well-formulated, to which most persons grant lip service at best. Where a code which was carried solely in the heads of nonliterate people was embedded in cements of religious sanctions and tightly knit relationships, that is, responded to with punishments automatically accorded either by supernaturals or by family, lineage, and community, did people often act against the code? An answer may be as follows. As societies became stratified, as supernaturals became less intimately identified with, bigger, more remote, more powerful and controlling, more like vacationing parental figures, and as lineage and community limits upon behavior attenuated, hypocritical and opportunistic lip service to ethical principles increased. Therefore, in food-gathering and economically primitive, unstratified agricultural societies ethics really worked. It worked less of the time in wealthier societies, to a point where individuals who adhered to it might be regarded as fanatics or deviants. All other persons used it in distinctive ways, but not to follow in ethical action. Indeed, they used it in order to make long-faced speeches and to present a public display of their integrity. They allowed ethics' items to limit or coerce them only when it did not bother them much to do so or when it was opportunistically prudent to behave ethically. In other words, individuals of wealthy and stratified societies accepted limits denoted by their professed ethical principles, not in order to act virtuously but in order to talk virtuously and to judge and control as if they were virtuous. They thereby maintained face and status and secured rewards. They acted in terms of what a philosopher might term "prudentialism." A psychiatrist might phrase their behavior as narcissistic and he would refer to corrupt superegos. The operational efficiency of moral principles had altered or deteriorated to a function of a wholly different kind. The function was to allow a prudent individual to add auras of respectability, integrity, and merit to himself. He also enhanced his sentiments of personal worth by admiring or sneering wisely, he presumed, at the few who remained severely moralistic.

On the other hand, citizens of wealthy and highly stratified societies did adhere more or less fully to innumerable minor ethical statements which were realized in mores or customs. Their limiting functions were potent. Again, these minor rules may be assembled in the course of prolonged field observations and by means of content analyses. A fair guess is that it may not be possible to accord them an orderly arrangement or logical structure, as in the possibly few instances of an explicit moral code which had taken on a certain patterning. However, connections of minor ethical statements with the rest of a sociocultural system and with personality structures were doubtless so extensive and important that many studies in a variety of sociocultural types should be designed so as to elicit them.

## Worldwide Values

Do any ethical principles appear globally, from food-gathering to modern urban-suburban societies? Let us see. Headhunting was bad in most but definitely not in all societies. So, too, were food cannibalism and, maybe, striking one's mate. These three, and doubtless a number of others, come fairly close, but not close enough, to universality. To be sure, each was condoned, if not rapturously accepted, in a number of districts. Adultery and poisoning were all right in many or most societies providing one was not caught. Giving seems to have been good universally, if recordings of people's words are regarded as definitive. But it is also necessary to document with cases. And when instances are listed around the world, it appears that there was a lot of variety in whom a person gave to, how much, when, why, and how much the people griped about it. An abstraction about giving is therefore really not meaningful. What people gave, when, and to whom depended on a sociocultural system. Love or acceptance of little children, even newborn babies, is another unusable abstraction because details of such behavior varied extraordinarily from one to another district. It is clear that a very few abstractions, abstract to the point of meaninglessness, can be offered. Each was realized in specific ways which were so encumbered with local contingencies that an always annoying protagonist of ethical relativity seems to have much evidence in his favor. Relativism is an unhappy finale for a citizen of western civilization who feels guilty and insecure without ethical absolutes to protect him from himself.

But ethical relativism is not a subject regarding which it is necessary or even advisable to be conclusive, because decision for or against it adds nothing to knowledge. What is necessary is to erect a theory about internalization and operations of diverse classes of values in different kinds of societies. Each ethical system with its major tenets and its inventory or sets of minor precepts flowed from and connected with a sociocultural system. The scientific task is never to show that this or that was profoundly right but it is to exhibit how it operated. Pursuit of universal standards to which all peoples adhered may have to await a world in which peoples everywhere live in much the same sociocultural web, one whose technological level is beyond that of today.

Anthropology cannot offer counsel about an array of ethical precepts to which everyone should adhere, although it is in the beginnings of research which may reveal the net of circumstance accountable for a particular people's concurrence about value ideals and for their egotistic prudence and foolishness. Anthropology can and should set forth at least one extremely important value. A few anthropologists can be found who would insist upon it with the greatest warmth. It is to respond, where possible, to nonwestern peoples' ethics and infractions of their own ethics with cool understanding rather than with culture-bound stereotypy, slander, and heat.

## Ethics as an Abstracted System

The history of classical Mediterranean and European sociocultural systems exhibits much philosophical specialist preoccupation with a sector of life that deals with value ideals. They have long been a subject of specialist inquiry among Euro-American theologians, too. They have been cut from the totality of western ideology in order to be accorded specialist attention. The vocabulary of every European language registers the fact of abstraction of a class of such items, with terms like morality, ethics, values, and ideals. Nonliterate cultures often, if not largely, lacked vocabulary terms that captioned a class of items of this kind. When Euro-Americans study nonwestern ethics they commit the familiar methodological fallacy of extrapolating a class of items from their own culture into cultures which perhaps lacked such a class. As for ethics, sets of ethical concepts and terms might have been lacking even in the many societies, maybe all societies the world over, where assigned elders upon definite occasions imparted values and where councils met to decide upon damages and penalties. Therefore, ethics may no more have constituted a macroclass of phenomena than the subjunctive mood comprised a class of morphemes and processes in a non-western language which lacked it in its grammar. So, too, ethics must be regarded as a special bulk class of features and functions in western civilization's sociocultural patternings. Functional, but not necessarily conceptual and structural, analogues of the class will be found in every nonwestern society. Another analogy, if the reader is puzzled by an analogy with grammar and the subjunctive mood, is invention. In western civilization invention receives conceptual realization and functions in the behavior of its specialist scientists and tinkerers. But in nonwestern societies creativity in gadgetry might not be conceptually or otherwise set apart, in the people's minds, from excellence in manufacture.

## Contradictory Values

In many cultures conflicting values stood side by side, even as in western civilization. Contradictory ideals very likely turned up more frequently in dense and stratified populations than in small food-gathering and comparably minute agricultural communities, where everyone internalized almost exactly the same ideology and everything else in a heritage. An undoubted presence of antithetical or inconsistent values in many societies which were not necessarily in process of rapid change points up a methodological issue. It is resolved by refusal to set up a class of ethical entities in a patterned ethical system where functionally only sentiments of approval and disapproval adhered to social relationships and customs. These sentiments sometimes displayed contradictions. They did so because no ethical philosopher was at work attempting to iron out inconsistencies. Indeed, in such an instance the culture lacked an integrated ethical system.

## Worth of an Ethics

The beauty or worth of a nonwestern people's ethics is another question which has interested a few Euro-Americans. The reader may anticipate an answer that some anthropologists have. It is much like their critical reaction to a nonwestern musical system which had complex content and style, connections of such features with the rest of the sociocultural heritage, and native composers, artists, and critics. Persons who wish to are free to hazard judgments about excellence in nonwestern musical compositions or performances before their own immersion in the totality of that sector of a culture. But anthropology is oriented toward building systems of scientific knowledge about cultural expressions and, therefore, has no central concern with Euro-Americans' esthetic or value judgments about a nonwestern art form. The worth of a nonliterate society's code of ethics is similarly no present concern of a scientist whose obligation is to add to knowledge about that code and its functioning. After all, the better it is understood, the closer a warrantable assessment of it can be made. But, with perhaps a few exceptions, comprehension of operations of nonliterate groups' values is too inchoate or superficial for good judgments about them at this time. And where is the calibrated ruler, the measuring stick, the universal set of values, which alone can justify appraisals? Is the need to judge others' values a displacement consequent upon gnawing doubt regarding values respected at home?

## SUGGESTIONS FOR FURTHER READING

A philosophically sophisticated but only programmatic and orientative recent work is by M. and A. Edel, *Anthropology and Ethics* (Springfield, Ill.: Thomas, 1959). An effort to analyze and contrast value systems is in O. von Mering, *A Grammar of Human Values* (Pittsburgh: University of Pittsburgh, 1961). Do not overlook R. Benedict's *Patterns of Culture* which offers a pioneer discussion, during the 1930's, of regional contrasts in both major world view premises and value ideals. A number of excellent field workers, for example, E. M. Albert, E. Z. Vogt, and J. M. Roberts, may be watched for their current or future work, together with researches by their students, on nonwestern value systems. Well-known older works, such as the once widely read L. M. Hobhouse, *Morals in Evolution*, appear to have suffered severely from the straitjackets of social evolutionism and nineteenth century comparative method.

# 20. LAW

## Definition of Law

Legal specialists in wealthy and stratified sociocultural systems have developed inventories of carefully worded statements about critical deviations from correct behavior, that is, from social norms and basic ethical canons. These statements list types of severely threatening trouble situations or conflicts which may occur between members of a society. The statements include more or less crisply worded punishments, sometimes called "negative sanctions," to be meted out to those who have behaved unethically or far too aberrantly and thereby have generated such trouble situations. Statements about trouble and means of resolution, and a wealthy society's customary ways of implementing them, constitute only a starting point for discussion of the subject of law. What about law, if we are not too culture-bound to identify it among food-gatherers and other preliterate peoples, also?

All peoples had customs, norms, right ways of relating to one another, value ideals, whether they were food-gatherers, economically simple agriculturalists, or otherwise strikingly different from the wealthiest sociocultural edifices. Statements about the totality of any sociocultural system's customs and canons about right behavior would fill books, even for economically most unimpressive groups such as those of native Australia. Study of the law embraces only a segment of all the statements about customs and ethics. This segment deals with jural or legal statements, those which treat of special kinds of intolerable behavior and customary means of response, whether by individuals, households, or whole communities.

The presence of judges, prosecutors, attorneys, and courts, together with an accumulation of cases in special volumes on the law, is not a requirement for recognition of presence of law in a small nonwestern society. An inventory of discoverable statements which imply or state important values and cite penalties, following precedents, for aberrant behavior which flaunts such values, appears to offer a sufficient criterion for the presence of law, if supplemented by an availability of means for carrying out the penalties. Every society the world over fulfilled this criterion. Law is, therefore, one of the universals both in social structure and cultural expressions. It was everywhere because its key functions appeared everywhere. The task is to depict and explain how it worked in every detail, even though types of machinery such as courts, prosecutors, and attorneys which appeared in the wealthiest civilizations were absent, and important components of law always overlapped or intertwined with the closely related sociocultural universal which was ethics.

A demand that special devices of the law such as were found in the wealthiest societies constituted the essence of law is analogous to a culture-bound or language-bound claim that a language had a grammar only if it displayed tenses, cases, conjugations, and declensions. Extrapolation of Europe's, China's, or Japan's institutionalized concomitants or other special features of operation of law, and reading them into depictions of law's expressive content, structure, and social functioning in an economically poor nonliterate society, is law-bound thinking. A lot of it is evident in writings of scholars of the law of western civilization.

Cultural anthropology requires that values, penalties, and most essential manner of operation or functioning of law be sought first, because they constitute the heart of this sociocultural phenomenon. They can be limned and explained in every society. Institutionalized proliferations or embroiderings such as courts, bailiffs, defense counsel, and juries, which were peculiar to one or a group of societies, are secondary matters. They were manifestations of wealth and specialization which sprouted in a rich socioeconomic soil.

Familiar in writings of students of law has been an allegation that so-called primitive societies were devoid of law as such because their customs or *mores* alone held people in line and kin groups rather than state machineries penalized for steps out of line. Such a point of view can inhibit examination of that sector of a heritage which comprised values about and apparatus for prevention and handling of insufferable behavior. If the premise is that law must be conceived of as broadly as anthropology envisions religion, art, or language, an avenue to its identification and separate study is left open. Superimpositions from the law of one or more rich societies which enjoyed attorneys, judges, and courts, or suffered from them, are not then intruded. The totality of the phenomenon can be examined and if it had some special institutions, structurings, or other features, it is possible to locate them.

It appears that law among nonliterate peoples can be chunked usefully and initially into major portions or macroclasses of features something as follows. One evident portion is the inventory of values which defined intolerable conduct. Here law connected with ethics. A second highly visible portion comprised individuals or groups which were accorded responsibility for responding, in the light of remembered precedents, and their manner of operation. A third portion contained penalties or other resolutions which they recommended and which they or others applied, always with physical coercion as a means ultimately available. These three portions of the law amounted to steps in resolution of severe trouble situations: one, something happened which the society or its government could not tolerate, digest, or handle with other customary means; two, it or its representatives decided what to do, guided by precedents; three, it or its representatives acted and, if necessary, utilized sharp teeth in accordance with the decision.

Decades of European scholars' work, which was focused on principles of law in one or another nonwestern society, display a culture-bound pressure to obtain that which then interested students of European jurisprudence. A result was that the dynamics of the law, the three gross steps noted above, in each such society remained obscure, even if field work might have sketched it.

## Method of Research

What is proper method of research on law in a nonliterate society? An analogy of method in nonwestern oral literature analysis may be instructive, with apologies lest its citation be tiresome. Presentation of observations about audience and recitalist behavior, comments on stylistic rules for beginning and ending myths, and a full inventory of their plots and motifs without verbatim recording and translation tell little about an oral literature in itself or as a functioning sector of sociocultural life. In general respects, a list of plots and motifs is like a list of normative rules and kinds of punitive action which many writers on nonwestern law have abstracted in their study of some nonwestern society. No matter how close to reality, such abstractions do not permit later scientists to reexamine data in order to check on the merit or validity of the abstractions. Basic depictive materials needed to portray the totality of a phenomenon are largely lost.

In research on a nonliterate people's law only a certain kind of case procedure appears capable of effecting an approach to fulfillment of requirements of scientific method. Apart from other merits, it allows subsequent recheck because of potential repeatability of instances of the phenomenon. And the procedure is, in broad respects, that for research in oral literature. There the requirement is to obtain as large a corpus of dictated myths or other recited forms as possible, with alternative versions and concomitant field question-and-answer commentary on each recital. Versions by both outstanding and less than outstanding recitalists should be obtained and discussions elicited from them. Scientific work on a nonwestern corpus of cases of law similarly requires presentation of a great many trouble cases. Each should be offered as closely as possible to a verbatim original. Tape recording would be advantageous. Each case should be supplemented painstakingly by field interrogation and annotative writing. Council elders, accused, accusers, vindicated, and uninvolved citizens should all be interviewed lest sketchings of cases receive skewing. Such requirements are minimal. Assuredly, they are also excessively severe because of the duration of field research required. Many scores, preferably hundreds, of trouble cases must be offered with utmost fullness, if in verbatim text and translation so much the better. Unhappily, such bare reporting is insufficient. A field worker must subsequently probe imaginatively into each case, in a question-and-answer procedure, to find out many additional things about principals, social relationships, ethical judgments, supernaturals, and everything else that tied in with the always relatively external description given in case text and translation. A most important and as yet neglected aspect of scientific field research in oral literature is the probing interrogation following a recital dictation. A most important tactic of scientific field research upon law in a nonliterate society is the question and answer work after a stark description of a case has been written down or taped. Of course, direct observation of the few current cases is excellent, but a hundred times as many cases which came up years before and are well recalled need to be described, even only partially, in order to supply something a little more nearly approaching the totality of the jural experience and heritage.

Cultural anthropology is so immature in its development of descriptive and taxonomic methodologies that it is hardly necessary to observe that there is not a single publication which exemplifies all portions of the method indicated for research on law among nonliterate groups. It is true that R. F. Barton in the Philippines and E. A. Hoebel in the United States, maybe a few others, long since pioneered creatively with their field resort to a descriptive case method in the first instance and their efforts, in the second, to place cases in a sociocultural setting. Question-and-answer probes subsequent to each case description, of kinds which facilitated identification and close analysis of minimal units of content, that is, of everything meaningful that was said and done, appear not to have been managed exhaustively for every case. But the field method of Barton and Hoebel is as close to ideal as that approached so far in study of almost any other type of cultural expression with the striking exception of anthropological linguistics' procedure.

## Religion and Law

Speculation about the first or later stages in changes in the ideology, structure, and functioning of law in early or nonwestern societies is never subject to proof or disproof. Guesswork by nineteenth century evolution-oriented writers about a religious origin of law was valueless because of its gross generality, its failure to point to causes, and the impossibility of disgorging evidence from the past. It would seem possible to generalize about functioning of law among economically simple food-gatherers if and when case reports of operation of law among them were many. Connections between law and religion among modern food-gatherers might then be indicated. But such deduced bonds would not offer warrant for extrapolation into remote eras.

Among modern food-gatherers, connections between law and supernaturals do seem to have varied greatly. In some groups resolutions of severe trouble situations were handled with secular rules by band or other assigned personnel, without intervention or implication of supernaturals in decisions. In other food-gathering groups supernaturals connected throughout, as kinlike sanctions for law and as aids to personnel who administered it. It would appear, then, that a rule of thumb about law among food-gatherers, probably all other socioeconomic types too, is that they supplemented secular rules, devices, relationships, or functionaries for handling of malefactors when wholly secular notions and means failed them. It was then that the always available projective figures who were kinds of especially resourceful, insightful, or powerful people were brought into the picture. In different wording, relationships between people were primary but, when especial difficulties arose in resolving certain kinds of troubles, projective people might be invoked. For example, in some nonliterate societies as in the northern Plains of North America, an accused who denied guilt in a case of murder was expected to take an oath of innocence. If he lied, a supernatural would surely punish or destroy him. This is an instance of efficient and just resort to projective figures in a society whose members numbered no skeptics who rejected all or many such beings. Religion and law connected, then, in such societies, but in differing degrees and ways. Only special analyses of each society may reveal how and why.

Because they lumped northwestern peoples of distinctive socioeconomic types together, earlier writers on law in nonwestern communities rendered it difficult, if not impossible, to add to that portion of a system of theory of law which denoted tendencies regarding ties between supernaturals and law. These tendencies or processes can be found only after discovery of the taxonomy of socioeconomic systems that is most appropriate for the purpose. It may well be, for example, that economically simple and advanced food-gatherers did not comprise two types for purposes of pointing up significant contrasts in connections between law and supernaturalism. Development of a method for studying law cross-culturally, therefore, may hinge, at least partly, upon determination of that kind of special classification of types of socioeconomic systems which can be used to lay bare contrasts in jural ideology and machinery.

At the moment, little can be done to develop a system of theory about law beyond stating a few premises. One of them controverts the old theory that law arose in religion. An acceptable premise is that law often connected with religion. Another not especially useful but related generalization may be offered. It is that supernaturals tended to be called into service when a social system lacked people or groups with prestige, organization, or coercive strength to do the legal job completely.

## Assessment of Law among Nonliterate Peoples

If an anthropologist had been successful in assembling a corpus of cases which he had observed in the field and augmented them massively with descriptions and discussions of bygone cases, he would be able to deduce principles in the law of the community. Besides, he could arrange his materials so as to conjoin the several cases, past and recent, to which the same principle had been applied. He would then be able to note rigidity or flexibility of employment of the principle and give and take in council, community, or judges' deliberations before a verdict.

The problem then arises whether or not to limit proper anthropological effort to analysis and reporting of what was done, or to go beyond the culture in order to offer some assessment of maturity of thinking and action, that is, of sophistication in settlements which most effectively reduced tensions and disposed of accused and litigants. Whatever an anthropologist may choose to write up in his report, his role as scientist would confine his labor to analysis of native law and legal practice.

No one may doubt that, at the present time, it is practically helpful to show also that even the economically lowliest peoples had law and sometimes administered it with exemplary patience, logic, and humane sophistication, as perceived from a culture-bound vantage point occupied by western ethics and jurisprudence. There seems little reason to question a likelihood that here and there in the nonwestern world a chief, lineage leader, council member, or judge solicited and examined evidence, digested arguments by litigants or their representatives, called in witnesses, engaged in logical thinking, and made generous and wise decisions which one may wish to compare with decisions of notable figures, such as Holmes and Cardozo, in the history of western courts.

Cross-cultural and therefore truly comparative jurisprudence would eventually possess great masses of tapes, translated materials, and annotative discussions from as many nonwestern peoples as can still be worked with. Such archives would permit cross-cultural knowledge of the law to be advanced toward a system of comparative theory. They would also permit evaluation of features of merit in jurisprudence in nonliterate societies, a worth that would reveal only the values present that agreed with western values, because cross-cultural judgments of merit are impossible before decision about values that are universal.

## SUGGESTIONS FOR FURTHER READING

E. A. Hoebel, *The Law of Primitive Man* (Cambridge: Harvard, 1954) offers a general and discursive introduction which is marred by some vestigia of old-fashioned orientations. Interesting descriptive studies of single groups, without really close analysis, include R. F. Barton, *Ifugao Law* (Berkeley: University of California, 1919), M. Gluckman, *The Judicial Process among the Barotse of Northern Rhodesia* (Glencoe: Free Press, 1955); K. N. L. Llewellyn and E. A. Hoebel, *The Cheyenne Way* (Norman: University of Oklahoma, 1941) and many others, especially by English and Dutch writers. Earlier and now out-of-date pioneerings of exemplary merit and interest include H. J. S. Maine, *Ancient Law*, which several publishers have reprinted from its first edition in the 1860's; and B. Malinowski, *Crime and Custom in Savage Society*, available in a paperback reprint over 30 years after its appearance (Littlefield, Adams, 1959).

# SUMMARY

Quests for cross-culturally usable delimitations or definitions of culture, personality, social structure, religion, ethics, art, law, government, a tribe, the state, warfare, indeed almost the entire inventory of interests and topics which occupy sociocultural anthropologists, appear to have suffered because of immature methods and knowledge. A definition which applies transculturally increases with aptness if what is defined is well described in its classes of content in various configurations and its variability the world over. Anyhow, definitions have so far served crudely and poorly except in examinations in college classes where an instructor's certainties exceeded bounds respected by a careful scientist. Definitions have been of slight use as guides to methods of rigorous description, arrangement, and discovery of sociocultural processes. Contributions to anthropology's descriptive knowledge or toward scientific maturation in the form of systematized theoretical knowledge have not often been furthered either with definitions or struggles to agree upon them. No sophisticated worker in a science would surrender time and opportunity to analyze carefully obtained evidences about a somewhat uncertainly delimited phenomenon in order to pontificate about various persons' definitions of that phenomenon. A definition should flow from or be rephrased by evidences, and they should not be omitted or distorted because of perceptions and limits granted by earlier definitions.

At the same time, a few anthropologists have usefully defined and thereby pointed to hitherto neglected, although perhaps not especially exactly demarked, sectors of sociocultural life as significant for knowledge. For example, during the 1930's, Professor Ralph Linton briefly discussed cross-cultural phenomena of role and status and thereby called attention to several areas of inquiry which warranted discrete studies. Each of these topics dealt with patently important structured subsystems of social relationships the components of which operated in distinctive and revealing ways. Provision of a tentative definition for each of these topics functioned to assist in the search for descriptive, cardinal, and distinctively patterned items which had usually failed to be perceived during earlier field researches.

One wonders, then, if a definition is worth pursuing only when it is required of college students taking an examination or when it summarily anticipates and tentatively locates an often crucial and structured segment of behavior not previously adequately recognized but found in some or all sociocultural systems.

The history of sciences which treat of transculturally present, structured, and salient phenomena has revealed rather intriguingly that facets of socio-cultural life upon which some of the earliest field researches were most intensively pursued were those which are among the earliest internalized and patterned during childhood. These include notably kinship and language. Lewis Henry Morgan discovered a century ago that in every society kinship relations displayed their own unique matrices. Today we know that about as soon as children learn their language, they also learn configurations of their relationships to kin and community. They somehow pinpoint each of the kinship and relationship units and they perceive the weaves composed of classes of units which constitute the warp and woof of their kinship and community relationship fabrics.

By the 1930's, it had become clear that during the ages from about 12 to 40 or more months every child perceives and incorporates several intersecting patterns of speech units. Mastery of the units and similar manipulation of each class of them allows the child to incorporate one after another and, indeed, rapidly all the other systems of behaviors, relationships, beliefs, and feelings.

Meantime, coterminous with learning of the language is a learning of appropriate body movements, made possible by reliable standing posture and release of forearms. It seems possible that understanding of the sector of body behavior hinges upon analysis of it into its significant units and that a few of them, for example the special manner of bringing food to the face, running, expectorating, and micturating, are peculiar to regions, not universal. They are culturally shaped in their features of difference. Few observations, to be sure, have been conducted in this subject although excellent pioneering in it characterizes Oceanian studies by Margaret Mead.

In short, language, relationships, and body or limb coordinations are among the first patterned systems whose units and sets of units are perceived and at once internalized.

Configurations of sociocultural materials of other kinds whose parts and smaller patterns receive incorporation in each child before five or six years of age are impressive in their numbers, the distinctiveness of their central contents, and very likely their diverse structurings.

A segment of culture called ethics begins to be internalized during the second year and in nonliterate societies appears to be pretty fully incorporated by six or seven. In food-gathering and very likely many of the economically primitive agricultural and pastoral peoples, the especially difficult to define segment of cultural heritage now dubbed as world view seems to be considerably, if not completely, internalized by six or seven. Doubtless it has its special classes of ideological units and fabriclike weaving of such classes. Contents and stylistic features of dance may also be incorporated early. They comprise a large cultural system which a young child engulfs in the process of observation of and participation with dancing elders. That most elaborate tapestry composed of details of scale, melody contours, rhythm, and vocal techniques is almost everywhere well internalized before six or seven years of age. Every nonwestern child has then incorporated a great many of the items and classes of items in humor, for it is in few societies, such as those of western civilization, that a large part of adult quipping and badinage may be withheld from children. Structured system after system, language, body manipulative behavior, kinship, community relationships, ethics, etiquette, world view, humor, music, dance, ritual, oral literature, and other kinds of relationships and expressive materials are, in a sense, poured into little people, one vast fabric after the other, one almost beside the other, one intertwined with the other and interconnecting in ascertainable ways. As children learn and receive approval for acquiring these systems and subsystems they advance toward self-confidence, feelings of familiarity with what is outside them, distinctive self-identity, and judgments of worth of self and others.

A few among a larger sociocultural system's special cultural fabrics may not be implanted, even in bare foundation ways with absences of details, until well after six or seven years of age. For example, government, law, theology, and warfare comprise most elaborate structures which may not quite reach younger children, especially so in richer agricultural and agricultural-pastoral societies.

Apparently what happens in each society is a series of childhood internalizations of its many intersecting systems and subsystems, whether they be social-organizational or expressive-cultural. Among food-gatherers and economically lowlier agricultural and pastoral peoples, such incorporation was speedy. It had to be. Bewildered, unsure, and meagerly competent persons of 13 or 15 years of age were a nuisance. Internalizations were largely built in, if not complete in essentials, by six or seven years of age. The years from then on until puberty featured rapidly progressive mastery and enrichment of each already imbedded pattern at the same time that a prepubescent was also in the beginnings of learning of productive techniques about foods, garments, containers, and gear. A not so gawky and flustered adultlike person emerged shortly after physiological puberty. Some final internalizings, notably a mature adult self-identity, world view, ethics, and law, might then be accorded special ritual observation.

Anthropological knowledge of a social structure and cultural heritage as a whole must remain slight until each patterned fabric such as economics, law-government, kinship, language, music, oral literature, or humor has received both genetic limning, that is, its manner of internalization has been described, and it has been granted what I have chosen to call "close analysis." The latter kind of minute inspection provides a tentative laying out of that fabric's classes of meaningful units and their patternings. Not least, it presents exactly the focus which can display their manner of internalization by children. Tragic deficiencies in anthropological studies since the 1920's therefore included two matters: one, failures to perceive the reality of many patterned systems apart from language structures and kinship—such materials indeed already enjoyed some attention; two, arid exorcisms of intensive ethnographic field studies by many anthropologists who had leading academic positions, and indifference to field explorations which might exhibit even beginnings of understanding of processes in child acceptance and internalization of special fabrics of expressive cultural phenomena. There was a general neglect of planning of field researches upon most sectors of cultural anthropology while a few facets of social structure were being examined.

Although the growing throng of anthropologists has continued to be interested principally in social organization, few exorcisms have been heard regarding manner of study of nonwestern oral literature, religious ideology, music, or language. Specialists in social organization have for the most part evinced only tepid curiosity in procedures of research upon expressive cultural systems and have to all appearances been willing to permit anthropological linguists, ethnomusicologists, folklorists, and others to conduct their kinds of studies without scoldings or even a modicum of confident advice. But the student should take note that social anthropologists have often displayed naïveté in their assessment of personnel, research methods, and results in cultural expressive subjects of inquiry. It is as if the cellists in the symphony orchestra took it upon themselves to make elementary pedagogic pronouncements upon the technique of the woodwinds and brasses. Social anthropologists are frequently overimpressed by verbiage written on cultural specialties and lack capacity to identify contributors and contributions to knowledge in such subjects. Many social anthropologists have continued their unconcern of three or four decades with the ignoring or evasion of research needed in a score of expressive cultural systems. It seems as if a gulf were widening between social and cultural anthropological specialties—an unhealthy condition, to be sure. It is as if great orchestral symphonies were being performed in public concerts by the cellos or violins and all the other instrument sections were more or less subtly told to stay at home.

At this early stage of knowledge in cultural anthropology and its component fields, it seems reasonable to urge that it is first necessary to ascertain just what is in each cultural system and subsystem, much as field workers in linguistics had led in revealing, by the 1930's, something of a language's principal intersecting structures such as phonemics and morphology. Disclosures of the universality of such patternings and their interconnections within languages permitted, for the first time, theoretically significant research, of kinds which have not yet been undertaken, on fundamental processes in child incorporation of language. Exposés of complexities in patternings within languages and of considerable differences in such patternings from language to language and region to region established a potential model, one only of a generic kind, for analyses within and comparisons of other expressive systems. A bare beginning had been made, of course, on nonwestern music, although utilization of a linguistic model for analysis of classes of units in a musical repertoire remained alien to the sad little handful of ethnomusicologists. The linguistic model so far has failed to receive employment in analyses of a score or more of other cultural systems, perhaps largely because of paucity of field-oriented cultural anthropologists and the circumstance that most anthropologists today are social anthropologists; they occupy themselves principally with social organization, acculturation, community studies, and some other specialties.

Actually, a linguistic model of a relatively limited array of form classes and units in them may also turn out to be deceptive or even dangerous for cultural anthropologists. A language's contents and structurings appear to be considerably simpler than many other expressive cultural fabrics. For example, even the little that is known about nonwestern oral literatures, humor, and music suggests caution in accepting language structurings as usefully analogous from the point of view of a criterion of probable number of form classes. Oral literature and humor, about which rather less is known than nonwestern music, appear to be extraordinarily elaborate fabrics. There is a chance that their interwoven classes of content and style units are saliently supplemented by far more of anarchic miscellanea than appears in exceptions to regularities that are found in every language. Furthermore, a child incorporates many different kinds of cultural systems almost simultaneously at a time subsequent to his acquirement of his language tool and all the systems at once connect in most elaborate ways with one another. The language model with its peculiarly clear-cut, almost crystalline, patterns and form classes offers slight help in its supply of suggestions as to how all the other intersecting fabrics internalize and operate. There are tremendous unexplored areas of inquiry here for cultural anthropology.

If cultural anthropology is seen in this fashion, as a barely initiated pursuit of the many fabrics within each of some thousands of nonliterate societies of most diverse kinds, of the ways in which those fabrics were learned, the results in kinds of people in those societies, and the ways the people usually quite unconsciously reshaped and altered their fabrics of cultural expressions, it develops that the science requires a thousand times as many investigators as it has at present. It needs them with dispatch before modernization and sociocultural changes have wiped out heritages which require analyses.

It also develops that some of the currently popular nonfield but library-based and other shortcut methods for making deductions about social and cultural phenomena among nonliterate peoples warrant concern. Cross-cultural studies which use publications now available on a few hundred sociocultural heritages have lately been ventured, as in the frequent employment of that repository known as the Human Relations Area Files whose archive materials repose in a score of American university libraries. The trouble is not in the indeed refined present-day method of cross-cultural comparisons. The problem arises in the quality of depictive data which can be examined in archives which were secured by field workers whose perceptions were shaped mostly by nineteenth century and very early twentieth century Euro-American outlooks and by pioneer teachers of that period. It is vital to understand that systems and subsystems of social structure and of cultural expressions can almost never be analyzed, structured, and connected with other sociocultural phenomena on a basis of archive reports of the kinds we have at present, in spite of the fact that some of the best of them have been placed in the Area Files. Attempts at structuring and display of ties of a theology here, a world perspective there, an oral literature of this people, or humor resorted to by that people, are like trying to formulate phonemic and morphological structures and all their connections and functions on a basis of a not very well transcribed and translated small volume of texts in a language of a group whose ethnography was unknown. Nor do ethnographic reports, or the Area Files archives, suggest satisfactorily how children incorporated their social patterns or cultural systems, because in no instances do these sources reveal fabrics and set forth the minimally contrastive units in those agglomerates. Cultural anthropology's library archives of the 1960's are therefore frighteningly overrated and frustratingly uneven. They lack essentials which only a few cultural anthropologists themselves are beginning to appreciate. Gaps in the field reports of even a Malinowski have been little understood. It has taken almost a century for cultural anthropology to advance toward vestiges of sophistication in what to look for, partly because it has failed to progress to the point of knowing how to identify the component parts of cultural phenomena and systems of expressive items and how to arrange or pattern them. British social anthropologists' verbigerations and cant about structure and function have turned out to be worthless for discovery of methodological steps which had to precede delineations of functioning of cultural materials. First things were not pointed to by these anthropological pioneers.

Cultural anthropology has certainly not begun to acquire what its most alert, scientifically sophisticated, and sensitive personnel now realize ought to be obtained. Malinowski did astonishingly well in his observations of Trobrianders when he was in the field with them from about 1914 to 1918. But it is shattering to list all the things he missed. Cursive descriptions such as he provided have to be supplemented and, indeed, framed around field-produced structurings of each aspect of social organization and each macroclass and microclass of expressive cultural materials. Even today a necessity for such method of field research and structuring escapes most investigators. The result is great gaps in field materials and an impossibility of filling voids without new field investigations.

A disheartening type of method, shortcut too, which has comically overawed many sociocultural anthropologists, especially those who have had little or no field experience among food-gathering peoples, is the a priori devising by one or another thaumaturgist of a mathematical model. It is paralleled by an implicit, certainly not a phrased, presupposition that superimposition of the magic model upon overrated ethnographic data, whether collected by Malinowski or anybody else, permits closer approach to depictions of reality, to revelations of regularities in social life, or to discoveries of child learning processes.

During the 1960's and for another decade or two, there may be no proper alternatives, in transcultural study of humor for example, to getting hundreds or some thousands of instances of a phenomenon within a single community and tearing the data into meaningful items and groupings of them. In linguistics there are still no possible means of circumventing field work analysis within each language before comparative work and reliable correlations can be ventured transculturally. Such labor must involve in each language production of its phonemic and morphologic structures in almost all their idiosyncratic details, regularities, and irregularities, before return back home from the field. If such unpostponed disentangling and exhibiting of sets and patterns in freshly obtained data is a *sine qua non* for understanding a linguistic or humor system, it seems fair to claim that each of 20 or more other internalized cultural systems and heaven knows how many subsystems have to be probed and patterned at once in the field, too, again for each culture. No comparative, correlation, or covariation studies which use frequently shabby reportings by earlier field workers, and which at best manufacture only a handful of statements which cannot be integrated into a beginning system of theory; no *Golden Bough* comparative method and no mathematically enormously sophisticated modern versions of that method—if it can be called a method; no will-o'-the-wisp frames composed of mathematical premises, can free contemporary cultural anthropology from a primary obligation to obtain, analyze, and formulate patterned systems about its always complex data right where they are, in field situations with living informants and interpreters and with theoretical sophistication as a principal resource of an humble investigator.

Respect for complexity, that is, a multitude of at once most elaborately structured and intricately interconnected cultural fabrics within each community, is a foundation premise for such observers and the science. Cultural anthropology has long since outgrown nineteenth century depreciatory concepts and terms such as "primitive," "crude," "wretched," "uncivilized," and "simple," although many of the personnel in anthropology cling to them like an old ham actor who continues to wear spats and a Windsor tie. The science no longer has important uses for simplistic and externally depictive notions like culture traits, culture areas, and diffusion. Nor may any culture be envisaged as a thing of shreds and patches, that is, a kind of anarchic chaos, as Professor Robert H. Lowie unhappily and almost destructively intimated a few decades ago. He was baffled by complexities regarding whose clarification methods of analysis and arrangement had not yet been discussed effectively among anthropologists, although linguistics and other behavioral sciences were becoming aware of advantageous new procedures. It is abundantly evident today that every food-gatherer and wealthier society has comprised both shreds and patches and a large number of interwoven social and cultural fabrics, that language is only one barely explored sample of webs of such a kind, and that it is simpler and more regularly patterned than most of them. The immediate task is to shelve concern about odds and ends and to move toward a more mature manner of delineation of all social or cultural items, their structurings, their connections, what they did to people, and how people learned, fashioned, and altered them.

These seem to constitute priorities in methods of research in cultural anthropology. It is now possible to descry a short initial stretch of the long road ahead toward scientific knowledge of all the world's kinds of peoples. Although global points of view about human nature, social life, and cultural activity and creativity cannot yet be granted by behavioral sciences, means of approaching ever closer to such vantage points are at hand for the asking, providing that anthropologists are willing to pay costs in unprecedentedly detailed analytic labors. Progress toward promontories which will allow sharply focused views of the world's societies and cultures will involve thrilling scientific journeys. Both social scientists and observant laymen can enjoy them. Even though rather technical comparative and dry mathematical validation methods will presently play a kind of counterpoint with much more exciting analytic and field studies, the discoveries, especially those about cultural expressions, will often be intelligible to children. They and everyone else will be led toward goals of global understanding and respect for cultural differences.

A central theme which runs through every chapter of this survey is its emphasis upon the newness, inchoateness, and immaturity in methods of research and state of global knowledge of cultural expressions. Cultural anthropology as a cluster of pure scientific disciplines is extremely young in spite of its age of one century. Everyone needs to appreciate that fact in order to stimulate cultural anthropology's development. There is nothing inherently difficult in understanding cultural anthropology's vistas, its positive assertions about the complexity and likely worth of cultural expressions in thousands of nonwestern societies, and its display of features of difference in the personality structures of the hundreds of mllions of people who grew up in such communities. Each pure science can and should be carefully translated and faithfully interpreted so that nonscientists, especially children, may benefit from those of its discoveries which minimize provinciality and erase prejudices and falsehoods that older generations tended to pass on to youngsters. Concepts of worldwide complexity and worth in the social relationships, cultural expressions, and psychological behavior of all nonliterate peoples can be illustrated and imparted effectively to children, where teachers themselves have comprehended and fully accepted such thoughts. Large chunks of both social and cultural anthropology, including psychological orientations at every point, can be dissected from the congeries of scientific disciplines which comprise general anthropology and then laid out with clarity for the education of very young people. It is a problem of selection and rephrasing. Most social and cultural anthropologists are so conditioned to employment of technical terminology and so anxious about criticism by scientific colleagues that it is impossible for them to change their customary manner of writing and talking for the sake of off-campus audiences and elementary and secondary school classrooms. But important insights, immediately applicable scientific discoveries, and humanitarian values are perfectly intelligible to seven-, eleven-, and fourteen-year-olds if arrayed in terms which they comprehend and if presented by globally oriented minds. Cultural anthropology could use hundreds of translators at once who understand method and theory in its several sciences and who also know how to speak to children enthusiastically, vividly, intelligibly, and without the slighest diminution in dignity. Unhappily, few such interpreters can be found today. Instead, schoolroom and other popular versions of fact and theory in the fields of cultural anthropology often amount to bowdlerized trash seasoned with nineteenth century nonsense about primitives, savages, and Stone Age peoples. School presentations of transcultural phenomena are generally decades behind the progress that the science has achieved.

Cultural anthropology, of course, has a potentially applied role as well as a role as pure science. It has enjoyed rapidly expanding ranks of pure scientists, specialists who pursue the truth whether in broadly depictive or problem-directed field researches or in comparative and correlation exercises which employ the Human Relations Area Files. Little that such scientists seek and learn in order to advance pure knowledge need remain hidden during the next decades from hundreds of millions of young people in schools the world over. Why should anyone grow up wholly provincial and ignorant about his fellow human beings? Why should anyone depreciate their worth and intricacies because teachers and elders have not understood something of the truth about different peoples?

In order to grant a perception of how far social and cultural anthropology have progressed, a contrast with an aspect of the history of astronomy may serve. A few generations ago, the numbers of galaxies in the universe were not indicated even hypothetically. In recent decades, a variety of research tools, including photography, radio astronomy, and mathematics, have served to advance knowledge of a few features of the only recently revealed myriads of galaxies. Anthropology is in one way more fortunate. There is a relatively low ceiling on the numbers of mutually unintelligible languages. They are not in the hundreds of millions or billions but a mere 3,000 or 4,000. And the sociocultural systems which displayed perhaps small, but nonetheless significant, contrasts doubtless numbered in recent times over 10,000, truly a large but not a staggering number. These systems have been tentatively arranged in types, just a very little like the galaxies which are presumably in one or another stage of evolution. Extremely few examples of each sociocultural type have been rather fully depicted for some facets of their complex manifestations, not quite like astronomy which has unfortunately been able to describe some things about just one galaxy, our own, and has been able to report very little indeed about any of the others. But that which is shared by astronomy and sociocultural anthropology is a progressive reaching out from a starting point which is home base. In astronomy that base is our own galaxy. In anthropology the base is western civilization and three or four that are almost comparable to it in wealth, such as Japan, China, and India. The history and future of sociocultural anthropology are in a sense a process of reaching out to a great many other sociocultural systems, eventually many hundreds, let us hope, so that each system may be comprehended on a basis of acceptance of its possibly equal complexity in spite of a kind of poverty in its materials, technology, and some related features. It is like the astronomers' constant additions to knowledge of the galaxies far out in space. Seen in this way, sociocultural anthropology, like astronomy, is in its bare beginnings.

# INDEX

*This book has been set on the Linotype in 10 point Janson, leaded 2 points, and 9 point Janson, leaded 1 point. Chapter numbers are in 36 point Deepdene; chapter titles are in 18 point Deepdene Italic. The size of the type page is 27 by 47 picas.*